BALANCED SCORECARD
STEP-BY-STEP

BALANCED SCORECARD
STEP-BY-STEP

Maximizing Performance and
Maintaining Results

Paul R. Niven

John Wiley & Sons, Inc.

Library of Congress Cataloging-in-Publication Data:

Niven, Paul R.
    Balanced scorecard step by step : maximizing performance
and maintaining results / by Paul R. Niven.
        p.   cm.
    Includes bibliographical references and index.
    ISBN 0-471-07872-7 (CLOTH : alk. paper)
    1. Organizational effectiveness—Measurement.   2. Performance—
Measurement. I. Title.
    HD58.9 .N58   2002
    658.4'013—dc21   2001006731

Printed in the United States of America.

10 9 8 7

For my parents, Bev and Jean Niven

Foreword

Dave Norton and I initially proposed the Balanced Scorecard 10 years ago.[1] Since that time, the concept has been adopted by all types of organizations—manufacturing and service, for-profit and not-for-profit, private and public—in virtually every developed and developing nation in the world. During these 10 years, the Balanced Scorecard has evolved from its initial purpose of an improved performance measurement system to become the basis of a new management system, one that aligns and focuses the entire organization on implementing and improving its strategy.

Norton and I documented this evolution and enhancement of the Balanced Scorecard concept through additional *Harvard Business Review* articles and two books.[2] But because of the rapid changes that have occurred in the past ten years, few practitioners beyond our small circle of consultants and project leaders have gained much experience with implementations that are at the current state-of-the-art. Paul Niven, through his experience as project leader at the excellent and highly successful implementation at Nova Scotia Power, and subsequently as a Balanced Scorecard consultant, is one of the few who can talk and write knowledgeably about how to make the scorecard happen in an organization. *Balanced Scorecard Step By Step* guides readers through the processes required for a successful Balanced Scorecard project. In addition, he shows how to become a strategy-focused organization by imbedding the Balanced Scorecard into critical organizational processes. The book provides an excellent complement to the two Kaplan-Norton books by explicating the details and processes that project leaders can follow to implement the Balanced Scorecard measurement and management system in their organizations. We are pleased to welcome this new book to the Balanced Scorecard literature. Niven's contribution will enable

---

[1]R. S. Kaplan and D. P. Norton, "The Balanced Scorecard: Measures That Drive Performance," *Harvard Business Review*, January–February 1992, 71–79.

[2]Kaplan and Norton, *The Balanced Scorecard: Translating Strategy into Action* (Boston: HBS Press, 1996); _____ *The Strategy-Focused Organization* (Boston: HBS Press, 2001).

many more organizations to achieve successful Balanced Scorecard implementations.

Robert S. Kaplan
Marvin Bower
Professor of Leadership Development, Harvard Business School
and
Chairman, Balanced Scorecard Collaborative

Acknowledgments

A friend and colleague once told me the best way for adults to learn is by speaking with other adults. This book represents years of conversations I have had with colleagues, clients, family members, friends, and innumerable other associates. And yes, I have learned and benefited greatly from each and every exchange of ideas.

This book would not have been possible, literally, if not for my editor at John Wiley & Sons, Tim Burgard, who approached me with the initial idea and has skillfully guided me through the entire process. I would also like to thank all of the clients it has been my pleasure to work with over the years, and those individuals kind enough to share their Scorecard journey with me, particularly Chuck Wehrwein and Valerie Mercer of the National Equity Fund, Andreas Schroeter of Westdeutsche Landesbank, Steve Mann at the County of San Diego, Ed Berkman of McCord Travel Management, Frank Vito at the Texas State Auditor's Office, and Henry Johnson from Scripps Health in San Diego.

Many past and present colleagues have helped shape this book as well. From KPMG Consulting I would like to thank Faisal Yousuf, Chris Kingsley, and Beckie Voss. From CSC Consulting, Mike Contino, Sue Gafner, Chris Reichner, and especially Bill Chandon with whom I've enjoyed many spirited discussions. A big thank you to former colleagues Jason Griffith and Wes Schaffer as well. My Scorecard initiation took place at Nova Scotia Power, and there I was very fortunate to be surrounded by amazing and talented people like Tina Whynot, Todd Bethune, Wanda Boutilier, and Bob Cyr. But most of all, I thank Nova Scotia Power's former CFO Jay Forbes—a great mentor and even better friend.

Finally, and most importantly, I would like to thank my wife Lois. While I wrote this book, she simultaneously acted as first line editor of the manuscript, chief supporter, dedicated community volunteer, and through it all, a constant source of encouragement and love.

Preface

Organizations in today's change-filled, highly competitive environment must devote significant time, energy, and human and financial resources to measuring their performance in achieving strategic goals. Most do just that, but despite the substantial effort and related costs, a recent survey found that only 35 percent of respondents rated their performance measurement systems as effective or very effective.[1] That, of course, means almost 7 out of every 10 organizations are feeling dissatisfied with their measurement efforts. Increasingly, organizations are reaching the conclusion that while measurement is more crucial than ever, their systems for capturing, monitoring, and sharing performance information are critically flawed. Today's systems in many ways bear a remarkable resemblance to their reporting ancestors. While the methods of modern business have transformed dramatically over the past decades, our systems of measurement have remained firmly mired in the past. At the root of our measurement misery is an almost exclusive reliance on financial measures of performance. While these systems were perfectly suited to the machine-like, physical asset-based nature of early industrial endeavors, they are ill-equipped to capture the value creating mechanisms of today's modern business organization. Intangible assets such as employee knowledge, customer and supplier relationships, and innovative cultures are the key to producing value in today's economy. Additionally, the role of strategy is more important today than it has ever been. Whether you're a high-tech newcomer or an established manufacturing veteran, the necessity of effectively executing strategy is crucial in an era of globalization, customer knowledge, and rapid change. But the sobering fact is that about 9 out of 10 organizations fail to implement their strategies. What is needed is a measurement system that balances the historical accuracy and integrity of financial numbers with today's drivers of economic success, and in so doing allows the organization to beat the odds of executing strategy.

The Balanced Scorecard has emerged as a proven and effective tool in our quest to capture, describe, and translate intangible assets into real value

---

[1]Performance Measurement Survey by the American Institute of Certified Public Accountants and Lawrence S. Maisel, 2001.

for all of an organization's stakeholders, and in the process allow organizations to successfully implement differentiating strategies. Developed by Robert Kaplan and David Norton, this deceptively simple methodology translates an organization's strategy into performance objectives, measures, targets, and initiatives in four balanced perspectives: Financial, Customer, Internal Processes, and Employee Learning and Growth (often simply referred to as Learning and Growth). While many organizations have used a combination of financial and non-financial measures in the past, what sets the Balanced Scorecard apart is the concept of cause and effect linkages. A well-constructed Scorecard will tell the story of an organization's strategy through a series of linked performance measures weaving through the four perspectives. The hypothesis reflecting strategy comes to life through the interplay and interdependencies among the financial and nonfinancial measures. Organizations around the globe have rapidly embraced the Balanced Scorecard and reaped swift benefits from its commonsense principles: increased financial returns, greater employee alignment to overall goals, improved collaboration, and unrelenting focus on strategy, to name just a few. To reap those rewards, however, an organization must possess the tools necessary to craft an effective Balanced Scorecard.

ABOUT THIS BOOK

In the mid-1990s I was working with an organization that, like so many others, was about to undergo significant change. The industry structure was changing, competitors appeared more nimble and threatening than ever, and customers were demanding better service with no price increases. A new strategy was developed that, if effectively implemented, would see the organization enhance employee skills, develop new processes, build loyal customers, and ultimately deliver breakthrough financial performance. But how could the strategy be successfully executed? The organization's chief financial officer investigated the Balanced Scorecard approach and determined it was the right tool at the right time. Acting as the executive sponsor for the initiative, he appointed me to lead a team charged with the responsibility for developing a new management system featuring the Balanced Scorecard as the cornerstone. Two years later his intuition paid off in a big way. Employee knowledge of strategy had increased significantly, internal processes were functioning more efficiently than ever, customer loyalty was on the rise, and, despite many adverse factors beyond the organization's control, financial returns were on target.

The organization described above is Nova Scotia Power, Inc. (NSPI), a Canadian electric utility company. As the results demonstrate, their Balanced Scorecard implementation was a great success and has been featured in case studies, shared at conferences throughout North America and beyond, and earned the organization a spot in the Balanced Scorecard Collaborative's Hall of Fame. Lessons learned from this pioneering organization are shared to illustrate many points in this book. As successful as the implementation was, it certainly was not without challenges. Our team quickly learned that building a Balanced Scorecard is far more than a "metrics project" but instead touches many disparate organizational processes. Building an effective team, generating support and enthusiasm for a change project, efficiently gathering and sharing data, coaching, training, and facilitating are just some of the many exciting and challenging tasks we faced. At that time, Balanced Scorecard literature and support services were at a nascent stage and we were left to our own devices when grappling with the many issues awaiting us. While the past number of years have seen a proliferation in Scorecard literature and related consulting and support products, few if any focus on the wide array of organizational activities that must accompany a winning Scorecard campaign. This book was written to fill the void existing between theory and application. Organizations embarking on a Scorecard effort must be aware of—and properly equipped with the tools to successfully navigate—the many potential pitfalls associated with a project of this magnitude. Based on my experience as a consultant along with extensive research, these pages guide the reader through the entire Balanced Scorecard process on a step-by-step basis. From determining your objectives for the Scorecard to testing your mission, to developing measures and targets, to placing the Scorecard at the center of your management system, to tips for sustaining your success, you'll find all this and more. Let's now take a look at how the book is organized and consider how you can use it to best suit your needs.

HOW THE BOOK IS ORGANIZED

Balanced Scorecard Step-by-Step is comprised of five parts, encompassing 14 chapters. Part One is entitled "Introduction to Performance Measurement and the Balanced Scorecard" and is designed to do just that—familiarize you with the field of performance measurement and provide a solid grounding of Scorecard background and principles. Chapter One elaborates on the discussion started in this introduction by examining how the Scorecard solves two fundamental modern business issues—reducing a reliance on financial performance measures and implementing strategy. In Chapter Two the rising prominence of human capital in today's enterprise is reviewed, and evidence presented that suggests the Scorecard methodology is here to stay.

Part Two of the book, "Step-by-Step Development of the Balanced Scorecard," provides you with a detailed review and description of the elements necessary to construct this new and powerful management tool. Chapter Three lays the foundation for the work ahead by examining objectives for a Balanced Scorecard, securing executive sponsorship, creating a team, and preparing a development plan. The core elements of any effective Balanced Scorecard—mission, values, vision, and strategy—are the subject of Chapter Four. You'll discover why each of these elements is crucial to the success of a Balanced Scorecard. With the Scorecard building blocks firmly in place, Chapter Five provides an in-depth view of what it takes to build indicators that act as a faithful translation of strategy. Determining which perspectives are right for you, gathering relevant background material, working with your executive team, and measures in each of the four perspectives are all covered in detail. Narrowing your performance measures down to a select few that weave together in a series of cause-and-effect linkages to describe an organization's strategy is the subject of Chapter Six. The final chapter of Part Two is titled "Setting Targets and Prioritizing Initiatives." The critical role of target setting and the Balanced Scorecard is presented along with a review of different types of targets. Ensuring that organizational plans and initiatives are aligned with the Balanced Scorecard and strategy is also given extensive coverage in Chapter Seven.

"Embedding the Balanced Scorecard in the Organization's Management System" is the title of the book's third part, and marks the Scorecard's transition from a measurement system to a strategic management tool. Aligning every employee's actions with overall organizational goals is the subject of Chapter Eight. This "cascading" of the Balanced Scorecard is critical should organizations hope to enjoy the benefits of greater employee knowledge of, and focus on, key organizational strategies. In Chapter Nine the role of the Balanced Scorecard in the budgeting process is examined. The chapter equips readers with specific techniques to align spending with strategy. The often challenging topic of incentive compensation is tackled in Chapter Ten. Readers will find a comprehensive review of critical compensation planning and design elements.

"Sustaining Balanced Scorecard Success" is the theme of Part Four. Frequent reporting of results is critical in gaining support of the Scorecard as an effective management tool. But should organizations buy one of the many performance management software packages available or build their own reporting solution? Chapter Eleven probes this question and offers several tools to be used when making the decision. A "new management review meeting" is also explained in the chapter. "Maintaining the Balanced Scorecard" is presented in Chapter Twelve. Business rules, processes, and procedures (including those for gathering data) necessary to embed the Scorecard in the fabric of organizational life are carefully reviewed. The Scorecard's "home" in the organization is also considered.

The Balanced Scorecard was originally conceived with the profit-seeking enterprise in mind. However, public-sector and not-for-profit organizations were quick to grasp the many advantages conferred by a Balanced Scorecard and have been adopting it almost since its inception. Part Five, "Balanced Scorecards, in the Public and Not-for-Profit Sectors and Concluding Thoughts" examines this rising trend in Chapter Thirteen, "Balanced Scorecards in the Public and Not-for-Profit Sectors." Readers from these sectors will learn that with some modifications the Scorecard architecture is ideally suited to their mission-driven organizations.

The important role of organizational change in securing a successful Scorecard effort is presented in the book's final chapter. There you will also discover the "top ten implementation issues" and receive guidance on the use of outside consultants when constructing a Scorecard.

This book can be used by organizations at any stage of Balanced Scorecard development. Those launching a Scorecard effort will of course benefit from the step-by-step advice guiding them from initial design to final product. But for organizations that have developed a Scorecard measurement system but have yet to transform it into a management system, Parts Three and Four will be most valuable. Finally, even organizations that have been using the Balanced Scorecard for some time will benefit from a review of the topics presented here. The techniques and advice presented can act as an audit of their own systems to ensure maximum effectiveness. To learn more about the topics covered in this book, and my ongoing work in Performance Management, please visit my web site at *www.primerusconsulting.com.*

Nearly 2,500 years ago the Greek playwright Euripides noted the importance of balance in our lives when he said, "*The best and safest thing is to keep a balance in your life, acknowledge the great powers around us and in us. If you can do that, and live that way, you are really a wise man.*" I truly believe the same applies to organizations.

Paul R. Niven
San Diego, California
September 2001

Contents

PART ONE

Introduction to Performance Measurement and the Balanced Scorecard

CHAPTER 1

Performance Measurement and the Need for a Balanced Scorecard

When you can measure what you are speaking about, and express it in numbers, you know something about it; but when you cannot measure it, when you cannot express it in numbers, your knowledge is of a meager and unsatisfactory kind.

—William Thompson (Lord Kelvin), 1824–1907

Roadmap for Chapter One The purpose of this opening chapter is to provide you with an overview of Performance Measurement and the Balanced Scorecard system. While you may be anxious to get right to the work of developing your new performance management tool, I urge you to spend some time on this chapter since it essentially serves as the foundation for the rest of the book. When you begin developing a Balanced Scorecard your organization will rely on you not only for advice on the technical dimensions of this new process, but also on the broader subject of performance measurement and management. You can enhance your expert credibility within the organization by learning as much as possible about this subject. This is especially important if your current function is one that typically does not get involved in projects of this nature. Think of this chapter as a primer for the exciting work that lies ahead.

The Balanced Scorecard assists organizations in overcoming two key issues: effective organizational performance measurement and implementing strategy. We begin the chapter by discussing performance measurement, and specifically our reliance on financial measures of performance despite their inherent limitations. From there we move to the strategy story and review a number of barriers to successful strategy implementation. With the issues clearly on the table we introduce the Balanced Scorecard and how this tool can overcome the barriers related to financial measures and strategy execution.

Our Balanced Scorecard overview begins with a look back at how and when the Scorecard was originally conceived. Next, we pose the question, "What is a Balanced Scorecard?" and elaborate on the specifics of the tool as a measurement system, strategic management system, and communication tool. In these sections you will be introduced to the theory underlying the Balanced Scorecard and the four perspectives of performance analyzed using this process. The chapter concludes with two important topics: the critical task of linking Balanced Scorecard measures through a series of cause-and-effect relationships, and finally, a discussion of what is actually meant by the word *balance* in the Balanced Scorecard.

TWO FUNDAMENTAL ISSUES

Welcome to your performance measurement and Balanced Scorecard journey. During our time together we will explore the many facets of this topic, and it is my hope that both you and your organization will be transformed as a result. As this book is being written, the Balanced Scorecard concept has been with us for just over 10 years. The Balanced Scorecard was born from a research study conducted in 1990 and has since become a critical business tool for thousands of organizations around the globe. In fact, recent estimates suggest that a whopping 50 percent of the *Fortune* 1000 has a performance management system (Balanced Scorecard) in place.[1] Before we discuss the nature of the Balanced Scorecard, let's examine its origins and attempt to determine just why it has become such a universally accepted methodology.

Two fundamental business issues have been greatly enhanced as a result of the Balanced Scorecard: the problem of effective organizational performance measurement and the critical issue of successful strategy implementation. In the following sections we'll examine both of these issues and then return to an overview of the Balanced Scorecard and discuss how it solves each. We'll begin with the subject of measurement—where we've been, what has changed, and where we're going (see Exhibit 1.1).

MEASURING ORGANIZATIONAL PERFORMANCE

Take another look at the quote from Lord Kelvin that opens this chapter: *"When you can measure what you are speaking about, and express it in numbers, you know something about it; but when you cannot measure it, when you cannot express it in numbers, your knowledge is of a meager and unsatisfactory kind."* Over the years I have seen a lot of quotes on measurement posted on walls and in binders, and some are great, like this Einstein admonition: *"Not everything that can be counted counts, and not everything that counts can be counted."* When

Exhibit 1.1 The Balanced Scorecard Solves Fundamental Business Issues

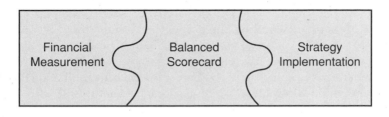

| Financial Measurement | Balanced Scorecard | Strategy Implementation |

you start the work of implementing your Scorecard project, it is a pretty good bet that at least one member of your team will have that quotation pasted somewhere in their workspace, and no wonder—the words are profound and revealing. But for sheer power of language I have to defer to the Lord Kelvin quote above. I love the words *meager* and *unsatisfactory*. To me, that paints a real picture of the importance of performance measurement. I don't know the specific date of Lord Kelvin's quote, but if we assume it was written around the middle of his life, say 1850, that is more than 150 years ago, and he is talking about the power and importance of measurement then. Measurement is every bit as important, no, more important than ever in today's environment.

While we are discussing sound bites, let's include one from the person many consider the greatest management thinker of our time, Peter Drucker. He suggests that few factors are as important to the performance of an organization as measurement, and measurement is among the weakest areas in management today. Is measurement really in such a deficient state? In 1987 a survey by the National Association of Accountants and Computer Aided Manufacturing-International (CAM-I) suggested that 60 percent of the 260 financial officers and 64 operating executives surveyed in the United States were dissatisfied with their performance measurement system.[2] The passage of time has apparently not improved the situation. More recent studies suggest that about 80 percent of large American companies want to change their performance measurement systems. The findings of these studies probably would not come as a great surprise to Bill Jensen. Jensen is the author of *Simplicity—The New Competitive Advantage*. In discussing performance management, Jensen suggests that most companies fail to provide employees with the information they need in a format and context that is relevant to their unique requirements. *"Working smarter means that any and all corporate data relevant to an individual's work should be available in formats that can be customized."*[3]

The research clearly demonstrates that many organizations both need and desire a change to their existing performance measurement systems, but is it possible to isolate any one key issue in the deficient state of performance measurement? Many would suggest the problem rests in our almost exclusive reliance on financial measures of performance.

Financial Measurement and Its Limitations

As long as business organizations have existed, the traditional method of measurement has been financial. Bookkeeping records used to facilitate financial transactions can literally be traced back thousands of years. At the turn of the twentieth century, financial measurement innovations were critical to the success of the early industrial giants like General Motors. That should not come as a surprise since the financial metrics of the time were the perfect complement to the machine-like nature of the corporate entities and management philosophy of the day. Competition was ruled by scope and economies of scale, with financial measures providing the yardsticks of success.

Financial measures of performance have evolved, and today the concept of economic value added (EVA) is prevalent. This concept suggests that unless a firm's profit exceeds its cost of capital, it really is not creating value for its shareholders. Using EVA as a lens, it is possible to determine that despite an increase in earnings, a firm may be destroying shareholder value if the cost of capital associated with new investments is sufficiently high.

The work of financial professionals is to be commended. As we move into the twenty-first century, however, many are questioning our almost exclusive reliance on financial measures of performance. Perhaps these measures would better serve as a means of reporting on the stewardship of funds entrusted to management's care rather than charting the future direction of the organization. Let's take a look at some of the criticisms levied against the overabundant use of financial measures:

- *Not consistent with today's business realities.* Today's organizational value-creating activities are not captured in the tangible, fixed assets of the firm. Instead, value rests in the ideas of people scattered throughout the firm, in customer and supplier relationships, in databases of key information, and cultures of innovation and quality. Traditional financial measures were designed to compare previous periods based on internal standards of performance. These metrics are of little assistance in providing early indications of customer, quality, or employee problems or opportunities.

- *Driving by rearview mirror.* Financial measures provide an excellent review of past performance and events in the organization. They represent a coherent articulation and summary of activities of the firm in prior periods. However, this detailed financial view has no predictive power for the future. As we all know, and experience has shown, great financial results in one month, quarter, or even year are in no way indicative of future financial performance.

- *Tend to reinforce functional silos.* Financial statements are normally prepared by functional area: Individual department statements are prepared and rolled up into the business unit's numbers, which are ultimately compiled as part of the overall organizational picture. This approach is inconsistent with today's organization in which much of the work is cross-functional in nature. Today, we see teams comprised of many functional areas coming together to solve pressing problems and create value in never imagined ways. Our traditional financial measurement systems have no way to calculate the true value or cost of these relationships.

- *Sacrifice long-term thinking.* Many change programs feature severe cost-cutting measures that may have a very positive impact on the organization's short-term financial statements. However, these cost reduction efforts often target the long-term value-creating activities of the firm such as research and development, associate development, and customer relationship management. This focus on short-term gains at the expense of long-term value creation may lead to suboptimization of the organization's resources.

- *Financial measures are not relevant to many levels of the organization.* Financial reports by their very nature are abstractions. Abstraction in this context is defined as moving to another level, leaving certain characteristics out. When we roll up financial statements throughout the organization, that is exactly what we are doing—compiling information at a higher and higher level until it is almost unrecognizable and useless in the decision making of most managers and employees. Employees at all levels of the organization need performance data they can act on. This information must be imbued with relevance for their day-to-day activities.

Given the limitations of financial measures, should we even consider saving a space for them in our Balanced Scorecard? With their inherent focus on short-term results, often at the expense of long-term value-creating activities, are they relevant in today's environment? The answer is yes for a number of reasons. As will be discussed shortly, the Balanced Scorecard is just that: balanced. An undue focus on any particular area of measurement will often lead to poor overall results. Precedents in the business world support this position. In the 1980s the focus was on productivity improvement, while in the 1990s quality became fashionable and seemingly critical to an organization's success. In keeping with the principle of what gets measured gets done, many businesses saw tremendous improvements in productivity and quality. What they didn't necessarily see was a corresponding increase in financial results, and in fact some companies with the best quality in their industry failed to remain in business. Financial statements will remain an important tool for organizations since they ultimately determine whether improvements in customer satisfaction, quality, on-time delivery, and innovation are leading to improved financial performance and wealth creation for shareholders. What we need is a method of balancing the accuracy and integrity of our financial measures with the drivers of future financial performance of the organization.

The Strategy Story

Strategy formulation is quite possibly the most discussed and debated topic on the business landscape. For generations of business leaders the development of a winning strategy was often seen as the key differentiator of organizational success. Executives, academics, and consultants alike, all searching for the panacea of a winning strategy, have shaped the subject and contributed to the debate. Their work over the years has not been unproductive, and in fact has led to the development of numerous schools of strategic thought. In *Strategy Safari*, Mintzberg, Ahlstrand, and Lampel identified 10 such schools. They document strategy setting as formal processes, mental processes, emergent processes, and negotiation processes, to name but a few.[4]

As with financial metrics, strategy has come under fire recently by those who suggest our dynamic and rapidly evolving business environment render a long-term strategy ineffective and almost instantly obsolete. Proponents of this school do not believe business has the luxury of pausing to develop a strategy and doing so creates a debilitating inflexibility. Not so, says Michael Porter, perhaps the world's best-known academic thinker on the subject of strategy. He takes an opposite view and suggests that strategy has never been more important. Profitability in many industries is under pressure as a result of the practices of some Internet pioneers. Porter suggests that these organizations have competed in a manner that directly contradicts the laws of effective strategy. Specifically, these organizations have:

- Focused on revenue and market share through heavy discounting, give-aways, and advertising rather than profits.

- Avoided the delivery of real value and instead concentrated on indirect revenue from advertising, and "click-through fees" from partners.

- Attempted to be all things to all markets by offering myriad products and services rather than making the difficult trade-offs associated with strategy formulation.

By ignoring the fundamentals of strategy, these companies have adversely affected their industry structures, making it more difficult for anyone to gain a competitive advantage. As a result, it is more important than ever for companies to distinguish themselves from their competition. Porter suggests sustainable competitive advantage through operational effectiveness, and strategic positioning holds the answer.[5]

Implementing Strategy

If we accept the premise that strategy formulation is as critical in today's fast-paced, rapidly evolving business environment as it ever was, then we can move to a more fundamental issue—the effective implementation of strategy. While the development of winning strategies has never been a simple task, the successful implementation of those strategies has been a much more daunting task indeed. A 1999 *Fortune* magazine story suggested that 70 percent of chief executive officer (CEO) failures came not as a result of poor strategy, but of poor execution.[6] Why is strategy so difficult for even the best organizations to effectively implement? Research in the area has suggested a number of barriers to strategy execution, and they are displayed in Exhibit 1.2. Let's take a look at these in turn.

The Vision Barrier

The vast majority of employees do not understand the organization's strategy. This situation sufficed at the turn of the twentieth century when value was derived from the most efficient use of physical assets, and employees were literally cogs in the great industrial wheel. However, in the information or knowledge age in which we currently exist, value is created from the intangible assets—the know-how, relationships, and cultures existing within

Exhibit 1.2   The Barriers to Implementing Strategy

Vision Barrier	People Barrier	Management Barrier	Resource Barrier
Only 5% of the workforce understands the strategy	Only 25% of managers have incentives linked to strategy	85% of executive teams spend less than one hour per month discussing strategy	60% of organizations don't link budgets strategy

Only 10% of organizations execute their strategy

Barriers to Strategy Execution

Adapted from material developed by Robert S. Kaplan and David P. Norton.

the organization. Most companies are still organized for the industrial era, utilizing command and control orientations that are inadequate for today's environment. Why is this the case when all evidence suggests a change is necessary? S.I. Hayakawa introduced a concept known as *cultural lag* over 50 year ago, and it goes a long way in explaining this organizational inertia. Hayakawa states, *"Once people become accustomed to institutions, they eventually get to feeling that their particular institutions represent the only right and proper way of doing things . . . consequently, social organizations tend to change slowly, and—most important—they tend to exist long after the necessity for their existence has disappeared, and sometimes even when their continued existence becomes a nuisance and a danger."*[7] Does this remind you of your company? If your structure is hampering employees' ability to understand and act on the firm's strategy, how can they be expected to make effective decisions that will lead to the achievement of your goals?

The People Barrier

Incentive compensation arrangements have been with us for quite some time, but have they been linked to the right things? Most systems provide rewards for the achievement of short-term financial targets, not long-term strategic initiatives. Recall the earlier admonition: What gets measured gets done. When the focus is on achieving short-term financial targets, clever employees will do whatever it takes to ensure those results are achieved. This often comes at the expense of creating long-term value for the firm.

The Resource Barrier

Sixty percent of organizations don't link budgets to strategy. This finding really should not come as a surprise to us because most organizations have separate processes for budgeting and strategic planning. One group is working to forge the strategy that will lead the firm heroically into the future, while independently another group is crafting the operating and capital budgets for the coming year. The problem with this approach is that human and financial resources are once again tied to short-term financial targets and not long-term strategy. I recall my days working in a corporate accounting environment for a large company. I was housed on the same floor as the strategic planners, and not only did our group not liaise regularly with them—we barely even knew them!

The Management Barrier

How does your executive team spend their time during their monthly or quarterly reviews? If yours is like most organizations, they probably spend the majority of their time analyzing the financial results and looking for remedies to the "defects" that occur when actual results do not meet budget expectations. A focus on strategy demands that executives spend their time together moving beyond the analysis of defects to a deeper understanding of the underlying value creating or destroying mechanisms in the firm.

THE BALANCED SCORECARD

As the preceding discussion has indicated, organizations face many hurdles in developing performance measurement systems that truly measure the right things. What is needed is a system that balances the historical accuracy of financial numbers with the drivers of future performance, while also assisting organizations in implementing their differentiating strategies. The Balanced Scorecard is the tool that answers both challenges. In the remainder of this chapter we will begin our exploration of the Balanced Scorecard by discussing its origins, reviewing the conceptual model of the Scorecard, and considering what separates the Balanced Scorecard from other systems.

Origins of the Balanced Scorecard

The Balanced Scorecard was developed by two men, Robert Kaplan, a professor at Harvard University, and David Norton, a consultant also from the Boston area. In 1990, Kaplan and Norton led a research study of a dozen companies exploring new methods of performance measurement. The impetus for the study was a growing belief that financial measures of performance were ineffective for the modern business enterprise. The study companies, along with Kaplan and Norton, were convinced that a reliance on financial measures of performance was affecting their ability to create value. The group discussed a number of possible alternatives but settled on the idea of a Scorecard featuring performance measures capturing activities from throughout the organization—customer issues, internal business processes, employee activities, and of course shareholder concerns. Kaplan and Norton labeled this new tool the Balanced Scorecard and later summarized the concept in the first of three *Harvard Business Review* articles, "The Balanced Scorecard—Measures that Drive Performance."[8]

Over the next four years a number of organizations adopted the Balanced Scorecard and achieved immediate results. Kaplan and Norton discovered that these organizations were not only using the Scorecard to complement financial measures with the drivers of future performance but were also communicating their strategies through the measures they selected for their Balanced Scorecard. As the Scorecard gained prominence with organizations around the globe as a key tool in the implementation of strategy, Kaplan and Norton summarized the concept and the learning to that point in their 1996 book *The Balanced Scorecard.*[9]

Since that time the Balanced Scorecard has been adopted by nearly half of the *Fortune* 1000 organizations and the momentum continues unabated. Once considered the exclusive domain of the for-profit world, the Balanced Scorecard has been translated and effectively implemented in both the not-for-profit and public sectors. These organizations have learned that by slightly modifying the Scorecard framework they are able to demonstrate to their constituents the value they provide and the steps they are taking to fulfill their important missions. Chapter Thirteen will take a closer look at how the Balanced Scorecard is being successfully implemented in both the public and not-for-profit sectors. So widely accepted and effective has the Scorecard been that the *Harvard Business Review* recently hailed it as one of the 75 most influential ideas of the twentieth century. Does all this whet your appetite for more? Let's now turn our attention to the tool itself and see what makes up the Balanced Scorecard.

What Is a Balanced Scorecard?

We can describe the Balanced Scorecard as a carefully selected set of measures derived from an organization's strategy. The measures selected for the Scorecard represent a tool for leaders to use in communicating to employees and external stakeholders the outcomes and performance drivers by which the organization will achieve its mission and strategic objectives. A simple definition, however, cannot tell us everything about the Balanced Scorecard. In my work with many organizations, and research into best practices of Scorecard use, I see this tool as three things: measurement system, strategic management system, and communication tool. (See Exhibit 1.3.) Let's take a look at each of these Scorecard uses.

Exhibit 1.3   What Is the Balanced Scorecard?

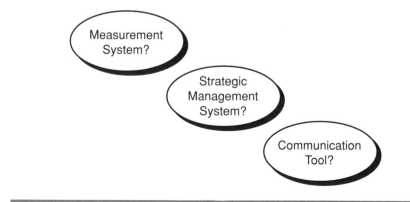

The Balanced Scorecard as a Measurement System

Earlier in the chapter we discussed the limiting features of financial performance measures. While they provide an excellent review of what has happened in the past, they are inadequate in addressing the real value-creating mechanisms in today's organization—the intangible assets such as knowledge and networks of relationships. We might call financial measures *lag indicators*. They are outcomes of actions previously taken. The Balanced Scorecard complements these lag indicators with the drivers of future economic performance, or *lead indicators*. But from where are these performance measures (both lag and lead) derived? The answer is your strategy. All the measures on the Balanced Scorecard serve as translations of the organization's strategy. Take a look at Exhibit 1.4. What is striking about this diagram is that vision and strategy are at the center of the Balanced Scorecard system, not financial controls as in many organizations.

Many organizations have inspiring visions and compelling strategies, but are often unable to use those beautifully crafted words to align employee actions with the firm's strategic direction. In his book *The Fifth Discipline*, Peter Senge describes this dilemma when he notes, *"Many leaders have personal visions that never get translated into shared visions that galvanize an organization."*[10] The Balanced Scorecard allows an organization to translate its vision and strategies by providing a new framework, one that tells the story of the organization's strategy through the objectives and measures chosen. Rather than focusing on financial control devices that provide little in the way of guidance for long-term employee decision making, the Scorecard uses measurement as a new language to describe the key elements in the achievement of the strategy. The use of measurement is critical to the achievement of strategy. In his book *Making Strategy Work*, Timothy Galpin notes "measurable goals and objectives"[11] as one of the key success factors of making strategy work. While the Scorecard retains financial measures, it complements them with three other, distinct perspectives: Customer, Internal Processes, and Learning and Growth.[12]

Perspectives

In this section of the chapter we will examine each of the four perspectives of the Balanced Scorecard. The use of the word *perspective* is intentional, and I believe represents the preferred method when discussing the Scorecard. You may hear others refer to the four "quadrants" instead of perspectives. The Oxford dictionary begins its definition of the word quadrant by describing it as a quarter of circle's circumference. The word reflects the number four and in that sense is almost limiting to the flexible approach inherent in the Scorecard. You may wish to have five perspectives

Exhibit 1.4 The Balanced Scorecard

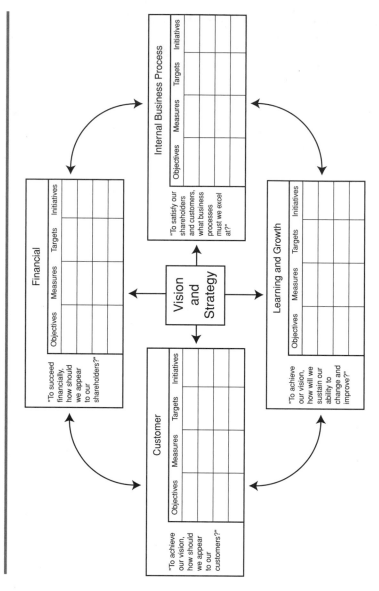

Reprinted by permission of *Harvard Business Review*. Exhibit from "Using the Balanced Scorecard as a Strategic Management System" by Robert S. Kaplan and David P. Norton, January–February 1996, p. 76. Copyright © by the Harvard Business School Publishing Corporation; all rights reserved.

or only three. Stick to the word *perspective* as it is more generic and merely reflects a viewpoint, not a fixed number.

Customer Perspective

When choosing measures for the Customer perspective of the Scorecard, organizations must answer two critical questions: Who are our target customers? and What is our value proposition in serving them? Sounds simple enough, but both of these questions offer many challenges to organizations. Most organizations will state that they do in fact have a target customer audience, yet their actions reveal an "all things to all customers" strategy. As we learned from Michael Porter earlier in the chapter, this lack of focus will prevent an organization from differentiating itself from competitors. Choosing an appropriate value proposition poses no less of a challenge to most firms. Many will choose one of three "disciplines" articulated by Treacy and Wiersema in *The Discipline of Market Leaders*[13]:

- *Operational Excellence.* Organizations pursuing an operational excellence discipline focus on low price, convenience, and often "no frills." Wal-Mart provides a great representation of an operationally excellent company.
- *Product Leadership.* Product leaders push the envelope of their firm's products. Constantly innovating, they strive to offer simply the best product in the market. Nike is an example of a product leader in the field of athletic footwear.
- *Customer Intimacy.* Doing whatever it takes to provide solutions for unique customers' needs help define the customer intimate company. They do not look for one-time transactions but instead focus on long-term relationship building through their deep knowledge of customer needs. In the retail industry Nordstrom epitomizes the customer intimate organization.

Regardless of the value discipline chosen, this perspective will normally include measures widely used today: customer satisfaction, customer loyalty, market share, and customer acquisition, for example. Equally as important, the organization must develop the performance drivers that will lead to improvement in these "lag" indicators of customer success. In Chapter Five we will take a closer look at the Customer perspective and identify what specific steps your organization should take to develop Customer measures.

Internal Process Perspective

In the Internal Process perspective of the Scorecard, we identify the key processes the firm must excel at in order to continue adding value for customers and, ultimately, shareholders. Each of the customer disciplines outlined above will entail the efficient operation of specific internal processes in order to serve the firm's customers and fulfill the firm's value proposition. Our task in this perspective is to identify those processes and develop the best possible measures with which to track our progress. To satisfy customer and shareholder expectations, you may have to identify entirely new internal processes rather than focusing your efforts on the incremental improvement of existing activities. Product development, production, manufacturing, delivery, and postsale service may be represented in this perspective.

Many organizations rely heavily on supplier relationships and other third-party arrangements to effectively serve customers. In those cases you might consider developing measures in the Internal Process perspective to represent the critical elements of those relationships. The development of performance measures for Internal Processes will be examined in greater depth in Chapter Five.

Learning and Growth Perspective

If you want to achieve ambitious results for internal processes, customers, and ultimately shareholders, where are these gains found? The measures in the Learning and Growth perspective of the Balanced Scorecard are really the enablers of the other three perspectives. In essence, they are the foundation on which this entire house of a Balanced Scorecard is built. Once you identify measures and related initiatives in your Customer and Internal Process perspectives, you can be certain of discovering some gaps between your current organizational infrastructure of employee skills and information systems, and the level necessary to achieve your results. The measures you design in this perspective will help you close that gap and ensure sustainable performance for the future.

Like the other perspectives of the Scorecard, we would expect a mix of core outcome (lag) measures and performance drivers (lead measures) to represent the Learning and Growth perspective. Employee skills, employee satisfaction, availability of information, and alignment could all have a place here. Many organizations struggle in the development of learning and growth measures. It is normally the last perspective to be developed and perhaps the teams are intellectually drained from their earlier efforts of developing new strategic measures, or they simply consider this perspective "soft stuff" best left to the Human Resources group. No matter how valid the rationale seems, this perspective cannot be overlooked in the development process. As mentioned earlier, the measures developed in the Learning and Growth perspective are really the enablers of all other measures on the Scorecard. Think of them as the roots of a tree that will ultimately lead through the trunk of internal processes to the branches of customer results, and finally to the leaves of financial returns. We will return to this important topic in Chapter Five.

Financial Measures

Financial measures are an important component of the Balanced Scorecard, especially in the for-profit world. The measures in this perspective tell us whether our strategy execution, which is detailed through measures chosen in the other perspectives, is leading to improved bottom-line results. We could focus all of our energy and capabilities on improving customer satisfaction, quality, on-time delivery, or any number of things, but without an indication of their effect on the organization's financial returns they are of limited value. Classic lagging indicators are normally encountered in the Financial perspective. Typical examples include profitability, revenue growth, and economic value added. As with the other three perspectives, we will return to have another look at financial measures in Chapter Five.

The Balanced Scorecard as a Strategic Management System

For many organizations the Balanced Scorecard has evolved from a measurement tool to what Kaplan and Norton have described as a "strategic management system."[14] While the original intent of the Scorecard system was to balance historical financial numbers with the drivers of future value for the firm, as more and more organizations experimented with the concept, they found it to be a critical tool in aligning short-term actions with their strategy. Used in this way the Scorecard alleviates many of the issues of effective strategy implementation we discussed earlier in the chapter. Let's revisit those barriers and examine how the Balanced Scorecard may in fact remove them.

Overcoming the Vision Barrier through the Translation of Strategy

The Balanced Scorecard is ideally created through a shared understanding and translation of the organization's strategy into objectives, measures, targets, and initiatives in each of the four Scorecard perspectives. The translation of vision and strategy forces the executive team to specifically determine what is meant by often vague and nebulous terms contained in vision and strategy statements, for example, *best in class, superior service*, and *targeted customers*. Through the process of developing the Scorecard, an executive group may determine that superior service means 95 percent on-time delivery to customers. All employees can now focus their energies and day-to-day activities toward the crystal-clear goal of on-time delivery rather than wondering about and debating the definition of superior service. Using the Balanced Scorecard as a framework for translating the strategy, these organizations create a new language of measurement that serves to guide all employees' actions toward the achievement of the stated direction.

Cascading the Scorecard Overcomes the People Barrier

To successfully implement any strategy it must be understood and acted on by every level of the firm. Cascading the Scorecard means driving it down into the organization and giving all employees the opportunity to demonstrate how their day-to-day activities contribute to the company's strategy. All organizational levels distinguish their value creating activities by developing Scorecards that link to the high-level corporate objectives. Cascading creates a line of sight from the employee on the shop floor back to the executive boardroom. Some organizations have taken cascading all the way down to the individual level, with employees developing personal Balanced Scorecards that define the contribution they will make to their team in helping it achieve overall objectives. Chapter Eight will take a closer look at the topic of cascading and discuss how you can develop aligned Scorecards throughout your organization.

Rather than linking incentives and rewards to the achievement of short-term financial targets, managers using the Balanced Scorecard have the opportunity to tie their team's, department's, or business unit's rewards directly to the areas in which they exert influence. All employees can now focus on the performance drivers of future economic value and what decisions and actions are necessary to achieve those outcomes. Chapter Ten will outline strategies for the linkage of Balanced Scorecard results to compensation.

Strategic Resource Allocation Overcomes the Resource Barrier

When discussing this barrier, we noted that most companies have separate processes for budgeting and strategic planning. Developing your Balanced Scorecard provides an excellent opportunity to tie these important processes together. When we create a Balanced Scorecard we not only think in terms of objectives, measures, and targets for each of our four perspectives, but just as critically we must consider the initiatives or action plans we will put in place to meet our Scorecard targets. If we create long-term stretch targets for our measures, we can then consider the incremental steps along the path to their achievement. The human and financial resources necessary to achieve Scorecard targets should form the basis for the development of the annual budgeting process. No longer will departments and business units submit budget requests that simply take last year's amount and add an arbitrary 5 percent. Instead, the necessary costs (and profits) associated with Balanced Scorecard targets are clearly articulated in their submission documents. This enhances executive learning about the strategy as the group is now forced (unless they have unlimited means) to make tough choices and trade-offs regarding which initiatives to fund and which to defer.

The building of a Balanced Scorecard also affords you a great opportunity to critically examine the current myriad initiatives taking place in your organization. As a consultant, when I visit a new client one of the laments I hear repeatedly from front-line employees is, "Oh no, another new initiative!" Many executives have pet projects and agendas they hope to advance, often with little thought of the strategic significance of such endeavors. More worrisome is the potential for initiatives from different functional areas to work against one another. Your Marketing department may be attempting to win new business through an aggressive marketing campaign, while independently your Human Resources group has just launched a new incentive program rewarding the Sales staff for repeat business with existing customers. Should the Sales team focus on winning new customers or nurturing current relationships? Initiatives at every level of the organization and from every functional area must share one common trait: a linkage to the firm's overall strategic goals. The Balanced Scorecard provides the lens for making this examination. Once you have developed your Scorecard, you should review all the initiatives currently underway in your organization and determine which are truly critical to the fulfillment of your strategy and which are merely consuming valuable and scarce resources. Obviously, the resource savings are beneficial, but more importantly, you signal to everyone in the organization the critical factors for success, and the steps you are taking to achieve them. Chapter Nine is devoted to a greater review of this topic and provides guidance on how you can link your budgets to strategy.

Strategic Learning Overcomes the Management Barrier

In the rapidly changing business environment most of us face, we need more than an analysis of actual versus budget variances to make strategic decisions. Unfortunately, many management teams spend their precious time together discussing variances and looking for ways to correct these "defects." The Balanced Scorecard provides us with the necessary elements to move away from this paradigm to a new model in which Scorecard results become a starting point for reviewing, questioning, and learning about our strategy.

The Balanced Scorecard translates our vision and strategy into a coherent set of measures in four balanced perspectives. Immediately, we have more information to consider than merely financial data. The results of our Scorecard performance measures, when viewed as a coherent whole, represent the articulation of our strategy to that point and form the basis for questioning whether our results are leading us any closer to the achievement of that strategy. As seen in the next section, any strategy we pursue represents a hypothesis or our best guess of how to achieve success. To prove meaningful, the measures on our Scorecard must link together to tell the story of or describe that strategy. If, for example, we believe an investment in employee training will lead to speedier product development cycles, we need to test that hypothesis through the measures appearing on our Scorecard. If employee training increases to meet our target but product development has actually slowed, then perhaps that is not a valid assumption and we should be focusing on improving employee access to key information. It may take considerable time to gather sufficient data to test such correlations, but simply having managers begin to question the assumptions underlying the strategy is a major improvement over making decisions based purely on financial numbers.

The Balanced Scorecard as a Communication Tool

The preceding sections have discussed the use of the Balanced Scorecard as a pure measurement system and its evolution into a Strategic Management System. There was considerable discussion about the power of the Scorecard in translating the strategy and telling its story to all employees— what might be called communicating. So why is an entire section (albeit a short one) necessary to outline why the Balanced Scorecard should be considered a communication tool? Simply because it is the most basic and powerful attribute of the entire system. A well-constructed Scorecard eloquently describes your strategy and makes the vague and imprecise world of visions and strategies come alive through the clear and objective performance measures you have chosen.

Much has been written in recent years about knowledge management strategies within organizations, and many schools of thought exist. One common trait of all such systems may be the desire to make the implicit knowledge held within the minds of your workforce explicit and open for discussion and learning. We live in the era of the knowledge worker—the employee who, unlike his organizational descendents who relied on the physical assets of the company, owns the means of production: knowledge. There may be no greater challenge facing your organization today than codifying and acting on that knowledge. In fact, Peter Drucker has called managing knowledge worker productivity one of the great management challenges of the twenty-first century.[15] Sharing Scorecard results throughout the organization provides employees with the opportunity to discuss the assumptions underlying the strategy, learn from any unexpected results, and dialogue on future modifications as necessary. Simply understanding the firm's strategies can unlock many hidden organizational capacities as employees, perhaps for the first time, know where the organization is headed and how they can contribute during the journey. One organization I worked with conducted employee surveys before and after the development of the Balanced Scorecard. Prior to implementation, less than 50 percent said they were aware of, and understood, the strategy. One year following a full Balanced Scorecard implementation, that number had risen to 87 percent! If you believe in openly disseminating information to your employees, practicing what some would call "open book management," then there is no better tool than the Balanced Scorecard to serve as your open book.

The Importance of Cause and Effect

If this book is your first introduction to the Balanced Scorecard concept, you may be saying to yourself, "We have lots of nonfinancial information: customer satisfaction, quality statistics, and employee morale data. I guess we're well on our way to the Balanced Scorecard." Not so fast! What really separates the Balanced Scorecard from other performance management systems is the notion of cause and effect.

The best strategy ever conceived is simply a hypothesis developed by the authors. It represents their best guess as to an appropriate course of action given their knowledge of information concerning the environment, competencies, competitive positions, and so on. What is needed is a method to document and test the assumptions inherent in the strategy. The Balanced Scorecard allows us to do just that. A well-designed Balanced Scorecard should describe your strategy through the objectives and measures you have chosen. These measures should link together in a chain of cause-and-effect relationships from the performance drivers in the Learning and Growth perspective all the way through to improved financial performance as reflected in the Financial perspective. We are attempting to document our strategy through measurement, making the relationships between the measures explicit so they can be monitored, managed, and validated. Here is a typical example of cause and effect: Let's say your organization would like to pursue a growth strategy. You therefore determine that you will measure revenue growth in the Financial perspective of the Scorecard. You hypothesize that loyal customers providing repeat business will result in greater revenues so you measure customer loyalty in the Customer perspective. How will you achieve superior levels of customer loyalty? Now you must ask yourself what internal processes the organization must excel at in order to drive customer loyalty and ultimately increase revenue. You believe customer loyalty is driven by your ability to continuously innovate and bring new products to the market, and therefore you decide to measure new product development cycle times in the Internal Process perspective. Finally, you have to determine how you will improve cycle times. Investing in employee training on new development initiatives may eventually lower development cycle time and is then measured under the Learning and Growth perspective of the Balanced Scorecard. This linkage of measures throughout the Balanced Scorecard is constructed with a series of "if–then" statements: *If* we increase training, *then* cycle times will lower. *If* cycle times lower, *then* loyalty will increase. *If* loyalty increases, *then* revenue will increase. When considering the linkage between measures, we should also attempt to document the timing and extent of the correlations. For example, do we expect customer loyalty to double in the first year as a result of our focus on lowering new product development cycle times? Explicitly stating the assumptions in our measure architecture makes the Balanced Scorecard a formidable tool for strategic learning.

Creating the cause-and-effect linkages between performance measures can prove to be the most challenging aspect of a Balanced Scorecard implementation. However, as with most endeavors the ultimate reward is worth the hard work since you will now have more than an ad-hoc collection of financial and nonfinancial measures. Instead, you will have developed a system that articulates your strategy, serves to communicate that strategy to all employees, and allows for ongoing strategic learning as you test and validate your model. We will return to this important topic in Chapter Six.

Balance in the Balanced Scorecard

As you develop the Balanced Scorecard in your organization, you may encounter some resistance to the actual term *Balanced Scorecard* itself. Some may believe the Balanced Scorecard represents the latest management fad sweeping executive suites around the nation and the mere mention of such a buzzword would preclude employees from accepting the tool regardless of its efficacy. This may represent a legitimate concern depending on the fate of previous change initiatives within your organization. Others may prefer Performance Management System, Scoreboard, or any number of monikers for the tool. It is important to consistently use the term Balanced Scorecard when describing this tool. The concept of balance is central to this system, specifically relating to three areas:

1. *Balance between financial and nonfinancial indicators of success.* The Balanced Scorecard was originally conceived to overcome the deficiencies of a reliance on financial measures of performance by balancing them with the drivers of future performance. This remains a principal tenet of the system.
2. *Balance between internal and external constituents of the organization.* Shareholders and customers represent the external constituents expressed in the Balanced Scorecard while employees and internal processes represent internal constituents. The Balanced Scorecard recognizes the importance of balancing the occasionally contradictory needs of all these groups in effectively implementing strategy.
3. *Balance between lag and lead indicators of performance.* Lag indicators generally represent past performance. Typical examples might include customer satisfaction or revenue. Although these measures are usually quite

objective and accessible, they normally lack any predictive power. Lead indicators are the performance drivers that lead to the achievement of the lag indicators. They often include the measurement of processes and activities. On-time delivery might represent a leading indicator for the lagging measure of customer satisfaction. While these measures are normally thought to be predictive in nature, the correlations may prove subjective and the data difficult to gather. A Scorecard should include a mix of lead and lag indicators. Lag indicators without leading measures do not communicate how targets will be achieved. Conversely, leading indicators without lag measures may demonstrate short-term improvements but don't show whether these improvements have led to improved results for customers and ultimately shareholders.

SUMMARY

The Balanced Scorecard assists organizations in overcoming two fundamental problems: effectively measuring organizational performance and successfully implementing strategy. Traditionally, the measurement of business has been financial; however, our reliance on financial measures of performance has come under criticism in recent years. Critics suggest that financial measures are not consistent with today's business environment, lack predictive power, reinforce functional silos, may sacrifice long-term thinking, and are not relevant to many levels of the organization. Successfully implementing strategy is another key issue facing the enterprise. Four barriers to strategy implementation exist for most organizations: a vision barrier, a people barrier, a resource barrier, and a management barrier.

The Balanced Scorecard balances the historical accuracy and integrity of financial numbers with the drivers of future success. The framework enforces a discipline around strategy implementation by challenging executives to carefully translate their strategies into objectives, measures, targets, and initiatives in four balanced perspectives: Customer, Internal Processes, Learning and Growth, and Financial. While originally designed in 1990 as a measurement system, the Balanced Scorecard has evolved into a strategic management system and powerful communication tool for those organizations fully utilizing its many capabilities. Linking the Scorecard to key management processes such as budgeting, compensation, and alignment helps overcome the barriers to implementing strategy.

An effective Balanced Scorecard is more than an ad-hoc collection of financial and nonfinancial measures. A well-crafted Balanced Scorecard should tell the story of the organization's strategy through a series of cause-and-effect linkages inherent in the Scorecard measures. The relationships are revealed through a series of "if–then" statements: If we increase customer loyalty, then we expect revenue to increase. Explicitly documenting the assumptions in your strategy through a cause-and-effect network of measures greatly enhances the opportunities for strategic learning at the executive level.

Finally, we stressed the importance of the word *balance* in the Balanced Scorecard. It represents the balance between:

- Financial and nonfinancial indicators
- Internal and external constituents of the organization
- Lag and lead indicators

NOTES

1. Robert S. Kaplan and David P. Norton, "On Balance," *CFO*, February 2001, p. 73–77.
2. Robert A. Howell, James D. Brown, Stephen R. Soucy, and Allen H. Seed, *Management Accounting in the New Manufacturing Environment* (Montvale, NJ: National Association of Accountants, 1987).
3. Bill Jensen, *Simplicity—The New Competitive Advantage* (Cambridge, MA: Perseus Publishing, 2000), 117.
4. Henry Mintzberg, Bruce Ahlstrand, and Joseph Lampel, *Strategy Safari* (New York: The Free Press, 1998).
5. Michael E. Porter, "Strategy and the Internet," *Harvard Business Review*, March 2001: 62–78.
6. R. Charan and G. Colvin, "Why CEOs Fail," *Fortune*, June 21, 1999.
7. S.I. Hayakawa and Alan R. Hayakawa, *Language in Thought and Action* (New York: Harcourt Bruce and Company, 1990), 171.
8. Robert S. Kaplan and David P. Norton, "The Balanced Scorecard—Measures that Drive Performance," *Harvard Business Review*, January–February 1992, 71–79.
9. Robert S. Kaplan and David P. Norton, *The Balanced Scorecard* (Boston: Harvard Business School Press, 1996).
10. P. Senge, *The Fifth Discipline: The Art and Practice of the Learning Organization* (New York: Currency Doubleday, 1990).
11. Timothy J. Galpin, *Making Strategy Work* (San Francisco: Jossey-Bass, 1997).
12. Kaplan and Norton, "The Balanced Scorecard—Measures that Drive Performance."
13. Michael Treacy and Fred Wiersema, *The Discipline of Market Leaders* (Reading, MA: Perseus Books, 1995).
14. Robert S. Kaplan and David P. Norton, "Using the Balanced Scorecard as a Strategic Management System," *Harvard Business Review*, January–February, 1996, 75–85.
15. Peter F. Drucker, *Management Challenges for the 21st Century* (New York: Harper Collins, 1999).

CHAPTER 2

Balanced Scorecard as an Enduring Management Tool

Roadmap for Chapter Two   Right now you may be holding this book, wondering if you should make the investment of the purchase price, and more importantly your valuable time in this concept, the Balanced Scorecard. You tell yourself that you have heard of the Scorecard, it's been around for a good long time, and just maybe its time is up! Could it go the way of other management panaceas that came before it? Well, I'm glad you are reading this because those are good questions to ask, and I would like the opportunity to answer them for you. This chapter will explore several items that contribute to the long-term value and in fact the continued growth of the Balanced Scorecard methodology. You can also share the findings in this chapter with key sponsors within your organization to gain support for the Scorecard initiative.

Value in most organizations is no longer a function of smoothly running physical assets, but rather it depends on the extraction, manipulation, and clever application of knowledge held by employees. The chapter begins with an examination of human capital and discusses the implications for measurement systems. It will show that the Balanced Scorecard is well suited to assist us in measuring the critical intangible assets within our organizations.

Although the Balanced Scorecard was originally designed with the for-profit world in mind, it has been successfully adapted by many public- and not-for-profit-sector institutions. In this section of the chapter we will consider the possibility that the Balanced Scorecard actually provides an even greater opportunity for the management of these organizations to measure what matters in achieving their missions. Whether you work in the public, not-for-profit, or private sector, you will find the discussion of new Balanced Scorecard applications interesting and beneficial.

With the acceptance of the Balanced Scorecard as a key management tool during the 1990s, many adopting organizations began searching for methods to communicate Scorecard results widely to all employees and use the tool as a cornerstone of their management systems. The low-tech solutions of the time were completely unprepared for such tasks. Fortunately, the software industry has answered the call by developing a number of excellent products that allow organizations to capture the full benefit of the Balanced Scorecard system. This section of the chapter looks at the evolution of these products and suggests they may be critical to the ongoing growth of the concept.

This chapter concludes with a short yet important discussion of the results organizations have achieved using the Balanced Scorecard system. The significant and consistent results gained by Scorecard organizations will prove the greatest impetus for the concept's continued growth.

THE RISING PROMINENCE OF HUMAN CAPITAL

What a difference 44 years can make. Writing in the *Harvard Business Review* back in 1957, Harvard Professor Malcolm P. McNair had this to say about organization's paying excess attention to their people: *"Too much emphasis on human relations encourages people to feel sorry for themselves, makes it easier for them to slough off responsibility, to find excuses for failure, to act like children."*[1] Can you imagine the reaction business leaders would have to this quote if it were uttered today? What was your reaction? If you are like most, you would probably completely disagree with McNair's pessimistic view and instead assert the now prevailing notion that an organization's people or its "human capital" represent the critical enabler in the new economy.

Chapter One discussed some of the limitations financial measures possess. Given these limitations and the growth in prominence of human capital, both the business and investment communities are placing ever-increasing emphasis on nonfinancial indicators of performance. Business leaders are now questioning their almost exclusive reliance on financial data and have begun to look at the operational drivers of future financial performance: customer satisfaction and loyalty, continuous innovation, and organizational learning, to name but a few. On the investor side, Wall Street has made it clear that nonfinancial data matters greatly to valuation and is growing in prominence all the time. A 1999 Ernst and Young study found that "even for large cap, mature companies, nonfinancial performance counts."[2] One of the study's findings suggests that, on average, nonfinancial criteria constitute 35 percent of the investor's decision. The researchers also found that "the more nonfinancial measures analysts use, the more accurate are their earnings forecasts."[3] But just what is human capital and why is it important to the future of the Balanced Scorecard?

Before terms like *human capital, intellectual capital,* and *intangible assets* entered the business lexicon, there was another metaphor sweeping across organizations—*the employee as asset.* Annual reports, press releases, and business literature were awash in statements proclaiming the great value companies placed in their human assets. By recognizing the value individuals bring to the firm, this metaphor represented a great improvement over the "employee as a cost object" philosophy that lay at the heart of the downsizing movement of the early 1990s. But consider the definition of an asset from our accounting studies: an object owned or controlled by the firm that produces future value and possesses a monetary value. Do we employees really fit that definition? Another school of thought has gradually developed that likens the employee as more of an investor of human capital than an asset to be controlled by the organization. Thomas Davenport cogently describes this new paradigm: *"People possess innate abilities, behaviors, personal energy and time. These elements make up human capital—the currency people bring to invest in their jobs. Workers, not organizations, own this human capital . . . and decide when, how, and where they will contribute it."*[4] Peter Drucker would label these investors *knowledge workers,* and suggest they hold the key to value creation in the new economy. For the first time in business history, the workers, not the organization, own the means of production—the knowledge and capabilities they possess—and they decide how and where to apply it.

Creating Value in the New Economy

Consulting organizations offer a good example of creating value from intangible rather than physical assets. Consultants don't rely heavily on tangible assets; instead, they provide value for clients by drawing on relationships with subject matter experts throughout the firm and knowledge from past client experiences to provide innovative solutions. Recently, a client I was working with encountered a problem in loading data for their new performance measurement software. Automatic data interfaces for the software (pulling data directly from source systems throughout their locations) would require significant human and financial resources to build and was not considered a viable option. The alternative of manual data entry was also deemed unacceptable as it would prove a time-consuming and non–value-added activity for system administrators. Our team was tasked with finding an innovative and cost-effective solution. We convened a team of experts on various subjects: the Scorecard software program, the Balanced Scorecard methodology, desktop software applications, and client data sources. The newly formed team brainstormed various approaches that would satisfy the criteria of cost efficiency and very limited manual data entry efforts. In the end we determined our best approach was to build a new data entry tool in a spreadsheet package. Data owners would enter their individual data in the spreadsheet and e-mail it to the system administrator, who would then automatically upload the information into the software. The spreadsheets were custom designed to contain only those measures for which each owner was accountable. This solution ensured that both criteria were satisfied. The new system would cost very little to develop and implement and would eliminate manual data entry for system administrators. It was not the physical assets that led to this innovative solution to a client's needs, but instead the skillful combination of an array of knowledge held by the individual team members.

The situation described above is happening in organizations around the globe as we make the transition from an economy based on physical assets to one almost fully dependent on intellectual assets. While this switch is evident to anyone working in today's business world, it is also borne out by research findings of the Brookings Institute. Take a look at Exhibit 2.1, which illustrates the transition in value from tangible to intangible assets. Since this research was completed, the pace of change has continued. Speaking on National Public Radio's *Morning Edition*, Margaret Blair of the Brookings Institute suggests that tangible assets have continued to tumble in value: *"If you just look at the physical assets of the companies, the things that you can measure with ordinary accounting techniques, these things now account for less than one fourth of the value of the corporate sector. Another way of putting this is that something like 75 percent of the sources of value inside corporations is not being measured or reported on their books."*[5] If you happen to be employed in the public sector, you may have noticed Ms. Blair uses the term *corporations* in the above quote.

Exhibit 2.1   The Increasing Value of Intangible Assets in Organizations

1982	1992	Today
		75%
	62%	
38%		

However, your organizations are being affected every bit as much as your corporate counterparts. The challenges represented by this switch are not going unnoticed in Washington. David M. Walker, Comptroller General of the United States, said in his February 2001 testimony to the U.S. senate that *"human capital management is a pervasive challenge in the federal government. At many agencies human capital shortfalls have contributed to serious problems and risks."*[6] In yet another demonstration of the importance of intangible assets, the Sloan School of Management at MIT and consulting firm Arthur Andersen recently announced the joint formation of the New Economy Value Research Lab. The think tank will study and develop quantitative valuations of the intangible assets Wall Street finds increasingly important in the new economy. Lab co-chair Richard Boulton says, *"Even the Coca-Colas and Disneys of the world are actually creating most of their value from assets that don't appear on their Balance Sheets."*[7]

This transition in value creation from physical to intangible assets has major implications for measurement systems. The financial measurements that characterize our Balance Sheet and Income Statement methods of tabulation were perfectly appropriate for a world dominated by physical assets. Transactions affecting property, plant and equipment could be recorded and reflected in an organization's general ledger. However, the new economy with its premium on intangible value–creating mechanisms demands more from our performance measurement systems. Today's system must have the capabilities to identify, describe, monitor, and provide feedback on the intangible assets driving organizational success.

Using the Balanced Scorecard to Measure Value in the New Economy

The value derived from intangibles is very different from that created by purely physical assets. Balanced Scorecard architects Kaplan and Norton have suggested a number of differentiating factors between the two[8]:

- *Intangible assets may not have a direct impact on financial results.* Investments in intangible assets may not in and of themselves lead to improved financial results. Think of an investment in customer service training for employees. It would prove very difficult to directly assess the impact of such training on the organization's operating results. More likely, the investment in customer service training would impact the quality of service being offered to customers that in turn would drive customer loyalty and ultimately financial returns. An investment in the intangible asset of improved employee skills may have a second- or third-order impact on financial success.

- *The value of intangibles is largely potential—it must be transformed.* In the industrial economy we could easily measure the impact of an investment in new machinery. Perhaps a new asset increases production capabilities by 20 percent, allowing the firm to increase order fulfillment and boost profits. Intangible assets present a more challenging case. Technology, employee skills, and empowering cultures must be transformed from the raw yet powerful forces they represent to actual value-creating opportunities.

- *Intangible assets require interdependence for success.* Isolated investments in intangible assets may provide little value to the organization. Instead, these assets must be bundled together to take advantage of their individual strengths. A firm's leadership style, culture, organization, skills, networks, and technology should all be forged together in order to draw the value from each.

When we look at the characteristics of intangible assets shown above, a common theme emerges. In order to extract real value from these assets, they must be transformed and linked together, creating a strong and coherent description of your strategy. How can this goal be best achieved? The last chapter described the importance of cause and effect as possibly the most important feature of a Balanced Scorecard system. The linkages between performance measures in a Balanced Scorecard allow us to offer a hypothesis of how the transformation of intangibles can lead to the fulfillment of our strategy and improved financial results. The Scorecard development process forces us to critically examine our strategy and describe how an investment in employee skills (in the Learning and Growth perspective) will affect business processes, customer issues, and, finally, financial performance. No other performance measurement system places this premium on the translation of strategy into the key value-creating components that will lead to its achievement.

Using the Balanced Scorecard methodology to describe the value of intangible assets is occurring at an increasing rate. Probably the best-known example is that of the Swedish-based organization Skandia. The *Business Navigator* became a supplement to their annual report beginning in 1994. The *Navigator* closely resembles the Balanced Scorecard, but rather than focusing on the traditional four perspectives, it uses five—financial, customer, process, human, and development and renewal. Developed by former Skandia Intellectual Capital Director Leif Edvinsson, the *Navigator* combines the academic Konrad theory (using nonfinancial indicators to monitor and present intangible assets) with the methodology embodied in the Balanced Scorecard. Measuring human capital will be discussed further in Chapter Five when we consider measures for the Employee Learning and Growth perspective of the Balanced Scorecard.

NEW APPLICATIONS ARE DRIVING CONTINUED GROWTH OF THE BALANCED SCORECARD

When the Balanced Scorecard was introduced in 1992, it represented a fairly radical departure from the prominent measurement systems of the time. Supplementing financial measures with the drivers of future financial performance and using a measurement hierarchy to describe an organization's strategy were novel concepts indeed. The first groups to embrace this new idea were for-profit organizations seeking to execute their strategies and ultimately deliver value to shareholders. The Balanced Scorecard provided an ideal tool to this audience. The series of interconnected performance measures on the Balanced Scorecards allowed profit-seeking organizations to effectively monitor the achievement of their strategies.

As the Balanced Scorecard concept gained notoriety and acceptance, both pundits and practitioners alike began to consider the applicability of the concept to other organizational forms. The need certainly existed. The Social Enterprise Program at Harvard University found that executives and board members of nonprofits consistently rated performance measurement as one of their top three management concerns.[9] The public sector was in need of new techniques as well. Passage of the Government Performance and Results Act in 1993 mandated that all federal departments start measuring results, and at the state and local level performance measures may soon be a requirement of the Governmental Accounting Standards Board. So does the Balanced Scorecard apply to these organizations? Scorecard architects Kaplan and Norton believe it does: *"While the focus and application of the Balanced Scorecard has been in the for-profit (private) sector, the opportunity for the Scorecard to improve the management of governmental and not-for-profit enterprises is, if anything, even greater."*[10] This is most likely the case since public-sector and not-for-profit organizations are truly mission driven and should be measured on how effectively and efficiently they serve their constituents. While many such institutions had strategy and mission statements before the Balanced Scorecard arrived, few had performance measurement systems to reveal whether the strategy was succeeding.

Implementing the Balanced Scorecard in public and not-for-profit sectors is not without challenges, however. Even basic issues such as terminology can be skewed toward a for-profit paradigm. Take, for example, the word *customer*. Who is the customer of a government agency? Who is served by a not-for-profit group? While this task is difficult, ultimately the critical examination of words like *customer* and *target* help these organizations determine exactly who it is they are attempting to satisfy and what critical drivers of performance they must excel at in order to do so.

Despite the challenges, a growing number of government and not-for-profit organizations have turned to the Balanced Scorecard and are achieving significant results. By rearranging the architecture of the Balanced Scorecard, they have found a means of articulating their strategies through measurement and gauging their success in achieving overarching objectives. Probably the best-known example of applying the Balanced Scorecard in a government setting is the city of Charlotte, North Carolina. The city uses the Balanced Scorecard system to translate five key strategic themes into performance measures across the four perspectives of the Scorecard. Additionally, the Balanced Scorecard has been cascaded through the organization at the business unit and employee level, and linked to the budgeting process. Mayor Pat McCrory had this to say about Charlotte's efforts: *"The Balanced Scorecard has helped me to communicate a strategic vision for the city to my constituents, the citizens, and to prospective businesses that are considering locating here. It helps the city manager focus on things that will have the biggest impact on the city."*[11] Chapter Thirteen will take a closer look at applying the Balanced Scorecard in the not-for-profit and public sectors: It will explore some of the specific challenges, suggest methods for developing your Balanced Scorecard, and look at other success stories.

THE EVOLUTION OF POWERFUL BALANCED SCORECARD SOFTWARE

In the mid-1990s, I was part of a team developing a Balanced Scorecard at Nova Scotia Power Inc., an investor-owned utility operating in the province of Nova Scotia, Canada. The award-winning Scorecard implementation was deemed a great success—we had built a high-level corporate Scorecard, cascaded it to business units and departments throughout the organization, and made the Scorecard the cornerstone of our management system by linking it to key processes such as budgeting and compensation. In fact, many Nova Scotia Power examples are used throughout this book. Early on in the implementation (after developing a Corporate Scorecard) discussions were held with team members on how this new and powerful strategic information would be reported to the executive team. Unfortunately, our options were quite limited. There were a few vendors offering software solutions, but they were new and unproven. Given these limited options in off-the-shelf Balanced Scorecard software packages, we actually considered developing our own tool with the help of an Information Technology consulting firm. We eventually settled on using a combination of paper reporting and the company's intranet to get results out to the organization.

The situation described above was typical of early Scorecard adopting companies as they struggled to find the right means to transmit this new wealth of strategically packed information to employees at all levels of the organization. Chapter One discussed the power of the Balanced Scorecard as a communication tool. Sharing information from across an entire organization using low-tech solutions is exceedingly difficult. Knowledge sharing and improved decision making result from the manipulation of data presented in the right context to the right people at the right time. While paper reports on spreadsheets represented an option to report Scorecard results to one (usually high) level of the organization, to truly harness the power of the Balanced Scorecard methodology, new robust reporting engines were required.

The lack of powerful reporting tools could have threatened the continued development of the Balanced Scorecard system as organizations struggled to find software solutions to keep pace with the advances made in applying this new methodology. Fortunately for all of us, the software industry has answered our call with a great number of products to fit every Balanced Scorecard implementation. With each succeeding generation of releases the functionality of these products reaches unprecedented heights. Awash in brilliant colors and amazing graphics, these tools not only perform the rather perfunctory task of reporting results, but also provide mechanisms for mapping strategies, displaying complex cause-and-effect linkages, and performing sophisticated "what if" scenario planning.

As organizations around the world continue relying on the Balanced Scorecard to effectively translate their strategic objectives, more and more will look to software providers for the tools they need to maximize the effectiveness of their efforts. In a recent survey conducted by the Balanced Scorecard Collaborative, "*nearly half the respondents stated that they expect to use commercially available Balanced Scorecard applications to report their results.*"[12] Aside from the numerous functional benefits to be derived from employing a software solution for the Balanced Scorecard, people simply seem to respond favorably to seeing their objectives and measures projected on a computer screen in front of them. This not so highly scientific observation results from my experience working with clients of all industries and sizes. In fact, this phenomenon occurs even before the Scorecard is built. As part of any Scorecard implementation effort, we spend a lot of time on education around key Balanced Scorecard concepts. I have given literally hundreds of these presentations and have had ample opportunity to limit my offerings to the truly essential concepts people need. Despite my best efforts, every group will at some point greet my enthusiastic teachings with glazed looks and heavy heads. "It couldn't possibly be me, could it?" I think to myself. But when I show them a mock-up of what their organization's measures might look like in a commercial software application, suddenly the room comes alive! Questions abound and the sense of anticipation becomes palpable as the group quickly sees the potential of this tool in getting their message across.

As is the case with many concepts in our world today, the evolution of the Balanced Scorecard methodology and the accompanying power of technology to enable and escalate those innovations will continue to propel the entire field of performance management forward to new and exciting heights. Chapter Eleven will take a closer look at this topic and help you determine the reporting requirements that are right for your organization.

BALANCED SCORECARD GETS RESULTS!

Nobody wants to invest their physical and emotional energy in a concept that will not stand the test of time. This chapter was written for that purpose, and outlines a number of reasons why the Balanced Scorecard is here to stay. It is very important that I share my evidence with you so that you can make an informed judgment on the future viability of this tool. Hopefully, you found the discussions on human capital, public and not-for-profit Balanced Scorecards, and software tools compelling and helpful in coming to your decision. But I probably could have made the chapter a whole lot shorter if I just told you the Balanced Scorecard gets results, plain and simple!

Since its inception in 1992 the Balanced Scorecard has been implemented in literally thousands of organizations of all types, sizes, and in every region of the planet. While some people naturally gravitate toward any new idea or concept regardless of its actual utility, most will only climb aboard once the idea has been proven and tested as effective. The Balanced Scorecard has done just that. In their latest book, *The Strategy Focused Organization*, authors Kaplan and Norton use part of the first chapter to describe a number of successful Balanced Scorecard organizations. Included are such well-known companies as Mobil, CIGNA, and Chase. Proving the Scorecard applies to smaller organizations or other sectors, they also discuss a Florida-based citrus grower (Southern Gardens Citrus), a university (University of California, San Diego), and a hospital (Duke Children's Hospital), among others.[13] You can find additional evidence of the Balanced Scorecard's acceptance and success by scanning most business periodicals that often contain references to the system and the organizations that are utilizing it to great benefit. If you need some empirical evidence supporting performance management, take a look at Exhibit 2.2. The studies illustrate the power of measurement to transform virtually every aspect of an organization. Measurement drives agreement on strategy and the communication of that strategy, leading to successful change efforts and ultimately improved financial performance. Everything on that chart is significant, but especially impressive is the percentage of measurement-managed organizations achieving success in their last major change effort—97 percent. That finding represents one of the outstanding benefits of the Scorecard system: the creation of a new language that galvanizes an entire organization toward the achievement of overall goals.

One last statistic: In a recent survey conducted by the Institute of Management Accountants, 90 percent of respondents said the Balanced Scorecard was worth implementing in their organization.[14] Are you ready

Exhibit 2.2   Performance Management Gets Results

	Measure of Success	Measurement-Managed Organizations	Non–Measurement-Managed Organizations
Performance	Industry leader over the past three years	74%	44%
	Reported to be financially ranked in the top third of their industry	83%	52%
	Success in last major change effort	97%	55%

	Measure of Success	Measurement-Managed Organizations	Non–Measurement-Managed Organizations
Culture	Agreement on strategy	93%	37%
	Communication of strategy	60%	8%
	Information shared openly and candidly	71%	30%

Adapted from John H. Ingle and William Schiemann, "Is Measurement Worth It?" *Management Review*, March 1996; and Morgan and William Schiemann, "Measuring People & Performance: Closing the Gap," *Quality Progress*, January 1999.

to take the Balanced Scorecard journey? These first two chapters have laid the groundwork for your trip by exploring the origins of the Balanced Scorecard, examining the model itself, and discussing why it will prove to be an enduring management tool. Now it is time to begin the work of developing a Balanced Scorecard for your organization.

SUMMARY

Current research suggests that approximately 75 percent of an organization's value is derived from intangible assets. These assets are different from our traditional view: They may not have a direct impact on financial results, they represent largely potential value, and they require interdependence. This transition in value creation from physical to intangible assets has major implications for measurement systems. The Balanced Scorecard with its focus on cause-and-effect linkages woven together to tell the story of the organization's strategy provides an ideal means for capturing and transforming the value of intangible assets.

Originally conceived with for-profit organizations in mind, the Balanced Scorecard has been successfully adapted by many public- and not-for-profit-sector institutions. In this context, the measures on a Balanced Scorecard should link together to drive the organization's mission. This differs from the for-profit model in which all measures ultimately lead to improved financial performance.

To capture the power of the Balanced Scorecard as a management system, organizations often require more than low-tech, paper-based solutions. The software industry has developed many Balanced Scorecard applications that support not only reporting but allow for sophisticated analysis, strategy mapping, and information sharing. Recent estimates suggest nearly half of all Scorecard-implementing organizations will pursue a commercially available software solution to support their efforts.

The Balanced Scorecard has been successfully implemented as a management tool in thousands of organizations. In a recent study by the Cost Management Group, the vast number of respondents believed it was worth implementing the Balanced Scorecard in their organization. The consistent and sustainable results achieved by organizations using the Balanced Scorecard serve as the best indicator of the concept's future growth and development.

NOTES

1. Malcolm P. McNair, "What Price Human Relations?" in "What Goes Around." *Harvard Business Review*, February 2001, 160.
2. Ernst & Young Center for Business Innovation, *Measures that Matter*, 1999.
3. Ibid., p. 13.
4. Thomas O. Davenport, *Human Capital* (San Francisco: Jossey-Bass, 1999), 7.
5. Interview on National Public Radio's *Morning Edition*, October 27, 2000.
6. Testimony by David M. Walker, Comptroller General of the United States before the Subcommittee on Oversight of Government, Management, Restructuring, and the District of Columbia Committee on Governmental Affairs, U.S. Senate, February 2001.
7. See "A Fact Factory for the New Economy," *Business Week*, February 7, 2000, 6.
8. Based on research presented by David P. Norton at the Balanced Scorecard North American Summit, New Orleans, LA, September 27, 2000.
9. Robert S. Kaplan, "Strategic Performance Measurement in Nonprofit Organizations," *Nonprofit Management & Leadership*, Spring 2001.
10. Robert S. Kaplan and David P. Norton, *The Balanced Scorecard* (Boston: Harvard Business School Press, 1996).
11. Pamela A. Syfert and Lisa B. Schumacher, "Putting Strategy First in Performance Management," *Journal of Cost Management*, November/December 2000, 32–38.
12. Laura Downing, "Progress Report on the Balanced Scorecard: A Global Users Survey," *Balanced Scorecard Report*, November–December 2000, 7–9.
13. Robert S. Kaplan and David P. Norton, *The Strategy Focused Organization* (Boston: Harvard Business School Press, 2001).
14. Mark Frigo, "2001 CMG Survey on Performance Measurement, Trends and Challenges in Performance Measurement," *Cost Management Update*, March 2001, 1–4.

PART TWO

Step-by-Step Development of the Balanced Scorecard

CHAPTER 3

Getting Started

Roadmap for Chapter Three   Victor Hugo once said, *"He who every morning plans the transaction of the day and follows out that plan, carries a thread that will guide him through the maze of the most busy life. But where no plan is laid, where the disposal of time is surrendered merely to the chance of incidence, chaos will soon reign."* If that's a little too long for you to commit to memory, try this one which was posted on the wall of a former colleague of mine, *"Plan your work, work your plan, your plan will work."* The point is that before we can develop and implement a Balanced Scorecard, we have to diligently plan the campaign ahead. There are a number of elements of this project that must be considered long before any metrics can be debated. This chapter will take a careful look at each of the building blocks of a successful Balanced Scorecard project. Specifically, we will explore the following: developing objectives for your Balanced Scorecard project, determining where to begin your efforts, the importance of executive sponsorship and how to secure it, building an effective team to carry out the work ahead, constructing a development plan for the Scorecard, and, finally, strategies for communicating the Balanced Scorecard project. Key pitfalls to avoid and strategies for your success will be provided to ensure that your project gets off to a great start.

PUT THE BIG ROCKS IN FIRST—DEVELOP CLEAR OBJECTIVES

I enjoy reading the work of Steven Covey. His writings have had a strong influence on my consulting work and my personal mission. In *First Things First,* Covey and his co-authors describe the concept of putting the big rocks in first. This is a method of determining the key priorities in your life and

ensuring that you address them before moving on to other pressing areas.[1]
When you begin your Balanced Scorecard implementation, you have to do
just that—put the big rocks in first. Consider this chapter your quarry for
the Balanced Scorecard. Perhaps the biggest rock is the one that outlines
your rationale for developing a Balanced Scorecard within your organization. Did your reason for building a Scorecard go something like this: You
read about the concept, saw it applied in other organizations you're familiar with, and felt the balance of financial and nonfinancial measurement
represents good business sense. Although this is certainly true, it is not a
sufficient reason alone for implementing a Balanced Scorecard.

On its own, even the most well-constructed Balanced Scorecard will not
instantly transform your organization. For positive change to occur the
Scorecard must be embedded in your management systems, becoming the
cornerstone for management analysis, support, and decision making. You'll
need to determine exactly why you are embarking on the Scorecard journey in order to ensure the Scorecard's transition from a measurement tool
to a management system. Exhibit 3.1 outlines a number of possible reasons
for launching a Balanced Scorecard effort. While this list provides valuable
information, it should not be seen as a shopping center for Scorecard objectives. Your organization should determine the precise motivation for
launching this tool based on your particular circumstances.

For the Scorecard to succeed it cannot be viewed as a one-time "now we
have a Balanced Scorecard" event. Determining your objectives in developing the Balanced Scorecard will go a long way in securing the evolution of
the tool in your organization. Conversely, the lack of a clear objective for
your Scorecard program may ultimately limit ifs effectiveness. For example,
some organizations may turn to the Balanced Scorecard in a time of great
crisis when an immediate turnaround is necessary for survival. A few key
objectives and measures on the Scorecard may provide a laser-like focus
during that battle, but how will the Scorecard survive once the organization
is out of life-threatening peril? When you have a well-understood, agreed-
upon, and widely communicated rationale for the project, you possess a
valuable tool in expanding the role of the Balanced Scorecard. Management and employees alike will view the development of measures in a Balanced Scorecard framework as the first of many stops on the road to a new
and powerful management system for the organization. The consensus
achieved from an overarching objective for the Balanced Scorecard greatly
assists your communication efforts as you focus and educate all employees
on the goals of the implementation. During the inevitable periods when
your Scorecard implementation experiences difficulty sustaining momentum, the focal point of your guiding objective can serve as a rallying cry to
reenergize and refocus the efforts of your team. Finally, the presence of
clear objectives will also be an invaluable tool in guiding the future work of

Exhibit 3.1   Rationale for the Balanced Scorecard

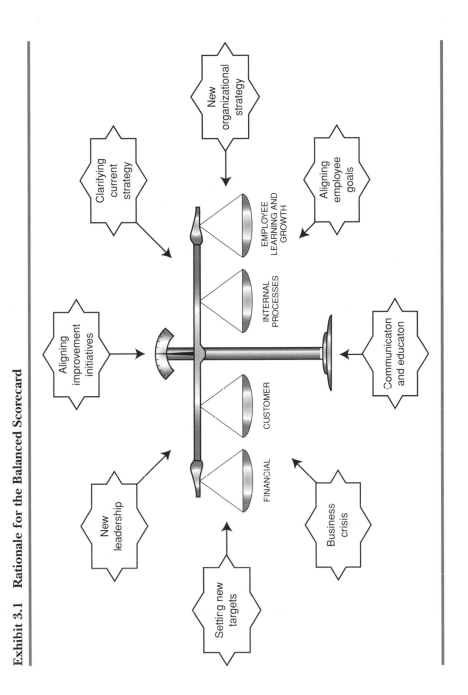

linking your Balanced Scorecard to management processes such as budgeting, compensation, and management reporting.

WHERE DO WE BUILD THE BALANCED SCORECARD?

Scorecard architects Kaplan and Norton have described the Balanced Scorecard as simple but not simplistic. This is the first of several times that reference will be used as we develop your Balanced Scorecard. Although the concept itself is relatively straightforward—balancing financial and nonfinancial measures to drive strategy—the execution of those tasks will involve many difficult deliberations on a wide variety of topics. We just described one such issue when we examined the objectives for developing a Balanced Scorecard. This section will explore another important subject requiring careful consideration: the choice of an appropriate unit in which to develop your first Balanced Scorecard.

Depending on the size of your organization you may be faced with a number of potential alternatives. If you work with a large organization, you could choose to begin your Scorecard at the top by developing a high-level corporate set of measures. Starting at the business unit or even shared service unit level (groups like human resources, information technology, etc.) would also represent possible options. Smaller organizations may have fewer choices but still must make the best decision in order to ensure success of the Balanced Scorecard program. Many organizations believe starting at the top represents the most logical choice, and frequently this is in fact the case. A Corporate Balanced Scorecard provides the means of communicating strategic objectives and measures across the entire organization. The focus and attention derived from these high-level metrics can serve to bring together disparate elements of the organization toward a common goal of implementing the strategy. The measures on the Corporate Scorecard then become the raw materials for cascaded Scorecards at all levels of the firm, producing a series of aligned measurement systems that allow all organizational participants to demonstrate how their day-to-day actions contribute to long-term goals.

Criteria for Choosing an Appropriate Organizational Unit

Before jumping to the conclusion that a Balanced Scorecard at the highest level is the best choice for you, we should consider a number of criteria for making this important decision. Several elements contribute to the selection of an appropriate organizational unit for your first Balanced Scorecard. Those criteria are shown in Exhibit 3.2. Let's consider each of these criteria in turn and then discuss a method for using them to make this important decision.

Exhibit 3.2   Seven Criteria for Choosing Where to Begin Your Balanced Scorecard

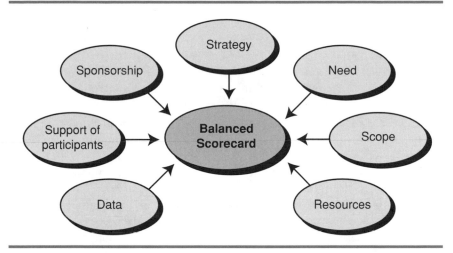

- *Strategy.* The single most important criteria in making your selection is whether the unit under consideration possesses a coherent strategy. After all, the Balanced Scorecard is a methodology designed to assist you in translating your strategy into objectives and measures that will allow you to gauge your effectiveness in delivering on that strategy. Without a strategic stake in the ground you're very likely to end up with an ad-hoc collection of financial and nonfinancial measures that do not link together to tell the story of your strategy. Without this linkage of cause-and-effect relationships articulated to describe your strategy, it will be difficult to determine whether improvements in one area of the Scorecard are producing the desired effects on other key indicators. In fact, detrimental effects may occur as you pursue a series of conflicting initiatives not linked to a clear strategy. Having said this, the lack of a clearly defined strategy certainly doesn't preclude you from building a Balanced Scorecard. It does mean you will construct a different *type* of Scorecard, one most likely focused on either key performance indicators or critical stakeholders. The importance of strategy to the Balanced Scorecard is examined in greater depth in Chapter Four.

- *Sponsorship.* The next section of this chapter will take a close look at the vital necessity of executive sponsorship for your Balanced Scorecard effort. For the purposes of this discussion, suffice it to say that if your leader is not aligned with the goals and objectives of the Balanced Scorecard and does not believe in the merits of the tool, your efforts will be severely compromised. An executive sponsor must provide leadership for the program in both words and deeds.

- *Need for a Balanced Scorecard.* The importance of clear objectives for the Balanced Scorecard program was discussed in the first section of this chapter. Based on that review, does the unit you're considering have an overarching goal or objective for their implementation? Is there a clear need for a revamping of their performance measurement system? In an excellent 1995 article, Vitale and Mavrinac outlined seven warning signs that could indicate a new system is needed.[2] Their signals for pending measurement change are outlined in Exhibit 3.3. Does the organizational unit you're considering display any of these signs?

- *Support of key managers and supervisors.* There is no doubt that executive support is critical for a Balanced Scorecard implementation to succeed. However, while executives may use Scorecard information to make strategic decisions, we also depend heavily on managers and first-line supervisors using the tool in their jobs as well. When the Scorecard is driven down to all levels through a process of cascading, the alignment and focus derived across the organization can lead to real breakthroughs in performance. Managers and supervisors make this happen with their understanding, acceptance, support of, and usage of the Balanced

Exhibit 3.3   Signs That You May Need a New Performance Measurement System

Time for a new performance measurement system?

Performance is acceptable on all dimensions except profit: A focus on quality and other measures has led to improvements in isolated areas, but not profits.

Customers don't buy even when prices are competitive: The problem may lie in your relative performance to competitors.

No one notices when performance measurement reports aren't produced: Data in the reports no longer contains meaningful information for decision makers.

Managers spend significant time debating the meaning of the measures: Measures must be clearly linked to strategic objectives.

Share price is lethargic despite solid financial performance: Wall Street needs to learn that you're investing in long-term value-creating activities.

You haven't changed your measures in a long time: Performance measures should be dynamic based on the organization's strategic direction.

You've recently changed your corporate strategy: All measures should link back to your strategy.

Adapted from Michael R. Vitale and Sarah C. Mavrinac, "How Effective Is Your Performance Measurement System?," *Management Accounting,* August 1995.

Scorecard. Not all members of these groups will demonstrate such a willingness to participate, however. While open criticism of new senior management initiatives is fairly rare, these managers and supervisors will often remain silent or demonstrate only mild enthusiasm, which workers quickly interpret as a questionable show of support for the program.[3] When choosing your organizational unit for the Balanced Scorecard, make an honest evaluation of the management team and supervisors you will be relying on for participation and support.

- *Organizational scope.* The unit you choose should operate a set of activities across the typical value chain of an organization. In other words, they should have a strategy, defined customers, specific processes, operations, and administration. Selecting a unit with a narrow, functional focus will produce a Scorecard with narrow, functionally focused metrics.

- *Data.* This criterion encompasses two elements. First, does this unit support a culture of measurement (i.e., would they be amenable to managing by a balanced set of performance measures)? While every group within a modern organization should rely on performance measures, for your first attempt you may wish to choose a unit with a history of reliance on performance measures. Second, will the unit be able to supply data for the chosen performance measures? This may be difficult to assess initially since at least some of the measures on your Balanced Scorecard may be new, with data sources as yet unidentified. However, if the unit has difficulty gathering data for current performance measures, they may be reluctant or unable to source the data you will ultimately require for your Balanced Scorecard.

- *Resources.* You can't build this new management system on your own. The best Balanced Scorecards are produced from a team of individuals committed to a common goal of excellence (see "Forming Your Team"). Ensure the unit you choose is willing and able to supply ample resources for the implementation. If your experience is like many that I have had, you will find people's time is something they vigorously defend, and rightly so.

Exhibit 3.4 is a sample worksheet you can use to determine the right organizational unit for your initial Balanced Scorecard effort. In this example, business unit "A" is being considered for a Scorecard implementation. Plotted along the left-hand side of the table are the seven criteria discussed above. In the next column, a score of out of ten is assigned for this unit against each of the criteria. The third column represents weights for each of the seven dimensions based on my judgment and experience. You may feel more comfortable assigning equal weights to each of the seven items, but clearly some areas, such as sponsorship and strategy, are imperative to success and should be weighted accordingly. The fourth column con-

Exhibit 3.4 A Sample Worksheet for Choosing Your Organizational Unit

Balanced Scorecard Project
Organizational Unit Assessment
Business Unit "A"

Criteria	Score (Out of 10)	Weight	Total Points	Rationale
Strategy	10	30%	3	This unit has recently completed a new strategic plan for the next five years.
Sponsorship	9	30%	2.7	New unit president has successfully utilized the Balanced Scorecard with two other organizations before joining us.
Need	5	15%	0.75	Results for this group have been excellent, and they may not see the need for this tool to sustain future efforts.
Support of Participants	7	10%	0.7	Young, energetic management group willing to experiment with new approaches.
Scope	8	5%	0.4	This unit produces, markets, and sells a distinct group of products.
Data	4	5%	0.2	Despite their success they have not utilized sophisticated performance measurement systems in the past.
Resources	4	5%	0.2	Unit is understaffed and will have difficulty finding resources for this project.
Total		100%	7.95	

Overall Assessment This unit scores a very high 7.95 out of 10 and is an excellent candidate for the Balanced Scorecard. The data and resource issues, while not insignificant, are mitigated by the strong leadership of the unit president, and the creation of a new strategic plan. Early education initiatives within this unit could focus on the value of the Scorecard as a means of sustaining results for the long term. This may reduce skepticism surrounding the implementation based on the past success of the unit.

tains the score for the unit within each criteria. Under "strategy" they were assigned a score of 10, which when multiplied by the weight for that category yields 3 total points. In the final column a rationale for the scores assigned is provided based on an assessment of the unit in the context of that specific criteria. It is important to document your decision-making process in order to validate it with others responsible for choosing the Balanced Scorecard organizational unit. Finally, a total score is calculated and an overall assessment provided. The overall assessment provides worksheet participants with the opportunity to discuss potential strengths and weaknesses of the unit, mitigate significant risks, and offer opinions on the viability of this group for the Balanced Scorecard project.

EXECUTIVE SPONSORSHIP—A CRITICAL ELEMENT OF ANY BALANCED SCORECARD PROGRAM

As a consultant and Scorecard practitioner I have had the opportunity to speak at and attend many performance management conferences. Some of the events focused on manufacturing organizations, some on the public sector, others on utilities, and many simply examined the topic of performance management in all industries. Speakers at these gatherings will proudly represent their companies' achievements in performance management, espousing their best practices and sharing lessons learned along the way. One common theme that runs through the presentation of every single successful implementing organization is the importance of executive sponsorship for their program. Presenter after presenter will tout the vital nature of a senior executive willing to give of his or her time and commitment to this endeavor. Kaplan and Norton believe senior management commitment is necessary for a number of reasons[4]:

- *Understanding of strategy.* Most middle managers lack an in-depth knowledge of the organization's strategy. Only the senior management team is able to effectively articulate an ongoing strategy.

- *Decision rights.* Strategy involves trade-offs between alternative courses of action, determining which opportunities to pursue, and more importantly, which not to pursue. Middle management does not possess the decision-making power to determine strategic priorities such as customer value propositions and related operating processes that are critical to the development of any Balanced Scorecard.

- *Commitment.* While knowledge of the enterprise's strategy is necessary, the emotional commitment of executives to the Scorecard program is the true differentiating feature of successful programs. Kaplan and Norton summarize this well: *"More important is the time spent in actual meetings where the senior executives debate and argue among themselves . . . . These meetings build an emotional commitment to the strategy, to the scorecard as a communications device, and to the management processes that build a Strategy-Focused Organization."*

In today's business environment where some chief executive officers (CEOs) have achieved icon-like stature and rock star fame, employees are watching more closely than ever for their leaders to signal what really matters in the organization. If senior management provides only shallow and casual support for the Balanced Scorecard, this demonstration will be rapidly translated by all employees as a sign the project probably is not worth their time and effort. Employees *"watch what the boss watches"*[5] and know what projects are likely to merit their attention. One organization I know of suffered as a result of missing senior management support. The project team stressed the importance of an executive sponsor at the outset of the project, but despite this important admonition they forged ahead without any single member of the senior team stepping forward to lead the implementation. They have since developed Scorecards throughout the organization and invested heavily in a software solution, but managers and employees alike now seem hesitant to use the tool without guidance on the ultimate purpose of the program being divulged from senior management. The implementation may eventually prove to be a great success, but if solid executive support had been present at the outset, they would already have been claiming victory.

Securing Executive Sponsorship

As seen in the preceding paragraphs, senior management support and leadership is a "must have" ingredient for a successful Balanced Scorecard program. Some organizations are very fortunate to have the Balanced Scorecard initiative result directly from executive intervention. Scripps Health of San Diego, California, is one such organization. Dr. Henry Johnson, Vice President, Clinical Measurement and Outcomes, traces the evolution of the Balanced Scorecard at Scripps to a meeting with new CEO Dr. Stan Pappelbaum in January 1998. *"Dr. Pappelbaum said he'd read about the Balanced Scorecard and it was something we needed to do."* Unfortunately, gaining the buy-in and support of senior leaders is not always this easy. Executives at the upper most ranks in the organization have myriad demands on their time and attention and like the rest of us they quickly filter out those ideas seemingly not worthy of their valuable resources. Clever people use many techniques to win the support of a senior manager for the Balanced Scorecard. Some of the most convincing methods include:

- *Look for a good fit.* If your senior management team is one that focuses almost exclusively on financial control systems to run your business, then the Balanced Scorecard probably will not offer natural appeal to them. You need to find senior executives who believe in the value, and indeed necessity, of balanced performance measurement and management. Senior managers who have gone through a strategic planning process designed to help them focus their efforts and define their objectives will also be more amenable to the Balanced Scorecard approach. Find the senior manager who fits this profile and make his or her door the first stop on your sponsorship tour.

- *Demonstrate results.* Senior leaders are charged primarily with achieving results for the organization. Appeal to this tenet of leadership life by outlining the many successes of other organizations pursuing a Balanced Scorecard approach. Success stories of Balanced Scorecard implementations abound in the business literature and at conference venues around the world. Testimonials from other senior executives are also very convincing, like this one: *"We've found the concept of the Balanced Scorecard incredibly useful, both as a framework for deciding which things we are really going to try and achieve, and as a way of showing people where we are going."*[6] Finally, the chances are pretty good that at least one of your competitors will be using the methodology, and perhaps even another geographic unit within your own organization. Document their success with the Balanced Scorecard and convince your leaders you can achieve even better results using this tool.

- *"Survey Says".* We all want to feel needed, and you can make your senior management feel very needed in the Balanced Scorecard by sharing a couple of key statistics on the implementations of other organizations. A Best Practices, LLC, study found that half of benchmark participants' CEOs took part in the process, and senior vice presidents and vice presidents participated 80 percent of the time.[7] In a study conducted for the Balanced Scorecard Report, respondents reported that CEOs, more than any other individual, were the sponsors of the Balanced Scorecard. Thirty-one percent of the organizations stated the CEO was their sponsor.[8]

- *Is danger lurking?* Take the proactive step of assessing your organization against the seven warning signs of performance measurement problems presented earlier in the chapter. Convincing evidence of issues in several of the categories should catch an effective executive's attention.

- *Educate.* To support any cause or idea, we must first accept it as meaningful or valuable. Meaning and value are derived from a comprehensive understanding of the subject. Senior managers follow the same constructs on their road to acceptance of new change initiatives. What this means to you is that you must provide your executive team with a well-designed and delivered presentation on performance management and the Balanced Scorecard if you hope to win their support. Let's discuss how this event might unfold. Prior to the session, you should consider distributing Balanced Scorecard literature to your executive team. Copies of books like this (couldn't resist a little plug), or good articles on the subject will help your audience prepare for the presentation to come. Hold the session itself if possible at an offsite location. Keeping distractions to a minimum will prove beneficial for all involved. To have an administrative assistant knock on the door and shuttle an engaged executive out of the room at a pivotal moment can be disastrous to your momentum. Consider using an outside consultant to deliver the actual material or at least participate in the event. There are a number of reasons for this. First, a well-trained consultant will have delivered countless presentations of this nature and use time-tested material. Second, and unfortunately, many times an outside voice will carry more weight with, and be assumed to have more credibility by, executives than will an internal one. This is a sad but true reality of modern organizational life. Finally, and perhaps most importantly, you are holding this event because you want to win the support of your executive team. An experienced consultant will have faced similar crowds many times and be well prepared to answer all queries and objections raised by the audience. Cogent and articulate responses here can translate to real support down the road. The actual agenda should include a two- to three-hour event structured as follows: 30 minutes on your organization and why a change is necessary (to keep pace with competitive forces, forge ahead, etc.), and 90 minutes on performance management and the Balanced Scorecard. Topics covered should include background information on the topic, a detailed review of the methodology, and case studies and success stories. Spend the final 30 to 60 minutes answering questions and soliciting support for the implementation. One final thing: Don't forget to feed them. I say that only half jokingly. If your culture is one in which food is present at all meetings, don't leave those sandwiches and cookies out of this session!

Securing senior management support for your implementation is difficult work, but the rewards are well worth the effort. At Nova Scotia Power the Balanced Scorecard was very fortunate to have the full and enthusiastic support of both CEO David Mann and chief financial officer (CFO) Jay Forbes. During the implementation virtually every memo originating from the CEO's office would begin with a sentence reading, "As you know the Balanced Scorecard is a key tool in the implementation of our strategic plan." These powerful and compelling words were backed up with consistent actions, such as discussing Scorecard progress at all management meetings and linking the tool to management processes throughout the organization. "Walking the talk" in this way was seen by employees as a true commitment to the Balanced Scorecard and provided the impetus for all groups within Nova Scotia Power to understand, accept, and begin using this powerful new tool.

Professor and consultant Rosabeth Moss Kanter has said that *"the most important things a leader can bring to a changing organization are passion, conviction, and confidence in others."*[9] As we know, the Balanced Scorecard is a change project and as such it needs the support and commitment of senior management as much as, if not more than, any other change initiative.

YOUR BALANCED SCORECARD TEAM

Throughout much of the twentieth century, a strongly held myth existed in the organizational world—that of a great man or woman working feverishly with tremendous dedication to solve any and all problems that stood between him or her and the organization's success. As with many things this myth lagged the reality of actual organizational life. How often during our life have we heard phrases like "two heads are better than one" or "none of us is as smart as all of us"? These words remind us of the power of groups to effectively accomplish tasks through the variety of skills and experiences represented by a collection of individuals. In reality, groups have been coming together to solve complex problems for centuries. For example, Michelangelo worked with a group of sixteen to paint the Sistine Chapel—truly a complex situation! Perhaps the complex, competitive, change-demanding world of today's organization is exposing the vulnerability of the "Lone Ranger" myth. Increasingly, organizations are developing self-directed work teams to solve the problems they face, and many compelling reasons support this movement. Teams strengthen the performance capability of individuals, hierarchies, and management processes. They are practical—most people and organizations can make teams work. Finally, teams get results. Your Balanced Scorecard implementation is well suited to a team approach. No single individual within your organization, including the CEO, will possess all of the necessary knowledge of strategy, markets, competitors, processes, and competencies to build a coherent Balanced Scorecard.

What Is a "Team"

Team is one of the many words in the modern business lexicon that can mean different things to different people. "It was a great team effort." "We have a real team in the finance department." Does the word *team* best represent the short-term efforts of a group of individuals tasked with achieving a specific project, or does it describe the long-term efforts of a group of people working together on common tasks?

In their book *The Wisdom of Teams*, Katzenbach and Smith offer this useful definition: *"A team is a small number of people with complementary skills who are committed to a common purpose, performance goals, and approach for which they hold themselves mutually accountable.*"[10] Let's examine this definition in the context of the Balanced Scorecard, beginning with the term *small number*. What exactly is a small number? The literature on teams often suggests that teams can range in size from 3 to 30. Studies of Balanced Scorecard implementations have demonstrated that a majority of organizations use 10 or more people in the Scorecard building process.[11] The key in choosing the appropriate number of people for your team lies in representing all the areas of your organization that you expect to be using the Scorecard. For example, if you're creating a high-level Corporate Balanced Scorecard, you should strive for representation from each of your business units. If your Scorecard effort is beginning at the business unit level, then key functional areas within the unit should have a presence on the team. Remember our earlier admonition—no one person has all the knowledge of strategy, markets, competition, and competencies to build an effective Scorecard. The knowledge you need to build an effective Balanced Scorecard resides in the minds of your colleagues spanning the entire organization. Additionally, by involving a number of people in the process, you increase the likelihood they will act as ambassadors of the Scorecard within their unit, thereby increasing knowledge and enthusiasm for the tool. So, a group effort is the clear choice for building your Balanced Scorecard, but if at all possible, you should attempt to keep your team capped at seven people or fewer. Anything larger will present logistical, facilitation, and consensus-building challenges.

Your team must contain a mix of *complementary skills*. In addition to different functional or business responsibilities, the complementary skills should encompass varied approaches to problem solving and decision making. It is also beneficial to have a mix of interpersonal skills on the team. Great teams thrive on a balance of personalities and skill sets. You are looking for people who are passionate about the cause at hand and are willing to vigorously defend their positions. This will sometimes lead to what a former colleague of mine calls *creative abrasion*, the very positive situation created when committed people seek to produce breakthrough results via the passionate and sometimes heated exchange of ideas and visions.

Teams come together when they are *committed to a common purpose and performance goals*. The purpose and goals represent more than a summation of the job descriptions of the individual members. They represent the creation of something new and powerful within the organization—in this case a Balanced Scorecard management system. To achieve that goal, all team members must put forth roughly equivalent contributions.

Successful teams work together using a *common approach*. This represents an important point in developing a Balanced Scorecard. To craft an effective Scorecard, all team members must be utilizing the same basic approach in their work. Imagine the outcome of your Scorecard effort if one of your team members were to suggest only financial measures based on her accounting background, while another suggested dozens of measures since that was the culture of her former employer. As previously discussed, differences of opinion and skills are healthy to team functioning; however, all members must commit to using a common approach of translating strategy into performance measures. That must be your guiding principle in building the Scorecard.

Commitment and trust in the team environment are fostered through *mutual accountability*. Business unit and functional representatives must place the Balanced Scorecard first on their priorities, not simply a campaign to advance their own cause. All members must be mutually committed and hold each other accountable for producing a Scorecard that truly does tell the story of the organization's strategy. If your Balanced Scorecard team shares a common approach and common purpose, then holding each other mutually accountable for results should be a natural occurrence.

Team Members—Roles and Responsibilities

In an ideal world your organization's executive team would take full responsibility for developing the Balanced Scorecard, investing the time and energy necessary to produce a product to guide the entire organization. If you are fortunate enough to enjoy this rare situation, you are to be congratulated—your Scorecard effort has a great head start. However, a more likely scenario is one in which you have the support of one or maybe two executives (perhaps you are a senior executive yourself) but you require other members of your organization to step up and assist in the effort of crafting your Balanced Scorecard. Don't despair, you can develop an effective Balanced Scorecard without your entire executive team working exclusively on the project. What you *do* need is at least one influential member of senior management working with the project team and liaising closely with the other executives. This individual must be well respected, possess in-depth knowledge of strategy, be considered a credible change agent, and ideally have the ear of the CEO. The other members of the team, while perhaps not executives themselves, must be "top lieutenants" of the business unit or functional areas they represent. In the boardroom you will need the full support of the entire executive group. Your teammates must win this support from their own executives by sharing information from the development process and "talking up" the power of the Balanced Scorecard within their own area. Between these representatives and the team's executive sponsor, your senior management team should always be up to date on what is occurring with the Balanced Scorecard project.

Let's look specifically at typical roles and responsibilities that should be present on your Balanced Scorecard team. As you probably surmised, a critical member of your team is the *executive sponsor*. This person will take own-ership of the Balanced Scorecard and, based on interactions with the se-nior executive team, will provide the necessary background on strategy and methodology to guide the team's work. A critical responsibility is maintain-ing constant communication with the senior management group, ensuring their ongoing commitment and support of the project. The sponsor must also take the responsibility of providing resources for the project and influ-encing other executives to do the same. The team will require both human and financial resources and will most likely face competition from other initiatives equally pressed for resources. Here the executive sponsor must possess the ability to clearly demonstrate the strategic significance of the Balanced Scorecard and why it warrants the allocation of scarce and valu-able resources. Finally, and most importantly, the sponsor must exhibit com-plete and enthusiastic support for the Balanced Scorecard in words and deeds. During the implementation phase your entire organization will take cues from the sponsor—does the sponsor appear legitimately committed to using this tool, are his or her words consistent with actions and policies they support? Obviously, the executive sponsor will have other duties calling out (maybe screaming, depending on the organization) during the process, but they must commit to regular attendance at team meetings to be seen as a truly committed and credible sponsor.

Building a Balanced Scorecard management system presents many chal-lenges. In this next role, your *Balanced Scorecard champion* or *team leader* has to face all the inevitable challenges and provide solutions that keep the team moving forward. The champion guides the process both logistically and philosophically by scheduling meetings, tracking progress, providing rel-evant background materials to team members, and offering subject matter expertise on the Scorecard concept. This individual should provide the thought leadership on Balanced Scorecard and performance management concepts that ensure the team is taking advantage of proven methodolo-gies and best practices. A potentially difficult aspect of this role is balancing the analytical requirements of Scorecard development with the interper-sonal skills of team building and conflict resolution. Team members look to the champion to provide both emotional and cognitive support, making the role all the more challenging. Given the demands, the champion must be a skilled communicator, able to liaise easily and comfortably with both executives and front line employees alike. Your champion should provide full-time support to the project and, as discussed in Chapter Twelve, should be in a position to support the Scorecard's development and linkage to management processes on an ongoing basis.

In many ways your sponsor and champion lay the groundwork for the Balanced Scorecard by providing background, context, and concept knowl-edge. The ultimate responsibility of translating those raw materials into an actual Scorecard falls on the shoulders of your core *team members*. This group will bring esoteric knowledge of their business unit or functional department to the table and provide critical input on Scorecard measures that apply to their areas. As stated earlier, they must also have the ability and opportunity to influence the executive to whom they report. Team members bring challenging issues and questions to their leaders, and also attempt to detect and deter any personal agendas that may be advanced to the detriment of the overall Scorecard effort. They balance the precarious issues of representing the best interests of their home area with the overall goal of creating an organization- or unit-wide Balanced Scorecard. As with all project participants, they must act as willing ambassadors of the Balanced Scorecard. During the implementation phase of the project, expect your team members to devote at least 50 percent of their time to this effort. Any potential team member who can offer only 10 to 20 percent of their time must be viewed with caution. Although they may carry valuable knowledge of their particular area, this must be weighed against the very negative lack of participation in the effort. Finally, to maximize the performance of team members, the team should share a geographic location. Commitment to the team increases with having team members work in the same geographic place.[12] Teams that work "shoulder to shoulder" form stronger relationships both professionally and personally, and these bonds tend to strengthen the team's work products.

The Balanced Scorecard represents a major departure in performance management for many organizations. Strategy, not financial controls, dictates the firm's direction, and the Scorecard creates a powerful new language for employee change. However, like any transformation, this one has its share of roadblocks. The inclusion of an *organizational change expert* on the Scorecard team can mitigate many of the change-related issues that arise during the implementation. Any major change initiative will bring to the surface a number of concerns from those affected. For example, how will this change affect my routines and processes? What does the organization expect from me as a result of this change? Is this change even necessary? Your organizational change resource can work with your team and projected users of the Balanced Scorecard to investigate the root causes of any concerns and design solutions to reduce, and hopefully eliminate, any potentially serious threats to the Scorecard's success. The role is very important but not required as a full-time resource to the team. Draw the change expert in at regular intervals to review progress and issues. Pay close attention to this topic during your own implementation. You may feel it is "soft stuff," but it is not the technology or the methodology that can cause these initiatives to fail—it is the people every time!

Exhibit 3.5 summarizes the roles and responsibilities of your Balanced Scorecard team.

Exhibit 3.5   Balanced Scorecard Team Roles and Responsibilities

Role	*Responsibilities*
Executive sponsor	• Assumes ownership for the Balanced Scorecard project • Provides background information to the team on strategy and methodology • Maintains communication with senior management • Commits resources (both human and financial) to the team • Provides support and enthusiasm for the Balanced Scorecard throughout the organization
Balanced scorecard champion	• Coordinates meetings; plans, tracks, and reports team results to all audiences • Provides thought leadership on the Balanced Scorecard methodology to the team • Ensures that all relevant background material is available to the team • Provides feedback to the executive sponsor and senior management • Facilitates the development of an effective team through coaching and support
Team members	• Provide expert knowledge of business unit or functional operations • Inform and influence their respective senior executives • Act as Balanced Scorecard ambassadors within their unit or department • Act in the best interests of the business as a whole
Organizational change expert	• Increases awareness of organizational change issues • Investigates change-related issues affecting the Balanced Scorecard project • Works with the team to produce solutions mitigating change-related risks

Training Your Team

For the majority of employees within your organization, the team you assemble will be the embodiment of the Balanced Scorecard. If the members do not appear as knowledgeable and credible sources of information, you can be certain that skepticism for the initiative will increase. Some team members may come to the project with a background in performance management and Balanced Scorecard concepts, while others may be experiencing their first exposure to these topics. Either way, to ensure a level playing field for the entire team you have to invest heavily in up-front training. Many believe in the power of training to improve business results. Former U.S. Secretary of Labor Robert Reich has said that well-trained and dedicated employees are the only sustainable source of competitive strength. No less eloquent, but definitely more colorful, Tom Peters chimes in on the subject of employee training with this thought: *"Companies that don't encourage employee education of all kinds are dumb!"*

Start your education efforts by preparing and distributing a comprehensive primer on the subjects of performance management and Balanced Scorecard. These topics are quite mature, and a rich and abundant supply of literature is available. Be sure to include the three seminal articles by Kaplan and Norton appearing in the *Harvard Business Review* from 1992 to 1996. There are literally hundreds of other articles and white papers to choose from, so narrow your search by including any documents that specifically reference your industry or implementation focus (corporate-wide versus business unit for example). A number of high-quality books have been published on these subjects as well, and you should consider providing at least one to each of your team members. Your team will also benefit from attending one of the many excellent conferences on performance management and the Balanced Scorecard. Again, you have the opportunity to tailor your training with your implementation by choosing an event focused on your industry type or implementation plan. They provide a very valuable exchange of ideas, challenges, and solutions.

A less conventional but no less beneficial method of training comes in the form of performance management "games." Many consulting and training organizations offer facilitated games that give participants the opportunity to learn about performance management skills while attempting to solve a real business issue. CSC Consulting has developed a game that introduces clients to the subject of performance management by tasking them with the challenge of producing a product in a quality fashion meeting all customer requirements. The two-hour facilitated simulation provides participants with the chance to see how performance indicators influence business success. Game participants value the experience and believe it creates many learning opportunities. The County of San Diego, California, is currently developing a Balanced Scorecard system, and Project Director Steve Mann took part in such a simulation game at the outset of the project. He believes games that focus on learning can bring people from disparate parts of the organization together and help build a strong team environment during the actual project. *"The game brings together people from different levels of the organization who will be working on the project team. In the game everyone is a beginner, and you can see people going through the learning process."*

Continuing with the theme of "learning by doing," your team should develop a Balanced Scorecard specifically for the Balanced Scorecard implementation. The purpose of this exercise is twofold. First, a pragmatic reason: Performance measures related to the project serve to keep the team focused on the critical tasks at hand. Your team will require yardsticks to gauge their implementation progress, and the Balanced Scorecard provides a powerful means for accomplishing this task. Second, developing the objectives and measures for their Scorecard gives team members a unique opportunity to engage in the mental gymnastics required to create an effective Scorecard. Who are our customers? What are their requirements? At what processes must we excel? What competencies do we require? These are all questions your team will be posing to others in your organization very soon, so it is perfectly appropriate that they go through the process themselves. Exhibit 3.6 is a sample Project Team Balanced Scorecard. Notice that in this example the financial perspective represents a constraint (i.e., budget dollars for the project) rather than an overall goal as it would in most profit-seeking enterprises. This is a good demonstration to the team of the Balanced Scorecard's flexibility.

YOUR BALANCED SCORECARD DEVELOPMENT PLAN

As with any major initiative you'll require a carefully crafted development plan to guide the work of your team. Every organization is different when it comes to the use of project plans. Some feel a highly detailed plan that

Exhibit 3.6   A Sample Balanced Scorecard for Your Implementation Team

Develop a Balanced Scorecard Meeting All Stakeholder Expectations	
Objectives	**Measures**
Customer — Maintain customer satisfaction; Increase Balanced Scorecard knowledge; Reduce revisions	C3—Executive satisfaction with Balanced Scorecard
	C2—Number of revisions per Scorecard draft
	C1—Percentage of surveyed employees aware of the Balanced Scorecard implementation
Internal — Share knowledge; Achieve milestones	I2 —Percentage of planned tasks completed on time
	I1—Number of Balanced Scorecard presentations given (all audiences)
EL & G — Increase skills; Access to tools; Ensure team involvement	E3—Percentage of identified resources available to the team (technology, Balanced Scorecard literature, etc.)
	E2—Percentage of team members attending advanced Balanced Scorecard training events
	E1—Percentage of team meetings with 100% attendance
Financial — Fiscal stability	F1—Variance to project budget

encompasses thousands of lines in Microsoft Project is the only way to capture all the necessary elements of the work. Others use less formal means, outlining only the most critical tasks and tracking them on MS Excel or Word documents. This section of the chapter will outline the key steps in developing your Balanced Scorecard based on experience and research. When creating your own plan, develop one that will be accepted by your team and sponsor based on the prevailing culture of your organization. The important thing is to include all the important elements of the project. Whether you display them as big chunks or decompose them into a thousand steps is up to you. One thing is certain—you will be spending lots of time in meetings while developing your Balanced Scorecard. For some suggestions on maximizing this time, see the box entitled "Meetings, Meetings, Meetings."

This entire book is a Balanced Scorecard development and implementation plan. After all, it is titled *Balanced Scorecard Step-by-Step*. For that reason the steps outlined below will present summary information of the task at hand to help you prepare your campaign. In subsequent chapters the steps will be translated into the many tasks necessary for your success.

The Planning Phase

Before you begin the work of building a Balanced Scorecard, you must lay the groundwork for the project. This chapter was written to help you do just that. To summarize, the planning phase includes the following steps, which are discussed in this chapter:

- Step 1: Develop objectives for your Balanced Scorecard.
- Step 2: Determine the appropriate organizational unit.
- Step 3: Gain executive sponsorship.
- Step 4: Build your Balanced Scorecard team.
- Step 5: Formulate your project plan.
- Step 6: Develop a communication plan for your Balanced Scorecard project.

Clients sometimes tease consultants because we tend to answer many questions with "It depends." This response is often necessary because much of the work we perform is a function of many variables often beyond our control. So it is with the caveat of "it depends" that timing is suggested for this and all phases of the project plan. If you have a full-time Balanced Scorecard champion leading the events outlined above, you should be able to accomplish them within four to six weeks. Take the necessary time to successfully complete these actions. Nothing is stopping you from developing a Balanced Scorecard without a communication plan or clear objectives

---

Meetings, Meetings, Meetings

It seems we spend more time than ever in meetings, but is the time well spent? There's a tale about Will Rogers being invited to sit in on a committee meeting of an organization that ordinarily didn't permit the presence of outsiders. When the meeting was over, Will remarked, *"I agreed to repeat nothing and I'll keep my promise. But I gotta admit, I heard nothing worth repeating."* You can't afford to have your Scorecard team members thinking, or worse yet, saying something similar after your meetings. And you will have meetings. Recent studies suggest that over 65 percent of Scorecard-implementing organizations used work meetings to accomplish their tasks. Here are a few things you can do to maximize the effectiveness of your Balanced Scorecard meetings:

- *Determine your purpose.* Are you holding the meeting to share information, generate ideas, and the like?

- *Determine desired outcomes.* What do you want to accomplish during the session? Ensure that everyone is aware of the desired outcomes when the meeting begins.

- *Evaluate attendance.* Nobody likes being invited to a meeting in which they have little to contribute. Determine who you need in attendance and simply distribute minutes to those who are not essential to achieving your outcomes.

- *Assign roles.* Determine in advance who will facilitate the meeting, who will act as the scribe, and who will fulfill the vital role of time-keeper.

- *Provide structured prework.* Provide attendees with relevant materials well in advance of the meeting and emphasize the importance of completing the prework.

- *Stay on time.* Get in the habit of starting and ending all meetings on time. Do not reward late comers by reviewing what they have missed.

Several excellent articles and books have been written on the topic of effective meeting management. For a simple and pragmatic look at the subject, see Thomas Kayser's 1990 book, *Mining Group Gold* (Serif Publishing).

---

for the implementation, but rest assured that your efforts will be severely compromised without these "stakes in the ground." When we discuss the Employee Learning and Growth perspective of the Scorecard, it will be described as the "enabler" of the other three perspectives. The planning phase of the project is similar in that it enables the development work to follow by clearly articulating what you plan to achieve, with whom, why, and how.

The Development Phase

Consider the steps presented below as a framework for your development of the Balanced Scorecard. As noted in the opening to this section, every organization is different and will want to emphasize different aspects of the Scorecard process. One of the many benefits of the Scorecard that has greatly contributed to its longevity and unabated growth is its flexibility in adapting to the constraints of every organization. Take advantage of that flexibility when constructing your plan.

Readers will note that a number of executive workshops are built in throughout the process. The importance of executive consensus throughout the development phase cannot be overemphasized, hence the inclusion of these checkpoints. However, it may prove virtually impossible to convene your senior management team this many times. If group meetings are not possible, ensure that your team members are frequently reporting to their "home" executives with team progress and gathering feedback from the executive that can be used to guide the future direction of the team's work.

- *Step 1: Gather and distribute background material.* The Balanced Scorecard is a tool that describes strategy. In order to fulfill this promise, your team must have ample access to background material on the organization's mission, vision, values, strategy, competitive position, and employee core competencies. Use internal resources such as your strategy and marketing groups to assist you with this effort. If you are publicly traded, many resources are at your disposal to garner information on past performance. Press releases, stories in the business media, and analyst reports will all provide valuable information.

- *Step 2: Develop or confirm mission, values, vision, and strategy.* Based on the information gathered in Step One, you should be able to generate a consensus of where your organization rests in terms of these critical items. If you do not have one or all of these Scorecard "raw materials," you will have to work with your executive team to develop them. Chapter Four provides a detailed review of each of these elements of an effective Scorecard.

- *Step 3: Conduct executive interviews.* The importance of executive involvement in the Scorecard process has been stressed. During this first interview with senior management, the team will gather feedback on the organization's competitive position, key success factors for the future, and possible Scorecard measures. Chapter Five provides a guide for your executive interview process.

- *Step 4: Develop objectives and measures in each of the Balanced Scorecard perspectives.* During this step, your team will determine which perspectives of the Scorecard are right for your organization and develop objectives and measures for each perspective based on a translation of your strategies. Chapter Five will discuss the many tasks associated with this step, including choosing your perspectives, identifying objectives, developing measures, refining measures based on key criteria, assigning ownership for results, and determining data requirements.

- *Step 4 (a): Executive workshop.* Gain senior management consensus on the objectives and measures developed by the team. Capture and incorporate any recommendations from the executive group.

- *Step 4 (b): Gather employee feedback.* Ultimately, you expect your Balanced Scorecard to provide information that allows all employees to determine how their day-to-day actions link to the organization's strategic plan. Therefore, you need to poll your managers and employees to ensure that they believe you have captured the critical elements of value to your whole organization. Chapter Six will describe methods for gathering employee feedback.

- *Step 5: Develop cause-and-effect linkages.* A good Balanced Scorecard must describe the strategy through a series of interrelationships among the measures you have selected. Chapter Six presents suggestions for accomplishing this fundamental and essential aspect of your Balanced Scorecard.

- *Step 5 (a): Executive workshop.* Establishing coherent and valid cause-and-effect linkages can prove challenging to even the most measurement savvy teams. What is most important in this step is the debate that will ensue among the senior management team as to the degree and timing of cause-and-effect relationships. It is during this discussion that we anticipate executives will—perhaps for the first time—see how their functional silo is a critical enabler of overall organizational success.

- *Step 6: Establish targets for your measures.* Without a target for each of your measures you will have no way of knowing whether improvement efforts are yielding acceptable results. The data from your metrics provides you with only half the picture. A target gives meaning to measure results by affording a point of comparison. However, setting targets may be among the most challenging aspects of your entire implementation. Many organizations have little actual practice or techniques for the establishment of meaningful performance targets. Chapter Seven explores this topic in greater depth and supplies advice for developing your targets.

- *Step 6 (a): Executive workshop.* The goal of this executive session is to gain final consensus on the Balanced Scorecard work product that has been developed by the team. At this point, the document should be ready for inclusion in the operations of the organization.

- *Step 7: Develop the ongoing Balanced Scorecard implementation plan.* The steps outlined above will get you from point zero to the development of a Balanced Scorecard measurement tool. The word *measurement* is stressed. The remainder of this book will focus on the evolution of that *measurement* tool to the cornerstone of your organization's *management system.* Parts Three and Four of the book provide you with the tools for linking the Balanced Scorecard to all key management processes within the firm. Cascading accountability for results to lower levels of the organization, linking budgeting and planning to strategic aims, aligning reward systems, and reporting results are all vital operations within your organization that can be positively impacted by the presence of an effective Balanced Scorecard.

Getting from Step 1 in the planning phase to Step 7 in the development phase can take anywhere from four to twelve months—I've seen both. The amount of time your organization expends on the project will *depend* (there is that word again!) on a number of factors: commitment of the executive team; allocation of resources to the project, size, and complexity of the organization for which a Scorecard is being built; and organizational readiness for a change of this magnitude. Exhibit 3.7 displays a possible timeline for both the planning and development phases.

COMMUNICATING YOUR BALANCED SCORECARD PROJECT

Chapter One described the Balanced Scorecard as a powerful communication tool, signaling to everyone in your organization the key strategies of success, and how you plan to achieve them. Many of us believe in the Balanced Scorecard system, and since you are reading this book you must be convinced of the tool's abilities as well. At this point it is a safe assumption that many people in your organization may not have even heard of the Balanced Scorecard. Those who do profess some familiarity with the concept may be completely skeptical of its ability to effect any real change. The Balanced Scorecard is a change project, and most change efforts struggle to succeed, with lack of communication being a chief cause of the potential failure. Professor and author John Kotter has said, "*Without credible communication, and a lot of it, employees' hearts and minds are never captured.*"[13] To their detriment, most organizations fail to heed this valuable advice and their change efforts are the worse for it. These challenges must be met head on during your implementation efforts if you expect employees to begin using this tool to make real business decisions. A carefully constructed communication strategy and plan will prove to be a great ally in the struggle to enlighten all employees and win support throughout your Balanced

Exhibit 3.7 Balanced Scorecard Project Timeline

	Week	1	2	3	4	5	6	7	8	9	10	11	12	13	14	15	16	17	18	19	20
Planning Phase																					
Step 1:	Develop objectives for your Balanced Scorecard.	▮																			
Step 2:	Determine the appropriate organizational unit.		▮																		
Step 3:	Gain executive sponsorship.			▮																	
Step 4:	Build your Balanced Scorecard team.				▮																
Step 5:	Formulate your project plan.					▮															
Step 6:	Develop a communication plan.					▮															
Development Phase																					
Step 1:	Gather and distribute background material.						▮														
Step 2:	Develop or confirm mission, values, vision, and strategy.						▮														
Step 3:	Conduct executive interviews.							▮													
Step 4:	Develop objectives and measures.											▮									
Step 4(a):	Executive workshop.												▮								
Step 4(b):	Gather employee feedback.													▮							
Step 5:	Develop cause-and-effect linkages.														▮						
Step 5(a):	Executive workshop.															▮					
Step 6:	Establish targets for your measures.																▮				
Step 6(a):	Executive workshop.																	▮			
Step 7:	Develop the ongoing Balanced Scorecard implementation plan.																				↑

Scorecard development process. You are about to invest tremendous effort into building a new management tool; do not let a lack of communication explaining the concept and the benefits it will produce derail that effort. Let's look at the elements of an effective communication plan you can use during your Balanced Scorecard implementation.

Objectives for Your Communication Plan

The consideration of a vision and objectives should be the starting point of your communication planning endeavors. Ask yourself why you are launching a communication plan and what you expect to achieve as a result. Is your primary focus on educating your key stakeholder groups or in winning the support of front-line employees? At Nova Scotia Power the Balanced Scorecard team used this vision to guide their communication efforts: *"To present the concepts of the Balanced Scorecard to the key constituents involved in both sponsoring and providing input to the project, and to provide all involved with regular updates regarding the team's progress during the implementation."* This simple statement provided the basis for all future communication efforts during the project. Your objectives should represent the unique attributes of your project and the culture of your organization, but in general most organizations include at least some of the following:

- Build awareness of the Balanced Scorecard at all levels of the organization.
- Provide education on key Balanced Scorecard concepts to all audiences.
- Generate the engagement and commitment of key stakeholders in the project.
- Encourage participation in the process.
- Generate enthusiasm for the Balanced Scorecard.
- Ensure that team results are disseminated rapidly and effectively.

When you begin your communication planning process, consider drawing on the resources of that most reliable of information sources—the company grapevine. Your project team was chosen on merits such as functional knowledge, influence in the group, and support for the Balanced Scorecard. It is doubtful that you selected any team members based on how plugged in they are to your organization's grapevine, but to discover what employees are really thinking about the change, the grapevine is possibly the most potent root of information. When launching your communication campaign, interview grapevine members and, when you are trying to influence opinion, establish open and honest relationships with them.[14]

Elements of the Communication Plan

The simplest way to devise your plan is by utilizing the "W5" approach—
who, what, when, where, and why. Each is discussed below in the context of
communication planning.

- *Purpose/message (what/why):* Describes the information content defined
  in the plan. All communication plans will contain "key messages" that
  must accompany information deliveries. Your Balanced Scorecard project
  may have a number of key messages, including how the Scorecard fits
  with strategy implementation, the role of the Balanced Scorecard in
  relation to other change initiatives, or the new management philosophy
  represented by the Scorecard. Other content defined in the communication plan may include timelines, project status, development issues,
  and education. Because the roles and responsibilities of your audience
  groups vary, the information messages should be tailored toward the
  target's role.

- *Audience (who):* The specific individuals or groups identified who will
  require messages during the project. Depending on the size and scope
  of your project, audiences will vary. However, plan to include your senior management team, steering committee if you are using one, middle
  management group, all employees, and your project team.

- *Frequency (when):* The timing of communication will depend on the needs
  of the audience groups. Those more heavily involved in the project will
  require more frequent communication. Having said that, recall John
  Kotter's admonition regarding the lack of frequent communication
  during change efforts. Do not risk losing the support and enthusiasm of
  any audience by limiting the amount of information they receive.

- *Delivery vehicle (where/how):* Describes the method chosen to broadcast
  the message and will depend on the needs of the audience. With today's
  technologies, choices of delivery vehicles are really just a function of the
  limits of your imagination. Consider any or all of the following as possibilities: face-to-face meetings, group presentations, project plans, newsletters, your intranet, workshops, brown-bag lunches, video presentations,
  message kits, e-mails, news bulletins, raffles and contests, pay-stub messages, demonstrations, road shows, and town-hall meetings.

- *Communicator (who):* The individual or group responsible for the content and distribution of the message. Again, the communicator will vary
  based on the message and the needs of the audience. For example, more
  formal communications will normally emanate from the executive sponsor, while a member of the project team may write newsletter articles.

What you decide to communicate is ultimately up to you, but there is
one thing you definitely should include in your communication plan—a

glossary of terms. Virtually every organization uses slightly different terminology to describe performance management terms. An *initiative* in one company might be known as an *objective* in another. *Critical success factors* at your shop may go by *key performance indicators* elsewhere. Semantics are important because in today's modern organization many employees referred to earlier as *knowledge workers* may have gone through a performance management initiative at another company using an entirely different vernacular. You want your Balanced Scorecard to foster teamwork, cooperation, and sharing of information. That will prove exceedingly difficult if your employees are speaking a different language than your project team. One organization I know of was nearing the end of a Balanced Scorecard project when at an important meeting of managers it became clear that the project team was using terms that held very different meanings in the minds of the managers. At that late hour the team had to embark on an extensive campaign to educate the entire management group on the vocabulary of the project and ensure that they shared common goals.

One final thought: Do not take the success of your communication efforts for granted. To ensure that communication activities are reaching targeted audiences, a communication effectiveness measurement effort is highly recommended. Survey target audiences regularly throughout the process, and assess your efforts on the following criteria:

- *No contact:* Has not heard of the Balanced Scorecard project
- *Awareness:* Has heard about the project, but doesn't know what it is
- *Conceptual understanding:* Understands the Balanced Scorecard and any individual effects
- *Tactical understanding:* Understands both the personal and organizational effects of the Balanced Scorecard
- *Acceptance:* Will support the Balanced Scorecard and the changes it will bring

A simplified communication plan is shown in Exhibit 3.8.

SUMMARY

A lot of valuable terrain was covered in this chapter, which, if followed, will pour a very solid foundation for your development efforts to follow. The chapter began with the challenge of articulating your specific objectives for developing a Balanced Scorecard. We discussed that clear goals for the Scorecard ensure a common focus during the implementation, increase communication efforts, and guide the future work of linking the Scorecard to management processes throughout the organization.

Organizations embarking on a Balanced Scorecard project often assume

Exhibit 3.8   A Simplified Communication Plan for Your Balanced Scorecard Project

Audience	Purposes	Frequency	Delivery Vehicle	Communicator
Executive team	• Gain commitment • Remove obstacles • Report progress • Prevent surprises	Biweekly	Direct contact	Executive sponsor
Management	• Convey purpose • Explain concepts • Report progress • Gain commitment	Biweekly	• E-mail • Management meetings • Articles	Champion/team members
All employees	• Convey purpose • Introduce concepts • Eliminate misconceptions • Report progress	Monthly	• E-mail • Newsletters • Town-hall meetings	Project team members
Project team	• Track progress • Assign tasks • Review expectations	Weekly	• Team meeting • Status memos	Champion

the logical starting point for their efforts is a high-level Corporate Scorecard. This may or may not be the case. We examined seven criteria for making the decision of where to begin your Scorecard effort: strategy, sponsorship, need, support of key managers, scope, data, and resources.

If there is one undeniable fact of organizational life, it is that no project will prosper or even survive without executive sponsorship. The Balanced Scorecard is no exception. You must find a willing and able senior executive who will act as an ambassador for your project. To secure executive sponsorship you must find a senior manager whose values are consistent with those of the Balanced Scorecard method, demonstrate the results this tool can offer, and educate your senior team on the subtleties of the methodology.

No single individual in your organization holds the necessary information to build an effective Balanced Scorecard. This effort must be accomplished through a group effort. We defined a *team* as a small number of people with complementary skills who are committed to a common purpose, performance goals, and approach for which they hold themselves mutually accountable. This definition was broken down to its component parts in the context of the Balanced Scorecard. Your team must include an executive sponsor, champion, work group members, and possibly an organizational change expert. For your team to construct an effective Scorecard they must possess the requisite knowledge of this tool. Team training may consist of literature reviews, conferences, and role-playing games.

The purpose of this book is to walk you through the sequential steps involved in developing a Balanced Scorecard. However, it is important that you build a plan that reflects the nature and scope of your initiative. Two key phases—planning and development—were examined, as well as the associated steps in crafting your Scorecard.

Finally, the importance of a communication plan for your Balanced Scorecard was discussed. Objectives of the plan include building awareness, providing education on key concepts, generating engagement and commitment, encouraging participation, generating enthusiasm, and providing results to interested parties. We used the "W5" approach of who, what, when, where, and why to draft the elements of our plan, and concluded the section by noting the importance of gauging the effectiveness of your communication efforts by following up with target audiences.

NOTES

1. Stephen R. Covey, A. Roger Merrill, and Rebecca R. Merrill, *First Things First* (New York: Simon & Schuster, 1994).
2. Michael R. Vitale and Sarah C. Mavrinac, "How Effective Is Your Performance Measurement System?," *Management Accounting*, August 1995, 43.

3. Janice A. Klein, "Why Supervisors Resist Employee Involvement," *Harvard Business Review,* September–October 1984.
4. Robert S. Kaplan and David P. Norton, *The Strategy Focused Organization* (Boston: Harvard Business School Press, 2000)
5. Robert Simons and Antonio Davila, "How High Is Your Return on Management?," *Harvard Business Review,* January–February 1998, 70.
6. Rebecca Macfie, "Six of Our Top Chief Executive Officers Tell the Independent How They Stay at the Top," *Independent Business Weekly,* April 2001, 8.
7. Best Practices Benchmarking Report, *Developing the Balanced Scorecard* (Chapel Hill, NC: Best Practices, LLC, 1999).
8. Laura Downing, "Progress Report on the Balanced Scorecard: A Global Users Survey," *Balanced Scorecard Report,* November–December 2000, 7–9.
9. Rosabeth Moss Kanter, "The Enduring Skills of Change Leaders," *Leader to Leader,* Summer 1999, 15–22.
10. Jon R. Katzenbach and Douglas K. Smith, *The Wisdom of Teams* (Boston: Harvard Business School Press, 1993).
11. Best Practices Benchmarking Report, *Developing the Balanced Scorecard.*
12. Jim Billington, "The Three Essentials of an Effective Team," *Harvard Management Update,* 1997.
13. John P. Kotter, *Leading Change* (Boston: Harvard Business School Press, 1996).
14. Susan Annunzio, "The Average Joe in the Know: How to Put the Grapevine to Work for You," *Journal of Employee Communication Management,* January/February 2001.

CHAPTER 4

Mission, Values, Vision, and Strategy

Roadmap for Chapter Four   Anyone who has ever built a new house knows that there are many things that must take place long before you ever cut a board or swing a hammer. First, you would conceive of the house you would like to live in and work with an architect to devise the plans that bring your images to life. Once you have the blueprint in place you can begin to assemble the materials you will need to actually construct your house: lumber, nails, plaster, pipes, and wires, among a host of other items. Only then can you erect a sturdy house that will withstand the elements and provide you long-lasting comfort and enjoyment. Developing a Balanced Scorecard is not unlike this exercise. The last chapter described the importance of planning your efforts, setting objectives, gaining executive support, determining where to begin, developing your team, and communicating your project. Once you have completed that, you have a blueprint for your Scorecard. Like our hypothetical house, you are now ready to gather your raw materials and start building your Balanced Scorecard. This chapter describes the raw materials you will need to construct a solid and sustainable Balanced Scorecard that will stand up to the volatile weather of the business environment.

The components of an effective Balanced Scorecard are your organization's mission, core values, vision, and strategy. This chapter will examine each of these building blocks in detail and consider what they are, how to determine their effectiveness, tips on developing them, and their vital linkage to the Balanced Scorecard. As a Scorecard practitioner you will need to determine whether the Balanced Scorecard you have developed is truly aligned with your mission, values, vision, and strategy (Exhibit 4.1). This chapter equips you with the tools to make that critical determination.

Exhibit 4.1   The Balanced Scorecard Translates Mission, Values, Vision, and Strategy

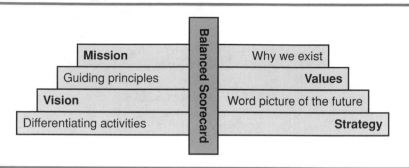

MISSION STATEMENTS

I decided to write this book to offer my experience with the Balanced Scorecard. As is always the case in life, the more you give the more you get. Crafting these pages has provided me with endless learning opportunities, and this chapter is a great example. Words like *mission, values, vision,* and *strategy* are business standards, widely accepted and (I thought) well understood. When I embarked on my research for this chapter I was quite surprised to discover the many and varied definitions of these terms, particularly *mission* and *vision*. Apparently, I am not the only one facing some confusion. In *The Dilbert Principle*, oft-quoted business sage Scott Adams has this to say about mission and vision: *"The first step in developing a vision statement is to lock the managers in a room and have them debate what is meant by a vision statement, and how exactly it differs from a mission statement. These are important questions, because one wrong move and the employees will start doing 'vision' things when they should be doing 'mission' things and before long it will be impossible to sort it all out."*[1] So, let's heed Scott's advice and sort this whole thing out before confusion reigns. What follows is my thinking on mission, values, vision, and strategy based on my experience and the work of many writers, theoreticians, and practitioners.

What Is a Mission Statement?

A mission statement defines the core purpose of the organization—why it exists. The mission examines the *raison d'etre* for the organization beyond simply increasing shareholder wealth, and reflects employees motivations for engaging in the company's work. David Packard captured the essence of mission very well in a 1960 speech to Hewlett-Packard employees: *"A group of people get together and exist as an institution that we call a company so they are able to accomplish something collectively that they could not accomplish separately—they make a contribution to society, . . . do something which is of value.*"[2] The mission attempts to capture the contribution and value that Mr. Packard so eloquently describes. Unlike strategies and goals that may be achieved over time, you never really fulfill your mission. It acts as a beacon for your work, constantly pursued but never quite reached. Consider your mission to be the compass by which you guide your organization. In today's hectic (to put it very euphemistically) business world, you need a star to steer by and your mission should provide just that.

Effective Mission Statements

Let's look at some characteristics of effective mission statements. These attributes should assist you if your organization does not currently use a mission statement. If you do have a mission, check it against these items to judge its effectiveness.

- *Inspire change.* While your mission doesn't change, it should inspire great change within your organization. Since the mission can never be fully realized, it should propel your organization forward, stimulating change and positive growth. Take, for example, the mission of 3M, which is *"To solve unsolved problems innovatively."* Such a simple and powerful mission is sure to lead 3M into many new and interesting fields as it attempts to solve the innumerable problems we face. Wal-Mart states its mission as *"Give ordinary folks the chance to buy the same things as rich people."* Retailing may look vastly different in 100 years than it does today, but you can bet that ordinary folks will still want the opportunity to acquire the same things as rich people!

- *Long-term in nature.* Mission statements should be written to last 100 years or more. While strategies and plans will surely change during that time period, the mission should remain the bedrock of the organization, serving as the stake in the ground for all future decisions.

- *Easily understood and communicated.* Nobody would argue that our modern organizational world is one awash in jargon. Buzzwords abound in offices around the world as we invent new and curious words and phrases to describe the world around us. While many people react negatively to buzzwords, some say they simply represent a sign of *"words in action and a culture on the move."*[3] Regardless of your opinion on the role of buzzwords in our modern life, they really have no place in a mission statement. Your mission should be written in plain language that is easily understood by all readers. A compelling and memorable mission is one that reaches people on a visceral level, speaks to them, and motivates them to serve the organization's purpose. You can actually consider your mission a valuable recruiting aid in attracting like-minded individuals to take up your cause.

Developing Your Mission Statement

The first question to consider when writing your mission statement is who should be involved in the process? There are different schools of thought on this subject. Some argue that the mission should be crafted by the CEO or some other executive, sent out for comments and revisions, and finalized without any meetings or committee involvement. Others believe the mission statement, with its inherent focus on capturing the hearts and minds of all employees, cannot possibly be drafted without employee involvement. Being the good fence-sitting consultant I am, I will come down somewhere on the middle in this debate. Chapter Three discussed the importance of executive involvement in the Balanced Scorecard. It was noted that executives were critical to the process of developing the Scorecard because most middle managers would lack the overall perspective demanded in creating the document. Mission statements are similar in that they require the broad and high-level thinking of an executive to consider the many possibilities available to the organization. Charismatic leaders often possess the enviable ability of crystallizing the organization's place and future goals in compelling terms to be shared with all employees. Do not deny yourself the opportunity of gleaning your executives' wisdom and foresight. At the same time, you should also involve as many people as possible in reviewing the draft mission statement. Let employees at every level of the organization have the chance to kick the tires of this most important of documents. The mission must serve to galvanize everyone toward an exciting future, and without involvement in the process commitment will be difficult if not impossible to acquire.

A very effective method for developing your mission is based on a concept known as the "5 Whys" developed by Collins and Porras.[4] Start with a descriptive statement, such as "We make X products or deliver Y services." Then ask, "Why is this important?" five times. A few "whys" into this exercise and you'll begin to see your true mission emerging. This process works for virtually any product or service organization. A waste management company could easily move from "We pick up trash" to "We contribute to a stronger environment by creatively solving waste management issues" after just a couple of rounds. A market research organization might transition from "provide the best market research data" to "contribute to customers' success by helping them understand their markets." Notice that with each round of "why" you will move closer and closer to your true reason for being as an organization, to the value or contribution you strive to create or make. This process is so powerful because it builds on the notion of *abstraction*— moving to a different level, leaving characteristics out. We humans are great abstractors, just ask anyone about himself and chances are the first thing you will hear is "I'm an accountant" or "I work in high-tech." We tend to let these descriptions or abstractions define us, and we perceive the world around us through that particular lens. Why not move down the abstraction ladder a bit and see yourself as a husband or wife, neighbor, churchgoer, movie lover, and so on. Doing so opens up a world of possibility in our lives. Similarly, most organizations focus intently on the micro details of their operations, failing to see the bigger issues that underly their purpose. The "5 Whys" force us to abstract to different levels, thereby leaving behind the myriad specific characteristics of our organizational being, and discovering our true meaning. Exhibit 4.2 shares the mission statements of a number of organizations.

Why a Mission Is "Mission-Critical" to the Balanced Scorecard

The Balanced Scorecard was not designed to act as an isolated management tool; instead, it is part of an integrated approach to examining our business and providing us with a means to evaluate our overall success. Above all, the Scorecard is a tool designed to offer faithful translation. What does it translate? The Scorecard decodes our mission, values, vision, and strategy into performance objectives and measures in each of the four Scorecard perspectives. Translating this "DNA" of our organization with the Balanced

Exhibit 4.2   Sample Mission Statements

Merck: To preserve and improve human life

American Institute of Certified Public Accountants (AICPA): To provide members with the resources, information, and leadership that enable them to provide valuable services in the highest professional manner to benefit the public as well as employees and clients

3M: To solve unsolved problems innovatively

Wal-Mart: To give ordinary folks the chance to buy the same things as rich people

Walt Disney: To make people happy

Hewlett-Packard: To make technical contributions for the advancement and welfare of humanity

Marriott: To make people away from home feel that they are among friends and are really wanted

Sony: To experience the joy of advancing and applying technology for the benefit of the public

Mary Kay: To give unlimited opportunity to women

Cargill: To improve the standard of living around the world

Scorecard ensures that all employees are aligned with and working toward the mission. This represents one of the great values of the Scorecard system. The mission is where our translating efforts begin. A well-developed Balanced Scorecard ensures that the measures tracked are consistent with our ultimate aspirations and guides the hearts and minds of employees in making the right choices.

When developing objectives and measures you must critically examine them in the context of the mission you have written for the organization to be certain they are consistent with that purpose. Would a measure of "market share of the richest 1 percent of Americans" make sense in light of Wal-Mart's mission? Probably not—in fact, it would reflect a fundamental shift in purpose. While Wal-Mart welcomes all shoppers—and certainly many price-conscious wealthy people shop there—it relies on a strategy of low prices to attract those who aren't "rich." 3M wants to "solve unsolved problems innovatively." If they develop a measure and target on their Scorecard to cut research, development, and training, would that be consistent with their core purpose?

You can build and implement a Balanced Scorecard without a mission statement for your organization. It would still contain a mix of financial and nonfinancial measures linked together through a series of cause-and-effect relationships, but consider the tremendous value and alignment you create when developing a Scorecard that truly translates your mission. If you do have a mission, make certain the Balanced Scorecard you develop is true to the core essence reflected in the document. If you don't have a mission statement, I would strongly encourage you develop one and see for yourself the focus and alignment you create when translating your mission into a Balanced Scorecard framework.

VALUES

What Are Values?

Competitive advantage can be derived from any number of sources in today's organizations. Superior strategies, innovative products, and exemplary customer service are just some of the many ways in which organizations seek to compete. But for some organizations it is the way they behave that makes the difference and provides the source of their strength. We have all experienced situations that demonstrate this—perhaps a hotel employee providing us with a missing essential from our travel bags or an amusement park worker who showed up to help at the exact moment before the combination of stress and joy (that only an amusement park can bring) became too much for us to bear. Chances are these acts did not result from reading the latest management guru's book or from a desire to get a bigger bonus.

No, they simply represent the way things get done at that organization—in other words, its values.

Values are the timeless principles that guide an organization. They represent the deeply held beliefs within the organization and are demonstrated through the day-to-day behaviors of all employees. An organization's values make an open proclamation about how it expects everyone to behave. In *Built to Last*, Collins and Porras suggest that visionary organizations decide for themselves what values to hold, independent of the current environment, competitive requirements, or management fads. They quote Johnson & Johnson CEO Ralph Larsen on values: *"The core values embodied in our credo might be a competitive advantage, but that is not why we have them. We have them because they define for us what we stand for, and we would hold them even if they became a competitive disadvantage in certain situations."*[5] "What we stand for" is an important part of the above quote. No universal set of right or wrong values exist; instead, each organization must determine or discover the core values that comprise its essence and hold importance to those within it. Organizations tend to have a small number of core values that truly reflect their very essence. A large number may indicate confusion between values and practices. While practices, processes, and strategies should change over time in answer to the many challenges that come our way, we expect values to remain the same, providing an enduring source of strength and wisdom.

In many organizations the core values represent the strong personal beliefs of the founder or CEO, for example, Walt Disney's belief in imagination and wholesomeness. Just as we would expect parents to exert great influence over the developing values of their children, it is the organization's leaders who set the tone for values within an organization. Therefore, leaders must constantly strive to not only develop appropriate values, but more importantly they must consistently mirror the values in their words and actions. As the Swiss philosopher Henri Amiel once said, *"Every man's conduct is an unspoken sermon that is forever preaching to others."*[6] One CEO who does a great job of living the company's values is Herb Kelleher of Southwest Airlines, which has been named the best company to work for in America by *Fortune* magazine. The values of maintaining a sense of humor and having fun at your job are two that are deemed critical by the CEO, and he ensures that these values are shared by the entire workforce through careful recruiting efforts.

Values-Driven Organizations

In reality, all organizations have a set of values. Author Richard Barrett recognizes this fact, but suggests that the declaration of the underlying values is key: *"The critical issue is whether these values are conscious, shared, and lived, or remain unconscious, and indiscussed. When values are not defined, the culture of the organization is subject to the vagaries of the personality of the leader.*"[7] Barrett goes on to suggest that if leaders are operating from self-interest, then the organization will do the same. However, if the personality of the leader is focused in higher levels of consciousness, then the organization will operate for the common good. We often associate positive values with the common good, holding certain beliefs and operating on them in the hope that our actions will result not only in economic profits but the improvement of society as well. Is there room in our modern economy, which often appears rather cutthroat to say the least, for an organization to do well by doing good, living its values? Some organizations are proving that is in fact the case.

J.W. Marriott has noted, *"The concept of making employees feel really good about themselves seems to be missing from many companies' philosophies."*[8] He understands that if employees feel confident and content, generally happy with themselves and the job, this positive attitude will translate to better service for guests. Marriott has determined that being good to people is not only the right thing to do for their employees, but makes good business sense. For that reason, *"Take care of Marriott people and they will take care of Marriott guests"* is one of their core values.

Another great example of running a company with values at the helm comes from the east coast of the United States—Tom's of Maine. Starting with a $5,000 loan from a friend, Tom and Kate Chappell began making products for home use that would not harm the environment. Beginning with the first nonphosphate liquid laundry detergent, they soon built a multimillion-dollar business supplying environmentally friendly personal care and wellness products. Founder Tom Chappell says, *"Your personal values can be integrated with managing for all the traditional goals of business—making money, expanded market share, increased profits, retained earnings, and sales growth. Not only can your personal beliefs be brought to work, they can work for you."*[9] The commitment to using natural ingredients in their products and serving customers and employees guides every decision made at the company. Tom's Statement of Beliefs, which serve as their core values, is shown in Exhibit 4.3.

A final example of values-driven organizations is provided by The Body Shop, an international skin and hair care retailer. The company was founded by Anita Roddick, who in 1976 began retailing homemade, naturally inspired products with minimal packaging. The organization rapidly evolved from one small shop in Brighton on the South Coast of England, to a worldwide network of shops, which now makes a sale every 0.4 seconds worldwide. The Body Shop has always believed that business is primarily about human relationships with its stakeholders—employees, franchisees, customers, communities, suppliers, and shareholders. The company continues to lead the way for businesses to use their voice for social and environmental change. Vocal against animal testing and the destruction of natural resources, The Body

Exhibit 4.3   Tom's of Maine Statement of Beliefs

WE BELIEVE that human beings and nature have inherent worth and deserve our respect.

WE BELIEVE in products that are safe, effective, and made of natural ingredients.

WE BELIEVE that our company and our products are unique and worthwhile, and that we can sustain these genuine qualities with an ongoing commitment to innovation and creativity.

WE BELIEVE that we have a responsibility to cultivate the best relationships possible with our co-workers, customers, owners, agents, suppliers, and our community.

WE BEIEVE in providing employees with a safe and fulfilling work environment, and an opportunity to grow and learn.

WE BELIEVE that our company can be financially successful while behaving in a socially responsible and environmentally sensitive manner.

Shop also provides support to communities in need through sustained trading relationships, not exploitation. Not content to simply state their values, The Body Shop has put them to the test by publishing a values report that details their performance on social, environmental, and animal protection issues. The company's 1997 values report scored the highest rating from SustainAbility, which compared the Body Shop's entry against approximately 100 company reports as part of the United Nations Environmental Program. SustainAbility refers to the 1997 Values Report as *". . . unusual in its efforts to integrate social and environmental reporting with considerable stakeholder engagement."* The Body Shop continues to reap the rewards of living their values—in 1999 it was voted the second most trusted brand in the United Kingdom and it continues to grow worldwide.

Establishing Values

This section is titled "Establishing Values" but actually the question "Can We Establish Values?" might be appropriate. After all, every organization has a set of values that are demonstrated every day, but do they reflect the true essence of the organization or simply the thinking of its current regime at the top? As noted previously, an organization's core values should not change, but should act as the guiding principles for the organization as it reacts to the world around it. While this is the case, we must also recognize that like virtually everything else, values within an organization will sometimes remain long after they cease to provide any benefit and in fact may become a hindrance to the ongoing success of the company. Some values may even prove unethical or unacceptable in the larger societal context. This does not suggest a wholesale change of values every few years to suit the current competitive landscape. It simply implies an honest evaluation of your organization and the recognition of which values truly represent the essence of your organization and are the keys to your enduring success.

The key to changing values and the underlying culture of an organization lies in open and honest identification of the current value systems that exist and are rewarded in the organization. One tool to help you in this endeavor was developed by Richard Barrett and is known as the *corporate value audit instrument*.[10] Individuals in the organization use three templates of values/behaviors to choose: the 10 values that best represent who they are (personal values), the 10 values that best describe how their organization/team operates (organizational values), and the 10 values they believe are most critical for a high-performance organization/team (ideal organizational values). This very illuminating exercise is used as a diagnostic tool to evaluate the strengths and weaknesses of existing values and culture. Organizations are able to assess the degree of alignment between personal values and existing and ideal organizational values, and identify the changes that are necessary to develop a successful and enduring value system. If you still need some assistance identifying values, author and consultant Jim Collins has developed a number of questions you can use to identify the core values in your organization[11]:

- What core values do you bring to work—values you hold to be so fundamental that you would hold them regardless of whether or not they were rewarded?

- How would you describe to your loved ones the core values you stand for in your work and that you hope they stand for in their working lives?

- If you awoke tomorrow morning with enough money to retire for the rest of your life, would you continue to hold on to these core values?

- Perhaps most important, can you envision these values being as valid 100 years from now as they are today?

- Would you want the organization to continue to hold these values, even if at some point one or more of them became a competitive disadvantage?

- If you were to start a new organization tomorrow in a different line of work, what core values would you build into the new organization regardless of its activities?

Once the current values are "on the table," with some careful planning and execution the organization can begin to substitute the values which truly represent their authentic character. Values are the collective principles held by the individuals that make up your organization, so when attempting to make changes you must begin with the individual and work to the group. The best way to accomplish this is through recruitment and selection of people who hold the values you desire for the organization. Skillful interviewing and reference checks will help you pinpoint those people.

Values and the Balanced Scorecard

The preceding section discussed the possibility of changing the values of an organization and the mechanisms for achieving this result. The Balanced Scorecard represents the best solution for broadcasting your values, reviewing them over time, and creating alignment from top to bottom in the organization. The real key is alignment, having every employee see how their day-to-day actions are consistent with the values of the company and how living those values is contributing to overall success.

Chapter Eight will discuss the concept of cascading the Balanced Scorecard—driving it down to lower levels of the organization while ensuring alignment throughout. Cascading allows employees at all levels to develop objectives and measures that represent how they influence corporate or business unit goals. The measures selected must be consistent with the values of the organization to ensure that everyone is headed in the same overall direction. Reviewing or "auditing" the measures on lower-level Scorecards provides a great opportunity to determine whether the values you espouse are really those held by your employees up and down the corporate hierarchy. If you value innovation, for example, but your business units have no performance measures tracking innovation or development, then perhaps they do not truly value innovation as a guiding principle of their operations. Conversely, if all lower-level Scorecards contain measures relating to customer service but this value is not captured on the high-level Corporate Scorecard, then perhaps you have missed a core value that is important to all of your employees.

Pragmatically, the Balanced Scorecard may also be used to track the extent to which your organization really lives its values. For organizations undergoing changes to values or suffering from turmoil, metrics that gauge adherence to stated values may be of great benefit. However, developing meaningful value-based metrics may prove challenging to even the most creative Scorecard builders. You could use "mystery shopper" or casual observation techniques to determine whether employees are behaving in accordance with your values. Calculating the percentage of employees who can recite your core values without prompting could also be used, but this would prove very difficult to track and may raise the ire of those being asked to spontaneously list the company's values. Another possibility is identifying behaviors consistent with your values and basing at least part of the annual performance appraisal on the demonstration of these behaviors by employees.

A final thought on values in the organization comes from Tom Morris. Writing in his book *If Aristotle Ran General Motors*, Morris has this to say about the importance of values at work: *"People who are personally reassessing their lives in light of their deepest values will not find it easy to settle for less than a work environment that respects and encourages those values. They will certainly not be able to flourish, to be and do their best, in conditions that have not been wisely developed with sensitivity to what deeply moves people and what most fundamentally matters to us all."*[12] Exhibit 4.4 displays the values of some large organizations with which we are probably all familiar.

VISION

What Is a Vision Statement?

Thus far, this chapter has discussed the importance of a powerful mission to determine your core purpose as an organization, and the values that you

---

Exhibit 4.4   Selected Statements of Values

General Electric
- Having a passion for excellence and hating bureaucracy
- Being open to ideas from anywhere and committed to working things out
- Living quality and driving cost and speed for competitive advantage
- Having the self-confidence to involve everyone and behaving in a boundless fashion
- Creating a clear, simple, reality-based vision and communicating it to all constituencies
- Having enormous energy and the ability to energize others
- Stretching, setting aggressive goals, and rewarding progress, yet understanding accountability and commitment
- Seeing changes as opportunity, not threat
- Having global brains and building diverse and global teams

Nordstom
- Service to the customer above all else
- Hard work and individual productivity
- Never being satisfied
- Excellence in reputation; being part of something special

Walt Disney
- No cynicism
- Nurturing and promulgation of "wholesome American values"
- Creativity, dreams, and imagination
- Fanatical attention to consistency and detail
- Preservation and control of the Disney magic

consider essential to achieving that purpose. Based on the mission and values, we now require a statement that defines where we want to go in the future. The vision statement does just that. The vision signifies the critical transition from the unwavering mission and core values to the spirited and dynamic world of strategy.

A vision statement provides a word picture of what the organization intends ultimately to become—which may be 5, 10, or 15 years in the future. This statement should not be abstract—it should contain as concrete a picture of the desired state as possible and also provide the basis for formulating strategies and objectives. A powerful vision provides everyone in the organization with a shared mental framework that helps give form to the often abstract future that lies before us. Vision always follows mission (purpose) and values. A vision without a mission is simply wishful thinking, not linked to anything enduring. Typical elements in a vision statement include the desired scope of business activities, how the corporation will be viewed by its stakeholders (customers, employees, suppliers, regulators, etc.), areas of leadership or distinctive competence, and strongly held values.

Do You Need a Vision Statement?

Virtually every organization in every industry has a vision statement. Despite their widespread use, however, it seems clear that *vision* has become one of the most overused and possibly least understood words on the business landscape. One of the biggest problems is that a vision statement can mean different things to different people. Deeply held values, outstanding achievement, societal bonds, exhilarating goals, motivational forces, and raisons d'etre are some of the many images conjured up by vision statements.[13]

In their book *Competing for the Future*, Hamel and Prahalad note that a wide variety of leaders from many walks of life have found themselves uneasy with the concept of vision. They warn of vision statements that simply reflect an extension of the CEO's ego and the inherent danger in this approach to visioning. However, they concede that every company needs a well-articulated view about tomorrow's opportunities and challenges. They choose the word foresight over vision. *"Vision connotes a dream or an apparition, but there is more to industry foresight than a single blinding flash of insight. Industry foresight is based on deep insights into the trends in technology, demographics, regulation, and lifestyles that can be harnessed to rewrite industry rules and create new competitive space."*[14] Others warn of the potential for a "dysfunctional" vision statement. For example, a vision statement could simply be wrong. Targeting the wrong opportunities or customers may create substantial corporate momentum toward the wrong future. This momentum could prove difficult to change. With many vision statements the very real danger of a lack of reality reflected in the document or an abundance of abstraction can create real problems for the organization. Additionally, so many vision statements are simply repositories for the latest buzzwords that they appear empty and shallow. Employees will greet such statements with cynicism and question the competence of the executives who drafted the document.

Despite the views reflected above, there is little doubt among the vast majority of organizations as to the value of a well-crafted vision statement. The power of a shared vision that is lived by all employees of the organization can provide a significant motivational force. John Kotter notes three important purposes served by a vision during a change process[15]:

1. By clarifying the general direction for change, the vision simplifies hundreds or thousands of more detailed decisions.
2. The vision motivates people to take action in the right direction, even if the initial steps are personally painful.
3. Actions of different people throughout the organization are coordinated in a fast and efficient way based on the vision statement.

Regardless of the size of your organization, a skillfully created vision statement not only describes what you are attempting to accomplish but will serve to inspire all employees to join you in meeting the challenges that lie ahead. Ralph Norris, CEO of ASB Bank suggests: *"It's a lot easier to hold a steady course in a volatile and uncertain market if the company has a clear corporate vision. I think every organization should have a vision of where it's going—otherwise anywhere will do."*[16]

Effective Vision Statements

Everything discussed in this chapter is critical to your organization and your Balanced Scorecard project. However, the vision may represent the most critical component because it acts as a conduit between your reason for being as reflected in the mission, the values representative of your culture, and the strategy you will put into execution to reach your desired future state. Without a clear and compelling vision to guide the actions of all employees, you may wind up with a workforce lacking direction and thus unable to profit from any strategy you put in place, no matter how well conceived. Let's look at some characteristics of effective vision statements:

- *Concise.* The very best vision statements are those that grab your attention and immediately draw you in without boring you from pages of mundane rhetoric. Often, the simplest visions are the most powerful and compelling, like Starbucks refrain of "2000 stores by 2000." If everyone in your organization is expected to act and make decisions based on the vision, the least you can do is create something that is simple and memorable. Consider it your organizational campaign slogan for the future.

- *Appeals to all stakeholders.* A vision statement that focuses on one group to the detriment of others will not win lasting support in the hearts and minds of all constituencies. The vision must appeal to everyone who has a stake in the success of the enterprise: employees, shareholders, customers, and communities, to name but a few.

- *Consistent with mission and values.* Your vision is a further translation of your mission (why you exist) and the values of underlying importance to your organization. If your mission suggests solving problems and one of your core values is constant innovation, a reference to innovation would be expected in your vision statement. In the vision you are painting a word picture of the desired future state that will lead to the achievement of your mission and ensure the two are aligned.

- *Verifiable.* Using the latest business jargon and buzzwords can make your vision statement very nebulous to even the most trained eye. Who within your organization will be able to determine exactly when you became "world class, leading edge, or top quality"? Write your vision statement so that you will know when you have achieved it. While mission and values will not change, the vision would be expected to change because it is written for a finite period of time.

- *Feasible.* The vision should not be the collective dreams of senior management, but must be grounded solidly in reality. To ensure that this is the case, you must possess a clear understanding of your business, its markets, competitors, and emerging trends.

- *Inspirational.* Your vision represents a word picture of the desired future state of the organization. Do not miss the opportunity to inspire your team to make the emotional commitment necessary to reach this destination. The vision statement should not only guide, but also arouse the collective passion of all employees. To be inspirational, the vision must first be understandable to every conceivable audience from the boardroom to the shop floor. Throw away the thesaurus for this exercise and focus instead on your deep knowledge of the business to compose a meaningful statement for all involved.

An inspirational vision statement is one of the greatest assets you can possess in your organization, and the rewards can be tremendous. Take the story of Albert Lai, a 19-year-old entrepreneur who, along with two other young business partners, sold his start-up mydesktop.com after just two years for over a million dollars. Lai suggests a clear vision and mission is critical for entrepreneurs wanting to build their business. *"Having unified vision and mission statements for your organization allows you to have a benchmark and touchstone for when you have to make decisions for the future. This will help when there are no clear answers, or for critical decisions that will fundamentally impact your products and services.*"[17]

Developing Your Vision Statement

The section on developing your mission statement began by suggesting that the first order of business is determining who should actually be involved in the process. Should the mission represent a brilliant flash of insight from an omniscient CEO, or should the entire executive team share the arduous task? Penning your vision statement offers a similar challenge, with no simple answers. Two methods for developing your vision statement are discussed next, which (as with mission statements) represent a compromise on the "either/or" thinking of just CEO involvement or the entire executive team.

1. *The interview method.* As you might have guessed, executive interviews are the key component of this technique for developing your vision. Each of the senior executives of your organization is interviewed separately to gather their feedback on the future direction of the organization. Use an outside consultant or facilitator to run the interviews. A seasoned consultant will have been through many interviews of this nature and have the ability to put the executive at ease, ensuring that the necessary information flows freely in an environment of trust and objectivity. The interview should last about an hour and include both general and specific (industry and organization) questions, as well as a mix of past-, present-, and future-oriented queries. Typical questions may include:

   • Where and why have we been successful in the past?

   • Where have we failed in the past?

   • Why should we be proud of our organization?

   • What trends, innovations, and dynamics are currently changing our marketplace?

   • What do our customers expect from us? Our shareholders? Our employees?

   • What are our greatest attributes and competencies as an organization?

   • Where do you see our organization in 3 years? 5 years? 10 years?

   • How will our organization have changed during that time period?

   • How do we sustain our success?

   The results of the interviews are summarized by the interviewer and presented to the CEO. At this point, the CEO will have the opportunity to draft the vision based on the collective knowledge gathered from the senior team. Once the draft is completed the entire team convenes and debates the CEO's vision ensuring it captures the essential elements they discussed during their interviews. You would not expect to have the first draft accepted by everyone, and that is the idea—involve the whole team in the creation process. However, by mandating the CEO with the initial responsibility for declaring the vision, you ensure her commitment to the vision and have a working draft from which to begin the refinement process. Once the team has hammered out the vision statement it should be reviewed and accepted by as many levels in the organization as logistically possible, and with today's technology that should include just about everyone!

2. *Back to the future visioning.* I enjoy working with clients on this technique. The exercise can be administered either individually or with a group. I personally like using it with groups as the initial attempt to develop a draft vision statement, but it also works well in individual settings. In describing the method I will assume a group session. Distribute several 3" x 5" index cards to each of the participants. To begin the session, ask the group to imagine that they awaken the next morning 5, 10, or 15 years in the future (your choice of time increment). In order to record their impressions of the future, they have each been given a disposable camera to capture important images and changes they hoped might take place within their organization. At the end of each day's adventure they must create a caption for the pictures they have taken during the day. Instruct the group to use the index cards you distributed to record their captions. By the end of the trip they have catalogued the future in detail. Give the participants about 15 minutes to imagine their trip to the future and encourage them to visually capture as much as possible in their minds' eye. Ask the group: "What has happened with your organization—are you successful?" "What markets are you serving?" "What core competencies are separating you from your competitors?" "What goals have you achieved?" Once the 15 minutes are up, you say: "Unfortunately, on the trip back to the present the reentry was a little rough and the pictures were destroyed" (more animated and comedic facilitators can have a field day with this section) "but fortunately for you the captions remain." Record the captions from the index cards on a flip chart or laptop computer and use them as the raw materials for the initial draft of a vision statement. I enjoy this approach to vision statement development because it challenges the participants to engage all of their senses in the process, not simply their cognitive abilities. Not only that, but it can be fun!

These are just a couple of methods that are very useful in developing a vision statement. Fortunately for all of us, abundant literature and practice exists on this subject and you have many resources at your disposal. Once you have developed your vision you will be amazed at the power it provides, and this is the case regardless of the industry in which you work. Michael Kaiser is President of the Kennedy Center for the Performing Arts in Washington, D.C. The power of vision is every bit as vital at this renowned performing arts center as it is at a manufacturing plant or high-tech laboratory. Mr. Kaiser explains: *"I think what leaders have to do is to provide a vision for the future. And what has been remarkable to me . . . is the power of a vision. If you can present (that vision) to people, either to people inside the organization who have been damaged or people outside the organization who have lost faith in what the organization can do, the power is remarkable."*[18]

Vision Statements and the Balanced Scorecard

When vision statements were described earlier in the chapter it was suggested that they normally include the desired scope of business activities, how the corporation will be viewed by its stakeholders (customers, employees, suppliers, regulators, etc.), areas of leadership or distinctive competence, and strongly held values. When writing a vision for the organization we are attempting to move away from a paradigm of "either/or" thinking to embracing the power of "and." It is no longer a matter of satisfying one group using certain competencies at the expense of another. The vision has to balance the interests of all groups and portray a future that will lead to wins for everyone involved. The Balanced Scorecard is the mechanism we use to track our achievement of this lofty goal. The principal tenet of the Scorecard is balance, and more accurately using measurement to capture the correct balance of skills, processes, and customer requirements that lead to our desired financial future as reflected in the vision. It works equally as well whether you are in the public or the not-for-profit sector. The challenge of making your vision a reality remains critical, and the architecture of the Balanced Scorecard can be molded to help you do just that.

The Balanced Scorecard will provide a new, laser-like focus to your business, and as such the potential problems represented by a misguided vision are significant. We have all heard terms like "What gets measured gets done," "Measure what matters," and many others. The Scorecard is essentially a device that translates vision into reality through the articulation of vision (and strategy). A well-developed Balanced Scorecard can be expected to stimulate behavioral changes within your organization. The question is: Are they the sort of changes you want? Be certain the vision you have created for your organization is one that truly epitomizes your mission and values because the Scorecard will give you the means for traveling first class to that envisioned future!

STRATEGY

As I write this chapter, my wife and I are preparing for a move to a new house. Fortunately, we are moving only about 12 miles, which greatly reduces the burden, but you still have to pack up your entire house room by room. Not a day goes by that I don't hear at some point, "When are you going to pack up your office?" You see, I am a packrat of sorts and have managed to hold on to virtually every article, book, and relevant (at least to me) scrap of paper that has come my way over the course of a lifetime. Aside from a pleasant diversion, you may be wondering what this has to do with the subject at hand—strategy. Well, as part of my research efforts for this book, I have catalogued most of my archives and have come to discover that a conservative estimate would reveal that about 90 percent of the documents have at least some reference to the concept of strategy. Where do I begin, and more importantly, will I ever be able to pack it all? This plethora of materials really should not come as a surprise since the field of strategy is undoubtedly the most chronicled subject in the world of business. What is amazing is that the disciplined study of business strategy has really been around only for a few decades, but in that time has spawned literally thousands of works. An additional challenge to discussing strategy is the fact that it has relevant connections with numerous other areas of study. Who among us does not know at least one person proudly displaying a copy of *The Art of War* in his or her office? Military strategy has been around for thousands of years. Historians, physicists, biologists, psychologists, and anthropologists, to name but a few, also contribute to the subject of strategy.

From the huge mountain of information that exists we must distill what is most critical to the discussion at hand. Developing a comprehensive strategy for your organization is beyond the scope of this book. Many well-written and cogent texts are available on the subject and in the section some of them will be cited. This section will focus on reviewing the common elements of strategy and, most importantly, will outline why strategy and the Balanced Scorecard must be woven together to get the maximum benefit from both.

What Is Strategy?

Henry Mintzberg, a prolific writer on the subject of strategy, provides this excellent synopsis of the subject to begin our discussion. *"My research and that of many others demonstrates that strategy making is an immensely complex process, which involves the most sophisticated, subtle, and, at times, subconscious elements of human thinking."*[19] The difficulty with defining strategy is that it holds several meanings, depending on the source. Some believe strategy is represented by the high-level plans management devises to lead the organization into the future. Others would argue that strategy rests on the specific and detailed actions you will take to achieve your desired future. To others still, strategy is tantamount to best practices. Finally, some may consider strategy a pattern of consistency of action over time. Rather than focusing on a stifling definition of this nebulous term, let's look at some of the key principles of strategy:

- *Understanding.* To get thousands of people in a large corporation or five people on a not-for-profit board moving in the same direction, they must all understand the strategy. How can the implementers of the strategy make sense of the thousands of choices before them if they don't have a firm grasp of the strategy? Leaders must act as teachers and evangelists.

- *Different activities.* Strategy is about choosing a different set of activities than your rivals, the pursuit of which leads to a unique and valuable position in the market.[20] If everyone were to pursue the same activities, then differentiation would be based purely on operational effectiveness.

- *Trade-offs.* Effective strategies demand trade-offs in competition. Strategy is more about the choice of *what not to do* than what to do. Organizations cannot compete effectively by attempting to be everything to everybody. The entire organization must be aligned around what you choose to do and create value from that strategic position.[21]

- *Fit.* The activities chosen must fit one another for sustainable success. Our assumptions about the business must fit one another to produce a valid theory of the business. Activities are the same—they must produce an integrated whole.[22]

- *Continuity.* Although major structural changes in the industry could lead to a change in strategies, generally they should not be constantly reinvented. The strategy crystallizes your thinking on basic issues such as how you will offer customer value and to what customers. This direction needs to be clear to both internal (employees) and external (customers) constituents.[23] Changes may bring about new opportunities that can be assimilated into the current strategy, for example, new technologies.

- *Various thought processes.* Strategy involves conceptual as well as analytical exercises.[24] As the Mintzberg quote at the outset of this section reminds us, strategy involves not only the detailed analysis of complex data, but also broad conceptual knowledge of the company, industry, market, and so on.

Using the elements discussed above as ingredients, an organization could literally cook up innumerable types of strategies, and over the years they have. In their book, *Strategy Safari*, Ahlstrand, Lampel, and Mintzberg offer 10 schools of strategic thought that have emerged in the ongoing practice of management.[25] These 10 categories are presented in Exhibit 4.5.

Exhibit 4.5   Ten Schools of Strategic Thought

Design School: Proposes a model of strategy making that seeks to attain a fit between internal capabilities and external possibilities. Probably the most influential school of thought, and home of the SWOT (strengths, weaknesses, opportunities, and threats) technique.

Planning School: Formal procedure, formal training, formal analysis, and lots of numbers are the hallmark of this approach. The simple informal steps of the design school become an elaborated sequence of steps. Produce each component part as specified, assemble them according to the blueprint, and strategy will result.

Positioning School: Suggests that only a few key strategics (positions in the economic marketplace) are desirable. Much of Michael Porter's work can be mapped to this school.

Entrepreneurial School: Strategy formation results from the insights of a single leader, and stresses intuition, judgement, wisdom, experience, and insight. The "vision" of the leader supplies the guiding principles of the strategy.

Cognitive School: Strategy formation is a cognitive process that takes place in the mind of the strategist. Strategies emerge as the strategist filters the maps, concepts, and schemas shaping their thinking.

Learning School: Strategies emerge as people (acting individually or collectively) come to learn about a situation as well as their organization's capability of dealing with it.

Power School: This school stresses strategy formation as an overt process of influence, emphasizing the use of power and politics to negotiate strategies favorable to particular interests.

Cultural School: Social interaction, based on the beliefs and understandings shared by the members of an organization lead to the development of strategy.

Environmental School: Presenting itself to the organization as a set of general forces, the environment is the central actor in the strategy making process. The organization must respond to the factors or be "selected out."

Configuration School: Strategies arise from periods when an organization adopts a structure to match to a particular context that give rise to certain behaviors.

Adapted from Henry Mintzberg, Bruce Ahlstrand, and Joseph Lampel, *Strategy Safari* (New York: The Free Press, 1998).

Strategy and the Balanced Scorecard—A Critical Link

A recent article discussing the execution of strategy in organizations began this way: *"Take this quick quiz. Question #1: Three frogs are sitting on a log. One decides to jump off. How many are left? You might think two, but the answer is three. One has decided to jump off. Question #2: Three companies have poor earnings. One decides to revitalize key product lines, strengthen distribution channels, and become customer intimate. How many companies have poor earnings? You get the idea: de-*

ciding and doing are two different things."[26] Although some organizations question the value of strategy, the vast majority consider strategy a mandatory component of success. The problem is not one of developing a strategy—numerous options are available for that task as we saw in the previous section. The fundamental issue is one of implementation, translating the strategy into terms that everyone understands and thereby bringing focus to their day-to-day actions. Recall from Chapter One that 70 percent of CEO failures are not the result of poor strategy, but rather poor execution.

The Balanced Scorecard provides the framework for an organization to move from *deciding* to live their strategy to *doing* it. The Scorecard describes the strategy, breaking it down into its component parts through the objectives and measures chosen in each of the four perspectives. The Balanced Scorecard is ideally created through a shared understanding and translation of the organization's strategy into objectives, measures, targets, and initiatives in each of the four Scorecard perspectives. The translation of vision and strategy forces the executive team to specifically determine what is meant by sometimes imprecise terms contained in the strategy, for example, *world class, top-tier service,* and *targeted customers.* Through the process of developing the Scorecard an executive group may determine that *world class* translates to zero manufacturing defects. All employees can now focus their energies and day-to-day activities toward the crystal clear goal of zero defects rather than wondering about and debating the definition of *world class.* Using the Balanced Scorecard as a framework for translating the strategy, these organizations create a new language of measurement that serves to guide all employees' actions toward the achievement of the stated direction.

A key attribute of strategy formation is performing a different set of activities than your rivals. By choosing a distinct set of related activities you have the opportunity to create unique value propositions for your customers and thus separate yourself from competitors. These activities must be reflected in the Balanced Scorecard, which should parallel the strategy. In other words, if you wish to distinguish yourself by engaging in a series of activities aimed at creating customer intimacy, then your Balanced Scorecard should reflect this strategic direction. We would expect to see linked measures through the four perspectives that when taken together, will drive this strategy. Measures related to service of targeted customers should appear prominently in the Customer perspective, linked to relationship management metrics in the Internal perspective, and customer knowledge measures in the Learning and Growth perspective. This chain of linked measures, which mirrors your chosen activities, is hypothesized to drive revenue growth in the Financial perspective. Again, the Balanced Scorecard provides the means to describe and articulate the activities separating you from your competition.

It is possible to develop a Scorecard-like system without a clear and concise strategy, and many organizations do just that. However, this mix of financial and nonfinancial measures is better termed a key performance indicator Scorecard or key stakeholder Scorecard rather than a Balanced Scorecard. The problem with this approach is that you simply cannot harness the true power of the Balanced Scorecard without a strategy driving its construction. Key performance indicator or constituent Scorecards lack the ability to align an entire organization around a set of complementary themes that drive the organization toward its overall vision and mission. Instead, they often reflect a number of good ideas that lack a coherent story or direction. The Balanced Scorecard and strategy truly go hand in hand. Kaplan and Norton sum up this subject very well: *"The formulation of strategy is an art. The description of strategy, however, should not be an art. If we can describe strategy in a more disciplined way, we increase the likelihood of successful implementation. With a Balanced Scorecard that tells the story of the strategy, we now have a reliable foundation."*[27]

SUMMARY

We are all aware of the power of semantics (i.e., meanings, in today's business world). The meteoric growth of technology devices has led to information sharing at warp speed around the globe. Although the spread of knowledge is admirable and ultimately beneficial to everyone, it often leads to confusion as people begin to substitute local meanings for universally accepted terms and phrases. Nowhere is that more evident than in the domain explored in this chapter, the often murky world of mission, values, vision, and strategy. This chapter has attempted to clarify these terms and provide you with tools to either develop or reexamine your current stance on each.

A mission defines the core purpose of the organization—why it exists. The mission captures the contribution and value an organization wishes to deliver to mankind, and provides a star to steer by in our turbulent world. An effective mission may be developed using the "5 Whys" technique, and should inspire change, be easily understood and communicated, and be long term in nature. The Balanced Scorecard allows an organization to translate its mission into concrete objectives that align all employees. The measures on a Balanced Scorecard must reflect the aspirations denoted in the mission statement to provide effective direction.

Values represent the deeply held beliefs within the organization, and the timeless principles it uses to guide decision making. Values are often reflective of the personal beliefs emanating from a strong CEO or leader. We often associate positive values with the common good—doing good for others while achieving organizational goals. Several organizations such as Disney, Marriott, and Tom's of Maine have proven that profits and societal contributions are not in conflict and use their values to derive a competitive advantage. Changing an organization's value systems represents a great challenge but may be accomplished by first openly and honestly identifying current values and providing the mechanisms that facilitate a transition to more appropriate values. The Balanced Scorecard provides organizations with a means of evaluating the alignment of values throughout the organization. The Scorecard may also be used to track the extent to which an organization is living its stated values.

The vision signifies our transition from the timeless mission and values to the dynamic and often messy world of strategy. The vision provides a word picture of what the organization ultimately intends to become. Although the need for a vision statement has been questioned, most organizations agree that it provides a critical enabler by clarifying direction, motivating action, and coordinating efforts. Effective visions appeal to all stakeholders, align with mission and values, and are concise, verifiable, feasible, and inspirational. Vision statements may be created through interviewing of senior executives, or by leading group "visioning" exercises designed to enlist the full involvement of your team. The vision statement balances the interest of multiple stakeholders in describing how the organization will create future value. The role of the Scorecard is to capture the correct mix of competencies, processes, and customer value propositions that lead to our desired financial future.

The study of business strategy has rapidly evolved over the past four decades, with numerous schools of thought emerging to proclaim the power of their insights. Effective strategy making involves combining a different set of activities than your rivals to produce value for customers. Devising strategy calls for the strategy maker to draw on both analytical and broad conceptual skills. Developing a strategy is one thing; successfully implementing it is another matter. Using the Balanced Scorecard, organizations have a great opportunity to beat the odds by translating their strategy into its component parts throughout the four perspectives. Strategy is then demystified as employees from across the organization are able to focus on the strategic elements they influence.

NOTES

1. Scott Adams, *The Dilbert Principle* (New York: Harper Business, 1996).
2. James C. Collins and Jerry I. Porras, "Building Your Company's Vision," *Harvard Business Review*, September–October 1996, 65–77.
3. Julia Kirby and Diane L. Coutu, "The Beauty of Buzzwords," *Harvard Business Review*, May 2001, 30.
4. Collins and Porras, "Building Your Company's Vision," 65–77.
5. Collins and Porras, *Built to Last* (New York: Harper Business, 1997).
6. Henri F. Amiel, *Amiel's Journey* (1852), Mrs. Humphry Ward (trans.) (Macmillan & Co., 1889).

7. Richard Barrett, *Liberating the Corporate Soul* (Boston: Butterworth Heinemann, 1998).

8. J.W. Marriott and Kathi Ann Brown, *The Spirit to Serve: Marriott's Way* (New York: Harper Business, 1997).

9. Tom Chappell, *The Soul of a Business* (New York: Bantam Books, 1993).

10. Richard Barrett, *Liberating the Corporate Soul* (Boston: Butterworth Heinemann, 1998).

11. Jim Collins, *Leader to Leader* (San Francisco: Jossey-Bass, 1999).

12. Tom Morris, *If Aristotle Ran General Motors: The New Soul of Business* (New York: Henry Holt and Company, 1997).

13. Collins and Porras, "Building Your Company's Vision," 65–77.

14. Gary Hamel and C.K. Prahalad, *Competing for the Future* (Boston: Harvard Business School Press, 1994).

15. John P. Kotter, *Leading Change* (Boston: Harvard Business School Press, 1996).

16. Rebecca Macfie, "Six of Our Top Chief Executive Officers Tell the *Independent* How They Stay at the Top," *Independent Business Weekly*, April 2001, 8.

17. Carly Foster, "Business Communications: "Envision Your Business, Realize Your Goals," *Canadaone.com e-zine*, October 1999.

18. Interview on National Public Radio's *Morning Edition*, March 26, 2001.

19. Henry Mintzberg, "The Fall and Rise of Strategic Planning," *Harvard Business Review*, January–February 1994, 107–114.

20. Michael E. Porter, "What is Strategy?," *Harvard Business Review*, November–December 1996, 61–78.

21. Ibid.

22. Ibid.

23. Keith H. Hammonds, "Michael Porter's Big Ideas," *Fast Company*, March 2001, 150.

24. E.E. Chaffee, "Three Models of Strategy," *Academy of Management Review*, October 1985.

25. Henry Mintzberg, Bruce Ahlstrand, and Joseph Lampel, *Strategy Safari* (New York: The Free Press, 1998).

26. Lawrence B. MacGregor Serven, "Can Your Company Actually Execute Its Strategy?," *Harvard Management Update*, May 1999, 3.

27. Robert S. Kaplan and David P. Norton, *The Strategy Focused Organization* (Boston: Harvard Business School Press, 2001).

CHAPTER 5

Developing Performance Objectives and Measures

Roadmap for Chapter Five   Bain and Company recently released the findings of their eighth annual management tools survey. The survey examines the usage, satisfaction, and effectiveness of 25 widely used management tools among senior executives across more than 30 industries. The Balanced Scorecard was cited as a leading instrument of success for these executives. Organizations around the world are turning to the Scorecard as a powerful means of implementing their strategies through the powerful language of measurement. This chapter will explore the concepts at the very core of the Scorecard system: developing performance objectives and measures.

The chapter begins by challenging you to determine the right perspectives for your organization since the traditional four may or may not be right for you. Once you have settled on your framework, you are ready to begin gathering background information for your Scorecard objectives and measures. We will explore where to find this information, what to look for, and how to gather input from your executive team.

Developing objectives and measures in each of the Scorecard perspectives is covered in detail in the chapter. We will probe the definitions of objectives and measures, consider the distinction between leading and lagging indicators of performance, outline techniques for conducting group sessions, and carefully review how you can develop effective objectives and measures that truly tell the story of your strategy.

CHOOSING YOUR PERSPECTIVES

Are the Four Perspectives Right for You?

This chapter will describe methods you can use to translate your strategy into objectives and measures in each of the Balanced Scorecard perspectives. The question is: How many perspectives will you choose for your Scorecard? Thus far, and for the remainder of the book, I speak exclusively of four perspectives: Financial, Customer, Internal Processes, and Employee Learning and Growth. But Kaplan and Norton themselves suggest that the four perspectives *"should be considered a template, not a straitjacket."*[1] Many organizations have followed this advice and developed perspectives for innovation, research and development, environment, suppliers, leadership, and the community.

The choice of perspectives for your Balanced Scorecard should ultimately be based on what is necessary to tell the story of your strategy and create a competitive advantage for your organization. When you examine your strategy and attempt to translate it, who or what are the key constituents necessary to describe it? The four perspectives are broad enough to capture most constituents; however, if you feel your organization claims a competitive advantage as a result of relationships or processes based on another constituency, you may consider adding a separate perspective for this group. For example, a manufacturing firm may rely heavily on suppliers in order to manage its operations to the maximum of efficiency. Adding a perspective devoted to supplier relations could make good business sense for this organization.

Capturing the key stakeholders who contribute to your organization's success is critical to your Balanced Scorecard. However, you should avoid simply including every possible contributor and designing a "Stakeholder Balanced Scorecard." Scorecards of this nature identify the organization's major constituents and define goals for each. Sears's initial Scorecard, which was constructed around three related themes, illustrates a Stakeholder Balanced Scorecard. The three themes were: "a compelling place to shop," "a compelling place to work," and "a compelling place to invest." Similarly, Citicorp used this architecture for its Scorecard—"a good place to work, to bank, and to invest."[2] These Scorecards focus on three key groups— employees, shareholders, and customers—but what is missing is the "how" of value creation that a truly Balanced Scorecard can provide. What value proposition will ensure that customers are satisfied and loyal? What processes must we excel at in order to drive this customer value proposition, and what competencies must our employees possess? These are the questions you must answer to develop a Balanced Scorecard that tells the story of your strategy and demonstrates how you plan to execute that strategy. It should be noted that both Sears and Citicorp went on to develop strategic

Balanced Scorecards that included insightful internal processes to complete the description of their strategies.

Let's not forget one of the many attractions of the original Balanced Scorecard—its brevity. A well-constructed Balanced Scorecard should tell the story of the organization's strategy through a relatively small number of measures woven together through the perspectives. As a communication tool, the Scorecard's ability to quickly and accurately transmit the organization's key drivers to a wide and broad audience is a fundamental benefit of the concept. So choose the number of perspectives that allow you to capture the key stakeholders of the organization and describe how you will ultimately serve each and thereby successfully implement your strategy. The true test is whether you can easily intertwine your perspectives to tell a coherent story. Stand-alone perspectives that describe a constituent group but fail to link together with the other perspectives do not belong on a Balanced Scorecard.

DOING YOUR HOMEWORK—REVIEWING BACKGROUND INFORMATION ON BALANCED SCORECARD RAW MATERIALS

Gathering and Reviewing Background Information

Each member of your Balanced Scorecard team will approach the project with certain preconceived notions regarding the nature of your business, its competitive position, future prospects, appropriate strategy, and measures. Level the playing field for your team by gathering and reviewing as much background material as you can find. You chose your team members based on their particular background and experience, but to build an effective Scorecard everyone must have access to the total pool of information that exists on your organization. Here are some of the sources of information you might consider:

- *Annual reports.* An invaluable source of information, your annual reports will not only contain detailed financial information but will also discuss your market position, key products, prospects for the future, and maybe even nonfinancial indicators of success.
- *Mission statement.* This may actually prove quite informative and possibly entertaining. Ask each member of your team to recite the organization's mission statement. After all, most organizations do have one, and after reading Chapter Four you should definitely have one.
- *Values.* Has your organization established its guiding principles?
- *Vision.* As with the mission, if you search hard enough you should be able to find a vision statement for your organization, or perhaps you

have just developed one. Does it reflect the current organizational reality?

- *Strategic plan.* The strategic plan is the motherlode of Scorecard building information. If you're fortunate enough to have a coherent strategic plan that is based on your mission, values, and vision, you are off to a great start in the process. Most organizations are not this fortunate and often have the Scorecard project delayed, or even derailed, as the organization struggles to produce a valid strategy.

- *Project plans.* If yours is like most companies, at any given time there will be dozens of initiatives swirling about, each vying for attention and resources. It's very important that you gauge which projects appear to be aligned with the strategy of the organization and have the support of influential executives. These initiatives may be candidates to remain as important action plans in achieving one or more Scorecard measures.

- *Consulting studies.* Consultants love to consume lots of paper and often leave behind treasure troves of valuable information. Regardless of what they have been studying at your organization, they most likely will have provided background information that will prove very helpful in your review process.

- *Performance reports.* You may not have a Balanced Scorecard, but every organization is run on some kind of management reporting system. Find and review at least a year's worth of these reports to determine what indicators of performance are currently deemed critical to the organization's success.

- *Competitor data.* Knowing what your competitors are doing and, if possible, what they're tracking may help you determine some of your own key objectives and measures. But remember the essence of strategy: doing different things than your rivals to create value. Do not simply copy the metrics of your competitors. They may have mature processes that focus on different aspects of the value chain than your organization, and hence their metrics would might actually prove counterproductive to your efforts.

- *Organizational histories.* Has anyone chronicled the history of your organization? If so, it will likely provide a wealth of information on why the organization was started (mission), what the founders valued, key lessons learned over the years, and a picture of the future.

- *Analyst reports.* If you are publicly traded analyst reports will provide an excellent glimpse into what the market values about your company. These documents often provide an abundance of statistical data as well.

- *Trade journals and news articles.* What is the business press saying about your organization? What you find here may have a strong impact on the measures you choose to influence public opinion.

• *Benchmarking reports.* Benchmarking is still quite popular, and many excellent studies are available on a wide variety of industries and functional specialties. While these documents provide good background and may stimulate discussion of potential measures, it is not a good idea to rely exclusively on them. Your Balanced Scorecard should tell the story of *your* strategy. The measures you choose to represent that strategy may in some cases mirror those of other organizations, but it is the determination of the key drivers for your particular organization that will ultimately differentiate you from your rivals.

The sources shown above are not intended to provide an exhaustive list, and in fact you may uncover several more. In determining where to search for information, and to further reinforce Scorecard fundamentals within your team, consider using the Balanced Scorecard architecture to assist you in identifying sources of material. For example, under the Financial perspective you would ask yourself, "Where might we find information relating to the financial performance of the organization?" From that question a number of candidates will likely spring to mind: annual reports, analyst reports, management reports, and the like. Exhibit 5.1 displays some of the sources you may discover under each element of the Balanced Scorecard.

What to Look for in Your Background Materials

The task of unearthing background material may appear somewhat daunting at first, but you will end up discovering more than you expected. While the information you collect will be informative, you should develop a plan to determine specifically what you hope to discern from your research. You will also require a repository for the prodigious amount of material you are sure to generate now and during the rest of the project. See the box on the next page on capturing this important information in a file structure.

One critical element to scrutinize is consistency. Are the documents providing a single view of the organization's mission, core values, vision, and strategies? Your Balanced Scorecard development depends on a shared understanding of those vital elements throughout the organization. If you find conflicting information, document it carefully and make the resolution of such discrepancies a goal of your executive interviews and workshop. Likewise, you will want to record any findings that suggest a strong and unified view on the mission, values, vision, and strategy. During the executive interview process you can confirm their ongoing validity.

Your review should also contribute several possible objectives and measures for each of the four Balanced Scorecard perspectives. Specific metrics will no doubt be sprinkled throughout the documents you review, and while you may not always find exact references to measures, the documents should

Exhibit 5.1   Using the Balanced Scorecard to Find Background Information

Financial	Customer
• Annual report • Performance reports • Analyst reports • Trade journals • Benchmark reports	• Marketing department • Trade journals • Consulting studies • Project plans • Strategic plan • Performance reports • Benchmark reports

Mission, Values, Vision, and Strategy

• Mission statement
• Values
• Vision statement
• Strategic plan
• Organizational histories
• Consulting studies
• Project plans

Internal Process	Employee Learning and Growth
• Operational reports • Manufacturing reports • Competitor data • Benchmark reports • Trade journals • Consulting studies • Project plans	• Human resources data • Trade journals • Core values • Benchmark reports • Consulting studies

---

A Filing System for Your Balanced Scorecard Project

No matter how small or large your organization, any project of this magnitude is sure to generate a lot of information. Simplify your efforts by creating both paper and electronic filing methods to capture, store, and share the knowledge you develop. Create binders and electronic file directories that mirror the specific steps in your project plan. For example, you may have a directory or binder titled "Background Information." Tabs in your binder and subdirectories on your computer could be labeled, "Executive interviews," "Strategy information," and so on.

The electronic filing is especially important since each member of your team will have preferred methods of naming and storing files. Develop a process everyone can agree on and insist that all relevant project files be posted on a shared drive that the whole team can access. Consider adding a date to every file created, or use another form of version control, to ensure that you are always working with the most recent copy of your document.

This may seem like a small and logical step, but it is often overlooked until an abundance of documentation has been created, and nobody seems to know where anything is located. Developing a Balanced Scorecard is tough enough; don't make it even more difficult by hampering your efforts through poor data management.

lead you in the right direction. For example, operational plans will include details of some key processes employed at your company. These will help you determine objectives and measures in the Internal Process perspective. Similarly, your research may produce information regarding core competencies that your organization hopes to leverage in the future. These competencies can help frame discussions of your Employee Learning and Growth perspective.

The concept of using the Balanced Scorecard as a strategic management system was introduced in Chapter One. Our goal in the evolution from a measurement system to a strategic management system is to make the Scorecard the cornerstone of management processes throughout the organization. Later chapters will detail the specific steps you will need to take to make this transition. For now, you should gather background material on your organization's key management processes such as budgeting and business planning, compensation design and delivery, and management reporting. An in-depth understanding of these processes will be very beneficial when you begin linking them to your Balanced Scorecard.

Conducting Interviews to Gather Executive Input

Once you have gathered sufficient background information, you are ready to synthesize your findings and confirm them through a one-on-one interview process with each member of the executive team. The importance of executive support for the Balanced Scorecard has been noted several times already, and is reiterated here. This is your first opportunity to work with the executive team on the Balanced Scorecard project. We all know how important first impressions are in business and in life. Ensure that you are prepared to show your executive team the value of this concept and the ability of your team to deliver results. Consider the following format for your interviews:

- *Review purpose.* Your executives should already be familiar with the Balanced Scorecard project; however, you should take the necessary time to explain the importance of soliciting their feedback in building an effective Scorecard. Outline with them (briefly) what you will be covering during the meeting, and the anticipated duration.

- *Mission, vision, values, and strategy.* Begin the interview by collecting executive input on these four critical elements of the Balanced Scorecard. Unless asked specifically, don't share what you have learned from your research. You are attempting to determine how your executives view these items and whether there is alignment among your senior team. The following questions may be used:

  - Has the mission for the organization been defined? If so, what is that mission?

  - What core values are essential in pursuit of the mission?

  - Has the organization developed a vision statement? If so, what is the vision?

  - What key strategies will lead us to the achievement of our vision?

  If the executive you are interviewing provides little in the way of details on these subjects or doesn't feel the organization really has any of the above, you will need to "redirect" the questions. Take the opportunity to probe the executive on her views of each by asking: "Why do you feel we exist as an organization (mission)?" "What core values do we hold?" "Where do you see us in 5, 10, or 15 years (vision)?" "What must we do to reach that desired future (strategy)?"

- *Performance measurement.* Use this component of the interview to accumulate the executive's thoughts on what objectives and measures are critical to the organization's success.

  - How will we achieve the strategies you just discussed?

  - What data or measures do you currently use to gauge success of the organization?

  - Do you have targets for the measures? If so, what are they?

  - What data or reports are most useful, and why?

  Of this set, the last question is particularly interesting. Most organizations are currently gathering an abundance of data, some of which is valuable, and some of which is completely disregarded. In the future, the Balanced Scorecard should be the focal report of management reporting. Find out what executives are watching now, what they like, and what they don't like.

- *Implementation issues.* In the final phase of the interview you hope to determine how well the executive understands the Balanced Scorecard and what must be done if the project is to succeed.

  - How would you rate your direct reports' knowledge of the Balanced Scorecard?

  - What would help enhance your team's understanding of this concept?

  - What are some of the barriers we may face in implementing the Balanced Scorecard, and how do we overcome them?

You'll notice from the first question in this set that I do not advocate simply asking your executives to rate themselves on Scorecard knowledge. What self-respecting executive in today's measurement-managed environment is likely to admit that he has never heard of the concept? Instead, ask them about their team. During the conversation you will be able to gauge whether the executive appears to be knowledgeable of the subject himself. If he says, "Well, Joe's former company did a high-level Scorecard, cascaded it from top to bottom, and used it to drive strategic learning through the management review process," then you will know that this executive probably has a pretty good grasp on the concepts. Plus, you can now casually slip in something like, "Sounds like you're pretty familiar with the Scorecard yourself. Have you experienced it before?" You will now be able to glean from the executive his direct Scorecard experience. Knowing which members of the executive team possess significant Scorecard knowledge is a great asset. These members of the senior team can act as sounding boards for your team's efforts and should be the first to provide leadership and support for the project.

Schedule the interviews for one hour, and limit your questions to about 10 to 15. You want your executives to be able to fully share their feelings on these subjects and don't want to cut them off in the middle of a thought to move on to another question. Some executive interviews have as few as two or three questions or as many as 40 (no kidding!).

In addition to interviewing members of your executive team, consider meeting with other influential people in the organization who may be in a position to increase the odds of a successful project. At some point you will be relying heavily on your information technology department to collect and disseminate data, so be sure and include them in the process. Finance, human resources, marketing, and operations will also be involved in the project. Don't use the same interview questions with these groups as you did with the executive team. The goal during those interviews is to inform the audiences of your project plans and win their support and assistance.

DEVELOPING YOUR OBJECTIVES AND MEASURES

Effective Translation Is the Key to Building Your Balanced Scorecard

Not to state the obvious, but why is it we require translators to tell us what someone we cannot understand is saying? Translation is necessary because we do not speak the language and therefore do not possess the ability to take action on what the person is saying based on our lack of comprehension. Think of the lexicon of the modern business organization. For the people on the front lines our "five-dollar words" must seem like a completely different language. Imagine sharing this gem at your next town-hall meeting: "If we leverage core competencies across the value chain and maximize synergistic opportunities among strategic alternatives, we may be able to reach EVA targets." How can someone who will leave that meeting and meet with a customer an hour later act on that statement? They can't. Given our choice of language, it is little wonder the effective implementation of strategy has been noted as the main cause of CEO failure in the United States. Employees require words that have meaning to them and will result in action, not confused inertia.

The next sections of this chapter will explore the faithful translation of your mission, values, vision, and strategy into language that motivates performance and ensures a shared understanding of the organization's goals. Translation means expressing something in other words, and the tools we use to do this are objectives and measures.

Take a look at Exhibit 5.2. This graphic is a representation of the development of our Balanced Scorecard. Chapter Four discussed mission, values, vision, and strategy in depth, and this chapter will explore how the Balanced Scorecard brings these concepts to life through the selection of objectives and measures. The arrows in the diagram indicate that the Scorecard is both a "top-down" and "bottom-up" process. We normally construct the Balanced Scorecard by starting at the top and translating mission, values, vision, and strategy. Equally important, however, is the bottom-up strategic learning that results from using the Balanced Scorecard. The objectives and measures we choose will tell the story of our strategy and over time the analysis of results will provide us with a gauge of the effectiveness of our implementation.

SETTING OBJECTIVES FOR THE BALANCED SCORECARD

What Are Performance Objectives?

Between your strategy, which defines the activities and choices you make to separate yourself as an organization, and the performance measures you

Exhibit 5.2   Translating with the Balanced Scorecard

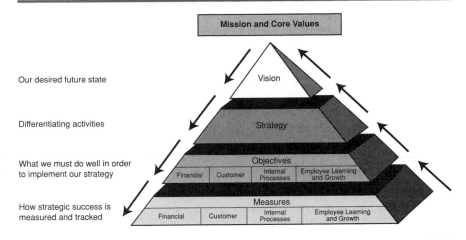

select to gauge your overall effectiveness, you require a set of performance objectives that describe what you must do well in order to execute your strategy. Objective statements are just that—concise statements that describe the specific things you must perform well if you are to successfully implement your strategy. The objectives you create will act as a bridge from the high-level strategy you've selected to the specific performance measures that you will use to determine your progress toward overall goals.

Developing Objectives

The best way to create performance objectives is to examine each perspective of the Balanced Scorecard in the form of a question. Challenge your team to consider these questions, and base your objectives on the responses you collect:

- *Financial perspective: What financial steps are necessary to ensure the execution of our strategy?* For example, if your organization is pursuing a cost-reduction or efficiency strategy, you may consider objectives such as "Lower our indirect costs" or "Increase revenue per employee." The objectives you choose in the financial perspective will be affected not only by the strategy you choose to follow, but also by the life cycle of your business. A growing business pursuing an efficiency strategy would be more concerned with revenue per employee, while a mature business may focus solely on cost reductions.

- *Customer perspective: Who are our targeted customers, and what is our value proposition in serving them?* The value proposition you select will ultimately drive the objectives and measures selected for this perspective. An organization pursuing a value proposition of customer intimacy may include objectives such as "Increase retention rates" and "Increase knowledge of customer buying patterns." Increasing customer satisfaction and loyalty are often found in the Customer perspective. As long as they reflect your value proposition, these objectives are perfectly appropriate. One caution, however: Don't limit yourself to purely "outcome" objectives, which these in fact are. The terms *lagging* and *leading* measures will be discussed a little later in the chapter, but for now just remember that an objective like "Increase customer loyalty" does not represent an isolated act. To increase loyalty you must engage in certain processes or behaviors that will ultimately lead to the goal of increasing loyalty among customers. In other words, what drives customer loyalty?

- *Internal Process perspective: To satisfy our customers and shareholders, at what processes must we excel?* One of the many benefits of the Balanced Scorecard is evident from your work in this perspective. Most performance systems tend to focus on the incremental improvement of current organizational processes, whereas the Balanced Scorecard—with its focus on strategy and the interplay among objectives and measures—may lead to the development of entirely new processes to drive customer and shareholder value. Consider, for example, an organization that chooses a Customer objective of "Lowering complaints." If, upon investigation, they discover no formal process for dispute resolution, they had better develop one quickly or achieving their overall objectives may prove very difficult! Objectives chosen for this perspective will often flow directly from those appearing in the Customer perspective. An objective of "Lower return rates" in the Customer perspective of a retail outlet may lead to "Work with 'A'-rated suppliers" in the Internal Process perspective.

- *Employee Learning and Growth perspective: What capabilities and tools do our employees require to help them execute our strategy?* Most organizations use the Employee Learning and Growth perspective to document issues relating to employee skills development. "Close skills gaps" and "Increase employee training" will appear frequently on a Balanced Scorecard. Although these are important objectives, do not forget to look beyond your employees to the tools they rely on to get their jobs done. Do they have access to the latest customer information on their computers? Are there processes in place to capture and share employee knowledge? These questions must be considered and represented in the objectives you choose for this perspective.

When developing your performance objectives, it helps to begin each with an action verb: increase, reduce, initiate, develop, lower, improve, become, achieve, and so on. The use of these verbs distinguishes the action-oriented nature of objectives from the sometimes static world of strategies by answering the crucial question of how the strategy will be executed. You may have a strategy of operational efficiency translated into the following objectives. We will execute our strategy of operational efficiency by lowering costs, increasing loyalty, reducing rework, and closing skills gaps.

Your objectives should motivate action, but they do not necessarily need to be quantitative in nature. Providing specific numerical representations of success is the domain of the performance measure, not the objective. Keep in mind that the Balanced Scorecard is about translation: translating the strategy into objectives, and then determining the best measure to track achievement of that objective.

Because your Balanced Scorecard team will be comprised of people from a variety of functional areas, you must ensure that everyone has a shared understanding of the objectives you have generated. Develop statements that clarify or describe the specific meaning of each objective. These statements should be one or two sentences long, just enough to capture the authentic intent of the objective but never so long as to discourage someone from reading them. For example, you may have an objective of "Closing skills gaps" under the Employee Learning and Growth perspective. As stated, this objective is somewhat vague and could be open to interpretation by those reading it. An accompanying statement might read: "We will close our skills gap by increasing strategic skills available to the organization through recruitment, training, and retention of key staff." Based on this articulation of the objective, you may develop performance measures around strategic skills, recruitment efforts, training, or retention. The statement describes how you will achieve the objective without detailing the specific steps necessary.

Develop Objectives and Measures First—Then Create Cause-and-Effect Linkages

Many articles and books on performance measurement, as well as consultants, advocate the development of linked objectives and measures through the four perspectives of the Scorecard. In other words, they suggest that you build your cause-and-effect linkages while developing objectives and measures. Theoretically, this sounds both expeditious and logical, but practically it has limitations. Interestingly, while the literature abounds with this advice, there is little in the way of techniques for successfully carrying out this particular process. That's because the actual work of sitting around a conference table and hammering out a coherent and logical story of your strategy through a series of linked objectives and measures is extremely difficult. My principal point of contention with the approach is that it can limit the creativity of the group in designing the powerful new performance measures that make the difference in driving your strategy. Often, the first performance driver for a particular objective or measure is chosen with little thought to the many alternatives which may exist. The work is simplified and more satisfying to all involved if you split the functions in two.

1. Develop objectives and measures for each of the four perspectives.
2. Create a description of your strategy from those, or completely new, objectives and measures.

Start your development process by brainstorming as many objectives and measures as your group can produce in each of the four perspectives. You chose your team based on their diverse backgrounds, functional specialties, and problem-solving abilities. Use a brainstorming session that allows the group to explore the full range of its creative abilities, motivating participants to draw on their complete spectrum of experiences. You will undoubtedly have dozens of potential objectives and measures in no time at all. Once you are ready to construct your strategy map of linked objectives and measures, you will have already created a virtual menu of options to choose from that reflect the experiences of the entire team. Your first brainstorming session may not capture every critical objective and measure, but will generate many possible alternatives for your consideration. During the building process you will have plenty of time to add new objectives and measures as they surface from team members, executives, literature reviews, research, and employees.

You will soon discover that Balanced Scorecard development is a very iterative process. Undoubtedly, your final Scorecard will not resemble your first draft in any way, and that's the way it should be since each successive version will more accurately depict your strategic landscape. This is another reason the two-step process of developing objectives and measures and then creating linkages is preferable to the alternative of completing the steps as one process. If you attempt to create a strategy map "from scratch" and later determine the objectives or measures are not well suited to your goals, or if your executive team feels they are not the right elements, you basically must start over from the beginning. With the brainstorming approach you have a vast supply of potential objectives and measures to "plug and play" into your strategy map until the appropriate balance is achieved. Let's review some tips on conducting effective sessions for generating objectives and measures.

Conducting "Objectives and Measures Generation Sessions"

The word *brainstorming* was intentionally left out of the title of this section. Although the brainstorming concept is very effective, some people feel trapped in these sessions and consider it stressful to generate ideas on demand. With that in mind, you may want to dub these meetings "idea generation sessions" or "hypothesis meetings"—anything you feel will produce interest and creativity within your group. Regardless of the moniker you put on the get-together, the end in mind is the generation of a large number of objectives and measures to tell the story of your strategy. Sessions of this nature are beneficial for a number of reasons. They:

- *Encourage creativity.* No idea is rejected during the meeting, and the open environment of sharing and mutual respect can often lead to breakthroughs in thinking.
- *Foster ownership.* The team you assemble owns this process until (and possibly after) the tool is put into production at your organization. Having all members participate in this session, putting forth their personal beliefs, will lead to a sense of ownership and commitment.
- *Level the playing field.* Undoubtedly, your team will include members from various levels of the organization. During these meetings everyone is on equal footing, and the sharing of ideas in a casual setting helps to build team cohesion.
- *Produce a large number of ideas.* Let's not forget why we are having the session! These meetings tend to produce a vast number of objectives and measures in a timely fashion. Some will obviously have more potential than others, but having a broad array from which to choose will assist your strategy mapping efforts to follow.

Like any meeting, these will require careful planning to produce successful results. Let's look at what should take place before, during, and after the meeting to ensure that your team generates mountains of potential objectives and measures for your Balanced Scorecard.

Before the meeting: Preparation is the key to success in any meeting situation. The first thing you have to consider is who will facilitate the session? Consistent with earlier recommendations, using an outside consultant or trained facilitator to manage the meeting is suggested. A good consultant or facilitator will be able to spark group thinking and apply proven techniques to ensure that you achieve your objectives. Schedule the sessions for a maximum of three hours. It is very difficult to sustain the type of momentum these gatherings require for more than three hours. Here are some other items to consider before your session:

- *Distribute materials in advance.* The Balanced Scorecard will translate your mission, values, vision, and strategy, so ensure that the team has received the most recent versions of each of these documents. In addition, pass around the information you gathered from your executive interviews.

- *Logistics.* If possible, the event should be held off-site to ensure that your team is not distracted by seemingly urgent activities taking place around you at the time of the meeting.

- *Prepare the room.* Regardless of where you stage your meeting, room preparation is key. Post the mission, values, vision, and strategy on large banners or pages at prominent locations around the room. Everyone in attendance should be able to clearly see these documents for easy reference. Also post any particularly interesting or relevant quotes heard during your executive interviews. The senior management team must ultimately own this tool, and therefore you want to ensure that their thinking is imprinted into everything you do. You must also have flip chart pages up and ready to capture input from the group. Have sheets prepared for each of the perspectives of the Scorecard, along with parking lot items and other issues. Finally, we all know the old saying "The devil is in the details." Make sure you have an ample supply of flip chart paper, Post-it notes, pens, and tape to capture it all.

During the meeting: Filmmaker Woody Allen is credited with saying *"90 percent of life is showing up."* I have really enjoyed many of Woody's cinematic efforts, but I have to disagree with him on that point—at least as it relates to your Balanced Scorecard meetings. Once your attendees "show up," it is then up to you to make sure everyone gets the most out of the session. You have done your homework, distributed your materials, and have assurances of perfect attendance at your meeting. Now let's look at what must take place during the session to guarantee a successful outcome.

- *Opening the meeting.* Your facilitator should thank everyone for attending, congratulate them on their efforts to this point, and clearly outline the challenging yet exciting work that lies ahead. She will also state her role in the session—that of objective facilitator. Objectives for the meeting should be presented, along with housekeeping items such as timing and amenities (if you're off-site). Finally, the session's ground rules will be presented. Although the session is meant to be casual, certain rules do apply—specifically, active participation by all participants, no rejected ideas, and adherence to the time limits.

- *Capturing ideas.* The facilitator kicks off the main portion of the meeting by reading the mission, values, vision, and strategies aloud to the group, along with anything else posted on the walls of the room. She then opens the floor up to ideas for potential objectives and measures in each of the four perspectives. As participants provide ideas they are captured on the flip chart page corresponding to the appropriate perspective of the Scorecard. Our first session of this type at Nova Scotia Power yielded over 100 potential objectives and measures in the initial 45 minutes. You will have great success as well, but inevitably every brainstorming session will eventually hit a creative brick wall. Here are a couple of suggestions to help get the creative juices flowing again. First, try introducing some physical activity into the meeting. One technique is known as *brainwalking*.[3] Have your team members get up from their chairs and walk around the room. As they pass the flip charts with objectives and measures, everyone is required to add at least one item to each list before they can sit down again. Just the physical activity and stretch afforded by this simple exercise can stimulate further creativity. Another idea to spice things up is the paper airplane method.[4] When the group appears a little fatigued, fold together a paper airplane and toss it in the air to someone nearby. Whoever is seated closest to the landing must provide an idea to the group. They then toss the plane in the air where it will land near someone else who has the same responsibility. If these little tricks of the trade don't work and your group appears very listless, you can always resort to a little cheating. Provide the facilitator with a list of possible objectives and measures you have found in benchmarking reports, reviews of trade journals, and so on. She can share a few with the group in an attempt to get them back on track. During the meeting your team may suggest that some objectives and measures can be linked together in a cause-and-effect relationship. Although strategy mapping is not the goal of this meeting, you will want to record any possible relationships among measures. Using different colored Post-it notes to denote possible linkages will be helpful. Conclude the meeting by summarizing the list of objectives and measures you have collected in each of the Scorecard perspectives. This gives participants the opportunity to clarify meanings and eliminate any items that may have been repeated.

After the meeting: Your team leader will have the responsibility of gathering the flip charts and having the material typed and distributed to the group. Any cause-and-effect relationships suggested during the meeting should also be documented for the group's review.

These sessions are a great way to foster a sense of teamwork and mutual accountability among your Balanced Scorecard team. While not every objective and measure appearing on your well-worn flip chart pages will ultimately appear on your Balanced Scorecard, they do provide a great head start and get your team accustomed to thinking in terms of the Balanced Scorecard perspectives and what it takes to effectively translate a strategy.

Refining Your Objectives

The session described above will undoubtedly result in dozens of possible objectives. How many objectives do you need, and how do you determine which to keep? The Balanced Scorecard is a powerful communication tool, signaling to everyone in the organization the key strategies for success and providing an opportunity for all employees to contribute to the achievement of those strategies. It is difficult to harness the communication power of the Scorecard if you have a multitude of objectives. Keep in mind that each objective on the Scorecard may result in two performance measures to accurately capture the intent of the objective. Therefore, if you want to keep your Scorecard limited to approximately 20 measures, you should have no more than 10 objectives. Try and limit the number of objectives to a maximum of three per each Scorecard perspective.

Once the team has had a chance to reflect on the objectives you have developed, hold a follow-up session. Depending on the number of objectives you have generated, you may need more than one meeting. During this meeting you will ask your team to vote on the objectives they believe should be included in your Balanced Scorecard. Each objective should be reviewed to ensure consistency with your mission, values, and vision. The objectives must also be examined to ensure that they represent a faithful translation of your strategy. Ask yourself: Will achievement of this objective lead to the successful execution of our strategy?

PERFORMANCE MEASURES—THE HEART OF THE BALANCED SCORECARD

What Are Performance Measures?

Earlier in the chapter when performance objectives were introduced, they were defined as concise statements that describe the specific things you must perform well if you are to successfully implement your strategy. But how do we know if we are in fact performing well on our objectives? Performance measures are the tools we use to determine whether we are meeting our objectives and moving toward the successful implementation of our strategy. Specifically, we may describe measures as quantifiable (normally, but not always) standards used to evaluate and communicate performance against expected results. However, no simple definition can truly capture the power that well-crafted and communicated performance measures can have on an organization. Measures communicate value creation in ways that even the most charismatic CEO's speeches never can. They function as a tool to drive desired action, provide all employees with direction in how they can help contribute to the organization's overall goals, and supply management with a tool in determining overall progress toward strategic goals. So measures are critically important to your Balanced Scorecard, but generating performance measures may not be as simple as you think. In a recent study by the American Institute of Certified Public Accountants, 27 percent of respondents stated "the ability to define and agree upon measures" as the most frequent barrier to implementing or revising a performance measurement system.[5]

This section will examine the powerful role of the performance measure in the Balanced Scorecard. The distinction between lagging and leading measures is our starting point, as it will prove essential in your measure development efforts. We will then dissect each of the four perspectives of the Scorecard, reviewing how to go about creating specific measures for each, and examining different types of measures we might encounter. Hopefully, after reading the following sections, your organization will not state *the ability to define and agree upon measures* as the biggest barrier to developing your performance measurement system.

Looking Back and Looking Ahead—Lagging and Leading Measures of Performance

I gave a presentation at a Software conference recently, and about halfway through the session I thought to myself, "I'm getting lots of questions today, and everyone is really attentive—hardly a yawn to be seen! I bet I'll get good reviews from this group." My thought was based on the premise that I desired good reviews from the group, and to get that positive feedback I had to hold the group's attention for the entire presentation period and encourage their active participation. In effect, I hypothesized that a low number of yawns and a high number of questions would lead to positive reviews on my evaluation sheets. In other words, the "yawn" and "question" measures were the performance drivers (leading indicators) of my overall evaluation score (lagging indicator). That is the key distinction between the two: Lag indicators represent the consequences of actions previously taken, while lead indicators are the measures that lead to—or drive—the results achieved in the lagging indicators. For example, sales, market share, and lost time accidents may all be considered lagging indicators. What drives each of these lagging indicators? Sales may be driven by hours spent with customers, market share may be driven by brand awareness, and lost time accidents may be driven by the safety audit scores. Leading indicators should predict performance of lagging measures.

Your Balanced Scorecard should contain a mix of leading and lagging indicators. Lagging indicators without performance drivers fail to inform us of how we hope to achieve our results. Conversely, leading indicators may signal key improvements throughout the organization, but on their own they do not reveal whether these improvements are leading to improved customer and financial results. Coming up with the lagging measures probably will not pose much of a challenge since our measurement language is awash in such indicators: sales, profits, satisfaction, and many others are common measures in use today. It is perfectly appropriate to feature a number of these lagging indicators on your Scorecard. While you may share such measures with many other organizations, your leading indicators are what set you apart by identifying the specific activities and processes you believe are critical to driving those lagging indicators of success.

The discussion of leading and lagging measures receives a lot of attention at performance management training seminars and in the Balanced Scorecard literature. Unfortunately, when it comes to actually developing good Balanced Scorecards, many organizations fail to closely monitor their mix of these important variables. While most people grasp the concept intellectually, they are hard pressed to actually develop leading indicators, and instead place a great reliance on lagging measures of performance. To overcome this issue, build the discussion of leading measures into all of your measurement dialogues. For example, during the "Measure Generation Sessions" discussed earlier, whenever someone suggests a lagging indicator of performance, the facilitator should say, "Good, now what drives performance for that measure?" When collecting measures on your flip charts, you should have two columns established: one for lagging indicators and a second for the leading measures that will drive your outcome measures. Lag and lead measures are contrasted in Exhibit 5.3.

Exhibit 5.3   Lag and Lead Performance Measures

	Lag	*Lead*
Definition	Measures focusing on results at the end of a time period, normally characterizing historical performance	Measures that "drive" or lead to the performance of lag measures, normally measuring intermediate processes and activities.
Examples	• Market share • Sales • Employee satisfaction	• Hours spent with customers • Proposals written • Absenteeism
Advantages	Normally easy to identify and capture	Predictive in nature, and allow the organization to make adjustments based on results
Issues	Historical in nature and do not reflect current activities; lack predictive power	May prove difficult to identify and capture; often new measures with no history at the organization

The Balanced Scorecard should contain a mix of lag and lead measures of performance.

MEASURES FOR THE FINANCIAL PERSPECTIVE

In Chapter One, the Balanced Scorecard was introduced as a method organizations can turn to for overcoming their almost exclusive reliance on financial measures of performance. A number of issues relating to financial measures were discussed:

- They are not consistent with today's business environment in which most value is created by intangible assets.

- Financial measures provide a great "rearview mirror" of the past but often lack predictive power.

- Consolidation of financial information tends to promote functional silos.

- Long-term value-creating activities may be compromised by short-term financial metrics from activities such as employee reductions.

- Most high-level financial measures provide little in the way of guidance to lower-level employees in their day-to-day actions.

Despite their apparent shortcomings, a well-constructed Balanced Scorecard is not complete without financial measures of performance. Scorecard practitioners recognize this fact, and most actually consider financial measures to represent the most important component of the Scorecard. One recent study indicated that 49 percent of organizations give financial measures higher importance than any other indicators.[6]

By using the Balanced Scorecard an organization has the opportunity to mitigate, if not eliminate entirely, many of the issues related to financial measures. For example, cascading your financial measures to lower levels of the organization provides an opportunity for all employees to demonstrate how their day-to-day activities contribute to the organization's overall strategy and goals, ultimately influencing financial returns. Financial measures should be part of any Balanced Scorecard, whether a private enterprise or not-for-profit or public-sector organization. This chapter will focus on financial measures for the private-sector world; however, Chapter 13 will discuss the use of this perspective in the not-for-profit and public sectors.

All measures selected to appear in your Balanced Scorecard should link together in a chain of cause-and-effect relationships that tell the story of your strategy. The financial measures you choose represent the "end in mind" for your story. Scorecard architects Kaplan and Norton put it this way: *"We start with the destination. What are we trying to achieve? . . . If you look at the logic of the Scorecard, the arrows all end up with financials."*[7] As "the destination," the measures in the financial perspective help to lay the groundwork for the selection of measures in each of the other three perspectives. As we develop linked measures in the customer, internal process, and employee learning and growth perspectives, we must ensure that their inclusion will lead to improved financial results and the implementation of our strategy. We could focus all of our energy and capabilities on improving customer satisfaction, quality, on-time delivery, or any number of things, but without an indication of their effect on the organization's financial returns, they alone are of limited value.

Choosing Financial Measures

Like all measures on the Balanced Scorecard, financial metrics should be derived as direct translations of the organization's strategy. Strategies are concerned with the differentiating activities that ultimately lead to success, and therefore we would expect a wide variety of measures in each of the Scorecard perspectives, including Financial. In practice, however, most organizations choose financial measures related to three areas: growth, profitability, and value creation.

At some point, most organizations will desire *growth* in markets served or revenues earned. Measures such as revenue from new products and share of target market are very useful to determine the fulfillment of this goal. While growth is often an objective, for the private-sector organization *profitability* is always a key criterion of success. Over the decades, our traditional accounting systems have developed numerous methods of calculating corporate profitability. Gross margin, net income, and profit as a percentage of sales are all typically used.

Although measures of growth and profitability are valuable, they cannot be relied on exclusively to tell the financial story of the enterprise. Take, for example, an organization that wishes to grow earnings. Expanding operations and investing in a new plant will undoubtedly accomplish this objective, but at what cost? *Value* is enhanced only if the expansion is profitable and achieves a return greater than the cost of capital. It is possible for a company to increase earnings and still destroy shareholder value if the cost of capital associated with new investments is sufficiently high.[8] To determine whether financial investments are truly creating value, many organizations have turned to the calculation of economic value added (EVA). Simply put, EVA equals a firm's net operating profit after taxes less a capital charge. Using EVA as a yardstick, many organizations now have a tool to evaluate the opportunity costs of various investment alternatives. For example, London-based Diageo PLC, which owns United Distillers & Vintners Limited, used EVA to gauge which of its liquor brands generated the best returns. The analysis determined that because of the time required for storage and care, aged Scotch did not generate as much profit as vodka, which could be sold within weeks of being distilled. As a result of the EVA analysis, management at United Distillers began to emphasize vodka production and sales.[9]

Not every organization will choose financial measures relating to growth, profitability, or value. Some, especially those in the financial and insurance industries, may choose indicators of risk management to complement other financial measures. Westdeutsche Landesbank is a German Wholesale bank represented in more than 35 countries worldwide. In developing financial measures at their New York City branch, West LB chose to augment their traditional financial measures of revenue growth and cost containment with a measure of risk-adjusted return on capital. This addition reflected the importance of risk management in their portfolio.

Some organizations will venture beyond their accounting systems and look to Wall Street to supplement their financial perspective. Measures of share price and market valuation are often found on Balanced Scorecards. Those working in organizations heavily reliant on innovation and human capital (who isn't?) may desire a financial measure capturing the value of their intellectual assets. As with all Balanced Scorecard measures, the key is alignment to one's strategy. The measures selected for the financial perspective will help set the course you take in determining measures for the rest of the Scorecard, so ensure that they reflect the goals in your strategic plan. Your measures should tell your individual story, but to help get you started a list of commonly used financial measures is provided in Exhibit 5.4.

Exhibit 5.4   Commonly Used Financial Measures

- Total assets
- Total assets per employee
- Profits as a % of total assets
- Return on net assets
- Return on total assets
- Revenues/total assets
- Gross margin
- Net income
- Profit as a % of sales
- Profit per employee
- Revenue
- Revenue from new products
- Revenue per employee
- Return on equity (ROE)
- Return on capital employed (ROCE)
- Return on investment (ROI)
- Economic value added (EVA)
- Market value added (MVA)

- Value added per employee
- Compound growth rate
- Dividends
- Market value
- Share price
- Shareholder mix
- Shareholder loyalty
- Cash flow
- Total costs
- Credit rating
- Debt
- Debt to equity
- Times interest earned
- Days sales in receivables
- Accounts receivable turnover
- Days in payables
- Days in inventory
- Inventory turnover ratio

MEASURES FOR THE CUSTOMER PERSPECTIVE

Most organizations have little difficulty in generating a multitude of customer measures. Customer satisfaction, market share, retention, and customer profitability will all surely surface during your measure generation sessions. However, if you look closely at these measures, they all reflect a bias toward actions already taken, and hence are what would be described as lagging indicators of performance. While each of these indicators is valuable, their results will reveal little until we know what actually drives their performance. In other words, what are their leading indicators? If customer satisfaction is plummeting, we need to know why—what is the driving force behind the decline? If profitability is on the rise, we need to surmise what has led to that serendipitous turn of events, and how we can sustain it. More than anywhere else in the Balanced Scorecard, the mix of lag and lead indicators is vital to the Customer perspective. Let's take a look at how we might develop our mix of lead and lag customer measures.

Using Your Value Proposition to Determine Leading Indicators

In the discussion of strategy in Chapter Four, the importance of a unique mix of complementary activities that drive customer value was noted. The customer value proposition describes how you will differentiate yourself and, consequently, what markets you will serve. To develop a customer value proposition, many organizations choose one of three "disciplines" articulated by Treacy and Wiersema in *The Discipline of Market Leaders*[10]:

- *Operational excellence.* Organizations pursuing an operational excellence discipline focus on low price, convenience, and often "no frills." Anyone who shops at Costco will recognize it as an operationally excellent company. Low prices and ample selection bring us back.

- *Product leadership.* Product leaders push the envelope of their firm's products. Constantly innovating, they strive to offer simply the best product in the market. Sony Corporation would be considered a product leader.

- *Customer intimacy.* Doing whatever it takes to provide solutions for customers' unique needs helps define the customer-intimate company. They don't look for one-time transactions but instead focus on long-term relationship building through their deep knowledge of customer needs. In the retail industry, Home Depot is a great example of a customer-intimate organization.

The value proposition you select will greatly influence the performance measures you choose since each will entail a different emphasis.

Measures of Operational Excellence

Treacy and Wiersema sum up the operationally excellent organization in one word: formula. These companies make hard choices to stay ahead of the competition: *"less product variety, the courage not to please every customer, forging the whole company, not just manufacturing and distribution, into a single focused instrument."*[11] Let's examine the performance measures these organizations may use to track their special combination of skills.

- *Price.* The core focus of most operationally excellent companies is a relentless pursuit of low prices. Wal-Mart, Costco, and Southwest Airlines all offer consistently low prices compared to their competition. Measuring product prices is critical to these organizations since it drives lagging indicators such as market share and satisfaction.

- *Selection.* These organizations realize that their customers do not expect them to supply every product under the sun—that would be a direct contravention of their "formula" for success. However, it's crucial for operationally excellent companies to ensure efficient inventory control to ensure that all products are available for customers. "Product availability," "inventory turnover," and "stockouts" would be closely monitored.

- *Convenience.* Operationally excellent companies strip away costs they perceive as not adding value for the customer. These costs may be tangible or intangible. Saturn provides a great example of an organization removing an intangible cost of doing business for its customers—the inevitable confrontation with the salesperson. Their no-haggle pricing makes it easy for customers to quickly determine the total cost of buying a car. "Customer complaints" relating to service or delivery represent a proxy of the convenience measure.

- *Zero defects.* When doing business with an operationally excellent company, customers anticipate zero defects, whether they're buying a Big Mac at any one of McDonald's thousands of restaurants, or expecting a package from FedEx. Streamlining operations and closely coordinating with suppliers paves the way for this lofty goal. "Manufacturing defect rates" or "service errors" will be carefully tracked.

- *Growth.* Value leadership is the mantra of the operationally excellent company. Raising prices for innovative products or providing heroic customer service would run counter to their efforts of providing seamless service and ultra-efficient operations. What they do want is growth in their chosen markets. These organizations have developed a winning formula and will expect to see "growth in targeted segments" as the proof of their success.

Product Leadership Measures

Product leaders are not content with a "new and improved" strategy; instead, they focus on creating an endless flow of innovative products that offer customers unmatched functionality. Making products that customers continually recognize as superior is the driving force behind these companies. Areas you might consider measuring if you are a product leader include:

- *Marketing is a must.* Product leaders will strive to promote strong brand images by supplying customers with products that offer enhanced functionality, save them time, and consistently outperform the competition. Because they are constantly innovating, product leaders may occasionally develop products for which the market is not quite ready. Treacy and Wiersema tell the story of the Remington company, which developed typewriters in 1874. Mark Twain bought one immediately and even invested in the company, but it took a full 12 years before the product caught on in the mainstream. "Brand awareness" could be used to ensure the market recognizes the many new products surfacing. Given their penchant for pushing the envelope of innovation product leaders might measure "help line calls per product" to determine the amount of interest, and possibly confusion, in their latest development.
- *Functionality.* We look to product leaders like Sony to offer consistently better functionality in all of their offerings. After all, it's not their price—which is most likely higher—or their threshold levels of customer service that bring us back. "Number of customer needs satisfied" may be tracked to ensure that expectations are being satisfied.

Measures for Customer Intimacy

Customer-intimate organizations recognize that their clients have needs beyond which their product alone can satisfy. They offer their customers a total solution that encompasses a unique range of superior services so that customers get the greatest benefit from the products offered. Attributes of customer-intimate organizations and the measures you might use to track your success should you follow the customer-intimate approach include:

- *Customer knowledge.* To succeed, every customer-intimate company requires a deep and detailed knowledge of its customers. To gauge staff knowledge, they may measure "training hours on client products." Sharing of knowledge is critical to the customer-intimate firm, and this metric also ensures that staff have the latest information available from their colleagues.

- *Solutions offered.* Customer-intimate firms also realize that customers are not turning to them for low cost or the latest product—it's the unmatched total solution they offer. To measure this attribute the customer-intimate firm will measure "total number of solutions offered per client."

- *Penetration.* At the height of IBM's success it was customer intimacy that assured their good fortune. The critical objective IBM legend Thomas Watson put forth to his staff was customer penetration or "share of targeted customer spending." The customer-intimate organization aims to provide complete solutions for its base and needs to ensure that these efforts are achieving success by deep penetration of accounts.

- *Customer data.* To offer the solutions only they can, these organizations also require abundant and rich data on their customers. "Percentage of employees with access to customer information" may be measured to track this key differentiator of success.

- *Culture of driving client success.* Employees of customer-intimate organizations feel they have succeeded when the customer has attained success—this is deeply rooted in their culture. An award from a cherished client as proof of their contribution is the greatest prize a customer-intimate company can receive. "Number of customer awards received" helps track this goal.

- *Relationships for the long term.* Customer-intimate organizations do not take a short view of any client relationships. Their goal is to build long-lasting unions during which they can increase their share of the clients business by providing unparalleled levels of knowledge and solutions. The relationship does not end when the sale is made, but is in fact just beginning. At Roadway Logistics, customers are assigned "directors of logistics development" who stay close to the process and often move to client locations. "Number of staff at client locations" could be a measure of the deep relationship these organizations maintain with their clients.

If you choose a customer-intimate strategy, the focus in your customer perspective will be on measures gauging your level of service to customers and the relationship you are attempting to cultivate with them. In addition to the measures noted above, "hours spent with customers" to track service and "number of referrals received from existing customers" as a proxy for relationship might be included.

Customer Satisfaction and Other Lagging Indicators of Customer Success

Determining your value proposition will go a long way toward helping you target particular customer segments. Customers looking for the latest products will most likely not find what they are looking for if you are focusing on a value proposition of operational excellence. Similarly, someone used to shopping at Wal-Mart may love the service at Nordstrom but be a little shocked at the prices. The idea of a particular group of customers may run counterintuitive to many of us who believe "a customer is a customer." However, the value proposition is about making hard choices. Now that you have made those choices and have considered some of the leading indicators of your success, you are ready to generate some core outcome measures of the customer perspective.

Most organizations will focus on a combination of the following metrics in their customer perspective: market share, customer profitability, acquisition, retention, loyalty, and that old standby, customer satisfaction. Although satisfaction may be the most popular metric suggested for this perspective (in one recent study 70 percent of respondents noted it appeared on their Scorecards[12]), it has come under criticism by many and should be carefully defined and crafted before making an appearance on your Scorecard.

Some pundits argue that satisfaction metrics were born in an era of poor quality when so many customers were dissatisfied that virtually any improvement in quality meant a boost to the bottom line. But as quality has improved, the link between satisfaction and the bottom line has become less clear.[13] A better proxy in today's environment may be the measurement of customer value, the market's evaluation of all the costs and benefits of using a particular product as compared to its alternatives. Service guru Ron Zemke, author of over two dozen books on service and related topics, refers to this as *pulse calls*, or measuring the pulse of customers. Ford-owned Kwikfit exemplifies this approach—their call center agents, unprompted, call thousands of customers every night and say, "You had your car serviced with us today. Do you have a minute to tell me how the experience was for you? Anything we could have done better?"[14]

Despite the drawbacks, customer satisfaction is still an important and valuable component of any customer perspective. Organizations need to know whether the value proposition they have worked so hard to perfect and measure with leading indicators is actually leading to happier customers who will return and do business with them once again. The key is tightly defining your satisfaction metric so that anyone evaluating your score can quickly identify its determinants and make appropriate decisions based on the results presented. Embassy Suites Hotels, the first all-suite upscale brand to enter the industry, carefully tracks customer satisfaction at each of its more than 150 hotels. Each location is judged on a guest satisfaction rating system in the form of surveys sent to customers from an outside survey company. Randomly selected past guests are asked to rate various aspects of their experience, including reservations, checkout, room service, quality of food, and overall service. These scores are an important component of the company's Balanced Scorecard, and locations achieving great success on satisfaction scores are publicly acknowledged.

Other Sources of Customer Measures

Choosing your value proposition and identifying your target customer segments will greatly enhance your efforts in developing measures for the customer perspective. However, they are not your only options. Other sources that can lead to measures you may wish to track include:

- *Financial objectives and measures.* Don't forget that the Balanced Scorecard should tell the story of your strategy from financial measures through the customer, processes, and employee capabilities you will need to achieve success. Once you have developed financial objectives and measures, ask yourself how they translate into customer requirements. For example, if you have a financial target of double-digit revenue growth, you may require greater customer loyalty or ambitious customer acquisition policies to achieve that goal.

- *The customer's voice.* The Internet is an incredibly powerful medium for spreading customer perceptions about your products and services, whether good or bad. Message boards and targeted sites across the vast universe of the web likely contain a host of references to your company and its offerings. Take advantage of this opportunity by listening to what your customers have to say about you, and then proactively defining yourself.

- *Moments of truth.* Any point at which a customer comes in contact with a business defines a moment of truth. The interaction can be either favorable or unfavorable and have a great impact on future business. Mapping these moments of truth provides you with an opportunity to isolate the differentiating features you offer and design metrics to track your success.[15]

- *Look to your channels.* Today's organization may serve customers in a number of ways, each with unique processes. Take the example of a retailer. They may offer shopping over the Internet, in retail stores, or by catalog. Each of these channels has specific processes and will entail different performance measures. For instance, when measuring checkout efficiency and speed in retail stores, error rates in keying items/prices into the register and the average length of a transaction might be monitored. Online, the same organization could monitor transaction ease by examining the number of fields into which the customer must enter information or the number of abandoned transactions. A catalog transaction would examine the number of rings it takes customer service representatives to answer calls and how long it takes to place the order.[16]

- *Work from the customer experience.* In *The Experience Economy,* Joe Pine and Jim Gilmore suggest that the economy is undergoing a shift to experiences in which every business is a stage and memorable events must be created for customers.[17] If you're like me you may have started your day with a trip to Starbucks or your favorite purveyor of coffee and shelled out anywhere from $2 to $5 for the pleasure. The company that harvested the beans probably received the equivalent of about one or two cents, but you just paid about 200 times that. Why? Because of the pleasurable experience the restaurant or coffee shop provided. Look at the experience you are designing for your customers and you will be sure to unearth a number of critical measures of success for the customer and all other perspectives of the Scorecard.

- *Customer relationship management (CRM) initiatives.* The customer intelligence market is growing rapidly. In the financial services industry, for example, Newton, Connecticut–based Meridien estimates that retail financial services companies will spend $6.8 billion this year on CRM. Tom Richards, author of the study "Measuring ROI: Yardsticks for Managing Successful CRM Strategies," suggests that industry needs to find better ways to determine how CRM helps profitability. Kathleen Khirallah, a senior research analyst at the TowerGroup research firm in Needham, Massachusetts, has an idea. She says companies should measure CRM with a Balanced Scorecard.[18] Your customer perspective should contain measures that track the effectiveness of your considerable investment in customer relationship management programs.

It is very important to include both lag and lead indicators in your customer perspective and the entire Scorecard for that matter. However, many Balanced Scorecard teams get way off track by endlessly debating what is a "lag" measure and what represents "leading" performance. Some members of your team will undoubtedly suggest that every measure is in effect "lagging" because it is historical in nature. We could argue the semantics of this topic forever, but in the end it comes down to choosing measures and asking yourself, "What drives this measure?" Whenever you choose one measure and can hypothesize a relationship with a related metric you believe drives the performance of the first measure, you have determined a lag and lead relationship.

Use the techniques above to help you generate measures for your own customer perspective. To get the creative juices flowing, a sample of customer measures is provided in Exhibit 5.5.

MEASURES FOR THE INTERNAL PROCESS PERSPECTIVE

Thus far in developing performance measures for the Balanced Scorecard we have defined our financial objectives and translated those into measures. We then determined our target customers and defined our value proposition in serving them. The value proposition assisted us in generating leading indicators of customer success, which we then supplemented with more traditional outcome measures (lagging indicators) such as customer satis-

Exhibit 5.5   A Sample of Customer Measures

- Customer satisfaction
- Customer loyalty
- Market share
- Customer complaints
- Complaints resolved on first contact
- Return rates
- Response time per customer request
- Direct price
- Price relative to competition
- Total cost to customer
- Average duration of customer relationship
- Customers lost
- Customer retention
- Customer acquisition rates
- Percentage of revenue from new customers
- Number of customers
- Annual sales per customer

- Win rate (sales closed/sales contacts)
- Customer visits to the company
- Hours spent with customers
- Marketing cost as a percentage of sales
- Number of ads placed
- Number of proposals made
- Brand recognition
- Response rate
- Number of trade shows attended
- Sales volume
- Share of target customer spending
- Sales per channel
- Average customer size
- Customers per employees
- Customer service expense per customer
- Customer profitability
- Frequency (number of sales transactions)

faction. To achieve our customer objectives, and ultimately our financial objectives, we must now develop performance measures to track the key internal processes and activities that support our customer value proposition. Firms will focus on the internal processes supporting their value proposition, but cannot simply ignore other supporting processes. For example, Home Depot provides excellent customer service and focuses on providing a complete solution to customer needs; however, they cannot ignore the procurement or logistics processes that distinguish the operationally excellent company. As with all things, the appropriate balance should be maintained. Let's examine each of the value propositions and determine which internal processes must be closely monitored to ensure success.

Customer Intimacy—Focusing on Customer Service

By providing an unparalleled mix of superior services that offer a total solution, the customer-intimate organization is able to move beyond simply providing a product or service to cultivating a lasting relationship with its clientele. Access to key customer information is a driving force in this endeavor. The more information the customer-intimate firm has about its customers, the better able it is to personalize, anticipate, and even predict customer patterns. A strong information foundation paves the way for this to occur. The information must provide users with a total view of the customer, must be integrated from all sources, be meaningful and actionable, and be user friendly.[19]

Organizations offering total solutions to their clients through unmatched knowledge must focus on a holistic view of the processes involved—marketing, selling, delivery, and service. Every customer "touchpoint" should have supporting performance measures that complement the entire process. For example, focusing only on marketing without a counterbalancing measure of postsale service may lead to more customers, but a lack of attention to service could also lead to more frustrated customers and increased defections.

With a base of customer information to work from it is now possible for the customer-intimate firm to measure critical supporting activities such as developing total solutions and providing advisory services.

Operational Excellence—Measuring the Supply Chain

No matter what type of business you are in, chances are you have heard a lot about improving your supply-chain practices. This rapidly growing field has gone from the backroom of most organizations to the Executive suite where leaders use the latest techniques to gain cost, quality, and service advantages over their competition. While ultra-efficient supply chain processes are the bread and butter of the operationally excellent company, every business organization can benefit greatly from measuring and improving this vital process. To learn about an interesting use of the Balanced Scorecard in the procurement area of supply-chain processes, see Exhibit 5.6, which describes Boeing's efforts to increase transactions with minority and women-owned businesses.[20]

A supply chain may be defined as *"a set of three or more organizations directly linked by one or more of the upstream and downstream flows of products, services, finances, and information from a source to a customer."*[21] Most of us think of the supply chain as comprising three main processes: sourcing and procurement, order fulfillment, and planning, forecasting, and scheduling. In industry after industry, supply-chain practices are becoming the key basis of competition, and little wonder since the stakes are very significant. In the U.S. auto industry, for example, the cost of purchased components, including inbound logistics, is 45 percent of total manufacturing and distribution costs.[22] Consider the impact even a 1 percent reduction would have on this $600 billion industry.

Unfortunately, performance measurement in the supply-chain field has not kept pace with today's world of interdependent business relationships. In fact, many organizations will focus on the optimization of particular supply-chain functions, often to the detriment of the overall process. Consider

Exhibit 5.6   Boeing Uses the Balanced Scorecard to Support Minority and Women-Owned Suppliers

The Commercial Airplanes Group of Aerospace leader Boeing is using their Balanced Scorecard to support a unique program designed to increase procurement of goods and services from minority and women-owned businesses. Under the "Business Direction" perspective of the Scorecard are two items. The first measures the percentage of subcontracting dollars to small businesses, small minority-owned businesses, and small women-owned businesses. The second tracks growth in the number of small and minority-owned and women-owned small business suppliers. Each line item receives a color corresponding to performance. Green means the procurement director is meeting the plan, yellow indicates caution, while red signals a plan not being achieved. If the measure score is either yellow or red, the procurement director meets with Boeing management to discuss what happened and how they can move the needle back to green performance.

Boeing awards about $15 billion in annual contracts to over 3,000 suppliers. This year their goal in the Commercial Airplane Group is to spend about 2% with minority-owned suppliers, 2% with women-owned suppliers, and 20% with small businesses. Prior to the launch of this initiative, which supporters call "cutting edge," there was no common set of performance metrics procurement directors could use to track their progress.

Adapted from Naomi R. Kooker, "Boeing Takes the Initiative," *Purchasing*, February 2001.

the company eager to reduce transportation costs, a key element of supply-chain logistics. Driving down these costs introduces local cost savings but may negatively affect order cycle time and consistency, increase damages, or generate more inventory. While transportation costs may go down, customer satisfaction and overall performance may suffer.[23] Another peril of supply-chain measurement is faulty data. In one in-depth study of 35 leading retailers, researchers found that the data at the heart of supply-chain management are often wildly inaccurate.[24]

How can we measure the supply chain to provide a competitive advantage? In *Keeping Score: Measuring the Business Value of Logistics in the Supply Chain*, the authors suggest a number of lessons for effective supply-chain measurement[25]:

- *Ensure consistency with strategy and value proposition.* Ensure that the metrics you use mirror your strategy and customer value proposition as each will entail a different supply-chain measurement focus. While this section focuses on the operationally excellent organization, as mentioned earlier, those pursuing customer-intimate or product leadership strategies must maintain threshold standards of supply-chain performance.

For example, when measuring the fulfillment process, operationally excellent companies will stress total delivered cost, order cycle time variance, accurate product selection, accurate invoicing, and timely and accurate availability of information. Supplier relationships are especially critical to the operationally excellent firm and must be captured through performance measures. Product leaders do not rely exclusively on supply-chain metrics but should monitor order cycle time and a damage-free product. Total delivered cost is not as critical for the product-leading company because its customers are willing to pay a little extra for the functionality its products offer. Finally, a customer-intimate organization would stress on-time delivery, order cycle time variability, transportation costs, complete orders (fill rate), approved exceptions, and availability of information. On-time delivery is crucial for the customer-intimate organization since its customers rely on it for exceptionally reliable service.

- *Truly understand customer needs.* Do not assume that you know what customers expect of you. As well, you must recognize that their needs will undoubtedly change over time.

- *Know your costs.* Deciding how much customer service to offer requires detailed cost information. Use the data to perform cost–benefit analyses.

- *Take a "process" view.* Define your measures at the process (procurement, fulfillment, scheduling), not the functional, level.

- *Focus on key measures.* You could generate hundreds of measures for the various supply-chain activities. Focus on key process measures. Functional- and activity-related metrics can be derived directly from these.

Those organizations that are able to effectively measure their supply-chain performance are sure to derive several benefits. First, supply-chain measures allow managers to highlight inefficient operations and reduce costs. As a result of more efficient supply-chain processes, organizations can anticipate improved service to customers. For instance, 3M was able to improve on-time delivery a whopping 32 percent over a three-year period with the help of a supply-chain measurement program. Also, insights into the costs of supply-chain activities provide managers with the information they need to make important decisions regarding what services and service levels to offer customers. Activity-based costing (ABC), a method of identifying cost drivers and assigning costs to activities rather than typical general ledger accounts, can be used in tandem with supply-chain measures to glean major insights into what activities in the supply chain are truly driving customer profitability. A number of supply-chain process measures are provided for your review in Exhibit 5.7.

Exhibit 5.7   Supply-Chain Process Measurements

Time	Cost
• On-time delivery receipt	• Finished goods inventory turns
• Order cycle time	• Days sales outstanding
• Order cycle time variability	• Cost to serve
• Response time	• Cash to cash cycle time
• Forecasting/planning cycle time	• Total delivered cost
• Planning cycle time variability	• Cost of goods
	• Transportation costs
Quality	• Inventory carrying costs
• Overall customer satisfaction	• Material handling costs
• Processing accuracy	• All other costs
• Perfect order fulfillment	• Information systems
• On-time delivery	• Administrative
• Complete order	• Cost of excess capacity
• Accurate product selection	• Cost of capacity shortfall
• Damage-free	
• Accurate invoice	**Other/Supporting**
• Forecast accuracy	• Approval exceptions to standard
• Planning accuracy	• Minimum order quantity
• Schedule adherence	• Change order timing
	• Availability of information

Source: James Keebler, Karl Manrodt, David Durtsche, and Michael Ledyard. *Keeping Score: Measuring the Business Value of Logistics in the Supply Chain* (Oakbrook, IL: Council of Logistics Management). Reprinted with permission.

Product Leadership—Innovating to Stay Ahead

Product leaders succeed by providing their customers with new and innovative products that offer unique functionality not available in competitors' offerings. The key internal process of the product leader organization is innovation.

Every organization's wish list would probably include greater innovation and more breakthrough ideas, but one company that truly lives in the "innovation fast lane" is IDEO. A true innovation factory, IDEO has created over 4,000 products, services, and environments for hundreds of clients. If you have decided to have your teeth whitened at BriteSmile, then you have been the beneficiary of IDEO innovation. Or if you visited "Workspheres," a collection of nine concepts that explore the theme of individuality in the context of corporate culture at the Museum of Modern Art in New York, you have enjoyed IDEO innovation. Founder and Chairman David Kelley typifies the IDEO culture when he says, *"Design is not a noun; it's a verb."*[26]

The IDEO approach is based on five interrelated phases of innovation: understanding, observing, visualizing, evaluating and refining, and implementing.

While you may be a long way from developing your four thousandth product, innovation is important for any product- or service-oriented organization. Tips for measuring the innovation process include:

- *Track successes.* An obvious performance measure of innovation is the number of new products or services launched within a given time frame.

- *And failure.* Not so obvious is the examination of your mistakes, but it is crucial to truly innovative organizations. Tom Kelley (brother of IDEO founder David Kelley) has chronicled the IDEO success story and suggests that IDEO's breakthroughs often come from doing things the wrong way! Not only can you learn and profit from your mistakes, but knowing when to say "enough is enough" and admit a mistake has been made is vital to the concept Peter Drucker calls *abandonment,* which is practiced by organizations fluent in the discipline of innovation.

- *Learn from lead users.* Researchers have discovered that many new products and services are originated and sometimes prototyped by users, and not manufacturers. These new products are often the brainchild of "lead users," a group well ahead of market trends with needs extending beyond those of the typical user. Identifying and working with your lead users gives you the opportunity to design the new products and services they may already be dreaming about. The Medical Surgical Markets Division at 3M is credited with introducing this process, and have been using it since 1996. Since that time the lead user process has been successfully tested in an additional seven divisions of the organization.[27]

- *Work in teams.* Two heads are better than one, five heads are better than two, and so on. Track the number of interdisciplinary teams working on generating breakthroughs at your organization. IDEO's teams feature specialists from many fields: human factors, cognitive psychology, business strategy, design planning, industrial design, interaction design, graphic design, architecture, mechanical and electrical engineering, software, and manufacturing.

- *Develop a pipeline.* Product leaders should see a steady stream of new ideas blossom as they perfect their innovation practices.

Measures of Good Citizenship

Thus far, our discussion of the internal process perspective has maintained a decided focus on what occurs within the four walls of the company. To conclude our look at this perspective, we must recognize that all organizations have important stakeholders and constituents beyond those four walls. Regulated industries such as utilities and telecommunications must maintain positive relationships with regulators and other governmental officials, and adhere to a number of environmental regulations. Additionally, all organizations must strive to be good corporate citizens in the communities in which they operate. Companies are beginning to realize that this is not only the right thing to do, but it makes good business sense. A study by the Conference Board of Canada found that 80 percent of Canadian managers feel that their company's good reputation goes a long way in recruiting and keeping good employees.

Those organizations required to follow guidelines regarding environmental or health and safety issues have a wonderful opportunity to use the Balanced Scorecard as a tool for moving from strict compliance to leadership. Take, for example, Nova Scotia Power (NSPI). As a regulated utility, NSPI must adhere to many environmental and health and safety guidelines enforced by various government agencies. When developing their internal process perspective, they used the Scorecard not simply to measure compliance with environmental regulations, but they challenged themselves to develop a measure and corresponding target that would establish them as environmental and safety leaders in the Canadian utility industry. An "environmental performance index" comprising a number of leading environmental indicators was constructed, which would guide NSPI's decisions on this carefully monitored aspect of their business. By including the index on the Scorecard, NSPI management signaled to the entire organization the importance of environmental stewardship and created a challenge for all employees to conduct their jobs in a manner that would positively impact this important indicator.

To prove successful over time a company both contributes to, and relies heavily on, the prosperity of the community. Although the organization is not solely responsible for the welfare of the surrounding community, it is incumbent upon them, and in their best interests, to monitor community success and ensure that they are contributing to the area's ongoing prosperity. Bob Nelson expresses this in his book, *1001 Ways to Energize Employees*. Bob says: *"These days the best organizations are involved in and contribute to their communities . . . It all boils down to helping find ways to make their communities better places to live, work, and do business through the sharing of resources, the labor of their employees, or just plain old-fashioned cash."*[28] In the book he chronicles a number of leading-edge organizations that have taken community involvement to a new level. One such company is Maryland spice manufacturer McCormick and Company. They open their plant one Saturday each year for "Charity Day." Employees work their normal shifts, but all wages are directed to the charity of the employee's choice. In the spirit of community caring, McCormick donates twice the employee's daily wage to the charity. You can monitor your community involvement by tracking donations to various charities, logging the number of hours employees spend volunteering (on company time), or counting the number of community-related partnerships you enter.

Exhibit 5.8 contains additional internal process measures for your consideration. The indicators shown are quite generic but will provide you with some guidance. Your challenge is to identify the unique processes that drive the customer value proposition in your organization, and define specific measures that tell your particular story. While all perspectives of the Scorecard will reveal some very individual measures, depending on the organization, it is the internal process perspective that normally contains the most "one-of-a kind" indicators. You'll also discover that unlike traditional performance management systems, which focus on the incremental improvement of existing processes, the Balanced Scorecard and corresponding measures in your financial and customer perspectives may lead you to entirely new processes necessary to achieve your strategic aims. Uncovering these *missing measurements*, as Kaplan and Norton term them, is often one of the most gratifying aspects of the Scorecard development process.

MEASURES FOR THE EMPLOYEE LEARNING AND GROWTH PERSPECTIVE

I recently had a conversation with a consultant (from a firm that shall remain nameless) regarding one of his current client engagements. He de-

Exhibit 5.8   Internal Process Measures

- Average cost per transaction
- On-time delivery
- Average lead time
- Inventory turnover
- Environmental emissions
- Research and development expense
- Community involvement
- Patents pending
- Average age of patents
- Ratio of new products to total offerings
- Stockouts
- Labor utilization rates
- Response time to customer requests
- Defect percentage
- Rework
- Customer database availability
- Breakeven time
- Cycle time improvement
- Continuous improvement
- Warranty claims
- Lead user identification
- Products and services in the pipeline
- Internal rate of return on new projects
- Waste reduction
- Space utilization
- Frequency of returned purchases
- Downtime
- Planning accuracy
- Time to market of new products/ services
- New products introduced
- Number of positive media stories

scribed the project as one of developing high-level performance measures and driving them to lower levels of the organization. "What are you measuring?" I enthusiastically asked. He replied they had decided to focus on financial and operational measures but were not developing employee and learning measures since "that stuff's going to happen anyway." *Wrong!* It is not going to just happen, you have to make a concerted effort to ensure that it does. If you don't, you will never really have a Balanced Scorecard or derive the benefits of the Scorecard system. As discussed in Chapter Two, the value creation in today's organization is overwhelmingly dominated by the influence of human capital. People—their knowledge and means of sharing it—are what is driving value in the new economy. Describing the activities that drive this value is the purview of the Employee Learning and Growth Perspective.

The measures of the Employee Learning and Growth Perspective are really the "enablers" of the other perspectives. Motivated employees with the right mix of skills and tools operating in an organizational climate designed for sustaining improvements are the key ingredients in driving process improvements, meeting customer expectations, and ultimately driving financial returns. Kaplan and Norton have noted that people often object to the placement of this perspective in Scorecard diagrams. Doesn't placing it at the bottom minimize its importance? Quite the contrary, the Scorecard architects say. It is at the bottom because it acts as the foundation for everything else above it. At a conference I attended some time ago, I heard Scorecard architect Bob Kaplan outline the strategy-mapping process. When he came to the Employee Learning and Growth perspective, he described it as the roots of a powerful tree which are the sources of support and nourishment leading to the blossoms of financial returns. His enthusiasm was tremendous throughout the talk, but there was a particular emphasis on this point as if to underscore its importance to sometimes incredulous audiences.

In case you are still not convinced of the importance of the "soft" measures, here are a couple of real-life examples that might influence your thinking on the subject.

- *The service profit chain at Sears.* Using econometric modeling techniques, Sears has quantified the linkage between employee satisfaction and financial performance. The company can now predict that for every 5 percent increase in employee satisfaction, they will see a corresponding 1.3 percent increase in customer loyalty three months hence. This spike in loyalty drives a 0.5 percent increase in revenue another three months down the road. In 1997, Sears predicted and achieved an incremental $200 million in revenues based on a 4 percent improvement in employee satisfaction.

- *Maister makes a point.* David Maister has chronicled the link between satisfied employees and financial returns in his new book *Practice What You*

Preach.[29] He was convinced that happy employees really do drive financial success and set about to find the actual proof of his suspicions. In 1999 he surveyed 5,500 employees of a large advertising and media conglomerate who were dispersed among 139 offices in 15 countries. His study found that a company could boost its financial performance by as much as 42 percent by raising employee satisfaction by 20 percent.

The stories outlined above illustrate the unequivocal link between employee performance and financial returns. Not only do the measures in the Employee Learning and Growth perspective lead to improved financial results for the organization, but it is through these indicators that we pave the way for sustaining that success over the long term. As the business environment inevitably changes, the enablers of future success described in this perspective will allow your organization to maintain flexibility and adapt to changing conditions.

There are a number of prerequisites that must be met if your employees are to positively contribute to organizational strategy. First, they must possess certain capabilities the organization deems critical to success. Second, employees must have the ability to manipulate knowledge through the use of physical and nonphysical tools. Finally, all employees must be motivated and acting in alignment with overall firm goals. Let's look at these areas and discuss potential performance measures for each.

Measuring Capabilities

Peter Drucker has suggested that any business can be as good as any other business. The only distinction is how it develops its own people. Suggestions for developing your most precious resource include:

- *Using core competencies to measure skill development.* The term *core competence* was coined by Gary Hamel and C.K. Prahalad in their immensely successful book *Competing for the Future.*[30] Over time, the phrase has evolved and now is described as *"an attribute or behavior that individual managers and employees must demonstrate to succeed at their particular company."*[31] The first step in the core competence process is identifying the differentiating competencies you need to achieve your strategy. Experts agree that the best way of doing this is to involve as many people as possible from all levels of the organization. Focus groups and interviews can be used to assess company needs and competence gaps. If you have not gone through this "competence inventory" process, it could represent a good first-year metric for your Scorecard. After all, you cannot evaluate your current staff against desired skills until you have catalogued those skills you deem as necessary to create a competitive advantage.

- *Using personal development planning (PDP) to boost competence holders.* Many organizations have introduced the idea of personal development planning to assist employees in generating goals. This is certainly an admirable effort; however, certain criteria must be stressed if PDPs are to prove beneficial to the employee or the organization. The principal issue is alignment to organizational strategic goals. The majority of personal goals in the plan should help the employee influence the achievement of the company's strategy. Goals in the plan should also be measurable and include specific action steps. At Nova Scotia Power, employees were encouraged to attend PDP workshops conducted jointly by outside consultants and company executives. Participants were coached on the elements of an effective plan and provided with binders containing a variety of useful information: company vision and strategy, capability definitions, planning guidelines, and worksheets. Once you have identified the core competencies you need to be a leader in your industry and your employees have developed plans that signal their contribution to your goals, you are ready to begin measuring. Track the percentage of employees who meet their personal development plan goals. Don't make it an annual measure. To motivate action on this important task, ask employees for quarterly or even monthly progress updates. You can also measure your "competency coverage ratio," which tracks the percentage of necessary skills you currently possess throughout your workforce. In other words, how many qualified employees do you have to meet your anticipated needs?

- *Encourage healthy lifestyles.* Experts suggest that over 50 percent of all mortality is related to lifestyle choices. Many organizations will include occupational health and safety measures in the employee learning and growth perspective, such as lost time accidents, workers' compensation claims, and injury frequency rates. However, enlightened companies are moving beyond these lagging indicators and attempting to offer employees an environment that facilitates and encourages them to adopt better lifestyles. Organizations pursuing this "health promotion" philosophy are attempting to create a win–win environment in which employees take responsibility for their own well-being and employers reap the benefits of lower lifestyle-related costs. Simple and low-cost solutions such as lunchtime walking clubs, weight-control programs, and health fairs have enabled one Southern Ontario auto parts company to institute a health promotion program for over 450 employees at a cost of only $30 per employee per year.[32] You can measure your health promotion initiatives by tracking the number of employees who take advantage of the program, or gauging employee attitudes regarding lifestyle choices. These measures may also be considered leading indicators of other popular learning and growth measures such as absenteeism, morale, and productivity per employee.

- *Measuring employee training.* Virtually every company will have at least one performance measure relating to employee training initiatives. And why not, since through training the organization gets better skilled workers who are more versatile, while employees learn new skills and gain new ways of seeing their work and how it affects overall success. The mistake most organizations make with training metrics is that they simply look at the raw amount of training offered, for example, number of training hours per employee. For training to prove effective, it must be linked to organizational goals and objectives, and companies should measure results of the training (i.e., the demonstration of new behaviors or skills, not just attendance). You should also encourage trained employees to share their newfound knowledge with their peers and networks in the company. Experts call this *third person teaching* and suggests that it offers many benefits to both the student and the teacher. For example, knowing you will have to share what you're learning will motivate most people to pay greater attention and capture more of the information they are receiving.

- *Employee productivity.* Investing in competency development and personal development planning should yield results in the form of greater productivity, and many organizations will measure just that. The problem with this measure, at least in its traditional form, is that it divides firm revenue by the number of employees. It is fairly easy to manipulate this ratio by reducing the number of employees, outsourcing entire functions, or increasing revenue in possibly unprofitable segments. Similar to the financial metric of economic value added, you should attempt to determine the value added per employee by deducting externally purchased materials from your numerator.

Tracking Employee Tools

Capabilities are a must for success in the new economy, but to achieve your goals employees must have access to certain physical and intangible tools to get their jobs done. Some of these tools, and how their impact on results might be measured, include:

- *The instruments of business.* A client I worked with recently was implementing a technology solution for their Balanced Scorecard program. Everything was going well until we found that a number of employees in off-site locations did not have computers on their desks; in fact, some didn't have voice mail on their phones. We could develop Scorecards for them, but many benefits of the program such as real-time reporting and decision-support would be very limited given their technology-deprived state. This may sound like an oversimplified performance measure, but you have to ensure that your employees have up-to-date and modern equipment if you hope to compete in today's economy.

- *Access to information.* For those associates fortunate enough to have the necessary equipment, you need to make certain they can also retrieve the right information. What percentage of customer-facing staff have the ability to access detailed customer information within 30 seconds of a customer interaction? You should determine what information is critical to employee decision making and develop a performance measure that tracks the percentage of employees who have this information available to them.

Motivation and Alignment

All the training and sharing of information in the world will accomplish little if employees are not motivated to perform their best or aligned with organizational goals. Considerations when measuring motivation and alignment include:

- *Employee satisfaction.* Perhaps the most common employee learning and growth measure is the employee satisfaction rating. The vast majority of organizations attempt to take the pulse of their organizations through annual surveys and use the findings to design better ways to do things. At least that's how it is supposed to work. Unfortunately, many employees believe the annual survey is a sham and waste of money, with the results gathering dust on a shelf and never acted upon. Satisfaction is a very valuable metric, so ensure that you use the data appropriately by swiftly acknowledging areas requiring improvement and developing action steps to improve them. You should also consider using the many technological tools at your disposal to gauge the mood of your employees on a more frequent basis. Corporate intranets and e-mail systems can be used to gather feedback from employees semiannually or quarterly. Given the pace of change in today's environment, you need the most up-to-date information from the front line if you expect to react quickly.

- *Alignment.* Your Scorecard should capture your strategy through the objectives and measures that make up your individual story. Chapter Eight will describe how to drive your high-level performance measures throughout the entire organization using the process of cascading. In the early stages of Balanced Scorecard implementation, a good alignment measure is simply the number of Scorecards produced within the organization. Once the performance management discipline becomes more mature you can refine the measure by analyzing individual Scorecards and assessing their "degree of alignment" (i.e., the percentage of measures directly relating to your strategic goals). Obviously, the target should be 100 percent. This is a great way to perform a diagnostic check on cascaded Scorecards.

Exhibit 5.9 provides some additional employee learning and growth measures you may consider for your Balanced Scorecard.

SUMMARY

This chapter marked a departure from the important foundation poured in earlier chapters to the actual development of objectives and measures comprising the core of your Balanced Scorecard system. As with the previous chapters, the material covered here now prepares us for the work that lies ahead—refining the Scorecard and using it as a management system.

Many people describe the Balanced Scorecard as a management framework. The perspectives you choose define the boundaries of your framework and should be selected to mirror your particular situation. Specifically, choose perspectives that allow you to capture the key stakeholders of your organization and describe how you will ultimately serve each, thereby successfully implementing your strategy.

Before you develop your objectives and measures, you have to ensure that you have gathered ample background material that will provide input

Exhibit 5.9   Employee Learning and Growth Measures

- Employee participation in professional or trade associations
- Training investment per customer
- Average years of service
- Percentage of employees with advanced degrees
- Number of cross-trained employees
- Absenteeism
- Turnover rate
- Employee suggestions
- Employee satisfaction
- Participation in stock ownership plans
- Lost time accidents
- Value added per employee
- Motivation index
- Outstanding number of applications for employment
- Diversity rates
- Empowerment index (number of managers)
- Quality of work environment
- Internal communication rating
- Employee productivity
- Number of Scorecards produced
- Health promotion
- Training hours
- Competency coverage ratio
- Personal goal achievement
- Timely completion of performance appraisals
- Leadership development
- Communication planning
- Reportable accidents
- Percentage of employees with computers
- Strategic information ratio
- Cross-functional assignments
- Knowledge management
- Ethics violations

to your decisions. You can use the perspectives of the Balanced Scorecard to assist you in detecting sources of this information. For example, considering the financial perspective will lead you to annual reports, analyst reports, and management reviews. When scouring your documents, look for consistency in the description of mission, values, vision, and strategy. Your executive team will provide valuable input into the process, and the best way to glean this information is through executive interviews. Conduct one-hour interviews to gather your senior team's thoughts on mission, values, vision, strategy, performance measures, and Scorecard implementation issues.

Performance objectives are concise statements that describe the specific things you must perform well if you are to successfully implement your strategy. Reviewing each of the Scorecard perspectives in the form of a question is the best way to develop performance objectives. For maximum impact, each objective should begin with an action verb and be no more than two or three sentences. Since each objective may result in the inclusion of two performance measures, attempt to limit your total number of objectives across the four perspectives to no more than twelve.

Use "objective and measure generation sessions" to develop potential objectives and measures for your Balanced Scorecard. These meetings help foster ownership for the process, build team cohesion, put members on equal footing, and produce a large number of potential candidates for your Scorecard. Cause-and-effect relationships among objectives and measures should be captured, but not stressed, during these meetings. It is more important to gather a broad array of possible Scorecard items now, and determine cause and effect as the next stage in the Scorecard building process.

Performance measures are the standards used to evaluate and communicate performance against expected results. They can be either lagging or leading in nature. Lagging measures normally denote the results of actions previously taken. Leading indicators predict the performance of the lagging indicators. A good Balanced Scorecard should contain a mix of leading and lagging indicators.

Financial measures are an important component of any Balanced Scorecard. These indicators tell us whether our strategy implementation and execution is leading to improved bottom-line results. Most organizations focus on the measurement of growth, profitability, and value in the financial perspective.

Leading indicators of customer performance are conveniently developed through the translation of your organization's "customer value proposition." Companies may focus on one of three disciplines: customer intimacy, operational excellence, or product leadership. Each will entail a different measurement emphasis. Determining the effect these leading indicators is having on our customer performance is measured by developing core outcome measures of customer success. Typical entrants include customer satisfaction, market share, and customer profitability.

The Internal Process perspective of the Scorecard describes the key processes and activities that ultimately drive customer and financial performance. Using the Balanced Scorecard as a management tool provides organizations with the opportunity to uncover entirely new processes in their pursuit of customer and financial outcomes. The value proposition outlined in the customer perspective will drive the choice of internal process measures. Customer-intimate organizations focus on customer knowledge and information technology capabilities. Efficient supply-chain operations are the critical enabler of the operationally excellent company. Product leaders will rely on the innovation process to drive customer outcomes.

If you hope to achieve substantial gains for customers and shareholders and improve internal processes, where do these gains emerge from? The measures in the Employee Learning and Growth perspective are really the enablers of the other three perspectives. These indicators ensure that you have employees who possess the right skills, can access the appropriate information, and are motivated and aligned with organizational goals. Effective employee learning and growth measures help sustain your ability to grow and improve as the business environment inevitably changes.

NOTES

1. Robert S. Kaplan and David P. Norton, *The Balanced Scorecard* (Boston: Harvard Business School Press, 1996).
2. Robert S. Kaplan and David P. Norton, "Transforming the Balanced Scorecard from Performance Measurement to Strategic Management," *Accounting Horizons,* March 2001.
3. Bryan Mattimore, *99 percent Inspiration: Tips, Tales, and Techniques for Liberating Your Business Creativity* (New York, NY: AMACOM, 1993).
4. Arthur B. VanGundy, *Idea Power: Techniques and Resources to Unleash the Creativity in Your Organization* (New York, NY: AMACOM, 1992).
5. Performance Measurement Survey by the American Institute of Certified Public Accountants and Lawrence S. Maisel, 2001.
6. Ibid., p. 15.
7. Robert S. Kaplan and David P. Norton, "On Balance," *CFO,* February 2001, 73–77.
8. Robert E. Quinn, Regina M. O'Neill, and Lynda St. Clair, *Pressing Problems in Modern Organizations (That Keep Us Up at Night)* (New York, NY: AMACOM, 2000).
9. Dawne Shand, "Economic Value Added," *Computerworld,* October 2000.
10. Michael Treacy and Fred Wiersema, *The Discipline of Market Leaders* (Reading, MA: Perseus Books, 1995).
11. Ibid., p. 63.
12. Performance Measurement Survey by the American Institute of Certified Public Accountants and Lawrence S. Maisel, 2001.
13. Mark Hochman, "Customer Satisfaction Measurements: An Answer to Yesterday's Problems?," *Harvard Management Update,* August 1999, 10.

14. Dourado, "Ten Steps to World Class," *Management Services,* March 2001, 14–16.

15. See Jan Carlzon, *Moments of Truth* (Cambridge, MA: Ballinger, 1987).

16. Terrence L. Foran and Arvin Jawa, "Golden Opportunity," *Catalog Age,* March 2001, 54.

17. B. Joseph Pine and James H. Gilmore, *The Experience Economy* (Boston: Harvard Business School Press, 1999).

18. Deborah Bach, "Most CRM Is a Leap of Faith," *American Banker,* May 2001, 9a.

19. Dennis Sparacino and Cindy O'Reilly, "Leveraging Customer Metrics for Strategic Decision Making," *Telemarketing and Call Center Solutions,* October 2000, 49–54.

20. Naomi R. Kooker, "Boeing Takes the Initiative," *Purchasing,* February 2001, 45.

21. J.T. Mentzer, W. DeWitt, J.S. Keebler, S. Min, N.W. Nix, C.D. Smith, and Z.G. Zacharia, "A Unified Definition of Supply Chain Management," Working Paper, University of Tennessee, 1999.

22. G.A. Mercer, "Don't Just Optimize—Unbundle," *McKinsey Quarterly,* No. 3, 1994.

23. James S. Keebler, Karl B. Manrodt, David A. Durtsche, and D. Michael Ledyard, *Keeping Score: Measuring the Business Value of Logistics in the Supply Chain* (Oakbrook, IL: Council of Logistics Management, 1999).

24. Anath Raman, Nicole DeHoratius, and Zeynep Ton, "The Achilles' Heel of Supply Chain Management," *Harvard Business Review,* May 2001, 25.

25. Keebler et al., *Keeping Score.*

26. Quote taken from IDEO's web site at *www.ideo.com.*

27. Eric vonHippel, Stefan Thomke, and Mary Sonnack, "Creating Breakthroughs at 3M," *Harvard Business Review,* September–October 1999, 47–56.

28. Bob Nelson, *1001 Ways to Energize Employees* (New York: Workman, 1997).

29. David Maister, *Practice What You Preach: What Managers Must Do to Create a High Achievement Culture* (New York: The Free Press, 2001).

30. Gary Hamel and C.K. Prahalad, *Competing for the Future* (Boston: Harvard Business School Press, 1994).

31. Marie Gendron, "Competencies and What They Mean to You," *Harvard Management Update,* September 1996.

32. Dr. Angela M. Downey, "Promoting Health on the Job," *CMA Management,* May 2001, 24.

Chapter 6

Finalizing Measures and Developing Cause-and-Effect Linkages

Roadmap for Chapter Six Performance measures are at the core of the Balanced Scorecard system. Chapter Five discussed methods for developing your indicators, and this chapter will explore how you can narrow them down to a select few that capture the true essence of your strategy. The vital topic of cause-and-effect linkages—telling your story through measurement—will also be covered in detail.

A number of criteria are available to help you determine which measures should comprise your Scorecard. Each will be reviewed to ensure that you select the right measures for your organization. Once you have arrived at your performance measures, we will consider whether you have an appropriate number to adequately track the execution of your strategy. Gathering data for your measures is a crucial and often challenging aspect of any Scorecard implementation. A performance measure data dictionary will be shared that assists you in capturing all the essential elements of your performance metrics. The measure section will conclude by considering how you can effectively gather feedback on your Scorecard from both your executive team and employee base.

Ralph Waldo Emerson said, *"Shallow men believe in luck. Strong men believe in cause and effect."* I can't imagine a more fitting quote to launch our adventures into the world of Balanced Scorecard cause and effect. Telling the story of your strategy through a series of linked measures is what really separates the Balanced Scorecard from other performance management systems. This important section will explore exactly why these linkages are critical to your Scorecard endeavors and how you can create an architecture of measures that tells your particular story. We will also examine the powerful role storytelling can have in complementing the linkages you create.

The chapter concludes by examining the future of your performance measures. Can we expect them to remain the same, or is change inevitable?

FINALIZING YOUR BALANCED SCORECARD MEASURES

At this point in your Balanced Scorecard implementation, you will have developed a multitude of potential measures in each of the Scorecard perspectives. Every one of those metrics will have a fan in at least one member of your team. Your challenge now is to cull the herd of possible measures down to the select few that accurately capture the essence of your strategy. Once you have a subset of lucky finalists, you are able to begin using them to construct the cause-and-effect linkages that comprise the map of your strategy. Let's begin our work by examining a number of criteria you can use to select the most well-suited measures for your organization. We will then discuss how many measures should appear on your Scorecard and methods of gaining feedback from both executives and employees.

Criteria for Selecting Performance Measures

One of the many benefits of the Balanced Scorecard is that it forces organizations to make difficult choices among a variety of alternatives. Choices regarding objectives, targets, and initiatives to achieve our targets must all be deliberated upon in developing a Scorecard that serves as the cornerstone of our management system. Nowhere is the process of making hard choices more evident than in the selection of performance measures. These measures are really the centerpiece of the Scorecard system and will provide the point of reference and focus for the entire organization. Here are several criteria that experience and research have proven to be effective in helping you evaluate and pick your measures.

- *Linked to strategy.* This one gets the vote for most obvious, but its importance cannot be overstated. The Scorecard is a tool for translating strategy into action through the performance measures that tell the story of your strategy. Choosing performance measures that do not have an impact on your strategy can lead to confusion and lack of clarity as employees devote precious resources to the pursuit of measures that do not influence the firm's overall goals. Having said that, you might have difficulty finding a direct link from every measure to your strategy. Most businesses will have a number of what we may term *diagnostic* performance measures that are important to the day-to-day efficient functioning of the business but do not seem to correspond directly to a strategy. These factors need to be monitored to ensure that the organization remains "in control" and is able to respond quickly to items that require immediate attention. Although these indicators are important, they are not necessarily strategic. Recall the discussion of value propositions in Chapter Five. An organization pursuing a customer intimacy strategy will devote the majority of its efforts to providing total solutions to customer needs through deep knowledge. This is their focus, but they cannot ignore logistics issues (operational excellence), or product functionality (product leadership). Maintaining threshold standards of performance in these areas may require the inclusion of performance measures on the Scorecard.

- *Quantitative.* There is often a temptation among Scorecard practitioners to include measures that rely on subjective evaluations of performance, for example, rating suppliers' performances as "good," "fair," or "average." Of course, the principal issue with this approach is that 10 people rating the same supplier may come up with completely different approaches and responses. However, if the same suppliers are evaluated on a percentage of on-time deliveries, the results are objective and convey the same meaning to all involved. Everyone knows what 10 percent connotes, but your definition of *average* and mine could vary significantly. If you are creative, virtually all performance measures can be calculated mathematically. For a medical services unit I worked with at a government agency, a key performance metric was the distribution of their trauma reports in a timely fashion. Their original measure was "Reports issued." In other words, a simple yes or no would suffice as the indication of performance. With a little tweaking, we improved the measure by restating it as "The percentage of trauma report recipients receiving the document on time."

- *Accessibility.* Kaplan and Norton often discuss the merits of "missing measures." Those are the performance measures you did not capture in the past, which came to light only as a result of the Balanced Scorecard development process. Undoubtedly, new and innovative measures are a wonderful benefit of the Scorecard; in fact, missing measures may signal that entire value-creating processes are not currently being managed. However, you should avoid selecting "wish list" performance measures, the type that require significant investments in information technology infrastructure to collect. You will learn fairly quickly that you must be pragmatic when selecting performance measures. I worked with one group recently who developed a Scorecard for their business unit that was considered by the group executive as the pride of the entire organization. When it came time to actually report the information, however, it turned out the data was completely uncollectable without significant investments in technology. This is not to suggest that you avoid new and innovative measures—just be sure to calculate the costs and benefits of their collection. Data requirements are discussed further in a following section covering measure dictionaries.

- *Easily understood.* Your ultimate goal should be to create a Scorecard that motivates action. It is difficult to do so when your audience does not grasp the significance of the measures you have selected. At a glance, Scorecard readers should be able to explain both the operational and strategic significance of every measure. The desired direction of movement of the measure should also be obvious. If your employees do not know whether a high value for the measure is good or bad, then you probably need to rethink it.

- *Counterbalanced.* Let's say you owned a fast food restaurant and were interested in improving your customer satisfaction scores. As we all know, these restaurants can become pretty crowded during peak hours, so you decide to increase staff and lower prices. The increased staff should be able to handle current and future demand created by your lower prices and will drive increased satisfaction. However, what effect will lowering prices and increasing staff have on your profitability? Chances are it will plummet in a hurry since you have increased your cost base and lowered your revenue. Some call this effect *sub-optimization* (i.e., the improvement of one or more measures at the expense of others). While your Scorecard will require that you make trade-offs and decisions regarding where to allocate resources, you do not want to create a situation in which focusing on certain measures actually hinders your ability to compete. In the case of our fast food establishment we would want to counterbalance our satisfaction rating with a measure of "revenue per employee." We need to ensure that despite our lower price structure, the resulting volume and efficiencies from increased staff are allowing us to maintain revenue targets.

- *Relevant.* The measures appearing on your Scorecard should accurately depict the process or objective you are attempting to evaluate. A good test is whether or not measure results are actionable. If some aspect of performance failed, you should be able to recognize the significance of the problem and fix it. This issue is demonstrated through the use of performance indices, which many organizations will use on their Scorecards. An index is a combination of several individual measures combined in some way to result in a single overall indicator of performance. Employee satisfaction may appear on your Scorecard as an index of the weighted–average performance of turnover, absenteeism, complaints, and survey results. Indices are a great way to quickly depict a number of performance variables in a single indicator, but they have some inherent weaknesses. First of all, they may obscure results and limit action. If turnover at your organization was at an all-time high but was given a low weight in your employee satisfaction index, you may never know there are issues since the overall index could appear to be on target. If key staff members are among those leaving the firm and you have not mounted a response, you may soon pay a heavy price in other areas of performance as reflected on the Scorecard. Indices also frequently fail to pass the "easily understood" criterion we discussed above. A "logistics" index appearing in the Internal Process perspective may contain valuable information but be baffling to those outside of the supply-chain side of the organization. Again, indices can provide very useful information, especially when you have a number of measures you would like to include but wish to keep your total Scorecard count limited. Based on the arguments above, however, their use should be limited to only a handful of your total at most.

- *Common definition.* Your Scorecard will likely contain a number of esoteric performance measures, and that is perfectly appropriate since it is your strategic story you are telling. However, problems occur when you place measures on the Scorecard that are loosely defined or not defined at all. On-time delivery may be a crucial metric, but what does on-time mean? You must specify the precise meaning of your performance measures and ensure that you have agreement from your entire team. Customer satisfaction could have a very different meaning for a team member from marketing than it does for someone from finance. The process of agreeing on measure definitions is yet another example of how the Scorecard building process brings seemingly disparate functions together as they work to ensure that the measures capture a meaning that allows all to contribute meaningfully to success.

Exhibit 6.1 is a worksheet you can use to choose among the performance measures you have gathered. List the measures under the appropriate perspective and rate each according to the criteria supplied. Rate each measure out of a possible 10 points on each of the individual criteria. For example, if you were to measure economic value added on your financial perspective, it may score a 10 for "accessibility" given the pure financial nature of the information. However, it could warrant a 5 or under on "ease of understanding" since most employees probably are not familiar with the metric.

How Many Measures on Your Balanced Scorecard?

This is a question frequently asked by clients when we begin developing Scorecards for their organizations. The interesting thing is that many orga-

Exhibit 6.1 Worksheet to Select Balanced Scorecard Measures

Balanced Scorecard Project—Measure Selection Worksheet

Measures	Linkage to Strategy	Ability to Quantify	Accessibility	Ease of Understanding	Counter-Balanced	Relevance	Common Definition	Total Points	Comments
Financial									
Measure 1									
Measure 2									
Measure 3									
Customer									
Measure 1									
Measure 2									
Measure 3									
Internal Process									
Measure 1									
Measure 2									
Measure 3									
Emp. L. & G.									
Measure 1									
Measure 2									
Measure 3									

Overall Assessment of Current Measures:

nizations are very concerned with creating too many measures but then go ahead and do just that! Since I have been working in the performance management arena, I have witnessed a steady rise in the average number of measures appearing on organizational Scorecards. Technology is a major contributor to the volume of performance measures. Several years ago when organizations had few reporting choices, they were more or less forced to minimize the number of measures they tracked given reporting limitations. With the rapid advent of functionality-rich Scorecard software we have available today, companies now have the ability to track literally hundreds or even thousands of measures throughout the organization. The question is: How many is too many? While no optimal or magic number of measures exists, there are guidelines you should follow to ensure that you have an appropriate number of measures for your organization.

The key to determining the number of performance measures is ensuring adequate description of your strategy across the four perspectives of the Scorecard. Telling your strategic story will require a sufficient mix of core outcome measures (lagging indicators) and performance drivers (lead indicators) scattered throughout the Scorecard. This is often a one-to-one relationship, but at times you may have two performance drivers for a single outcome measure. Assuming it were one to one, your Balanced Scorecard would require eight measures. A one-to-two relationship implies 12 measures. Add the fact that some performance objectives require more than one measure and you will quickly be up to 20 or more indicators. Most Scorecard practitioners and consultants have settled on a figure of 20 to 25 measures as being appropriate for your highest-level Balanced Scorecard. Benchmarking studies of Scorecard implementations across a variety of industries have returned similar findings. Don't be constrained by these numbers, however. If you require 30 measures to adequately describe your strategy, do so. Similarly, if you can tell your story in 15 measures, do not add measures that do little more than pad the Scorecard.

The other frequently asked question is whether the measures should be equally dispersed across the four perspectives. Again, what matters most is ensuring that the measures describe your strategy in a way that is transparent to anyone reading the Scorecard. The following distribution of measures would be expected in most high-level Balanced Scorecards:

- *Financial.* Three or four measures of anticipated financial results. The organization should be very clear on its financial goals and not require a large number of metrics.
- *Customer.* Five to eight measures. Your value proposition will dictate the composition of your measures. The customer perspective will normally have a large number of leading indicators.
- *Internal process.* Five to ten measures. In this perspective, you have identified the key processes you must excel at in order to continue adding

value for customers and financial stakeholders. Processes may span the entire organization, resulting in a greater number of measures.

- *Employee Learning and Growth.* Three to six measures. These measures act as the enablers of the other three perspectives. They are often the most difficult to isolate and agree upon.

Creating a Performance Measure Data Dictionary

You have now evaluated all your measures and have selected a set you are ready to share with your executive team, and later your fellow employees throughout the organization. But before you do that, you need to catalog them in a measure "data dictionary." The dictionary definition of the word *dictionary* reveals the following, "book that lists . . . the topics of a subject." That is precisely what you are crafting in this step of the process—a document that provides all users with a detailed examination of your Balanced Scorecard measures, including a thorough list of measure characteristics. Creating the measure data dictionary is not a very glamorous task, but it is an important one. When you present your Balanced Scorecard to executives and employees alike, they will undoubtedly quiz you on the background of each and every measure. "Why did you choose this measure?" "Is it strategically significant?" "How do you calculate the measure?" "Who is responsible for results?" These and numerous other queries will greet your attempts to share your Scorecard with colleagues. The data dictionary provides the background you need to quickly defend your measure choices and answer any questions your audience has. Additionally, chronicling your measures in the data dictionary provides your team with one last opportunity to ensure a common understanding of measure details.

Exhibit 6.2 provides a template you can use to create your own measure dictionary. There are four basic sections of the template you must complete. In the first section, shown at the top, you provide essential background material on the measure. The second section lists specific measure characteristics. Calculation and data specifications are outlined in the third component of the dictionary. Finally, in the bottom section, you provide performance information relating to the measure. Let's examine each of these sections in some detail, using the example provided in Exhibit 6.2.

Measure Background

At a glance, readers should be able to determine what this measure is all about and why it is important for the organization to track.

- *Perspective.* Displays the perspective the measure falls under.

Exhibit 6.2 Balanced Scorecard Measure Dictionary

Perspective: Customer	*Measure Number / Name*: C01 / Customer Loyalty Rating	*Owner*: D. Ferguson, VP Marketing
Strategy: Revenue growth	*Objective*: Increase customer loyalty	
Description: The customer loyalty rating measures the percentage of surveyed customers stating they prefer our products to competitor offerings, and will purchase our products again. Our research indicates that loyal customers make more frequent purchases and tend to recommend our brands to others. Therefore, we believe increasing customer loyalty will help us achieve our strategy of revenue growth.		
Lag/Lead: Lag	*Frequency*: Quarterly	*Unit Type*: Percentage	*Polarity*. High values are **good**
Formula: Number of quarterly survey respondents answering yes to survey questions 5: "Do you prefer our products to competitor offerings?" **and** #6: "Will you purchase our products again?" **divided** by the total number of surveys received.		
Data Source: Data for this measure is provided by our survey company, "SST." Each quarter they perform a random survey of our customers and provide the results electronically to our marketing department. Data is contained in the form of MS Excel spreadsheets (MKT SURVEY.xls, lines 14 and 15). Data is available the 10th business day following the end of each quarter.		
Data Quality: High—received automatically from third-party vendor	*Data Collector*: I. Hashem, Marketing Analyst	
Baseline: Our most recent data received from SST indicates a customer loyalty percentage of 59%.	*Target*: Q1 2001: 65% Q2 2001: 68% Q3 72% Q4 2001: 75%	
Target Rationale. Achieving customer loyalty is critical to our revenue growth strategy. The quarterly increases we're targeting are higher than in past years but reflect our increased focus on loyalty.		
Initiatives:	1. Seasonal promotions	
	2. Customer relationship management project	
	3. Customer service training	

- *Measure number/name.* All performance measures should be provided a number and name. The number is important should you later choose an automated reporting system. Many will require completely unique names for each measure, and since you may track the same measures at various locations or business units, a specific identifier should be supplied. The measure name should be brief but descriptive. Again, if you purchase software for your reporting needs, they may limit the number of characters you can use in the name field.

- *Owner.* Not only does the Balanced Scorecard transmit to the entire organization what your key strategies for success are, but it also creates a climate of accountability for results. Central to the idea of accountability is the establishment of owners for each and every measure. Simply put, the owner is the individual responsible for results. Should the indicator's performance begin to decline, it is the owner we look to for answers and a plan to bring results back in line with expectations. In the example shown, a specific individual is listed as the owner of the measure. However, some organizations feel more comfortable assigning ownership to a function and not a person. They rationalize that while people may come and go, functions tend to remain, and assigning the ownership to a function assures that the responsibilities inherent in the task are not lost when a new person comes on board. This argument has merits, but I recommend you use actual names rather than functions. Not that people will hide behind their titles, but seeing your name associated with the performance of a key organizational measure will tend to promote more action and accountability than will a job function.

- *Strategy.* Displays the specific strategy you believe the measure will positively influence.

- *Objective.* Every measure was created as a translation of a specific objective. Use this space to identify the relevant objective.

- *Description.* After reading the measure name, most people will immediately jump to the measure description, and it is therefore possibly the most important piece of information on the entire template. Your challenge is to draft a description that concisely and accurately captures the essence of the measure so that anyone reading it will be able to quickly grasp why the measure is critical to the organization. In our example we rapidly learn that customer loyalty is based on a percentage, what that percentage is derived from (survey questions), and why we believe the measure will help us achieve our strategy of revenue growth (loyal customers buy more and recommend our products).

Measure Characteristics

This section captures the "meat and potatoes" aspects of the measure you will need when you begin reporting results.

- *Lag/lead.* Outline whether the measure is a core outcome indicator or a performance driver. Remember that your Scorecard represents a hypothesis of your strategy implementation. When you begin analyzing your results over time, you will want to test the relationships you believe exist between your lag and lead measures.

- *Frequency.* How often do you plan to report performance on this measure? Most organizations have measures reported on a daily, weekly, monthly, quarterly, semiannual, or annual basis. However, I have seen unique time frames such as "school-year" for one government agency. Attempt to limit the number of semiannual and annual measures you use on your Scorecard. A measure that is updated only once a year is of limited value when you use the Scorecard as a management tool to make adjustments based on performance results.

- *Unit type.* This characteristic identifies how the measure will be expressed. Commonly used unit types include numbers, dollars, and percentages.

- *Polarity.* When assessing the performance of a measure, you need to know whether high values reflect good or bad performance. In most cases, this is very straightforward. We all know that higher income and customer loyalty is good, while a high value for complaints and employee turnover reflects performance that requires improvement. However, in some cases the polarity issue can prove quite challenging. Take the example of a public health organization. If they choose to measure caseload of social workers, will high values be good or bad? A high number of cases per social worker may suggest great efficiency and effectiveness on the part of the individual workers. Conversely, it could mean the social workers are juggling far too many clients and providing mediocre service in an attempt to inflate their caseload numbers. In cases like this, you may want to institute a "dual polarity." For example, up to 25 cases per social worker may be considered good, but anything over 25 would be a cause for concern and necessitate action.

Calculation and Data Specifications

Information contained in this section of the dictionary may be the most important, yet most difficult to gather. To begin reporting your measures, precise formulas are necessary, and sources of data must be clearly identified.

- *Formula.* In the formula box, you should provide the specific elements of the calculation for the performance measure.

- *Data source.* Every measure must be derived from somewhere—an existing management report, third-party vendor–supplied information, customer databases, the general ledger, and so on. In this section you should rigorously attempt to supply as detailed information as possible. If the information is sourced from a current report, what is the report titled, and on what line number does the specific information reside? Also, when can you access the data? If it is based on your financial close process, what day of the month can you expect final numbers? This information is important to your Scorecard reporting cycle since you will be relying on the schedules of others when producing your Scorecard. The more information you provide here, the easier it will be to begin actually producing Balanced Scorecard reports with real data. However, if you provide vague data sources or no information at all, you will find it exceedingly difficult to report on the measure later. A warning—spend the time you need to thoroughly complete this section. Some Scorecards proceed swiftly through the development stage only to stall at the moment of reporting because the actual data could not be identified or easily collected.

- *Data quality.* Use this area of the template to comment on the condition of the data you expect to use when reporting Scorecard results. If the data is produced automatically from a source system and can be easily accessed, it can be considered "high." If, however, you rely on an analyst's word document that is in turn based on some other colleague's Access database numbers that emanate from an old legacy system, then you may consider the quality "low." Assessing data quality is important for a couple of reasons. Pragmatically, you need to know which performance measures may present an issue when you begin reporting your results. Knowing in advance what to expect will help you develop strategies to ensure that the data you need is produced in a timely and accurate fashion. Data quality issues may also help direct resource questions at your organization. As discussed earlier, one of the benefits of the Scorecard is in the "missing measures" it often helps you unearth. If the information is truly critical to strategic success, then perhaps the organization should invest in systems to mine the data more effectively.

- *Data collector.* In the first section of the template the owner of the measure was identified as that individual who is accountable for results. Often, this is not the person we would expect to provide the actual performance data. In our example, D. Ferguson, the VP of Marketing, is accountable for the performance of the measure, but Marketing Analyst I. Hashem serves as the actual data contact.

Performance Information

In the final section of the template we note our current level of performance, suggest targets for the future, and outline specific initiatives we will use to achieve those targets.

- *Baseline.* Users of the Balanced Scorecard will be very interested in the current level of performance for all measures. For those owning the challenge of developing targets, the baseline is critical in their work.

- *Target.* Some of you may be saying right now, "At this point in the process we haven't set targets, that's the next chapter, so what do we do?" That is very true; targets will be covered in Chapter Seven. However, some of your measures may already have targets. Perhaps a goal of 15 percent return on equity is clearly outlined in your latest analyst reports or lowering emission levels at your plants by 5 percent is legislated by your state government. Wherever targets exist, use them now. For those measures that do not currently have targets, you can leave this section blank and complete it once the targets have been finalized. For those of you who do have at least some targets, list them based on the frequency of the measure. In this example, quarterly customer loyalty targets are shown. Some organizations may find it difficult to establish monthly or quarterly targets and instead opt for an annual target, but track performance toward that end on a monthly or quarterly basis.

- *Target rationale.* As above, this will apply only to those measures for which you currently have a performance target. The rationale provides users with background on how you arrived at the particular target(s). Did it come from an executive planning retreat? Is it an incremental improvement based on historical results? Was it based on a government mandate? For people to galvanize around the achievement of a target, they need to know how it was developed and that while it may represent a stretch, it is not merely wishful thinking on the part of overzealous executives.

- *Initiatives.* At any given time most organizations will have dozens of initiatives or projects swirling about. Often, only those closest to the project know anything about it and any possible synergies between initiatives are never realized. The Scorecard provides you with a wonderful opportunity to evaluate your initiatives in the context of their strategic significance. If an initiative or project cannot be linked to the successful accomplishment of your strategy, you have to ask yourself why it is being funded and pursued. Use this section of the template to map current or anticipated initiatives to specific performance measures. Chapter Seven will return to the subject of initiatives.

Conducting an Executive Workshop to Share Balanced Scorecard Measures

The executive workshop is an exciting event during which you will unveil your newly created Balanced Scorecard measures to the senior team of your organization. While this may be the first time the entire group is convened to specifically review and debate your performance measures, it should in no way be their first exposure to your proposed measures. As noted in Chapter Three, your project's executive sponsor holds the responsibility of maintaining constant communication with the senior management group, ensuring their ongoing commitment and support of the project. To supplement the efforts of your sponsor, each of your Scorecard team members should have created an ongoing dialogue with their "home" executive in order to gather their feedback and engender support.

Preparing for the Workshop

The key to a successful executive workshop is preparation. Long before the conference room door shuts and you are in front of a captive group of executives ready to pounce on your every word, you should have supplied them with the information they need to make the session productive and successful. The following paragraphs will outline the specific components of a Scorecard packet that should be hand-delivered to each executive by the appropriate team member approximately one week in advance of the meeting. A week should give even the busiest of executives ample time to review and digest the material.

Open the document with a section describing the *methodology* your team has followed in developing the Scorecard. The methodology outlines the steps you have taken to this point and the overall process you employed. You might begin by clearly stating that you pursued a Kaplan and Norton Scorecard approach, a modified Baldrige approach, and so on. Next you can discuss how you uncovered the background material you used for the Scorecard, the number of interviews held, and number of potential objectives and measures identified before settling on this current group. Any particular challenges you encountered should also be reported in this section. The problems you have faced to this point may be harbingers of future complications. Your executives should be made aware of these problems and be able to provide possible solutions to avert similar occurrences as the project continues.

The next section of the document should contain some form of *graphical representation* of the Scorecard—a one-page rendering that contains all of the performance measures shown in relation to each of the four Scorecard perspectives. This will provide a valuable reference source during the workshop. Following your Scorecard diagram, readers should see the contents of your Balanced Scorecard *measure dictionary*. To make an informed choice regarding measures and provide appropriate feedback, your executives need the specific details that comprise each of the measures. The last page(s) of this section should contain a list of the performance objectives and measures you originally conceived of but later eliminated based on your evaluation techniques described earlier in the chapter. There may be objectives or measures your executive group believes are critical to the organization's success despite the issues you identified during your evaluation.

As a prelude to the cause-and-effect linkage work that lies ahead, you should create a one-page, high-level summary of how the measures you have selected will work together to help you achieve your strategic goals. At Nova Scotia Power, this one-page summary was called "Value Creation Through Strategy," and it provided the executive team with insights into how using the Scorecard would lead to value creation for the organization. The summary also reiterates the critical nature of cause and effect in Balanced Scorecard success. The objectives and measures are not isolated indicators, but when woven together they create a powerful means of describing the organization's strategy. Nova Scotia Power's Value Creation summary is shown in Exhibit 6.3.

Your executive packet should also contain a *project timeline* demonstrating the work that has been completed and the status of what remains to be done. In any major change project it is very important to celebrate successes along the way, and comments made in the "work completed" section of the timeline allow you to tout your many accomplishments to this point. Based on the success you have shown, you now possess additional ammunition when canvassing the executive team for further support in meeting your final project timelines.

Conclude your document with a section outlining any and all resources your team has used in their work. List books, articles, videos, company information, web sites, and the like. Not only will this show your tenacity in producing a great product, but it may inspire otherwise uncommitted executives to conduct some additional research of their own, thereby increasing their personal knowledge and acceptance of the Balanced Scorecard.

Conducting the Workshop

As in any meeting, the structure of the executive workshop is very important to a successful result. You need defined roles, a clear agenda, and specific desired outcomes if you expect the meeting to be a success.

Invite your entire project team to attend and participate in the meeting. They will prove invaluable in answering specific questions regarding measures they proposed or those for which they provided detailed background information. The meeting should be co-facilitated by your executive sponsor and Balanced Scorecard team leader. The sponsor opens the meeting, reviews the agenda, and establishes the desired outcomes. He should also make a very brief presentation (two or three slides) outlining the benefits to be derived from using the Balanced Scorecard. Some may consider this repetitive, but I am a strong believer in the "mere exposure effect." The more a group is exposed to an idea, the greater is the likelihood they will

Exhibit 6.3 "Value Creation through Strategy" at Nova Scotia Power Inc.

The Balanced Scorecard is a strategic management system which tracks NSPI's performance from four key, balanced perspectives. The Scorecard combines the historical accuracy of financial information with the operational drivers of future success. We have identified key strategies in each of the Scorecard perspectives. However, success cannot be achieved in any one isolated area. Our strategies link together to form a value chain that stretches from our employees to internal processes, to customers, and ultimately to our shareholders. The "value chain" is discussed below in the context of each Scorecard perspective, and corresponding strategy. For continuity, the reader should begin with the Employee Learning and Growth area, and work up through the chain.

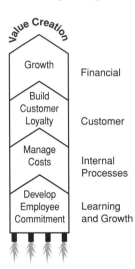

Financial: Measures in this perspective display whether our strategy implementation and execution are leading to improved bottom line results. All measures selected for the Balanced Scorecard should link in a series of cause and effect relationships back to improved financial performance. Our strategies and measures signify our commitment to maintaining the confidence of the investment community balanced with our desire to grow our business in new and exciting ways.

Customer: By focusing on the key processes that drive value for all constituents, we'll be in a position to meet our goal of moving well beyond satisfied customers to loyal customers. When developing measures for the customer perspective, it's important to include not only the core outcome measures such as customer loyalty rating, but also measures which demonstrate the company's customer value proposition. The measures we've selected for this perspective represent a solid combination of these key elements. Among other things, our customers value reliability and price. These leading indicators appear on our scorecard as drivers of customer loyalty.

Internal Processes: What are the key processes we must excel at in order to continue providing value for all stakeholders? That is the question posed by the Internal Processes perspective. Once employees have the commitment, infrastructure, and skills to perform, they will be in a position to contribute to the environment of continuous improvement which is necessary to sustain competitive advantage in today's marketplace. Our focus will be on continuously improving the productivity of our workforce, developing innovative customer offerings, and ensuring we're optimizing the utilization of our capital assets. All of this will be done with sensitivity to our commitment of sustainable economic development. To that end we will continue to expand and improve our efforts to improve environmental performance.

Learning and Growth: If we plan to achieve ambitious targets for our customers, shareholders, and internal processes, how will we meet these challenges? Measures in this perspective are the enablers of the other three perspectives. Our aim is to create an environment which encourages employee commitment. For only through the dedicated commitment of our workforce will we achieve our goals. How will we accomplish this? By focusing on and measuring success in key areas such as: safety, competencies development, and effective communication. We'll give our employees not only the physical tools to make better business decisions, but equally as important we'll deliver the training necessary to ensure all employees have the knowledge base to continue adding value to their positions.

begin to understand and support it. Following the short Scorecard briefing, the team leader will conduct the meeting and rely on the sponsor and team members to provide additional support and clarifying information.

The agenda for the meeting should flow directly from the information packet you distributed to the executive team. To begin, the team leader will share a brief presentation outlining the methodology followed in developing your Scorecard. At that point, you will be ready to take an in-depth look at your performance measures. Work through the four perspectives beginning with Financial and concluding with Employee Learning and Growth. Executive comments on each of the measures can be captured on flip charts and in notes taken by members of your team. Your senior management team may suggest changes to any element of a measure, description, formula for calculation, frequency, and so on. They may even offer input on prospective targets. Once all of the measures in a perspective have been discussed and debated, the executive team should vote on which will remain on the Balanced Scorecard. As noted earlier, they may wish to include measures your team had originally developed but later eliminated, or they may suggest entirely new measures.

After the meeting, your team will need to reconvene and make the necessary adjustments to the Scorecard based on changes from the executive group. You should now have a very solid draft to begin mapping your cause-and-effect linkages. The final hurdle to cross is sharing the draft Scorecard with your fellow employees and gaining their buy-in and support of the tool.

Gathering Employee Feedback on the Balanced Scorecard

Ultimately, you expect your Balanced Scorecard to provide information that allows all employees to determine how their day-to-day actions link to the organization's strategic plan. Most experts will tell you the executive of your organization must own the Balanced Scorecard if it is to be effective in generating results. That is true, but while executives may own the Scorecard, it is the employees who must accept the tool and be willing to use it if you hope to achieve any of the breakthroughs this concept can bring. It is on a day-to-day, decision-by-decision basis at the front lines of commerce that your battle of Scorecard success will be fought and won or lost. The rise of human capital is mentioned frequently throughout this book. If you truly believe that employee knowledge makes the difference in achieving organizational victory, do yourself an immense favor and find out what employees think about your Scorecard before you ask them to use it as a management tool.

Here are three methods you can employ to capture what your employees think about your Balanced Scorecard:

1. *Conduct a Balanced Scorecard "open house."* The County of San Diego, California, has instituted a wide-ranging performance management program to better serve the citizens of this sixth most populated county in the United States. They began their efforts by developing Balanced Scorecards for the Health and Human Services Agency (HHSA). With a budget of over $1 billion and 5,000 employees, HHSA is larger than many corporations. Given the diverse nature of services offered throughout the agency, HHSA asked each of its program areas to develop Balanced Scorecards that demonstrated how they successfully serve their customers. A Balanced Scorecard project team made up of county personnel and consultants worked with each program to develop Scorecards over a four-month span. Once preliminary Scorecards were built, the team looked for a way to share what had been developed with all employees and gather their feedback. They decided to hold what they termed *validation sessions*. Four sessions were held—two in the morning and two in the afternoon. Upon entering the conference room, participants were greeted by project staff and given a folder to hold the information they would gather during the event. Each session was kicked off with a short presentation from the project team leader. He provided an overview of the project, benefits to be derived from performance management, and the work that lay ahead. Once the presentation concluded, participants were free to roam the large room and visit any one of the several booths manned by project team members. Each booth featured a number of different Scorecards that the participants could review and discuss with the team. A kiosk was also set up, giving employees the opportunity to take a test drive of the Scorecard software that would be used to report results. Feedback forms were distributed and participants were encouraged to provide their input to the team. The event was a great success since employees from across the agency had the chance to participate in the evolution of performance measures and see how other groups within HHSA were measuring their outcomes.

2. *Use your intranet.* Take advantage of the widely available technology that currently exists within your organization by broadcasting Scorecard updates over your intranet. A presence on your internal web should be established that contains information updates on Scorecard progress, performance management presentations, quotes from executives on the value of the Balanced Scorecard, and frequently asked questions. Once you have a draft Scorecard, post it on the intranet and ask employees to send their comments via e-mail to the project team, or create a chat room and post all comments received on the Balanced Scorecard project. It is always important to foster as much conversation about the Scorecard as you possibly can since these informal exchanges may lead to breakthroughs in knowledge. Using the intranet is a very efficient way of

gathering feedback from a large number of people in a short period of time.

3. *Hold management meetings or town halls.* If you hold regular meetings that bring together your entire management team, use that venue to share the draft Scorecard. Devote time to providing Scorecard background, the methodology employed in building the Scorecard, and what has been developed thus far. You should also prepare the audience for the challenges awaiting them, for example, developing their own Balanced Scorecards, and using the system to run their businesses. Breakout sessions by business group are a good way to have managers start thinking about the benefits the Balanced Scorecard will bring to their group. During breakouts, specific business groups and departments will be able to assess how well the current Scorecard measures capture their concerns and competitive advantages. Town-hall meetings can also be a great way to share what you have developed with a large number of employees. To accommodate schedules, you will undoubtedly have to schedule a number of these sessions to ensure that everyone has the chance to participate. The key is sharing of information at these sessions and gathering feedback, so ensure the dialogue is not one-way but instead fosters communication between employees and the project team. Whether you conduct management meetings or town halls, attempt to have an executive open the meeting. This shows senior management support for the concept and may help convince incredulous staffers that the Scorecard is in fact here to stay!

CAUSE-AND-EFFECT LINKAGES—TELLING YOUR STRATEGIC STORY

As discussed in Chapter One, the best strategy ever conceived is simply a hypothesis of those who wrote it on behalf of the organization. It represents their best guess as to an appropriate course of action, given the best available knowledge concerning the environment, competencies, competitive positions, and so on. What is needed is a method to document and test the assumptions inherent in the strategy. The Balanced Scorecard allows us to do just that. A well-designed Balanced Scorecard should describe your strategy through the objectives and measures you have chosen. These measures should link together in a chain of cause-and-effect relationships from the performance drivers in the Learning and Growth perspective all the way through to improved financial performance as reflected in the Financial perspective. We are attempting to document our strategy through measurement, making the relationships between the measures explicit so they can be monitored, validated, and managed.

Why Cause-and-Effect Linkages Are Critical to the Balanced Scorecard

If you have followed my advice to this point, you should now have a collection of objectives and measures in each of the four perspectives. What you do not have is a Balanced Scorecard. There is one final hurdle to cross before you can make that claim, and it can be difficult to overcome for many organizations—the process of linking your measures through a series of cause-and-effect relationships that unite to describe your strategy.

Developing a series of measures that weave together in the description of your strategy allows the organization to not only measure the implementation of its strategy, but also describe the all-important "how" of value creation. The cause-and-effect linkages or "strategy maps" serve as the recipe of your success. Kaplan and Norton explain. *"Strategy implies the movement of an organization from its present position to a desirable but uncertain future position. Because the organization has never been to this future place, the pathway to it consists of a series of linked hypotheses. A strategy map specifies these cause and effect relationships, which makes them explicit and testable."*[1] Cause-and-effect linkages outline the specific path you will follow to achieve your strategy. Without this series of connections, you are left with nothing more than an ad-hoc collection of financial and nonfinancial measures. Some may argue that a group of financial and nonfinancial measures is still better than a total preoccupation with one element of success, such as quality or revenue. That may be, but without linkages being defined between measures, you still have not articulated the "how" of your strategy execution. That can be accomplished only through the chain of cause and effect evident in your strategy map.

Cause-and-effect linkages also serve as a highly effective diagnostic tool to examine your newly created Balanced Scorecard. Consider the following scenario. You have decided to pursue a revenue growth strategy and are in the process of reviewing the measures that comprise your Balanced Scorecard. In order to achieve your revenue growth targets as stated in the financial perspective of the Scorecard, you choose to measure customer loyalty in the customer perspective. You hypothesize that loyalty is a function of developing new products and services for your customers; hence, you measure innovation in the internal process perspective of the Scorecard. Upon reviewing your employee learning and growth perspective, you discover that employee satisfaction is the only metric being evaluated. While satisfied employees may well have a greater proclivity toward creativity and thus develop new products, you have included no measures that describe the tools employees will require for creative breakthroughs. Satisfaction could be derived from any number of sources. Perhaps you have instituted a four-day workweek, launched an on-site day care center, or started providing subsidized lunches. Any of these initiatives could lead to greater satisfaction. But will they lead to increased productivity and innovation? To complete your link of cause-and-effect measures, perhaps you should have included a performance measure tracking the percentage of employees possessing key competencies you need to produce new products for your markets or monitored employee access to the latest technology to design and implement breakthrough solutions. Only by analyzing the chain of cause-and-effect linkages can you begin to see possible gaps or missing ingredients in your recipe of success.

Cause and effect implies a connectedness between seemingly disparate elements of the organizational story. Speaking of U.S.-based organizations, psychologist Abraham Maslow suggested that organizations are "embedded" in their immediate communities; this immediate community is embedded in the larger community, which in turn is embedded in the country, which is embedded in the Western world, and so on. He notes that these are all functional relationships in the sense that demonstrable causes and effects can be listed and can be listed by the thousands. Interestingly, the idea of connections extends far beyond the organizational world in which most of us dwell. In fact, the natural world that surrounds us provides the best example of individual elements working together to produce a stronger, more complete whole. In her thought-provoking book *Leadership and the New Science*, Margaret J. Wheatley describes the elegant inner-workings of the natural world and describes the new science in which systems are understood as whole systems, with attention paid to relationships within those networks. Her work has implications for our present concern in this chapter. Consider these powerful statements drawn from her book. *"We cannot understand a system by looking only at its parts. We need to work with the whole of a system, even as we work with individual parts or isolated problems."*[2] *"If we hold awareness of the whole as we study the part, and understand the part in its relationship to the whole, profound new insights become available."*[3] And finally, *"To make a system stronger, we need to create stronger relationships."*[4] Sound familiar? She could easily be describing the notion of cause and effect as it relates to the Balanced Scorecard. We cannot understand our business by simply examining each of its component parts. While working with each of the parts, we must see the organization as a coherent whole. The relationships we describe on our strategy maps represent the binding force that makes the entire system stronger and leads us to the achievement of our strategy.

Developing Cause-and-Effect Linkages

The cause-and-effect linkages we build in our Balanced Scorecard are telling the story of our strategy. *Story* is a key word in that sentence. To effectively harness the communication power of your cause-and-effect linkages, you need both the graphical map and a short accompanying narrative articulating that map. Let's begin by considering how we should create our graphical map, then we will turn our attention to the words that will draw the entire organization into your Scorecard efforts.

Recall from Chapter Five the suggestion that you first develop performance measures, and then construct a map consisting of a series of cause-and-effect relationships. Assuming you have done that, you should now have a host of performance measures in each of the four perspectives from which to choose when constructing your map. The following paragraphs will outline how you can create your strategic story through those measures. When developing your strategy map, you may find that some of the measures you have created just do not fit into the tale you are weaving. You should not feel that the effort expended in designing those measures was a waste of time. In fact, there is a good chance they may be appropriate for the lower-level Scorecards you will be creating when you begin cascading (see Chapter Eight). Alternatively, they may be considered "operational" or "diagnostic" measures and tracked outside of the Balanced Scorecard. Another possibility when devising your map is the addition of entirely new measures in order to make your strategic story coherent. Here we see the true value of the mapping process as it forces you to carefully consider the measures that will reflect a faithful translation of your strategy.

A good Balanced Scorecard should contain a mix of core outcome measures (lagging indicators) and the performance drivers that lead to improved performance on those metrics (leading indicators). When building your cause-and-effect linkages, begin by creating a story from your lagging indicators of performance in each of the four perspectives. The results-oriented nature of these measures makes them very amenable to combining in a logical sequence, beginning with financial aspirations and tunneling downward through customer, internal process, and ultimately, employee learning and growth measures. Once you have created a logical architecture of lagging measures spanning across the four perspectives, you can consider the leading indicators of performance for each. Don't be concerned if the leading indicators of performance will not easily link together through the four perspectives. These measures are the differentiators of performance for your organization in achieving its core outcome measures, and as a result we would expect them to be very esoteric. As Margaret Wheatley reminded us, we must look at the individual parts as they relate to the whole of the system. While the performance driving lead indicators may not appear to be linked or belong to a common theme, when examined in the context of the entire Scorecard system (including the lagging indicators they support), we see that they supply a powerful fuel to drive the entire Scorecard engine.

The development of cause-and-effect linkages is demonstrated in Exhibit 6.4. Imagine for a moment that you have created an award-winning Scorecard for your organization, and have enjoyed the process so much that you decide to go into business for yourself consulting to other organizations on

Exhibit 6.4   Cause-and-Effect Linkages in the Balanced Scorecard

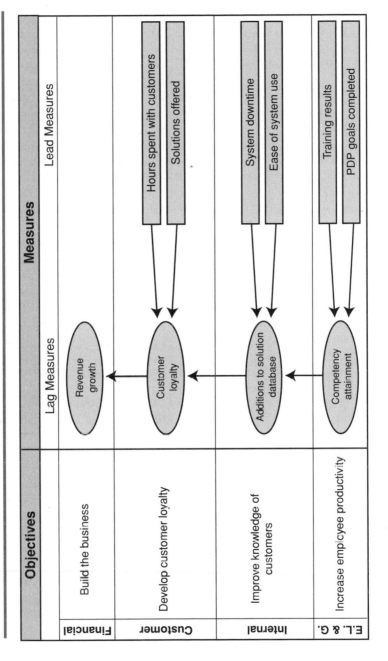

how to develop performance management solutions. "Using detailed customer knowledge to serve midmarket organizations" is the strategy you choose to pursue. Your basis of competition is not a leading-edge product or a superefficient operational style. No, you are offering clients your knowledge, experience, and the total solutions that arise from blending the two. The strategy map shown in Exhibit 6.4 could represent a condensed Scorecard for your organization. Work from the top down, beginning with the financial perspective, and examine how this map was constructed.

The financial perspective provides the destination we are ultimately trying to reach through measuring our performance. In this case, since your consulting firm is new, you believe it is necessary to build your business, and thus the measurement of revenue growth is appropriate. You hypothesize that revenue can be grown if you have a strong base of loyal customers who return to you for additional services. Customer loyalty is the logical choice for a lagging measure of performance. Now you ask yourself, "What drives loyalty for my company?" You have focused on customer intimacy as your value proposition and, therefore, providing total solutions to your clients is crucial to succeed. Being recognized as an organization with abundant solution offerings will certainly assist in generating loyal customers. To develop your solutions you need to know as much as you can about your customer base—their challenges, opportunities, competitive environment, and so on. Accomplishing this task will require spending time at client locations learning directly from them, and thus you measure "hours spent with customers."

With financial and customer measures chosen, you now turn your attention to the critical internal processes you must excel at in order to meet expectations. Consistent with your value proposition of customer intimacy, you recognize the importance of strategic information regarding client needs as the driver of customer loyalty. You develop a solutions database and track the number of additions to the system as your lagging internal process measure. However, you realize that the system will not populate itself. If the database is going to serve as a key tool in driving customer loyalty, then employees must be motivated to use it consistently. You hypothesize that ease of use and system downtime will drive the number of additions to the system. Employees need to feel that the system is reliable, and at the same time entering data into the system cannot be seen as a burdensome task offering no rewards. Finally, you need to consider what employee learning and growth measure will lead to an increased number of additions to the solutions database. You feel that employees who possess the right mix of competencies necessary to provide total solutions to client needs are in the best position to contribute to the database. Therefore, you measure "competency attainment" as a lagging indicator of employee learning and growth success. Like many organizations, you invest heavily in training to develop critical competencies within your staff. However, unlike many organizations, you do not simply monitor training hours or classes attended. You look for specific examples of behaviors that model the training received. "Training results" is a leading indicator of competency attainment. In addition to training, all employees have developed personal development plans (PDPs). You believe that successfully completing plan goals will also lead to increased competency attainment.

You have now created a strategy map consisting of a linked series of performance measures through the four perspectives of the Balanced Scorecard. This map represents your best guess as to what it will take to achieve your strategy. It also serves as a great tool in aligning employee actions with overall organizational goals and testing the execution of your strategy. Exhibit 6.5 displays a number of questions to ask yourself that will assist you in developing your cause-and-effect linkages.

To maximize the effectiveness of a strategy map's communication ability, you need to create the accompanying story that brings the map to life in the minds of your employees. The next section of the chapter will explore the tremendous power of storytelling in communicating your strategy and ensuring alignment throughout the organization.

Exhibit 6.5   Questions to Ask When Building Cause-and-Effect Linkages

Financial

Do the financial objectives and measures describe how we will satisfy shareholder expectations of our organization?

Internal Process

- Have we identified the key internal processes we must excel at in order to meet customer and financial expectations?
- Will the achievement of these measures lead to improved customer and financial results?

Customer

Do the customer objectives and measures reflect the value proposition we will pursue to achieve our financial goals?

Employee Learning and Growth

Do the employee learning and growth objectives and measures describe the skills, information infrastructure, and alignment that will enable us to excel at our internal processes?

Overall Questions

- Do we have an appropriate mix of lagging and leading measures on our Scorecard?
- To sustain our improvement, the Scorecard should contain measures that will lead to short-, intermediate-, and long-term value creation. Have we considered the timing of our linkages?
- Does this Balanced Scorecard tell the whole story of our strategy?

Using Storytelling to Bring Your Linkages to Life

"A picture says a thousand words" is something we have all heard many times in our lives. Your completed strategy map is certainly capable of telling a thousand words. The problem is that every person viewing the map may generate an individual set of words based on their unique interpretation of the picture you have presented. Creating a story to accompany your strategy map takes any guesswork out of the scenario for your employees. The story forces you, the writer, to clearly articulate the assumptions inherent in the map and supply precious details such as the timing and magnitude of the relationships you have identified. For example, your map could display brand awareness in the Customer perspective being a function of targeted marketing efforts measured in the Internal Process perspective. What is the nature of this relationship (i.e., how long before investments in targeted marketing lead to improved brand awareness)? Additionally, what is the magnitude of the relationship? Will a 10 percent increase in marketing yield a corresponding 5 percent increase in brand awareness? Your strategy map story compels you to make the nature of all cause-and-effect linkages clear so that everyone reading the map understands the direction in which you are headed.

Why are stories so effective? Because they tend to captivate us, engage us, and draw us into the subject. Social historians suggest that stories are a critical force in holding societies, families, and cultures together. Human intelligence and memory are also strongly affected by stories. From stories a child learns to *"imagine a course of action, imagine its effects on others, and decide whether or not to do it."*[5] Researchers have confirmed that a story-based style leads to improved learning and memory. In one interesting study, American history textbooks were translated to a story format. Students recalled up to three times more from the story-based books than they did when reading traditional textbooks. Some organizations have already recognized the power of storytelling in strategic planning and other critical business functions. 3M is one such company. *"Stories are a habit of mind at 3M, and it's through them—through the way they make us see ourselves and our business operations in complex, multidimensional forms—that we're able to discover opportunities for strategic change. Stories give us ways to form ideas about winning."*[6]

Whether it's a spooky tale of ghosts and goblins spun around a crackling campfire or the latest Hollywood blockbuster you can't wait to see, every story adheres to a basic format—conflict, transition, climax, close.[7] Your strategic story should contain the same elements. *Conflict* implies defining the current situation, analyzing your market, and discussing the current tensions that make change inevitable. This is the "burning platform" section of the story, explaining why it is imperative that you change to stay ahead of the competition. The *transition* phase of your narrative introduces the Balanced Scorecard system, provides an overview of the methodology, and supplies evidence of its success. Your objectives for launching a Balanced Scorecard would also be found in the transition phase. Your story's *climax* describes the performance measures you've chosen, and lucidly outlines the cause-and-effect relationships that will drive your performance. It is here that you provide the reader with sufficient background on the assumptions you have made in drafting the map. *Close* your narrative with a discussion of how you believe the Balanced Scorecard you have crafted will lead to the successful execution of your strategy and bring you closer to your mission and vision.

The biggest challenge in creating your story is in making it clear and compelling, yet brief. The story should complement the strategy map, not overshadow it. The two elements must work together to draw the reader into the sphere of strategic thinking necessary to achieve success in your market. Every organization has different attention spans, and you will have to determine the optimal length of your story. For some companies, it may be condensed to a single page, while others may find that employees are willing to invest in reading a five-page document. A document of three pages is best—one page for the graphical map and two pages for the accompanying story.

A strategic story can be a powerful galvanizing force within your organization. The commitment and excitement of every employee from the executive suite to the shop floor will be enhanced through the telling of your unique tale. You have described what it takes to win and made it tangible through your story, plus you have given people an opportunity to locate themselves in this drama and ensure they are involved in its successful resolution. You will be amazed at what a good story can do.

Strategy Maps in Action—McCord Travel Management

McCord Travel Management is one of the largest full-service travel management firms in the United States. Based in Chicago, the company has sales of more than $725 million and a staff of over 950 travel professionals. In 1998, McCord embarked on a Scorecard implementation and quickly realized the importance of a strategy map in telling their strategic story. Ed Berkman, Senior Vice President of the Business Process Group, recalls a meeting early in the process that solidified in his mind the necessity of linking strategy with day-to-day employee actions. *"I had a meeting with about 250 travel agents and asked them, 'What is our vision?' They enthusiastically replied, 'We get it right, one traveler at a time.' Next I asked what they did. 'I take reservations' and other functions were stated. Then I asked, 'Why do you do it?' You could have heard a pin drop. There was clearly a gap between our vision statement and what people did on a day-to-day basis. Strategy had not been communicated down."*[8] Based on that meeting, Ed knew it was time to put in place a system that would provide all employees with the opportunity to demonstrate how they contribute to McCord's overall strategic goals.

After successfully launching a pilot Balanced Scorecard project in the eastern region of their Business Travel Management Group, it was time to launch the Scorecard at the corporate level. Exhibit 6.6 displays McCord's corporate strategy map, including their key objectives in each of the four Balanced Scorecard perspectives. While the number of objectives on the map is relatively high compared to most organizations, McCord wanted to ensure they told their story in a compelling and coherent way. Executives believed that each of the objectives shown on the map was a critical ingredient to their success. McCord President and CEO Bruce Black recognizes the value of the Scorecard in aligning employee actions with company strategy. *"A key feature of the Balanced Scorecard . . . is its ability to bridge the gap, holistically, between strategic goals set by executive management and the frontline staff whose daily performance is absolutely critical to reaching those goals."* [9]

Using the strategy map as a measurement, management, and communication tool has allowed McCord to move ever closer to achieving their strategies of being seen as customer intimate by their clients and concurrently increasing profits. The results have been impressive; a 186 percent increase in earnings before interest, taxes, depreciation, and amortization (EBITDA), reduction in management fee pricing to customers, a 17 percent reduction in indirect expenses, and reduced cycle time in all key areas. Ed Berkman believes the Balanced Scorecard and accompanying strategy map have been significant contributors to McCord's success. *"Once employees understand their jobs do connect to a vision and it's part of an overarching strategic direction the company wants to achieve the benefits are huge."* [10]

Restoring Your Organizational Voice with Strategic Conversations

In the groundbreaking book *The Cluetrain Manifesto*, the authors suggest all markets are conversations and people around the globe are flocking to the Internet because it offers them the opportunity to exercise their voice and their passion through conversations. [11] The World Wide Web allows anyone, anywhere, at any time to start a conversation and establish a global dialogue on virtually any topic imaginable. When people begin to connect on a personal level, wonderful, profound things begin to take place, and learning is facilitated in a way no training session could ever duplicate. Developing a strategy map detailing the cause-and-effect linkages in your Balanced Scorecard is your opportunity to start strategic conversations throughout the organization.

The Balanced Scorecard tells the story of your strategy and reflects the hypothesis you have chosen in the pursuit of your goals. When results begin to accumulate as you report on your Scorecard measures, you can question and challenge the assumptions inherent in your plan. Perhaps you believed that employee training would lead to greater innovation. Has that happened, and to the magnitude you assumed? Or customer loyalty increased 10 points. Have you seen a corresponding increase in return on capital employed as you anticipated? Rather than treating any deviations from planned results as defects in need of immediate correction, you can instead devote your attention and managerial skill to questioning the validity of the assumptions that underlie your cause-and-effect linkages throughout the Scorecard. What if customer loyalty increased, but return on capital employed remained the same? Would you abandon any further investments in loyalty programs? As discussed earlier, the focus should now be on the relationships within the entire system that is the Balanced Scorecard. In the case of customer loyalty, after scanning the environment, examining what your competitors are doing, and canvassing your organization, you may believe there is still a correlation between loyalty and return on capital, just not to the order of magnitude you originally conceived.

Many of the cause-and-effect linkages you forge may lack true statistical significance, especially in the short term. Do not let that deter you from capturing the real value to be derived from this system. More often than not it is the conversations spawned by questioning assumptions that leads to real breakthroughs. The Balanced Scorecard should lead to as many questions as it does answers, and in today's world in which intellectual capital drives corporate value you want your employees constantly asking strategic questions. Let your employees' voice be heard by encouraging an active dialogue questioning the assumptions that comprise your Scorecard.

DO PERFORMANCE MEASURES REMAIN THE SAME?

Before we end our discussion of performance measures we must consider the question of their longevity within the Balanced Scorecard. "Will we have the chance to change our measures?" and "Should measures change?" are two of the most frequently asked questions once an organization has launched a Balanced Scorecard program. Some people fear that once they commit to measuring a certain element of performance, they are obligated to keep that measure as long as the Scorecard is in existence. That is definitely not the case.

The Balanced Scorecard is designed to be a dynamic tool, flexible and capable of change as conditions warrant. Over time, you can expect a number of changes to take place within the realm of your measures. In the most extreme case, you may abandon a strategy you have pursured based on Scorecard results that prove much of your hypothesis was invalid. In that case, you would likely develop a new strategy for your organization and select new and corresponding measures that acted as direct translations of

Exhibit 6.6 Strategy Map for McCord Travel Management

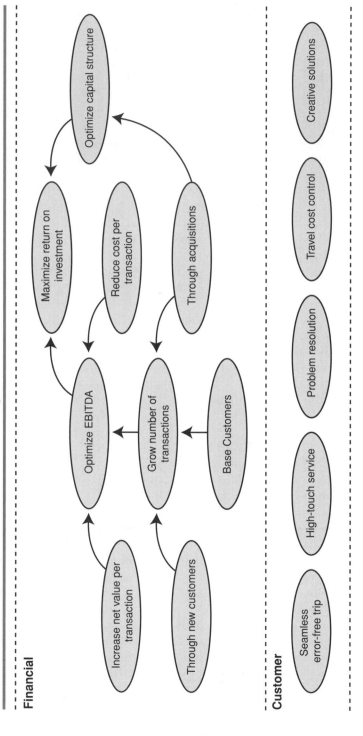

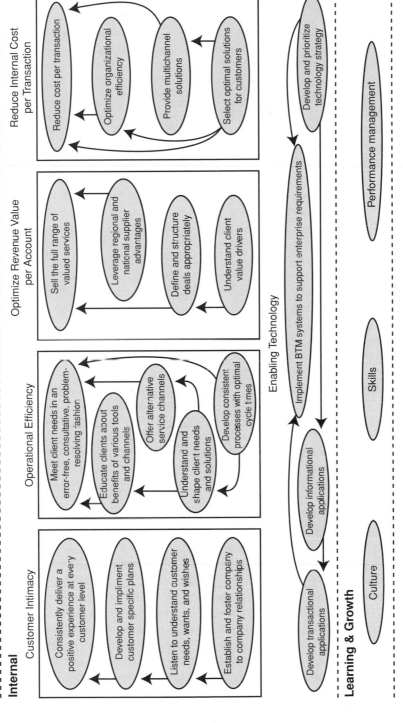

Internal

Customer Intimacy

- Consistently deliver a positive experience at every customer level
- Develop and implement customer specific plans
- Listen to understand customer needs, wants, and wishes
- Establish and foster company to company relationships

Operational Efficiency

- Meet client needs in an error-free, consultative, problem-resolving fashion
- Educate clients about benefits of various tools and channels
- Offer alternative service channels
- Understand and shape client needs and solutions
- Develop consistent processes with optimal cycle times

Optimize Revenue Value per Account

- Sell the full range of valued services
- Leverage regional and national supplier advantages
- Define and structure deals appropriately
- Understand client value drivers

Reduce Internal Cost per Transaction

- Reduce cost per transaction
- Optimize organizational efficiency
- Provide multichannel solutions
- Select optimal solutions for customers

Enabling Technology

- Develop and prioritize technology strategy
- Implement BTM systems to support enterprise requirements
- Develop informational applications
- Develop transactional applications

Learning & Growth

- Performance management
- Skills
- Culture

175

the new strategy. Even if you do not completely renounce a current strategy you should review your performance measures at least annually in conjunction with your planning events (strategic planning, business planning, budgeting, etc.). Measures should be evaluated to ensure that they are still valid in light of current and anticipated business conditions, and are able to remain as key chapters in your strategic story.

Many organizations tend to make subtle changes to measures as they gain experience with the Balanced Scorecard system. The method of calculation may change to better capture the true essence of the event under investigation, or the measure's description may be enhanced to improve employee understanding of its operational and strategic significance. You may also change the frequency with which you collect performance data. For example, you may have attempted to track employee satisfaction monthly, but the logistics of gathering the data simply proved too challenging. In that case, you would not forsake this important indicator—rather, you would simply change the reporting period to something more amenable to measurement. Changing your performance measures is yet another way to tap into the collective knowledge of your organization. Be sure to advertise the fact that you are about to consider measure changes for the coming fiscal year, and give the entire employee base the opportunity to provide feedback regarding beneficial adjustments.

The caveat regarding such changes is this—don't alter your measures simply because you do not like the current crop or the results are not what you expected. The Balanced Scorecard is about learning—learning about your strategy, learning about the assumptions you have made to win in your marketplace, and learning about the value proposition you have put forth. Sometimes you will not necessarily enjoy what your measures are telling you, but as we discussed earlier, do not simply treat these alterations from plan as defects, instead use them to question and learn about your business.

SUMMARY

This chapter explored techniques for accomplishing the often difficult tasks of finalizing your performance measures and creating a series of cause-and-effect linkages that tell the story of your strategy.

Creating a Balanced Scorecard of performance measures requires making difficult choices among a vast number of possible metrics for evaluating strategy. Fortunately, there are a number of criteria you can employ to assist you in making your decision. Scorecard measures should be linked to your strategy, be quantitative, accessible, easily understood, counterbalanced, relevant, and based on a definition shared by all involved. Each potential measure should be evaluated in the context of all criteria to determine which will comprise your Scorecard.

As the Balanced Scorecard methodology continues to gain prominence, the number of measures tracked by most organizations has increased steadily. The advent of functionality-laden software, which facilitates the tracking of thousands of measures, has contributed greatly to the proliferation in the number of measures. The key in determining the appropriate number of measures for your Scorecard lies in their ability to coherently and completely capture your strategic story. Some organizations may require as few as a dozen measures, while others will require 25 or more. Research of Scorecard practitioners across a variety of organizations has revealed most use between 20 and 25 measures for their highest-level organizational Scorecards.

Performance measure data dictionaries chronicle all the relevant aspects of your indicators, allowing everyone to learn, at a glance, the nature of your measures. You should create a dictionary that includes the following sections for each measure: background, characteristics, calculation and data elements, and performance information.

Before considering your measures final they must be reviewed and validated by both your executive team and your employees. Conduct an executive workshop to gather the feedback of your senior team. To ensure you meet your objectives distribute information packets to executives in advance of the meeting. The document should contain information regarding your Scorecard methodology, a graphical representation of your measures, measure dictionaries, a project timeline, and a review of the resources you used to create your Scorecard. When it is time to hold your review session, all members of your team should participate. The meeting will be co-facilitated by your executive sponsor and team leader.

While your executives must own the Balanced Scorecard if it is to catch on at your organization, your entire group of employees must understand the tool and be involved in its development if they are to be expected to use it as a management tool. Conducting "open houses," using your intranet, and holding town-hall meetings are all methods you can use to gather Balanced Scorecard input from your employees.

Cause-and-effect linkages of measures in your Scorecard combine to describe the strategic story of your organization. They outline the specific path you'll follow to achieve success with your strategy, and describe the "how" of value creation derived from your combination of measures. The linkages also serve as a diagnostic tool, allowing you to ensure that the measures you've selected for your Scorecard combine in such a way as to fully and coherently describe your chosen strategy.

Cause-and-effect linkages are best developed by working top down from the financial perspective through the Customer, Internal Process, and ultimately, Employee Learning and Growth perspectives. Within each perspective we identify the lagging indicators of success and the corresponding drivers of performance (leading indicators), which lead to successful outcomes.

Stories have always engaged and captivated us and have been a major contributor to learning. Using storytelling allows you to articulate the specific assumptions throughout your series of linked performance measures. All the essential elements of a good story should accompany the map of your strategy—conflict, transition, climax, and close.

When we begin analyzing results from our Balanced Scorecard, we can examine the relationships that depict our strategy rather than focusing on individual elements of performance. Considering the results we have achieved in the context of these relationships allows strategic conversations to emerge throughout your organization. Deviations from plan are no longer simply considered defects, but are instead examined in the context of the relationships between measures and the assumptions we made regarding those relationships.

Measures on the Balanced Scorecard will evolve and change over time. Change may come in the form of entirely new strategic directions that require corresponding measures, or could be more subtle. Organizations will often adjust measure descriptions, methods of calculation, or frequency of collection as the performance management system advances in maturity.

NOTES

1. Robert S. Kaplan and David P. Norton, "Having Trouble with Your Strategy? Then Map It," *Harvard Business Review*, September–October 2000, 167–176.
2. Margaret J. Wheatley, *Leadership and the New Science* (San Francisco: Berrett-Koehler, 1999).
3. Ibid., p. 143.
4. Ibid., p. 145.
5. William Calvin, "The Emergence of Intelligence," *Scientific American*, October 1994.
6. Gordon Shaw, Robert Brown, and Philip Bromiley, "Strategic Stories: How 3M is Rewriting Business Planning," *Harvard Business Review*, May–June 1998, 41–50.
7. Bill Jensen, *Simplicity—The New Competitive Advantage* (Cambridge, MA: Perseus Publishing, 2000).
8. Interview with Ed Berkman, July 3, 2001.
9. From McCord Travel Management's web site, *www.mccord.com*. Originally appeared in the Forum section of *Business Travel News*.
10. Interview with Ed Berkman, July 3, 2001.
11. Rick Levine, Christopher Locke, Doc Searls, and David Weinberger, *The Cluetrain Manifesto* (Cambridge, MA: Perseus Publishing, 2000).

CHAPTER 7

Setting Targets and Prioritizing Initiatives

Roadmap for Chapter Seven When we began our Balanced Scorecard journey together, I described this tool as three things—measurement system, strategic management system, and communication tool. This chapter will provide the final pieces required to create your Balanced Scorecard measurement system and communication tool—setting targets and prioritizing initiatives. It will also lay the foundation for our next challenge—instituting the Balanced Scorecard as the cornerstone of your managerial processes.

The strong human desire to meet a predetermined goal has been with us since time immemorial. Many centuries ago, Seneca said, *"If a man knows not what harbor he seeks, any wind is the right wind."* Oliver Wendell Holmes weighed in on the subject with this piece of wisdom, *"The great thing in this world is not so much where we are, but in what direction we are moving."* Sure, Seneca and Holmes are erudite gentlemen, but their advice cannot compete with this pearl from that wisest of all sages, Yogi Berra, *"If you don't know where you are going, you might wind up someplace else."* Although these quotes represent vastly different times, places, and perspectives, what they do have in common is the focus on a future destination—in other words, a target. Balanced Scorecards need performance targets to fully tell your strategic story. Without a corresponding target, your performance data lacks the feedback necessary for analysis and decision making.

This chapter will examine the critical role of targets in the Balanced Scorecard. Organizations may pursue different types of targets associated with specific time frames. We will look at three possible target time frames you may use with your Balanced Scorecard, as well as supporting organizational elements, to ensure that they motivate the right performance. Setting targets is never a simple chore, but this chapter will outline a process of using your cause-and-effect linkages to facilitate the target-setting pro-

179

cess and provide several sources of target information. As with performance measures, your targets should be subject to a formal review process, and we will consider some techniques you can employ to ensure that your targets receive appropriate feedback.

Initiatives describe specifically how a performance target will be met—the action steps, processes, projects, and plans that will bring the targets to life. At any given time, most organizations will be pursuing a multitude of different initiatives. The vital consideration is whether the initiatives are helping you meet your strategic goals. We will examine organizational initiatives in the context of the Balanced Scorecard, as well as a four-step process for ensuring you have the right initiatives in place to support the achievement of your strategy.

EVERY BALANCED SCORECARD NEEDS TARGETS

Like many people, I love golf. The game cast its spell on me when I was 16 and I have been a hopelessly optimistic hacker ever since. Mark Twain called golf "a good walk spoiled" but I can't get enough of it. When I started thinking about how to begin this chapter, my mind wandered to the golf course. Imagine playing a round of golf without flags and holes. At what would you aim? How far would you try and hit the ball, and in what direction? I suppose you could step up to the first tee box, place your ball on a tee and take a mighty swing. Wherever the ball landed would be good enough and you could go on to the next hole—maybe even with a smile on your face. But how do you know if your game is getting any better? What is the standard? Flags and the holes in which they are placed provide us with something to aim at, something on which we can place our attention and unwavering focus. By aiming at the flag and counting the strokes to put the ball in the hole, we have a means of judging our performance against a predetermined standard called *par*. And we love the challenge of attempting to make par. Of course, we humans have always had a desire to meet our goals and succeed. Cultures around the globe, including ancient Peruvians and Egyptians, believed that writing out a goal in advance would help ensure a positive outcome. Using primitive colors, they created renderings on the walls of caves that represented their goals.

We have come a long way from drawing on the inside of cave walls, but our desire to succeed by meeting a challenge has remained the same. Like a golf course without flags or holes, the Balanced Scorecard is incomplete without a set of targets to motivate and inspire breakthrough performance. Targets make the results derived from measurement meaningful and tell us whether we are doing a good job. An on-time delivery percentage of 65 percent really doesn't tell us much unless we consider that performance in the light of our desired results. It is only by combining our actual performance with a target that this feedback becomes meaningful. Our on-time delivery rate of 65 percent takes on a lot more relevance when we learn the industry standard is 80 percent and our chief competitors all have percentages hovering in the high seventies. Armed with this knowledge we see that our rate requires improvement if we are to compete effectively in the marketplace. We might now set an aggressive target of 85 percent on-time delivery for the coming year. As performance data accumulates, it is now imbued with meaning in the context of the target, and we can evaluate trends and make decisions regarding how to make certain we meet or exceed that target. Predicting future results is also facilitated by monitoring our results as compared to the target. And finally, accountability is fostered by assigning ownership for results to an individual responsible for achieving the target.

Using performance targets is a standard and accepted procedure among Balanced Scorecard practitioners. One study found that 93 percent of respondents *"employed quantitative goals that have been directly aligned with Scorecard measures."*[1] In case you're wondering why it wasn't 100 percent, some organizations will use targets of a subjective nature, ratings such as "fair" or "average," for example. As we discussed in Chapter Six, this practice should be avoided whenever possible as it is always preferable to apply a quantitative standard in order to maximize objectivity.

Different Types of Targets

A target can be defined as a quantitative representation of the performance measure at some point in the future (i.e., our desired future level of performance). The word *future* is key to the notion of targets. When developing targets, we can choose to evaluate performance against a goal just for this month, quarter, or year, or we could develop an even longer-term objective requiring additional effort and performance. This section will examine three types of targets you can employ, each associated with a different time frame.

Long-Term Targets: Big Hairy Audacious Goals (BHAGs)

On May 25, 1961, President Kennedy made this bold proclamation: *"This nation should commit itself to achieving the goal, before this decade is out, of landing a man on the moon and returning him safely to earth."*[2] This statement represents the best essence of a "Big Hairy Audacious Goal" or "BHAG." *Built to Last* authors Jim Collins and Jerry Porras coined this term to describe the seemingly outrageous objectives that organizations establish as powerful mechanisms to stimulate progress.[3]

The idea behind a BHAG is that it will dramatically shake up an organization by throwing at it a monumental challenge that cannot be achieved through business-as-usual operations, but will instead require tremendous effort. BHAGs, as evidenced by their dramatic challenges, are necessarily long-term goals with a clear and compelling finish line toward which all energies can be focused. Most would take between 10 and 30 years to successfully accomplish. The long time frame serves two purposes. First, a worthy BHAG is unlikely to be met in a year or two. The extreme challenge it represents will take many years to conquer. For example, Citibank's BHAG of attaining 1 billion customers worldwide may take many years considering they currently have about 100 million customers. Second, an extended time horizon ensures that executives do not sacrifice long-term results for the sake of achieving a short-term goal.

When Jack Welch took control of General Electric, he made this now famous dictum: *"To become #1 or #2 in every market we serve and revolutionize this company to have the speed and agility of a small enterprise."*[4] There is no room for doubt in that statement. Anyone reading it will arrive at the same conclusion and be motivated to make things happen or risk possibly dire consequences. That is the essence of a BHAG—clear and compelling, often consisting of only one or two sentences but making the anticipated results abundantly clear.

Midrange Targets: Stretch Goals

Whereas BHAGs reach out and grab the entire organization, serving as a unifying focal point for one immense goal, stretch targets normally apply to a wider variety of activities. Essentially, we are taking the BHAG and breaking it down into its component parts. Becoming number 1 or number 2 in every market GE serves requires specific targets to be met in every phase of the business. That's where stretch targets come into play. Stretch targets are set three to five years in the future and while they are not quite as dramatic or outrageous as BHAGs, they do represent discontinuous operations. Moving customer loyalty from 40 percent to 75 percent over a three-year period would constitute a stretch target, as would doubling stock price or inventory turnover.

Consider the story of Honeywell. In February 1995, when Michael Bonsignore assumed the role of chief executive officer (CEO), he faced a very difficult situation. *Business Week* warned that investors were becoming impatient and the board was upping pressure to show results. Lackluster financial numbers from 1994 put major demands on the new CEO to right the ship. One of Bonsignore's first acts was to establish a powerful stretch target of achieving $10 billion in annual revenue by the year 2000, a remarkable goal for a company that had not produced much more than $6 billion in over a decade. Bonsignore later recalled, *"I wanted to send a very strong signal to the organization. We were gonna do something different or die trying."*[5] Despite initial resistance by Honeywell executives, the organization eventually rallied around the target and set about to achieve it. By 1999, Honeywell had achieved sales of $9.9 billion. The establishment of a powerful stretch target helped orchestrate this impressive turnaround.

Short Term: Incremental Targets

We all know that a journey of 1,000 miles begins with a single step. So it is with the incremental performance target. These goals are normally established on an annual basis for each of the measures appearing on the Balanced Scorecard. They provide a quantitative goal for our measures and allow us to gauge our progress toward stretch goals and, ultimately, BHAGs. Incremental targets act as an early warning system, providing timely feedback relating to the achievement of our desired future state as represented in stretch targets and BHAGs. Most organizations use annual targets; however, greater benefits can be derived by aligning targets with the reporting frequency of performance measures. For example, you may wish to measure targeted market share on a quarterly basis. Your target for the year is 50 percent, but you may be able to break that down to 40 percent for the first quarter, 44 percent in the second, 48 percent in the third, and finally, 50 percent at year end. Having targets for each of the quarters endows actual results with more meaning for decision making since you can now make valid comparisons between actual and targeted results.

Are All Three Target Types Necessary?

Based on the discussion in the preceding section, we see that the three classes of targets can work together in shaping an organization's future. BHAGs set the desired long-range future vision, which is then decomposed into a number of stretch goals. Feedback on the attainment of stretch goals is received by analyzing performance results in the short term. Ideally, targets should be constructed relating to each time period. However, in practice, this is infrequently done, at least during the early stages of a Scorecard implementation. Just establishing incremental performance targets can often prove to be a significant challenge, especially considering the fact that a number of performance measures may be brand new with little in the way of baseline data to support a logical target. Items to consider when establishing each type of target include:

- *BHAGs need organizational support systems.* Achieving a BHAG will take many, many years, possibly even decades. One surefire way to derail a BHAG is to put in place management systems that not only don't support the achievement of the BHAG, but actively work against it. Compensating executives on short-term profit while simultaneously pursuing a BHAG of revolutionary growth is a contradiction that will ensure that the latter goal is never reached. To help organizations reach the lofty realms of their BHAGs, author Jim Collins describes *catalytic mechanisms* as the link between performance and objectives. Catalytic mechanisms *"transform lofty aspirations into concrete reality. They make big, hairy, audacious goals reachable."*[6] Collins uses the example of 3M, which urged its scientists to spend 15 percent of their time experimenting and inventing in the area of their own choice. This mechanism was designed to ensure innovation and creativity remain as the hallmark of 3M.

- *Make stretch targets realistic.* While seemingly outlandish claims and goals that seek to galvanize an organization are the domain of the BHAG, stretch targets must be firmly rooted in reality to be accepted. Imagine hiring a personal trainer to help you achieve your fitness goals. After one workout together your brawny teacher notes, "Someday you could compete in the Olympics." You feel pretty good about that until the leviathan's next utterance, "So tomorrow we're going to get you ready by bench-pressing 400 pounds 10 times." Unless you're a trained weightlifter, that goal clearly is not rooted in reality, and rather than motivating you, it may deter you from even showing up at the next session! Unfortunately, many organizational stretch targets seem to be chosen with as little rigor as our hypothetical example. Instead of lifting some ridiculous amount of weight, the equally nonsensical goal is zero manufacturing defects in one month or doubling net earnings in six months. Even if employees were somehow motivated to achieve such goals, they are often ill-equipped to do so since they lack the knowledge, tools, and means necessary to produce. For stretch targets to prove effective, they must balance the perilous line between motivation and reality. Additionally, as with BHAGs, you must put in place management systems that complement the achievement of your stretch targets.

- *Let the games begin—incremental performance targets. Increment* means added amount, and when organizations create targets of this nature that is very often what they do—add (or subtract) a small amount to the previous year's number. Increase sales by 5 percent, lower supplies expense by 10 percent, and so on. The question is: What is an appropriate number to add or deduct? Some managers become very adept at developing targets they camouflage as stretch when they know very well they can achieve them with a minimum of effort. This can be very dangerous because it may appear from inside that the organization is attempting to continuously improve, when in fact it is merely a charade and competitors are improving at a much quicker rate. All targets on the Balanced Scorecard should be subject to a rigorous review process to ensure that the numbers suggested are actually meaningful targets that represent significant effort to achieve. Rather than accepting targets at face value, managers and executives must quiz the target setter, questioning his assumptions, generating alternatives, and generally determining that the target is the result of careful analysis and not meticulous game playing.

Not every measure on your Scorecard will have an associated big, hairy, audacious goal. That would prove nearly impossible to manage and could lead to a diffusion of priorities throughout the organization. However, you should attempt to develop stretch targets for each of your measures. These stretch targets will play an important role when you link the Balanced Scorecard to your organization's budgeting process (discussed in Chapter Nine). Of course, incremental targets should also form a part of your Scorecard. For every measure, you must form a picture of where you want to be in three to five years and the incremental steps you'll take to get there.

Cause-and-Effect Linkages Make the Impossible Possible

Chapter Six discussed the use of storytelling to convey the assumptions contained within your strategy map. Using a story-based approach forces the writer to clearly articulate the assumptions inherent in the map and supply details such as the timing and magnitude of the relationships between measures. Your strategy map story compels you to make the nature of all cause-and-effect linkages clear and understandable to anyone reviewing the map. Using the linkages you have identified throughout the map and relying on the magnitude of correlation you expect, you are able to create targets that help you achieve the breakthrough performance you desire.

Let's say you have a financial stretch target of increasing return on equity (ROE) by 20 percent over the next three years. Initially, that may not appear feasible in the hearts and minds of the managers who will be charged with making it happen. However, using a unique and powerful combination of leading and lagging indicators spanning the four perspectives of the Scorecard as the ingredients, you will be able to successfully achieve that goal. Your challenge now is to determine the right mix of targets that will turn that dream into reality. By plugging in different targets for each of your indicators, you have the ability to determine the optimal combination of events that lead to the fulfillment of your overall financial target. You may have hypothesized that an increase in employee satisfaction of 5 percent will drive a corresponding 10 percent improvement in defect rates, which in turn drive 6 percent improvements in customer satisfaction, which leads to a 5 percent improvement in ROE. After reviewing a number of different scenarios, the right mix of targets will emerge. In their first book, Kaplan and Norton describe the case of Kenyon Stores. They used this scenario planning process to decompose a high-level financial stretch target into a series of smaller objectives that, taken together, enabled them to achieve their financial goal of doubling revenues.[7]

Putting this into practice will most likely take some time in your organization. Just developing a series of cause-and-effect relationships can be difficult enough without the added burden of developing opinions on the strength of correlations. Consider this a possible enhancement to your Scorecard model as your performance management discipline evolves and becomes more stable and mature.

Sources of Target Information

Many organizations encounter serious difficulty developing targets for their measures. In certain cases, managers appear hesitant to commit themselves to an actual target they will be bound to honor and judged against. However, it is often simply a case of the measure being brand new with no baseline to work from or a lack of potential sources of target information that holds people back. I can't help you too much with the first point, but can assist on the latter. Here are a number of places you may find information that will help you create targets for your particular measures.

- *Employees.* You should never forget that those closest to the action are in the best position to provide information on what it takes to exceed stakeholder expectations. No matter what type of business you are in, your employees have a unique glimpse into the customer experiences and internal processes that drive value throughout the organization. Involving employees in target setting will also help increase buy-in and support for the Balanced Scorecard as a management tool.

- *Trends and baselines.* A trend analysis or other statistical techniques will help you establish a baseline projection if past data exists. This baseline data can be used to help you predict future levels of performance under conditions similar to those experienced in the past. That is a key point. If your organization or industry is subject to increasing levels of volatility, incremental improvement from previous baselines may not be enough to sustain profitable performance. Trends work best when you are in a period of relative stability.

- *Executive interviews.* When you met with your executives earlier in the process, they may have shared with you what they felt was a required level of performance to achieve success. Similarly, your executive workshops, conducted throughout the process of developing a Scorecard, will likely yield potential Scorecard targets.

- *Internal/external assessments.* If you have recently gone through any kind of strategic planning process, you have undoubtedly conducted an assessment of strengths, weaknesses, opportunities, and threats (SWOT). Information from these assessments will help you determine appropriate targets to maximize opportunities and minimize threats.

- *Feedback from customers and other stakeholders.* Expectations from these important groups may yield information you can use when establishing performance targets. Customers may have explicit or implicit standards to which they expect all vendors to adhere. Involving stakeholders in the target-setting process also demonstrates your commitment to working with everyone involved with your enterprise to produce mutually beneficial results. Recall our earlier discussion of customers rating your performance on the Internet. Don't miss this opportunity to engage your customers in a dialogue about what constitutes great performance in their minds.

- *Industry averages.* There are a number of credible agencies that monitor the performance of virtually all industries. J.D. Power and Associates comes to mind when thinking of the automobile industry. Your organization is most likely affiliated with some industry or trade association that may have valuable information regarding performance across your industry on selected metrics. Be careful to ensure that any data you use is consistent with your methodology for measurement. Many organizations follow vastly different methods of calculating even the most common performance measures.

- *Benchmarking.* Examining best-in-class organizations and attempting to emulate their results is effective to a point. It is very important to try and achieve the same level of success as the star performers in your industry, but benchmarking has a downside as well. First of all, most organizations will simply focus on one element of operations when conducting a benchmarking study—perhaps innovation processes, month-end closing processes, or call center operations. The problem with this approach is that the best-in-class company you are studying probably has a number of different activities it combines to drive a unique mix of value for customers (the essence of strategy as espoused by Michael Porter). Copying just one element of this formula may lead to isolated improvements in that area but fail to bring about breakthrough financial performance. Additionally, the organizations you review may have different customers, processes, and resources. Perhaps they allocate significant human and financial resources to the process under the microscope, and that is what accounts for their success.

Getting Approval for Your Targets

Your executive team should own the responsibility for approving the targets appearing on your highest-level Balanced Scorecard. Ultimately, it is the executives who own this tool and they must feel that the goals on the Scorecard represent exceptional performance, which will require great effort and collaboration to successfully accomplish. Approving targets is yet another opportunity for your senior team to break out of their functional silos and demonstrate how their particular role in the organization contributes to overall success. The team must ensure that the targets displayed on the Scorecard will combine to produce the breakthrough financial results they anticipate. If the VP of Manufacturing commits to tremendous gains in supply-chain activities, and the VP of Sales extends a willingness to produce unheard-of sales increases, you would expect a correspondingly high target from the chief financial officer (CFO). Again, each part of the Scorecard and each member of the senior management team is part of the larger system, the greater whole that is made stronger through the power of relationships.

Chapter Six noted the importance of gathering employee feedback on your performance measures. While employees will not approve your highest-level Scorecard targets, they must have the opportunity to review them and provide feedback. The last thing you want is for employees to perceive your targets as edicts issued from on high with no regard to the toll they will exact on those who have to do the actual work. Employee concerns regarding targets, their viability, and likelihood of success should be captured and fed back to senior management. Even if the executive team decides that a controversial target must remain in the Scorecard to produce the results you desire, they can take the opportunity to communicate their decision to the staff and explain why the inclusion of this particular target is critical to the successful achievement of the strategy. To win at this Balanced Scorecard game, you must take advantage of every single opportunity to educate, communicate, and motivate your staff.

PRIORITIZING ORGANIZATIONAL INITIATIVES

To this point you have developed a Balanced Scorecard of linked objectives and measures telling the story of your strategy, and have populated the model with targets that will lead you to unparalleled success. But you are not finished yet. The last piece in the puzzle of using the Balanced Scorecard as a measurement system is the development and prioritization of initiatives that will help you achieve your targets. Initiatives are the specific programs, activities, projects, or actions you will embark on to help ensure that you meet or exceed your performance targets. The target is your "end in mind" for the performance measure, and to get there you need to determine what investments in initiatives are necessary to guarantee a positive outcome.

If yours is like most organizations, there will be no shortage of initiatives underway at any given time. Employee empowerment, ISO 9001, facilities upgrades, growth initiatives local area network (LAN) modernization, and customer relationship management are all examples of the myriad projects that could be swirling about your organization right now. The interesting thing about most organizational initiatives is the broad spectrum of disciplines and processes they intend to influence. In addition to a wide variety of focal points, they are probably each sponsored by a different manager or executive and executed with independent human and financial resources. The question of interest to us is this: Are they strategic in nature? Every initiative at your organization will undoubtedly drive local improvements in the area it is focused on improving. Chances are it would not have been sponsored if that was not the case. But are the improvements you will derive actually leading to the fulfillment of your Balanced Scorecard targets and hence your strategy? A critical examination of your current initiatives may yield interesting insights. You may find that you simultaneously have too many initiatives and too few![8] An abundant number of projects gaining support may not be geared toward any specific element of your strategy, while concurrently the actions you need to take in order to achieve your Scorecard targets may not be represented with a single initiative.

When developing your Balanced Scorecard, you undoubtedly developed many performance measures that had never before been contemplated at your organization. This is particularly the case with the leading indicators of success, the drivers of future financial performance. Your performance-driving lead measures are the unique ingredients of your recipe for success and are not easily duplicated by competitors. If the measures themselves are new, then it is a sound bet that no initiatives are currently under consideration to ensure the success of these measures. Every original metric you uncover could mean you have a corresponding strategic process not being managed, or not being managed effectively. A value proposition of customer intimacy, for example, necessitates processes ensuring deep customer knowledge housed within the Internal Process perspective of the Scorecard. If, upon examination, you have developed innovative new measures for capturing customer knowledge but not the associated activities or processes to support the measures, then you really have no way to meet your targeted expectations. To do so will require launching explicit initiatives that support the new managerial processes and measurements. Let's look at a method you can use to ensure that you have the right initiatives in place to support your Scorecard measures.

Ensuring That You Have the Right Initiatives in Place

In case you need a little incentive to complete your trek through this arduous terrain of initiative prioritization, here is a metaphorical carrot. Establishing the initiatives that are truly providing support in your pursuit of strategic goals is one of the best and easiest ways to gain a quick economic pay-back from a Balanced Scorecard project. Think about it: You probably have dozens of initiatives competing for scarce human resources, even more scarce financial resources, and the ultimate in scarce resources—the time and at-tention of senior management. Projects that are not helping you achieve your strategy are not only counterproductive, but the excess use of human and financial capital could be causing you to rapidly lose ground to your competitors. Eliminating nonstrategic initiatives by using the laser-like lens of the Balanced Scorecard will quickly translate to freeing up valuable re-sources that can be funneled into projects that create real value and lead to competitive advantage.

There are four steps that will lead us to the promised land of strategic initiatives. They are:

1. Perform an inventory of all current initiatives taking place within the organization right now.
2. Map those initiatives to the objectives of our Balanced Scorecard.
3. Consider eliminating nonstrategic initiatives, and develop missing ini-tiatives.
4. Prioritize the remaining initiatives.

Let's consider each of these steps in more detail.

• *Developing an inventory of current initiatives.* To make an informed deci-sion regarding which initiatives are strategic and which are not, you must first gather information on all projects currently underway throughout the organization. This will mean searching under a lot of rocks because you may find initiatives in every far-reaching corner of the organization. Your executive team should be able to provide excellent input on cur-rent initiatives since each project will most likely have an executive spon-sor. Managers and specific department heads will also be aware of cur-rent initiatives which affect them. Your strategic planning department may keep a detailed listing of all projects taking place at any given time, and such a document will prove invaluable to you. Finally, the account-ing department may be keeping tabs on project-related costs and be able to provide you with a roster of current initiatives. To aid in the decision-making process that will follow, ensure that you have the initiative's name, the objective to be achieved from the project, projected costs, any dis-counted cash flow analysis performed, anticipated timeline, and names of people involved.
• *Mapping initiatives to your strategic objectives.* Armed with an exhaustive accounting of the initiatives currently underway, you are now ready to map those projects to the objectives you have identified in each of the

four perspectives of your Scorecard. It sounds easy enough—take an initiative and look at in the context of each objective. If it contributes to the achievement of an objective, you mark it as such. If it does not, you leave that grid empty. However, simply evaluating the initiative based on its name may be problematic. Perhaps the title does not reflect the true nature of the tasks being undertaken or there are ancillary activities that do in fact support strategic objectives. Perform an appropriate amount of due diligence when completing this step. The first thing to do is determine specifically what you classify as "strategic." Every organization will have a definition of this term. Carefully review the information you gathered during your inventory step to ensure that you have an adequate understanding of the true goals of each and every initiative. Speak to the sponsors, project team members, and those affected by the initiative to ensure that you have determined its full scope of activities and potential results. Each initiative should include supporting documentation to assist you in making this important decision. Those initiatives that are not fortified with critical information such as linkage to strategy, resource requirements, and net present value analysis are prime candidates for elimination in our next step. It will be very difficult to avoid having a little subjectivity creep into your analysis, but as previously discussed, strategy is messy business and often considered as much an art as a science. Exhibit 7.1 displays a template that will assist you in identifying which initiatives map to specific objectives. On the left side of the document, you will list your strategic objectives as they appear on your Balanced Scorecard. The upper portion of the template provides space to record your initiatives. In our example, only one initiative—facilities beautification—cannot be directly linked to a strategic objective on the Balanced Scorecard.

- *Eliminating nonstrategic initiatives and developing missing initiatives.* After thoughtfully judging the strategic value of each initiative, you must give serious consideration to canceling or reducing in scope those that do not contribute to the achievement of your strategy. Again, this is easier said than done. Every initiative will have a number of ardent supporters throughout the company who will most likely resist any attempts to destroy what they have built. Not only are resources on the line here, but relationships and perceived power as well. The diplomatic skills of your Balanced Scorecard executive sponsor will be called into action during this delicate step. Before simply abandoning those initiatives that do not appear to add strategic value, dig a little deeper and investigate the possibility of consolidating projects that taken individually do not lead to the fulfillment of strategy, but when combined with others have synergistic possibilities that could translate to strategic breakthroughs. Should you require new initiatives to fill the void created by new performance measures, develop them on a solid foundation. Ensure that there is an

Exhibit 7.1 Mapping Initiatives to Objectives

Perspective	Objectives	Benchmarking	Maintenance Overhaul	ISO 9002	Frequent Purchase Program	IT Tools and Training	360 Feedback	Global Communication	Partner Program	Just-in-Time Mfg.	Decision Training	Facility Beautification	New Pricing Programs
Financial	Grow revenue												●
	Increase asset utilization	●								●			
Customer	Increase partnering								●				
	Build loyalty				●								
	Grow market share				●								
Internal Process	Develop customer information					●							
	Reduce downtime		●	●									
Employee Learning and Growth	Develop core competencies							●					
	Increase empowerment						●				●		

192

executive willing to sponsor the new initiative, clearly defined plans and project scope, a legitimate budget, and the commitment of resources necessary to successfully complete the initiative.

- *Prioritize strategic initiatives.* Now that you have a definitive number of initiatives you consider strategic, you must rank them in order to make resource allocation decisions (assuming you don't have unlimited financial and human resources!). Chapter Nine will discuss the role of initiatives in the budgeting process in greater detail, but for now let's consider how you can make a rational decision between competing alternatives. The key is basing the decision on a common set of criteria that will determine the most appropriate initiatives given your unique priorities. Obviously, the initiative's effect on driving strategy is the chief concern, but you cannot ignore investment fundamentals like cost, net present value, and projected time to complete. Essentially, every initiative should have a valid business case to support its claim as being necessary to achieve your strategy. Once you have drafted business cases for each of the initiatives, you can use a template similar to that shown in Exhibit 7.2 to assist in making the prioritization decision. Each criterion you choose is assigned a weight, depending on its importance within your company. The assignments are subjective; however, strategic importance should always carry the greatest weight in the decision. Next, each initiative must be scored on the specific criteria listed in the chart. You may use ratings of between zero and ten, or if you prefer a wider scale, use zero to one hundred. I've used zero to ten in my example. Before assigning points to each, you must develop an appropriate scale. For example, a net present value (NPV) of greater than $2 million may translate to 10 points. NPV of $1.75 million yields 9 points, and so on. Involving more than one executive on a full-time basis may translate to a score of 2 points in the resource requirements section since their involvement could impose a heavy burden on the organization. Develop scales that work for you; however, to ensure mathematical integrity, a high value should always represent preferred performance. Those initiatives generating the highest scores should be approved and provided budgets to ensure their timely completion. Notice in our example, initiative 1 generates a higher total score than initiative 2 despite the latter's impressive scores on five of the six criteria. The reason for the discrepancy is the critical variable of strategic linkage. Initiative 1 demonstrates a strong linkage to strategy while number 2 is missing that connection. We will return to the topic of initiatives and budgets in Chapter Nine.

The Rewards Are Worth the Effort!

Developing and prioritizing initiatives to support your Balanced Scorecard can be one of the most difficult aspects of the implementation. As I dis-

Exhibit 7.2 Prioritizing Balanced Scorecard Initiatives

Criteria	Weight	Description	Initiative #1		#2		#3		#4	
			Points	Score	Points	Score	Points	Score	Points	Score
Linkage to stragegy	45%	Ability of the initiative to positively impact a strategic objectives	7	3.2	1	.45				
Net present value	15%	Present value of initiative benefits discounted 5 years	5	.75	10	1.5				
Total cost	10%	Total dollar cost including labor and materials	5	.50	10	1.0				
Resource requirements (key personnel)	10%	Key personnel needed for the initiative including time requirements	8	.80	10	1.0				
Time to complete	10%	Total anticipated time to complete the initiative	8	.80	10	1.0				
Dependencies	10%	Impact of other initiatives on the successful outcomes anticipated with this initiative	3	.30	10	1.0				
			6.4		6.0					

cussed earlier, making these decisions can affect long-standing relationships between different functional areas, and result in negative perceptions of organizational power wielding. However, this important task can also provide you with the first of many opportunities to show the economic value of the Balanced Scorecard by highlighting those initiatives which legitimately lead to the fulfillment of your strategy and those that merely soak up precious resources. Aligning initiatives with strategy also greatly facilitates the use of the Balanced Scorecard as a strategic management system by providing a method of linking the budgeting process with strategy and strategic planning. Finally, clarifying and prioritizing is yet another opportunity to utilize the Scorecard as a means of increasing accountability. Every initiative will have an executive sponsor who feels passionate about the project and strongly believes it will yield tremendous results. Using the Balanced Scorecard to validate your investments allows you to confirm or deny those beliefs on the part of your senior team.

Many organizations are already beginning to harness the value of aligning initiatives with strategy by using the Balanced Scorecard. Wachovia Corporation is a $76 billion financial holding company. Founded in 1879, they serve customers through a network of 754 banking offices in five states. Lawrence Baxter is a Wachovia executive vice president and head of the Winston-Salem company's e-business division. Among his responsibilities are developing online strategy, orchestrating corporate e-commerce support, directing Wachovia's web site, and deploying new technologies. Baxter explains Wachovia's methodology for making difficult decisions on competing online opportunities this way: *"We've developed an underlying set of focal points that are in keeping with the philosophy of the Balanced Scorecard . . . (We've) developed a set of criteria, or filters, through which every online project is evaluated. They are quite recognizable concepts, such as Will this project add revenue? Will it reduce expenses? Will it retain current customers and acquire new ones? Does it align with the overall strategy of both the company and the relevant lines of business?"*[9] Wachovia also utilizes a postinitiative metrics system to illuminate project economics and foster accountability for results.

Chapter Five discussed the fact that a good Balanced Scorecard contains a mix of leading and lagging indicators of performance. Lagging indicators without performance drivers fail to inform us of how we hope to achieve our results. Conversely, leading indicators may signal key improvements throughout the organization, but on their own they do not reveal whether these improvements are leading to improved customer and financial results. Targets and initiatives are similar in that one without the other simply will not lead us to the results we desire. A target without supporting initiatives is missing the "how" of meeting our performance goals. However, initiatives without targets do not signal whether the results we have achieved are what we expected or commensurate with any predetermined standards. Developing targets and initiatives can prove challenging, but with the tools and techniques outlined in this chapter, you will be well on your way to developing goals and associated supporting initiatives that will ensure your Balanced Scorecard tells your story complete with how you will ensure a happy ending!

SUMMARY

Developing performance targets and supporting initiatives complete the work of building a Balanced Scorecard that tells the story of your strategy and acts as a powerful measurement system and communication tool. This chapter explored the role of targets and initiatives and considered methods to ensure that our strategy was well served from our selection of these important Scorecard elements.

Targets make the results derived from measurement meaningful and tell us whether we are doing a good job. Performance data without associated targets has no meaning or context that can be used to evaluate performance and make decisions. Many organizations will use a combination of three distinct yet related target types, each with a corresponding time frame. Big hairy audacious goals, or BHAGs, are long-term targets that act as compelling mechanisms used to guide organizations toward tremendous breakthroughs. Given their often seemingly outrageous nature, a BHAG will normally take 10 to 30 years to complete. To really galvanize employees in the pursuit of a BHAG, organizations will require supporting organizational systems. Catalytic mechanisms are one such system. They represent specific processes geared toward stimulating the achievement of a BHAG. Stretch targets also promote discontinuous operations but are based on a shorter time frame, normally three to five years. Many organizations will develop a stretch target for each of the performance measures appearing on their Balanced Scorecards. To prove effective the stretch target must represent a great challenge, but must also be rooted in reality. Incremental targets are the (normally) annual targets that, if achieved, will lead to the fulfillment of stretch targets. They serve as the guideposts to the larger goals represented by stretch targets. Managers will sometimes attempt to "game" the system by developing targets that appear to represent a huge challenge but in reality are easily achievable.

The cause-and-effect linkages on your Balanced Scorecard will work together to tell the story of your strategy. By considering the magnitude of relationships between the measures, you have an opportunity to use these maps in developing targets. The optimal targets necessary to achieve exceptional results for shareholders or customers can be developed by plugging in different options and determining their effect on the relationships documented in the strategy map.

There are a variety of information sources available for establishing performance targets. Employees, trend analyses, executive interviews, assessments, stakeholder feedback, industry averages, and benchmarking are all possible origins of potential targets. Once targets have been set, they should be reviewed by employees but approved by your executive team.

Targets may supply much needed motivation, but achieving your goals requires the activation of specific initiatives. Initiatives represent the projects, processes, action steps, and activities you engage in to ensure successful measure outcomes. Most companies suffer from an abundance of initiatives with little relation to the organization's strategy. Paradoxically, the Balanced Scorecard may lead to the development of additional initiatives. However, these new initiatives will prove necessary to achieve the strategic goals of the organization.

Four steps are necessary to ensure that you have the right initiatives in place at your organization. First, develop an inventory of all initiatives currently underway. Gather information on project costs, expected benefits, linkage to strategy, key players, and timelines. Next, map those initiatives to the objectives appearing on your Balanced Scorecard. Be sure to work closely with initiative supporters to be certain you know the specifics of each project before making a decision as to its strategic relevance. Third, eliminate, consolidate, or reduce in scope those initiatives that are not contributing to your strategy. Develop initiatives to support the new Balanced Scorecard measures never before used at your organization. Finally, prioritize your strategic initiatives. Each should have a corresponding business case that will provide an objective basis for making the decisions.

Prioritizing your Scorecard initiatives is a difficult but important task. One of the key benefits emerging from the process is the identification of projects that truly drive strategic results and those that simply drain resources. Highlighting this potentially expensive difference by using the Scorecard as a lens demonstrates the economic value to be derived from the Balanced Scorecard.

NOTES

1. Best Practices Benchmarking Report, *Developing the Balanced Scorecard* (Chapel Hill, NC: Best Practices, LLC, 1999).
2. Daniel J. Boorstin, *The Americans: The Democratic Experience* (New York: Vintage Books, 1974).
3. James C. Collins and Jerry I. Porras, *Built to Last* (New York: Harper Business, 1997).
4. Robert Slater, *The New GE* (Homewood, IL: Richard D. Irwin, 1993).
5. Martin Puris, *Comeback* (New York: Times Business, 1999).
6. Jim Collins, "Turning Goals into Results: The Power of Catalytic Mechanisms," *Harvard Business Review*, July–August 1999, 71–82.

7. Robert S. Kaplan and David P. Norton, *The Balanced Scorecard* (Boston: Harvard Business School Press, 1996).
8. Robert S. Kaplan and David P. Norton, *The Strategy Focused Organization* (Boston: Harvard Business School Press, 2001).
9. Steve Klinkerman, "Testing the Waters," *Banking Strategies,* May/June 2001.

PART THREE

Embedding the Balanced Scorecard in the Organization's Management System

CHAPTER 8

Cascading the Balanced Scorecard to Build Organizational Alignment

Roadmap for Chapter Eight Now that you have built a Balanced Scorecard that eloquently describes your strategy, it's time to take it to the streets! Okay, maybe not the streets, but at least to the corridors and cubicles of your company. The next task in our Scorecard journey is to use the high-level Scorecard you have created as a template for the creation of aligned Scorecards from top to bottom within your organization. This chapter will describe how you can do just that and along the way ensure that all employees are pursuing goals that are consistent with, and lead to, the achievement of your strategy.

Most of us today are knowledge workers and as such we look for meaning and contribution to form an integral part of our working lives. Cascading the Balanced Scorecard provides a means of fulfilling this creative expression on the part of employees by allowing them to develop objectives and measures linked to overall organizational goals. For successful cascading, everyone in the organization must possess a solid understanding of the objectives and measures that make up the highest-level Scorecard. We will examine what it takes to ensure that your organization has that all-important understanding. From that point forward, it is a matter of influence. How do lower-level units and groups influence those high-level Scorecard indicators? We will look at how to develop aligned Scorecards and explore examples from organizations that have been through it already.

The entire organization stands to benefit from cascading the Balanced Scorecard. To that end, we will investigate how you can develop Scorecards for your shared service units and even drive the Scorecard down to the individual employee level.

All the Scorecards you develop must link back to overall objectives if you are to derive value from this process. The chapter concludes with a discussion of how you can effectively review and evaluate the Scorecards produced from ever corner of your company.

WHAT DOES "CASCADING" THE BALANCED SCORECARD MEAN?

Before describing the techniques and processes necessary to properly cascade your Balanced Scorecard, I should describe what is meant by the term. Cascading refers to the process of developing Balanced Scorecards at each and every level of your organization. These Scorecards align with your organization's highest-level Scorecard by identifying the strategic objectives and measures lower-level departments and groups will use to track their progress in contributing to overall company goals. While some of the measures used may be the same throughout the entire organization, in most cases the lower-level Scorecards will include measures reflecting the specific opportunities and challenges faced at that level. Many successful practitioners have made their highest-level Scorecards just the first piece in a program that links all employees from the shop floor to the executive boardroom through a series of cascading Balanced Scorecards.

Cascading the Balanced Scorecard Links All Employees to Your Strategy

In his book *Simplicity*, Bill Jensen suggests that a leading cause of work complexity is unclear goals and objectives.[1] You are probably thinking you have that problem licked since you have taken the initiative and developed a Balanced Scorecard with very clear objectives and measures that work together to tell your unique strategic story. Not so fast. Jensen goes on to note that another major contributor of work complexity is lack of alignment of goals.[2] Now things get interesting, don't they? Does your organization have clear alignment of goals from top to bottom? Do the people answering the phones at your company know how their day-to-day actions are contributing to the achievement of the company's strategy? What about a midlevel manager in sales—would she know? Does anyone below the executive ranks have a clear idea of how they support the organization's overall goals? In a large number of organizations the answer is no. Employees go about their business, performing duties in accordance with job descriptions that may be long overdue for updating, all the while having very little knowledge of how what they are doing is helping the organization achieve its objectives.

Even for those organizations that have developed Balanced Scorecards, there may be severe alignment issues hampering their desire to outperform rivals. Some people subscribe to the notion that a Balanced Scorecard is the exclusive domain of the senior management team. Lower-level employees are welcome to look at the measures on the Scorecard, maybe even learn from them, but their performance can be monitored by other systems such as the performance review process. Organizations that believe this are betting on the superiority of awareness over alignment, but unfortunately for them that is simply not the case. Will mere awareness of corporate strategy, objectives, and measures lead to improved decision making on the front lines of the organization? Probably not. How does awareness of a customer intimacy strategy help a customer service representative deal with an irate customer that demands immediate satisfaction? It doesn't.

All employees require the opportunity to demonstrate how their specific actions are making a difference and helping the company fulfill its strategic objectives. The best way to do this is by cascading the Balanced Scorecard to every far-reaching level of the organization. When we cascade the Scorecard—driving it down to lower levels in the company—we provide a line of sight for all employees from their day-to-day actions back to the lofty aims espoused in the strategic plan. As an employee, strategy is no longer some poorly understood treatise formulated by senior management, but is instead transformed into specific objectives and measures I need to achieve in order to make a meaningful contribution to success. And that is precisely what every single employee in your organization wants more than anything else— to make a contribution. This particular time in organizational history is one of the knowledge worker. These highly skilled purveyors of talent differ from their organizational ancestors in one key respect. Unlike earlier workers who depended on the organization to supply machines and other modes of production, these workers carry the means of production—their knowledge—with them. Peter Drucker has suggested that in this era of the knowledge worker, employees should be considered volunteers. A volunteer does not provide her valuable knowledge, skills, and experience for the hope of tremendous monetary reward or personal advancement. Very often, volunteers crave that which eludes them in their nine-to-five world—meaning and contribution. A lack of alignment between personal objectives and corporate strategy obscures the hope of finding true meaning and contribution in work. Cascading the Balanced Scorecard helps restore this possibility by providing every employee, regardless of function or level, with the opportunity to demonstrate that what they are doing is indeed critical to the overall efforts of the organization.

Not only does the cascading process align employee actions with strategy, it is consistently cited as a key factor in the success of Balanced Scorecard programs. For example, when I worked with Nova Scotia Power we used a large management meeting to unveil the newly developed Corporate Balanced Scorecard. In addition to using the opportunity to educate and communicate, we solicited feedback on the Scorecard and requested input regarding what it would take to ensure a successful implementation throughout the entire company. A large number of responses indicated that in order for the Scorecard project to prove successful it must be taken to the shop floor. Our audience recognized that while a high-level Scorecard is critical for decision making at the executive level and provides a wonderful communication tool, all employees need a similar mechanism to ensure that they act in alignment with overall strategy. Subsequent client engagements have reinforced this insight. Successful Scorecard implementers know that those on the front line must embrace and use this tool if it is to reach the level of effectiveness it is capable of achieving. Cascading the Scorecard allows you to reach your entire organization and supply them with the means of answering the critical question, "How do I add value and make a meaningful contribution to our success?" The answer lies in the objectives and measures embedded in Balanced Scorecards throughout your organization.

THE CASCADING PROCESS

Exhibit 8.1 displays the cascading process typically followed by most organizations. The highest-level Balanced Scorecard, often that used for the organization as a whole, is the starting point of cascading efforts. The objectives and measures contained in that Scorecard are then driven down to the next level in the organization, which will often comprise individual business units. At the third level of cascading, specific departments and groups develop Balanced Scorecards based on the Scorecards "in front" of theirs—in this case, the business unit Scorecard. The final level shown is that of team and personal Balanced Scorecards. Organizations cascading to this level will gain the maximum value from the Balanced Scorecard by ensuring that all employees, regardless of function or level, have developed objectives and measures that align with overall organizational objectives.

The diagram outlined in Exhibit 8.1 should be considered *descriptive* and not *prescriptive*. If you have begun your efforts within a specific business unit of your organization, that Scorecard would comprise your highest-level card and you would cascade based on the objectives and measures it contains. Similarly, you may work in a public-sector or not-for-profit organization and use different terminology to describe the various levels of your organization. Again, focus on the theory of cascading rather than the specific words contained in the diagram. The process works equally well whether you work in a large *Fortune* 1000 company, a local community group, or a state government agency. The following sections will examine the specific steps of the cascading process in further detail.

Exhibit 8.1   The Cascading Process

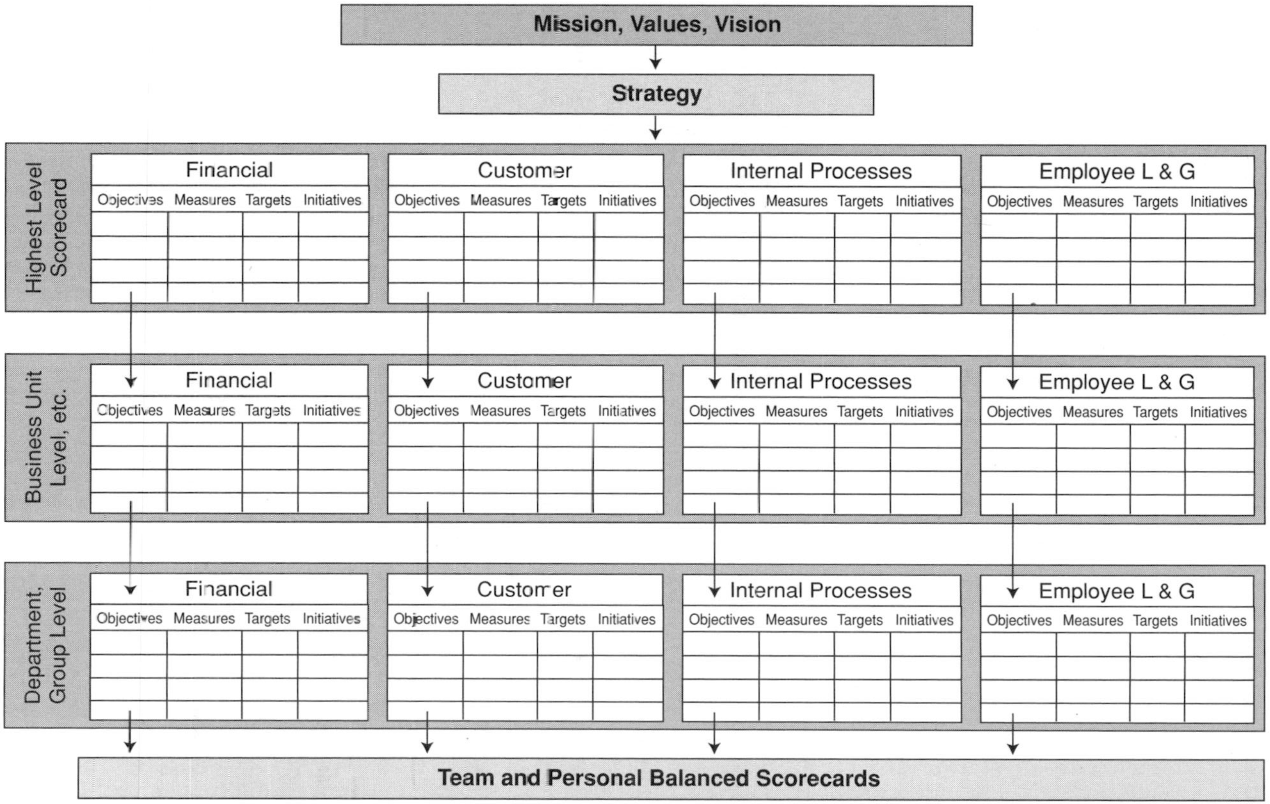

Understanding Is Key to the Highest-Level Balanced Scorecard

The cascading process begins at the top with your highest-level Balanced Scorecard. The first seven chapters of the book outline how you should go about creating this document, so the specifics of the Scorecard will not be examined here. This section emphasizes the importance of employee knowledge and understanding of the objectives and measures that make up the high-level Scorecard.

Your highest-level Balanced Scorecard identifies the key measures of success that weave together in a series of cause-and-effect relationships to tell the story of your strategy. It is absolutely imperative that everyone in the organization understand the strategic significance of these measures before they begin creating their own Balanced Scorecards. This is particularly true for those individuals who carry the responsibility of leading the development of Scorecards at lower levels of the organization. If these individuals do not possess a solid knowledge of the high-level objectives and measures, it will be very difficult for them to construct Scorecards that are truly aligned to the organization's high-level goals.

Flawed assumptions occasionally cause companies to inadvertently sabotage their own efforts when they reach this step in the Scorecard process. There are organizations that believe lower-level employees are incapable of understanding critical value-creating activities and processes that ultimately drive success. Executives in these firms maintain that topics ranging from economic value added to customer segmentation to supply-chain best practices are the sole domain of the executive boardroom and employees are merely the actors hired to play out the drama they have masterfully orchestrated. Nothing could be farther from the truth. In fact, successful organizations question this assumption and spend the necessary time and money to educate employees on these concepts with outstanding results. Consider as an example the innovative Brazilian firm Semco. Employees in this company, often cited for its creativity and innovation, participate in virtually every facet of organizational life, from choosing real estate to designing manufacturing facilities to determining their own pay. CEO Ricardo Semler strongly believes the driving force of productivity is motivation and genuine interest and that is spawned from trusting employees to perform their jobs in ways that make sense to them.[3]

To ensure that employees of your organization understand the objectives and measures appearing on your high-level Balanced Scorecard, you should embark on a significant communication and education program. Chapter Six discussed three possible ways of gaining employee feedback on your Balanced Scorecard. These methods can also be used to communicate and educate your staff on the specifics of your strategy as embodied in the Scorecard. The three methods are summarized as folows:

1. Conduct a Balanced Scorecard "*open house.*" Follow the example set by the County of San Diego, California, during their Balanced Scorecard project. Invite employees to attend an open house during which the Balanced Scorecard is shared, discussed, reviewed, and critiqued.

2. Use your *intranet.* Post your new Balanced Scorecard on the intranet and include background on the strategic and operational significance of the measures, quotes from executives on the value of the Balanced Scorecard, and future plans for cascading your measures throughout the entire company.

3. Hold *management meetings or town halls.* If you hold regular meetings that bring together your entire management team, use that venue to educate your team on the Scorecard you have created. *Town-hall* meetings can also be a great way to share what you have developed with a large number of employees.

Creative Scorecard practitioners will undoubtedly find many other methods of educating staff on the Balanced Scorecard. Brochures, videos, and inserts accompanying pay stubs are just a few of the many ways in which you can take the opportunity to explain the inner workings of your Scorecard to interested employees.

Focus on "Influence" at the First Level of Cascading

Once you feel comfortable that employees have gained a sufficient understanding of your high-level Scorecard, you can begin the process of having them develop Balanced Scorecards that outline their own contributions to the organization's success. The key to creating aligned Scorecards is the concept of influence.

A dictionary might define the word *influence* as the ability to produce an effect, and that is exactly what we have in mind when cascading the Balanced Scorecard. All employees should have the chance to produce an effect on the organization's outcomes. Their forum for doing so is the Balanced Scorecard. When developing Scorecards at this first level of cascading, the relevant question to guide the proceedings is this: "What can we do at our level to help the organization achieve its goals?" The Scorecards you create at this level will align with the high-level Card but will not necessarily contain the same measures. That is a key point warranting some attention. Many people consider cascading a simple exercise of "chopping up" high-level objectives into bite-sized pieces scattered throughout the organization. That approach might work for certain financial metrics such as revenue or costs, but how do you reasonably allocate customer loyalty or new product development? An effectively cascaded Balanced Scorecard is not one that simply contains bits and pieces of the highest-level Scorecard. High-level organizational measures could be completely meaningless to the people working at lower rungs of the organizational ladder. A better approach is to carefully examine the high-level Scorecard and determine which of the objectives and measures you can *influence* at this level of the organization.

Nova Scotia Power Inc., the Canadian electric utility discussed throughout the book, started their Balanced Scorecard program by first creating a high-level Corporate Scorecard that told the story of their strategy as they prepared for looming deregulation in the Canadian utility industry. To ensure that all employees had the opportunity to participate in the fulfillment of their strategy, they subsequently cascaded the Balanced Scorecard to all levels of the organization. Over 100 Scorecards were created, spanning the executive team at corporate headquarters to the shop floor at power plants. An example of their cascading efforts is shown in Exhibit 8.2. The example shows how a business unit selected measures based on the Corporate Balanced Scorecard. Targets shown are for illustrative purposes only.

Take a look at the middle portion of Exhibit 8.2, the Customer Service and Marketing Balanced Scorecard. This level of the organization represents the first level of cascading at Nova Scotia Power. To build an effective Scorecard the Customer Service and Marketing business unit carefully reviewed the Corporate Balanced Scorecard and determined which of the objectives and measures on that Scorecard they could influence. In the example presented, one measure appearing on the corporate Balanced Scorecard was "Customer Loyalty Rating." The Customer Service and Marketing Business Unit was obviously interested in this critical indicator and felt they could positively influence its outcome. Therefore, they chose to develop a performance measure on their Balanced Scorecard that would indicate how they thought they could successfully move the needle on this measure at their level. But take a close look at the measure they developed. First of all, while the Corporate objective and measure appeared in the Customer perspective, the measure developed by Customer Service and Marketing was better suited to the Internal Process perspective of their Scorecard. The objective they chose mirrored the corporate objective, but the new measure better captured how they could *influence* the corporate indicator of Customer Loyalty Rating. The business unit knew from their research that a number of key customer processes contained specific bottlenecks and issues that were consistent sources of customer dissatisfaction. They felt that by redesigning the most troublesome of those processes they would be able to positively influence Customer Loyalty Rating at the corporate level. Following the technique of determining which corporate objectives and measures they could influence allowed the Customer Service and Marketing business unit to create a Balanced Scorecard that demonstrated to the entire company how they would contribute to Nova Scotia Power's success.

Exhibit 8.2   Cascading the Balanced Scorecard at Nova Scotia Power Inc.

Corporate Scorecard			
Perspective	Objective	Measure	Target
Customer	Increase Customer Loyalty: Move beyond "satisfied" to "loyal" customers.	Customer Loyalty Rating: A composite index of earned customer loyalty.	75%

Customer Service and Marketing Scorecard			
Perspective	Objective	Measure	Target
Internal Processes	Increase Customer Loyalty: Move beyond "satisfied" to "loyal" customers.	Redesigned Customer Processes: Number of redesigned customer processes and services.	5

CS&M Information Technology Scorecard			
Perspective	Objective	Measure	Target
Internal Processes	Effective Desktop Support: Provide effective desktop support for CS&M employees.	Service Requests: Number of desktop service requests completed.	500

When developing Balanced Scorecards for this (or any subsequent) level of the organization, you should not expect each group to influence every objective and measure appearing on the high-level Scorecard. Organizations derive value by combining the disparate skills of all employees within every function, and therefore each group will rightly focus on the objectives and measures over which they may exert an influence. Having said that, a major benefit of the cascading process is watching creativity bloom throughout the organization as groups begin to contemplate how they might contribute to an organizational goal once considered well outside their sphere of influence. One organization making that discovery is McCord Travel Management, which was discussed in Chapter Six. When individual agents at McCord were confronted with the challenge of developing Balanced Scorecard performance measures based on corporate objectives and measures, the task seemed daunting indeed. How could they influence these high-level organizational outcomes from which they seemed so far removed? With facilitation and coaching, this group soon learned they could influence many of the critical indicators of McCord's Balanced Scorecard. For example, at first glance most agents probably would not suggest they could have an impact on a financial objective such as "Increase Net Value per Transaction." Upon further examination and discussion, however, the agents learned they could in fact help McCord achieve this objective. By directing clients to vendors with whom they (the clients) had a preferred contract, the agents could generate additional commission income for both McCord and the client while lowering the cost of the ticket for the traveler by using the preferred vendor discount rate. A true win–win arrangement. The percentage of transactions with preferred vendors became a key measure on agents' Scorecards.

The Importance of Influence Continues with Lower-Level Scorecards

Depending on your organizational architecture, the next level of cascading you engage in could be to the department, group, or team level. As discussed earlier, you may use different terminology to describe the various levels that exist within your company. However, regardless of the name, the principle of influence remains the same. At this level within the organization, Scorecards should be based on those to whom these groups report. We would not expect an individual marketing department, for example, to develop a Balanced Scorecard based on the Corporate Scorecard. More likely, the Marketing group's indicators would be derived from the Sales and Marketing business unit's Balanced Scorecard. To illustrate this point let's continue with the example outlined in Exhibit 8.2. The Customer Service and Marketing business unit (CS&M) of Nova Scotia Power has developed a Balanced Scorecard based on the objectives and measures they can influence on the Corporate Scorecard. Customer Service and Marketing is comprised of a number of smaller groups, one of which is Customer Service and Marketing Information Technology (IT). When developing their Scorecard, the employees of CS&M IT looked to the business unit's Scorecard to determine which of the objectives and measures they could impact. When reviewing the Scorecard, they saw that CS&M was measuring "Redesigned Customer Processes." The IT group is not directly involved in redesigning customer processes, but they feel they can positively influence this objective. For the CS&M team to redesign a number of key customer processes, they will rely heavily on desktop support functions as they experiment with new and innovative ideas. The IT group recognizes this and hypothesizes that by quickly and accurately completing service requests they will enable the CS&M business unit to achieve their goal of redesigning troubled customer processes.

The measures in each of the three Scorecard excerpts of Exhibit 8.2 are not identical, but they are *aligned*. Employees of the IT group within CS&M know that by efficiently turning around service requests they are not only assisting the business unit in achieving its goals but are also making a key contribution to the corporate objective of improving customer loyalty. Similarly, senior management within Nova Scotia Power can rest assured that employees at the front lines now have goals that are consistent with the corporation's objectives.

In addition to different performance measures, lower-level Balanced Scorecards will most likely contain a greater number of measures. The measures that describe your strategy in the Corporate Balanced Scorecard are often very high-level abstractions (brand awareness, employee satisfaction, etc.) with many details left out of the picture. As you move to lower levels of the organization, the specifics necessary to achieve success on the corporate measures are filled in as part of the business unit, department, and team Scorecards. Filling these gaps may require more than a one-to-one measure relationship. In the Nova Scotia Power example, the CS&M IT group may require two or even three measures to adequately ensure that they assist the business unit meet its goal of redesigning customer processes. The challenge, of course, is finding an appropriate number of measures. Some groups within your organization may influence a large amount of measures and therefore require substantial numbers on their Scorecard. Use the criteria presented in Chapter Six to help you finalize the measures appearing in all cascaded Scorecards.

Assisting the Development of Aligned Balanced Scorecards

In every organization there are people who have a natural affinity toward the Balanced Scorecard and the method of management it entails, and those who view it as yet another panacea being forced down their throat by an overzealous senior management team. Regardless of where the majority of employees fall in your company, one thing is certain—they will require assistance in developing their Balanced Scorecards. Here are a couple of tips that will help you ease the cascading process:

- *Provide clear accountabilities, guidelines, and personal assistance.* The Balanced Scorecard may be the most elegantly simple and logical tool to ever grace a business magazine, but managers and employees who have never built a Scorecard may feel a good deal of trepidation. To help them through the process, it is important to have developed some helpful devices up front. Discuss the Scorecard whenever possible, distribute it to all employees, share articles and books that provide useful information, and, most importantly, develop templates they can use to guide them through the process of developing their own Balanced Scorecard. Helping them also includes the provision of clear accountabilities and timelines so that they know exactly what is expected of them and when. But the single most critical thing you must do is provide personal assistance. Share the expertise that resides on your Balanced Scorecard team across your organization. Your team can lead training sessions on Scorecard concepts and then act as facilitators during the development of Balanced Scorecards. The Scorecard and functional knowledge they possess will be an unbeatable combination.

- *Use business plans.* The highest-level Balanced Scorecard at your organization was the product of a careful translation of your unique strategy. As you cascade the Scorecard to successively lower levels of the organization, you will not find specific strategies, missions, and visions. What most groups do have is a business plan since the practice of developing annual plans is well established in most organizations. These business plans can be an invaluable source of information to help business units, departments, and teams develop their Scorecards. Most plans will contain information on key processes, objectives, initiatives, and costs. Once the Balanced Scorecard becomes embedded in the management system of your organization it may replace business plans.

Shared Service Balanced Scorecards

Shared service groups are what some call *corporate resources* or *corporate staff.* Human resources, accounting and finance, and information technology are all examples of shared service units housed in virtually all organizations. These departments provide specialized services to the business units and corporate entity they serve, and should do so at a cost and level of quality superior to external vendors. There, as Shakespeare put it, is the rub. Are your shared service groups providing services at a cost and quality level that outperforms third-party vendors supplying similar services? A Balanced Scorecard takes these groups to task and monitors their performance to ensure that the services they provide are assisting the business units to achieve their strategic objectives.

Since most shared service units do not have a specific strategy, but instead focus on meeting the needs of their internal customers, they sometimes find it difficult to begin the Scorecard development process. Lacking a specific strategy, they wonder what should form the basis of their Balanced Scorecard. For that reason, organizations often negotiate service-level agreements (SLAs) between business units and shared service groups. These documents spell out in detail the level of service required by the business unit on specific processes and products supplied by the shared service unit. Costs, objectives, and key indicators of desired performance are also included. The SLA now forms the basis of Scorecard development for the shared service unit. Not all organizations will be large enough to require formal SLAs between business units and shared service groups. Lacking a formal SLA, shared service units may follow the advice outlined earlier in this chapter. By reviewing business unit Scorecards, the shared service group can determine which objectives and measures it can most directly influence and develop its own performance measures based on those indicators. The highest-level Scorecard in the organization may also contain measures that the shared service group can directly impact. For example, if a goal of improving employee turnover appeared on the Corporate Scorecard, the human resources group would be expected to develop cascaded performance measures to make this a reality.

Given the flurry of outsourcing activity underway in most large organizations, the Balanced Scorecard is an ideal method for shared service units to demonstrate the unique value they contribute to the organization. Producing positive results on Scorecard measures exhibits a rationale for their continued existence. Beyond this very pragmatic reason for cascading the Scorecard to shared services, there lies a deeper and more compelling justification. Employees of these groups often feel very little connection to the overall strategy of the organization. Whereas those in manufacturing may see the actual product being developed, and marketers work diligently to create demand, those in shared service groups often have little visibility into the products and services that drive the organization. Cascading the Balanced Scorecard provides this much-needed line of sight, allowing employees within shared services to see the connection between their work and the overall strategy of the organization.

Personal Balanced Scorecards

Very few organizations excel at the task of developing meaningful goals and objectives for individual employees. In fact, the annual performance appraisal process is one fraught with issues for both management and employees alike. Companies will expend significant energy in promoting a formal appraisal process, issuing memos, providing templates with information on the competencies and behaviors they desire to see, and training employees on how to develop an effective plan. However, there is often little follow-up beyond this initial splash of activity. When discussing the performance appraisal process with new clients, I am often greeted with rolling eyes and shaking heads. Even organizations that do follow up on the appraisal process and hold review sessions with employees are invariably behind schedule. This critical activity involving the most precious of resources tends to get pushed to the back burner. When we critically examine the process at most organizations, there is little wonder why this sorry state of affairs exists. Very often, the performance ratings are completely subjective and based purely on a manager's or supervisor's limited view of employee performance. This does little to engender trust on the part of employees, and instead makes them suspicious of the process. Throughout the performance period there is infrequent feedback to employees, and when they get feedback it concerns outcomes and results, not behaviors. But the most egregious omission of the process is the lack of alignment between personal and organizational goals. Employees have little or no idea how success on their performance review will positively impact the company's success.

Cascading the Balanced Scorecard to the individual employee level can mitigate, if not entirely eliminate, many of the issues found with the normal performance appraisal process. The many benefits to be derived from having employees develop their own personal Balanced Scorecards include:

- *Builds awareness of the Balanced Scorecard.* Developing Scorecards at the individual level provides yet another opportunity to share with all employees the principles and techniques inherent in the Balanced Scorecard system.

- *Generates commitment to the Scorecard.* There is little doubt that increased involvement in virtually any activity will tend to increase commitment to that cause. So it goes with the Balanced Scorecard. Having employees learn about the Scorecard and develop their own series of linked objectives and measures will certainly boost support from this critical audience.

- *Increases comprehension of aligned Scorecards.* In order to craft their individual Scorecards, employees must first understand the objectives and measures appearing in all cascaded Scorecards from the high-level organizational Scorecard to the business unit Scorecard to their team or department's card. Thus, cascading supplies an outstanding training opportunity.

- *Offers a clear line of sight from employee goals to organizational strategy.* Developing personal Balanced Scorecards that align to team or department Scorecards allows every employee to demonstrate how their specific actions are making a difference and leading to improved overall results.

- *Builds support for the goal-setting process.* Using the Balanced Scorecard can breathe new life into often tired and irrelevant employee goal-setting processes.

The format you follow for personal Balanced Scorecards is limited only by your imagination. Exhibit 8.3 provides one possible version of a template your employees can utilize to develop personal Balanced Scorecards. This template is based on the cascading efforts of an electric utility organization. In the document three key areas are merged—cascaded Scorecards, incentive compensation, and personal development plans. To maximize educational and practical value, the document is split into two pages. Page 1 serves the important purpose of outlining mission, vision, and strategies and establishing a line of sight for the employee. The remainder of the page illustrates the cascading Scorecards relevant to that individual. Summarized versions of the organizational, business unit, and departmental Balanced Scorecards are provided. Displaying this individualized cascading demonstrates the cascading that has led to this point and greatly facilitates the completion of the personal Balanced Scorecard on page 2.

While we might consider page 1 a learning page, page 2 has a more specific purpose—allowing the individual employee to define the specific objectives and measures they will pursue to help their department reach its objectives, supply potential incentive awards, and outline the action steps they will take to achieve success. Linking the Balanced Scorecard to compensation is discussed further in Chapter Ten. Here are the specific steps that must be taken to complete page 2 of the template:

1. The individual must develop the objectives, measures, and targets that comprise his or her individual Scorecard. By displaying all linked Scorecards on page 1, with discussion and coaching the development of personal goals should flow quite smoothly.

2. The individual must then select the appropriate weights for each measure when determining his or her incentive possibilities. The manager or supervisor will have final approval on the weights and associated targets, ensuring that they appear reasonable and challenging but attainable. The perspectives are also weighted to denote the areas in which the employee is able to exert the most influence. In this example, perspective weights are equal. Employee targets are discussed further in the review of the Balanced Scorecard's role in compensation (Chapter Ten).

3. Finally, the employee may begin to construct a personal development plan (PDP) based on the goals established on their Scorecard. This document may or may not replace the need for a formal PDP, but it will certainly facilitate the development of that document by identifying the key areas of focus for the individual.

The creation of personal Balanced Scorecards completes the chain of linked Scorecards from "the boardroom to the back room," and in so doing can also incorporate the key elements of incentive compensation and competency attainment.

Exhibit 8.3 Personal Balanced Scorecard Template—Page 1

Name:	Department:	Date Covered:

Mission: Provide low-cost energy to help our communities prosper   *Vision:* Be the #1 energy supplier by 2010

Utilize state-of-the-art technology and human capital principles to drive profitable growth

Perspective	Corporate Scorecard	Business Unit Scorecard	Department Scorecard
Financial	F1. Return on Equity	F1. Manageable Cost Reduction F2. Lower Service Agreement Costs	F1. Lower Administrative Spending F2. Rationalize Capital Spending F3. Increase Miscellaneous Revenue
Customer	C1. Customer Loyalty Rating C2. Sales Volume	C1. Customer Loyalty Rating C2. Outage Performance Index	C1. Customer Loyalty Rating C2. Meeting Commitments C3. Meter Reading C4. Call Centre Performance C5. Reliability Index
Internal Process	IP1. Environmental Performance IP2. Number of new products and services	IP1. Environmental Performance IP2. Service Quality Programs in place	IP1. System Maintenance IP2. Inspections IP3. Service Quality Programs
Employee Learning & Growth	E1. Safety Rating E2. Employee Commitment Rating E3. Employee Development	E1. Number of Accidents E2. Employee Commitment Rating E3. Employee Development	E1. Number of Personal Accidents E2. Number of Vehicle Accidents E3. Employee Commitment Rating E4. Employee Development

Exhibit 8.3 Personal Balanced Scorecard Template—Page 2

Department Manager—Personal Balanced Scorecard

Perspective	Objective	Measure	Weight	Threshold	Midpoint	Stretch	Related PDP Goals
Customer 25%	Customer loyalty	Presentations to local trade groups	40%	10	15	20	• Develop 5 new professional contacts this year. • Join 2 trade associations
	Outage reliability	Plant visits	60%	20	30	50	
Employee Learning and Growth 25%	Safety	Departmental injuries	60%	2	1	0	• Attend safety training course
	Develop skill sets	% Employees completing education	15%	80%	90%	100%	• Complete facilitator training
	Develop skill sets	Complete Personal Development Plan	10%	—	—	—	• Complete PDP by mid-year
	Employee commitment	Departmental commitment rating	15%	75	80	85	• Support employee volunteer efforts
Internal Process 25%	Meter reading and meter changes	% on-time readings	50%	90%	95%	100%	
	System maintenance	Conduct plant audits	50%	25	40	45	
Financial 25%	Minimize administrative spending	Local costs	55%	Budget	Budget less 1%	Budget less 2%	• Complete 2 courses in finance
	Grow revenue	Increase departmental miscellaneous revenue	45%	5% increase	10% increase	25% increase	• Lead departmental brainstorming sessions on revenue enhancement

217

This section focuses almost exclusively on the benefits employees can derive from developing personal Balanced Scorecards—knowledge of the Scorecard system, understanding of organizational objectives and measures, and alignment with overall goals. However, senior managers also have much to gain from this process. Cascading to this level allows managers to gain a high level of visibility into the specific actions contributing to, or detracting from, overall organizational results. Take the case of McCord Travel Management. Senior Managers at this travel organization monitor a productivity index which tracks the number of tickets issued per hour by individual agents. The measure appears on McCord's Corporate Balanced Scorecard but is also cascaded down to the individual agent level. When actual results began to lag expectations, senior managers looked to their cascading Balanced Scorecards for an answer. Examining regional performance (the first level of cascading) on the productivity index provided little information because most areas were producing similar results. However, when McCord managers examined specific site Scorecards, they found some very interesting deviations that were driving the high-level corporate outcome. It turns out that agents who catered to professional service firms (attorneys, accountants, consultants) were producing consistently lower results than other groups. When questioned, they noted that clients from these firms were frequently changing plans, which made it difficult to actually issue a ticket. Without the questions spawned by the Balanced Scorecard, McCord senior management could have made the faulty and dangerous assumption that these sites were simply poor performers and taken inappropriate action. Armed with the knowledge gleaned from cascaded Balanced Scorecards, managers were able to adjust the targets to more accurately reflect the nature of clients served by different McCord sites. McCord Senior Vice President Ed Berkman sums up the benefits of cascading the Balanced Scorecard: *"The key benefit of cascading is allowing everyone to know of their importance in the overall strategy of the company and that they are an active and critical part, and it's not just lip service, it's real."*[4]

Reviewing and Evaluating Cascaded Balanced Scorecards

Depending on the size of your organization, you may develop dozens of cascaded Balanced Scorecards at all levels of the company. The benefits of alignment and increased knowledge cannot be overstated, but danger may lurk if you do not carefully monitor the Scorecards being created. Unrealistic targets, missing measures, and departments working against each other may all result if you do not have a review and evaluation process in place to ensure truly aligned Balanced Scorecards. A two-phased approach ensures that your Scorecards are telling a consistent story throughout the company.

Your Balanced Scorecard team should hold the initial responsibility of personally reviewing the cascaded Scorecards created within their specific business units. Based on their experience, your team has the requisite knowledge to effectively critique objectives and measures, ensuring consistency in form and approach across the organization. Once business units and departments have distributed their Scorecards, the Balanced Scorecard team can review them and later hold sessions with the submitting departments to discuss refinements and improvements.

Once groups across the company have had the chance to make adjustments to their Scorecards based on your team's input, you are ready to open them up to the real test—that of their peers. The open house approach used by the County of San Diego is an excellent means of gathering the feedback of a significant number of people in a fun and organized fashion (see Chapter Six). Invite employees to review the Scorecards of their peers and offer their suggestions for clarification and improvement. The first point in that sentence—clarification—is significant. Despite their best efforts to make Scorecards clear and concise, it is difficult for individual groups not to create Scorecards with esoteric words and phrases. Employees from other areas of the company will be quick to assess the readability of colleagues' Scorecards and open up the possibility of rewording or changing specific items to make them more understandable to a wide audience. Another exciting outcome of these scorecard sharing sessions is the learning that often occurs. In the modern business enterprise there are a multitude of interdependencies within groups that serve to propel the company forward. Some are explicit and widely known, whereas others are implicit. Sharing objectives and measures on Balanced Scorecards often motivates business units and departments to critically examine their relationships and challenge other groups to provide measures that impact their working relationship. For example, there may be internal customer–supplier relationships that need to be documented on Balanced Scorecards. Sharing Scorecards also inspires creativity as groups will build on the measures shown in others' Scorecards to make modifications and improvements to their own efforts.

Things to look for when reviewing the cascaded Balanced Scorecards at your organization include:

- *Linkage to related Scorecards.* Don't forget, the key principle here is cascading—driving the Scorecard to lower levels in the organization. Each Scorecard should contain objectives and measures that influence the next Scorecard in the chain.

- *Linkage to strategy.* The Balanced Scorecard is a tool for translating strategy. The measures appearing on cascaded Scorecards should demonstrate a linkage to the organization's overarching strategy.

- *Appropriate targets.* Target setting can be a difficult exercise requiring significant professional judgment. Ensure that cascaded targets will lead to the fulfillment of higher-level targets throughout the chain of linked Balanced Scorecards.

- *Coverage of key objectives.* The chief tenet of cascading is that of influence. For example, what can we do at our level to influence our business unit. Scorecard? Not every group will influence every high-level objective, but across the company the complete population of highest-level objectives should receive adequate coverage.

- *Lag and lead indicators.* Cascaded Scorecards should contain an appropriate mix of lagging and leading indicators of performance.

Cascading—Final Thoughts

No matter how you employ the Balanced Scorecard system, it can produce tremendous benefits—as a measurement system, strategic management system, and communication tool. But cascading, if implemented effectively, may pay the biggest dividends of all. Driving the Scorecard to every level of the company signals to each employee what the key drivers of success are at your company and provides them with the opportunity to define how they contribute to that success. You also create a consistent language in the company—the lexicon of measurement that guides action and can lead to breakthrough results. Leading Scorecard practitioners are recognizing the value of cascading as evidenced by a recent study, which found that over 60 percent of participating organizations were driving the Scorecard to lower levels.[5] Allowing every employee to participate in setting meaningful objectives and measures can lead to a flourishing spirit of involvement and partnership that leads to amazing results for everyone involved.

SUMMARY

This chapter described how you can involve your entire workforce in the Balanced Scorecard process by using the highest-level Scorecard as a template for producing aligned Scorecards throughout the company. Cascading refers to this process of developing Scorecards at all levels of your firm. These Scorecards align with your organization's highest-level Scorecard by identifying the strategic objectives and measures lower-level departments and groups will use to track their progress in contributing to overall company goals.

Developing a high-level organizational Scorecard is a great way to gauge your success in meeting strategic objectives and generate awareness of strategy on the part of your employees. But will mere awareness of organizational strategies lead to change at all levels of the company? To maximize the effectiveness of the Scorecard, every group should have the opportunity to develop linked Scorecards that demonstrate how they are contributing to the company's goals.

To successfully cascade the Balanced Scorecard, everyone in the organization must understand the operational and strategic significance of the objectives and measures appearing on the Scorecard. Organizations may use a combination of communication and education efforts to ensure that this understanding is present before attempting to cascade the Scorecard. The essence of cascading the Scorecard to lower levels of the organization is captured in the word *influence*, that is, the ability to produce an effect. Strategic business units should examine the highest-level organizational Scorecard and ask, "What can we do at our level to help the organization achieve its goals? Which objectives and measures are we in the best position to influence?" Departments and groups within business units must ask a similar question: "What can we do at our level to help the business unit achieve its goals? Which of their objectives and measures can we influence?" The Balanced Scorecard team must be actively involved in the cascading process if it is to be effective. Training, facilitation, and coaching are necessary for groups that may be encountering Scorecard development for the very first time.

Shared service units (corporate staff) should also be encouraged to develop Balanced Scorecards. To assist these groups in building Scorecards, many organizations encourage business units and shared service units to enter into service-level agreements. These agreements specify the outcomes expected by the business unit (the customer) and form the basis for the development of shared service unit Scorecards. Lacking formal service-level agreements, shared service units may build Scorecards by examining how they influence business unit or even high-level organizational outcomes.

Personal Balanced Scorecards represent the final frontier of cascading. Driving the Scorecard down to the individual level, allowing employees to craft the goals they will track that spell their contribution to overall success. Both the employee and the organization stand to benefit from developing Scorecards at the employee level. Employees gain a greater insight into overall strategy and their role in its fulfillment, while the organization receives a rich abundance of potential data from which to glean new insights.

Cascading may create dozens of Balanced Scorecards within your company. Their value is enormous, provided they align with overall goals and tell a consistent story. To ensure that this is the case you should launch a rigorous review and evaluation process in conjunction with your cascading efforts. Once again, your Balanced Scorecard team will be called on as the first line of defense, reviewing Scorecards and working with groups across the company to refine, modify, and improve their offerings. Inviting feedback from your employee base is also an excellent way to engender cooperation, information sharing, and commitment to the Balanced Scorecard.

NOTES

1. Bill Jensen, *Simplicity: The New Competitive Advantage* (Cambridge, MA: Perseus Publishing, 2000)
2. Ibid., 26.
3. Ricardo Semler, *Maverick* (New York: Warner Books, 1993).
4. From interview with Ed Berkman, July 20, 2001.
5. Best Practices Benchmarking Report, *Developing the Balanced Scorecard* (Chapel Hill, NC: Best Practices, LLC, 1999).

CHAPTER 9

Using the Balanced Scorecard to Strategically Allocate Resources

Roadmap for Chapter Nine   Very few people have much good to say about budgets and the budgeting process employed at most organizations. Former Secretary of Defense Frank C. Carlucci once said, *"The budget evolved from a management tool into an obstacle to management."* Management heavyweight and former General Electric CEO Jack Welch contributed to the subject by suggesting, *"Making a budget is an exercise in minimalization. You're always getting the lowest out of people, because everyone is negotiating to get the lowest number."* There is little doubt that the budget process, which was designed about 80 years ago and has remained virtually the same ever since, is due for transformation. This chapter will explore the budgeting process, examining specific issues and offering possible methods to improve this most long-standing of organizational traditions.

The chapter begins with a look at some of the issues plaguing the budget process as it currently stands. A chief concern from the standpoint of this book is the very disturbing fact that few organizations make an attempt to link budget spending to their strategy. In the past they may not have possessed the tools to forge this link; however, the Balanced Scorecard now provides the means for making this critical connection. Given the budget process's many problems, it is not surprising that organizations have begun to tinker with and, in some cases, totally abandon the practice altogether. We will look at some of the current trends in "new budgeting."

The bulk of our work in this chapter is devoted to the examination of how the Balanced Scorecard can be used to effectively drive the budgeting process. This analysis begins with an overview of the roles of cascading and initiative setting. At that point, a five-step process of linking budgets to strategy through the careful use of the Balanced Scorecard is presented. The chapter concludes by considering some of the many benefits to be derived by using the Balanced Scorecard to lead the budgeting process.

BEMOANING THE BUDGET

We are all well aware of the dizzying pace of change in the modern organizations we populate. Everything seems to be going at warp speed, with all indications that it is only going to get faster and more chaotic in the years ahead. But, as I write this it is summer, and even for the most harried of modern employees this cherished season will often trigger a slightly slower pace and relaxed attitude. Some companies still even practice that seemingly ancient rite of four-day workweeks during the "lazy" days of summer. So perhaps you too slip into a comfortable summer groove and are able to enjoy the long days (even if they are spent at the office), but beware, *it* is probably right around the corner. What is this potentially horrific *it* to which I am referring? The much dreaded annual plan and budget document, that's what. If your company is like most, and assuming you have a December 31 fiscal year end, you will probably receive a 40- or 50-page manual designed to kick-start the annual budgeting process around mid-August. After several months of paper pushing, mind-numbing analysis, and endless game playing, you just might have something worthy of presenting to your Board of Directors. If you are really lucky, they might provide their approval before you are sipping champagne to ring in the New Year. If you think I'm exaggerating, think again. A Hackett Benchmarking study conducted in 1998 found that the average organization invests more than 25,000 person days per billion dollars of revenue in the planning process, and the average time to develop a financial plan is four and a half months.[1]

The often loathsome budgeting process most companies follow today is not significantly different from the original technique developed about 80 years ago to help the early industrial giants like DuPont and General Motors control their costs. Back in those days companies operated in a vastly different environment from that to which you and I have become accustomed. Customer choice was virtually unheard of—we have all heard Henry Ford's famous dictum when discussing customer choice and the Model T: *"They can have any color they want, as long as it's black."* Additionally, globalization certainly wasn't an issue since businesses operated almost exclusively in their local area, and fiscal environments were relatively stable. The consistent thread running through the business processes of the day was control. Senior management developed plans, and employees were expected to carry them out with complete adherence to routine, repetitive steps.

Control reports depicting deviations from the carefully crafted plans were fed back up the chain of command, and new orders were issued to treat these defects.

The world of business we inhabit today is vastly removed from that of our organizational ancestors. Globalization means intense competition in all industries, where customers have virtually unlimited choice and access to information. Fiscal environments are less stable, and the rate of change is frenetic, to say the least. We are also attempting to evolve from the age of control to one of empowerment. In this environment, the once vaunted budget is often out of date almost immediately after it is produced. But like so many relics of a bygone era, the traditional budget remains. Not only does the current budgeting process stand in direct opposition to many of the forces driving the modern enterprise, but its execution is often seriously flawed. Consider the following:

- Sixty-six percent of surveyed *CFO* magazine readers believe their planning process is influenced more by politics than by strategy.[2]
- In a 1998 *CFO* survey, 88 percent of respondents stated they were dissatisfied with budgeting.[3]
- For many companies, planning processes are not yet fully utilized as decision-making functions and are hampered by excessive levels of detail, extended cycle times, and a focus on the wrong information.[4]
- Sixty percent of organizations do not link budgets to strategy.[5]

Politics and gaming the system seem to go hand in hand with the budgeting process at many companies. At one firm I worked for some time ago, everyone in our department had a strange sense of pride stemming from the fact that our boss's budget negotiation skills were highly regarded throughout the company. He knew his way around the ins and outs of the game, that's for sure. "Promise less and ask for more" was his mantra, and it seemed to work since our targets always seemed comfortably achievable. Looking back, I realize the many problems he was creating. The incessant game playing inevitably protracted an already interminably long budgeting process, virtually guaranteeing that nothing would be established before the start of the following year. And was he really protecting us? No, his weak targets merely served to limit our need to exercise creativity and search for breakthrough solutions. No doubt there are those in your organization who are masters of the budgeting game as well.

Perhaps the most frightening shortcoming of the current budget process is reflected in the fourth point above—60 percent of organizations do not link budgets to strategy. Think about that for a minute. The budget spells out in painstaking detail what the organization expects to receive and what they will spend in the months ahead. In effect, this allocation is a strong signal of what they truly value. If spending is not aligned with the strategy, then just what is that demonstrating about priorities, and how does the budget bring the organization any closer to achieving its strategic goals? As disturbing as the 60 percent statistic is, it really should not come as a surprise to us. Most organizations have separate processes for business planning and budgeting and strategic planning. The strategic planners are busy crafting the plan that will elevate the firm above its competitors, while another group is independently developing the operating and capital budgets for the coming year. The problem with this approach is that human and financial resources are linked to short-term financial targets as espoused in the budget and not to the goals of the strategy. Most of Chapter Eight discussed the merits of alignment, and as troubling as a lack of staff goal alignment is, unfocused spending is equally problematic. Fortunately, by utilizing a cascaded series of Balanced Scorecards, your organization can overcome many of the problems presented by today's budget process. A little later in the chapter, techniques for using the Balanced Scorecard to drive the budgeting process will be described, but before that let's take a look at some other current thoughts surrounding the revision of this often challenging organizational task.

BANISHING THE BUDGET

Fueled by the many limitations of budgeting's current state, the topic has not been without considerable study and debate. Perhaps the greatest depth of knowledge and experience comes from a group known as the Beyond Budgeting Round Table (BBRT). Formed as a result of a partnership with the Consortium for Advanced Manufacturing International (CAM-I), this group's quest is the development of management processes appropriate for the modern enterprise. Not surprisingly, they see budgets as a major bane to the effective operation of all companies. Since its inception in 1998, the BBRT has seen the participation of over 50 (mostly large European) organizations, but has also attracted member companies from the United States and South Africa.

The primary focus of the BBRT's research is based on the answer to a fundamental question: How are leading companies that have abandoned, radically changed, or significantly deemphasized their centralized planning and budgeting processes now fulfilling their well-established purposes?[6] The answer, as supported by their research findings, is that leading organizations have developed new performance and management processes that eradicate a reliance on budgets and instead focus on creating adaptive organizations based on empowerment and accountability. The BBRT's poster child for corporate success without budgets is the Swedish bank Svenska Handelsbanken. This 510-branch bank, founded in 1871, has consistently delivered leading financial performance despite changing economic tides. BBRT white paper authors Jeremy Hope and Robin Fraser believe former Handelsbanken President Dr. Jan Wallander has been key to the bank's enduring success. *"(Dr. Wallander) is a real visionary who could see that the way large organizations were being managed was fundamentally flawed."*[7] The key to his success? According to Dr. Wallander himself, it was radical devolution supported by the dismantling of the budget model. During his tenure Wallander powerfully transformed the Handelsbanken culture by attacking bureaucracy and top-down controls, and freeing individual managers to make decisions concerning their businesses. Continuous improvement at the bank is now driven by pressure to outperform competitors and peers on key measures of performance. Annual budgets and plans are nowhere to be found. The results have been impressive—costs are lowest in the industry, employee turnover is practically nonexistent, and a rate of 25 percent compound total shareholder return has been achieved over the past 18 years. Other organizations following the BBRT's methodology have also fared well with *"early indications from over 200 companies showing that there is a statistically significant correlation between the BBRT model and competitive success."*[8]

Rather than dismantling the budget process entirely, many organizations have turned to the concept of rolling forecasts to strike a compromise between the need for planning and the desire for flexibility. Rolling forecasts generally extend six quarters into the future and allow a stronger integration of planning and budgeting than the typical calendar year budget. Each quarter, the plan is reviewed and executives are able to change directions or fund strategic projects based on current business conditions. Managers are likely to support rolling forecasts since they provide them with much-needed flexibility in taking advantage of new opportunities as they arise. That is one of the key advantages of the rolling forecast. Often, an organization will spot an opportunity in midyear, but the set-in-stone budget, which has already allocated every penny of discretionary spending, will not allow for the funding of what could turn out to be a competitive advantage for the firm. Despite their advantages, critics of the rolling forecast do exist. They contend that rolling forecasts are time consuming to prepare and may not completely eliminate the politicking and in-fighting that so often characterizes the budgeting process.

Some organizations have actually decided to embark on a Balanced Scorecard project in order to retool, or even replace, the budgeting process. SKF, a leading manufacturer of rolling bearings employing 44,000 people, is one such company. In 1995, with dissatisfaction for the budget process growing ever stronger, SKF turned to the Balanced Scorecard in order to *"replace the budget, which was perceived as having largely negative effects, while still retaining the positive features of a budget, e.g. setting targets and discipline in meeting commitments."*[9] Even if you are not quite ready to completely banish the budgeting process from your managerial landscape you would likely benefit from tinkering with or reengineering parts of the process. Let's now turn our attention to how you can use the Balanced Scorecard to align the allocation of resources with your strategy.

STRATEGIC RESOURCE ALLOCATION
WITH THE BALANCED SCORECARD

Exhibit 9.1 provides an overview of the steps necessary in linking the Balanced Scorecard to the budgeting process. Most of this will look very familiar since the preceding eight chapters of the book covered most of these items in detail.

Based on the organization's mission, vision, values, and strategy, a high-level organizational Scorecard is built. That Scorecard contains a series of linked objectives and measures that use cause-and-effect relationships to tell the story of the organization's strategy. Focusing on the high-level Scorecard, business units, departments, shared service units, and perhaps even individual employees develop their own aligned Balanced Scorecards documenting how they will influence the achievement of corporate goals. Each of these cascaded Scorecards will contain not only objectives, measures, and targets in each of the four perspectives, but they should also include the initiatives each group will pursue in order to successfully meet their targets. These initiatives will entail the allocation of resources, which are quantified and used to form the basis of budget submissions. Sounds simple enough, right? Let's break down these steps, beginning with the crucial topic of cascading.

Cascading Balanced Scorecards Sets the Stage for Strategic
Resource Allocation

Recall the worrisome statistic that 60 percent of organizations do not link budgets to strategy. Just for a moment let's give those organizations the benefit of the doubt. There is a good chance they did not have the means necessary to link their budgets to strategy. Being the typical top-down, command and control organization, they issued directives from senior management and asked business units and departments to develop budgets supporting those plans. So that is what they did—using the same old politics and game playing that saw them through previous budget seasons. Without Balanced Scorecards, the business units and departments had little ammunition in displaying how they could impact an overall strategy. With a Balanced Scorecard, however, the story changes significantly. Now units and

Exhibit 9.1   Linking the Balanced Scorecard to Budgeting

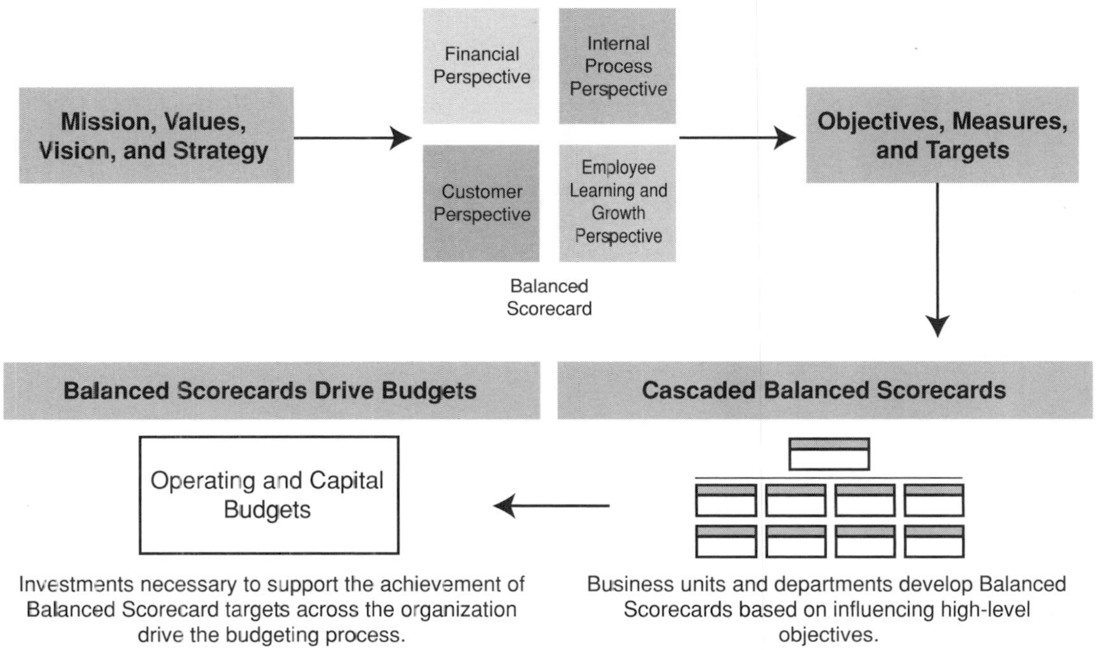

Mission, Values, Vision, and Strategy

Objectives, Measures, and Targets

Balanced Scorecard

Financial Perspective

Internal Process Perspective

Customer Perspective

Employee Learning and Growth Perspective

Balanced Scorecards Drive Budgets

Cascaded Balanced Scorecards

Operating and Capital Budgets

Investments necessary to support the achievement of Balanced Scorecard targets across the organization drive the budgeting process.

Business units and departments develop Balanced Scorecards based on influencing high-level objectives.

229

departments from across the firm develop meaningful objectives and measures that are a direct translation of Scorecards from higher levels.

A hallmark of the cascading process is the inclusive nature of the task. No Scorecard can be effectively built in isolation. It is only through the involvement of all those with a stake in the outcomes that valuable Balanced Scorecards emerge. The same principle readily applies to budgeting. With a Balanced Scorecard as the guide, managers are wise to solicit feedback and involvement of every employee when developing budgets. Some have done just that. For example, at Supertel Hospitality, a Norfolk, Nebraska, hotel franchiser with 63 properties, everyone participates in creating yearly budgets. Housekeepers are even asked to project how much linen and other supplies they will need and make a budget for those items. Chief financial officer (CFO) Tony Beatty says the process contributes to lower turnover and higher profits.[10] At Canadian telecommunications company TELUS, employees in the operator services division are being assigned budget responsibility in an effort to reduce the unit cost of operator-assisted calls. Management says the response has been "unbelievable," with more than 10 percent being cut off the cost structure. *"Just engaging people in making decisions is rewarding in itself."*[11]

The cascaded Balanced Scorecards emerging from every facet of the organization allow all employees to understand the firm's direction and participate in ensuring a successful outcome. Employees now possess an all-important line of sight between what they do every day and how those actions affect organizational outcomes. The logical next step is determining what initiatives must be undertaken to meet Scorecard targets. It is the Scorecard initiatives that forge the powerful link between budgets, Scorecards, and, ultimately, strategy.

Balanced Scorecard Initiatives—The Glue that Binds Budgets to Strategy

Chapter Seven defined initiatives as the specific programs, activities, projects, or actions you will embark on to help ensure that you meet or exceed your performance targets. Initiatives are designed to close the gap between current performance and that embodied in the stretch targets established. The target is your "end in mind" for the performance measure, and to get there you need to determine what investments in initiatives are necessary to guarantee a positive outcome. *Investments* may be the key word in that sentence; after all, what is a budget if not an exercise in determining appropriate investments—in people, processes, technology, and the like? The key is ensuring that the initiatives you decide to fund are strategic in nature and will help you achieve the goals you have set to propel the organization forward.

Funding nonstrategic initiatives is not only a waste of valuable financial resources, but will undoubtedly consume another precious resource—the time and attention of already busy managers.

STEPS IN LINKING BALANCED SCORECARDS TO BUDGETS

The remainder of the chapter will outline the specific steps you can follow to ensure the budget you establish reflects your strategy. But first a word on timing. Even if the budget process at your organization is crying out for reengineering, and you are very anxious for the Balanced Scorecard to come heroically to the rescue, it may not be feasible during year one of your implementation. If you are introducing the Scorecard for the first time, that alone will supply a major challenge to the status quo of operations at your company. As previously discussed, the Scorecard introduces a whole new framework for management that places strategy, not financial controls, at the center of the organizational universe. Gaining the support and commitment of your entire workforce will take some time, and attempting to forge a link between budgets and Balanced Scorecards, no matter how great the potential rewards, may be a bit much for the typical company bandwidth to absorb. Most organizations wait until the Scorecard management process is more mature and accepted as part of the overall management strategy of the organization. Of course, the time necessary to achieve this will vary and be different with most every organization. As a general rule, you need a high-level Scorecard and a series of cascaded Balanced Scorecards to effectively execute the budget/Balanced Scorecard link. This can often be accomplished during year two of your implementation. However, if you have developed Scorecards throughout the organization during year one of the implementation and believe your company is ready for more positive change, by all means take advantage of your momentum and make the hugely beneficial link of Balanced Scorecards to budgets.

Step 1: Plan Ahead

You probably already have a well-established budget process that includes a very thick document, which is distributed to all budget preparers throughout the company. Use that device, plus a variety of other communication forums, to get the word out about the "new" budgeting process that is driven by the Balanced Scorecard. Audiences around the company must be prepared for what lies ahead—the new processes and methods you will use to generate budgets that align spending with your strategy. As with every other aspect of the Balanced Scorecard we have reviewed, it is imperative that you provide ample assistance to those responsible for developing budgets. Once again, your Balanced Scorecard team should form the first line of assistance, providing training, guidance, and support.

Step 2: Develop or Refine the High-Level Organizational Balanced Scorecard

The organizational Balanced Scorecard sets priorities for the company as a whole, describing to everyone the key objectives and measures that signal success. All subsequently cascaded Scorecards will align with the measures appearing on this Balanced Scorecard.

Step 3: Build Cascaded Balanced Scorecards

Business units, departments, teams, and individuals develop Scorecards that demonstrate how they can influence higher-level objectives and outline the specific indicators they will track. The Scorecards must include both targets necessary for breakthrough performance and the specific initiatives that require funding to make certain those targets are met. Ideally, the budget should support year one targets in a series aimed at achieving the stretch goals you developed for each performance measure. (See Chapter Seven for a review of target setting.)

Each initiative appearing on the Scorecard should include a reference to the associated strategy it supports; this is the case regardless of the organizational level the Scorecard represents. Even at department and team levels, Scorecard initiatives should link back to overall organizational objectives. Initiatives should also provide clearly stated resource requirements (i.e., the operating and capital dollars needed to fully support them). This leads to a question: Will the Balanced Scorecard for a specific business unit or department contain all the resource requirements necessary to operate the group. In other words, should typical budget line items, such as salaries, benefits, supplies, travel, and the like, be split up among the initiatives appearing on the Balanced Scorecard? There are different schools of thought on this subject. Kaplan and Norton suggest that organizations should follow a method of *dynamic budgeting*, which represents the combination of operational and strategic budgeting.[12] The operational budget is used to support the allocation of resources necessary for recurring operations, whereas the strategic budget directs spending on the key initiatives designed to close the gap between current and desired performance on critical strategic drivers. Kaplan and Norton contend that most of an organization's spending will be determined by the operational budget as a result of the large base of products and services currently existing within the firm. Others suggest that only one budget be used and that it should contain the entire mix of operational and strategic elements necessary to reflect a true picture of the organization. Following this route forces the organization to critically examine current operations in light of budget requests and determine how operational expenses are linked to strategic requests. This is obviously easier said than done, but there are tools to assist in the calculation. Activity-based management techniques are one way to examine current operations and determine which activities actually drive costs within the organization. Using an activity view of organizational expenses may facilitate the allocation of current operations to strategic initiatives.

Proponents of the "one budget" school also suggest that simply thinking in terms of the linkage between current expenses and strategy will foster important conversations within the organization and motivate managers to contemplate how their day-to-day actions are contributing to strategic results. Your choice of budgets will depend on the ability to accurately assign ongoing costs to strategic initiatives, past attempts at changing the budget process, and the feeling of senior executives on the subject. The process I describe works equally well for a strategic budget or one budget encompassing both operational and strategic elements.

Related to the preceding discussion is an equally vexing issue. How can you ensure that senior management will fund initiatives aimed at improving the leading indicators of performance, the often "softer" measures such as employee retention and customer satisfaction? As discussed in Chapter Seven, every initiative should be supported by a valid business case that includes how the initiative impacts a strategic goal, as well as the cost, timing, resources, and dependencies involved. Applying these criteria to a nonfinancial indicator of performance might be challenging but certainly not impossible. Take the case of Fidelity Investments. Practice Management Vice President Colleen Catallo and her team developed a number of innovative measures such as management depth, employee retention, and work climate, all aimed at improving employee performance. To support requests for funding the team demonstrated what was "broken" at the organization, how the new measures would fix it, what it would cost, and the expected savings from making the repairs. In effect, they outlined the return on investment (ROI) for each measure.[13] Your initiatives, whether they relate to hard or soft measures, should be accompanied by supporting documents that provide a justification for funding. To level the playing field, everyone should use the same basis of evaluation when rationalizing initiatives. Whether it is discounted cash flow analysis, internal rate of return, payback period, total costs, or a host of other potential yardsticks, the key is to apply them uniformly across the organization. See Chapter Seven for more help prioritizing initiatives.

Step 4: Compile Results

The budget process generates a lot of paper, no doubt about it. Even in this so-called era of the paperless organization, the annual budgeting season exacts a heavy toll on the tree population. Hundreds of spreadsheets producing reams of analysis and countless iterations of budget submissions serve to keep printers and photocopiers humming from August to December. In virtually every section of this book I have described problems and then described how the Balanced Scorecard can step in and save the day. Not this time. At least during the first year, using the Scorecard to drive the budget process will definitely require some paper. Budget preparers must be provided with templates they can complete to make the ultimate job of compiling all spending requests a little easier. You can attempt to do this electronically, but unless you are very advanced in the ways of paper conservation you will be receiving most of your submissions on good old-fashioned eight and a half by eleven. The light at the end of the tunnel starts to appear in year two as the process matures. Those preparing budgets should become increasingly comfortable with methods of filing Scorecard-related budget submissions electronically. Exhibit 9.2 displays a simplified template that groups may use to record their budget submission.

In this example, the mortgage lending department of a bank has outlined three initiatives they believe are crucial in achieving a 75 percent Customer Loyalty Rating. Keep in mind that this illustration shows just one measure from the group's Scorecard. They will have many more, hence the paper! Everything shown in Exhibit 9.2 must have backup documentation for support (i.e., the detailed Balanced Scorecard for mortgage lending, a breakdown of the specific elements comprising the initiative, and the related costs). These details are necessary for executives to make an informed decision regarding which initiatives to fund and which to defer.

Once all groups have submitted their proposals, budget requests may be summarized according to specific Balanced Scorecard strategies or objectives. Exhibit 9.3 provides a potential form designed for that purpose. Here we see that one of our fictional bank's strategies is to become customer focused. To do that, they have developed three objectives on their Balanced Scorecard—increase customer loyalty, increase customer confidence, and increase flexible solutions. The next column shows the bank's current performance on each of those objectives. Customer loyalty is green, which signals acceptable performance; customer confidence is yellow, which raises a flag of caution; and flexible solutions is red, meaning it is performing below target. The last two columns provide a rollup of budget requests from around the organization related to the objectives. Executives can use this simple form to determine where the majority of spending requests are being directed and take action to ensure an appropriate balance in the allocation of resources. In the example presented, we see that customer loyalty is

Exhibit 9.2. A Simplified Budget Submission Form

			Resource Requirements	
Measure	Target	Initiatives	Operating	Capital
Customer Loyalty Rating	75%	Account Officer Training Program	$250,000	$175,000
		Affiliate Marketing	$125,000	$350,000
		Customer Information System	$150,000	$750,000

Business Unit/Department: Mortgage Lending

Exhibit 9.3   Budget Requests by Balanced Scorecard Strategy

Corporate Strategy: Become Customer Focused

Objective	Current Scorecard Status	Budget Request Operating $000s	Budget Request Capital $000s
Increase customer loyalty	Green	$XXM	$XXM
Increase customer confidence	Yellow	$XXM	$XXM
Increase flexible solutions	Red	$XXM	$XXM
Percentage of total spending		44%	38%

currently green, meaning it is performing at a satisfactory level. Executives must determine how much they are willing to spend to sustain this performance. Similarly, they must determine how much to commit to flexible solutions, which is currently performing below their expectations. Customer confidence is currently displaying yellow or cautionary performance. How much should be spent to bring it in line with targeted expectations?

Step 5: Finalize the Budget

Once you have tallied the budget requests that have been generated from groups around the organization, you will undoubtedly encounter a gap— or perhaps it's a chasm the size of the Grand Canyon. This gap to which I am playfully referring is the difference between what you know you can afford to spend, still meeting reasonable return on equity estimates, and the total of requests submitted by budget-hungry business units and departments. This is when things get interesting and the real value of using the Balanced Scorecard to drive budgets comes to the fore.

To finalize the budget, each business unit leader should make a formal presentation to fellow executives outlining the budget submissions from his or her group; what they encompass, why they are strategically significant, and how they will positively impact Scorecard targets. Everyone in attendance during these presentations will be aware of the gap that exists between desired and possible spending, and this sharing of information will be critical in helping the executive team process information, engage in productive dialogue, and make decisions regarding which initiatives are truly strategic and necessary. At this point the process becomes iterative, with executives reviewing and questioning the proposals, attempting to determine which are worthy of inclusion in the budget. To ease the decision-making process somewhat, you may wish to develop an internal ranking system for the initiatives you propose. A simplified rating system may be devised to represent the potential impact of removing a specific initiative on the Balanced Scorecard. For example, a "1" might indicate an initiative that could be eliminated and have minimal impact on the ability of the group to achieve it's target. A "2" might translate to an initiative that could be cut, but with a definite effect on the group's chances of meeting targeted expectations. Finally, those initiatives given a "3" could represent those initiatives that are deemed as crucial to the successful achievement of Scorecard targets. The ratings will be necessarily subjective, but they will serve as a powerful impetus for conversations centered on establishing spending priorities.

Benefits of Using the Balanced Scorecard to Drive the Budgeting Process

The methods and techniques described in this chapter may at first glance appear very simplistic; in fact, you may consider them too simplistic to work in your organization. The simplistic approach advocated here is done so intentionally. We often benefit from questioning our exceedingly complex processes and getting back to the core purposes represented by our actions. What is the fundamental purpose of a budget? To allocate scarce resources among a variety of possible alternatives. What better way to do that than to use the Balanced Scorecard that is a direct and faithful translation of our strategy. Only those initiatives that provide a meaningful contribution to the fulfillment of strategic objectives should be undertaken. Many organizations are beginning to embrace the possibility of simplicity in organizational life, and questioning the core purposes of all corporate actions. For a number of years Nova Scotia Power has conducted its annual budgeting process on a model similar to that which I describe here. Rather than missing the complexity, most of those involved welcome the elegant ease of linking the Scorecards to budgets. One senior director suggested, *"This is the best budget process we've ever had. I simply develop a Scorecard, show what invest-ments I need to fulfill my targets and submit that for approval.*" Other benefits accruing to those who choose to let the Scorecard lead the way for develop-ing budgets include:

- *Reinforces your key strategies.* Rather than taking last year's budget and adding a certain percentage, the Balanced Scorecard puts strategy at the center of the budget cycle. Making strategy synonymous with bud-get dollars is a great way to get a lot of people to stand up and take notice. Your organization is a double winner. In order to prepare effec-tive budgets, managers and employees must develop a firm grasp of the essence of the strategy, thereby increasing organizational knowledge and learning. Second, and equally important, the budgets submitted demonstrate how individual groups plan to have a real impact on the strategy.

- *Reduces game playing.* When you institute a system like the Balanced Scorecard, which features strategy as the key principle, it reduces the likelihood of the typical game playing of normal budgeting efforts. Forc-ing everyone to demonstrate a direct link between their spending plans and the strategy puts all the cards on the table, so to speak. Asking for a little more and promising a little less just will not cut it in this environ-ment sparked by producing commitments that display real strategic value.

- *Leads to cooperation.* For any retooling of the budgeting process to work, managers must switch their mindset away from trying to hit their own personal budget numbers and toward a team approach focused on meet-ing the organization's strategic objectives. The Scorecard facilitates this switch in direction by encouraging an open dialogue among all involved on what is the optimal mix of spending that will achieve broad corpo-rate goals. In fact, increased cooperation and sharing of information is one of the key benefits to be derived from this process. Prior to using a Scorecard-led approach, managers may be unwilling to share spending plans, fearing that any inappropriate disclosure could lead to a reduc-tion in funds. With the Scorecard in place, managers are encouraged to explore synergies among groups and look for ways that everyone can achieve their individual goals, which when aggregated will translate to a win at the organizational level as well.

- *Facilitates learning.* Organizations should carefully review the results achieved from budget decisions. A "postaudit" or review should be con-ducted to determine whether the anticipated effect on Scorecard tar-gets from a certain initiative did in fact produce the expected benefit. Similar to the Scorecard itself, which is based on management's hypoth-esis of the relationship among performance measures, funded initiatives represent a hypothesis. They must be subjected to the same rigorous testing as Scorecard objectives and measures to ensure that the theory behind the initiatives is valid and producing results.

SUMMARY

The budgeting process that exists in most modern enterprises is strikingly similar to the techniques originally developed over 80 years ago. At that time markets were stable, customer choice was nonexistent, and companies competed in local areas only. Given these circumstances, budgets served very well in their primary function as control tools for the early industrial pioneers.

Today, as we move from control to empowerment as the central guiding force of organizations, many are questioning our reliance on this seemingly antiquated tool. Today's budgeting and planning process is burdened by time-consuming details, game playing, and general dissatisfaction on the part of executives, managers, and employees alike. However, the most troubling aspect of this process is the lack of alignment between spending as outlined in the budget and organizational goals as demonstrated in the strategic plan. As organizations have grown over the past decades, separate functions have emerged to control what should be interdependent processes. Strategic planners focus on developing plans to lead the organization into the future, while business planners and budgeters independently develop operating and capital plans.

Budgets have increasingly come under the microscope in recent years, and some organizations have taken radical action to improve their processes. The Beyond Budgeting Round Table (BBRT) suggests new performance and management processes that eradicate a reliance on budgets and instead focus on creating adaptive organizations based on empowerment and accountability. Rolling forecasts have been hailed by proponents as a vast improvement over the typical budgeting process. These (generally) six-quarter forecasts provide flexibility to executives anxious to take advantage of emerging opportunities. While an improvement, rolling forecasts are not a panacea for the budgeting process. They are time consuming and may not eliminate the game playing and turf protection typical during budget time.

The Balanced Scorecard can be used by organizations to develop budgets that place strategy at the center of the process. Spending is dictated by the ability to influence strategic goals rather than a simple recalculation of the previous year's submission. Five steps are necessary in utilizing the Balanced Scorecard to drive the budgeting process. During step 1, organizations must plan their attack and widely communicate their intention of having the Scorecard lead the budgeting process. Balanced Scorecard team members must be active in the education and communication efforts that follow. In step 2, a high-level organizational Scorecard should be developed (or updated) to begin the actual process. This document provides the necessary means for the development of cascaded Scorecards throughout the firm, which forms the basis of step 3. These Balanced Scorecards include not only objectives and measures, but also the targets and initiatives necessary to achieve success on Scorecard indicators. The investments needed to support the initiatives are used in making budget submissions that directly impact strategy. During step 4, results are compiled from across the organization. Executives can use simple tools to ensure that spending is appropriately balanced on the critical success factors imperative to driving the strategy. The budget is finalized during an iterative process of analysis and dialogue in step 5. Executives advance their spending requirements and engage other senior management in discussions regarding the strategic impact of their requests.

Allowing the Balanced Scorecard to be at the forefront of budget development offers many benefits. Key strategies are reinforced as a result of the knowledge and analysis necessary to draft budgets linking spending to organizational objectives. Game playing is significantly reduced since budget preparers must clearly demonstrate a connection between spending appeals and strategy. Not only are politics mitigated, but cooperation is fostered. Business units and departments seek synergies to ensure that their funding is approved. Finally, learning is accelerated as organizations use actual Scorecard results to begin questioning the assumptions surrounding initiatives in the budget.

NOTES

1. Hackett Benchmarking Solutions, *www.thgi.com*, 2001.
2. Cathy Lazere, "All Together Now," *CFO*, February 1998.
3. Russ Banham, "Revolution in Planning," *CFO*, August 1999.
4. Hackett Benchmarking Solutions, *www.thgi.com*, June 14, 2001.
5. Robert S. Kaplan and David P. Norton, *The Strategy Focused Organization* (Boston: Harvard Business School Press, 2001).
6. Jeremy Hope and Robin Fraser, "Beyond Budgeting White Paper," CAM-I Beyond Budgeting Round Table, May 2001.
7. Ibid., p. 12.
8. Ibid., p. 3.
9. Nils-Goran Olve, Jan Roy, and Magnus Wetter, *Performance Drivers* (New York: John Wiley & Sons, 1999).
10. "High Performance Budgeting," *Harvard Management Update*, January 1999, 1.
11. Ibid., p. 3.
12. Robert S. Kaplan and David P. Norton, *The Strategy Focused Organization* (Boston: Harvard Business School Press, 2001).
13. Tad Leahy, "Budgeting on the Softer Side," *Business Finance*, April 2001.

CHAPTER 10

Linking Rewards to Performance: The Balanced Scorecard and Compensation

Roadmap for Chapter Ten   An anonymous sage once noted *"Money is the root of all evil,"* to which George Bernard Shaw wittily retorted, *"Lack of money is the root of all evil."* I think we can probably all point to evidence of both. Regardless of where you stand on this issue, one thing is clear—organizations have in the past and will continue in the future to reward excellence with the allocation of monetary rewards. This chapter will investigate how the Balanced Scorecard can be profitably linked to your incentive compensation system.

We begin by tackling an age-old question: What motivates people in the workplace? Is it the fulfillment resulting from a job well done that drives satisfaction, or does the promise of a regular paycheck bring us back day after day? We'll see that the increasing use of incentive compensation plans can pay dividends for your Balanced Scorecard program by providing additional education and support opportunities.

More than any other aspect of the Balanced Scorecard, the linkage to compensation is extremely variable and customizable. A seemingly endless stream of possible programs will greet every organization making the decision to tie rewards with performance. This chapter includes an overview of the critical planning and design elements you must consider when constructing your own Balanced Scorecard link to compensation. The choice of design is ultimately yours; however, the chapter also provides you with a number of alternatives currently in use at leading Scorecard organizations.

A QUESTION OF MOTIVATION

I have a friend who loves to work on old cars. Nothing makes him happier than getting up at the crack of dawn on a Saturday morning, taking a hot cup of coffee out to the garage, and settling in under the hood of his latest project. He gets lost in the challenge of rusty old parts that lie before him and before he knows it the sun is setting. Nobody is paying him to spend his time in the garage toiling endlessly over beaten-down cars that will never produce a dime of revenue. No, he does it purely for the joy it brings in him. In other words, he is intrinsically motivated to perform the work. Now to get me out there is another matter entirely. Someone would have to offer a very large reward for me to spend my Saturdays cooped up in an old garage surrounded by dilapidated auto parts. So, I guess you could say I would require extrinsic motivation to perform the same work.

The debate over intrinsic versus extrinsic rewards and motivation has been raging for decades. Intrinsic rewards may produce fulfillment and a sense of pride, while extrinsic rewards hold the possibility of sharpening our focus on what must be done in order to succeed. Interestingly, there is a significant body of evidence suggesting that extrinsic rewards can impede intrinsic motivation. Classic studies involving students have demonstrated that those paid to participate in an experiment showed less enthusiasm than those who volunteered. The group without pay actually continued to work and share interest in the experiment after it ended. Similarly, studies have shown that children displaying an interest in reading may actually reduce the number of books read when offered a monetary inducement to read more books. Applying the debate to the organizational world means reducing it to a fundamental question: Why do people work? Is it rewards (i.e., money and other forms of compensation) that provide the impetus for our daily trek to the workplace? Or do we perform our duties out of a sense of self-fulfillment and pride? Most pundits suggest that the latter is the prevailing rationale for engaging in work. They suggest that while extrinsic motivators may work in the short term, their long-term viability is very limited since they fail to satisfy basic human needs such as fulfillment and meaning. I have mixed feelings on this topic. On the one hand, I know from personal experience (as do all of you) that working on an interesting and meaningful project with dedicated and talented people who share common goals is extremely rewarding. As Robert Louis Stevenson said in 1882, *"When a man loves the labor of his trade beyond any question of success or fame, the gods have called him."* On the other hand, I have a mortgage payment that comes due every 30 days, and "meaning and fulfillment" don't mean a thing at the bank! The discussions and arguments over this topic will most likely continue for decades to come.

You may or may not subscribe to the merits of extrinsic rewards, but the fact is, more and more companies are turning to reward systems as they look to gain an advantage over competitors. A 1999 study by compensation consultants Towers Perrin found that 40 percent of 770 American companies surveyed offer some form of incentive-based compensation to all their employees, not just salespeople or executives. In a consistent finding, Hewitt Associates discovered that 78 percent of surveyed businesses have at least one type of variable pay plan in place, up from 70 percent in 1999 and 47 percent in 1990.[1] This increase in variable pay plans could have a positive impact on the acceptance of the Balanced Scorecard at your organization. In a recent study of leading Balanced Scorecard adopting companies, the author found that *"Surveyed companies . . . have been most successful in securing high levels of awareness and acceptance of the Balanced Scorecard at the executive level. Awareness and acceptance among business unit leadership was also shown to be high, but at the management, professional and operational/support levels, greater difficulty was clearly being experienced in reaching satisfactory levels of acceptance."*[2] Cascading the Balanced Scorecard will obviously alleviate this deficiency of awareness, but linking the Scorecard to compensation is another powerful means of substantially boosting employee knowledge and support of the Scorecard.

Thirteen of the fifteen companies included in the study referenced above have linked pay to their Balanced Scorecard system. While each used different processes and specific programs, they all share a common belief that aligning employee rewards with the achievement of Balanced Scorecard measures is a powerful mechanism for generating focus on what is important to the organization. This is especially the case for lower levels of the company where clear lines of sight between daily employee actions and overall goals are sometimes blurry at best. Linking the Balanced Scorecard to your compensation system makes crystal clear what is valued and what outcomes are necessary to achieve performance rewards.

Some will argue that aligning rewards to Balanced Scorecard targets provides merely extrinsic motivation and could possibly hamper innovation, creativity, and fulfillment. A more optimistic and pragmatic view illuminates another possibility. Linking the Scorecard to compensation is simply an added bonus (pun intended) that completes a true win–win arrangement. Simply developing the Balanced Scorecard and sharing it with employees across the organization holds the strong prospect of increasing intrinsic motivation. Employees, possibly for the first time, now have the opportunity to gain an in-depth knowledge of the company's strategy and define the role they will play in its achievement. Brainstorming performance measures, developing strategy maps, and questioning the hypothesis that underlies the Scorecard are all intellectual tasks that serve to amply stretch the cognitive and organizational abilities of every employee participating in any level of Scorecard development. There is little doubt that knowledge and involvement are powerful levers in enhancing intrinsic motivation. The Balanced Scorecard offers the possibility of both. Providing extrinsic rewards should not lead to the erosion of motivation produced by developing the Balanced Scorecard. Rather, it acts as a laser, focusing the attention of all employees on the critical drivers of organizational success. The two motivational factors work together in this scenario. Involving all employees in the development of Balanced Scorecards increases intrinsic motivation, which is used to develop breakthrough solutions in the achievement of Scorecard targets. Exceeding the targets then translates into performance rewards to be shared by all those who made the valuable contributions necessary for success.

DESIGN ATTRIBUTES TO CONSIDER

No two Balanced Scorecard implementations will be completely alike. Each and every organization choosing to use the Scorecard system will manipulate the tool to fit individual culture, current managerial processes, and the state of organizational readiness for such a major change initiative. Linking the Scorecard to compensation will result in even greater individual differences. Historical pay preferences, possible presence of union contracts, and the variety of job classes are but a few of the many factors affecting the incentive pay decision. To assist you in designing a system that is customized for you, here are a number of design issues for your consideration. Readers should note that all references to compensation contained thus far and in the remainder of the chapter signify *variable* or *incentive* compensation. Base salary is normally not affected by the Balanced Scorecard.

Planning the Compensation Link

* *Purpose.* What is the overall purpose of your linkage of compensation to the Balanced Scorecard? What specific behaviors are you attempting to encourage or discourage? How will the new pay plan affect the culture of the organization? Having an overarching purpose in mind will help guide your efforts in a direction that best suits your individual needs.

* *Communication.* Steven Covey has referred to employee compensation as "rice bowl" issues. Messing with someone's rice bowl, whether in a positive or negative vein, is bound to stir up a lot of interest. There tends to be an air of controversy surrounding even the most well-intentioned compensation schemes, so it is in your best interests to communicate the specifics of the plan to your entire employee audience as soon as the plan is developed. Actually, even before the plan is developed, it should be reviewed and discussed with employee focus groups. You must ensure that the perception among employees is that the plan is fair and equitable. Communication efforts not only enlighten everyone as to the

compensation plan, but may also be used to demonstrate the value and benefits to be derived from using the Balanced Scorecard as a key component of your overall management system.

- *Development.* Who will be involved in the development of the new program? As with all other aspects of the Balanced Scorecard, you should attempt to involve a variety of participants in the design of your new pay program. The different perspectives and functions represented will help ensure that the new process is perceived as fair and equitable throughout the company. Perceived fairness is an issue that should not be taken lightly. Research of pay programs at a variety of companies has demonstrated that employees are more concerned with the equality and fairness represented by the program than they are with the actual amount of monetary rewards available.

- *System review.* There is a lot at stake with your compensation plan, and it is certain to be closely watched by all employees once up and running. Make it clear from the outset that you plan to review the entire program within 12 months of its initial launch. Stating this intention in a forthright manner from the beginning will send a strong signal that you are committed to making any necessary adjustments to ensure that the plan functions as anticipated in a manner assuring everyone's best interests. This way, if modifications must be made, they will not be perceived as changing the rules in midstream or subjectively altering the program to stack the deck in management's favor.

Design Elements

- *Timing.* You may be anxious to link rewards to performance and consider establishing the bond in the first year of your implementation. However, there are a number of issues you must ponder prior to launching the program. The primary concern relates to the measures you have selected for your initial Balanced Scorecards. As previously discussed, the performance measures represent a hypothesis, or your best guess, as to what it will take to execute your strategy. Most organizations make changes to their original Scorecard objectives and measures in an ongoing effort to fine-tune their cause-and-effect linkages. Linking pay to measures that may or may not stand the test of time is a dangerous proposition. Employees will be motivated to achieve the targets you establish, and, as we've all heard, "you get what you measure." Can you afford to pay for results that do not necessarily assist you in fulfilling your strategic objectives? Another issue is data collection. The Scorecard will often result in developing brand new performance measures for which a reliable data source is currently unavailable. Obviously, you do not want to link rewards to measures you cannot accurately report. In addition to the possibility of inaccurate data, you may not have the requisite systems to manage the pay program. Variable compensation is among the least automated items on a typical profit and loss statement, but given the potentially volatile swings of payouts you need methods of accurately tracking your compensation liability.

- *Involvement.* Will every employee be eligible for participation in the new pay program, or is involvement limited to certain categories of your staff? Many organizations will pilot the linkage of compensation to the Balanced Scorecard with their executives. This approach certainly has merit since the senior team was most likely involved in the development of the Scorecard and has a vested interest in the outcomes of all performance measures. However, as discussed earlier, it is often the lower levels of the organization that lack awareness and knowledge of the Balanced Scorecard. Extending the pay program to all employees greatly enhances the likelihood of increasing knowledge and advocacy of the Balanced Scorecard. Related to the issue of involvement is the question of whether incentive pay should be awarded to individuals or groups. Awarding individuals recognizes outstanding achievement and can motivate excellent performance in the future. However, most organizations today rely heavily on interdependence and the sharing of information across the enterprise. Rewarding individuals in this environment could potentially impede the knowledge sharing and collaboration necessary to generate innovative solutions. Practitioners are mixed on this point. Some provide only group rewards in an effort to stimulate teamwork and collective accountability, while others provide a mix of individual and team rewards.

  - *Number of performance measures included.* Psychologists suggest that we humans have difficulty concentrating on more than seven items at any given time. Have you ever noticed how many things seem to involve the magical number seven? *The Seven Habits of Highly Effective People* and seven deadly sins, for example. Does this mean we should limit to less than seven the number of performance measures linked to compensation? Some would say yes and suggest that a lesser number of measures is yet another method of sharpening focus on the critical drivers of success. However, if the Balanced Scorecard is well constructed, the number of measures tied to compensation should be irrelevant. A good Balanced Scorecard tells the story of your strategy through a series of cause-and-effect relationships running through the four perspectives. If the tale you have woven is tight and seamless, then employees should be able to concentrate on any number of measures since they know how each affects the overall story you are telling through measurement.

- *Perspectives of measures.* Not only is the number of measures linked to compensation an element for consideration, but the type of measure must also be contemplated. Will you attach rewards to the achievement of only the most verifiable and objective indicators, normally represented by financial measures? Or will meeting targets of measures located in other perspectives also lead to rewards? In one study focusing on the linkage of compensation to the Balanced Scorecard, it was discovered that leading Scorecard organizations are aligning rewards with measures from all four perspectives. However, the weights assigned to each perspective were not always equal. Most respondents applied a heavier weight to financial measures, which averaged about 40 percent of the potential reward. The Customer, Internal Process, and Employee Learning and Growth perspectives were weighted approximately 20 percent each.[3] Deciding to include nonfinancial measures in your calculation can heighten the challenges associated with the process. While you would like your nonfinancial indicators to focus on outcomes, a key benefit of the Scorecard is the articulation of leading indicators of performance that are not always outcome based. For example, you may hypothesize that "hours spent with customers" is a leading indicator of "repeat purchases." However, aligning compensation with "hours spent with customers" could lead salespeople to amass unnecessary time with non-purchasing customers simply to boost the chance of receiving an incentive award. Incentives should be balanced so that both leading and lagging indicators of performance are appropriately represented and lead to the outcomes you desire.

- *Measure timing.* Another measure-related consideration is whether rewards should be linked to short-term or long-term performance. Some argue that the Balanced Scorecard is a tool for sustaining success over the long term (obviously, I agree with this assessment as this book's subtitle will attest), and thus a true indication of success is best measured by examining enduring accomplishment. Additionally, by linking rewards to long-term success, there is no incentive to sacrifice long-term benefits for the sake of achieving a short-term gain. Others point to the motivational benefit of providing more frequent rewards along the path to long-term prosperity. Proponents of this camp will suggest that generating positive Scorecard results and sharing the rewards with employees on an annual or even more frequent basis serves to strengthen the commitment of all organizational participants to the achievement of strategic goals.

- *Performance thresholds.* There are those who believe that paying incentive goals on individual measure results when overall organizational objectives have not been met obscures the focus needed from all employees. For that reason, some organizations will not pay any rewards unless a predetermined standard or cap is met. Normally, this hurdle is represented by a high-level financial objective such as return on equity. This approach ensures that all employees know very well what the key driver of success is for the organization and helps them align their efforts in exceeding it. However, the problem with this course of action is that employees may feel bitter or resentful if, for reasons beyond their control, a high-level financial objective has fallen short while other performance goals are met.

- *Funding.* Don't forget this very pragmatic element of any compensation plan—from where does the money flow? Will the potential payouts associated with exceeding Scorecard targets be funded from the firm's budget, or do you expect savings generated from the Scorecard to "self-fund" the incentives? And just how much do you plan to offer in incentives? Involving both your executive team and the professionals in your human resources department will help you develop solutions to these issues.

METHODS OF LINKING THE BALANCED SCORECARD TO COMPENSATION

As noted earlier in the chapter, you have virtually unlimited choices when making a link from the Balanced Scorecard to compensation. The many permutations and combinations of award triggers, measures, and potential outcomes is staggering. Organizations pursuing this link will undoubtedly travel many different routes, but all arrive at the same conclusion—aligning rewards with Scorecard results leads to increased attention on the critical drivers of the organization. Let's examine some of the methods used to combine Scorecard measures and compensation.

Basing Rewards on Overall Results

The simplest method of tying Balanced Scorecard performance to rewards is using the highest-level organizational Scorecard as the barometer of success and arbiter of bonuses. Under this scenario, a certain percentage of incentive compensation is available to employees should the organization achieve some or all of its goals. Each measure on the high-level Scorecard is assigned a weight, with total weights across the four perspectives summing to 100 percent. Financial targets often receive a higher weight, reflecting the value management continues to place on achieving fiscal success. As results are tracked, percentage payouts are calculated and distributed. Depending on the level of program sophistication, this allocation of rewards may take place monthly, quarterly, semiannually, or annually. Here is an example of how the program might work. Let's say an organization is willing to extend a 10 percent annual bonus (of base salary) to employees based on Scorecard results. The company tracks a total of eight measures across the four perspectives, as shown Exhibit 10.1.

Final results are reported at year end, and the employee bonus is calculated as shown in Exhibit 10.2.

Exhibit 10.1   Sample Targets

Perspective	Measure	Target	Weight
Financial	Return on equity	15%	30%
	Revenue growth	25%	10%
Customer	Customer satisfaction	75%	15%
	Repeat purchase percentage	80%	5%
Internal Processes	On-time delivery	90%	10%
	Manufacturing efficiency	85%	10%
Employee Learning and Growth	Competency attainment— percentage of employees gaining three new competencies	70%	12%
	Employee turnover	5%	8%

Exhibit 10.2   Sample Payout

Perspective	Measure	Target	Weight	Actual	Payout
Financial	Return on equity	15%	30%	16.5%	3.0%
	Revenue growth	25%	10%	20%	0
Customer	Customer satisfaction	75%	15%	77%	1.5%
	Repeat purchase percentage	80%	5%	75%	0
Internal Processes	On-time delivery	90%	10%	85%	0
	Manufacturing efficiency	85%	10%	85%	1.0%
Employee Learning and Growth	Competency attainment— percentage of employees gaining three new competencies	70%	12%	75%	1.2%
	Employee turnover	5%	8%	4%	0.8%
	Total Payout				7.5%

The organization achieved its return on equity target and, since it makes up 30 percent of the total weight of all measures, employees will receive 3.0 percent of their bonus based on that result. Based on the positive Scorecard results achieved the total award sums to 7.5 percent of base salary. In this example, the payout is conducted annually. However, to ensure that employees remain locked in on overall goals the organization would be wise to provide regular (perhaps monthly) feedback on Scorecard results.

The simplicity of this method makes it very transparent and ideal for communication to the entire workforce. As Scorecard results are monitored throughout the year, they form the basis for strategic conversations from top to bottom within the firm. Issues associated with this technique include the degree of stretch involved in the targets and the lack of any thresholds that must be achieved before bonuses are awarded. Using this method of incentive compensation, it is conceivable that employees will receive a bonus whether or not the firm achieves its overall financial objectives. This could send a message inconsistent with the theory of the Balanced Scorecard, which asserts that positive results on measures in the lower perspectives will drive improved financial performance.

Driving the Link to All Levels of the Organization

Many Scorecard-adopting organizations put tremendous energy into establishing the all-important line of sight from individual action to overall goals. This process of cascading not only informs employees of how they can influence results, but also serves as a powerful mechanism for using the Balanced Scorecard as a true strategic management system. Chapter Nine reviewed how a series of cascaded Balanced Scorecards may be used to launch the strategic allocation of resources, ensuring that budget requests align with strategy. This section will discuss the use of cascaded Scorecards as the springboard for making a connection between the Scorecard and compensation. In contrast to the approach discussed in the previous section, which relied on overall corporate results to dictate bonus allotments, using the cascading technique aligns awards with results that hit closer to home for employees. Cascading displays how individual employees are able to influence higher-level goals, and the associated compensation link demonstrates the rewards that await outstanding performance at the business unit, department, or individual level.

Nova Scotia Power Inc. is one organization that used the cascading method of linking the Balanced Scorecard to compensation. The utility's Scorecard implementation had proven very successful even from the earliest stage of development. However, managers continually noted that until the new system was linked to paychecks it would never become "real" in the minds of most employees. Senior management took this advice to heart and developed a system of incentive compensation that aligned rewards with the successful achievement of Balanced Scorecard targets.

The first level of compensation cascading at Nova Scotia Power took place when each member of the executive team developed a Personal Balanced Scorecard based on the Corporate Scorecard. The weights assigned to each perspective and associated measures were relatively balanced; however, each executive overweighted those areas in which he was best able to contribute. For example, the vice president and chief financial officer (CFO) developed a Scorecard with representative measures in each of the four perspectives, but the Financial perspective and related measures were assigned the greatest weight given the nature of the CFO's work and its impact on these critical indicators. Similarly, the vice president of sales and marketing overweighted the Customer perspective. Scorecards developed at the executive level contained a mix of measures, some pulled directly from the Corporate Balanced Scorecard and others describing how the executive would influence the corporate indicators. Rather than using one target for each measure, three were developed, with each exemplifying increasing degrees of stretch. Percentages of base salary were linked to each, representing its degree of difficulty. A threshold target stood for minimum acceptable performance on the measure. No incentive compensation would be paid on a measure for which the threshold was not achieved. Midpoint targets represented better-than-average performance and therefore warranted increased rewards. Finally, stretch targets were considered best in class and required significant effort to be met. Therefore, additional incentives awaited their achievement.

Balanced Scorecards were then developed at the business unit, department, and individual level of the organization. As with the executive Scorecards, every group or individual assigned weights to each perspective and measures and developed corresponding threshold, midpoint, and stretch targets. All Scorecard measures and targets were reviewed and approved by management to ensure adequate coverage of corporate strategic themes and achievable yet challenging targets. Nova Scotia Power wanted to leave no doubt in employees' minds that meeting their return on equity target was critical for the ongoing success of the organization. Therefore, they decreed that no incentive awards would be paid unless the corporation met this financial target. This message served to galvanize employees around meeting their own Scorecard targets, which they knew from cascading experience would help drive the overall corporate results.

Competency-Based Pay

Compensation firm Towers Perrin has reported that while only 8 percent of surveyed organizations currently use competency-based pay systems, a whopping 78 percent plan to implement such a system in the near future.[4] As the world of work continues to evolve from machines to knowledge, the focus on competencies appears to make sense. Organizations have squeezed practically every last drop out of process improvement and reengineering. What is left is the greatest source of productivity enhancements of all: human knowledge. Competency-based systems with their painstaking attention to the attributes and behaviors necessary to effectively compete in today's environment can drive the changes organizations require to succeed. Basing pay on competencies is a dramatic shift from the old world of seniority-dependent pay.

As we saw in Chapter Five when discussing the Employee Learning and Growth perspective, all employees can use the Balanced Scorecard to track the addition of key competencies. As a logical extension, incentive compensation may be directed toward the acquisition of competencies. Employees who can demonstrate they have been able to add new competencies to their repertoire are allotted an incentive award. One potential drawback is the concern that an exclusive focus on competencies may lead to lesser concentration on actual performance results. Therefore, a caveat when considering this approach is that pay for competencies be balanced with results, especially in the short term. Other measures on the Balanced Scorecard can be used to provide a balance between new skills and attributes and the results they collectively produce.

GAINSHARING

Gainsharing is an improvement system that relies on employee actions to enhance organizational results. Key measures of performance are developed, and targets for improvements or cost savings are agreed upon. Any savings generated from the improved results are shared with employees through incentive bonuses. Gainsharing experts suggest that organizations engaging in this technique *"must be willing to engage in at least some form of employee involvement that shares business information, educates employees in the economics of business, and encourages suggestions. Without moving information, knowledge, and power downward, it is unlikely that a significant line of sight will develop and that the plan will be successful."*[5] Sounds to me like they're describing the need for a Balanced Scorecard to make gainsharing work. The Scorecard involves employees in its design, provides unlimited educational opportunities, encourages suggestions through the questioning of assumptions, and creates a powerful line of sight.

Performance measures developed for the Balanced Scorecard can serve as the guiding force behind a gainsharing program. Each of the four perspectives may contain measures that have an economic element and can be used to drive cost savings throughout the organization. As Scorecard results are tracked over time, any savings can be distributed to employees in the form of incentive compensation.

Points Programs

For some companies the idea of a cash-based incentive program makes great sense, but their union contracts prohibit the use of such tools. In these circumstances, creative teams have developed innovative ways of recognizing employee and organizational success without distributing the usual monetary award. Kaplan and Norton describe the case of Texaco Refinery and Marketing Inc. (TRMI).[6] Constrained by their union agreements, this organization turned to a points program to reward success. Points, each with a par value of $1, were awarded based on plantwide, work group, team, and individual results. The accumulated points could be redeemed for merchandise, travel, and retail awards. Results were swift and dramatic. In the very first year of the plan, two plants set records for utilization, expense reduction, and safety.

SUMMARY

On the meaning of success, prolific inventor Thomas Edison once said, *"One might think that the money value of an invention constitutes its reward to the man who loves his work. But speaking for myself, I can honestly say this is not so . . . I continue to find my greatest pleasure, and so my reward, in the work that precedes what the world calls success."* This is an eloquent description of what we now refer to as intrinsic motivation, the derivation of meaning and satisfaction from the joy of the task at hand. At the other end of the motivation spectrum is extrinsic motivation. Performing a task for the promise of a reward is characteristic of the extrinsically motivated individual. Despite the inspiring citation offered by Mr. Edison, the fact remains that an increasing number of organizations are offering monetary incentives to reward outstanding performance. If these rewards are extended to all levels of an organization, they can support the Balanced Scorecard by providing another means of focusing employee attention on the select drivers of success. The Scorecard often provides intrinsic motivation since it illuminates for employees how they can influence and contribute to high-level strategy. Extrinsic rewards can supplement this knowledge by supplying incentives to achieve stated objectives.

Pay is a sticky subject at many organizations. Whether they are deemed to pay too little or (rarely) too much, significant attention is paid to the compensation scale. As a result, most companies will devise a linkage between the Balanced Scorecard and their compensation system that is customized to meet unique challenges and needs. There are several planning and design components that must be considered before attempting to link the Scorecard to compensation. Planning aspects include the purpose of making the bond between your Scorecard and compensation systems, how you'll communicate the program, who designs it, and how it will be reviewed and judged. When designing the system, several other considerations must be made. The timing is an important decision. Will the Scorecard be linked to compensation in your first year of implementation or will you wait until the program is more stable and mature? Since many organizations will adjust their initial Scorecard measures, it may be prudent to forge a bond between the Scorecard and compensation in your second year. When selecting performance measures that will be tied to compensation, you must consider the number, perspective, and timing. The establishment of thresholds, which must be met before any rewards are paid, is another possibility to be discussed. Finally, you must determine how you will fund your incentive plan. Awards may be part of your budget or self-funded through savings generated from Scorecard results.

The most convenient method of linking the Scorecard to compensation is basing payouts on the results achieved with your high-level organizational Scorecard. This approach is ideal for communicating the Balanced Scorecard and elevating the importance of organizational indicators. However, it does little to reward outstanding performance at the business unit, department, or individual level. To alleviate this shortcoming, organizations may develop lower-level Scorecards and use them as the basis for a link to compensation. This way, all employees have the chance to show how their actions are leading to improved results and are rewarded for their local efforts. The Balanced Scorecard can also be used for incentives relating to competency-based pay systems and gainsharing methodologies. In both cases, performance measures from the Balanced Scorecard provide the potential means for the allocation of rewards. For those organizations unwilling or unable to offer monetary rewards, the option exists of distributing points to employees based on Scorecard results. Points are accumulated throughout the year and may be redeemed for merchandise, travel, or retail rewards.

NOTES

1. Jennifer Kaplan, "Sun Uses Incentive Compensation to Boost Supply-Chain Performance," *CFO.com*, March 26, 2001
2. Todd Manas, "Making the Balanced Scorecard Approach Pay Off," *ACA Journal*, Second Quarter 1999.
3. Ibid.
4. Marie Gendron, "Competencies and What They Mean To You," *Harvard Management Update*, September 1996.
5. Edward E. Lawler III, *Rewarding Excellence* (San Francisco: Jossey-Bass, 2000).
6. Robert S. Kaplan and David P. Norton, *The Strategy Focused Organization* (Boston: Harvard Business School Press, 2001).

PART FOUR

Sustaining Balanced Scorecard Success

.

CHAPTER 11

Reporting Balanced Scorecard Results

Roadmap for Chapter Eleven   Despite best efforts and intentions, the development of a Balanced Scorecard does not guarantee its use in guiding day-to-day decision making. Frequent reporting of results, however, can bring the Scorecard to the organizational forefront, drawing the attention of all employees. But how to report the Scorecard? Do you rely on paper-based reports or venture into the ever-expanding world of Performance Management software to find the solution? This chapter will explore the critical choice of how to report Scorecard results.

The earliest Scorecard users counted on good old-fashioned paper reports to supply the information contained in their Scorecards. Despite this very low-tech solution, many early adopters achieved great success. However, as the use of the Scorecard has grown and expanded from a measurement system to a strategic management system and communication tool, many users have turned to technology.

Prolific science fiction author Arthur C. Clarke once noted, *"Any sufficiently advanced technology is indistinguishable from magic."* One look at the impressive array of Scorecard software tools on the market today and you will probably agree. With the many bells and whistles available in today's products, making an informed decision can be a great challenge. To assist in that endeavor, we will examine a number of criteria to help you wade through the choices. We will also take a look at what's around the corner in the world of Scorecard technology and some potential issues that can crop up when utilizing a software solution.

Technological solutions are not for everyone. Some organizations will feel more comfortable pursuing other forms of reporting, while some may simply not wish to commit the extensive financial and human resources necessary when investing in a software solution. We will look at other options and discuss what some organizations have done in lieu of technology.

The chapter concludes with an examination of how you can use the Balanced Scorecard reporting system to eliminate redundant reports and become the cornerstone of your management review meetings.

AUTOMATING THE BALANCED SCORECARD

When the Balanced Scorecard was developed and began to gain favor in the early 1990s, there were less than a handful of software vendors providing tools to automate this revolutionary management tool. Still, many organizations took advantage of the Balanced Scorecard's elegantly simple methodology and achieved tremendous results. These pioneers blazed the Scorecard trail using nothing more than spreadsheet-based paper reports with some color graphs mixed in to spice things up a bit. They proved that you do not need sophisticated tools and a big budget to benefit from the Balanced Scorecard. But then again, the Scorecard methodology had not matured and entered its period of greatest sophistication at that point. Most practitioners relied on the Scorecard as a new and improved measurement system but had yet to tap the huge potential of the Scorecard as a strategic management system and communication tool.

By the mid to late 1990s, the Balanced Scorecard landscape had changed dramatically. Organizations began to cascade the Scorecard from top to bottom, attempting to align all employees with overall goals, and linkages from the Scorecard to budgets and compensation were also more frequently reported. The old paper-based reporting systems that had been established with the first Scorecards simply could not meet the challenges represented by these innovative Scorecard extensions. As is always the case, creative and adaptive organizations recognized this opportunity and were quick to supply new and elaborate automated Scorecard software solutions to fill the void. Scorecard practitioners of all sizes welcomed the options, functions, and add-ons provided by these vendors with open arms. And why not, since the new software facilitated even greater focus and attention on the many benefits to be derived from using the Scorecard system. It appears that more and more organizations will embrace performance management technology in the days ahead. In one recent study, 51 percent of companies surveyed said that technology changes were anticipated in the next 12 to 18 months.[1]

Automating your Balanced Scorecard provides a number of benefits and maximizes its use as a measurement system, strategic management system, and communication tool. The advanced analytics and decision support provided by even the simplest Scorecard software allow organizations to perform intricate evaluations of performance and critically examine the relationships among their performance measures. Automation also supports true organizationwide deployment of the tool. Cascading the Scorecard across the enterprise can often lead to the development of dozens of Scorecards if not more. Without the use of an automated solution, managing the process and ensuring alignment is extremely difficult. Communication and feedback can also be dramatically improved with Scorecard software. Commentaries used to elaborate on a specific measure's performance may spawn a companywide discussion and lead to creative breakthroughs based on collaborative problem solving made possible only through the wide dissemination of Scorecard results. Information sharing and knowledge are also enhanced by the software's ability to provide relevant links to interested users. A hyperlinked measure may be just the beginning in the user's journey to a variety of knowledge-enhancing sites, including the mission statement, the latest comments from a valued customer, or the results of a much anticipated benchmarking study.

Choosing Balanced Scorecard Software

As discussed above, the past few years have seen the number of companies providing Balanced Scorecard software increase substantially. The market has become increasingly competitive, with large enterprise resource planning (ERP) vendors, midsize software enterprises, and small niche players each vying for a share of this ever-enlarging market. The choice of which vendor will supply your software is one of the most difficult and important decisions you will be forced to make during your Scorecard implementation. There is a lot on the line here, not only the effective reporting and analysis of your Scorecard measures, but equally vital, the acceptance of the tool by your workforce. Adding to the challenge is the fact that software selection can be a very esoteric business and most of us probably do not count this skill among our core competencies. Obviously, you will rely heavily on your information technology (IT) colleagues to help guide you through the dizzying maze of choices you are about to encounter. To supplement the assistance you receive from the IT folks, below you will find a host of criteria to consider when making your decision.

Design Issues—Configuration of the Software

This section will examine a number of the Scorecard software set-up and design elements.

- *Time to implement.* Software programs for the Balanced Scorecard can run the gamut from simple reporting tools to sophisticated enterprise-wide management solutions. Therefore, major differences exist in the time and resources necessary to implement the system. You must determine what your thresholds are in terms of timing and resource requirements necessary to have the system up and running.

- *Various Scorecard designs.* This book focuses exclusively on the methodology of the Balanced Scorecard; however, you may at some point wish to track other popular measurement alternatives such as the Baldrige criteria, total quality management (TQM) metrics, or any number of different methodologies. The software should be flexible enough to permit various performance management techniques.

- *User interface/display.* Most Balanced Scorecard software features a predominant display metaphor. It may use gauges similar to those on the dashboard of a plane or automobile, boxes that are reminiscent of organizational charts, or color-coded dials. Some of these simply look better (i.e., more realistic and legitimate) than others. That may sound insignificant, but remember, you are counting on your workforce to use this software faithfully and if they find the instrumentation unrealistic, or worse, unattractive, that could significantly impact their initial reaction and ongoing commitment.

- *Number of measures.* As stated earlier in the book, most Scorecard practitioners are (on average) increasing the number of measures they track. This is a result of new software tools that allow unlimited measures to be entered. Too many measures can distort an organization's focus and blur what is truly important. However, your software must be equipped with the flexibility to handle a significant volume of measures to accommodate tracking results from across the organization.

- *Strategies, objectives, measures, targets, and initiatives.* As the backbone of the Scorecard system, you should be able to easily enter all of the above elements in the software. Additionally, the functionality of the tool should permit you to link objectives to perspectives, measures to objectives, targets to measures, and initiatives to targets.

- *Cause-and-effect relationships.* Your Scorecard software should provide a means of demonstrating the cause-and-effect linkages that describe your strategy. Capturing these strategy maps with compelling and easy-to-understand graphics is critical should you hope to benefit from the information sharing and collective learning to be derived from the Balanced Scorecard.

- *Multiple locations.* The software should accommodate the addition of performance measures from a variety of physical and nonphysical locations.

- *Descriptions and definitions.* Simply entering names and numbers into the software is not sufficient for communication and eventual analysis. Every field in which you enter information must be capable of accepting textual descriptions. Upon launching the software, the first thing most users will do when looking at a specific performance indicator is examine its description and definition.

- *Assignment of owners.* The Scorecard can be used to enhance accountability only if your software permits each performance indicator to be assigned a specific owner. Since you may also have another individual acting as the owner's assistant and yet another as data enterer, it is beneficial if the software provides the ability to identify these functions, as well.

- *Various unit types.* Your performance indicators are likely to come in all shapes, sizes, and descriptors from raw numbers to dollars to percentages. The tool you choose must permit all measure types.

- *Appropriate timing.* Not all performance indicators will be tracked with the same degree of frequency. An item like sales could be tracked annually, quarterly, monthly, weekly, or even daily, while employee surveys are most likely conducted and reported only once or twice a year. However, you may wish to view past performance in different time increments than originally reported. For example, you may wish to view on-time delivery (reported monthly) annualized for the past two years. Your software should provide this flexibility.

- *Relative weights.* All measures on the Balanced Scorecard are important links in the description of your strategy. However, most organizations place greater emphasis on certain indicators. Perhaps financial measures are vital at the outset of your implementation. A good Scorecard tool should permit you to weigh the measures according to their relative importance.

- *Aggregate disparate elements.* That description sounds a little complicated, but it simply means that your program should deliver the ability to combine performance measures with different unit types. This can best be accomplished with the use of weighting (see above). Measures are accorded a weight that drives the aggregation of results regardless of the specific unit type of each indicator.

- *Multiple comparatives.* Most organizations track performance relative to a predefined target, for example, the budget. However, it may be useful to examine performance in light of last year's performance, relative to your competition, or a best-in-class benchmarking number. Look for the software to allow a number of comparatives.

- *Graphic status indicators.* At a glance, users should be able to ascertain the performance of measures based on an easy to understand status indicator. Many programs take advantage of our familiarity with red (stop), yellow (caution), and green (go) metaphors.

- *Dual polarity.* For the software to produce a color indicating measure performance, it must recognize whether high values for actual results represent good or bad performance. Up to a certain point, results might be considered good, but beyond a certain threshold they may be a cause for concern. For example, it may be perfectly appropriate for a call center representative to answer 15 calls an hour, but responding to 30 may indicate the representative is rushing through the calls and sacrificing quality for the sake of expediency. The software solution should be able to flag such issues of "dual polarity."

- *Cascading Scorecards.* Users should be able to review Balanced Scorecards from across the company in one program. Ensure that your software allows you to display aligned Scorecards emanating from throughout the organization.

- *Personal preferences.* "My" has become a popular prefix in the Internet world, with "My Yahoo," "My Home Page," and so on. The information age has heralded a time of mass customization. And so it should be with your Balanced Scorecard software. If desired, users should be able to easily customize the system to open with a page displaying indicators of importance to them. Having relevant information immediately available will greatly facilitate the program's use.

- *Intuitive menus.* Menus should be logical, easy to understand, and relatively simple to navigate.

- *Helpful help screens.* Some help screens seem to hinder users' efforts as often as helping them. Check the help screens to ensure that they offer relevant, easy-to-follow information.

- *Levels of detail.* Your software should allow users to quickly and easily switch from a summary view of performance to a detailed view comprising a single indicator. Navigating from data tables to summary reports and back to individual measures should all be easily accommodated. The user community will demand this functionality as they begin actively using the tool to analyze performance results.

Reporting and Analysis

Any software solution you consider must contain robust and flexible reporting and analysis tools. This section will explore a number of reporting and analysis factors to be considered during your selection process.

- *Drill-down capabilities.* A crucial item. The tool must allow users to drill-down on measures to increasingly lower levels of detail. Drill-down might also be considered in the context of strategy maps, which should be easily navigable at the click of a mouse.

- *Statistical analysis.* Your software should include the facility of performing statistical analysis (e.g., trends) on the performance measures making up your Balanced Scorecard. Additionally, the statistics should be multidimensional in nature, combining disparate performance elements to display a total picture of actual results. Simply viewing bar charts is not analysis. Users require the opportunity of slicing and dicing the data to fit their analysis and decision-making needs.

- *Alerts.* You will want to be notified automatically when a critical measure is not performing within acceptable ranges. Alerts must be built into the system to provide this notification.

- *Commentaries.* Whether a measure is performing at, above, or below targeted expectations, users (especially management) need to quickly determine the root cause of the performance and be aware of the associated steps necessary for sustaining or improving results. Commentary fields are essential to any Scorecard software program and most, if not all, include them.

- *Flexible report options.* "What kind of reports does it have?" is invariably one of the first questions you will hear when discussing Scorecard software with your user community. Ours is a report-based and dependent culture, so this should not come as a surprise. What may in fact come as a surprise is the wide range of report capabilities featured in today's Scorecard software entries. Test this requirement closely because, simply put, some are much better than others. An especially important area to examine is print options. We purchase software to reduce our dependency on paper but as we all know it does not necessarily work that way. Ensure that the reports will print effectively, displaying the information clearly and concisely.

- *Automatic consolidation.* You may wish to see your data presented as a sum, average, or year-to-date amount. The system should possess the flexibility to provide this choice.

- *Flag missing data.* At the outset of their implementation, most organizations will be missing at least a portion of the data for Balanced Scorecard measures. This often results from the fact that the Scorecard has illuminated entirely new measures never before contemplated. The software program should alert users to those measures that are missing data, whether it is for a single period or the measure has never been populated.

- *Forecasting and "what-if" analysis.* Robust programs possess the capability of using current results to forecast future performance. It is also very useful to have the ability to plug in different values in various measures and examine the effect on related indicators. This what-if analysis provides another opportunity to critically examine the assumptions made when constructing the strategy map.

- *Linked documents.* At a mouse click users should have the ability to put measure results into a larger context by accessing important documents and links. Annual reports, CEO videos, analyst reports, discussion forums, and a variety of other potential links can serve to strengthen the bond between actual results and the larger context of organizational objectives.

- *Automatic e-mail.* To harness the power of the Balanced Scorecard as a communication tool, users must be able to launch an e-mail application and send messages regarding specific performance results. Discussion forums or "threads" may develop as interested users add their perspective on results and provide insights for improvements.

Technical Considerations

This section examines hardware and software technical dimensions associated with your software selection.

- *Compatibility.* Any software you consider must be able to exist in your current technical environment. Most employ client/server technology and will run on Windows 95, 98, 2000, XP, and NT.

- *Integration with existing systems.* Data for your Balanced Scorecard will probably reside in a number of different places. Financial data from your general ledger, customer information from your customer relationship management (CRM) system, and other measures from an ERP system. Your software should be able to extract data from these systems automatically, thereby eliminating any rekeying of data. Users who appear reluctant to use the Scorecard software will often point to redundant data entry as a key detraction of the system. Therefore, a big win is delivered should you have the ability to automatically extricate information with no effort on the part of users.

- *Accept various data forms.* In addition to internal sources of data, you may collect performance information from third-party providers. The software should therefore contain the ability to accept data from spreadsheets and ASCII files.

- *Data export.* Sometimes getting information out is as important as getting it in. The data contained in the Balanced Scorecard may serve as the source for other management reports to boards, regulators, or the general public. A robust data export tool is an important component of any Scorecard software.

- *Web publishing.* Users should have the option of accessing and saving Scorecard information using a standard browser. Publishing to both an internal intranet and the Internet is preferable.

- *Trigger external applications.* Users will require the capability of launching desktop programs from within the Balanced Scorecard software.

- *Cut and paste to applications.* Related to the above, users may wish to include a graph or chart in another application. Many programs will provide functionality enabling users to simply copy and paste with ease.

- *Application service provider (ASP) option.* An ASP is a company that offers organizations access to applications and related services over the Internet that would otherwise have to be located in their own computers. As IT outsourcing grows in prominence, so does the role of ASPs. A number of Scorecard software vendors now offer this service, which gives anyone direct access to the Balanced Scorecard for a monthly (normally) fee based on the number of users.

- *Scalability.* This term describes the ability of an application to function well and take advantage of changes in size or volume in order to meet a user need. Rescaling can encompass a change in the product itself (storage, random-access memory [RAM], etc.) or the movement to a new operating system. Your software should be scalable to meet the future demands you may place on it as your user community and sophistication grow.

Maintenance and Security

Ensuring appropriate access rights and ongoing maintenance are also important criteria in your software decision. Elements to consider include:

- *System administrator access.* Your software should allow for individuals to be designated as system administrators. Depending on security (see below), a number of these users may have access to the entire system.

- *Ease of modification.* Altering your views of performance should be facilitated easily with little advanced technical knowledge required.

- *Control of access to the system.* My proclivities are toward open book management with complete sharing of information across the enterprise. Organizations practicing this participative form of management give it glowing reviews for the innovation and creativity it sparks among employees. The Scorecard facilitates open sharing of information both through the development of a high-level organizational Scorecard and the series of cascading Scorecards that allow all employees to describe their contribution to overall results. However, not all companies share this view and many wish to limit access to the system. Therefore, a software program should allow you to limit access to measures by user and develop user groups to simplify the measure publishing process.

- *Control of changes, data, and commentary entry.* Related to the above, not all users will necessarily be required to make changes, enter data, or provide result commentaries. Only system administrators should have the power to change measures, and only assigned users will have access to entering data and commentaries.

Evaluating the Vendor

Chances are you will be presented with a wide array of software choices from both industry veterans and upstarts you have never heard of. Either way, performing a little due diligence on the vendor is always a good idea.

- *Pricing.* As with any investment of this magnitude, pricing is a critical component of the overall decision. To make an informed decision, remember to include all dimensions of the total cost to purchase and maintain the software. This includes the per user license fees, any maintenance fees, costs related to new releases, training costs, as well as salaries and benefits of system administrators.

- *Viability of the vendor.* Is this provider in for the long term or will any vicissitudes of the economy spell their demise? As I write this, we are experiencing a significant economic downturn, which may have a direct effect on the number of players competing in this market in the months and years ahead. After reading this book, you know that financial information is like looking in the rearview mirror, but nonetheless you should ask to see the vendor's audited financial statements to assess their financial position and growth potential. Since they are in the business of providing Scorecard software, you would expect them to steer their own course using the Balanced Scorecard. Ask them to review Scorecard results with you. For reasons of confidentiality, they may have to disguise some of the actual numbers, but you should still glean lots of valuable information on the organization's future prospects.

- *References and experience.* By examining the profiles of past clients, you can determine the breadth and depth of experience the vendor has accumulated. While no two implementations are identical, it will be reassuring to know the software company has completed an installation in an organization with some similarity to yours, whether it is the same industry or a comparably sized organization. References are especially important. When discussing the vendor with other organizations that have been through the process, quiz them on the vendor's technical skills, consulting and training competence, and ability to complete the work on time and on budget.

- *Postsale service.* You will inevitably have many bumps in the road as you implement your new reporting software. Bugs hidden deep in the program will be detected, patches will be required, and thus a lifeline to the vendor is crucial. How much support are they willing to offer, and at what cost? Do you have a dedicated representative for your organization or are you at the mercy of their call center? These are just a couple of questions to ask. And never forget that software companies owe a lot to us, the users. New functions and features are very often the product of intense lobbying on behalf of function-starved users who sometimes end up knowing more about the product than the vendor. So don't be shy with your requests!

Exhibit 11.1 displays an easy-to-use template that will assist you in ranking various software choices. This example includes only the configuration and design elements; however, you can expand it to include all aspects of the decision. In this example, the configuration and design items have been weighted at 50 percent of the total decision. Specific elements comprising the category are listed in the first column, and the competing vendors are shown in the third, fourth, and fifth columns. Each vendor is accorded a score out of a possible 10 points demonstrating how well it satisfies each element of the decision. For example, vendors 1 and 3 each have short times to implement and are awarded 10 points. Vendor 2 has a slightly longer implementation horizon and is allotted 9 points. Once all evaluations have been made, the points are totaled for each vendor. In this example, vendor 3 has scored perfect 10s on all points and therefore receives the full 50 points available.

What's Next in Scorecard Applications?

It is exciting to imagine where the future of Balanced Scorecard applications may take us. It was not long ago that people began discussing the desirability of linking human capital modules to Scorecard software, and presto, there you have it. The latest generation of Scorecard tools can align specific investments in people to the execution of strategic business objectives, coordinate collaboration between employees and managers in monitoring the goals, and even support related personal development plans.

On the technical side, several industry players have banded together in an effort to develop extensible markup language (XML) standards for Balanced Scorecard applications. XML is a flexible way to create common information formats and share both that format and related data on the World Wide Web, intranets, and elsewhere. Applying XML standards to Scorecard applications would allow for seamless integration between those applications, thereby simplifying information sharing and analysis among previously disparate tools.

Another dramatic technical innovation is the use of wireless devices to keep the ultrabusy executive ever apprised of breaking Scorecard results.

Exhibit 11.1   Software Evaluation Template

Criteria	Weight	Vendor 1	Vendor 2	Vendor 3
Configuration and design	50%			
Time to implement		10	9	10
User interface/display		9	7	10
Various Scorecard designs		8	8	10
Number of measures		8	7	10
Strategies, objectives, measures,				
targets, and initiatives		9	9	10
Cause-and-effect relationships		5	6	10
Multiple locations		9	7	10
Cascading Scorecards		9	5	10
Descriptions and definitions		8	5	10
Assignment of owners		7	6	10
Various unit types		10	8	10
Appropriate timing		10	8	10
Relative weights		10	5	10
Aggregate disparate elements		9	5	10
Multiple comparatives		8	5	10
Graphic status indicators		10	5	10
Personal preferences		6	5	10
Intuitive menus		5	5	10
Helpful help screens		8	5	10
Levels of detail		9	5	10
Total		167	125	200
Total Points		41.75	31.25	50.00

Emerging wireless Internet technologies are allowing software vendors to market tools that will zap the latest return on equity (ROE) or customer satisfaction numbers right to your handheld cellular phone, pager, or personal digital assistant (e.g., Palm Pilot). For those who can't stand being out of the information loop for even a nanosecond, this could be the ultimate "must-have" tool.

Aside from the mind-boggling technological breakthroughs that seem to be occurring on practically a daily basis, the evolution of the Balanced Scorecard and related software tools may spawn another innovation—creative partnerships. In October 2000, Software vendor CorVu and Hilton Hotels Corporation announced an alliance to develop and market a global, web-based performance measurement solution for the hospitality industry. Look for more ventures of this nature in the days to come as Scorecard software users begin to realize they know almost as much about the software as the vendor, and way more about their industry! Putting two and two together, they suspect a market could exist for an industry-specific tool, and they are in a unique position to create it.

Technology Caveats

A recent study indicated that 5 percent of Scorecard users select a technology solution before designing their Balanced Scorecard, and about 29 percent design the Scorecard and choose technology at the same time.[2] There are serious dangers associated with these approaches. When technology is chosen before or concurrently with the design of the Scorecard, it can *become* the Balanced Scorecard in the minds of the user community. The term *Balanced Scorecard* is relegated to generic status and is considered a task performed by the latest software acquisition. Of course, it is actually the other way around—the software is just an enabler or facilitator of the enhanced use of the Scorecard. Choosing software prior to developing the Scorecard also presents a distinct possibility that valuable training resources will be diverted from Scorecard education to the acquisition of software skills. Some organizations go through very rote Scorecard education sessions, discussing only the four perspectives and the system's departure from traditional financial-based measurement systems. Very little training is conducted on the art of selecting strategic measures and developing strategy maps; instead, the focus is shifted to developing proficiency in using the new software. These organizations pay a heavy price when attempting to mold the Scorecard into their management processes. So little time and attention has been paid to the fundamentals of the Balanced Scorecard and how to create and effectively use it that they often find themselves having to start all over again when users demonstrate that they simply don't "get" how this new system works.

Many software packages are now offering "libraries" of performance measures that users may choose among to rapidly develop and begin reporting a Balanced Scorecard. The trade-off of speed for careful reflection frightens me. A great deal of value from the Balanced Scorecard is derived from the often difficult, but always rewarding, process of thoughtfully and faithfully translating a strategy into the objectives and measures necessary to see it successfully implemented. Further, strategy is about differences, doing different things, and combining different activities to drive a unique mix of value. The measures you choose must represent your organization's individuality. Sure, there may be some measures you share with many other companies, but the real differentiators are the new measures that you hypothesize as driving future results. Will a predefined library contain exactly the measures that describe who you are as an organization? Probably not.

Technology greatly facilitates accountability in an organization, but on the darker side provides the opportunity for abuse and inappropriate evaluations. Many users will shy away from an automated Scorecard solution because of the frightening glare cast by red lights that indicate sub-par performance! They fear, and probably with sufficient reason, that managers and supervisors will strike with great vengeance at the first hint of red emerging from their computer monitors. If the Scorecard solution you choose is to be accepted by your user community and actually used in day-to-day operations, your management team must be trained to treat deviations not as opportunities for severe punishment, but as signals for potential learning and growth. How frequently we read in the business literature that greatly admired and successful organizations don't treat failure as reason for punishment, but instead turn it around and look for ways to learn from mistakes and improve future prospects. Yet, many managers still seemed poised to attack at the first sign of problems. Use the results generated from the Balanced Scorecard and reported in your software as constant chances to learn about and question your strategy, not as opportunities to pass around the corporate dunce cap.

Developing Your Own Reporting System—Building Rather Than Buying

Automated Scorecard solutions offer a great many benefits and are becoming more sophisticated all the time, but they don't come cheap. Deploying a system across the entire organization can cost several hundred thousand dollars. Add the inevitable consulting, training, maintenance, and new release fees and you could soon be looking at seven digits. For smaller organizations, and larger companies attempting to control their spending, it is simply cost prohibitive, and they are forced to search for other methods of reporting Scorecard results. As noted earlier, the original Scorecard practitioners relied heavily on paper-based reports with some later graduating to intranet applications, and they achieved great results. So, fortunately, for the vast number of smaller enterprises out there, the procurement of Scorecard software is not a prerequisite of success.

With today's desktop publishing tools, even the humblest paper-based Scorecard report can resemble a glossy business publication. Text, graphics, and numbers may all be formatted to artistically represent the organization's business while also delivering valuable Scorecard results. Exhibit 11.2 displays the paper Balanced Scorecard developed by the Hydro Power Production Group of Nova Scotia Power, Inc. They used this simple, yet highly descriptive and creative, paper report as an education and communication tool for all employees. I especially like the many hydro references contained on the page—the dam, faucets, and water drops. Paper-based tools are especially well suited to reporting the highest-level orga-

Exhibit 11.2 Nova Scotia Power Inc's. Hydro Group Balanced Scorecard

Our Vision: To be the customer's choice in energy and services

Our Strategies:

Develop Employee Commitment — Build Customer Loyalty — Cut Costs — Build Business

Our Perspectives:

Employee Learning & Growth	Customer	Internal Processes	Financial

Employee Learning & Growth:
- Safety Loss Control
- Safety All Injury
- Employee Commitment
- Employee Development

Customer:
- Customer Loyalty Community
- Customer Loyalty Environment
- Customer Loyalty Sustainability

Internal Processes:
- Reliability
- Operating
- Manageable Costs
- Capital Approval
- SBUs

Financial:
- Return on Investment
- Growth

Our Success:

Legend
- Off Target
- Within 5% of Target
- On Target

271

nizational Balanced Scorecard. Many senior executives still cling to the comfort of paper over the vast unknown housed within their computer, so a paper Scorecard report may be enthusiastically received. However, when you attempt to take the Scorecard from the boardroom to the shop floor and cubicles of your organization, paper probably won't cut it. The potentially hundreds of performance measures scattered across dozens of Scorecards require a more virtual world to ensure that the raw information they contain can blossom into the fruit of organizational knowledge. To solve this dilemma, many organizations will turn to their intranet. At a relatively low cost, Scorecard results can be easily displayed and manipulated on the company's net, encouraging collaboration and group problem solving to take place without the attendant costs and responsibilities of a formal Scorecard software solution. Chapter Three introduced you to Scripps Health of San Diego, California. This five-hospital system decided very early in their Scorecard implementation to harness the power of the corporate intranet. With the help of a webmaster they created a site dedicated to the Balanced Scorecard. Clicking on any of the main page's color-coded performance measures takes interested employees to a screen dedicated to that particular measure. There they find a discussion of why the measure is important to Scripps, its purpose, and associated target. Including a data source on the page ensures that Scripps management is able to increase accountability for accurate and timely reporting of results. Perhaps of greatest interest to most users is the performance graph for the measure. It depicts performance over time and is accompanied by a commentary describing current and anticipated results. The informative site has been a great success, logging several thousand hits per quarter, and provides further evidence that high-priced software is not necessarily essential for sharing Scorecard results.

Before you decide to completely forgo any thoughts of investing in Scorecard software, remember that building your own solution is not without some significant issues. Perhaps the biggest barrier is data entry. With some programming, the vast majority of automated tools connect to current organizational systems, automatically drawing measure data and performing necessary calculations. Homegrown systems, however, require manual data feeding to churn out Scorecard reports. Should you cascade your Scorecard across the company, this data entry could go from a minor task to a major burden requiring hundreds of hours to complete. Plus you will have to design a system to gather the data and will undoubtedly encounter resistance from those unwilling or seemingly unable to supply the data for their measures. Finally, manual data entry brings with it the attendant risk of inaccurate data being entered into the system. Quality control will consume additional time and energy.

Ultimately, the decision to automate or not will depend on a number of factors. Your organization's readiness to implement and administer the system, the amount of resources you are willing to commit, sophistication of your Scorecard, and, of course, the cost are all elements of the decision.

THE NEW MANAGEMENT MEETING

The vast majority of organizations produce far more reports than fast-paced executives and managers could ever hope to find the time to read. Of course, it is not just a function of time, but also of content. A common scenario played out in companies everywhere is the production of reports that have been produced for years, despite the fact that the so-called information they contain is no longer relevant given new competitors, strategies, and value propositions. I recall my days as a Financial Analyst at a large manufacturing organization. I spent about four days a month producing two mammoth reports that were widely distributed to the management team. My accompanying cover letter always concluded with the line, "If you have any questions, please call me." My phone never rang. At this organization, as is the case in most, no one questioned why the reports should exist. It was easier to simply give them a cursory glance and toss in the recycling bin. So it is not surprising that a common protest during Scorecard implementations is the possibility of this tool's adding yet another layer to an already complex management reporting system.

The arrival of the Balanced Scorecard signals the perfect opportunity to conduct a thorough analysis of the reports currently produced at your organization. Those that do not complement the Scorecard, adding another dimension to your description of strategy, should be eliminated. Using the Balanced Scorecard, you can also make a clean break from the traditional management meeting with its dependence on financial results and budget variances. The Scorecard should be used to herald a new paradigm, one in which strategy drives the meeting agenda, not financial results. An added bonus is that meeting frequency and duration can actually decrease as a result of these radical but strategic changes. With the Scorecard in place, strategic feedback is continuous. This is especially the case if the organization is employing an automated solution. All employees have a line of sight from singular action to overall goals and make decisions accordingly. Rather than conducting lengthy meetings on a monthly basis, managers might convene quarterly and examine current Scorecard results in light of strategy. The focus shifts from a blaming culture attempting to ferret out who is responsible for the decline in revenue or gross profit to a collaborative environment in which managers work together to critically examine the relationships among measures and learn from the collective results that have been achieved.

The new management meeting should be attended by anyone who has accountability for the results of a performance measure. At the highest level of the organization, every measure should be assigned an executive as owner. However, there may be others in the organization with a deep and significant impact on results. In the spirit of learning, collaboration, and team problem solving championed by the Scorecard, those individuals should also be in attendance. The agenda will focus primarily on results of Scorecard performance measures and discussing the impact of those results on the hypothesis reflected in the strategy. Working from the top (financial) down will help facilitate the cause-and-effect discussion that follows. Participants can discuss and debate whether results confirm the strategy, whether changes are necessary, and the impact of strategic initiatives on outcomes. Meetings of this nature should not be confined to the executive boardroom. Every business unit, department, and work group should have a Balanced Scorecard and use it as the focus of review meetings. At lower levels of the company, these meetings once again provide an opportunity to underscore the critical importance of the Scorecard in meeting strategic objectives, and how the tool can be used to help all groups define their unique contributions.

SUMMARY

As the use of the Balanced Scorecard has evolved from a measurement system to a strategic management system and communication tool, many organizations have looked to technological solutions in an effort to take advantage of advanced Scorecard techniques. Software packages provide advanced analytic and decision support tools, allow for wide dissemination of strategic information, and encourage innovation and team problem solving. Choosing a software provider can prove to be one of the most difficult tasks in the entire Scorecard implementation. Elements of the decision include design and configuration issues, reporting and analysis tools, technical considerations, maintenance and security, and vendor assessments. The latest tools offer human capital modules and the ability to broadcast Scorecard results using wireless applications.

Despite the many advantages to be gained from a technology solution, it must never take the place of the collaborative effort necessary to craft a Balanced Scorecard describing your specific strategy. Technology is an enabler of the Scorecard, expanding its use and creating unlimited opportunities for knowledge sharing and strategic breakthroughs.

With the help of desktop publishing tools, those organizations not wishing to pursue a software solution have the capability of creating polished reports distilling Scorecard information to the entire organization. As a next step, many will use their organization's intranet as a means of communicating Scorecard results and facilitating information sharing and learning.

The Balanced Scorecard should not contribute to an organization's management reporting burden. In fact, the reporting regimen should be rationalized in light of the Scorecard's presence. Existing reports must be placed under the microscope of strategy to determine whether they own a rightful place in the company's reporting space. The new Scorecard reports form the basis for innovative management meetings that revolve around strategic learning gleaned from Balanced Scorecard results. Managers from across the organization use the Scorecard as the organizing platform for thought-provoking meetings in which measure results are assessed in light of their contribution to the company's ongoing efforts to implement its strategy.

NOTES

1. Performance Measurement Survey by the American Institute of Certified Public Accountants and Lawrence S. Maisel, 2001.
2. Laura M. Downing, "The Global BSC Community: A Special Report on Implementation Experiences from Scorecard Users Worldwide," presented at the Balanced Scorecard North American Summit, New Orleans, September 2000.

CHAPTER 12

Maintaining the Balanced Scorecard

Roadmap for Chapter Twelve   In an earlier chapter I mentioned that my wife and I were in the middle of a move. Well, we've settled comfortably into our new house now and recently had our backyard landscaped. Nothing extravagant, mostly lawn with some shrubs and trees. Oh, but that lawn—I can't help staring at that grass for at least a few moments every day. It's just so pristine, vibrantly green, and healthy looking. But can you imagine what that same perfect lawn would look like after a few weeks with no mowing, watering, or fertilizer? Now consider the condition of your freshly minted Balanced Scorecard without a similar level of ongoing maintenance. To reach its full potential as an integrated strategic management system, the Scorecard must be carefully maintained and nurtured. This chapter will explore the "care and feeding" of your new performance management system.

The adoption of business rules, processes, and procedures will assist the Scorecard in making the transition from measurement system to management tool. Among a host of considerations, organizations must evaluate how the Scorecard fits into long-term strategic planning, how and when new Scorecards will be developed, under what circumstances measure changes will be considered, and how it will ultimately link to management processes like budgeting and compensation. Gathering and reporting data is also central to the Scorecard, and effective techniques must be created to ensure that this process is seen as beneficial and not burdensome. Once organizations decide what must be done to make the Scorecard a regular part of ongoing operations, they must then decide who will do what and where the Scorecard function will ultimately reside. The chapter outlines key Scorecard roles and provides guidelines to help you determine who should own the Balanced Scorecard.

THE BALANCED SCORECARD IS NEVER "COMPLETE"

Renowned leadership expert John Kotter has written extensively on the field of organizational change and what it takes to sustain a major change initiative. In his book *Leading Change*, he says, *"Major change often takes a long time, especially in big organizations. Many forces can stall the process far short of the finish line: turnover of key change agents, sheer exhaustion on the part of leaders, or bad luck."*[1] The Balanced Scorecard is not a metrics project, a technology project, or a human resources program. More than anything else, the Balanced Scorecard represents a major change initiative and as such can fall prey to any of the issues suggested by Kotter. Key change agents are critical to the success of any effort but are absolutely vital to the hopes of institutionalizing the methods of the Balanced Scorecard. Without a person (or team) leading the refinement and continued development of the Scorecard system, it can easily be derailed, with managers slipping comfortably back into their former practices. Change agents will be discussed further in the "Key Roles" section of the chapter. Executives, with many important initiatives on their plates, can become overwhelmed with the tides of change. The Balanced Scorecard could pay the price of their fatigue through a lack of attention and modeling necessary to set the proper tone throughout the organization. And yes, even bad luck can victimize Scorecard efforts. Software that simply will not work as guaranteed and inexperienced consultants who promise more than they can deliver are just a couple of examples of unfortunate circumstances that may conspire to sabotage your carefully planned efforts. Perhaps the single biggest Scorecard pitfall to be avoided, however, is lack of maintenance. The Scorecard, like any major change, must be constantly nurtured for a significant period before it takes root within the culture and ongoing management practices of the organization.

Beyond sustaining momentum, the Balanced Scorecard is never really complete because your business is never really complete. Is there ever a point at which you can stop and say, "Well this is it, we've done it all, there's nothing left to conquer, looks like smooth sailing ahead." No, because the environment in which you operate is constantly changing. New competitors enter the marketplace rapidly and from all over the globe, the wide and swift availability of knowledge is causing customers to be more demanding than ever, and employees insist on satisfying and challenging roles that make a real contribution to success while simultaneously providing quality of life. All of these forces will affect your Balanced Scorecard, but fortunately this tool is not only capable of flexibility, but in fact that could be its chief identifying characteristic. As conditions change, current strategies will be severely tested, and new strategies may be called into action. Strong relationships thought to exist among measures may prove specious and necessitate the adoption of new indicators. The Scorecard is malleable enough to handle such changes and will serve as a valuable tool while you navigate the changing course that is your business. The question is, how do we ensure that the Scorecard remains a viable tool and is fully entrenched in the management system of your organization so that it can be looked to as a guiding and trusted compass during periods of change? Maintenance, nurturing, and building on the current Scorecard base provides the answer. This care and feeding is comprised of establishing business rules and processes for effective Scorecarding operations, putting the right people in place to further the transition to this new method of management, and finding a home for the Balanced Scorecard. Each of these items will be examined in this chapter. This is critical work, as Kotter reminds us: *"Whenever you let up before the job is done, critical momentum can be lost and regression may follow."*[2]

MAINTAINING THE BALANCED SCORECARD

Establishing Balanced Scorecard Policies, Procedures, and Processes

The title of this section reminds me of the old command and control days of business that featured a heavy emphasis on rules and process controls to ensure strict adherence to steadfast procedures. Of course, the Scorecard is more representative of the new business paradigm characterized by open information sharing, collaboration, empowerment, and team problem solving. Unfortunately, simply developing a Scorecard will not magically transform your organization into a paragon of enlightened management practice. To become part of everyday life in the organization, your Scorecard will require some business rules, processes, and procedures to ensure smooth functioning, especially in the early stages of implementation. Specific areas to address once your Scorecard system is up and running include:

- *Long-range strategic planning.* What is the role of the Balanced Scorecard in the organization's long-term strategic planning efforts? It should be at the forefront of strategic planning; however, after initial development of a Scorecard, some organizations will revert back to their previous methods. Work with your strategic planning team to define the Scorecard's role in the process on a go-forward basis, assuring it will remain the key tool in effective execution of strategy.

- *Annual Scorecard development.* The Balanced Scorecard is designed to be a flexible and dynamic tool, adjusting to the changes occurring in your business. At least annually, your Balanced Scorecard should be tweaked to describe the continuing saga of your strategy. Do not wait until the last minute to put together a schedule, surprising already overworked managers around the firm. Compose a timeline early in the process giving everyone involved ample time to formulate a Balanced Scorecard that thoroughly displays how they contribute to overall success.

- *Reporting dates.* The wide distribution of Scorecard production dates is critical. There is a strong possibility that at least some of your Scorecard data will not come directly from source systems. That data will need to be collected and entered into your reporting system, whether it is automated or not. Those responsible for providing data must be aware of the timelines associated with reporting and the importance of timely and accurate data submission. Your executive team will be relying on the data, so don't be shy about including that veiled threat in any correspondence you produce when on the hunt for data.

- *Terminology.* Does the word *objective* have the same meaning for an executive, a midlevel manager, and a customer service representative? If you want to use the Scorecard to create a new language of measurement, it should. You will have to grapple with terminology issues earlier in your implementation, however. Creatures of habit that we are, some folks may tend to migrate back to previous definitions.

- *Roles and responsibilities.* Determine who is accountable for administering the Scorecard system in the organization and the accompanying responsibilities. This will be discussed in greater depth in the "Key Roles" section of the Chapter.

- *Thresholds of performance.* When using the Scorecard as a measurement system, organizations compare actual performance against a predetermined benchmark. That comparative may be a budget amount, last year's number, a best-in-class number, or a stretch target. Regardless of the comparative you choose, the relative ranges of performance must be established. Perhaps "green" performance is anything meeting or exceeding the target. "Yellow" may represent an actual amount within 10 percent of the target, and "red" could mean anything greater than a 10 percent variance. Performance thresholds are bound to stir a little controversy. Some will consider them too strict, while others counter that they are slack and do not promote breakthrough action. My recommendation is to err on the conservative side at least in the first year. Give people the opportunity to become accustomed to this new way of managing before imposing strict thresholds demanding exemplary performance.

- *Changing objectives, measures, and targets.* Under what circumstances will you allow a midyear change in any of these performance indicators? Targets are especially vulnerable since many organizations lack a strong target-setting competence, and initial attempts are either too difficult to achieve or too easy. Only in clear cases of a misguided objective, measure, or target should changes be permitted. Perhaps the calculation of a measure is leading to dysfunctional decision making or the target's perceived difficulty is demotivating to employees. In these situations, a change may be warranted. This topic will be examined in greater detail when we discuss "Updating the Scorecard's Core Elements" a little later in the chapter.

- *Timetable for Scorecard linkages to management processes.* You may or may not wish to cascade the Scorecard and link it to budgeting and compensation during the first year of your implementation. At the very least, you should have a plan for future development. Consider it the Balanced Scorecard "master plan" describing where you expect to take the Scorecard in the future and the requirements to make that happen. Even if linkages are not occurring during year one, the dialogue to facilitate future transformation should be taking place.

Gathering Data for the Balanced Scorecard

Gathering and entering data into your Scorecard reporting system can often present unique challenges. The first issue you face is whether or not the data is even available. One of the strongest benefits of the Scorecard is its ability to highlight the "missing measures" that drive future results. Identifying these indicators is one thing, gathering the supporting data is another. You may not have the systems or tools in place to harvest the data at the outset of your implementation. In fact, estimates vary but you can probably expect to be missing between 20 and 30 percent of your data as you begin to report results. This absent data should not dictate any delay in reporting the Scorecard. Focus on the measures you do have and spend the necessary time and effort to develop processes for acquiring outstanding data.

Have you ever considered a career in law enforcement? I ask because when attempting to have measure owners submit their Scorecard data you may feel like the "Balanced Scorecard Police." Like the highway patrol officer pulling over a contrite speeder, you will hear every excuse in the book. "The source reports haven't been produced yet," "I'm waiting for one more number from accounting," "I was on vacation last week and am still catching up!" Some are legitimate and may signal that a redesign of processes is necessary, while others are downright outrageous, "Aliens studying twenty-first century earthly organizational practices beamed down and stole it." Cajoling, persuading, and even threatening will only go so far. The only reliable method of ensuring a smooth data-gathering process is to make it as painless and simple as possible for those affected. Even if you are using a relatively low-tech reporting solution, you can build automated links into the gathering process, making it easier for those involved to send their much-needed data. Designing and distributing a customized measure template will go a long way toward assuring compliance among data owners. Exhibit 12.1 is a data collection form you can customize for your performance

Exhibit 12.1 Balanced Scorecard Data Collection Form

Measure Owner: K. Tobin
Data Owner: S. Chezenko

| Measure Name | Perspective | Description | Actual Results | | | Commentary |
			July	Aug	Sept	
Number of calls received	Customer	Total number of calls logged in the call center during the month	3,000	3,500	3,750	Call volume is steadily increasing as anticipated. Advanced training and the addition of one staff person should enable us to handle up to 5,000 calls per month by year end.
Number of one-call resolutions	Customer	Number of customers for which all issues were resolved during the first call	50	60	45	Result is deceiving. A lower number of one-call resolutions was logged during September; however, this is a result of fewer complaints being registered by callers.

measures. Develop a form for each owner of Balanced Scorecard measures, and distribute them electronically for completion or further distribution to a data owner. If you don't have an e-mail system, you can always print the forms and distribute them using the interoffice mail or via fax. In this example, data is requested for the month of September; however, previous submissions are also displayed to provide relevant background and facilitate a performance commentary. Once completed, the form should be sent by e-mail back to the Balanced Scorecard system administrator, who will enter the data into the Scorecard reporting tool. Should you choose an automated solution to report Scorecard results, you may be able to import data directly from the form into the software, and depending on the functionality offered by the program you may even have the capability to directly import the narrative supplied in the commentary columns. Using this simple form and taking advantage of your e-mail system for distribution greatly reduces any burden on measure owners. They simply open the e-mail attachment, fill in their performance information, and send the form back. Not only does the process make it easier for those responsible to supply data, but Scorecard administrators will also appreciate the existence of just one form of template. Rather than attempting to translate data scribbled on the back of business cards, or read barely decipherable faxes, the administrator can easily transfer data from a common form to the reporting tool.

Updating the Scorecard's Core Elements—Objectives, Measures, and Targets

As previously discussed, the Balanced Scorecard is designed to be a dynamic tool, flexible and capable of change as necessitated by business conditions. Over time, you can expect a number of changes to take place within the realm of your objectives, measures, and targets. At the far end of the possibility spectrum you may decide to abandon a strategy you have pursued based on Scorecard results that disclaim much of your hypothesis. In that extreme case you would likely develop a new strategy for your organization and likewise select new and corresponding objectives, measures, and targets that acted as direct translations of the updated strategy. Even with today's shorter strategic shelf lives, you would not expect to make wholesale changes to objectives, measures, and targets each and every year. However, it is a very good idea to critically examine the Scorecard at least annually and determine if its core elements are still appropriate in telling an accurate strategic story. Results of a best practices benchmarking study suggest a majority of Scorecard practitioners do just that. In the study 62 percent of participants updated their Balanced Scorecards annually. Fifteen percent updated every six months, while 23 percent updated every three months.[3] Make the annual Scorecard review process part of the normal planning cycle that occurs at most companies. Organizations engage in strategic planning, budgeting, and business planning every year. The Scorecard can be slotted in with these activities and take its rightful place as a key management process.

Expect many subtle changes to be made with objectives and measures as experience is gained using the Balanced Scorecard system. Objectives may be reworded to more accurately represent their core purpose or to clarify potentially confusing terminology. Similarly, measures could be subject to changes in the method of calculation to better capture the true essence of the event under investigation, or the description may be enhanced to improve employee understanding of operational and strategic significance. You may also change the frequency with which you collect performance data. For example, you may have attempted to track employee satisfaction monthly, but the logistics of gathering the data simply proved too challenging. In that case, you would not abandon this important indicator, rather you would simply change the reporting period to something more amenable to measurement. Any change in a measure has a potential impact on the corresponding target. This is especially the case should you make changes to formulas or calculations. Additionally, targets may change to reflect more realistic goals or conversely, something more challenging.

Updating your performance objectives, measures, and targets is yet another way to tap into the collective knowledge of your organization. Be sure to involve as many employees as possible to ensure any changes reflect organizationwide interests. Surveying employees is an excellent method of gathering their feedback on Scorecard use and potential improvements. Exhibit 12.2 displays a 10-question survey that can be administered to employees at least annually to ensure the critical feedback and knowledge they possess is collected. Employees should answer the survey questions with their specific group or department in mind. The senior executive team would assess the high-level organizational Scorecard. In addition to asking questions, the survey also includes a space for employee comments and recommendations for Scorecard improvements. In this example, the surveyed employee gives her group's Scorecard 38 out of a possible 50 points. Any total over 35 would be considered positive; however, the composition of the scores provides as much insight as the aggregate. In this case, for example, the Scorecard appears to be working very well in its intended capacity of informing employees about organizational strategy and providing a line of sight. It also appears this group reviews their results on a regular basis and uses the information to identify future improvement initiatives. However, it is also clear this employee is not happy with the reporting tool being used, the cause-and-effect linkages are not clear and, as evidenced by her comments, Scorecard results are not stimulating organizationwide discussions. This input is invaluable as managers and employees look to develop future iterations of their Scorecard. Customers and suppliers also have a stake in

Exhibit 12.2   Balanced Scorecard Employee Survey

Question	Score
Use of the Balanced Scorecard in my group has helped increase my knowledge of the organization's strategy.	5
Our group's Balanced Scorecard measures clearly demonstrate how we contribute to the achievement of overall organizational goals.	5
Our measures represent an appropriate balance among the four Balanced Scorecard perspectives.	4
Our measures are linked in a series of cause-and-effect relationships.	3
My input was sought during the development of our group's Balanced Scorecard.	4
In our group we review Balanced Scorecard results on a regular basis.	4
The reporting tool we use is efficient.	3
Managers and employees are held accountable for achieving Balanced Scorecard results.	4
Analyzing Balanced Scorecard results allows our group to identify potential improvement initiatives.	4
Discussing Balanced Scorecard results with colleagues has increased my knowledge of their function(s).	2
Total Score	**38**

Additional Comments:

1 would like to know more about the use of the Scorecard in other groups within the company. How are results reported, and can those results be shared with all employees?

your performance and would probably be flattered and impressed should you consult them regarding possible updates to the Scorecard.

As stated in Chapter Six, the caveat regarding such changes is this—don't alter your measures simply because you don't like the current crop, or the results are not what you expected. The Balanced Scorecard is about learning—learning about your strategy, learning about the assumptions you have made to win in your marketplace, and learning about the value proposition you have put forth. Sometimes you won't necessarily enjoy what your measures are telling you, but your challenge is to use these deviations from plan as opportunities for learning, not simply as defects in need of remedy.

Key Balanced Scorecard Roles

Chapter Three introduced the critical roles necessary to make the Balanced Scorecard implementation a success. Let's revisit a number of those roles within a new context—making the Scorecard an ongoing success to maximize your performance and maintain results.

The theme running through this chapter is simple—Balanced Scorecards are not necessarily self-sustaining. Development and progress must be constantly nurtured in order for meaningful results to be derived. The critical player in the Scorecard's ongoing development is the *Balanced Scorecard champion* or *team leader*. Someone in the organization must be equated with the Balanced Scorecard and seen as both its ambassador and thought leader. Everything we have reviewed thus far in this chapter will require leadership. Steering the course of discussions around policies and procedures, evaluating possible measure changes, and providing insight on data acquisition strategies all need a strong leader. The Scorecard champion is that someone. With a unique mix of communication and leadership skills, the champion is the recognized Scorecard subject matter expert, coaching leaders and managers alike on Scorecard concepts and how the tool can best be utilized to achieve breakthrough results. But it is more than guiding discussions and setting policies, it is the five-minute conversations in the hallway about last month's Scorecard results, or the distribution of an article about the latest Scorecard techniques, or the presentation to a group of administrative assistants who previously felt out of the "Scorecard loop" that really make the difference. In a word, it is communication. The champion artfully communicates how the Scorecard is making a difference now and can forge new ground in the future through innovative uses as a strategic management system. Unilever is an organization recognizing the importance of this position. Colin Sharp, Strategy into Action project manager, notes, *"We've created a position to implement the [Scorecard] process and support it through its early years. This has been a critical role."*[4] The most logical candidate for the role is the individual filling the position during your initial implementation. This person will have already carved inroads in the credibility roadways of the organization and be seen as "Mr. or Ms. Balanced Scorecard." Asking the person to assume the role full-time and give up, or at least scale back, their former responsibilities probably will not require extensive coaxing. I have been part of a number of implementations during which the Scorecard champion so enjoyed the role they asked to make the position a permanent move. I am absolutely convinced the assignment of a full-time Balanced Scorecard champion is a key differentiator of successful Balanced Scorecard implementations. The knowledge, continuity, and constant communication offered by the position cannot be beaten.

The other truly indispensable Scorecard role is that of *executive sponsor*. Everything chronicled in Chapter Three regarding this role applies on an ongoing basis as well. The Sponsor provides new information on strategy and plans, maintains constant communication with other members of the senior team, and continues to supply enthusiastic support for the Balanced Scorecard. All senior executives must share an ownership interest in the Balanced Scorecard if it is to reach its full potential. The executive sponsor works to make this happen by constantly engaging other members of the senior team in dialogue addressing the benefits and future direction of the Scorecard. As the Scorecard program grows and matures, the executive sponsor is counted on to share your enlightened management concepts with colleagues and networks of other executives. Depending on where responsibility for the Scorecard ultimately resides in the organization (see "Who Owns the Balanced Scorecard" below), it would be convenient and beneficial to have the Scorecard champion report directly to the executive sponsor. The clear line of communication resulting from this relationship would ensure the latest Scorecard developments are funneled to the executive suite where swift action can be taken to leverage opportunities and remove obstacles.

Balanced Scorecard *team members* were integral in the original development of the Balanced Scorecard, but the role of this group will change as the Scorecard develops. Rather than hands-on Scorecard building, the task of the team evolves to information and best-practice sharing. Team members are convened on a regular basis and use the opportunity to review what the Scorecard has meant in their units or groups. Valuable input is supplied in the form of tips, effective Scorecard processes, and issue resolution strategies. The team should also be used as a proving ground for your latest Scorecard ideas. When linking the Scorecard to budgeting or compensation, for example, team members are able to provide a unique perspective on what will be necessary to make the transition a success in their business unit or group. Some organizations will migrate from a Balanced Scorecard team to a steering committee comprised of the champion, executive sponsor, other senior executives, and certain members of the original team. This group carries a more formal mandate of establishing Scorecard policies and charting future development.

A role we did not consider when developing the Balanced Scorecard, but which is crucial to long-term success, is that of the *system administrator.* This term is normally associated with the individual administering a packaged software solution but may also apply if you develop your own reporting solution. Depending on the sophistication of your reporting tools the Balanced Scorecard champion may be able to competently fill this role. However, should you purchase an automated solution an administrator will most likely be required. The system administrator holds the ultimate responsibility of scheduling results reporting, ensuring Scorecard data is gathered on a timely basis and entered accurately into the tool. They also make changes to Scorecard elements (objectives, measures, and targets), provide technical support to users, upgrade to new versions of software, and supply training. Liaising closely with the Balanced Scorecard champion and executive sponsor, the administrator plays an important part in defining the Scorecard's role in management review sessions. Whether it is transparencies displayed on an overhead projector or the latest Scorecard software, the technology that supports Scorecard reviews must function properly to bolster credibility for the new process. Most commercially available software packages will provide material spelling out in detail the requirements of a system administrator.

Who Owns the Balanced Scorecard?

We have considered the roles necessary to ensure the Scorecard is embedded in the management systems of the organization; now we must find a home for the Scorecard function, and more specifically the champion and system administrator. Team members will continue reporting to their business unit head, and the executive sponsor remains in her senior management position, but to whom will the champion and system administrator report? Before we answer that question, let's consider why it is in fact critical to find a home for the Scorecard function. At this point in the process the Balanced Scorecard may still be viewed as a "project" and not an ongoing way of managing the business. Without a solid foundation and clear ownership, it will be very difficult to erase this perception and it may become solidified in the minds of employees. Of course, the word *project* connotes an image of something generally temporary in nature that over time, and with significant effort, is achieved or considered complete. But as we have seen the Balanced Scorecard is never really complete since it must flow with the changing tides of your business, helping steer the course as conditions inevitably change. If the Scorecard is thought of as complete, the desire and incentive to report results and use them in making business decisions is greatly reduced, and over time serious gaps may develop in measurement and reporting. In contrast, providing the Scorecard with a functional home changes the paradigm and shifts the Scorecard to a permanent, legitimate business operation on its way to becoming ingrained in the fabric of everyday organizational life.

The leading candidate in the race for Scorecard custodial rights is the finance function. In one recent study, participants were asked which functional area is responsible for managing their company's performance measurement system. Sixty-seven percent replied Finance.[5] My experience echoes this finding. The vast majority of Scorecard implementations on which I have been engaged concluded with the responsibility for ownership and ongoing development resting with finance. With its place at the center of the organization's information processing and distribution function, finance may have always represented a legitimate choice for Scorecard ownership.

Recent developments in the field have made their bid for Scorecard owner-ship even stronger. *"The information age calls for Finance to play a new role—architect of the enterprise . . . The traditional focus on control and compliance activi-ties must be replaced by strategic, economic, tactical, and performance measurement leadership . . . Why Finance? Finance has the highest level of access to information, strategy, economic targets, and internal process activities."*[6] It's clear that finance professionals have begun embracing new roles in the organization, shed-ding the burdensome, and often non–value-added, corporate policeman persona in favor of a powerful and dynamic new look that places strategy and business partnership at its core. The Balanced Scorecard, with its holis-tic and collaborative nature, fits like a glove in this new finance paradigm.

Before you rush down the hall and place the "Balanced Scorecard Owner" sash over the shoulder of your finance leader, remember that every organi-zation and every Balanced Scorecard implementation are unique. Finance may be a great home for the Scorecard in many organizations, but your finance function may still be mired in the old control and compliance frame-work and have yet to experience the benefits occurring from developing business partnership relationships. If that's the case you will probably find the people intensive, knowledge sharing, collaborative features of the Scorecard aren't a great fit for your finance function. Perhaps the strategic planning or human resources function fits the bill in your organization. If so, place Scorecard responsibilities there. The bottom line (pardon the fi-nance function pun) is this: you're looking for a home in which the execu-tive leader believes in the management theory captured by the Scorecard and is willing to actively support, develop, refine, and evangelize the tool. The right person could be in human resources, marketing, manufacturing, strategic planning, or finance. As always, it is the characteristics of the leader, not the functional title, that really matter.

SUMMARY

By viewing the Balanced Scorecard as a one-time metrics or systems project some organizations fail to take advantage of the many attributes the system has to offer as a strategic management system. Through proper guidance and maintenance, the Scorecard will become the cornerstone of the organization's management system. Making this transition requires the con-sideration of how a number of Scorecard-related tasks will fit into current and anticipated management models. These include:

- The Scorecard's role in long-range strategic planning
- Annual Scorecard development
- Reporting dates
- Terminology

- Roles and responsibilities for Scorecard development
- Thresholds of performance
- Changing Scorecard elements
- Linking the Scorecard to management processes

Strategies for effectively and efficiently collecting and loading performance data into a Scorecard reporting tool must be developed if the tool is to be accepted and used by employees. Whether or not an automated Scorecard solution is pursued, the data gathering process is enhanced by the use of customized collection templates.

A majority of Scorecard practitioners update their Scorecard on an annual basis. As conditions change and Scorecard learning intensifies, many companies will make changes to performance objectives, measures, and targets. The adjustments could reflect a change in strategic direction, or a simple clarification to an otherwise confusing indicator.

All the key players involved in the initial design and development of the Balanced Scorecard have a role to play in its ongoing evolution. The Balanced Scorecard champion's role takes on expanded prominence as this individual uses communication skills and Scorecard knowledge to coach and train executives, managers, and employees alike on the benefits to be derived from an even greater reliance on the Balanced Scorecard methodology. A new function emerges as the Scorecard grows—the system administrator. This individual controls the vital function of ensuring timely and accurate reporting of Scorecard results.

The finance function is the predominant home of the Balanced Scorecard in most organizations. As the purveyors of company information and with their unique view into strategy, processes, and economic events, this function often makes a very logical choice. However, the ultimate test for Scorecard ownership is an executive willing to actively use, support, and help shape the future direction of the Scorecard as a key strategy execution tool of the organization.

NOTES

1. John Kotter, *Leading Change* (Boston, MA: Harvard Business School Press, 1996).
2. Ibid., p. 133.
3. Best Practices Benchmarking Report, *Developing the Balanced Scorecard* (Chapel Hill, NC: Best Practices, LLC, 1999).
4. Charles Birch, "Balancing Act," *Australian Accountant*, March 2001, 50.
5. Performance Measurement Survey by the American Institute of Certified Public Accountants and Lawrence S. Maisel, 2001.
6. Mark J. Morgan, "A New Role For Finance, Architect of the Enterprise in the Information Age," *Strategic Finance*, August 2001.

PART FIVE

Balanced Scorecards in the Public and Not-for-Profit Sectors and Concluding Thoughts on Scorecard Success

CHAPTER 13

Balanced Scorecards in the Public and Not-for-Profit Sectors

Roadmap for Chapter Thirteen Employees of public-sector and not-for-profit organizations may be concerned that only one chapter of this entire book is devoted to their worlds. The good news is that almost everything covered in the book to this point is applicable to both a public-sector and a not-for-profit environment, with some modifications. This chapter will discuss those required modifications and outline the particular challenges awaiting Scorecard developers in government and not-for-profit organizations.

How do you feel about your elected representatives? Your first reaction may not be entirely positive, but it is probably a good deal rosier than the views of writer and editor H.L. Mencken who once said, *"I believe that all government is evil, and that trying to improve it is largely a waste of time."* Don't hold anything back, Henry! The fact is government *can* be improved, and tools like the Balanced Scorecard are key weapons in the arsenal of change. The chapter begins with a review of performance measurement initiatives in the public sector that have led to the emergence of the Balanced Scorecard as a viable governmental improvement tool.

Neither public-sector nor not-for-profit organizations look to financial rewards as their ultimate show of success. Instead, they seek to achieve lofty missions aimed at improving society. As mission-focused organizations, they must change the architecture of the Balanced Scorecard, elevating the role of the mission and customers, and reducing the influence of financial indicators. We will examine how the Scorecard geography differs for public-sector and not-for-profit applications.

The Balanced Scorecard has found a home in many not-for-profit and government agencies, but the task has not always been easy. A number of implementation challenges await managers looking to institute a Scorecard solution. The chapter reviews several issues in detail and offers advice on overcoming many of the associated pitfalls. A growing number of agencies have overcome the difficulties of developing a Scorecard in the public and not-for-profit sectors and are using the tool to align all employees with the mission. We will chronicle one such Balanced Scorecard pioneer and share the secrets of their success.

PUBLIC-SECTOR USE OF THE BALANCED SCORECARD

Performance Measurement in the Public Sector

Do you remember much about 1993? Here are some pop culture and news flashbacks to jog your memory. At the box office, *Jurassic Park* clawed its way to the top en route to raking in over $350 million worldwide. A future movie smash, *The Bridges of Madison County*, was the number one book of the year. Whitney Houston controlled the pop charts, winning Grammys for album of the year (*Bodyguard* soundtrack) and record of the year (*I Will Always Love You*). In sports, Michael Jordan led the Chicago Bulls to a 4–2 series win over the Phoenix Suns. On the real news front, 80 people died in the Davidian compound fire in Waco, Texas; the Menendez brothers were about to live their 15 minutes of fame as a result of their highly publicized murder trial; and, finally, William Jefferson Clinton became the 42nd president of the United States.

It is that last bit of news that is of concern to us. President Clinton wasted little time shaking things up in the federal government. On August 3 of that year he signed into law the Government Performance and Results Act (GPRA). The act required that federally funded agencies develop and implement an accountability system based on performance measurement, including setting goals and objectives and measuring progress toward achieving them. But more than that, it sought to effect a fundamental transformation in the way government was managed by placing greater emphasis on what was being accomplished as opposed to what was being spent. As radical a departure as this seemed to represent, it was not without precedent. Back in the 1960s the Program Planning and Budgeting System (PPBS) was introduced to the government as an extension of a successful Department of Defense application. Zero-based budgeting and management by objectives (MBO) replaced PPBS as the programs de jour of the 1970s, and the 1980s saw the rise of productivity improvement and quality management. In 1988, a President's Quality Award was established. The new program was closely aligned with the Malcolm Baldrige National Quality Award and focused on customer-driven quality, continuous improvement and learning, and employee participation and development, among a host of criteria. Once Mr. Clinton assumed control of the oval office in 1993, he was anxious to leverage the new focus on quality with the performance improvement ethic he championed during his tenure as Arkansas governor in the 1980s. In March 1993, he appointed Vice President Al Gore to head a six-month study on what had to be done to further improve government performance. "Creating a Government That Works Better and Costs Less" was the resulting report, which eventually led to the development of the "National Partnership for Reinventing Government." All of which leads us back to August 1993 and the signing of the GPRA. Under the new act, all federal agencies are required to develop mission statements, overall outcome-related goals, internal performance goals and objectives, and measures to be used to evaluate progress toward those goals and objectives.[1]

The goals and ideals embodied in the GPRA are noble and make great sense, but movements of the past had similar objectives and soon faded from sight. The question is: Will the GPRA go the way of previous governmental attempts at results-oriented operations? Several pieces of evidence suggest things are different this time. A critical difference between the GPRA and earlier ancestors is the fact that it is a *law*, a creation of both the president and Congress. Unlike presidential directives that tend to begin and end with the term of the current president, the GPRA is meant to endure. In fact, current President George W. Bush has already sent signals that his administration will focus on making government "results-oriented." In April 2001, the Bush administration announced that agencies will be required to submit performance-based budgets for selected programs during the fiscal 2003 budget cycle. This is the first time agencies have been forced to tie spending to performance goals. Another pillar of GPRA and performance measurement strength is the changing tide of public funding. For many decades funding was stable or even growing, but today budgets are shrinking and programs must clearly display the value they create. With the advent of mass communication, today's citizenry is better informed than at any other point in history. Knowledge possessed by constituents equates to a demand of accountability on the part of government. More than ever, people want to know how their hard-earned dollars are being spent and whether the allocation of funds is helping to promote wide-ranging social benefits. Perhaps the key difference between earlier attempts at measuring public-sector performance and today's programs is the recent rise of the performance management discipline in the private sector. Since Kaplan and Norton's first Balanced Scorecard article appeared in a 1992 edition of the *Harvard Business Review*, thousands of organizations across the globe have turned to this dynamic and effective method of gauging organizational success. The tidal wave of information available at the click of a mouse has also led to the swift and efficient dissemination of information on emerging practices in performance management. Public-sector managers have practically unlimited resources from which to draw when researching best practices on the latest performance management techniques. Since the mid-1990s, "Performance Measurement in Government" publications, resources, and conferences have sprung up around the country.

Results-based management certainly is not limited to the federal sector; it is finding its way into local government as well. Recent studies show that 34 percent of counties with populations over 50,000 and 38 percent of cities with populations over 25,000 use some type of performance measurement system.[2] State and local governments that voluntarily embark on performance measurement systems are probably just staying slightly ahead of the curve. Many experts believe the Government Accounting Standards Board (GASB) will soon require these jurisdictions to provide "service efforts and accomplishments," which are tantamount to performance measures.

This new way of managing in the public sector is just beginning to gain a critical mass and will most likely come into its own in the years ahead. Rather than bemoaning the radical new culture represented by performance measurement, public-sector managers are wise to embrace this movement and the many benefits it confers. Employing performance measurement techniques allows public-sector managers to clearly demonstrate to legislators and citizens alike the value their programs bring to constituents. Tracking that value comes from the development of meaningful, outcome-based indicators that can be used to gauge the effectiveness of program success. In an age of declining budgets, those managers turning to performance measurement have the tools to clearly outline how the allocation of funds to their program will make a difference to the people ultimately affected by the service delivery. Public-sector employees are also beneficiaries of the performance measurement revolution. Like their private-sector brethren, these employees are now able to shift their focus from rote, nonstrategic activities to the processes and initiatives that drive a meaningful contribution toward program success. The knowledge and information sharing provided by the Balanced Scorecard makes this possible. For these and many other reasons early public-sector Scorecard practitioners report that the results of developing a Balanced Scorecard are worth the effort. But—and this is a big but—they note there is a great deal of effort involved. The next section will examine how the architecture of the Balanced Scorecard must be adjusted to fit the public-sector model.

Building a Balanced Scorecard to Fit the Public Sector

Public-sector use and acceptance of the Balanced Scorecard continues to increase at a steady pace. Little wonder since these organizations are able to exact the same Scorecard benefits private-sector companies have enjoyed

since the early 1990s. However, the Balanced Scorecard was originally designed with the profit-seeking enterprise in mind and its basic framework
must be modified for public-sector organizations to utilize it to full advantage. Exhibit 13.1 displays a public-sector Balanced Scorecard model. We
can use this diagram to differentiate between private- and public-sector use
of the Scorecard.

Strategy remains at the core of the Scorecard system, regardless of whether
it's a government agency, *Fortune* 500 company, or a mom and pop store.
However, government organizations often have a difficult time cultivating a
clear and concise strategy. While many attempt to develop statements of
strategy, they amount to little more than detailed lists of programs and initiatives used to secure dollars from legislative funding bodies. As a result,
early governmental Scorecard efforts focused primarily on internal measures of efficiency and quality with little regard to the ultimate goal of serving citizens. A review of the history books is revealing. As noted in the preceding section, the 1980s and early 1990s saw a rise in prominence of the
quality movement in government circles, the effects of which strongly influenced performance measurement. Clearly, public-sector organizations need
to supplement the goals of strategy with higher-level objectives describing

Exhibit 13.1   Public-Sector Balanced Scorecard

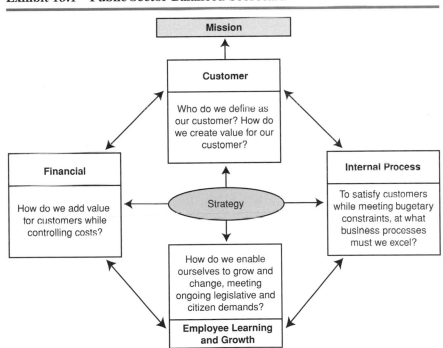

why it is they exist, and ultimately what they hope to achieve. In other words, they need to describe their mission. "Reducing illiteracy," "Decreasing the incidence of HIV," and "Increasing public safety," are all examples of goals we would expect public agencies to espouse, but they are not strategies. They are missions, providing the motivating force for action within the public-sector agency. These overarching objectives must be placed at the top of the government Balanced Scorecard to guide the development of performance measures that will lead to their fulfillment. With its position at the top of the Scorecard, the mission clearly communicates to all why the organization exists, and what they are striving to achieve.

A clear distinction between private- and public-sector Balanced Scorecards is drawn as a result of placing mission at the top of the framework. Flowing from the mission is a view of the organization's customers, not financial stakeholders. Achieving a mission does not equate with fiscal responsibility and stewardship; instead, the organization must determine who it aims to serve and how their requirements can best be met. In the profit-seeking world, companies are accountable to their capital providers (shareholders) for results, and they monitor this accountability through the results attained in the financial perspective of the Scorecard. Not so in the public sector. Here the focus is on customers and serving their needs in order to accomplish the mission. But the question of "who is the customer" is one of the most perplexing issues that government Scorecard adopters face. In the public sector, unlike the for-profit world, different groups design the service, pay for the service, and ultimately benefit from the service. This web of relationships makes determining the customer a formidable challenge for many public-sector managers. Establishing the real customer in many ways depends on your perspective. The legislative body that provides funding is a logical choice, as is the group you serve. However, think about that group you "serve." Would law enforcement agencies consider the criminals they arrest their customer? You could probably make a case for that. Conversely, many would argue that constituents are the ultimate beneficiaries of policing activities and are therefore the real customers. Fortunately, the Balanced Scorecard does not force you to make this difficult decision. Including all customers is permissible and possible using the public-sector Scorecard framework. Not only is it possible, it's desirable since meeting the mission will most likely entail satisfying disparate customer groups, each of whom figure in your success. Each group of customers identified will likely result in different measures appearing in the other three perspectives of the Scorecard. Once public-sector executives and managers have made their way through this tangled maze, the job of choosing performance measures in all perspectives becomes much simpler.

In the public-sector Scorecard model, financial measures can best be seen as either enablers of customer success or constraints within which the group must operate. The ultimate goal of the government agency is to fulfill their mission and customer requirements, not achieve financial success. However, financial metrics still have an important place in the overall framework. Working efficiently and creating value at lowest cost will be of critical importance in any organization, regardless of its status. Determining the costs of services rendered can lead to important conclusions and dramatically affect funding decisions. Government organizations, like their colleagues in the private sector, are increasingly looking to activity-based management techniques to assist them in establishing the true drivers of costs and how best to minimize total outflows in the future. Applying disciplined cost control methods and tracking detailed financial metrics can be a particularly painful thorn in the side of many public-sector managers, however. Consider those working in the field of human services, such as adoption or family services. They will suggest, with merit, that you can't put a price on placing a child in a supportive and loving home or reuniting a child with parents who have successfully completed a counseling program and show tremendous promise for the future. Skillful Scorecard practitioners must coach the reluctant managers to see that financial measures are not necessarily at odds with their nonfinancial goals but are intended to balance the ultimate goal of serving customers with fiscal accountability and responsibility.

Internal process measures in the public sector should derive from the value proposition reflected in the Customer perspective. What key processes must be executed flawlessly to increase the likelihood of achieving customer success? The notion of a value proposition is often new to public sector agencies that are often more accustomed to simply meeting budgets and not creating any significant control issues. As noted above, a legacy of government quality programs has been the reliance on measures of internal efficiency and quality with little regard to the effect these metrics have on the ultimate goal of meeting customer performance yardsticks and ultimately the mission. However, public-sector agencies need not depend exclusively on delivering operational excellence propositions, but with strong vision and captivating leadership can develop customer intimacy or even product leadership goals. Internal Process measures may also be generated from the increasing trend of government organizations contracting with third-party vendors and partnering with providers to meet customer needs. Performance measures should be crafted to track this important development.

To meet the objectives established in the Internal Process, Financial, and Customer perspectives, government agencies must develop metrics in the Employee Learning and Growth area that will enable such positive outcomes. Motivated employees with the right mix of skills and tools operating in an organizational climate designed for sustaining improvements are the key ingredients in driving process improvements, working within financial limitations, and ultimately driving customer and mission success. Government organizations normally do not experience much difficulty in populating this perspective, and will in fact flood it with metrics relating to everything from training programs to diversity initiatives to telecommuting pilot projects. Not to suggest these aren't important, but this perspective cannot simply act as a repository for every human resources initiative currently taking place. New measures must be developed that track the effectiveness of training programs, examine and attempt to fill the skills gap, establish the existence of information flows, and monitor the organizational climate.

Cascading Is Critical

Throughout this book we have discussed the importance of cascading the Balanced Scorecard, driving it to lower levels and thereby giving everyone the opportunity to define their contribution to the organization's success. As vital as cascading is in the private sector, it may be even more critical in public-sector applications of the Balanced Scorecard.

Among the many goals and benefits of cascading is the alignment that is created from top to bottom of the organization. Given the vast web of inter-dependencies existing within most public-sector agencies, alignment may be considered less a benefit of cascading and more of a necessity for Scorecard success. Achieving a high-level objective such as "Reducing child poverty" cannot be done through the actions of one group and captured in the objectives and measures of a single Scorecard. As customers move through the government system, availing themselves of the many services it offers, they rarely receive one-stop shopping. A more likely scenario is the acquisition of assistance from a variety of independent, yet closely related program providers. A family attempting to secure health insurance for their children could simultaneously be interacting with government health insurance specialists, immunization providers, and family counselors. Each of these groups play a vital part in helping the family achieve its goal of receiving insurance for their children, and therefore, each must document this contribution in the form of performance measures on the Balanced Scorecard. Taken cumulatively, the actions of program providers across the enterprise will move the agency ever closer to achieving its overall mission. Just as with the private sector, cascading will also increase the opportunities for government agencies to work collaboratively in solving problems and fulfilling their important mission.

Issues in Public-Sector Balanced Scorecard Development, and Ideas on Overcoming Them

As the old saying suggests, nothing worth having comes easy. So it is with developing a Balanced Scorecard in the public sector. One of the best attributes of the Balanced Scorecard is its simplicity. But remember, simple does not equate to simplistic. Applying this sophisticated tool requires rigor and discipline in any organizational structure, but the public sector offers some unique challenges. This section will explore those issues and offer some possible solutions to help you get the most from your Balanced Scorecard implementation.

- *What I do is not measurable.* This is perhaps the most common lament of public-sector managers and employees alike. Health and social services agencies are the most vocal, and with good reason. Helping drug-addicted individuals get back on their feet, attempting to ensure that all poor children have health insurance, reducing disease rates, and reuniting troubled families are all outcomes that are subject to a wide variety of influences making them difficult to measure. The key word in that last sentence is *outcomes.* Each of the examples cited is a long-range (usually) goal the government is working diligently to achieve. Many suggest that such outcomes are impossible to measure since they can take years to accomplish, involve a variety of contributors, and are subject to many variables out of the control of the public-sector agency. Trying to convince a dedicated social services manager that his or her work should be captured under the framework of the Balanced Scorecard can be one of the toughest tests to face even the most tenacious Scorecard facilitator. To overcome the challenge, public-sector agencies must distinguish between *outcomes* and *outputs.* Consider outputs the short- or medium-term substitutes for long-range outcomes the agency hopes to achieve. The hypothesis you are putting forth under this scenario suggests that short-term success on the outputs will eventually lead to long-term success on the outcomes. For example, measuring the reduction of HIV rates in a community may be difficult and subject to myriad influences. However, as an output measure, tracking the number of high-risk individuals attending awareness presentations may over time help stem the growth of HIV rates. Not all substitute measures will be perfect surrogates for the outcome under question, but they will at least allow for a benchmark to be established and more importantly will stimulate conversation, information sharing, and learning among those involved in tracking the measure. After all, without measuring, how can you determine whether progress is being made in meeting social goals? Public-sector agencies must begin to consider possible cause-and-effect relationships and start accumulating data that can be used to, at the very least, generate better questions, and at the most, lead to some insightful answers. As performance measurement systems in the public-sector become increasingly sophisticated, creative managers are beginning to find ways to measure many things that were considered unmeasurable. The city of Sunnyvale, California, has been a pioneer in the field of government performance measurement. They recently launched an initiative to measure perhaps the granddaddy of the unmeasurables—quality of life. Their eight-point initiative focuses on performance measures encompassing community safety; high-quality education; a healthy and sustainable environment; efficient and safe transportation systems; quality, diverse, and affordable housing; community pride and involvement; a diverse and growing economy; and a community with diverse cultural opportunities.

- *Results will be used to punish.* Most of the people I know who are unhappy in their current jobs have at least one thing in common. When they perform well there is no praise awaiting their achievements, but when things go wrong the boss is on their back faster than the disappearance of a politician's campaign promises. Unfortunately, this negative conditioning tends to occur quite frequently in public-sector ranks and can be a huge issue in the successful implementation of a Balanced Scorecard initiative. Two things need to happen in order to turn the tables on this problem. First of all, executives and managers have to be trained, coached, begged, pleaded, and coached some more about the dangers inherent in this practice. The Scorecard introduces new practices, new performance measures, and new ways of thinking about the business. It's all about a hypothesis of how what you do today will affect what happens tomorrow. Sometimes it does not play out exactly as planned, but that's life. Poor performance results cannot be treated as defects but must be seen as opportunities for discussion and learning about the business. The manager who enters a staff meeting declaring "Okay, we missed all our targets last quarter, what does that say about our current value proposition and strategy?" will go a long way toward cementing the Scorecard as an accepted business tool. Not only do executives and managers have to change their behaviors, but those affected by Scorecard results must also start acting differently. It is incumbent upon them to turn the tables on their supervisors by using below par performance results to demonstrate the need for new funding or new initiatives, not as an excuse to run and hide, waiting for the inevitable axe to drop. Software tools provide a great opportunity for defending performance by allowing commentaries to be entered regarding measure results. Ultimately, this like so many of the issues we will discuss, is a cultural issue, and cultural issues cannot be solved overnight. Only through the persistent and sustained efforts of a committed group of executives, managers, and employees will changes to organizational culture break through.

- *What is the mission?* In his book *Measuring Up*, author Jonathan Walters notes the dilemma faced by the U.S. Forest Service who are supposed to *"see the efficient killing of trees and the careful protection of wildlife."*[3] In this scenario, what is the Forest Service's true mission, and how do they go about developing performance measures? Many government agencies may feel similar pressures of being pulled in a number of different directions rendering a clear and concise Scorecard nearly impossible. Lacking clear direction, leaders facing such contradictory forces must make an effort to determine what they feel is the guiding mission of the organization and develop performance measures accordingly.

- *The public won't understand negative results.* Freedom of Information and Public Records legislation dictates that most if not all data relating to a public-sector performance management system must be released to any citizen requesting the information. The function of these laws is noble, permitting the public to see how the government is performing its functions, but very understandably they are a concern to public-sector Scorecard adopters. Not only can results be taken out of context, but below-target performance can be easily served up on the front page of the newspaper as evidence of the government's total incompetence. It is little wonder that many public-sector agencies shun the development of stretch targets, since they know that failure to achieve them could end up on the 6 o'clock news. There is no simple resolution to this issue. Inviting members of the public and media in to your office and explaining the virtues of the Balanced Scorecard would be impractical and probably viewed with great skepticism. Despite the challenge posed by freedom of information acts, public-sector organizations that have embarked on a Scorecard journey feel the risk of greater performance offered by this tool outweighs the potential for public and media confusion.

- *Why invest in something that will only last with the current administration?* We all know that common political practice dictates an incoming administration disavow itself of everything their predecessor's initiated, whether good or bad. A performance measurement program can certainly be the victim of such political whims, and cause even the most ardent supporter to have second thoughts about investing precious energy toward its success. However, unlike other programs that may come and go, performance measurement is here to stay from administration to administration. The Government Performance Results Act, as we know from our earlier reading, is a law, which means that it is definitely here to stay. And at lower-levels of government, elected officials are receiving more pressure than ever from constituents who demand they be accountable for results. Performance measurement systems are the tools they need to demonstrate results. Gaining the support of elected officials is similar to having senior executives in the for-profit world lend their encouragement and acceptance, and is not easy. One method of securing sponsorship is involving them in the development of performance measures since *"elected officials who participate less in the design of performance measures are also less likely to support them."*[4] Education and training are also beneficial since even the basic concepts of performance measurement and the Balanced Scorecard may be relatively foreign to elected officials.

- *Culture of not trusting business solutions.* Public-sector organizations tend to be quite wary of the latest business fads sweeping boardrooms across the nation. They argue that the esoteric and socially relevant nature of their work makes such models inappropriate for their operations. Beyond distrust there could lie an element of fear since business solutions normally represent very new turf for the typical public-sector employee. This view is changing and will continue to do so as the line between business and government practices continues to blur. In the meantime, public-sector agencies must avail themselves of any system that holds the promise of helping them achieve their mission, whether it emerges from within or from their business brethren. The Balanced Scorecard with its growing number of public-sector success stories should not be subject to as much criticism and skepticism as many business techniques.

- *No burning platform for change.* In the for-profit world companies will sometimes turn to the Balanced Scorecard in a time of great crisis when a change is not only desirable but necessary for the very survival of the enterprise. Development of a core group of performance measures can galvanize all employees and rally them around the outcomes necessary to ensure they live to see another day. Government organizations do not normally face this dilemma since going out of business is not really an option. Therefore, it is often more difficult for a Balanced Scorecard program to take hold in such an environment. However, having your function outsourced to a third-party (private-sector) provider is an option these days, as is continued scrutiny from taxpayers on how their dollars are being spent and what results are coming of those investments. Employees must be constantly aware of the challenges they face and how the Scorecard can demonstrate value to taxpayers and result in self-preservation!

- *Technical constraints.* Although things are changing, it is safe to say that most public-sector agencies lag behind their for-profit counterparts when it comes to having the latest technological tools. This can pose a problem for your Balanced Scorecard, especially if you choose to use an automated software tool. One government organization developed an excellent Scorecard system, but when it came time to begin reporting results they discovered that several key managers with responsibility for measures did not have computers. That made it a little tough to generate data and discuss the results. The sheer cost involved in establishing a performance measurement project can also be a deterrent to public-sector agencies. From software to training to consultants, the fees can rapidly escalate.

- *Staff skills.* The government has its share of analysts and those folks handy with a calculator and spreadsheet, but for many the analytical tools of business are a completely foreign language. Government employees often possess specialized skills that enable them to perform their jobs at a very high level of competence. However, for a law enforcement officer, public health nurse, or emergency medical system administrator, those skills probably do not include complex data analysis. To gain the advantages offered by the Balanced Scorecard, employees must be able to analyze and learn from the results generated by their performance measures. Fortunately, the Balanced Scorecard is not rocket science and the subtleties of the technique can be mastered by anyone with the requisite training and dedication to learn. Unfortunately, education, critical as it may be, is often lacking in public sector Scorecard implementations. Anxious to start measuring, many organizations will hold a cursory briefing session explaining the Scorecard as a metrics project and then charge everyone in attendance to develop a Scorecard that tells the story of what they do and how that contributes to overall outcomes. That is sort of like telling me that surgery is about cutting someone open, removing (or adding) something, and sewing him back up. Does that qualify me for brain surgery? Time and energy must be invested up front in detailed Scorecard training to ensure that those involved have the skills necessary to build effective Scorecards and benefit from the results achieved.

- *Developing innovative measures.* Since the idea of performance measurement is new to many public-sector organizations they are very likely to gravitate toward the familiar when developing performance measures. Some groups will already be responsible for submitting quarterly or annual information to funding bodies and will simply reword those requirements in an effort to populate the Scorecard perspectives. Sometimes these metrics are valid, but often they are not. If they are not effective measures, how can they motivate performance? Scorecard developers must be reminded that it is the new or missing measures that often provide the greatest value on the Scorecard. By defining the customer, determining what processes must be maximized to satisfy the customer, what financial constraints are present, and what employee skills are necessary, the public-sector manager can open a new world of creative performance measures that tell a strategic story.

- *Can't show the money!* From Scorecard architects Kaplan and Norton to for-profit practitioners around the globe, all agree that for cultural change to be secured in an organization the Scorecard should at some point and in some way be linked to compensation. Government agencies for the most part do not have this critical lever of Scorecard acceptance. Tight budgets, labor contracts, and a host of other potential problems conspire to make this option exceedingly difficult to execute. Difficult but not impossible. The City of Charlotte, North Carolina, has instituted a program that pays staff a reward based on the achievement of Scorecard targets, so there is proof it can be done. In the absence of monetary rewards, public-sector managers may turn to the intrinsic rewards emanating from the Scorecard. Increased knowledge, learning, satisfaction, and possible increases to budget allocations being just a few.

Those are just some of the issues you may encounter when developing a Balanced Scorecard for your public-sector organization. But before you throw your hands up in utter defeat, all is not lost. There are brave pioneers who have blazed a winning trail before you, and the next section will look at one such Scorecard overachiever that is sure to inspire you.

The Texas State Auditor's Office

The Texas State Auditor's Office (TSAO) supports the Texas legislature and is responsible for auditing the executive branch agencies entrusted with state funds for the provision of services to the state's 20 million citizens. Audits and analyses conducted by the TSAO help to determine how effectively and efficiently agencies manage their funds toward the achievement of desired outcomes. The group operates out of Austin with 237 staff and an operating budget of $14 million. The paragraphs that follow will explore why the TSAO turned to the Balanced Scorecard, the process they followed, the role of technology in their implementation, benefits resulting from the Scorecard, challenges in implementations, and keys to their success.

The Balanced Scorecard at the TSAO got its start in the same way that many such initiatives originate. A director, Deborah Kerr, happened to read about the concept in the *Harvard Business Review*, was impressed with what she read and wanted to share it with managers. Over a series of "lunch and learn" sessions, the Balanced Scorecard at the TSAO was born. The time was late 1998 and although the TSAO felt they were doing a lot of things right, they could not always reproduce their success on a consistent basis. As manager Frank Vito puts it, *"We were tired of managing by miracles."* The group felt that if they could only identify what they were doing right and repeat it, while simultaneously determining what they were doing wrong and correct it, they could achieve more consistent and sustainable results. The Balanced Scorecard with its emphasis on mission, strategy, and organizational learning seemed a perfect fit.

Even before the TSAO chose the Balanced Scorecard they took the proactive step of looking into the future world of auditing and considering what their role might be in the new environment. Analyzing the current environment, external factors, and potential changes, the group determined that a new mission and strategies were necessary if they were to successfully navigate the terrain awaiting them in the not-so-distant future. "Actively provide government leaders with useful information that improves accountability" became the simple but powerful new mission of the TSAO. The mission was then decomposed into three key strategies.

1. *Providing assurance services.* The focus of assurance services is accountability. The TSAO will not only provide traditional financial and performance audits, but develop the skills and offerings necessary to conduct the audits of the future which may include assessing the accuracy and security of information and systems, and providing web security certifications.

2. *Provide management advisory services.* Assistance is the hallmark of management advisory services. The newly formed team provides assistance and information to state government clients attempting to identify weaknesses and develop improvement strategies. Doing so reduces overall risks in the State.

3. *Provide education services.* The operating environment of the future promises to be more complicated, and the TSAO's goal in education services is making managers aware of these risks and providing tools for dealing with them.

With the new mission and strategies in place, the TSAO turned to the Balanced Scorecard as a means of measuring progress toward their goals. Their first task was to rearrange the architecture of the Balanced Scorecard to a framework that fit their situation as a public-sector organization. Since serving public needs, and not making a profit, was their chief concern the TSAO created a mission perspective to appear at the top of their Balanced Scorecard. All other performance measures flowed directly from serving the mission as shown in Exhibit 13.2.

A four-step process was used to develop Balanced Scorecards throughout the TSAO over an 18-month period. The process is outlined in Exhibit 13.3. Balanced Scorecards were developed for each of the three TSAO strategies that aligned with the office's overall Scorecard. Support units then developed their own cascading Scorecards to demonstrate how they would meet the needs of internal customers. Finally, project managers and team members constructed Scorecards consistent with TSAO's strategies. These projects are the specific audits performed by the TSAO and represent an innovative use of the Balanced Scorecard in an auditing environment. Frank Vito explains. *"Every project has unique objectives, and if you look at those objectives as a mission then you can translate it using the Balanced Scorecard. With the Scorecard project teams started to look at customers, key processes, and the skills of their team. They used the Balanced Scorecard as a management tool."*[5]

Exhibit 13.2   Using the Balanced Scorecard to Measure the Mission at the Texas State Auditor's Office

We acheive our mission through establishing working relationships with and meeting the needs of our customers.

We establish working relationships with and meet the needs of our customers through efficient, high-quality internal processes.

We establish efficient, high-quality internal process by acquiring and developing the skilled employees needed to do the work.

We acquire and develop the skilled workforce by effectively managing our appropriated funds.

Mission

Customer Focus

Internal Processes

Learning and Knowledge

Financial

Exhibit 13.3   Developing the Balanced Scorecard at the Texas State Auditor's Office

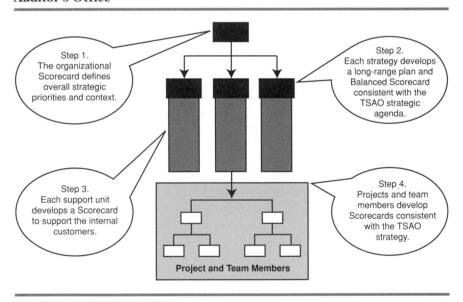

Step 1.
The organizational Scorecard defines overall strategic priorities and context.

Step 2.
Each strategy develops a long-range plan and Balanced Scorecard consistent with the TSAO strategic agenda.

Step 3.
Each support unit develops a Scorecard to support the internal customers.

Step 4.
Projects and team members develop Scorecards consistent with the TSAO strategy.

Project and Team Members

With Scorecards in place throughout the TSAO, benefits of the project began to accrue almost immediately. Cascading the Balanced Scorecard helped every employee understand how they contribute to the achievement of the mission and what was necessary of them to actively participate. The TSAO also showed an early commitment to using the Scorecard as a strategic management system by "throwing away" the old management meeting agenda and replacing it with the Balanced Scorecard. Manager, Frank Vito explains the results. *"In the past our meetings focused on how things were going, what problems we had and what fires had to be put out. Now we put the Scorecard on the screen at the beginning of the meeting and focus on the story being told by our strategy."*[6]

Technology played a strong role from the beginning of the TSAO implementation. They chose a performance management software called pb views as their automated solution. Frank Vito maintains that technology was a strong contributor to the Scorecard's success by providing real-time detailed feedback on performance, facilitating learning and culture change, and enabling the TSAO to expand performance measurement to all levels of the organization.

No change effort of this magnitude is completely void of challenges and the TSAO encountered their share of difficulties along the path to Scorecard success. Many managers agreed with the Scorecard concept in theory, but when it came time to put that theory into practice by developing their own Scorecards, they were suddenly hesitant. Some blamed difficult technology while others claimed a lack of time. The project team also spent considerable time explaining that "red" (indicating less than targeted performance) was not bad, but instead signaled an opportunity for improvement and learning. In a fun and creative attempt to deemphasize the negative connotations associated with red, they used the color in every way they could. Red fonts, red folders for distributing Balanced Scorecard materials, you name it. With training, coaching, and involvement of the state auditor, the red stigma began to fade.

In yet another demonstration that public-sector Scorecard development has much in common with private-sector attempts, the TSAO cite commitment from the top, involvement and ownership, continuous improvement, communication, and training as keys to a successful implementation. And they know something about success. In July 2000, the Association of Government Accountants recognized the TSAO Balanced Scorecard efforts by presenting them with a Best Practices award. The Society of Human Resource Management (SHRM) also lauded the TSAO's efforts when recognizing their implementation as one of the four most successful Balanced Scorecard implementations in the country. In addition to these accolades, let's not forget that the Scorecard solved the TSAO's original problem—it provided the means for identifying what they were doing right and repeating it, while also helping them determine what they were doing wrong so that they could correct it. No more managing by miracles!

DEVELOPING BALANCED SCORECARDS IN NOT-FOR-PROFIT ORGANIZATIONS

One of the issues identified with applying the Balanced Scorecard to public-sector groups was the possibility of no "burning platform for change" necessitating the development of a performance measurement system. The same cannot be said of not-for-profit organizations. Clearly, the landscape facing most not-for-profits is changing rapidly, signaling the need for transitions to take place. Among the chief threats is the increasing number of competitors each vying for scarce donor contributions. Further, contributors increasingly demand that a high percentage of their donations actually reach recipients and are not gobbled up by administration costs. In such an environment, even not-for-profits with the noblest of missions are forced to examine their managerial practices in search of methods ensuring they are able to continue meeting the needs of the many constituents relying on their help each and every day. With increasing frequency, not-for-profits are turning to performance measurement techniques, and specifically the Balanced Scorecard, to meet the challenges they face.

In a number of ways the public-sector and not-for-profit Balanced Scorecards share a great resemblance. Neither organization claims financial objectives as their reason for being, but instead looks to serve constituent needs in both a humane and efficient manner. For that reason, mission—not financial objectives—appears as the overarching objective of the measurement effort. Customer objectives are next, followed by internal processes, financial, and employee learning and growth (some place financial at the bottom of the framework). The two groups also share many of the same issues impeding the successful development of a Balanced Scorecard: results that are not easily measurable, lack of control over variables, and technical constraints, to name just a few.

While many similarities exist between the two groups, not-for-profits face some issues that make the development of Balanced Scorecards particularly challenging. One such challenge is the background, experiences, and motivation of most not-for-profit employees. Many enthusiastically choose to join these organizations at reduced salaries for the chance to work on a cause or mission toward which they feel very passionate. Often, their previous training and experience is in closely related fields, which makes them great candidates for success. These attributes are undoubtedly a tremendous asset to the not-for-profit as it works to fulfill its mission, but may be a liability when launching a performance measurement effort. As distrustful as public-sector employees may be of businesslike solutions, not-for-profit employees share not only the lack of trust but, for the most part, will have virtually no prior exposure to efforts of this ilk. Lack of knowledge and potential distrust leave a huge void for fertile imaginations to fill with negative perceptions toward the measurement effort. The lack of trust and knowledge can manifest itself in a variety of ways, including the insistence that a performance measurement initiative is time consuming and will drain resources from all important service delivery, which renders the effort unworthy of attention. Not-for-profit executives and managers, perhaps more than those of any other organizational type, must invest extraordinary effort at the outset of measurement projects explaining the background of the methods to be used, the process to be followed, and the benefits to be derived. Only through constant communication (which is a must in any implementation) will not-for-profit employees be expected to really understand and embrace these tools.

A characteristic differentiating not-for-profits from most other organizational types is the premium they place on involvement and group decision making. Unfortunately, this seemingly positive trait can be a double-edged sword. On the upside, nothing builds buy-in and support faster than including a wide range of employees in the Scorecard building process. Engaging employees in the development of innovative performance measures that will lead to the achievement of their mission can unleash reserves of creativity previously unknown in even the most enlightened organizations. However, not-for-profit organizations can have a tendency to take this inclusive atmosphere a little too far. It's not that including a wide range of people in developing measures is inherently bad, but when you try to please everyone and make every decision based on consensus, trouble comes to a boil very quickly. In an environment where everyone's opinion is sought and attempts are made to satisfy all, the end result can be diffusion of responsibility, confusion around measures and objectives, and a stifling proclivity toward apathy. This sounds harsh, but it happens. Not-for-profit executives with the best of intentions attempt to develop Scorecards based on the wants and needs of all but end up with a product that pleases and inspires no one. To overcome this problem, executives and managers must exercise strong leadership. Encouraging input and involvement is one thing, but leaders must make it clear that they own the organizational Scorecard and will make the final decision on what measures are critical to the not-for-profit's ability to meet its mission. Doing so clearly communicates the organization's direction to all employees, but does not preclude active and participative dialogue between leaders and staff.

Implementing the Balanced Scorecard offers many opportunities to a not-for-profit organization in spite of the hurdles that must be cleared. Increased focus on the mission, accountability for results, and alignment of human and financial resources toward overall objectives can all result from the development of a Balanced Scorecard. Kaplan and Norton have even gone so far as to suggest that *"the opportunity for the Scorecard to improve the management of governmental and not-for-profit enterprises is, if anything, even greater."*[7] If that is the case, and when you consider there are over one and a half million not-for-profit organizations registered with the Internal Revenue Service here in the United States, the opportunities for improvements to those organizations and thus society at large is staggering.

SUMMARY

The passage of the Government Performance and Results Act (GPRA) put all public-sector employees on notice that a transformation was about to take place in the way government operations are managed. The new focus is on what is being accomplished, not how much is being spent. All federally funded agencies must now develop performance measures documenting their accountability for results. Unlike public-sector performance measurement efforts of the past, the GPRA is here to stay. Its status as a law guarantees that, but growing public pressure for results and the increasing use and sophistication of performance management tools also provide harbingers of its staying power. Results-based government is not limited to the federal level, but is catching on at both the state and local levels as well. Public-sector managers are quickly recognizing the many benefits of performance measurement using the Balanced Scorecard. Demonstrating value to legislators and citizens and aligning all employees toward the achievement of their missions are just two of the many advantages of the system.

Early governmental performance measurement initiatives focused almost exclusively on measuring quality improvement and process efficiency. Doing so led to isolated improvements but did not inform the agency as to whether they were fulfilling the socially relevant mission their constituents and legislators expected them to achieve. Recognizing the importance of measuring the mission, public-sector organizations have reorganized the Balanced Scorecard by placing the overarching goals and objectives represented by the mission at the top of the framework. Customer requirements, not financial objectives, are critical to meeting the mission, and therefore the Customer perspective is also elevated in the public and not-for-profit sectors. Internal Processes, Employee Learning and Growth, and even Financial metrics are still important and have a place on the Balanced Scorecard.

Solving the issues facing our modern society cannot be accomplished through even the most heroic acts of any single government agency. Cooperation and collaboration are crucial in meeting the goals in today's public-sector environment. Cascading the Scorecard takes on increased prominence in public-sector applications since it provides an opportunity for disparate governmental agencies to collaborate, share information, and learn from each other through the discussion and dissemination of Balanced Scorecard results.

Developing public-sector and not-for-profit Balanced Scorecards presents some unique challenges not often encountered in the profit-seeking enterprise. Activities that seem "unmeasurable," conflicting or confusing missions, public misperceptions of results, staff background and skills, and fickle elected officials are just some of the many problems that must be conquered. Despite the challenges, an ever-expanding group of agencies have built Scorecards and are benefiting from the new management practices it heralds.

NOTES

1. Carl G. Thor, "The Evolution of Performance Measurement in Government," *Journal of Cost Management,* May/June 2000, 18–26.
2. Evan Berman and Xiao Hu Wang, "Performance Measurement in U.S. Counties: Capacity for Reform," *Public Administration Review,* September/October 2000.
3. Jonathan Walters, *Measuring Up* (Washington, DC: Governing Books, 1998).
4. Ibid., p. 10.
5. From interview with Frank Vito, August 24, 2001.
6. Ibid.
7. Robert S. Kaplan and David P. Norton, *The Balanced Scorecard* (Boston: Harvard Business School Press, 1996).

CHAPTER 14

Concluding Thoughts on Balanced Scorecard Success

Roadmap for Chapter Fourteen   Do you remember those college days when you knew you had amassed enough marks to pass a course so you decided to skip the last few classes? Tempting as it may be, let's not have a repeat of history here because we still have some work to do before you get your "A" in Balanced Scorecard.

Chapter Three introduced the role of an organizational change expert, and this chapter will take a much closer look at the important work to be performed by this individual. Following our look at change activities necessary to secure Scorecard success is a review of the "Top Ten" Balanced Scorecard implementation issues. If you hurry, you can still organize an office pool to guess number 1. Many organizations will determine that building a Scorecard is better done with the assistance of experienced management consultants. The chapter provides a number of criteria to be considered when choosing a consulting partner.

THE IMPORTANCE OF ORGANIZATIONAL
CHANGE CONCEPTS

Between 50 and 80 percent of large change initiatives fail to meet expectations. This startling statistic is relevant to us because, as we know, the Balanced Scorecard does not represent a measurement project but is instead the very essence of a change effort. Not only does an organization's measurement system change as a result of the Scorecard, but if the initiative is to prove successful, the fundamental management processes guiding the company will be dramatically altered as well. The Balanced Scorecard represents a major departure in performance management for many organizations. Strategy, not financial controls, dictates the firm's direction, and the Scorecard creates a powerful new language for employee change. As is the case with strategy, it is not the change effort itself that tends to cause the failure but the execution of that change that will always derail the effort.

Effective organizational change is every bit as challenging as successful implementation of a new strategy. Judging by the square footage devoted to the topic at bookstores, most managers would agree with that assessment. Dozens of books and hundreds of articles are devoted to this vexing yet utterly critical management challenge. While cracking the code of change is far beyond the scope of this book, outlining some key change issues that require thought and planning is not. In Chapter Three, the organizational change expert was introduced as a member of the Balanced Scorecard implementation team. Let's now consider some of the key issues that will require the change expert's attention and knowledge as you attempt to develop a Balanced Scorecard system.

- *Why is this change necessary?* Organizations will often announce a sweeping change program that will ultimately effect everyone in the organization but neglect to share the necessity of the change and related objectives. Employees, being human beings after all, will fill any such communication void with rumors, and chances are they will not be overly positive. Not only will the rumors support a negative rationale for the change, but they will most likely attribute downright nasty motives to the executives who cooked up the whole scheme. Rationale for the change and associated objectives must be clearly stated at the outset of the project if there is any prospect of gaining employee support. Referencing Chapter Three once again, "developing objectives" was the very first topic mentioned. If employees are expected to rally around the Scorecard, they must first recognize the need for a change and the rewards to be achieved by successfully implementing it.

- *What do you expect from me as a result of this change?* Clarity of expectations can be an absolute make-or-break issue when attempting to successfully manage change. What impact will Scorecard reporting have on managers and employees? How does it affect routine processes? Will it disrupt personal relationships? These and several other questions will naturally flow from a review of expectations. Scorecard planners must be proactive in determining what is expected of all employees once the Scorecard is up and running.

- *Compatibility with culture and values.* Some organizations have a strong and proud history of managing by measures while others have been content to focus on a few key drivers to monitor their ongoing activities.

Introducing the Balanced Scorecard into a culture with no past reliance on, or knowledge of, advanced measurement techniques may be very difficult.

- *Support systems for completing the change.* When developing a Balanced Scorecard, organizations must ensure that resources and support systems are in place to help ensure a successful outcome. Employees will be wary to lend their energy and support to any endeavor lacking in the necessary resources to see it through to completion.

- *Confidence of employees.* Organizations have long memories, especially for past failures. If previous attempts at change have delivered frustration instead of results, then current endeavors may be plagued from the outset with a lack of confidence. Optimism and belief on the part of employees that the change can be wrought is crucial. Confidence tends to boost energy and propel everyone toward achievement, while a lack of belief can lead to organizational apathy.

These are some of the issues that affect the success of a change program. There are no easy fixes or answers for any of the issues, as each is a product of the unique culture residing within every organization. However, recognizing you have problems and developing potential solutions goes a long way toward a smooth Scorecard implementation. At the outset of a Scorecard effort, effective organizational change facilitators should assess staff members spanning the organization's ranks, from executives to managers to front-line employees, in an effort to capture the perceptions held regarding the critical success factors. Armed with that knowledge, the facilitator can work with other members of the Scorecard team to develop action plans and programs aimed at mitigating the potentially negative effects associated with the issues identified.

The only way to stack the change deck in your favor is to perform a comprehensive assessment of opinions and perceptions held at all levels of the organization, and take appropriate action based on what you find. Being proactive is always a positive trait but is absolutely crucial here. Waiting too long can prove disastrous to your Scorecard efforts. As a final warning, remember it is not technology or methodologies that cause change efforts to fail—it is almost always "people" issues.

TOP TEN BALANCED SCORECARD
IMPLEMENTATION ISSUES

In this book I have attempted to provide a comprehensive guide on what it takes to successfully implement the Balanced Scorecard. My optimistic belief is that by following the advice found here your organization can successfully evade many of the pitfalls known to be hazardous to your Scorecard's health. Some of the problem areas are so pervasive, however, that they merit further attention and review before you launch your campaign. Here are my top ten Scorecard implementation issues. It is my sincere hope that your organization is able to elude the perilous grip of each and every one.

Number 10: Premature Links to Management Processes

The transition from a measurement system to a strategic management system is a natural evolution for a successful Balanced Scorecard. Embedding the Scorecard into management processes such as budgeting and compensation allows organizations to tap the full potential of this dynamic framework. However, premature attempts to forge these links may cause a swift decline in Scorecard momentum. A major culprit here is the link of Scorecard measures to compensation. Employee attention and focus is undoubtedly heightened thanks to this powerful lever, but exercising it too soon can produce many unintended side effects. For one thing, the measures linking the Scorecard to compensation may be unproven and lead to dysfunctional decision making on the part of managers looking to cash in. Targets are also an issue, especially for new measures. An aggressive target may be perceived as unattainable and unrealistic, causing employees to lose any motivation they may have had to achieve it. However, a target easily achieved will do little to foster breakthrough performance. Should the compensation link come under fire, employees, managers, and executives alike may be quick in assigning blame to an inherent shortcoming of the Scorecard system itself rather than properly shouldering the responsibility for an ill-conceived compensation scheme.

Number 9: Lack of Cascading

This issue actually warrants a higher placement than number 9 but is stationed here because it does not apply to every organization. Some small companies or business units within a larger entity may develop one Balanced Scorecard that is sufficient for guiding the actions of the entire workforce. Organizations of any appreciable size, however, must cascade the Scorecard from top to bottom if they hope to gain the advantages offered by this system. Front-line employees are so far removed from organizational strategy that a high-level Scorecard, while providing a modicum of learning and motivation opportunities, will do little to shepherd daily activities. It is only by cascading the Scorecard to all levels of the organization and allowing every employee to describe how they contribute to the organization's overall success that true alignment can occur.

Number 8: Terminology

We've all heard the famous Shakespeare quote, *"What's in a name? That which we call a rose by any other name would smell as sweet."* Roses maybe, but key performance indicators don't smell a thing like objectives, yet many organizations will use the two terms to describe the same thing. Think of a choir with different song books, or a football team with 20 playbooks—both are sure recipes for disaster behind the mike or on the gridiron. And so it is with the Balanced Scorecard. Everyone needs to be speaking the same language if measurement is to be used in guiding change within an organization. I have been in meetings taking place months into a Scorecard project when it suddenly becomes painfully obvious that not everyone in the room is on the same page. Translating strategy into measures is hard enough, but when you realize you can't even agree on the same language it can be very disheartening indeed.

Number 7: No New Measures

Taking an existing group of measures and placing them into conveniently predefined perspectives does not a Balanced Scorecard make. Yet the temptation to do just that is sometimes overwhelming for organizations. In an effort to comply with the latest management fiat, groups quickly and easily assemble the same performance measures they have always used and dutifully tuck them into the four perspectives thinking they have developed a brand new Balanced Scorecard. After several months of reporting, the group will inevitably question the necessity of the Scorecard since results are about the same as always. As we have seen from our discussion of measures in Chapters Five and Six, and elsewhere, it is most often the new and "missing measures" and their interplay with other indicators that drive the value emanating from a Balanced Scorecard. Many of the measures needed to tell the story of the strategy may already be present, but in the vast majority of cases they must be supplemented with new and innovative metrics to ensure the execution of strategy.

Number 6: Consistent Management Practices

The Scorecard, as reflected by its name, represents a new paradigm of balance within an organization: balancing the needs of internal and external stakeholders, balancing short-term opportunities with long-term value creation, balancing lag and lead indicators of performance, and, of course, balancing financial and nonfinancial indicators. A surefire method of promoting premature Scorecard death is to actively promote balanced measures while concurrently rewarding behaviors that reflect decidedly nonbalanced ideals. A good example is attempting to manage by the Balanced Scorecard yet compensating executives solely on short-term financial performance. The message sent with this practice is clear—we may say that nonfinancial indicators are important, but we all know that money really matters most. Many organizations will similarly tout teamwork and collaboration as the critical differentiators of their success while openly promoting individuals based on personal achievements only. Effective use of the Balanced Scorecard dictates a genuine commitment to developing and engaging in managerial processes that are consistent with the holistic goals inherent in the Scorecard itself.

Number 5: Timing

Both ends of the time spectrum may be sources of Scorecard issues, the long and short of it if you will. Let's start with the long. Some organizations will not unveil their new Scorecard until every measure has been developed, data sources confirmed, and results ready to pour in. Since as many as 30 percent of measures may be missing when the Scorecard is developed, they could be waiting a long time! Scorecard benefits such as collaboration, information sharing, and group learning do not depend on having every single measure in place. The Scorecard should be launched once a critical mass of performance measures is available. The dialogue that ensues from reviewing Scorecard results more than compensates for the lack of a complete card. At the opposite end of the spectrum are those organizations that attempt to have a Scorecard up and running in ridiculously short periods of time. Often, organizations will attempt to compress the time frame when using consultants. They feel that the experience and methodologies offered by their hired guns should ensure a completed product in no time at all. There is little doubt the advent of Scorecard technology and the rich body of literature available to practitioners have served to significantly reduce Scorecard development times. However, developing a Balanced Scorecard complete with requisite cause-and-effect linkages weaving together disparate measures to tell your strategic story cannot be completed overnight. Nor should it be. Reaching consensus on strategy, translating the strategy, developing objectives, measures, and targets takes significant effort. Often, the best results are achieved when organizations take the necessary time to let the ideas and discussions germinate, moving from concept to reality, and in so doing producing innovative new measures and solutions.

Number 4: No Objectives for the Balanced Scorecard Program

This issue was previously discussed at the beginning of this chapter but bears mentioning here as well. As organizations around the globe experience the multitude of benefits from Balanced Scorecards, the concept has gained wide acceptance and approval as a management tool. With its heavyweight status confirmed, some organizations will adopt the Scorecard simply because it seems like the right thing to do. Certainly, it is the right thing to do, but that in no way excuses an executive team from determining the specific objectives it has in mind when turning to the Scorecard. What problem will the Scorecard solve in the organization? If there is no answer to this fundamental question, or worse yet, if it has not even been contemplated, the Scorecard is sure to suffer the ignominious fate of organizational inertia. A lack of guiding objectives often results from having the Scorecard developed as an "add-on" to another large-scale change project. Perhaps an enterprise resource planning initiative or a customer relationship management program is underway. Consultants may suggest that the Scorecard is a logical extension of these efforts and should be immediately implemented. With no clearly articulated goal for the program, it can be easily misunderstood and ultimately ignored until it simply fades from view.

Number 3: No Strategy

It is extremely difficult to implement a strategic management system without a strategy. At the very core of the Scorecard concept is the organization's strategy—guiding all actions and decisions, and ensuring alignment from top to bottom. A Scorecard can be developed without the aid of a strategy, but it then becomes a key performance indicator or stakeholder system, lacking in many of the attributes offered from a true Balanced Scorecard. Having said that, the processes involved in building a Balanced Scorecard may help a company "back in" to its strategy as a result of detailed and empassioned discussions surrounding performance measures necessary to stimulate breakthrough performance.

Number 2: Lack of Balanced Scorecard Education and Training

In their haste to build Scorecards, the vast majority of organizations sacrifice the up-front effort of providing meaningful and detailed Scorecard training to those expected to use the system. Awareness sessions are held, during which the Scorecard is trumpeted as a measurement system featuring financial and nonfinancial measures, but little is offered regarding the many subtleties and complexities of the model. It is often the deceptive simplicity of the Scorecard that makes people very susceptible to the false notion that in-depth training is not required. Believing that the Scorecard can be simply mastered, the organization will sponsor high-level training and then trust their employees' business instincts to kick in and fuel the development of powerful new performance measures. The cost of this decision will manifest itself in poorly designed Scorecards, lack of use, and weak alignment within the organization. Take the necessary time at the beginning of the project to develop a comprehensive Scorecard curriculum that includes background on the concept, your objectives in implementing it, typical problems, success stories, and project details.

Number 1: No Executive Sponsorship

Are you surprised? I didn't think so. For a while I debated whether lack of education and training should be the number one issue but concluded that with tenacious leadership and support a Scorecard project could ultimately succeed despite a lack of training at the outset. Without executive sponsorship, however, the effort is most likely doomed. So it remains the number one Balanced Scorecard implementation issue. Chapter Three provides a detailed review of executive sponsorship, including a number of methods for gaining support, and I urge you to review it carefully should you be lacking executive sponsorship for your project. Many Scorecard elements will take place in stages—first strategy is deciphered and translated; objectives, measures, targets, and initiatives are then developed; the Scorecard is cascaded throughout the organization; and, finally, it becomes embedded in the organization's managerial processes. Executive support and sponsorship is the common thread that connects the entire end-to-end process. Without a strong and vocal leader present at each and every juncture, the effort can quickly stall. Simply put, nothing can take the place of an energetic and knowledgeable executive willing to work tirelessly toward the cause of advancing the Balanced Scorecard.

USING CONSULTANTS TO DEVELOP THE BALANCED SCORECARD

After reading this book and digesting the findings of other research, I am sure you will agree that developing a Balanced Scorecard promises to bring great rewards but is certainly no simple task. Given the complexity of the development process, many organizations will turn to consulting companies for assistance. Even for small organizations there are many independent consulting companies and individuals suitably equipped to provide assistance. Hiring consultants is often a prudent decision since a quality firm may bring with it implementation experience, proven methodologies for completing the work in a timely fashion, and objective advice. Consultants also offer a quality sometimes in short supply during the implementation period—credibility. Senior management may be more receptive to the Scorecard when it is co-developed by outside "experts." But consulting help does not come cheap; in fact, developing even a high-level organizational Scorecard may cost several hundred thousand dollars, depending on the scope of the work and the particular consulting organization. And while consulting firms may lend credibility to the Scorecard from a senior management perspective, they may not engender the trust of employees who consider them overpaid and lacking in sufficient knowledge of the organization to complete an acceptable work product. The decision of whether to use consultants can be very difficult. Should you feel consulting help would benefit your Scorecard project, here are a number of factors to consider when selecting a firm.

- *Balanced Scorecard experience.* Given the popularity of the Balanced Scorecard, virtually every management consulting firm will suggest they have a performance measurement offering and will boast substantial experience from previous implementations. However, similar to our discussion of terminology a little earlier in the chapter, their conception of a Balanced Scorecard and yours may be miles apart. Through presentations and discussions you may discover that what they call a Balanced Scorecard is really an executive information system designed to supply the senior team with important business metrics, but lacking in leading indicators and cause-and-effect linkages. Be sure the firm you select is able to supply the Balanced Scorecard product you have in mind. This brings us to prior success. Most consulting firms will proudly advertise their past accomplishments at big-name organizations and offer glowing testimonials from satisfied clients. Be sure to perform an appropriate amount of due diligence here to ensure that those clients really are satisfied with the work performed and the final outcome of the project.
- *Look for a range of skills.* As we saw in the review of Balanced Scorecard team members presented in Chapter Three, developing a Scorecard requires a broad range of skill sets. The team assembled by your consulting partner should also have a diverse and complementary array of competencies. The entire team should be comprised of skilled communicators able to liaise easily and comfortably with all levels of staff. Some

members should be gifted presenters and trainers to ensure that the concepts behind the Scorecard are delivered clearly and cogently. Others should possess strong facilitation skills in order to capably manage the often (and necessary) conflict-filled Scorecard development sessions. Analytical skills are a must for combing through data and potential measures, and, finally, the team should possess members with enough technical skills to work effectively with your own information technology group.

- *Cultural fit.* This is an important and often overlooked quality when one is selecting a consulting firm. Your organization has a certain culture, as does each and every consulting company. We often read about the importance of cultural fit when two companies are planning a merger; in fact, conflicting cultures can sometimes even prove to be a deal breaker in these negotiations. Although you will not be permanently joined with the consultants you choose, they will be an extremely important part of your organization during the development of your Scorecard. Look past the sales presentations and testimonials to the real people you will be dealing with every day. Will they be compatible with the culture of your organization? Will executives and front-line staff alike be willing to work with them? Only you can answer this important question.

- *Knowledge transfer.* A key component of every work plan devised by consulting firms will be sufficient and timely knowledge transfer from the consultants to the employees of the contracting organization. Knowledge transfer implies just that—a passing of knowledge on key concepts and techniques from the consultants to the clients. However, in their zeal to complete the project on time and on budget, consultants may inadvertently sacrifice knowledge transfer activities in favor of more tangible work efforts. Organizations pay a heavy price when this occurs. As the consultants are walking out the door, they leave behind an organization bereft of the skills and knowledge necessary to sustain the momentum that was so difficult to achieve. Ensure that any consultants you work with will devote the necessary time to a comprehensive sharing of Scorecard knowledge.

FINAL THOUGHTS

Since its inception only 10 years ago, the Balanced Scorecard has had a profound effect on the practice of management around the world. The transition from antiquated industrial age methods to information age necessities dictated the emergence of new reporting tools. Heeding the call for new and innovative systems, the Balanced Scorecard quickly ascended the ranks of influential management tools. As Scorecard practitioners have tinkered with, experimented on, modified, and improved the methodology, it has only become stronger and more adaptable as a management system. The broad acceptance of the methodology is reflected in recent estimates suggesting that upwards of 50 percent of *Fortune* 1000 organizations have developed Balanced Scorecard systems. That, of course, means a corresponding 50 percent have not. And what of the thousands of small and medium-size enterprises, government agencies, and not-for-profit organizations spanning the globe? Clearly, the potential for future growth and development of the Balanced Scorecard is dramatic. Fortunately for all of us, the work continues, and the most exciting breakthroughs are most likely still ahead of us. It is organizations like yours, ready to embark on the Scorecard journey, that will write the next chapters in the life of this powerful and dynamic system. I thank you and wish you great success.

SUMMARY

It seems the only constant in today's organization is, ironically, change. The demands of twenty-first-century business dictate that organizations constantly adapt to new conditions or risk perishing. Unfortunately, the record of successful change in most organizations is dismally low. To ensure that the Balanced Scorecard does not suffer the fate of previous attempts at change, companies must engage in a number of organizational change activities. Rationale for the change must be clearly communicated, along with what will be expected of employees once the Scorecard system is initiated. Organizations must also determine how compatible the Scorecard is with current culture and to what extent employees have confidence the tool can be successfully implemented. Change facilitators can assess employee perceptions on key change issues and work with Scorecard team members to devise mitigating strategies.

Many organizations will fall prey to at least one of the top ten Balanced Scorecard implementation issues. They are: premature links to management processes, lack of cascading, terminology use, no new measures, consistent management practices, timing, no objectives for the Scorecard, no strategy, lack of training and education, and no executive sponsorship.

Consulting organizations have been quick to develop Scorecard offerings in conjunction with the tool's rapid growth. While consulting engagements are costly and not all employees relate well with "outsiders," they can provide a number of significant benefits. Proven methodologies, past Scorecard implementation successes, and speedy development times are just a few of the advantages awaiting those organizations hiring consultants. Before making the decision to hire consultants, organizations should consider the firm's actual implementation experience, skill sets offered, cultural fit, and knowledge sharing commitment.

About the Author

Paul R. Niven is a Management Consultant and noted speaker on the subjects of Performance Management and the Balanced Scorecard. As both a practitioner and Consultant he has developed successful Performance Management systems for clients large and small in a wide variety of organizations, including Fortune 500 companies, public sector agencies, and not-for-profit organizations. He may be reached at (760) 918-5990.

Index

Pollution Prevention

A Practical Guide for
State and Local Government

Edited by
David T. Wigglesworth

LEWIS PUBLISHERS
Boca Raton   Ann Arbor   London   Tokyo

Library of Congress Cataloging-in-Publication Data

Wigglesworth, David T.
    Pollution prevention: a practical guide for state and local
government / David T. Wigglesworth.
    p. cm.
    Includes bibliographical references and index.
    ISBN 0-87371-654-X
    1. Pollution. 2. Local government. 3. State governments.
  I. Title.
TD177.W53   1993
363.73′56—dc20   93-12193
                                                    CIP

PRINTED IN THE UNITED STATES OF AMERICA
1 2 3 4 5 6 7 8 9 0
Printed on acid-free paper

Dedication

This book is dedicated to the staff and management of the Alaska Department of Environmental Conservation and other environmental professionals actively working to prevent pollution. All book royalties eligible to the editor will be donated to the National Roundtable of State Pollution Prevention Programs.

About the Editor

David T. Wigglesworth is currently Chief of the Alaska Department of Environmental Conservation Pollution Prevention Office. Prior to this assignment, he was an Environmental Protection Specialist with the U.S. EPA Pollution Prevention Office. He also served as Deputy Director of Alaska Health Project where he established and managed the Waste Reduction Assistance Program (WRAP) for small business. Mr. Wigglesworth is the author of *Profiting from Waste Reduction in Your Small Business*. He has been an active member of the National Roundtable of State Pollution Prevention Programs since 1986 and has just completed a three-year term on the National Advisory Board to the Roundtable. Mr. Wigglesworth is a graduate of Harvard University with a degree in Visual and Environmental Studies. He and Nancy, his wife, currently reside in Anchorage, Alaska.

Preface

Preparing this handbook was satisfying for me both personally and professionally. Perhaps the most enjoyable aspect of this project was the opportunity to work collectively with my peers in the field of pollution prevention and to reestablish relationships with other colleagues with whom I used to work directly.

At first, I thought I would undertake this effort myself, but quickly rejected the idea for many reasons. Competing priorities for my personal time contributed to this decision, and because the field is changing so rapidly, it is virtually impossible for any one person to keep tabs on all the activities, projects, and trends. This is particularly evident in the area of pollution prevention funding policies. Upon completion of this book, it is evident that more emphasis is placed on issues concerning state pollution prevention programs than the concerns of local government. I encourage local program managers to consider preparing additional works that explore local pollution prevention program needs in greater detail.

I would like to thank all the contributing authors for assisting me with this effort and for taking the time to prepare excellent chapters. Additional thanks goes to Matt Knutson for his assistance in preparing some of the book figures, Sally Edwards for reviewing selected chapters, Skip Dewall, Elise Hoffman, and the editors of Lewis Publishers for their interest in publishing this book in the first place, and to Jim Labeots and Chris Richardson of CRC Press, Inc. for their assistance. A very special thanks goes to Sarah Araki for helping me with some of the final editing details. And last, but not least, a hearty thanks to my wife Nancy for encouraging me to finish this effort and for reminding that weekends are not just for writing books!

This handbook contains many examples for incorporating pollution prevention into the things state and local environmental personnel do. It suggests that pollution prevention practices can be integrated into the fabric of environmental programs. Yet, this book also implies that pollution prevention practices and policies are far from being firmly rooted in the framework of these programs and that the federal government will retain influence over the development of these programs. It is my hope that policy and decision-makers at the federal, state, and local level seize today's opportunities to foster and sustain innovative activities focusing on eliminating pollution rather than controlling it after the fact. Given today's environmental problems, the limitations of our current environmental protection framework, and associated pollution control costs, is there really any choice?

—**David T. Wigglesworth**

Introduction

The use of our air, land, and water resources as disposal media for our waste products is a tradition in most environmental protection programs. Today, this practice is being questioned by the public, government, industry, and elected officials. The environmental protection paradigm centered on controlling pollution after it has been created is now being challenged by an emerging view rooted in preventing pollution at its source. *Pollution Prevention: A Practical Guide for State and Local Government* explores this changing paradigm within state and local government environmental protection programs.

This book is not about pollution prevention success stories or a description of different state programs, nor does this book provide an exhaustive analysis of state and local pollution prevention integration efforts. This is due in part to the fact that many of these activities are currently in progress. Moreover, increasingly creative solutions will be developed and implemented as local and state agencies come to grips with the limitations of simply treating and disposing of waste and the limitations on available resources to correct environmental problems after the fact. In addition, this book does not take an in-depth look at federal pollution prevention activities such as incorporating prevention into the federal rule-making process.

Rather, this handbook focuses on current efforts to integrate prevention into local and state agency functions. It provides useful guidance for local and state environmental officials to more clearly understand the obstacles, opportunities, and techniques to incorporate prevention into their day-to-day functions.

Contributing authors provide suggestions based on practical experience and on methods to incorporate pollution prevention into inspections, permits, enforcement action, technical assistance, training, voluntary initiatives, pollution prevention partnerships, and agency budgets. Case study examples and resources for additional assistance are also provided.

Issues concerning the role of agency personnel in fostering pollution prevention are discussed. Other issues concerning redirecting funds toward pollution prevention, coordination among diverse agency programs, measuring progress, conducting pollution prevention training, labor-based pollution prevention activities, and the federal government's impact on state and local prevention efforts are explored.

This book is divided into four sections for purposes of organization and to provide the editor with the opportunity to introduce broad topical areas in the book. Effort was made to link related topics in each chapter through direct reference in applicable chapters. The editor and the chapter authors worked together to refine the scope of each chapter. However, the contents of each chapter are the opinions of its author and do not necessarily represent the views of the editor, other chapter authors, and their employees.

Above all, this book is intended to be a practical "how to" resource to assist local and state environmental protection personnel to identify opportunities to participate in this changing environmental paradigm. Whether our role is as an innovator, supporter, facilitator, leader, or evaluator, we have an enormous obligation and responsibility as environmental professionals to help foster this transition from pollution control to pollution prevention. The editor and contributing authors hope this book will help you.

Quick Reference to Each Chapter

SECTION I: STATE AND LOCAL POLLUTION PREVENTION FRAMEWORK

Chapter 1: The Federal Agenda: Impact on State and Local Pollution Prevention Efforts

This chapter explores the influence that the federal pollution prevention agenda has in determining the nature and extent of state and local pollution prevention activities. While state and local programs have considerable flexibility, the federal government still has significant influence over how these programs develop.

Chapter 1 is written by William Ross, Principal of Ross and Associates; and Chris Konrad, Junior Associate, Ross and Associates. Ross and Associates is an environmental policy consulting firm located in Seattle, Washington.

Chapter 2: Factors Contributing to the Development of State Programs: A Case Study

State pollution prevention programs show considerable variety. Some are firmly established and have healthy budgets, while others operate with a single person without consistent funding. This chapter explores some of the factors contributing to the development of state programs through a closer look at the growth of the North Carolina Pollution Prevention Pays program.

This chapter is written by Gary E. Hunt, Director of the Office of Waste Reduction, North Carolina Department of Environment, Health, and Natural Resources, Raleigh, North Carolina.

Chapter 3: Factors Contributing to the Development of Local Programs

Many local government or community-based pollution prevention programs are started without legislative mandates. Typically, these programs are started voluntarily and championed by government staff, individuals, the public, and/or local business. Some local governments are motivated to develop pollution prevention programs because these strategies help retain and encourage business development. This chapter explores more fully why and how local programs get started. It also considers the factors that contribute to a sustained local program.

This chapter is written by Linda G. Pratt, Pollution Prevention Program Manager, San Diego County Department of Health Services, Hazardous Materials Management Division, San Diego, California; and Anthony Eulo, Executive Director of the Local Government Commission, Sacramento, California.

SECTION II: TOOLS FOR INTEGRATION

Chapter 4: Facility Inspections — Obstacles and Opportunities

Regulatory compliance can be achieved by companies utilizing pollution prevention strategies. This chapter explores the obstacles and opportunities for incorporating pollution prevention into agency inspection programs. It argues that agencies do not have to alter the central purpose of agency inspections — regulatory compliance — as agencies seek to incorporate prevention into these activities.

This chapter is written by Timothy J. Greiner and Paul H. Richard, Massachusetts Office of Technical Assistance, Boston, Massachusetts, and Lee A. Dillard, Massachusetts Department of Environmental Protection, Boston, Massachusetts.

Chapter 5: Incorporating Pollution Prevention into Facility Permits

Agency permitting programs provide enormous opportunity to foster pollution prevention programs within industry. Many states are piloting pollution prevention permitting initiatives. Some include pollution prevention as a permit condition, while others build pollution prevention into the project design and permit application phase. This chapter discusses emerging pollution prevention permitting activity and provides useful tips for environmental agencies considering this activity.

This chapter is written by David Teeter, U.S. Environmental Protection Agency, Region 10, Seattle, Washington.

Chapter 6: Incorporating Pollution Prevention into Enforcement Actions

Enforcement actions are another "tool" environmental agencies can use to motivate industry to adopt pollution prevention practices. This chapter explores one aspect of the enforcement process — the settlement agreement. These agreements can be used to require industry to conduct pollution prevention opportunity assessments, conduct pollution prevention training, and incorporate pollution prevention into management policy.

This chapter is written by David Hartley, Chief of the Technology Clearinghouse, Office of Pollution Prevention and Technology Development, California Department of Toxic Substances Control, Sacramento, California. Mr. Hartley was past Chair of the National Roundtable of State Pollution Prevention Programs.

Chapter 7: Incorporating Pollution Prevention into Facility Planning

In some states, companies are now required to develop and implement pollution prevention plans. These new requirements, often called "toxic use reduction planning" or "facility planning," are an emerging pollution prevention tool for environmental agencies. Escalating environmental management costs, in addition to concerns about environmental quality and public health, have spurred states to pursue these new requirements. This chapter describes the issues surrounding facility planning requirements, providing useful advice for state and local agencies considering this pollution prevention option.

This chapter is written by David Rozell, Oregon Department of Environmental Quality, Toxic Use Reduction Program, Portland, Oregon.

Chapter 8: Promoting Pollution Prevention Through Technical Assistance

State and local pollution prevention programs typically strive to establish strong technical assistance programs. Technical assistance programs provide valuable information and advice to business and the public about methods to reduce waste. This chapter describes some of the critical components of a technical assistance program and basic day-to-day considerations in running an effective program.

This chapter is written by David Kidd, M.S., P.E., Instructor of Environmental Technology and Engineering, Linn-Benton Community College, Linn-Benton, Oregon. Mr. Kidd was the former Program Manager for Alaska Health Project's Waste Reduction Assistance Program (1989–1990).

Chapter 9: Conducting Pollution Prevention Training Programs

Training is an important aspect of any state and local pollution prevention program. Pollution prevention training is used to motivate industry, agency staff, management, and others to consider pollution prevention technologies and techniques. It is also used to convey specific technical information about industry-specific pollution prevention options and conducting pollution prevention facility assessments. This chapter explores these issues and provides useful tips for those developing and conducting their own pollution prevention training.

This chapter is written by Terry Foecke, Executive Director of the Waste Reduction Institute for Training and Applications Research (WRITAR), Minneapolis, Minnesota.

Chapter 10: Measuring Pollution Prevention Progress

Developing methods to measure pollution prevention progress is a difficult challenge confronting state and local environmental agencies and the federal government. High expectations for pollution prevention programs and declining revenue for all environmental agencies are putting considerable pressure on programs to justify their existence from a programmatic and resource perspective. This chapter outlines a process state and local environmental agencies can use to determine how to measure progress. Central to this process is the identification of measurement needs and linking these needs with appropriate measurement methodology.

This chapter is written by David Dellarco, U.S. Environmental Protection Agency, Region 10, Seattle, Washington.

Chapter 11: Securing Resources to Support Pollution Prevention Programs

State and local pollution prevention programs often have difficulty in sustaining prevention services beyond initial funding levels, frustrating state and local agency attempts to develop core prevention programs. This chapter explores an emerging trend to redirect funds from core federal media program grants to support state pollution prevention initiatives.

This chapter is written by David T. Wigglesworth, Chief of the Alaska Department of Environmental Conservation, Pollution Prevention Office, Juneau, Alaska.

SECTION III: POLLUTION PREVENTION PARTNERSHIPS

Chapter 12: Fostering Voluntary Pollution Prevention Initiatives

Voluntary initiatives are an important part of any local or state pollution prevention effort. These activities are driven by an entirely different set of incentives than those used within the regulatory process. This chapter takes a look at these incentives as they have been found to operate within the Green Star Program — a cooperative pollution prevention effort between business, government, and environmental groups. This program recently attained national recognition through receipt of the EPA Administrators' Award for excellence in pollution prevention.

This chapter is written by Megan Benedict, Green Star Program Director, Anchorage Chamber of Commerce, Anchorage, Alaska.

Chapter 13: Regional Pollution Prevention Partnerships

Partnerships in pollution prevention have also been fostered on a regional (geographic) basis. These activities have assisted government and industry address issues concerning capacity assurance, pollution prevention technical assistance, and information sharing. This chapter explores the factors contributing to regional partnerships through a closer look at the cooperative efforts taking place in the Pacific Northwest. EPA Region 10, British Columbia, and the states of Oregon, Washington, Idaho, and Alaska have all been working together over the past several years to foster active state pollution prevention efforts and develop regional efforts such as the Pacific Northwest Pollution Prevention Research Center.

This chapter is written by David Teeter, U.S. Environmental Protection Agency, Region 10, Seattle, Washington.

Chapter 14: Labor-Based Pollution Prevention Initiatives

The literature cites the importance of worker involvement in the development and implementation of pollution prevention programs (within an industry and an agency). However, little is written describing the techniques and opportunities for worker-based programs. This chapter provides an excellent investigation into the interest workers have in pollution prevention programs, provides examples of worker and union-based activities, and suggests how state and local environmental agencies might foster greater worker-based programs.

This chapter is written by Mark D. Catlin, Industrial Hygienist, Occupational Medicine Program, University of Washington, Seattle, Washington.

SECTION IV: POLLUTION PREVENTION RESOURCES

Chapter 15: Selected Pollution Prevention Resources

There are a multitude of resources to help state and local environmental protection agencies develop pollution prevention programs. The Environmental Protection Agency (EPA) has stimulated the growth of many of these resources. This chapter describes selected organizations providing technical and financial assistance. A brief summary of federal grant programs that may offer flexibility for pollution prevention projects is presented. Finally, federal and state pollution prevention contacts are also provided.

This chapter is written by David T. Wigglesworth, Chief of the Alaska Department of Environmental Conservation Pollution Prevention Office, Juneau, Alaska.

Contributors

Megan Benedict
Director
Green Star Program
Anchorage Chamber of Commerce
Anchorage, Alaska

Mark Catlin
Industrial Hygienist
Occupational Medicine Program
Harborview Medical Center
University of Washington
Seattle, Washington

David Dellarco
Pollution Prevention Policy Analyst
U.S. EPA Region 10
Seattle, Washington

Lee A. Dillard
Executive Office of Environmental
  Affairs
Massachusetts Department of Environ-
  mental Protection
Boston, Massachusetts

Anthony Eulo
Executive Director
Local Government Commission
Sacramento, California

Terry Foecke
Executive Director
Waste Reduction Institute for Training
  and Applications Research
  (WRITAR)
Minneapolis, Minnesota

Timothy J. Greiner
Executive Office of Environmental
  Affairs
Massachusetts Office of Technical
  Assistance
Boston, Massachusetts

David Hartley
Chief
Technology Clearinghouse
Office of Pollution Prevention and
  Technology Development
California Department of Toxic
  Substances Control
Sacramento, California

Gary E. Hunt
Director
Office of Waste Reduction
North Carolina Department of
  Environment, Health, and Natural
  Resources
Raleigh, North Carolina

David Kidd
Instructor
Department of Environmental
  Technology and Engineering
Linn-Benton Community College
Linn-Benton, Oregon

Chris Konrad
Junior Associate
Ross & Associates, Environmental
  Consulting Ltd.
Seattle, Washington

Linda G. Pratt
Pollution Prevention Program
  Manager
San Diego County Department of
  Health Services
Hazardous Materials Management
  Division
San Diego, California

Paul H. Richard
Executive Office of Environmental
  Affairs
Massachusetts Office of Technical
  Assistance
Boston, Massachusetts

William Ross
Principal
Ross & Associates, Environmental
  Consulting Ltd.
Seattle, Washington

David Rozell
Pollution Prevention Coordinator
Oregon Department of Environmental
  Quality
Toxic Use Reduction Program
Portland, Oregon

David Teeter
Chief
Planning and Outreach Section
Water Division
U.S. EPA Region 10
Seattle, Washington

David T. Wigglesworth
Chief
Alaska Department of Environmental
  Conservation Pollution Prevention
  Office
Anchorage, Alaska

Contents

SECTION I: STATE AND LOCAL POLLUTION
PREVENTION FRAMEWORK

SECTION III: POLLUTION PREVENTION PARTNERSHIPS

SECTION IV: POLLUTION PREVENTION RESOURCES

SECTION I:

STATE AND LOCAL POLLUTION PREVENTION FRAMEWORK

Introduction

Diversity perhaps best describes pollution prevention activity at the federal, state, and local level — diversity in terms of program services and emphasis, and in terms of program origin and funding levels. By taking a look at the current federal pollution prevention agenda and factors contributing to the development of state and local programs, this section provides policy-makers with useful information to consider when attempting to build a sustained pollution prevention framework. Several factors emerge as important to the successful development of state and local programs:

- the development of a program "vision" and program plan
- the existence of program champions
- top level commitment
- strong technical assistance services
- the creation of partnerships and teamwork both within and outside of government
- an established trust with industry
- incentives for industry to consider pollution prevention
- regional cooperation and partnerships
- departmental reorganization to increase visibility and authority of the program
- incorporation of pollution prevention programs into the base budget of the agency
- emphasis on effectively targeting limited resources for priority concerns and striving for quick results
- an understanding of and a commitment to the amount of time and energy required to move environmental programs away from pollution control and toward pollution prevention
- development of new approaches to measuring success

As the federal pollution prevention agenda develops and exerts its influence on state and local programs, it will be important to make certain the flexibility and diversity these programs currently enjoy are retained in order to meet the needs of local conditions. Moreover, policy-makers examining state and federal pollution prevention frameworks should take note of the factors contributing to successful programs.

CHAPTER 1

The Federal Agenda: Impact on State and Local Pollution Prevention Efforts

Bill Ross and Chris Konrad

1.1 INTRODUCTION

In light of the many innovative public policies to prevent pollution being developed at state and local levels, the federal government still has considerable influence in determining the nature and extent of state and local pollution prevention activities. This federal influence is exerted through the existing public policy and regulatory framework for environmental issues of all types, as well as an emerging federal pollution prevention agenda. The existing policy framework and the emerging federal agenda now offer opportunities for state and local governments to design policies and programs based on pollution prevention, *provided* these state and local governments continue to fulfill their other regulatory duties. While the continued development of a national pollution prevention policy may very well further legitimize pollution prevention approaches to solving environmental problems, extensive federal participation in driving pollution prevention through the public policy framework might also result in decreased flexibility or acknowledgement of current state and local pollution prevention efforts.

1.2 FEDERAL POLLUTION PREVENTION AGENDA

The public sector's efforts to protect environmental quality grow each year in terms of resources and complexity, but environmental problems persist in spite of these increasing efforts. Consequently, federal, state, and local governments have begun to develop innovative public policies, based on pollution prevention, to deal with the imperative presented by the remaining environmental problems.

A federal pollution prevention agenda has emerged pertinent in terms of the opportunities it provides to state and local governments and the direction it sets for national pollution prevention policies. Much like the developing state and local pollution prevention efforts, the federal agenda departs from the existing policy and regulatory framework with a broad scope of applications and new approaches to environmental protection. Simultaneously, the federal agenda is limited by pollution prevention's relatively recent introduction into the existing public policy framework. As a result, the federal government has concentrated its efforts to date primarily on ad hoc pollution prevention efforts, with the exception of some initiatives to integrate pollution prevention into existing regulatory activities.

1.2.1 Scope

The domain of pollution prevention is potentially as wide as the domain of the federal government, though to date, the federal pollution prevention agenda has been defined primarily by the Environmental Protection Agency (EPA), Department of Agriculture, Department of Defense, and Department of Energy.

Of all federal agencies, EPA is notable for the scope of its pollution prevention activities. Pollution prevention has been afforded its own place in the agency's administrative structures through the newly created Office of Pollution Prevention. All EPA regions have initiated pollution prevention activities. The EPA has also participated with private organizations in the creation of new institutions such as the American Institute for Pollution Prevention and the Pacific Northwest Pollution Prevention Research Center. Many of the EPA's program offices contribute to its pollution prevention agenda including water, air, toxic substances, solid waste, pesticides, policy, research and development, and enforcement.[1]

In addition to the range of EPA program offices and regions pursuing pollution prevention, pollution prevention has been applied to EPA functions from research to regulation. Research at the Risk Reduction Engineering Laboratory, grants from the Small Business Innovative Research program, and technical information via the Pollution Prevention Information Clearinghouse foster the development of private sector pollution prevention projects. As regulatory development can intentionally and unintentionally create incentives for or against pollution prevention, EPA has taken the opportunity to integrate pollution prevention into new regulations such as perchloroethylene emission controls for dry cleaners which mandate maintenance and record keeping procedures to prevent solvent loss.[2] Enforcement actions recently have used pollution prevention projects in settlements, and in the future, environmental permitting of new projects may have an increased emphasis on multimedia and pollution prevention issues.[3]

Other federal agencies also help create the federal pollution prevention agenda. The Department of Agriculture's Low Input Sustainable Agriculture (LISA) program funds research, implementation, and training projects focusing on reducing soil erosion and limiting agricultural use of fertilizer and pesticides. The Department of Defense (DOD), which formally initiated pollution prevention with its "Hazardous Materials Pollution Prevention Directive" in 1989, focuses its efforts on two areas of action: prevention of the pollution DOD facilities generate and revision of procurement so that suppliers to DOD rely less on hazardous materials and processes.[4]

Like DOD, the Department of Energy has developed pollution prevention plans for its hazardous waste generating facilities. Both departments have applied techniques from private sector pollution prevention efforts by incorporating process and waste audits, hazardous materials and waste accounting, management initiatives, better housekeeping, source substitution, and process modifications in their facility plans.

1.2.2 New Approaches

New approaches to protecting environmental quality are integral to promoting pollution prevention, and four of these approaches characterize the federal pollution prevention agenda. While EPA still relies primarily on technology-based regulation of single medium pollutants, it also now attempts to foster pollution prevention through voluntary, educational, consumer-oriented, and inter-agency/program activities.

Voluntary Pollution Prevention

Voluntary programs are a distinguishing feature of the current federal pollution prevention agenda. Generally, these programs focus on major point sources of pollution or large energy users. Three types of voluntary pollution prevention programs are being developed or administered by EPA.

One of the most notable is the "33/50 program" aimed at reducing the industrial releases of 17 target chemicals. Under this program, EPA has asked for voluntary commitments by the 600 largest industrial emitters of the target chemicals to reduce their emissions of these chemicals by 33% by 1992 and by 50% by 1995. Epitomizing a flexible and voluntary approach, the "33/50 program" allows participating companies to choose their preferred methods for reducing releases (which need not be source reduction) and provides no regulatory consequences for failure to meet the goals. EPA, though, has given the "33/50 program" a high profile and will publicize companies' annual progress toward their commitments.

Another EPA program, "Green Lights," exhibits a similar approach in which EPA seeks energy reduction commitments from the private sector. Under "Green Lights," EPA educates businesses about cost-effective, energy-efficient lighting systems and then garners agreements from them to install such systems.

The early reduction/alternative emission limitations provision of the Clean Air Act Amendments is the second type of voluntary program. Under this provision, a facility that is required to control its emissions of air toxins can be granted a six year compliance extension from the final source control standards if that facility reduces its emissions of air toxins by 90% before the final source control standards are issued. While initial participation is strictly voluntary, EPA considers any facility's specific commitment to the reductions as enforceable.[5]

EPA's enforcement activities have demonstrated a third type of voluntary approach to pollution prevention. In some cases of Toxic Substances Control Act (TSCA) and Emergency Planning and Community Right to Know Act (EPCRA) violations, the defendants and EPA have agreed to include commitments by the defendants to implement specific pollution prevention activities in the settlements as partial relief for the original violations and as supplemental projects to mitigate related environmental problems.[6] States are also looking to enforcement settlements as a way to drive more pollution prevention.

Pollution Prevention Education

Educational programs, targeted to industries and household consumers, contribute another approach to the federal pollution prevention agenda. EPA's Office of Research and Development (ORD) has published a series of guides for specific industries, describing applicable pollution prevention techniques and suggesting ways to implement pollution prevention activities. ORD, through its "consumer product comparative risk project," also has examined life-cycle analysis as a tool for educating consumers about the environmental implications of their choices.[7]

The Pollution Prevention Information Clearinghouse is an EPA network that disseminates information about public and private pollution prevention research, programs, and activities. Other EPA-supported efforts include workshops and newsletters that focus on pollution prevention and aim to educate both the regulatory community (federal, state, and local) and industry about the latest breakthroughs in pollution prevention programs and technologies.

Consumer-Oriented Pollution Prevention

By adopting consumer-oriented approaches, the federal government attempts to tackle pollution by aiming even further "up stream" than just the sources of output-related pollution. Executive Order 12780, signed on October 31, 1991, reiterates the 1984 requirement that federal agencies procure recovered materials when possible and revise specifications to give preference to recovered materials.[8]

Through initiatives in each branch of the military and the Defense Logistics Agency, the DOD is attempting to revise its procurement specifications to reduce its demand for hazardous materials and processes and to account for the environmental life-cycle costs of materials up-front.

The Federal Trade Commission and EPA participate in consumer-oriented pollution prevention by examining manufacturers' "recycled and recyclable" claims and by proposing guidelines on such claims.[9] As discussed, EPA also is investigating life-cycle analysis to inform consumers about the environmental differences between products.

Inter-Agency/Inter-Program Pollution Prevention

Federal implementation of pollution prevention policies that are multimedia in nature requires cooperation of various agencies and programs, which otherwise operate independently. While federal agencies have not been explicitly reorganized to capture the multimedia and cross-jurisdictional dimension of pollution prevention, there are examples of recent attempts to coordinate different agencies on pollution prevention projects.

The DOD and EPA have cooperated on the Waste Reduction Evaluations at the Federal Sites program in which military installations are assessed for pollution prevention opportunities. Additionally, geographic targeting of environmental protection has led to cooperation among federal agencies. In the Great Lakes basin, EPA, U.S. Fish and Wildlife Service, and state agencies are cooperating on pollution prevention and habitat conservation efforts. Finally, EPA and the Department of Agriculture are jointly sponsoring a grant program for education, research, and development of projects concerned with agriculture and environmental issues.[10]

One of the most imposing challenges of integrating pollution prevention in the federal government is coordinating programs within EPA. In an attempt to foster multimedia, inter-program approaches, EPA has defined a series of regulatory "clusters." The clusters are collaborative efforts by program offices to coordinate regulatory development as a way to address specific issues beyond the scope of single program offices. For example, the "pulp and paper cluster" is a group of program offices working to control dioxin emissions from pulp and paper mills, and the "groundwater cluster" is focused on sharing information among the variety of program offices concerned with groundwater.

1.2.3 Piecemeal and Ad Hoc Nature

Since bureaucracies integrate new ideas slowly, the federal pollution prevention agenda has been advanced in a piecemeal and ad hoc manner relative to the extent of the changes implied by full acceptance of pollution prevention by the federal government. While EPA's "Pollution Prevention Strategy" indicates the agency's resolve to reorient the agency to prevent pollution, the strategy appears to fall short in some cases as it tends to fit pieces of pollution prevention into the agency's existing duties. For example, EPA invests in state pollution prevention programs through its competitive and limited grant program, but it is only beginning to address the integration of pollution prevention into other aspects of the federal-state relationships like State-EPA Agreements. These annual agreements define the overall allocation of resources and performance goals for state environmental agencies authorized to implement federal programs.

While the federal government is encouraging single media programs to integrate pollution prevention into their activities, it has not yet embraced multimedia approaches through State-EPA Agreements. EPA has included aspects of pollution prevention during regulatory development, permitting, and enforcement, but the orientation of regulatory programs largely remains on single medium, point source control of existing pollutants. Overall, EPA's pollution prevention initiatives are only beginning to develop long-term ramifications for the agency's basic functions.

Like EPA, other federal agencies have initiated ad hoc activities, but have neglected to develop pollution prevention strategies commensurate with their authority. For example, the Departments of Energy and Transportation have demonstrated little vision in promoting pollution prevention alternatives to the current energy and transportation systems and the environmental problems that have been created by the nation's demand on those systems.

In recognition of its progress to date, EPA has limited latitude to change its fundamental mission without congressional endorsement and has pushed pollution prevention into as many or more areas as state and local agencies have. While many states have made "a leap of faith" as they initiated permanent regulatory, monitoring, or technical assistance pollution prevention programs that in some cases will dramatically change basic agency operations, this type of change is generally initiated by acts of a state legislature. The federal agenda is unlikely to develop more comprehensive programs until pollution prevention advances further through congressional initiatives of this type.

1.2.4 Statutory Progress

The impetus for pollution prevention has been an indirect result of much of the nation's environmental legislation. While the major statutes addressing pollution control and management in a specific medium (i.e., Resource Conservation and Recovery Act, Clean Water Act, and Clean Air Act) acknowledge some role for prevention as a national policy or a goal for public sector programs,[11] they and other statutes provide a strong incentive for pollution prevention by adding expenses and responsibilities for properly managing existing pollution.

Another statute that indirectly pushed pollution prevention forward, the Superfund Amendments and Reauthorization Act (SARA), created an effective climate for states to initiate pollution prevention programs. Under SARA, states are required to demonstrate that they have sufficient capacity to manage all of the hazardous waste generated within their borders lest they lose cleanup funding.[12] By reducing the need for management capacity, pollution prevention provides states with one alternative to attempting to site hazardous waste management facilities within their borders or to enter into interstate agreements with states that have excess management capacity.

Congress first emphatically endorsed hazardous waste minimization in the 1984 reauthorization of the Resource Conservation and Recovery Act (RCRA).[13] The act, the Hazardous and Solid Waste Amendments of 1984, introduced pollution prevention into the hazardous waste regulatory scheme; it stipulates that hazardous waste generators must have a waste minimization program in place and that they must report the results of their waste minimization efforts as part of the Biennial Report.[14]

Since 1984, the direct references to pollution prevention have expanded in federal legislation. The Pollution Prevention Act of 1990 is notable among federal statutes in this regard; it overtly supports pollution prevention, and it directs EPA to implement pollution prevention activities. In particular, the act advances the following five approaches:

- funding of state technical assistance programs
- integration of pollution prevention into EPA activities (e.g., regulatory analysis to facilitate source reduction, EPA staff training)
- establishment of a pollution prevention information clearinghouse
- reporting on pollution prevention activities as an addition to Toxins Release Inventory reporting

As is evident, these approaches are largely nonregulatory with the exception of the reporting requirement and EPA review of regulations "to determine their effect on source reduction."[15]

Other statutory references to pollution prevention, however, have had a regulatory orientation. Principally, the Clean Air Act Amendments (1990) introduced pollution prevention into a number of regulatory arenas including the development of source control standards for air toxins, the schedules for complying with the air toxins standards, the marketing of vehicle fuel, and the manufacture and operation of vehicle fleets.[16] In addition to explicitly providing for a role for pollution prevention, the amendments expanded a novel economic tool for pollution control — SO_2 emission allowances — which may indirectly promote prevention as utilities search for less expensive alternatives to purchasing emission allowances or installing pollution control equipment.

As the nation's environmental statutes are reauthorized in the future, the emphasis of pollution prevention in regulatory programs will likely grow. Under this scenario, media-specific regulatory programs would adopt pollution prevention as the next frontier of required environmental activity — i.e., an activity to be monitored and enforced at large point sources of pollution. The fate of multimedia and nonregulatory approaches will depend, then, on such factors as how aggressively the Pollution Prevention Act is implemented, the tack of the Office of Pollution Prevention, and, generally, the ability of EPA, its program offices, and other agencies to become involved in regulatory, educational, and economic activities that transcend media-specific pollution control approaches.

1.3 FEDERAL POLICY FRAMEWORK IMPACT ON STATE AND LOCAL GOVERNMENTS

The federal government's historical participation in the existing public policy and regulatory framework is a useful guide in understanding the impact the federal agenda has and will have on state and local pollution prevention activities. While the federal agenda demonstrates many different types of pollution prevention activities, the federal policy and regulatory framework dictate the changes that can occur to the public sector's administrative functions.

1.3.1 Statutes, Regulations, and Programs

Traditionally, the federal government has reacted to environmental problems by Congress passing statutes intended to control pollution of a single medium or to solve isolated environmental problems.[17] As well, the statutes typically target large point sources. There are numerous examples of statutes that define environmental problems in terms of one medium or that respond to one manifestation of what might be larger environmental problems.[18]

These patterns in federal statutes contravene two tenants of pollution prevention: first, hazardous substances contribute to environmental problems at various points in their life cycle (i.e., manufacture, transport, use, and release), not just as waste or pollution releases; second, preemptive action is the most effective way to address most environmental problems. The discontinuity between the character of pollution prevention and the character of existing federal environmental statutes restricts the extent to which pollution prevention is currently incorporated into federal activities. Furthermore, the discontinuity will likely continue as the federal agenda struggles with implementing multimedia and proactive programs that concentrate on pollution prevention.

Regulatory development and implementation comprise the next steps in the federal policy framework. Typically regulations reflect statutory perspectives, and in the case of environmental regulations they focus on pollution control and management in a single medium. More often than not, federal regulations have concerned only large point sources. At the regulatory level, change is typically demonstrated by the addition or deletion of regulations, but not the development of a new tack. The framework can integrate pollution prevention in terms of protocol, but it will miss multimedia and nonregulatory aspects of pollution prevention. Pollution prevention's lack of a strong enforcement ethic to date further limits its acceptance by the existing regulatory framework that it is founded upon.

The last phase of federal participation in the framework comes when programs are implemented to administer regulations. In this phase, the impact of federal policy is made manifest at the state and local level as the responsibility for program implementation shifts to state and local governments. The shift in responsibility at this phase results from statutory intent through funding additions or deletions and through guidance delineating what state and local governments are to do in order to keep their delegated responsibility. The development of federal policy, as it feeds into this process, will define many legal and financial parameters for state and local governments attempting pollution prevention activities.

The federal government is showing flexibility by allowing pollution prevention activities to be supported through state-EPA grants. To receive grants, states agree to perform specific tasks outlined in a workplan that traditionally focuses on regulatory activities. Demonstrating flexibility, the EPA drafted supplemental guidance for the 1993 fiscal year, providing principles whereby states' media programs can propose to allocate resources to pollution prevention activities through the development of annual workplans.

The principles do not restrict states, but recognize the importance of integrating pollution prevention in program activities whenever feasible. EPA emphasizes that states should consider the pollution prevention results of options when making decisions. In the guidance, the agency supports states that establish pollution prevention research and education focused on pollution prevention techniques. The guidance also acknowledges the importance of measuring the success of pollution prevention efforts. To support these prevention activities, the guidance suggests that EPA afford states greater flexibility in workplan outputs, targets, and deadlines. While EPA is giving state governments a signal that pollution prevention can be a priority among other duties for media programs, a number of policy issues have not been resolved. Notably, it remains to be seen how federal policy will support states' multimedia pollution prevention efforts.

1.3.2 Capacity for Change

The existing federal policy framework may be limited in its capacity to nurture the full range of approaches conducive to preventing pollution, due to structural differences between the current policy and regulatory framework, and pollution prevention. Structurally, the single medium or single issue reactive regulatory approach is deeply rooted in existing regulations, statutes, and bureaucracy with few opportunities for innovation, whereas pollution prevention suggests a multimedia, proactive and less emphatically regulatory approach.

Pollution prevention policies are often flexible as they give generators of pollution the option of preventing generation as an alternative to pollution control.

The emphasis of pollution prevention programs can be educational in that they provide technical assistance to industries, require generators to consider prevention alternatives, and inform consumers about product choices. Finally, policies based on pollution prevention emphasize broader environmental concerns than traditional regulatory policies in terms of the impact of releases, the time-scale of those impacts across the life-cycle of products, and the focal points for policies (i.e., a facility rather than a pipe, a region rather than point sources, and consumers and producers rather than just producers).

Given the existing policy framework and the distinct nature of pollution prevention, the changes required to realize the full potential of pollution prevention will require statutory initiatives. Such statutory initiatives, however, will be difficult to foster, given the current approach to environment regulation.

1.4 CHALLENGES AND OPPORTUNITIES

The federal government's pollution prevention agenda will undoubtedly impact the duties of state and local governments as well as create opportunities for expanded pollution prevention activities. Given the current federal pollution prevention agenda, state and local governments can approach the development and implementation of pollution prevention policies in three ways.

1.4.1 Participating in the Federal Agenda

While many of the activities and programs described in this chapter are attributed to the federal government, there is room for state and local governments' participation. For example, in Wichita/Sedgwick County, Kansas, the County Department of Community Health, state Department of Health and Environment, EPA Region 7, and local industries are cooperating in an attempt to achieve dramatic reductions in waste emissions in the county. Following the lead of the "33/50 program," Sedgwick County generators who were too small to be included in the national "33/50 program" plan on voluntarily reducing emissions of 17 priority chemicals 38% by 1992 and 55% by 1995.[19]

Following this lead, state and local governments can integrate elements from the federal pollution prevention agenda into their policy development. Using federal assistance and expertise, state and local governments can perform the following:

- participate in EPA grant programs that offer financial assistance for initiating new programs or developing pollution prevention techniques
- explore innovative regulatory initiatives that use pollution prevention in permitting, inspections, and enforcement actions and model new initiatives after them
- learn about successful public and private efforts that have prevented pollution generated by specific industries or processes, and apply the lessons to their industries and generators

- open a dialogue with the regulated community to discuss federal and state regulations and how pollution prevention can be a long-term strategy for compliance
- identify areas of cross-jurisdiction with federal agencies and work with those agencies to develop coordinated policies that will most efficiently prevent pollution
- participate in the National Roundtable for State & Local Pollution Prevention Programs

EPA, state, and local governments are developing significant experience with pollution prevention. As well, many agencies have developed resources that can provide information about pollution prevention technologies and programs. Given the breadth of the federal agenda, any state or local government will likely be able to find federal activities appropriate for their environmental priorities and can work to expand or develop these activities in their area.

1.4.2 Complementing the Federal Agenda

Prevention is proving to be effective at addressing point sources of pollution that have been the primary foci of federal regulation. But state and local governments face a spectrum of environmental issues that have not been addressed by the federal agenda. Pollution prevention policies can empower state and local governments with new tools for managing environmental problems that have resisted traditional regulation: nonpoint sources that result from our collective actions of a large number of small and/or mobile sources.

At first glance, these problems appear vast. They result from our demand for housing, transportation, manufactured goods, services, agricultural products, and energy. Pollution prevention, however, provides at least one measure for comparing policy options when state and local governments face decisions in these arenas. State and local governments interested in pollution prevention for nonpoint sources can acknowledge, in their full range of their activities, a preference for pollution prevention and for those projects that will prevent pollution.

An initial approach to complementing the federal agenda is to note those areas where federal agencies are taking the lead (e.g., point source emissions of SO_2). State and local governments can then assess their other responsibilities for environmental protection, establish some sense of priority among them, and apply pollution prevention policies to these outstanding problems that might best respond to state and local initiatives.

1.4.3 Stretching State And Local Agendas

In many ways, state and local governments are already stretching the limits of current pollution prevention policy. For example, a number of states have statutes that compel industries to consider pollution prevention options. There are many opportunities for state and local governments to address their particular environmental concerns through innovative policies that develop the following:

- new structures for environmental protection such as multimedia facility permitting, inter-agency and regional collaboration, and public-private partnerships for research and technical assistance
- new approaches to environmental protection including facility planning and accounting for pollution prevention, chemical bans, education of industries and the public about their ability to prevent pollution, and market-based incentives for encouraging prevention

State and local governments should recognize that these structures and approaches may represent a substantial change from existing regulatory structures and approaches. Consequently, they may require reorganization of program offices, training of staff, and dedication of management to their success.

While stretching the limits of environmental policy may prove to be effective in protecting the environment, state or local governments attempting innovative policies should consider the following four aspects where the federal government can and will play an important role:

- Federal programs can provide valuable information to state and local governments for planning pollution prevention efforts.
- Innovators run the risk of being out of alignment with federal programs and should be aware of the possibility that the federal government may call for some level of national uniformity in regulating pollution prevention in the future.
- New programs will likely need to demonstrate their efficacy especially to existing and potential sources of funding. Measuring success in fostering pollution prevention is at its infancy and will grow in importance if pollution prevention is to get more than marginal funding.
- State-EPA agreements may be useful for institutionalizing pollution prevention if a state can achieve the necessary flexibility (e.g., establish new performance targets for pollution prevention activities and shift resources from previous targets). As mentioned, EPA is demonstrating increasing flexibility in the grant process to allow states to pursue pollution prevention.

1.5 CONCLUSION

The federal pollution prevention agenda, as it becomes manifest in the federal policy and regulatory framework, may begin to drive more pollution prevention activities at a state and local level. Regardless of the direction the federal agenda takes, state and local governments will do well to stay informed of federal activities. They can learn from federal experiences of integrating pollution prevention into existing responsibilities. They can participate in innovative federal pollution prevention programs. They can benefit from federal assistance for pollution prevention projects. Finally, they can develop their own policies to prevent pollution that will complement the focus of current federal programs and stretch beyond the limit of current federal policies to address the environmental problems they find to be most urgent.

The remaining chapters in this book explore these challenges and opportunities in greater detail. Efforts to incorporate pollution prevention into voluntary initiatives and the regulatory process are described herein. Additional resources are provided in Chapter 15.

1.6 REFERENCES

1. Hampshire Research Associates, Inc. "Progress on Reducing Industrial Pollutants," U.S. EPA, Office of Pollution Prevention, EPA 21P-3003 (October 1991).
2. "First Air Toxins Rule under CAA Includes Pollution Prevention Provision," *Pollut. Prev. News* (January 1992), p. 1.
3. "Pollution Prevention Strategy," U.S. EPA, p. 26.
4. Pollution Prevention Information Clearinghouse. "Federal Program Summary," U.S. EPA.
5. "Proposed Rules on Early Reductions of Toxic Releases Under Clean Air Act," *Environ. Rep.* 22(7):459 (1991).
6. U.S. EPA Docket No.: TSCA-89-H-17; TSCA-90-H-03; and EPCRA-I-90-1007.
7. Hampshire Research Associates, Inc., p. 154.
8. 42 U.S. Code 6962.
9. "Agency Hears Public Comment on Proposal To Offer Guidance on Green Marketing Claims," *Environ. Rep.* 22(29): 1669 (1991).
10. Hampshire Research Associates, Inc., p. 185.
11. Clean Air Act, Section 101(c), states, "A primary goal of this act is to promote [public sector activities] for pollution prevention." Resource Conservation and Recovery Act, Section 1003(b), states, "National Policy. The Congress hereby declares it to be the national policy of the U.S. that, wherever feasible, the generation of hazardous waste is to be reduced or eliminated as expeditiously as possible." Clean Water Act, Section 101(b), recognizes the responsibility of states to prevent pollution.
12. Comprehensive Environmental Response, Compensation, and Liability Act, Section 104(c)(9).
13. Hazardous and Solid Waste Amendments of 1984, PL 98-616.
14. 42 U.S. Code 3002(b).
15. 42 U.S. Code 13103(b)(2)g.
16. Clean Air Act Amendments of 1990, PL 101-549.
17. "Reducing Risk: Setting Priorities and Strategies for Environmental Protection," Science Advisory Board, U.S. EPA, SAB-EC-90-021 (September 1990), p. 3.

The federal government's participation in public policy does occasionally deviate from these patterns. Congress found, as stated in Section (2)(a)(2) of the Toxic Substances Control Act, that unreasonable risks to human health and the environment resulted from multimedia exposure to many chemicals during "manufacture, processing, distribution in commerce, use, or disposal." The scope of the Superfund Amendments and Reauthorization Act of 1986 is also multimedia as the act stipulates reporting of inventories for hazardous chemicals and their releases to all media. The National Environmental Policy Act (NEPA) demonstrates a proactive approach to solving environmental problems. Though not specifically focused on pollution, the NEPA requires federal agencies to assess the environmental degradation that will result from proposed federal projects before the actual degradation occurs. Compared with the bulk of reactive, single issue federal legislation, TSCA, SARA, and NEPA are exceptions.

18. Three statutes exemplify the reactive, single medium/single issue approach the federal government has attempted to use to solve environmental problems: the Clean Water Act of 1977; the Comprehensive Environmental Response, Compensation, and Liability Act (CERCLA) of 1980; and the Safe Drinking Water Act of 1974.

19. "Fact Sheet 33/50 Project, Sedgwick County, Kansas," U.S. EPA, Region 7 (July 29, 1991).

CHAPTER 2

Factors Contributing to the Development of State Programs: A Case Study

Gary E. Hunt

2.1 INTRODUCTION

Since the mid-1980s, an ever-increasing number of states are taking the innovative approach of encouraging pollution prevention rather than the treatment of pollution. Traditional regulation of pollution through standards, permits, regulation, and other negative incentives has been shown to be only part of the answer to environmental protection. As more and further-reaching regulations were developed, it became evident to industry and state governments that the end-of-pipe treatment was not the total answer. The reduction of waste through source reduction and recycling is an important part of any waste management strategy. In the rush to develop traditional "end-of-pipe" regulations, this simple approach was overlooked. It was "rediscovered" in the early 1980s and has since become the watchword of state governments, the EPA, environmental groups, and industries.

North Carolina is the recognized state leader in developing and implementing a multimedia pollution prevention program. The history of how this program came into being is one of perseverance, timing, and luck. From 1981 when the pollution prevention concept started to take root in North Carolina, through 1984

0-87371-654-X/93/$0.00+$.50
© 1993 by Lewis Publishers

when the Pollution Prevention Pays program (PPP program) was first funded, and finally up to today, there has been constant change and growth. All along the way, there were many chances for the program to have been stopped. However, the pollution prevention concept has grown greatly since it was first voiced in 1981. Now it has been embedded in a division level office, which has developed a world-wide reputation.

This chapter will follow the development and implementation of the pollution prevention concept in North Carolina including the development of the PPP program. This, hopefully, will identify some of the pitfalls to avoid and some of the key approaches to try in establishing a similar effort. It must be noted that there was no legislation setting up the PPP program; the actual implementation of the program was accomplished because a few people chose to take some risks and push the concept. As the chapter will tell, while these people believed in the PPP concept, they did not all agree on how it should be implemented.

2.2 ESTABLISHMENT OF THE NORTH CAROLINA POLLUTION PREVENTION PAYS PROGRAM

The exact time when the PPP concept was first introduced into the state is now lost. However, in 1980 considerable discussion was under way regarding the management of waste, especially hazardous waste. Recommendations of the Governor's Waste Management Task Force resulted in passage of the Waste Management Act of 1981. Intended as a strong policy statement that hazardous wastes should be kept out of landfills, the statute reads, "The General Assembly of North Carolina hereby finds and declares that prevention, recycling, detoxification, and reduction of hazardous wastes should be encouraged and promoted."

During this time, the Governor's Board of Science and Technology was working on a toxic chemical management project. The staff became interested in waste reduction through publications on the PPP concept written by Dr. Michael Royston.[1,2] Based on these works and the growing interest in waste management within the administration, the Board of Science and Technology applied for and received a grant from the Mary Reynolds Babcock Foundation in November of 1981 to undertake a PPP educational effort. This two phase program consisted of a symposium on the philosophy, technology, and economics of pollution prevention and developing mechanisms for the implementation of the pollution prevention concept into the state's government and industries. The conference was held in May of 1982 and brought together about 150 people from industry, government, academia, and the public. Speakers included Dr. Royston, representatives of 3M, Dow Corning, Ciba-Geigy, J.P. Stevens, as well as representatives of university and government agencies. A wide range of technical and policy issues were presented and discussed.[3]

This was the first high level waste reduction conference in the United States and brought together some of the world's experts in the emerging field of pollution prevention. This gathering provided the catalyst and energy needed to establish the PPP concept in North Carolina. It started a growing interest in developing a pollution prevention program within state government. However, two different approaches started to develop. One was backed by the research community and favored a pollution prevention research center within the university system. The other favored a nonregulatory pollution prevention technical assistance program within the regulatory agencies. Both efforts moved forward, and it was not until 1984 that one approach took control.

2.3 REGULATORY AGENCY ACTION

During the summer and early fall following the conference, the Department of Natural Resources and Community Development started to develop a plan to establish a pollution prevention effort. The secretary of the department endorsed this effort, and it was spearheaded by the Division of Planning and Assessment and the Division of Environmental Management (DEM). DEM houses the regulatory programs for air, water, and groundwater quality. Realizing that other groups were also working on developing a program, DEM moved quickly in October of 1982 and wrote an implementation plan by the following month. One reason DEM was interested in the pollution prevention concept is shown by the following statement from the plan's introduction:

> "Reduced pollution and improved environmental quality are the twin goals to be gained by the division supporting the Pollution Prevention Pays (PPP) concept. This is a good program because environmental quality can be improved while at the same time industry can realize savings — a win-win situation. Such a positive approach to environmental protection can go a long way toward reducing pollution and improving the Division's acceptance and effectiveness among the regulated community."[4]

The plan was a 20 month, 2 person year effort to develop and implement a pollution prevention program into DEM. It contained the following five key components:

- Develop expertise in the PPP area. This includes a resource person(s) within the division to provide technical and policy assistance on waste reduction.
- Incorporate a PPP philosophy within division programs in dealing with municipalities and industries. This included incorporating the pollution prevention concept into the planning, permitting, and enforcement process.
- Develop an educational program to promote the PPP concept. Under this element were such activities as a newsletter, outreach efforts such as conferences and workshops, and publishing case studies.

- Establish a prototype pollution baseline and environmental indices to measure success of the project. This element recognized there must be a way to measure the success of the pollution prevention effort. It was proposed that the current data collected by the media programs be used for such a measurement effort.
- Develop incentives to encourage industries and municipalities to reduce pollution. There were a number of specific proposals made including tax credits for major reducers and an awards program.

This detailed action plan included many of the program elements that would later be incorporated into other states' pollution prevention programs. (In fact, some of the specific ideas are still trying to be put into place today in North Carolina.) One key element is that the program was always envisioned to be multimedia, though some of the tasks had a water quality flavor because it was written by Water Quality staff in DEM. While the program would be located in DEM, it would work in cooperation with the two agencies which oversaw the hazardous waste management programs in North Carolina, the Governor's Waste Management Board and the Department of Human Resources' Division of Solid and Hazardous Waste.

The administration designated DEM as the lead agency for implementing the state's PPP program. The plan was adopted and put into action over the course of the next year. A number of initiatives were undertaken by the DEM and the Division of Planning and Assessment to build the foundation necessary for a successful program. This ranged from something as simple as putting the phrase "Pollution Prevention Pays" onto all DEM letterhead, to co-sponsoring the first of a series of industrial specific waste reduction workshops, to putting the necessary bureaucratic structures in place. By the end of 1983, these early efforts culminated in the transfer of a position from the Planning and Assessment Division to become the director of the PPP program. The program's first director was Roger Schecter. He would lead the program for the next seven years. From the beginning, the PPP program was multimedia and nonregulatory. The director of the PPP program reported directly to the director of DEM in order to sustain its multimedia focus and remain nonregulatory.

During 1984, the PPP program developed many of its now well known program elements. This included an information clearinghouse, collections of case studies, a matching grant program for industry, and outreach efforts. The director spent much of his time developing the program's infrastructure and base of support both within and outside the division. The major event this year was the funding (by the legislature) of the PPP program for FY-85 (July 1984 to June 1985). The program received $116,000, which included an engineering and a clerical position, as well as funds for a matching grant effort. The significance of this is that the PPP program was now a line item in the division's annual budget and as such would be much more likely to maintain continual funding. This was the last legislative funding increase the PPP program would receive until FY-93 (July, 1992). By the end of 1984, the two positions were filled, and the program now had a three-person staff.

2.4 RESEARCH COMMUNITY ACTIONS

Based on the results of the 1982 conference and its ongoing hazardous waste management research efforts, the Governor's Board of Science and Technology requested and received $300,000 from the legislature for a Pollution Prevention Research program, starting in July, 1983. The board, as well as many in the research community, defined pollution prevention more broadly than is accepted today. Its focus was alternatives to the landfilling of waste, due to the growing public attention on the management of hazardous waste. Thus the research agenda included waste reduction technologies, health and environmental effects of toxic chemicals, waste management facility siting, hazardous waste stream composition, and waste reduction workshops. Part of the function of the Board of Science and Technology is to develop and oversee new research initiatives and is not itself a research organization. Thus the Pollution Prevention Research program it was starting would eventually be spun off, possibly to some sort of research center.

At the same time as these research funds were appropriated, the legislature also empowered the Legislative Research Commission to study the "desirability and feasibility of creating a Pollution Prevention Pays Research Center in North Carolina." This effort was assigned to the Hazardous Waste Study Commission. Starting in October of 1983, the commission heard proposals from a wide range of state agencies, universities, and environmental groups. During this, the commission heard the following:

> "...discussion of how a pollution prevention research center might be structured: whether as a loosely knit information network of state agencies and boards and voluntary participants from industry; a research referral operation focusing on liaison between industries seeking effective methods of pollution prevention and university or other research organizations which might, on a contract basis, perform the necessary research; an extension service operation with small central staff and a series of regional operations; or a major centralized facility..."[5]

Because of the diversity of viewpoints, the committee asked the various interested parties to work together to develop a proposal, with the major caveat that it would not involve extensive commitment of funds. This proposal was mainly prepared by the staff of the PPP program and the Board of Science and Technology working with university representatives. One of the major findings of the report is that there was not enough information available to identify the research needs nor how to best structure an institutional link between industry, state government, and the center. Additionally, it was found that the current pollution prevention research and technical assistance efforts would eventually provide this information. Based on these and other findings, the report contains the following four major recommendations:[6]

- The Department of Natural Resources and Community Development should be the lead agency in pollution prevention efforts, and it is recommended that the General Assembly endorse a program within the department that incorporates a number of identified technical assistance and educational efforts.
- The Board of Science and Technology should continue its pollution prevention research efforts.
- Pollution prevention workshops should be funded through the Board.
- A pollution prevention research project at North Carolina State University should be initiated to investigate waste reduction opportunities in the chemical industry and should be supported by $145,000 in funding for this effort.

The first three of these recommendations were already under way, and the final one was never funded by the legislature.

This report did several things to help the pollution prevention program. First, it legitimized the establishment of the multimedia, nonregulatory PPP program within the Department of Natural Resources and Community Development. Second, it formed the basis for the continuation of the PPP research program by the Board of Science and Technology. Third, it effectively stopped the university community from obtaining state funding for a pollution prevention research center. From now on, the only source of state appropriated research funds would be through the Board of Science and Technology. Since the pollution prevention program staff helped manage these funds, it allowed the program to coordinate all state-supported pollution prevention research. This enabled the program to coordinate technical assistance and educational and research activities in order to address areas of greatest need. Also this allowed the research to address short-term needs of industry to resolve current problems, rather than the long-term basic research advocated by the university community.

This last statement really shows the difference between the goals of the research community and the PPP program. One reason the PPP program has been so successful is it has been able to provide industry with simple approaches to reduce their waste, the so called "low hanging fruit." This is critical as industry needs answers to current problems. If there are no available solutions, then that is an area for more short-term applied research. The state's funds for pollution prevention are just too limited to tackle any major long-term basic research projects.

2.5 IMPLEMENTATION OF THE POLLUTION PREVENTION CONCEPT

The funding of the PPP program in July of 1984 stimulated the growth of a pollution prevention philosophy in North Carolina. While everyone in state government had voiced support for the concept, actually getting it under way was another matter. As with any new program, there were logistic and institutional problems that had to be overcome. However, the unique aspect of this program is that it requires a cultural change. For an organization that had always looked at single media end-of-pipe solutions, this requires a radical shift in focus. The first reaction to this idea is support, as long as it does not mean more work or cost more money. One of the goals of the program has always been to institutionalize the PPP concept into all aspects of state environmental actions and policies. After 10 years of effort, that level of integration still has not been met. However, through constant discussion and contacts with state agency and legislative staffs, this goal is beginning to be met. This is a key function of any pollution prevention program and is one reason why state programs must be located in or work closely with state environmental agencies.

By early 1985, the PPP program had developed all of the basic program elements that are still in place today. These include an information clearinghouse, general technical assistance, onsite technical assistance, matching industrial grants, outreach/training, and research. Each of these will be discussed in more detail later. However, there have been a number of changes in the program over the years as it matured.

One of the first activities of the program was to develop the necessary information sources and publications for a strong technical assistance effort. This had to be done before any mass mailing of brochures or grants announcements, in order to ensure there was some level of information available. In collecting this data, it became apparent that a number of other states were also developing similar programs. Thus the PPP program, along with the Board of Science and Technology, invited other state programs to a meeting in Raleigh in March of 1985 to exchange waste reduction information, set up a network, and try to avoid duplication of efforts. This small group became the core for the National Roundtable of State Pollution Prevention programs, which currently has a membership of over 400.

The program was so successful some of the regulatory staff became frustrated with always being the "bad guys" while the PPP program always got the glory. This was somewhat overcome in later years through working with the regulators and training them on waste reduction. However, in 1987 the Hazardous Waste Management Branch established a group to provide generators with regulatory, waste management and waste reduction assistance. This group, known as the Technical Assistance and Support Unit, focused on the waste minimization aspects of RCRA. While there were some "turf battles" in the beginning, this three-person unit provided a valuable source of information to the state's hazardous waste generators. It was phased out in 1990 when some of its resources were transferred to the newly created Office of Waste Reduction, described later in this chapter.

In FY-87 (July 1987 to June 1988), the pollution prevention research funds were transferred from the Board of Science and Technology to the pollution prevention program. However, they were reduced from 300,000 to $150,000. In the next fiscal year, the funds were restored to $300,000. This transfer now gave the program control of the state's pollution prevention research effort. Over the years, these funds were concentrated on waste reduction educational efforts and demonstration projects.

In 1989, the program received a federal EPA grant to develop a multimedia waste tracking system. This grant added two people to the current staff of four. (One additional position had been transferred in 1986 from the Water Quality Section to focus on waste reduction opportunities for wastewater dischargers.) This EPA grant allowed the program to link together all the state's environmental data bases including Toxic Release Inventory Reports, hazardous waste generator annual reports, as well as water quality and air permit information and monitoring data. This allows the program to track reduction and cross-media transfers and to help target the program's limited resources.

Also in 1989, a key piece of legislation was passed that established waste reduction planning and reporting requirements for hazardous waste generators and most water and air quality permit holders. This was given to the PPP program to implement. Since there were no funds appropriated with the legislation, the implementation of these provisions has been slow. Rules should be put into place sometime in 1993. This law has raised questions on how the program can stay nonregulatory. While procedures are being developed to keep the program out of the regulatory and enforcement areas, it may put a little more regulatory slant on the program's activities. This legislation also mandated that a pollution prevention program be established in the Department of Natural Resources and Community Development. What this provision did was to make legal what the department did five years earlier. This was done to protect the program from having to justify its funds each year.

2.6 EXPANDING REGIONAL COMMITMENT

In 1989, a joint project was undertaken with EPA Region IV and Tennessee Valley Authority to establish a Waste Reduction Resource Center of the Southeast. This center was placed in the PPP program's offices because of the extensive knowledge and resources on waste reduction available. The mission of the center is to provide free technical support and training to the eight state pollution prevention programs in the region. This resource center includes a staff of four retired engineers and one clerical position. The center has provided the PPP program with many benefits including the following:

- additional resources support
- contact with activities in other Region IV states
- increased knowledge of waste reduction options
- needed technical support

Since 1984, the pollution prevention program has been reorganized a number of times within the department. This all culminated in April of 1990 when

Governor Martin established the Office of Waste Reduction. This new division level agency brought together all the waste reduction activities going on within the just-consolidated Department of Environment, Health, and Natural Resources. This included the PPP program, hazardous waste reduction activities, and municipal solid waste reduction efforts. The staff was expanded by transferred positions and rebudgeting of existing grant monies to fund a total of 13 positions. The office now has two programs: the pollution prevention program, which addresses multimedia industrial waste and the Solid Waste Reduction program, which addresses municipal solid waste. The office's major function is still to provide nonregulatory technical assistance. However, its mission has been expanded to include developing policies needed to implement waste reduction related requirements in several major environmental laws.

In FY-93 (July 1992 to June 1993), the legislature provided additional funds to the office. This was the first funding increment for the state's waste reduction effort since the PPP program was first funded in 1984. The office now has a staff of 19 and a budget of over $1,200,000. These expanded resources significantly increase the ability of the office to provide the needed level of technical assistance and education.

2.7 OVERVIEW OF KEY PROGRAM ELEMENTS

The state's pollution prevention effort has developed six basic assistance elements: an information clearinghouse, general technical assistance, on-site technical assistance, outreach and training, matching grants, and research. These have been covered in depth elsewhere.[7] The following discussion will highlight some problems encountered and their solution.

2.7.1 Information Clearinghouse

A growing information data base in the office's library provides quick access to literature sources, contacts, audio-visuals, and case studies on waste reduction techniques. More than 3000 references on waste reduction methods have been identified and organized by industrial category and entered into an electronic data base.

This collection primarily serves as a resource for the office's staff. While it is open to the public, it is rarely used by anyone outside of the office. Over the years, only a small percentage of the publications are ever really used. The best ones are usually identified by the staff and used repeatedly. Also, so much of what is put into the technical assistance reports comes from daily contacts with industry facilities and previous experience and is not in the published literature. Thus a technical assistance program can get along with a core reference library of key documents. This approach was used by the Waste Reduction Resource Center when they identified the best documents in each major industrial category and provided copies to each of the waste reduction programs in Region IV. However, in order to stay current, recent journals and other literature must be reviewed by the technical assistance staff.

2.7.2 On-Site Technical Assistance

Comprehensive technical assistance is provided directly through staff visits to facilities. During an on-site visit, program staff collect detailed process and waste stream information and consult with personnel on current management practices. The collected information is analyzed, and a series of waste reduction options are identified. A short report outlining the management options is prepared for the facility. The report package includes such supporting documentation as literature, contacts, case studies, and vendor information.

On-site technical assistance is one of the program's most requested services. However, it is also the most time and staff intensive. An average on-site assistance takes about 40 hours to complete, with the actual visit lasting one day. Two people conducting the actual site visit will greatly enhance the quality of the report and actually reduce delivery time. To make sure the facility is truly interested in waste reduction, a presite assessment form is sent to the company requesting background information. A visit will not be scheduled until the data is returned. This increases the efficiency and quality of the visit and also eliminates firms that are not really interested in waste reduction enough to collect the needed data. Nine months after the report is sent, a follow-up survey is sent in order to find out what the company has done, how much waste was reduced, and how effective were the program's services.

Concerns relating to client confidentiality are an issue many new programs attempt to resolve. Again this has never been a problem in North Carolina. The companies are advised that the files are open to the public, and thus the report does not contain or need to contain any confidential data. Additionally, a draft copy of the assistance report is sent to the client for review, and a request is made to note any confidential information they want removed. However, confidential information is very rarely encountered. Many of the secrets in manufacturing center on adjustments in a piece of equipment and not the general process itself. Also, the problem of companies not requesting help because they are afraid of being "turned in" does not seem to be a valid issue in North Carolina. This is because they have worked hard to get the message across that they are nonregulatory. The number of requests for assistance has increased by about 50% each year, thus many companies must believe the program can be trusted.

2.7.3 Matching Grants

Since 1985, the PPP has been giving out matching grants to industry for the implementation of waste reduction efforts. Over 100 projects have been funded, totaling over $1 million. A dollar for dollar match is required, but the average is three private sector dollars to one public sector. Thus the program is able to significantly leverage private sector support for pollution prevention. Up to $15,000 in matching funds can be used to support individual projects. About 10 to 15 grants are given out each year. This is where most of the state's pollution prevention research grant money is spent.

These demonstration projects have produced some of the best waste reduction information available from the program. These are real world demonstrations of innovative waste reduction options. They have produced better and more timely results than many of the university based research efforts. These grants are also one of the best ways to get information about the program out to industry. Every year an announcement for the next round of grants is mailed to all hazardous waste generators, direct and indirect wastewater dischargers, and toxic release inventory reporters. In each letter is a list of the program's services along with the announcement. This mailing results in increased inquiries for technical assistance and first time callers who did not know the services were available.

2.8. SUMMARY

Implementation of the pollution prevention concept in the state of North Carolina has come a long way since it was first introduced in 1981. However, there is still a lot further to go. The concept must become part of all state and industrial environmental policy and actions. When government and industry begin to look at waste management systems and see opportunities to reduce pollution, we have finally arrived.

State pollution prevention programs must provide the atmosphere and mind set for this change. It is sometimes a frustrating and uphill battle, but the North Carolina experience has shown it can be done. The program had no legislative basis, limited funds, numerous bureaucratic barriers, and turf battles, yet it has developed into a world class waste reduction effort. Central to this effort were a few dedicated people and a unique vision and desire to make it happen.

2.9 REFERENCES

1. Royston, M. *Pollution Prevention Pays* (Oxford: Pergamon Press, 1979).
2. Royston, M. "Making Pollution Prevention Pay," *Harv. Bus. Rev.* (November/December 1980).
3. Huisingh, D. and V. Bailey. *Making Pollution Prevention Pay — Ecology with Economy as Policy* (Oxford: Pergamon Press, 1982).
4. Division of Environmental Management. "Incorporating the Pollution Prevention Pays Concept within the Division of Environmental Management — A Plan of Action," Raleigh, NC (1982).
5. Hazardous Waste Study Commission. *Creation of a Pollution Prevention Pays Research Center in North Carolina,* Raleigh, NC (1984).

6. Ibid.
7. Schecter, R. "Pollution Prevention," *Pop. Gov.* (Winter 1987).

CHAPTER 3

Factors Contributing to the Development of Local Programs

Linda G. Pratt and Anthony Eulo

3.1 INTRODUCTION

The decade of the nineties can be characterized as "business as *unusual*," especially for local government environmental managers. Instead of viewing problems narrowly, independent of their connections to other problems and organizational units, managers are using a more holistic approach to address environmental problems. This transition from the "old" compartmentalized decision-making approach to the new cross-program (and media) approach has been fostered by the concept of pollution prevention. Simply stated, pollution prevention builds bridges between the diverse concerns associated with economic viability and the environmental quality. Local governments are motivated to adopt pollution prevention programs because such programs are an effective tool for successful environmental strategies that foster economic competitiveness. As seen from the eyes of many local government officials, pollution prevention strategies become one of business retention providing an opportunity to thread environmentally sensitive development practices into the fabric of local government and the community. Local environmental service agencies have a wonderful opportunity to catalyze interactions that will bring about policy and procedural changes to promote a healthy environment and a healthy economy.

3.2 BARRIERS TO LOCAL PROGRAMS

If implementing pollution prevention strategies is considered integral to maintaining quality of life at the local level, then why have so few local government programs been initiated? The reasons are clear:

*   Risk. It requires a commitment from many agencies/organizations to stretch beyond established boundaries and collaborate; for all that effort, there are no guaranteed results.
*   Resource constraints. During a time of budget shortfalls and associated project cuts, there is tremendous competition for existing staff and funding. State and federal governments have not developed programs to sustain funding for local programs beyond initial start-up.
*   Justification. Evaluating the effectiveness of pollution prevention programs can be a frustrating experience because the results are typically long-term and do not fall neatly into the typical quantitative measurement mode.
*   Increasing demands. The complexity and sheer number of environmental laws and regulations often place managers in a reactive mode, unable to expend resources for developing "nonmandated" programs (typically of most pollution prevention programs).

Complicating these issues further is that agencies that have taken action to incorporate pollution prevention have typically done so without *coordinating* with their "sister" agencies. The action taken to achieve environmental goals of one agency has often shifted the environmental burdens to other media and agencies. This lack of coordination often prohibits a net overall reduction of pollutants entering the environment, results in a confused and frustrated industry, and leaves local agencies wondering which agency is accountable and whether prevention programs are effective.

3.3 HOW DO LOCAL PROGRAMS GET STARTED?

How do local programs get started, given the many hurdles that need to be overcome and the fact that many are started without legislative mandates? An individual or organization to "champion" the program is critical, as well as the ability to effectively market creation of the program. In attempting to start a local program, there is value in studying traditional corporate approaches to marketing a product: identifying the customer, designing information that meets the needs of the customer, and effective promotion of the product or service. The objective of a good promotion/marketing campaign is to *inform, remind,* and *persuade* the customer to *respond* to the product or service being offered. Successful programs are started by strategically identifying program "customers."

The local realities of each region dictate who the various customer(s) should be, but there are some general categories that remain constant. *Clear and visible executive support is essential.* Without top level commitment, efforts to develop a pollution prevention program will not appear credible. Therefore, agency management, elected officials, and policy-makers should always be considered key customers. External to the agencies and organizations involved, the first-line customers are business representatives. Finally, design the project so that it can be useful to the general public. After all, the ultimate goal is to instill the pollution prevention ethic into all sectors of the community, resulting in a cleaner and safer environment.

How can pollution prevention compete for resources with more established programs? The issue of justifying the "worthiness" of a pollution prevention program requires serious consideration of the "WYMIWYG Principle," which is the acronym for "What You Measure Is What You Get." What we choose to measure and how we measure affect performance.

There are a number of criteria that can be quantitatively measured in pollution prevention programs such as the number of onsite assessments conducted, workshops presented, phone calls received, etc. However, one of the most important components is the coordination between agencies, the cross-training, and the slowly evolving behavioral changes in all sectors of the community. This cannot be measured quantitatively, and it is not a short-term project. Consequently, pollution prevention activities do not easily conform to typical measurement tools. Two of the challenges that must be addressed in order to secure resources for pollution prevention programs are as follows:

- reaching the agreement that traditional program effectiveness measures may not be suitable for justifying pollution prevention programs
- designing new methods for success measurement

3.4 WHO ARE THE PROGRAM "CHAMPIONS"?

While there are a few examples of local programs being mandated, most local programs are created voluntarily. Champions of these programs include elected officials, government staff, the public, and local business.

3.4.1 Elected Officials

Some elected officials have initiated a pollution prevention program in their community. This has been done by either introducing a formal resolution or ordinance that establishes a program, inserting program funds into the budget, or working "behind-the-scenes" with staff. The elected officials' motivation is sometimes driven by public policy concerns, i.e., wanting to address or prevent a problem, and sometimes driven by the need for compromise, i.e., interest in establishing a "win-win" program for their business and environmental constituents. As mentioned in Chapter 1, EPA's "33/50 program" and "Green Lights" initiative offer two examples of so called "win-win" programs.

Regardless of the elected officials' motivation, their involvement is usually limited to the initiation of the program. Program implementation is left to staff.

3.4.2 Staff Initiated

Staff initiated programs are the most common type of pollution prevention program in local governments. While programs can literally be started by anyone from line staff to city managers, first-level supervisors (those supervising staff that do not have supervisorial responsibilities) seem to be commonly involved. While local government staff can initiate pollution prevention programs by either bringing the issue up to the local governing body for approval or forging ahead with a program without formal approval, it should be noted that successful and sustained efforts are usually formally recognized by the governing body.

Pollution prevention programs can generate staff appeal by providing the opportunity for staff to be more creative and innovative than is typically allowed in the "routine" bureaucratic setting. Local government staff are keenly aware of the need to enhance working relationships between government and industry. Helping businesses understand the financial and environmental benefits of pollution prevention, and working with them to implement such a program offers yet another motivating factor for local government management and staff to dedicate resources to improve the level of service provided to their "customers".

3.4.3 The Public

Programs are sometimes established to directly address the concerns of the public or public interest groups. Increasing public demand for a cleaner environment has driven the development of local and state programs. The initial state pollution prevention facility planning laws were, in many instances, the result of citizen pressure and activism (see Chapter 7).

3.4.4 Legal Mandates

In unusual circumstances, it may be possible for a local government to have a pollution prevention program mandated. The unique environment of the San Francisco Bay, characterized by high urbanization with slow mixing and dilution, has caused the San Francisco Regional Water Quality Control Board to mandate that specific sanitation agencies establish pollution prevention programs.

In another example, air quality agencies are beginning to recognize that sanitation facilities emit large quantities of volatile organic compounds. Sanitation agencies may soon be required to reduce these emissions, which may become a *de facto* pollution prevention mandate.

3.4.5 Local Business

Local business groups and trade associations have either developed programs directly for their members or joined a "team" of agencies to support an overall local program. San Diego County's program mentioned later in this chapter and the Green Star program highlighted in Chapter 15 underscore the valuable role of business in developing, organizing, and funding local programs. Business associations, such as the Chambers of Commerce, realize that good pollution prevention programs, business development, and business retention go hand-in-hand. Joint programs between business and government offer an opportunity to build bridges between diverse groups and enhance communication providing benefits to the community well beyond the pollution prevention program itself.

3.5 WHAT MAKES A PROGRAM LAST?

Regardless of how a program is initiated, it will not last long if it does not have several key attributes. The following list represents a number of attributes that contribute to a pollution prevention program:

- political commitment
- dedicated staff
- politically sensitive staff
- strong ties to the business community
- effectiveness/results
- adequate funding and resources
- dedicated activists
- team building

3.5.1 Political Commitment

The locally elected officials, whether or not they had a hand in establishing the program, should be periodically updated about its progress and results. This keeps them in touch with this "benefit" their agency is providing local businesses and ensures that they will at least be familiar with the program when making budgetary decisions.

Sometimes, program managers will lose the support of their own agency's upper management, and upper management will recommend reducing or eliminating a program. The continued interest of elected officials cannot only remedy proposed cuts, but also prevent them from occurring.

3.5.2 Dedicated Staff

Having staff that are interested in the pollution prevention program and dedicated to its success is the single most important attribute a program can have. No matter how interested an elected governing body is, a pollution prevention program will not flourish without the commitment and dedication of the local staff.

It is often advisable to involve many agencies in the effort. In this way, the program can be more comprehensive and more efficient. In addition, by involving many agencies, the work can become small parts of many people's jobs — as opposed to a major portion of a few people's jobs. This spreading of the work load prevents the program from crumbling when one key staff person changes jobs.

3.5.3 Politically Sensitive Staff

Program staff must continually be aware of the local politics and work to generate positive political interest in the program. Opportunities to directly involve elected officials and/or upper management should be sought out and pursued. People directly involved in a program have a greater sense of ownership and will be more likely to support its existence and expansion. Workshops, conferences, and outreach materials can be employed to involve elected officials.

Staff must recognize the need to develop strong ties to the business community. Including business leaders in designing and evaluating a government sponsored pollution prevention program establishes an important partnership. Ultimately, this may result in additional support for the expansion and existence of the program.

The success of pollution prevention activities initiated by both government and industry should be documented. These may be best reported in a "success story" format. Promoting these successes to upper management, elected officials, and to the media is fundamental to heightening the visibility of the program which may create additional support.

3.5.4 Effectiveness/Results

No matter how well connected a program is politically, it needs to achieve results in order to last. As previously mentioned, program managers need to carefully consider how much time will be spent on quantifying results. Program measurement has the potential to drain away huge amounts of resources. Program managers, however, cannot ignore this task. Some programs rely on anecdotal evidence on a few case studies — rather than trying to develop a number representing the "total amount of pollutants that were not generated as a direct result of the program." Establishing adequate measures to determine program success is not easy and may vary from community to community. First, identifying the reasons for measuring progress will help a community define the methods to collect the information necessary to measure progress. See Chapter 10 for more details on this topic.

3.5.5 Adequate Funding and Resources

Most programs are typically funded through one-time grants and/or shared costs. That is, local (and state) programs generally do not have a secure and stable funding base, unlike other more traditional environmental programs.

The viability of any program is directly linked to a stable resource base. Developing strong ties with industry and forming partnerships with other organizations provide a constituency to ensure a local program survives the budget process. Long-term funding opportunities for local government include fee for service, tax support, private contributions and in-kind support, and internal set-aside programs in which a certain percentage of the budget from other environmental programs is tapped to support the pollution prevention program. See Chapter 11 for more details on this topic.

3.5.6 Dedicated Activists

Dedicated activists can supply the energy needed to keep a program going. One activist, a long-time member of a citizen/staff committee in a rural county, is largely responsible for their program existing and lasting over the years. By continually representing the need for pollution prevention programs in the community, this activist has gotten the county to establish the program and kept it operating.

3.5.7 Team Building

The cross-media nature of pollution prevention requires an interdisciplinary approach to creating and sustaining a program. Broad participation from agency programs, business, and the public makes the difference between the success and failure of a local program. Teams encourage communication and problem-solving. They allow everyone to be involved in a process where team member ideas influence decisions. Moreover, teams are effective at clearly defining problems and brainstorming solutions.

Figures 1, 2, and 3 are taken from *Adhocracy, The Power to Change,* by Robert H. Waterman Jr. The basic premise of his book is that ad hoc organizational forms are the most powerful tools for effecting change. If done well, a team can get wonderful results without uprooting sound bureaucratic infrastructure. Readers are encouraged to consider the information presented in these tables and develop teams to sustain local pollution prevention efforts.

For Executives

Your main job is to create the process for effective problem-solving, not to solve the problem yourself. Therefore, your role at this stage is crucial.

- If you are the chief executive, you should probably never lead project teams. The same applies if you report directly to the chief executive.

- Make yourself available to your team on the first day of the project. Block time for regular interaction, which, depending on the importance of the effort, might mean getting together daily, weekly, or monthly--certainly no less frequently than once every quarter. Your role is to pay attention and act as coach, to help the team cut across traditional organizational boundaries, to encourage it to think boldly, and to ensure that it has the necessary resources.

- Match the scope of the task force activity to the breadth of your own responsibilities. If solving the problem correctly requires company-wide involvement, then the chief executive has to be involved and supportive. The project team should be responsible to an executive who has the power to make it happen.

- Be fussy in picking task force leaders and in helping them select task force members. Reach down in the organization to find promising people.

- Provide the financial resources necessary to make adhocracy work. In the rush to downsize and de-layer, most companies don't have the human resources to make adhocracy work as well as it should. If you agree that rapid change is here to stay and that team efforts work only when staffed with good people, then it's hard not to conclude that there is such a thing as being too lean and too mean.

- Learn how to contribute to or effectively manage project teams. Create a special training program that teaches the techniques of group problem-solving, conflict resolution, listening skills, effective confrontation, coaching and the like.

- Don't start projects until you are committed to their importance. The two horns of today's organizational dilemma are the need to change and to decide where to allocate scarce resources. Focus is pivotal to adhocracy.

Figure 1. Role of executives.

For Team Leaders

Take on a project only when you hear clear noises from top managers, at the outset, that they will get involved and stay involved.

- Concoct ways to keep top management's attention. From the start, plan regular reporting sessions to the sponsoring executive and the steering committee. If executive involvement is waning, recommend the project be cut short or redirected.

- Don't fret excessively about leading peers. Your job is to make sure the process works. You are not supposed to have the answer. Even if you think you do, it's best kept to yourself for awhile.

- Use the team-leader experience as a way of building your own leadership skills. Give enough direction to ensure the team is getting results and meeting schedules, but spend most of your time listening to and encouraging others.

- Negotiate with management for the best people you can find, and make sure the makeup of the team covers the breadth of the problem. Ask for and use the power to replace a team member who isn't up to muster.

- Obtain from upper management a clear understanding about the resources available to the team. If you don't think they're adequate, tell top management right away.

- Commit only to budgets, schedules and goals you feel are realistic. The perception of your success will depend on management's expectations.

Figure 2. Role of team leaders.

For Team Members

You will not have much influence in getting projects off to the right start, but you can do a few things to help ensure later success.

- Do your best from the outset to understand the issue from top management's point of view. If you don't have the information or exposure to do that, ask for it.

- Look at the assignment as a unique learning opportunity. You'll get exposed to points of view, parts of the organization, people and skills you would see in no other way.

- Make sure everyone in the process recognizes your full-or-part-time commitment to the team. After establishing the proper replacement and support at your usual job, make a clean break. Don't clandestinely use the old job as an excuse to put off project work.

- Talk back to the boss. Don't be nice and agree to serve on teams you feel are destined to fail. If you're being asked to do the impossible, say so.

Figure 3.   Role of team members.

3.6 CASE STUDIES IN PROGRAM EVOLUTION: SUCCESS AND FAILURE

The following are case studies on how different local programs have evolved. Specific identifiers have been left out due to requests for confidentiality. This section ends with a more detailed accounting of San Diego County's Pollution Prevention Program — a nationally recognized local program. For more complete descriptions of the programs, refer to the guidebook, *Ten Model Local Government Programs for Reducing Hazardous Waste*, Local Government Commission, 909 12th Street, Suite 205, Sacramento, CA 95814.

3.6.1 Case Study #1

This city started a program primarily at the direction of a local activist. Minimal staff interest and political commitment were obtained. For a short time, city inspectors handed out pollution prevention information. When the staff member was reassigned, the program died. This program lacked nearly every attribute needed for success.

3.6.2 Case Study #2

This program was initiated formally by a city council member who generated the interest and involvement of program staff. The council member made sure upper management was supportive of the program and continued to show political commitment. An innovative ordinance was passed by the city council. The program progressed for several years. In 1991, however, a key staff member was promoted and was no longer involved in the effort. The replacement staff member was not quite as capable as the original staff member, and the program suffered. Efforts to energize this program are now under way. The strong political commitment present in this community will be enough to keep the program alive. The program will not flourish, however, until staff are given additional resources and implement the program with enthusiasm.

3.6.3 Case Study #3

This program, housed in a small, rural county, was initiated in 1989. A solid and hazardous waste committee comprised of citizens, elected officials, and county staff directs the effort. The interest and energy of one activist is primarily responsible for this program existing. Given the budget woes faced by the county and the onslaught of mandates not at all related to pollution prevention, it is quite remarkable this program still exists. The ongoing presence of this activist and her continual networking in the community keep the program moving forward. This is a rare example of a program surviving without strong political commitment or dedicated staff.

3.6.4 Case Study #4

This program is a testament to what can happen with extreme staff dedication. Initiated with a grant, the program did not develop a supporting network strong enough to keep it fully operational when the grant ran out. Instead of giving up, program staff sought out additional funds and have used those funds to further build up the program. Program staff have worked on building up political commitment, increasing their support in the business community, and involving staff from other agencies in the effort. There is a good chance the program will continue when the grant funds run out. Unfortunately, despite these efforts, it is likely the program would die if the key staff person were to leave.

3.6.5 Case Study: San Diego County

San Diego County encompasses more than 3900 square miles and has a population of more than 2.4 million. Within its boundaries are a blend of traditional heavy industrial manufacturing, "high-tech" research and development facilities, military installations, and a variety of small businesses. The volume of hazardous waste generated on a yearly basis is approximately 100,000 tons. The administration and enforcement of environmental laws and regulations have been compartmentalized into the following three agencies:

- hazardous materials management
- industrial waste control
- fair pollution control

The County Department of Health Services, Hazardous Materials Management Division (HMMD) has been empowered to enforce pertinent state and federal hazardous materials laws and regulations. Industrial waste control is performed by five independent programs, each being unique in its field of inspection protocol, permit issuance procedures, and the industrial discharge limitations. The local Air Pollution Control District has the task of protecting public health by achieving and maintaining air quality standards throughout San Diego County.

The Technical and Educational Assistance Model (TEAM) Project is coordinated by the HMMD. The project does *not* focus on compiling technological advancements for source reduction, but rather on behavioral factors that can influence change. While the benefits of pollution prevention are rarely disputed, there remains a need for a "cultural change" to overcome many institutional barriers that exist in firmly established government agencies.

Since the inception of the TEAM Project in December 1990, the program has been enriched through the participation of many agencies and associations. The cooperative effort is driven by the conviction that working together, the people can have a significant impact on the quality of the environment of San Diego County. The program has expanded its outreach so that it now benefits from the active participation of representatives from environmental regulatory agencies, economic development agencies and associations, trade associations, and a privately owned utility. Team players include the following:

- San Diego County Department of Health Services, Environmental Health Services, Hazardous Materials Management Division
- Industrial Waste Control Programs:
  City of San Diego, Metropolitan Industrial Wastewater Program
  Encina Wastewater Authority, Source Control Program
  City of Oceanside Water Utilities Dept., Industrial Waste Pretreatment Program
  County Department of Public Works, Liquid Waste Division
- San Diego County Air Pollution Control District
- County Department of Public Works, Solid Waste
- City of San Diego Economic Development Division
- California Department of Commerce
- San Diego Economic Development Corporation
- California Association of Local Economic Developers
- Economic Policy, Administration and Coordination Program, San Diego County Chief Administrative Office
- San Diego Community Awareness and Emergency Response (CAER) Association
- Industrial Environmental Association of San Diego
- San Diego Gas and Electric Company

The greatest success with the TEAM Project in San Diego County is the opportunities it provided to "get our foot in the door" to meet with representatives of many agencies and organizations that traditionally do not exchange information. It has been an invitation for more cooperative ventures between various levels of government and industry. These meetings have evolved into partnerships that foster a comprehensive outreach program for the community on pollution prevention. The lesson learned is that pollution prevention is not a "stand-alone" program, but rather, it can be successfully woven into the fabric of many existing educational outreach programs. Certainly the bias may be different for each agency or organization, but the message is clear that pollution prevention can bridge the issues of environmental quality and economic competitiveness.

Measurable accomplishments of the TEAM Project include the following:

*   The successful development of *Guide to Environmental Service Agencies* exemplifies the cooperative spirit of each agency to advocate pollution prevention strategies. It is the first brochure that illustrates to the business community that multi-agency coordination does take place and cohesive information is available.
*   The Multi-Agency Cross Training Workshop was very significant in elevating the level of understanding of each agency's responsibilities and providing a much broader perspective for staff to consider. It is strongly recommended that each county or region design a similar session for those staff who are routinely in contact with the public.
*   The symposium "Environmental Solutions" illustrated to the industrial community that issues associated with business retention are not being ignored by local government. The theme "Welcome to San Diego. Please Stay," was warmly appreciated by those who had the impression environmental regulatory agencies were eager to have businesses leave the county. The symposium brought together a broad base of resources from which could be extracted information and assistance on how to target the policy-making system and be part of the solution, economic assistance, cost-saving incentives for energy efficiency and technology transfer, and projections for future trends in regulations.

The design and evaluation of the Pollution Prevention Program activities are ongoing. It is clear the program will continue to serve as a catalyst for establishing partnerships for pollution prevention throughout many sectors of the community.

It would be a disservice to conclude that pollution prevention activities have been easily integrated into the established industry inspection program. This has been the greatest challenge. The institutional barriers that must be addressed include the following:

*   Time. During routine compliance inspections, staff are overburdened with enforcing the mandated federal, state, and local laws and regulations. This workload is not streamlined and is certainly not diminishing.
*   Measurements. One of the current measurements for assessing program effectiveness is enumerating the number of compliance inspections completed. Likewise, this

criteria is also used for staff performance evaluations. Consequently, there is little incentive to spend extra time during each inspection to discuss pollution prevention opportunities because the number of completed inspections may very well decrease.

- Inconsistent expectations. Agency management and staff are not clear as to what level of technical expertise is appropriate to provide to business. At what point does the advice pose potential liability problems for the agency? Additionally, the business representatives are not clear as to what assistance they can consistently rely on from government agencies. Industry representatives apparently are more receptive to the information when it is delivered outside of a compliance inspection. By so doing, the issue of pollution prevention remains the priority of the visit and does not become diluted to the point of being forgotten.

3.7 CONCLUSIONS: BE A LEADER

Be a leader! There has not yet been a successful pollution prevention program that "just happened." Someone has had to take the initiative to call the first meeting, to pull together the first statement of issues, and to advocate the philosophy of preventing pollution as the most desirable environmental management option.

Clarify the "local realities," and decide what needs to be done to begin an integrated pollution prevention program. Key questions to consider include the following:

- What is the current level of pollution prevention activity within your region?
- What are the most significant sources of pollutants into the environment?
- What agencies/organizations are currently providing assistance to the business community?
- What can be done to establish formal lines of communication or enhance existing cooperative efforts with those agencies/organizations?
- What resources are available for collaborative educational outreach activities, and how can those resources be most efficiently leveraged?
- What is the level of support from management, and what are their expectations of an integrated pollution prevention program?

Be thorough in your evaluation of the "local realities," but *do not* allow an excessive evaluation process to prohibit action. The program will not be perfect upon inception, so be flexible to changing needs. Recognize the *process* of collaborating to develop a strategy is just as valuable as the final product. This is a long-term planning process; the success of which cannot be measured by quantum leaps, but by incremental steps.

Take advantage of the information already developed by programs across the nation. Much of the groundwork has been done, and this foundation can serve to enhance the ability of local, state, and federal agencies to promote a consistent strategy that will reduce the volume of pollutants released into our environment.

3.8 FOR FURTHER READING

1. Pratt, L., J. Orttung, and S. Kephart. "The Technical and Educational Assistance Model (TEAM) Project: Local Government Perspectives from San Bernardino, San Diego and Ventura Counties," California State Department of Toxic Substances Control, Alternative Technology Division (April 1992).
2. Waterman, R. H. Jr. *Adhocracy, The Power to Change* (Whittle Direct Books, 1990).
3. Kanter, R. M. *The Changemasters, Innovation for Productivity in the American Corporation* (Simon and Schuster, Inc., 1983).
4. Rosenau, M. D. Jr. *Successful Project Management* (Wadsworth, Inc., 1981).
5. Lele, M. M. and J. N. Sheth. *The Customer is Key* (John Wiley and Sons, Inc., 1987).

SECTION II:

TOOLS FOR INTEGRATION

Introduction

The previous section focused on the federal pollution prevention framework and the factors contributing to the development of state and local programs. The chapters in this section explore opportunities for incorporating pollution prevention into the functions of local and state environmental agencies.

Regulatory and nonregulatory opportunities exist to incorporate pollution prevention into the programmatic functions of state and local environmental agencies (e.g., inspections, permitting, enforcement, etc.). Effective utilization of these depends on many factors including, but not limited to the following:

- the commitment of agency management to pollution prevention integration efforts and the trade-offs that may be necessary to initiate these efforts
- a willingness on the part of media programs to move beyond the traditional regulatory framework
- communication and teamwork between the media programs, industry, and the public
- a federal pollution prevention framework that supports local and state innovation in this area
- resources to sustain these efforts

Readers should note that the ability to incorporate pollution prevention into existing agency functions such as enforcement settlement is also influenced by whether or not a state implements its own environmental programs under its own laws. State and local governments that simply implement federal programs in cooperation with EPA may have less opportunity for innovation in this area. State and local programs are advised to consult with EPA pollution prevention contacts prior to implementing new policies or guidance in this area. This will help avoid any possible conflicts in the future and will provide an opportunity to share and transfer information on these topics.

CHAPTER **4**

Facility Inspections — Obstacles and Opportunities

Timothy J. Greiner, Paul H. Richard, and Lee A. Dillard

4.1 INTRODUCTION

Pollution prevention will soon be a part of every inspector's job. In 1989, the EPA Office of Enforcement developed guidance for making enforcement settlements that include pollution prevention measures and incentives.[*] Since then, over 20 states have passed pollution prevention bills. In 1991, the EPA Office of Solid Waste issued a policy statement on the role of compliance inspectors in encouraging waste minimization/pollution prevention.[**] This growing legal and policy mandate signals a deeper integration of pollution prevention into regulatory programs.

---

[*] "Final Action Plan on Pollution Prevention and Enforcement", memorandum from Edward E. Reich, Acting Assistant Director, Office of Enforcement and Compliance Monitoring, (June 30, 1989).

[**] "Policy Statement: The Role of RCRA Inspectors in Promoting Waste Minimization," memorandum from Bruce Diamond, Director, Office of Waste Programs Enforcement, (September 1991), OSWER Dir. #9938.10.

45

Integrating pollution prevention into the facility *compliance inspection* need not compromise the legal or administrative purpose of the inspection — to identify noncompliance with applicable regulations, standards, and permits. Inspectors and the regulated community need to understand that pollution prevention strategies, in preference to recycling, treatment, and disposal strategies, provide effective means for firms to achieve compliance with existing environmental standards while frequently improving economic competitiveness.

Pollution prevention is not, in our minds, a substitute for compliance with environmental discharge standards rather, it is the preferred strategy for acheiving and sustaining compliance. From the regulatory agency's perspective, pollution prevention compliance inspections are a tool that the regulatory agency uses to attain better environmental protection.

This chapter suggests approaches to integrating pollution prevention into environmental compliance inspections. Integration into enforcement, permitting, and other regulatory activities is covered in other sections of this book. This chapter argues that successful integration requires the agency to adopt pollution prevention objectives, refocus inspection activity, and provide resources and training to inspectors so they may identify and communicate pollution prevention opportunities during an inspection. The chapter addresses the question of how inspectors may give pollution prevention advice without exposing themselves or the agency to liability if a firm implements pollution prevention changes that fail. The chapter is meant to be a practical guide to integrating pollution prevention into an agency's compliance inspection program.

4.2 FOUR FEATURES OF INTEGRATING POLLUTION PREVENTION INTO A COMPLIANCE INSPECTION PROGRAM

To successfully integrate pollution prevention into its compliance inspections, an agency must train inspectors to change the way they perform inspections. This includes training inspectors to think differently about the sources of and solutions to compliance problems. This section reviews what we believe are the four basic features of a pollution prevention compliance program: (1) adopt pollution prevention as a program objective and management responsibility, (2) provide agency personnel with training and resources, (3) focus inspection activity to encourage pollution prevention, and (4) communicate potential pollution prevention opportunities to industry.

4.2.1 Adopt Pollution Prevention as a *Program Objective* and *Management Responsibility*

No matter how much informal support there is for pollution prevention, successful implementation requires that the agency formally adopt pollution prevention as a program objective. It need not be a legislative objective, i.e., required by law, it may be administratively determined.

Commitment from the top is a necessary condition for successful integration of pollution prevention objectives. Furthermore, managers at all levels need to analyze and plan ways to accomplish prevention objectives and be made responsible for their attainment.

4.2.2 Provide Agency Personnel with *Training and Resources*

Integrating pollution prevention into inspections requires staff support in the form of training and resources. Inspectors need training on industrial processes and pollution prevention methods. Inspectors need extra time to learn about pollution prevention and incorporate it into inspections.* Inspectors need resources — such as extra time, supervisory support, and access to pollution prevention information — to experiment with some of the pollution prevention tools outlined in this chapter.

4.2.3 Focus *Inspection Activity* to Encourage Pollution Prevention

Inspectors must inspect the facility differently when they incorporate pollution prevention objectives into their work. In addition to investigation of standard compliance issues, inspectors must focus on whether the manufacturing process generates waste, why the process generates waste, where the waste goes, and whether the waste stream can be reduced. This method of inspecting the process provides the inspector with pollution prevention insight to solving compliance problems.

4.2.4 Communicate Pollution Prevention Opportunities to Industry

With some exceptions, inspectors cannot require firms to modify manufacturing processes. They can however promote and communicate the benefits of pollution prevention such as saving money, reducing regulatory burden, and improving product quality. Later in this chapter we discuss guidelines for communicating specific pollution prevention opportunities to industry.

4.3 POLLUTION PREVENTION TOOLS

This section reviews tools or methods for encouraging pollution prevention that inspectors may utilize during an inspection. They are grouped here into tools for:

---

* Chapter 6 reviews some of the pollution prevention training methods and resources agencies use to train their staff.

- general education and communication about pollution prevention
- identifying specific prevention opportunities

The methods we discuss require no additions or changes to regulations and all are currently in use in federal, state, and local agencies.

4.3.1 General Education and Communication about Pollution Prevention

In this section we discuss various ways that inspectors can provide general education and communication about pollution prevention during an inspection. They are:

- distributing general "how to" and resource information
- emphasizing prevention
- making the case for prevention

These tools cost little to implement in terms of staff training and support.

Distributing General "HOW TO" and Resource Information

Distributing prevention information is the easiest way for an inspector to include pollution prevention in their inspection. The information may be promotional — such as a flyer on the state technical assistance program — or specific to the industry — such as one of the U.S. EPA *Guides to Pollution Prevention.*[*] Distributing information requires very little effort and can be performed once the inspector receives introductory pollution prevention training.

Emphasizing Prevention

Emphasizing prevention during the opening meeting and right on through until the close of an inspection lets the firm know the importance of prevention to the regulatory agency. Firms look for hints as to what satisfies the inspector. Therefore, an inspector's deliberate references — such as stating their intent to inspect the manufacturing process as well as compliance at the end-of-pipe — can motivate firms to devote resources to prevention.

Making the Case for Prevention

Inspectors can make the case for prevention by pointing out the potential

---

[*] A list of PP information sources is located in Chapter 16: Resources for Assistance.

benefits of implementing prevention strategies. The benefits include (1) reducing regulatory, waste treatment, and disposal costs; (2) improving product quality; (3) reducing worker risk; (4) reducing other potential liability; and (5) achieving sustained compliance. Inspectors may also communicate negative incentives. As the example below illustrates, stressing the likelihood of stricter future regulations may prompt industry to take pollution prevention measures today.

> *Painting operation*
> [Inspector]: "The new Clean Air Act places greater restrictions on VOC (volatile organic compound) emissions. Although you won't be affected for a few years, you could look into non-solvent, low-VOC paints such as powder paints and aqueous paints. If you're able to reduce your VOC emissions below the 50 ton threshold, you will not have to perform an expensive BACT (best achievable control technology) analysis."

4.3.2 Identifying Specific Prevention Opportunities

The following tools require somewhat more investment in staff training, materials development, and management support. They are (1) giving prevention advice, (2) identifying prevention opportunities, (3) writing process-based inspection reports, and (4) conducting facility-wide inspections.

Giving Prevention Advice

As inspectors gain expertise in identifying pollution prevention opportunity, they should convey their insights to the firm. For conveying these insights, inspectors may cite an example where another, unnamed, company successfully implemented a similar pollution prevention change.

But inspectors must be careful when giving advice to firms on ways to prevent pollution. Inspectors must give the advice such that it is neither binding in any way nor related to compliance with regulations since doing so may jeopardize the enforcement process. The EPA Office of Waste Programs Enforcement (OWPE) recommends inspectors give limited basic advice in an informal way.[*] The following examples, adapted from the OWPE, show how to and how not to give pollution prevention advice:

> *Metal working industry*: (good example)
> "At another company, I saw that they had substituted the use of sulfur-based cutting oils with aqueous coolants. They were happy with the switch since it extended their tool life, increased throughput through their tools, and saved them money. They also cut down on their waste generation. I don't know all the details but you can call these technical assistance people who can probably help you out. Their phone number is ..."

---

[*] "Policy Statement: The Role of RCRA Inspectors in Promoting Waste Minimization."

Adhesives industry: (good example)
"If you seal the area around the drum while you are filling it with solvents, you will greatly reduce the amount of solvent that escapes into the air. It'll probably save you money and give you fewer emissions in your plant to worry about."

The next example shows advice that is too specific, endorses a specific product and appears binding for compliance:

Parts cleaning: (bad example)
"You shouldn't use this chlorinated solvent here. Many firms have switched to Natur-Clean, an aqueous oil remover. You should switch too. It may save you a lot of money and will reduce your regulatory burden."

If there are problems later with compliance or the firm tries the substitute and it fails, the firm may use the inspector's specific language to challenge an enforcement action.

Pollution Prevention Checklists

The Alaska Department of Environmental Conservation has developed a pollution prevention checklist for inspectors.[*] The primary benefit of a checklist is that it ensures that agency inspectors are collecting uniform pollution prevention information and asking a minimum of pollution prevention-related questions.

The shortcomings of a checklists are twofold. First, they cannot be tailored for the myriad of different types of processes inspectors see in the field. Inspectors may restrict themselves to the questions on the checklist and not develop their own questions, tailored to the specific process they are inspecting. Thus, they may miss opportunities. Secondly, checklists are too often used as a substitute for pollution prevention employee training.

Uncovering Prevention Opportunities

An inspector can uncover potential pollution prevention opportunities without being an expert in the manufacturing process in question. Rather than become an expert, the inspector needs to develop two skills: (1) learn where to look in the process and (2) learn how to ask the right kind of exploratory questions.

The first place to look for pollution prevention opportunities is at points in the manufacturing process. This is where the firm uses hazardous substances and generates waste. Spills, leaks, out-dated manufacturing equipment, and poor worker practices are the easiest opportunities to observe.

---

[*]   "Waste Minimization Checklist for Hazardous Waste Inspections," Alaska Department of Environmental Conservation, Solid and Hazardous Waste Section.

Open-ended Questions	Closed Questions
"Why are you using a solvent here?"	"Do you have to use that solvent?"
"How is this waste being generated? Would you show me where it comes from?"	"Is there any way to reduce waste from this process?"
"What other materials have you tried here? What were the results of your efforts?"	"Have you tried to substitute other materials?"

Figure 1. Pollution prevention questions.

More complex opportunities are revealed by asking open-ended questions about the manufacturing process. Open-ended questions, as opposed to closed questions, get detailed responses. They get the firm to think about and reconsider their manufacturing methods. Open-ended questions help to identify problems, which is the first step in finding solutions. Figure 1 lists examples of open and closed questions.

Process-Based Inspection Reports

The use of process-based inspection reports helps the inspector identify, collect, and organize pollution prevention information. Process-based inspection reports were piloted in the Massachusetts Blackstone Project.* At the onset of an inspection, Blackstone inspectors divided the facility's operations into discreet manufacturing processes. Then for each manufacturing process, Blackstone inspectors collected the following information:

- description of process
- list of inputs
- process flow diagram
- description of waste streams by media
- record of violations by media
- pollution prevention opportunities

Figure 2 on the following page contains an excerpt from a Blackstone inspection report for one of eight manufacturing processes at a metal plating facility.

The format of process-based inspection reports meshes well with the tools we've already discussed in this chapter. To gather the process-based inspection reports information, inspectors must walk through the process, examine piping,

---

MANUFACTURING PROCESS: Zinc Cyanide Rack Plating Line.
See flow diagram for details on automatic rack plating line. Tank dumps and rinse waters are pretreated at waste water treatment unit before discharging to sewer.

SUBSTANCES:
-cleaner NaOH (4,000 gal, 3,000 gal, 3,000 gal tanks)
-muriatic acid HCl (3,000 gal and 700 gal tank)
-ZnCN (in soln in 15,000 gal tank)
-nitric acid (.5% soln in 700 gal tank)
-chromate dip - Cr^6 (700 gal)
-water soluble lacquer

MANUFACTURING PROCESS FLOW DIAGRAM:

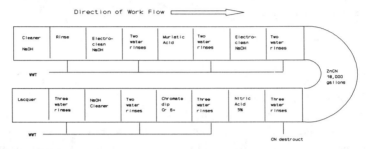

WASTE STREAMS:
WATER:
Alkaline and acids go to batch tank. Chrome goes to chrome reduction to reduce Cr^6 to Cr^3, then to batch tank. ZnCN goes to CN destruct tank. Then all water discharges go to pH adjust and then sewer. Total plant flow ranges form 62,000 - 111,000.
Violations: no operator daily log, O&M manual not updated, pH meter calibrated only monthly.

HAZARDOUS WASTE:
F006 sludge shipped to Stablex, Quebec. Manifest copies available. Have land ban attmnt. About 30,000 to 40,000 lbs sludge goes to Stablex ea. shipment (10x/yr)
Violations: no signs, no impermeable surface, not secured. Also, no notification of change in generator status from SQG to LQG.
Satellite Accumulation: None

AIR:
Violations: "Room" exhaust at ZnCN tank area; sharp odor noted near tanks.

SOURCE REDUCTION OPPORTUNITIES:
-they have converted 2 countercurrent rinse tanks - looking into counter current flow at nitric acid rinsing tanks.
-looking into alkaline Zinc to replace cyanide.
-substitution of Cr^3 for Cr^6.

Figure 2.   Process-based inspection reports.

and checking chemical feed systems to determine where and why waste is being generated. During the process review, inspectors may spot opportunities, give pollution prevention advice, and stress future restrictions on releases from the process. Process-based inspection reports integrate the pollution prevention tools we've describe in this chapter thus far.

Facility-Wide Compliance Inspections

Facility-wide compliance inspections, where one or more inspectors conduct full compliance inspections for all media during a single facility inspection, are used by only a few states.* Massachusetts piloted the approach in the aforemen-

Total Number of Firms	Number Implementing Source Reduction	Number Implementing Recycling	Number Implementing Treatment
11	8	2	1

Figure 3. Pollution prevention and agency coordination.**

tioned Blackstone Project. Facility-wide inspections were performed by one to three inspectors representing five different programs: air, hazardous waste, toxics release inventory (TRI), water inspectors, and the local publicly owned treatment works (POTW). The Blackstone Project provides the most readily available source of information on the facility-wide approach.

The Blackstone Project produced four important findings. First, coordinating inspectors from different programs and agencies insured that all environmental requirements were inspected and the full weight of noncompliance was brought to bear on the company through enforcement that encouraged prevention. Secondly, coordinated inspections helped insure that changes to prevent pollution in one media did not shift the pollution to another media. Thirdly, since individual media inspectors did not visit the facility separately, the Massachusetts Blackstone inspections took fewer person-hours per inspection than the equivalent traditional inspections. Lastly, when different media coordinate and promote prevention, firms get a strong signal to shift more resources towards preventing pollution before it gets generated. In the three cases where the Massachusetts DEP required firms to *evaluate* pollution prevention changes as part of an enforcement action, all three firms chose to implement pollution prevention changes to attain compliance. As Figure 3 illustrates, when agencies promoted pollution prevention and coordinated with one another, the firms were likely to institute pollution prevention changes.

Limited experience with the facility-wide inspection shows it to be an effective way to facilitate pollution prevention.

---

* Many states and five EPA regions have or are currently developing multimedia checklists that enable inspectors to identify certain common or especially threatening violations in programs other than their own. For example, a water inspector may observe a firm improperly managing its hazardous waste. The inspector may record the suspected violation and inform the RCRA program section chief. The use of multimedia checklists can improve an inspector's ability to check compliance with all environmental media, but multimedia checklists are generally not used to identify and communicate pollution prevention opportunities.

** Involved agencies: Massachusetts Department of Environmental Protection, Massachusetts Office of Technical Assistance (formerly the Department of Environmental Management), and the Upper Blackstone Water Pollution Abatement District. Based on a survey of 28 central Massachusetts firms. "FY 91 Report on the Blackstone Project," Massachusetts Department of Environmental Protection, forthcoming.

4.4 USING POLLUTION PREVENTION INFORMATION
FOR *ENFORCEMENT*

Inspectors can incorporate pollution prevention information recorded during an inspection into enforcement actions. Inspectors use the information to prompt the violating firm to examine pollution prevention strategies and compare these strategies with end-of-pipe treatment. Frequently, pollution prevention brings firms into compliance, improves their manufacturing process, and saves money. While end-of-pipe solutions also bring firms into compliance, they may transfer waste from one media to another instead of preventing it. Chapter 5 of this book examines integrating pollution prevention into enforcement.

4.5 INTEGRATING POLLUTION PREVENTION INTO INSPECTIONS

In this chapter we introduced several pollution prevention tools for inspectors. We purposely laid out the tools in this chapter from easiest to most complex. As inspectors and their managers become more comfortable with simple tools, they could proceed to complex ones such as collecting pollution prevention information using flow diagrams and facility-wide inspections.

But attempts to integrate pollution prevention into inspection protocols will likely founder without the features we outlined at the start of the chapter — adopt pollution prevention as a program objective and management responsibility, provide agency personnel with support and resources, focus inspection activity to encourage pollution prevention, and communicate potential pollution prevention opportunities to industry. With the four features, the pollution prevention tools we've outlined here can be successfully institutionalized into an agency's inspections.

CHAPTER 5

Incorporating Pollution Prevention into Facility Permits*

David Teeter

5.1 INTRODUCTION

Early public sector pollution prevention programs were largely built upon technical assistance. Technical assistance not only addressed legitimate needs; it also reflected attitudes about how much government pollution prevention efforts can or should intrude into the private sector — especially industry's decision-making about the production process. Government should not tell the private sector to change their processes or chemical usage or, worse yet, tell a facility how to manufacture their products. The logic went as follows. In order for agency prevention efforts to be effective, they must focus on providing either information or incentives to facilities through agency programs sufficiently distant from their regulatory arms; regulatory approaches would accomplish little other than to create resistance. The facility owners, not government, know best whether and

---

* Please note that the comments and opinions expressed here are those of the author alone and do not represent those of the U.S. EPA.

0-87371-654-X/93/$0.00+$.50
© 1993 by Lewis Publishers

how to integrate pollution prevention into their environmental programs and strategies.

Public sector pollution prevention programs have evolved a great deal over the past five to seven years. Technical assistance programs have grown and matured, but due to legislative mandates, frequently have moved in a regulatory direction. Mandatory facility pollution prevention planning requires plan development and submission, while at the same time leaving it largely to the facility to identify, evaluate, prioritize, and implement prevention facility options.

Use of the facility permitting process to promote pollution prevention can be quite different; in this case an agency is integrating prevention into a primary regulatory function. Promoting pollution prevention through the permitting process is intriguing, and it presents opportunities for agencies and facilities. There are obstacles, as well. This chapter reviews some of the emerging programmatic trends in pollution preventive permitting. It highlights some of the issues confronting agencies as well as some of industries' perspectives on requiring use of prevention in the permitting process. Finally, it includes summary observations about the role and effectiveness of this tool.[1]

Readers should not assume this chapter summarizes all relevant efforts undertaken by government agencies to incorporate prevention into the permitting process. Relevant examples may have been overlooked. The main objective in writing this is to provide the reader with a sense of "what's happening" and the opportunities and issues to be addressed if the permitting process is to be an effective place to promote pollution prevention.

5.2 WHY BUILD POLLUTION PREVENTION INTO PERMITTING?

Strong enforcement of environmental requirements promotes pollution prevention. The costs of compliance and the potential liabilities facing those who handle hazardous substances and release toxic air emissions have highlighted the economic benefits of reducing waste at the source. If this is the case, and if technical assistance is an incentive for facility pollution prevention, then what additional value does use of the permitting process add to pollution prevention program development and integration?

5.2.1 Reasons for Agency Use of the Permitting Tool

Following are a few of the reasons why agencies have elected to use the permitting process to promote pollution prevention:

*   Use permitting authorities can induce facilities to prepare pollution prevention plans. About half of the states currently have no facility planning legislative mandate, nor does the EPA. Agency permitting authorities may enable them to negotiate facility plans with permittees.[2] This forces facilities to look higher than just emissions

management or disposal on the waste management hierarchy — to prevention. Agencies still tend to provide focused technical assistance in conjunction with mandatory planning.

- The pollution prevention plan itself can become an enforceable part of the permit and discourage cross-media pollution transfers. Integration of pollution prevention into permitting can become a force on which to base allowable facility environmental releases emanating from hazardous materials use and waste generation. This is especially the case where multimedia permits are contemplated such as in New Jersey (discussed later).
- It forces different media programs within an agency to work together to coordinate their permitting activities and priorities. It also enhances the role of the pollution prevention coordinator. Coordinated permitting can provide certain permitting program efficiencies, though this point is widely debated because of the disparate requirements permit writers must enforce in their specific media programs.
- Finally, use of the permit to promote pollution prevention further institutionalizes this concept into agency programs, giving traditional regulatory program personnel a stake in prevention. It broadens the perspectives of permit writers, drawing more than technical assistance staff into the overall pollution prevention effort.

5.2.2 Company or Facility Perspectives

Facility[3] feelings about promotion of pollution prevention through the permitting process are probably best described as ambivalent. Companies have accepted facility planning requirements in many states, seeing these as preferable to more prescriptive alternatives. Facility planning leaves decision-making authority in their hands. They also recognize the intuitive logic of consolidated permitting; it can both consolidate their application requirements and reduce their reporting requirements.

On the other hand, facility officials have natural concerns about use of regulatory programs — including permitting — to require pollution prevention, including the following:

- a fear that their pollution prevention plan will become an enforceable permit condition, in effect obligating them to these actions which can affect how a product might be manufactured
- a fear that this regulatory approach will create just one more rigid requirement that might stifle innovation and limit flexibility; will government merely endeavor to create rigid technology standards once they have these plans in hand?
- concern that government is overstepping its legitimate statutory authorities
- concerns about disclosure of business or trade secrets

From the point of view of industry, the proper role of government pollution prevention programs is promotion and incentive building.[4] Facilities already have sufficient economic incentives to encourage institutionalization of pollution prevention, and government ought to reinforce and reward such behavior. Technical assistance, recognition programs, and requirements that induce the facilities to undertake pollution prevention planning can reinforce these economic incentives;

regulatory pollution prevention does not, however, and therefore may be challenged by the facility.

Many public agencies recognize the need to forge a new form of partnership with facilities through their pollution prevention programs. A few different approaches are being tried that use the permitting process, however. These are outlined in the next section.

5.3 REVIEW OF SOME AUTHORITIES ENABLING POLLUTION PREVENTION IN PERMITS

Authorities available through the air, water, and waste programs all present certain opportunities to integrate prevention into the permitting process. These potential authorities are highlighted below.

5.3.1 Clean Air Act (as Amended in 1990)

Clean Air Act permitting opportunities can be used in a few ways to promote pollution prevention. Most significant of these is probably the new source review. Prevention can play a role through the review and evaluation of processes during the course of new source permit development and issuance, though the focus is based upon technology-based standards. Focusing upon technology standards versus performance-based incentives presents certain disincentives for source reduction, however. Availability of proven off-the-shelf treatment technology may create strong economic incentives for a facility to use treatment, rather than source reduction alternatives, which may take time to develop and test. Furthermore, promulgation of new regulations may be required to either create or alter a treatment standard, both of which may create major disincentives for innovation.

5.3.2 Clean Water Act

The Clean Water Act also includes provisions enabling use of the permit process to promote pollution prevention. Among the opportunities available are the following:

- Industrial waste discharge permits. Publicly owned treatment works (POTW) having problems meeting their own discharge standards or difficulties with metals content in their treatment sludges may request that industrial dischargers promote source reduction as a principal "pretreatment" strategy. Permit writers reviewing the pretreatment process can work with the facility to promote review and evaluate prevention alternatives.
- The National Pollution Discharge Elimination System (NPDES) permit — direct discharge permits. Pollution prevention in the water program has so far been most frequently pursued through the NPDES permitting process. One section of the Clean

Water Act in particular has been most utilized — Section 304(e), which pertains to best management practices (BMPs). BMPs are most frequently procedural methods aimed to achieve specific goals. They are usually designed to be flexible and allow alternative means to accomplish these ends. Though BMP plan requirements do not specifically promote pollution prevention, the plan requirements themselves include many of the same elements as a pollution prevention plan: facility evaluation, good housekeeping practices, preventive maintenance and record keeping, employee training, and company/plant commitment to implementation. This tool could be customized to promote pollution prevention versus treatment strategies, whether for an industrial facility or a POTW.

5.3.3 Resource Conservation and Recovery Act

The 1984 Amendments to the Resource Conservation and Recovery Act (RCRA) encourages use of the permitting process to promote pollution prevention. These 1984 Amendments (called the Hazardous and Solid Waste Amendments, or HSWA) established waste minimization as the most desirable form of hazardous waste management.[5] The statute also directed the development of regulations applicable to all hazardous waste generators shipping wastes offsite and to those generators who also treat, store, and dispose of their wastes onsite (called TSDs). Two basic requirements are laid out in this statute:

*   The generator shall have a program in place to reduce the volume or quantity and toxicity of such waste to the degree determined by the generator to be economically practicable (Section 3002 (b)).
*   The proposed method of treatment, storage, or disposal is that practicable method currently available which minimizes the present and future threat to human health and the human environment (Section 3002(b)).

Section 3005 applies this standard to generators that are also TSDs, stating, furthermore, that all permits issued for those TSDs must contain a provision requiring the same certification listed above (Section 3005(h)).

These statutory standards have been promulgated into regulations applicable to generators and generators who also use onsite TSD facilities. The provisions include the following:

*   Permitted owners and operators of these TSD facilities must include in their operating record an annual certification that they have a program in place to reduce hazardous waste "to the degree determined by the permittee to be economically practicable." They must certify that the proposed method of treatment meets the public health protection threshold laid out in the statute.[6]
*   Owner/operators must also include in their biennial reports to EPA "a description of the efforts taken during the year to reduce the volume and toxicity of wastes generated." The report must describe the actual changes in generation realized during this year in contrast to other years. A signed certification by the owner/operator is required.[7]

A few major issues have arisen regarding these provisions: (1) the definitional question of what constitutes "minimization" versus source reduction; (2) a question as to the ultimate enforceability of these provisions, given the fact that the facilities really self-certify and determine what is "practicable;" and (3) questions regarding the meaning of "program-in-place."

To help address this third issue, EPA developed Draft Guidance in the June 12, 1989 Federal Register, *Guidance to Hazardous Waste Generators on the Elements of a Waste Minimization Plan*.[8] These structural elements are essentially the same as those found in many of the state facility planning laws and requirements. The guidance also leaves decision-making authority in the hands of the generator/permittee.

5.3.4 State Requirements

State pollution prevention requirements vary in terms of basic approach and the extent to which they are nonregulatory in flavor. State programs can generally be categorized as follows:

*   those states with facility planning requirements (most requiring establishment of targeted quantitative goals within the plans)
*   programs lacking statutory facility pollution prevention planning authority, but which are creatively exploring other authorities to promote pollution prevention facility planning (A few have utilized permitting to promote pollution prevention)
*   those states with no programs at all
*   those with facility planning programs, but which are also integrating prevention into their traditional regulatory programs
*   those with legislation requiring facility-wide multimedia permitting integrating pollution prevention plans into the permit

State programs also vary in the extent to which their regulatory programs simply adopt federal standards or pursue their own legislative and regulatory agenda as delegated programs.

5.4 EMERGING TRENDS IN USE OF THE PERMITTING PROCESS TO PROMOTE POLLUTION PREVENTION

There are various regulatory tools that agencies can use to promote or "require" pollution prevention: the inspection process, use of penalty mitigation in enforcement actions, use of broad agency mandates, and the permitting process itself. This section outlines two basic approaches being tried by public sector agencies to build pollution prevention into the permitting process.

The first approach uses single media permitting program regulatory authorities and permitting opportunities. The second option attempts to integrate pollution prevention into multimedia permits. Each of these is discussed in turn, along with the associated issues raised.

5.4.1 Use of Single Media Permitting Requirements

Some states' environmental programs, along with several EPA Regional Offices, are integrating pollution prevention into the permitting process of individual media programs. Of the authorities available to these agencies, the hazardous waste requirements have been most frequently utilized. A number of observations stand out regarding experience so far with the permitting process.

Agencies have taken two basic approaches. They may try to negotiate pollution prevention requirements as a condition of the permit itself. Alternately, they may use the requirement to request information about facility prevention activities, but market pollution prevention without attempting to negotiate specific conditions into the permit itself.[9] Some initial observations about these efforts include the following:

- Whether built into a permit or not, these efforts are primarily designed to make pollution prevention planning mandatory. These are largely "regulatory" equivalents to mandatory facility planning. Planning and some reporting are required, but the decision-making is left to the facility itself.
- The planning process itself is emphasized, not specific technology fixes or regulatory requirements that must be met.
- Most of these efforts also place a high premium upon technical assistance and may, as in mandatory facility planning, link these efforts to technical assistance.
- Some focus only on certain wastes or emissions, whereas others request/require that the facility consider not only environmental releases/wastes, but also hazardous substance usage (per *Superfund Amendments and Reauthorization Act,* Title III, Sections 312 and 313).
- Agencies emphasize different parts of the "requirements" — the certification itself, reporting requirements, elements of the pollution prevention plan, prevention measures and assessments, or program evaluation.
- The pollution prevention results are a little unclear, since some of these efforts only recently got under way or resultant permits were only recently negotiated. Will the results encourage multimedia prevention or reflect cross-media transfers of pollutants?

5.4.2 Issues Associated with Use of Single Media Permits

Agencies seeking to incorporate pollution prevention into single media permitting authorities should consider a number of questions:

- Are they hoping for too much based on vague or limited mandates? Remember, the RCRA program-in-place requirement, though quite useful, is effectively unenforceable because of the self-certification nature of the generator/TSD's obligation.

- Are they overstepping their own mandates? This could lead to challenges and make the complicated life of the permit writer that much more difficult.
- How do we ensure these efforts — facility and program — can be undertaken, given generally tight resource levels? Facilities should be governed by the pollution prevention opportunities afforded by addressing these requirements, not the costs and uncertainties associated with this process. Useful guidance on pollution prevention plan preparation is extremely important in this regard. Agencies should also recognize and be willing to invest the resources necessary to address the following significant costs: the transaction costs in permit discussions, the training necessary, the time and effort necessary to develop guidance and outreach packages, and the enormous time and effort potentially necessary to review facility plans and evaluate the plan options.
- Will these efforts result in fuller and more effective integration of pollution prevention into agency activities? Use of the permitting process itself will be most effective if the separate media programs are, at a minimum, coordinating efforts. Realize this too takes time and effort. It is more than likely to slow down the permitting process as well.
- Will use of the permitting process change the role of the permit writer? Depending on the agency permitting requirements, the permit writer's role could be largely unchanged; it could call for more of a "helping" role in understanding how to assess opportunities; or it could demand they become experts on pollution prevention technologies and opportunities.
- Will a facility facing other media permit requirements in coming years really have an effective incentive to look cross-media and develop pollution prevention approaches, or will the technology-based nature of many of the requirements encourage adoption of treatment options?
- Will these efforts produce real results? This requires that the agency act to ensure solutions are truly prevention, not cross-media shifts of contamination. It requires that agencies target their activities — which industries are most important to address — and it requires that reasonable tools be developed and made available with which to track and measure progress.

5.4.3 Use of Multimedia Approaches

Integration of pollution prevention into multimedia permits has certain appeals and apparent advantages over use of single media permits:

- It allows development of "facility-wide" approaches to both pollution prevention and emission controls/limits.
- It requires agency staff to work and coordinate their effort.

There are few examples of programs emphasizing pollution prevention through multimedia permitting. One is discussed below. New Jersey's Pollution Prevention Act requires implementation of a pilot program in facility-wide permitting with 10 to 15 facilities. The state environmental agency hopes to use the permitting process as the driving force on which to base allowable emissions and overall use of hazardous substances at a facility. A few elements of the New Jersey pilot are worth highlighting:

- A pollution prevention plan is required for each facility. The planning process itself requires inventory of all emission sources affecting all media. Source reduction opportunities are emphasized, though not required. The facility identifies opportunities, sets priorities, and evaluates projects based on waste contribution, portion of chemical usage, and health and environmental risks. Many of these are common to other state nonregulatory facility planning programs. Unlike these programs, however, the plan itself is part of the permit, and the source reduction implementation schedule becomes an enforceable permit condition.
- A pre-pilot phase has been developed to work out the "process" itself and develop the teamwork necessary to implement the pilots at the selected facility. A permit team approach has been developed and includes staff from each of the media programs and the pollution prevention program who will lead it. Out of this will come the procedures necessary for preparing and issuing facility-wide permits.
- The results of the pilot program will be provided to the governor and the legislature.

The New Jersey approach seems reasonably well thought out and merits follow-up and evaluation as it is implemented.

5.4.4 Issues Associated with Use of Multimedia Permits

Few states appear to have followed New Jersey's lead, although several (including California, North Carolina, Massachusetts, and Oregon) have multimedia permitting initiatives. EPA has no authorities enabling it to pursue this path.

The issues confronting the use of a multimedia permit approach emphasizing pollution prevention are not unlike those outlined for the single media programs:

- Are the resource demands justified? Multi-program coordination poses major challenges, can take lots of time, and is not encouraged through current legislation. Media programs each have distinct requirements and timetables applicable to facilities. Permit writers and enforcement staff are directed to enforce these requirements. The staff will need to become familiar with each other's requirements. All of this adds to their workload and the complexity of these permits.
- In light of these pre-existing single media requirements, does a facility have a strong incentive to choose source reduction versus treatment, especially when proven treatment technologies may be readily available?
- Will use of the permitting process add anything over and above what general facility planning legislation can provide? The heart of the whole effort is the facility pollution prevention planning process, but will this form of government involvement do anything more than mandate planning to encourage facility prevention activities? The New Jersey experiment does link all the levels of the waste management hierarchy and puts pressure on facilities to choose source reduction to reduce emissions and chemical use. Time will tell.

5.5 CONCLUSION

Government environmental agencies are beginning to use traditional agency programs and tools including the facility permitting process to promote pollution prevention. The preceding discussion has highlighted some mandates available to agencies, emerging trends, as well as some of the issues associated with use of the permitting process, or a permit, to promote pollution prevention.

Government programs should tap those things motivating companies to develop and use pollution prevention strategies. There are already strong economic drivers in place (e.g., compliance costs, disposal costs, the threat of liability, increased knowledge of particular options available for processes or facilities). Government programs can further contribute to facilities' adoption of pollution prevention programs through provision of technical assistance, awards programs, and support of pollution prevention research. Finally, mandatory facility planning, particularly when it is linked to technical assistance, is likely to result in more frequent use of source reduction.

What will use of the permitting process add to this? Use of the permitting process to require facility pollution prevention planning can be quite helpful. Integration of pollution prevention into the permitting process can also help in other ways:

- It effectively reinforces source reduction and communicates commitment.
- It brings the permit writer into the pollution prevention advocacy process.
- It facilitates cross-media coordination (the New Jersey pilot merits particular attention).

Education and training are essential for these staff; however, it is not presuming to make them technical experts, but to help them identify and look for opportunities to reduce wastes.

Looking to the permit process to produce enforceable permit conditions of a "regulatory" flavor, may not be as successful especially if they require adoption of traditional technology-based solutions. Agencies ought to promote and reinforce facility innovation ("continuous improvement"), not force adoption of a single alternative.

Over time, pollution prevention successes in specific industries and processes will probably be sufficiently documented to justify a set of minimum expectations and perhaps even initial technology or performance standards. That is years away, however. In the meantime, use of the permitting process itself is likely to yield more results — for less investment — than a pollution prevention command-and-control orientation.

5.6 REFERENCES

1. The opinions expressed in this article are the personal views of the author and do not reflect any agency position.
2. Authorities are available through the air, water, and waste programs.
3. Regulated facilities include not only private sector operations, but also government facilities.
4. A possible exception might be selective use of enforcement authorities to require certain facility pollution prevention actions as part of an enforcement settlement.
5. The Pollution Prevention Act of 1990 took this one step further by explicitly making source reduction the top of the federal waste management hierarchy.
6. 40 CFR 264.73(b)(9).
7. 40 CFR 264.75 (h–j).
8. These elements include top management support, characterization of waste generation, full cost accounting, encouragement of technology transfer, and program evaluation.
9. For instance, some states and EPA Regional Offices have emphasized the "program-in-place" RCRA requirements. They have concentrated on the *institutional* features outlined in the EPA generator guidance.

CHAPTER 6

Incorporating Pollution Prevention into Enforcement Actions

David Hartley

6.1 INTRODUCTION

Government environmental programs must have access to and utilize all existing tools to assure that businesses that generate wastes are informed, supported, and encouraged to eliminate or reduce their waste generation. This chapter considers methods to incorporate pollution prevention into the enforcement settlement process. The settlement agreement is an effective regulatory tool in assisting industry with the implementation of pollution prevention technologies, strategies, and programs.

6.2 WHAT IS A SETTLEMENT AGREEMENT?

The responsible regulatory agency has several options for obtaining compliance when facilities are found to be out of compliance with governing laws and regulations. Criminal, civil, and administrative actions are the most common regulatory actions taken to obtain compliance. Criminal actions are taken for the

0-87371-654-X/93/$0.00+$.50
© 1993 by Lewis Publishers

most severe violations, knowingly endangering public health and the environment. These types of violations usually result in court actions that focus on imprisonment of the violator and cessation of facility operations. Civil and administrative actions are used for violations of a less severe nature (i.e., storage of incompatible wastes, improper drum labeling, record keeping violations, etc.). They afford an excellent opportunity for negotiating a mutually agreeable settlement prior to filing the action with a court of law. The settlement agreement is a legal document. It usually lists conditions for mitigating the violations and may contain provisions for paying fines and implementing some form of pollution prevention.

Precedence for including pollution prevention activities in settlement agreements has been set by many state programs, and more recently in policy established by the U.S. EPA (issued on February 12, 1991).[1] The U.S. EPA Office of Enforcement (OE) issued this policy statement to encourage the use of the settlement process to identify and implement pollution prevention activities. The policy emphasizes the need for a continued strong enforcement program that can further the goals of pollution prevention. In order to provide a common term of reference, OE uses the term "supplemental environmental project" to describe pollution prevention activities included in settlement agreements.

6.2.1 Settlement Agreement Process

Most facilities breaking the law recognize the utility of a quick settlement, rather than enduring a protracted legal battle. The settlement agreement provides the vehicle for avoiding lengthy court battles for determination of guilt. In addition, it can provide environmental benefits beyond what can be secured solely through the collection of fines if it is carefully crafted and executed. For regulatory programs that routinely administer enforcement actions, willingness and desire are the major requirements needed to perform settlement agreements.

Settlement agreements usually consist of the following two step process:

1.   the *Corrective Action Order and Complaint for Penalty,* which specifies the violations and penalties
2.   the *Settlement Agreement and Order,* which specifies actions to be taken to mitigate the violations, together with any terms and conditions for supplemental environmental pollution prevention projects

6.2.2 Corrective Action Order and Complaint for Penalty

The first step in the settlement agreement process is to notify the facility that it is in violation of specific laws and/or regulations. An example of a typical corrective action order and complaint for penalty is included as Appendix 1.

The corrective action order specifies the sections of the laws or regulations that have been violated and lists the specific violations (Determination of Violations). A compliance schedule listing the specific actions that must be implemented to abate the violations is also included. Correction of the violations is mandatory and is typically not given monetary credit in the settlement agreement.

The next step is assessment of a penalty. Monetary penalties are typically assessed as a punitive deterrent for future violations. The monetary penalty, which is imposed in addition to the requirement to correct the violation, is the "bargaining chip" that can be negotiated for conducting supplemental environmental pollution prevention projects. The penalty is usually based on the seriousness of the violations and should be defendable by the governmental agency. Some agencies attempt to determine the amount of the penalty by calculating the monetary savings that occurred as a result of being out of compliance. For instance, if a facility stored hazardous wastes onsite for longer than the 90 days allowed, without filing for a permit, the facility may have saved $50,000 in transportation and disposal costs. Thus the penalty may be assessed at $50,000, and some portion of that penalty may be negotiated for the performance of some form of pollution prevention.

After the penalty is listed, the respondent is provided with a "right to a hearing." This section provides an ideal point to introduce the potential for supplemental environmental projects.

It should be noted that some governmental agencies are very adamant about not offering supplemental environmental project opportunities in the Corrective Action Order and Complaint for Penalty. Some agencies feel this process may "reward" a facility for being in violation of laws or regulations, since pollution prevention can reduce waste handling costs and add to the facility's competitiveness. Moreover, some agencies collect fines to support the regulatory programs. Others argue they do not have the time or resources to perform supplemental environmental projects in the settlement agreement process. These arguments are classic institutional barriers to pollution prevention that must be overcome in order to assure that industries do everything possible to eliminate or reduce the generation of wastes. In most cases, if a facility proposes to implement some form of pollution prevention that will reduce the generation of hazardous pollutants, most agencies will entertain the proposal. In addition, some agencies require that industry pay the fine and conduct a pollution prevention project, thereby avoiding the concerns mentioned above.

6.2.3 Settlement Agreement and Order

The Settlement Agreement and Order is a negotiated document specifying the terms and conditions of the final settlement. A model of the Settlement Agreement and Order including supplemental environmental pollution prevention language is attached as Appendix 2.

The Settlement Agreement and Order usually contains the waiver of hearings, compliance with legal requirements, liabilities, specifics on communication (i.e., reporting), termination of obligations, and a detailed explanation of the proposed supplemental environmental pollution prevention project. It is extremely important to craft this document in such a way that it lays out in detail the exact project parameters, time lines, deliverables, and consequences of failure to act. The best advice for agencies interested in performing supplemental environmental pollution prevention projects is to involve the agency legal counsel in the process as early as possible. The legal counsel will be able to craft the legal language that can prevent future liabilities or problems.

An important consideration that should be included in a settlement agreement is "an admission of guilt." While settlement agreements do not inherently require an admission of guilt, a settlement with no such admissions cannot be used in a future action to show recurring violations if the need arises. This is important in setting penalties in subsequent enforcement actions and any actions to suspend, revoke, or deny a facility permit. In order to assure that a violator's past performance can be fully considered in any future enforcement actions, a compromise admission can be included as follows:

> Respondent does not admit the allegations made in the enforcement order except as follows: respondent admits the facts alleged in the enforcement order for purposes of any subsequent action brought by the (government agency) within five years of the date the violations are alleged in the enforcement order to have occurred.[2]

6.3 EXAMPLES OF SUPPLEMENTAL ENVIRONMENTAL PROJECTS

The most effective method for obtaining good supplemental environmental projects is to ask the facility to submit a proposal. The facility operator or environmental manager typically knows of technologies or strategies that will eliminate or reduce the generation of hazardous pollutants at the facility. Additionally, the facility's environmental manager may have wanted to conduct various pollution prevention feasibility studies for such things as product substitutions or process modifications, but was unable to do so because of a lack of support from corporate officials. The settlement agreement can provide the environmental manager with the opportunity to open the wish list. Do not overlook this avenue.

6.3.1 Case Studies of Supplemental Environmental Projects

The U.S. EPA, Office of Pesticides and Toxic Substances, published a listing of pollution prevention projects negotiated in settlement agreements.[3] The following are abbreviated examples of a few of those projects:

- Balzers, Inc. of Hudson, New Hampshire, manufactures high technology vacuum equipment for film processing and cryogenic equipment for laboratories. The company failed to report freon-113 emissions in violation of the Federal "Emergency Planning and Community Right-to-Know Act" § 313 (EPCRA). The proposed penalty was $17,000. However, Balzers agreed to replace its freon-based cleaning system with a water-based system and pay a reduced penalty of $8500. Switching to water-based cleaning at both its New Hampshire and California facilities will cost the company $56,000. In this example, the penalty was reduced by half, and the company matched the credited penalty with an additional $47,500. The net result was the elimination of freon emissions from its cleaning operations.
- Seekonk Lace Company of Barrington, Rhode Island, was found in violation of EPCRA § 313 for failure to report emissions of acetone. The proposed penalty was $25,000; however, Seekonk negotiated a credit of $10,000 by agreeing to eliminate its use of acetone. The company instituted a mechanical method for separating nylon and acetate threads, eliminating more than 250,000 pounds of acetone per year. The total cost of the project was estimated to be $95,000.
- Madico, Inc. of Woburn, Massachusetts, received a proposed penalty of $50,000 for failure to report emissions of methyl ethyl ketone (MEK) under EPCRA § 313. The company received a credit of $20,000 towards the penalty for implementing process modifications and material substitutions that reduced the use of toluene by 90% and MEK by 50%. The company now uses ultraviolet and infrared radiation to aid in the application of scratch resistant coatings on polyester films. The total cost of the project was estimated at $49,000.
- Andrew Corp. of Orland Park, Illinois, received a proposed penalty of $84,000 for alleged reporting violations of EPCRA § 313. The company agreed to a final penalty of $15,000 and agreed to implement a material substitution project that would eliminate the use of 52,000 pounds of 1,1,1-trichloroethane and 15,000 pounds of phosphoric acid per year. The company switched from the toxic cleaners to water-based cleaners for a total cost of $190,693.

Following is a list of potential supplemental environmental projects that may be proposed in settlement agreements.

6.3.2 Pollution Prevention Audits

In states that do not have mandated facility planning (pollution prevention planning) laws (see Chapter 7), the settlement agreement can require a facility to conduct a comprehensive audit of its waste generating processes. This will identify options available for implementation of pollution prevention technologies and strategies. In states that require facility plans, a review of the plan can quickly identify pollution prevention options that may have been identified but were not implemented. In most cases, the identified options are not implemented because of financial considerations. The settlement agreement can be used to make the option "economically feasible." This approach provides the facility with some flexibility to pick and choose the options felt to be most viable for implementation within the dollar range specified in the settlement agreement. Examples of technologies that could be credited are installation of a counter-current rinse system in a metal plating operation, drip plates, mechanical hoists, etc. In most cases, it is best to let the facility recommend the technologies they feel they can implement.

Allowing the facility to propose projects and technologies has the added benefit of relieving the regulating agency of potential liabilities associated with mandating technologies that may not perform optimally. The liability issue is an important consideration, which is often cited as the reason regulators are unwilling to agree to technology development and implementation in the settlement agreement process. As stated previously, a well crafted settlement agreement, developed by competent legal counsel, can eliminate potential liabilities associated with failed technologies that may have been proposed in the settlement agreement. Additionally, the regulator should never try to act as the technical consultant to industry. The regulator's role should simply be that of the facilitator for the settlement agreement process (see Chapter 4).

6.3.3 Feasibility Studies

Feasibility studies for process modifications or product substitutions can be labor intensive, lengthy, and costly and are therefore not given serious consideration by many small to medium sized facilities. The settlement agreement can be used to encourage the facility to experiment and explore pollution prevention options. Examples of feasibility studies that may be conducted by facilities are testing water-based bonding primers for metals that can be used to replace solvent-based primers, switching from solvent-based cleaning systems to aqueous systems, switching from solvent-based printing inks to soyoil-based inks, etc.

6.3.4 Good Housekeeping Options

For small to medium sized facilities, it may be desirable to direct a facility to implement simple management options that can lead to reductions in waste generation. Examples include full cost accounting systems to determine the true cost of waste generation; inventory controls such as just-in-time purchasing of raw materials, first-in-first-out inventory controls, and bar coding systems for tracking raw material inventories and wastes; waste segregation procedures to improve recyclability, etc.

6.3.5 Management Options

The settlement agreement can be used to direct a facility to establish management policies for implementation of pollution prevention options. Examples of management policies could be establishing employee teams to research and recommend pollution prevention options, employee incentive programs, employee recognition programs, etc.

6.3.6 Training

Specific language can be written into settlement agreements that directs the environmental manager or facility operator (and in some cases the owner or CEO) to attend and obtain certificates from university extension programs offering hazardous materials management programs. Additionally, in-house training programs can be required for introducing pollution prevention concepts to the employee work force. Training programs can be developed and offered to the facility's vendors, clients, or small Mom-and-Pop facilities.

6.3.7 Community Outreach

Environmental public awareness projects can include developing publications, broadcasts, seminars, etc., to educate the community on the roles of the consumer in preventing pollution. Developing and funding household hazardous waste collection programs for the local community tend to provide high visibility, win-win projects.

6.3.8 Other Projects

The facility may be directed to provide funding to a nonprofit pollution prevention technical assistance program (university-based or other). Funding of university-based pollution prevention research has also been proposed as a settlement agreement option. Other innovative projects can range from local habitat preservation and restoration projects to purchasing large tracts of threatened rain forests in third world countries.

6.4 OBSTACLES TO IMPLEMENTATION OF POLLUTION PREVENTION IN THE SETTLEMENT AGREEMENT PROCESS

Perhaps the single most significant obstacle that must be overcome in order to utilize the settlement agreement process to encourage pollution prevention is the lack of commitment on the part of agency management. State and local surveillance and enforcement staff must be given the time and opportunity to receive pollution prevention training. Surveillance and enforcement inspectors have traditionally been trained to look for violations of laws and regulations. Inspectors have not been trained to look for opportunities to assist facilities in eliminating and reducing the generation of hazardous pollutants. Additionally, inspectors have been trained to control the releases of hazardous pollutants after they have been generated and have limited knowledge of the potential for the elimination of toxic pollutants prior to generation.

Other obstacles focus on the "bean counting" concept. Program personnel must meet a workload standard by conducting a certain number of inspections per year or collecting a certain amount of fines and penalties. If "bean counting" is a necessary part of a programs' measure of success, then a workload standard for pollution prevention can be formulated. Examples of pollution prevention "beans" can be as simple as allocating an extra 15 minutes per inspection to fill out a questionnaire or discuss pollution prevention opportunities or as complex as establishing a fixed number of settlement agreements that will contain pollution prevention components.

Time constraints are often cited as obstacles to negotiating settlement agreements. The process of development, negotiation, and follow-up of final agreements can require a considerable time commitment. However, if agencies believe preventing pollution is equally or more important than regulating the management of the pollutants after they are generated, then sufficient time can be allocated in the annual workplans for these types of activities. Additionally some federal grants provide incentives for conducting pollution prevention. Settlement agreements can be included as deliverable products in the grant workload standards.

Environmental regulatory personnel must remember the primary mission of an environmental regulatory program is to protect the public health and prevent the degradation of the environment. One way to protect the public's health and the environment is to eliminate or reduce the generation of toxic pollutants. Pollution prevention, while not a panacea, is an important component of any program. What better way to regulate a facility than to provide it with the opportunity to eliminate the generation of toxic pollutants. This message must be conveyed to regulatory program personnel through training and a firm commitment from high level managers.

The U.S. EPA Office of Waste Enforcement issued a memorandum on September 12, 1991, titled "The Role of RCRA Inspectors in Promoting Waste Minimization" that clearly encourages the enforcement inspectors to incorporate the prevention concept into their everyday workload.[4]

6.5 CONCLUSION

Environmental professionals have a unique opportunity to protect public health and the environment by assuring that pollution prevention is institutionalized into all aspects of their work. Including pollution prevention into settlement agreements is just one example of the role regulatory agencies can play in promoting the prevention ethic. Precedence has been set for integrating pollution prevention into the work of the regulatory inspectors (see Chapter 4). EPA policies have clearly stated that this is a desirable goal. All that is needed is the desire and the willingness to devote time that would otherwise be spent regulating waste that has already been generated, to preventing the generation of those wastes.

6.6 REFERENCES

1. Strock, J. M. "Policy on the Use of Supplemental Enforcement Projects in EPA Settlements," U.S. EPA memorandum (February 12, 1991).
2. Soo Hoo, W.F. "Admissions of Guilt in Enforcement Actions," California Department of Toxic Substances Control, Management Memo #90-2 (December 24, 1991).
3. Dawes, K. A. "Pollution Prevention Through Compliance and Enforcement, A Review of OPTS Accomplishments," U.S. EPA Report-22T-1002 (January 1992).
4. Diamond, B. "The Role of RCRA Inspectors in Promoting Waste Minimization," U.S. EPA memorandum (September 12, 1991).
5. "Pollution Prevention 1991, Progress on Reducing Industrial Pollutants," U.S. EPA, Office of Pollution Prevention, EPA 21P-3003 (October 1991).

6.7 APPENDICES

6.7.1 Appendix 1: Model Corrective Action Order and Complaint for Penalty

Introduction

Parties. The (government agency) issues this Corrective Action Order and Complaint for Penalty to (facility name), an Ohio Corporation herein referenced as respondent.

Site. Respondent generates, handles, treats, stores, and/or disposes of hazardous wastes at the following site: (facility address).

Generator. During times relevant herein, respondent was a generator of the following hazardous pollutants: epoxy resin, oil sludge, methyl ethyl ketone, sodium hydroxide, etc.

Determination of Violations

The (government agency) has determined that respondent has violated, is violating, or threatens to violate (specific laws or regulations, i.e., TSCA, EPCRA § 313, etc.) and other specified provisions as follows:

1. Respondent violated (Title, Section) in that respondent failed to file a 1987 Biennial Report with the (government agency).
2. Respondent violated (Title, Section) in that respondent failed to label hazardous waste barrels with the words "Hazardous Waste."
3. Respondent violated (Title, Section) in that respondent stored hazardous waste onsite for over 90 days without a permit.
4. Respondent violated (Title, Section) in that respondent failed to separate incompatible wastes from each other by means of a dike, berm, wall, or other device.

Schedule for Compliance

Based on the foregoing DETERMINATION OF VIOLATIONS, IT IS HEREBY ORDERED THAT:

1. Respondent shall immediately label all hazardous waste containers with the words "Hazardous Waste" and all other applicable information.
2. Respondent shall immediately ensure that no hazardous wastes are stored onsite for more than 90 days without a permit.
3. Within 15 days of the effective date of this order, the respondent shall separate incompatible wastes by means of a dike, berm, wall, or other adequate device.

Penalty

Based on the forgoing DETERMINATION OF VIOLATIONS, the (government agency) sets the amount of respondent's total proposed penalty at $75,000.

Right to a Hearing

You may request a hearing to challenge the Order and Complaint by contacting the (government agency) within 10 calendar days. A portion of the penalty may be waived for "supplemental environmental (Pollution Prevention) projects" at the sole discretion of the (government agency). Contact the (government agency) for information on supplemental environmental projects within 10 days.

Effective Date

This Order and Complaint is final and effective ten days from the date it is served to you, unless you request a hearing within the ten-day period.

Failure to Respond

Failure to respond to this order within 10 calendar days will result in this case being referred to the (District Attorney, Attorney General, etc.) for immediate legal prosecution.

6.7.2 Appendix 2: Model Settlement Agreement and Order

Introduction

On (date), the (government agency) served a Corrective Action Order and Complaint for Penalty to (facility name). The (governmental agency) now settles that proceeding upon the terms and conditions set forth in this Settlement Agreement and Order ("Order").

Corrective Action Order and Complaint for Penalty

The Corrective Action Order and Complaint for Penalty issued herein alleges that (facility name) violated several provisions of (law or regulation) with respect to its operations at the facility. The Corrective Action Order and Complaint for Penalty seeks penalties and directs certain corrective actions by (facility). A copy of the Corrective Action Order and Complaint for Penalty is attached as Exhibit A.

Settlement of Disputed Claims

(Facility name) and (government agency) enter into this order pursuant to a compromise and settlement of disputed claims for the purpose of avoiding prolonged and complex litigation with respect to the Corrective Action Order and Complaint for Penalty and in furtherance of the public interest.

This Order constitutes full settlement of the violations alleged, but does not limit (government agency) from taking appropriate enforcement actions concerning violations other than those alleged in the Corrective Action Order and Complaint for Penalty.

Nothing in this Order is intended or shall be construed as an admission of any violation of law or any issue of fact. Notwithstanding the above, the (government agency) may without prejudice assert the allegations made in the Corrective Action Order and Complaint for Penalties prior violations in any proceeding, brought on or before (five years) to deny, suspend or revoke any permit, registration or certificate applied for or issued to (facility name). In any such proceeding, the (government agency) shall have the burden of proof of establishing the occurrence of such alleged prior violations.

Waiver of Hearing

By signing this Order, (facility name) waives any right to a hearing on the Corrective Action Order and Complaint for Penalty.

Basic Settlement

(Government agency) and (facility) agree to settle this proceeding for $95,000 as follows:

(Facility) shall pay civil penalties to (government agency) in the amount of $75,000 within (ten) days of entry of this Order. Said payments shall be made by certified or cashiers' check.

Within 60 days of entry of this agreement, (facility) shall begin to conduct a study of the feasibility of using water-based adhesive bonding primers as replacements for solvent-based adhesive bonding primers (the feasibility study). The (facility) shall spend not less than $20,000 conducting the feasibility study as specified in the feasibility study proposal submitted by (facility). (Facility's) obligations with respect to the conduct of the feasibility study, its obligations in the event that it is unfeasible to conduct the feasibility study, and the nature of the feasibility study to be conducted are described more fully in the document entitled, "The Feasibility Study," which is attached hereto as Exhibit B and is incorporated by this reference as though fully set forth herein. Any failure on the part of (facility) to conduct the activities described in this paragraph, and in

Exhibit B to this order, within the time periods specified, shall constitute a violation of this agreement, and the (facility) shall pay to (government agency) $20,000 upon receipt of written notice.

Compliance with Applicable Laws

(Facility) shall carry out this Order in compliance with all federal, state, and local requirements.

Modification of Order

This Order may only be modified upon the written approval of the parties hereto.

Termination of Obligations

This order shall terminate on (date specified for completion of the feasibility study) upon completion of the requirements specified in the Order. In the event (facility) has not completed the requirements by the specified date, the Order shall not terminate, and the (facility) shall pay the $20,000 specified in this Order.

Communication

All communication pursuant to this Order shall be sent to the following: (list names and addresses of all parties in the agreement).

(Government Agency) Not Liable

The (government agency) shall not be liable for any injury or damage to persons or property resulting from acts or omissions by (facility name) or their employees, agents, affiliated corporations, representatives, or contractors in carrying out activities pursuant to this Order, including the exhibits hereto, nor shall (government agency) be held a party to or guarantor of any contract entered into by (facility name) in carrying out activities pursuant to this Order, including the exhibits hereto.

Retention of Jurisdiction

In the event that (facility name) fails to comply with this order, (government agency) may apply to the Superior Court for an order enforcing the terms of this Order and any other relief that may be appropriate.

Entry of this Order

Each of the signatories hereto certifies that he or she is fully authorized to enter into this Order, to execute it on behalf of the party he or she represents, and legally bind that party.

Regulatory Changes

Nothing in this Order shall excuse (facility name) from meeting any more stringent requirements that may be imposed by changes in relevant or applicable legislation or regulation.

CHAPTER 7

Incorporating Pollution Prevention into Facility Planning

David Rozell

7.1 INTRODUCTION

Several states have adopted pollution prevention facility planning statutes that direct industrial facilities to examine their processes for potential reductions in chemical use and/or hazardous waste generation. Although still in the initial stages of implementation, all of the state models center on businesses using a prescribed planning process to assess their chemical usage and hazardous waste generation and then develop reduction options and goals.

It is this prescribed process of discovery, in conjunction with a strong management commitment, that has helped some facilities substantially reduce, if not eliminate, many toxic chemicals and waste streams from their operations. This has reduced their costs, increased worker safety, and reduced environmental risks.

Facility planning, however, is not a panacea. There are inherent problems for both industry and government to overcome including measurement, funding, and commitment. This chapter explores the issues surrounding facility planning laws, providing useful insight for state and local governments considering similar requirements.

0-87371-654-X/93/$0.00+$.50
© 1993 by Lewis Publishers

7.2 BACKGROUND

In August 1989, the first facility planning laws in the nation were passed by Oregon and Massachusetts. These innovative pollution prevention initiatives (the Toxics Use Reduction and Hazardous Waste Reduction Act in Oregon and the Toxics Use Reduction Act in Massachusetts) represent the first attempts by grass roots organizations in these states (OSPIRG in Oregon and MassPIRG in Massachusetts) to work with both the regulatory agencies and their regulated communities toward making fundamental changes in the way business and industry think about their products and industrial processes.[1] Instead of the traditional command and control regulation of industrial pollution, these laws, for the first time, required manufacturing facilities to investigate and then plan for the implementation of technologies and management practices that reduce the use of toxic chemicals and the generation of hazardous wastes before they became a management or disposal problem.

In their search for new approaches to environmental problems, these states and 14 others have begun a regulatory experiment that the other states, the United States Congress, and the EPA are watching closely.

Factors contributing to the rise of facility planning laws vary between states. Oregon pursued facility planning legislation for the following three primary reasons:

- The ever increasing use of toxic chemicals in manufacturing posed a continued threat to worker safety and public health in general.
- The escalating generation of hazardous wastes increased the threat of spills and long-term environmental damage as well as presented long-term liability issues for companies.
- States were being asked to administer an increasing number of federal regulations while regulatory budgets continued to shrink.

On September 1, 1991, the first facility plans were developed by Oregon industrial facilities. Much of what is included in this chapter is based on the experience gained in implementing the program by industry and staff of the Oregon Department of Environmental Quality. Other references are noted where appropriate.

7.3 WHAT IS FACILITY PLANNING?

Facility planning is designed to move an industrial plant (1) to increase its awareness of chemical usage and hazardous wastes generated, (2) to foster a commitment to chemical and waste reduction as a corporate ethic, (3) to conscientiously evaluate the reduction options for their specific operations, and (4) to voluntarily commit to specific reduction implementation strategies and numeric reduction goals.

In most facility planning statutes, industry is required to develop a plan and notify the state that it has been completed or actually submit the plan, or an executive summary of the plan, to the regulatory agency. Most facility planning statutes target facilities required to report annually under EPA's Toxics Chemical Release Inventory (SARA Title 313) program. This data on chemical usage is used to decide whether a facility must develop a plan. In some statutes, hazardous waste generators are included in the universe of facilities that must prepare reduction plans.[2]

While states have taken the lead in industrial facility planning, local governments have also been involved. California and New York have examples of local government activities in this area primarily focusing on technical assistance. But local governments can also use their regulatory authority over POTW. Owners and operators of POTWs, because of their knowledge of industrial effluent, are uniquely qualified to deliver pollution prevention services to the users of these facilities, and facility planning can assist them in this activity.[3]

7.3.1 The Plan

The contents of a pollution prevention facility plan generally include the following elements and practices:

- a written policy statement that clearly affirms management's commitment to toxic chemical and/or hazardous waste reduction
- an in-depth assessment of toxic chemicals used in, and/or the hazardous wastes generated from, the production process (This usually includes data on the types, amount, and hazardous constituents of toxic substances and hazardous waste streams as well as where and why these chemicals are used and what hazardous wastes are generated.)
- the in-depth review of potential reduction options for toxic chemical use and hazardous wastes generation
- the evaluation of costs associated with the use of toxic chemicals and the generation of hazardous wastes. This usually includes the following:
  the cost of purchasing chemical
  the cost of disposal
  the cost of storage
  the cost of waste treatment
  the cost of environmental compliance and liability
- an employee awareness and training program that involves staff in the planning process as well as the implementation of the plan
- an analysis for reduction options that identifies which options are technically and economically feasible
- numeric reduction or performance goals for chemicals used and/or wastes generated
- a schedule for the implementation of those selected options and the achievement of the performance goals

Seen from a larger perspective, the planning process has but two parts. The first part requires management to create a fertile ground for reduction planning and implementation through a strong policy statement, a deliberate employee awareness and training program, an effective cost accounting system, and finally,

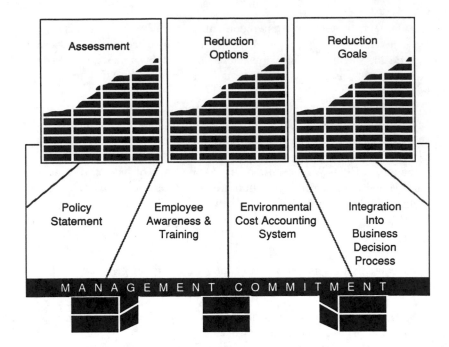

Figure 1.   Facility planning model. Strong management commitment is mandatory for a successful Toxics Use Reduction facility planning program.

a sincere commitment to building a pollution prevention ethic by integrating the concept into daily business practices and procedures. The second part is the technical assessment, development of options, and the establishment of reduction goals. Without strong management commitment in the first part, the goals set in the second part cannot be achieved. See Figure 1.

7.4 DOES FACILITY PLANNING WORK FOR INDUSTRY?

There is little experience or data, to date, on how well these programs work. However, based on the formal review of 39 Toxics Use Reduction and Hazardous Waste Reduction plans in Oregon as well as individual interviews and discussions with many other industry representatives, it is possible to make the following statements regarding program effectiveness:

- Management commitment to the facility planning and implementation processes is the single most important success factor. With it, the plan is a powerful and successful tool for toxic chemical and hazardous waste reduction. Without that support, the plan is not likely to be implemented.
- In medium to small facilities, the planning process has developed information and a new sense of awareness about their processes and procedures that have lead to inefficiencies and waste.

- The requirement that the plan be reviewed by the senior facility manager elevates its importance and raises the visibility of environmental regulations and the opportunities for pollution prevention. The attention and support of management are key to getting a plan implemented.
- Facility planning, when accomplished as outlined above, lets the facility determine what alternatives it will implement, offering an opportunity for creative responses instead of prescriptive technical fixes.
- When there is a true management commitment, facility planning creates a forum for discussion between management and employees about how to increase chemical efficiency and worker safety. This vests the employees in the outcome and usually leads to greater awareness and motivation.
- Most facilities that have implemented pollution prevention facility plans have seen costs decrease and generally feel that they are reducing the impact of or actually avoiding more stringent environmental command and control regulations.

7.4.1 Problems

Since states are in the early stages of pollution prevention facility planning, there are still many things to be learned. However, even at this early stage, several problems for industry in the implementation of these plans can be identified:

- It is impossible to legislate corporate commitment. Therefore, facility planning programs will always result in different levels of commitment and consequently different levels of reduction between facilities.
- In some cases, other environmental regulations may actually inhibit creative solutions to hazardous waste management issues. As an example, under the Resource Conservation and Recovery Act (RCRA), industry has found it extremely difficult, if not impossible, to reuse certain industrial wastes as a substitute for a commercial chemical product.[4]
- In most cases, the success of a program is directly dependent on the amount of new command and control regulations promulgated from the state or EPA. Limited capital and staff resources will inevitably be focused to avoid violations and fines at the expense of facility planning implementation.
- Although a few companies are doing an exemplary job of developing a reduction measurement system, true reduction measurement is very difficult for even these with the current tools available and impossible for the rest. This, however, generally does not lessen the reduction commitment of these facilities because success can also be measured as a function of the number of reduction options that have been implemented. This keeps them moving toward their goal, even when they cannot actually measure progress quantitatively.

7.5 DOES FACILITY PLANNING WORK FOR GOVERNMENT?

As part of an integrated regulatory scheme with command and control regulations, pollution prevention facility planning has several benefits for state and local governments:

- Since most facility planning laws are founded in chemical use reductions, they are multimedia (air, water, and solid and hazardous waste). This creates the opportunity to coordinate information and activities at an individual facility across traditional environmental programs.
- In theory, more pollution prevention is achievable per government dollar through facility planning efforts than by technical assistance site visits alone.
- For the facility, the planning process generally results in a clearer understanding of why chemicals are used and waste is generated within a particular operation. This new information almost always translates into more efficient operations. This additional information, in many cases, also increases compliance with command and control regulations.
- The reduction in the amount of chemicals used and wastes generated within a facility is environmentally and socially beneficial.

7.5.1 Problems

Although pollution prevention facility planning has several benefits for government, some issues should be addressed before a local or state government decides to enact such legislation:

- Quantitative measurement of pollution prevention is difficult at best and may be meaningless, due to the data inaccuracies. Will a state or local government be willing to promote a program that is difficult to evaluate?
- Since the implementation is dependent almost totally on industry, the success of a facility planning program is more likely if there is a good relationship between industry and the state or local agency responsible for the program implementation.
- A strong environmental enforcement program is a very good motivator to implement facility pollution prevention plans. In fact, some Oregon facilities have reported that they were motivated to do pollution prevention more to reduce their regulatory burden than because of any other factor.
- Some states have had difficulty in funding facility planning programs. At a minimum, staffing resources are necessary to monitor and report on what industry is implementing and to track chemical use and hazardous waste generation on a statewide level. Funding for these activities will always be difficult if these programs must compete with traditional command and control programs for limited resources.

7.6 CONCLUSION

In conjunction with strong traditional permitting and enforcement programs, facility planning can provide an additional tool for local and state governments that improves worker safety and reduces risks to public health and the environment.

Facility planning, while not a panacea, can be a powerful tool in showing businesses the links between chemical use, releases to the environment, and industrial process efficiency.

For state and local governments, it provides an additional tool that will reap environmental benefits beyond the traditional command and control programs, a benefit to everyone.

7.7 REFERENCES

1. Sugarman, Q. Personal communication, Oregon State Public Interest Research Group (July 1992).
2. Freeman, Harten, et al. "Industrial Pollution Prevention: A Critical Review," *J. Air Waste Manage. Assoc.* 42:618 (1992).
3. Ibid.
4. Byers, R. L. "Regulatory Barriers to Pollution Prevention," *J. Air Waste Manage. Assoc.* 41:418 (1991).

CHAPTER 8

Promoting Pollution Prevention Through Technical Assistance

David Kidd

8.1 INTRODUCTION

The following chapter describes the fundamental components of a technical assistance program and how these programs can foster pollution prevention. This chapter is divided into three sections covering the following:

- the basic pieces that need to be in place to operate a technical assistance program
- the basic day-to-day considerations in running an effective program
- methods for conducting assessments of businesses

A strong technical assistance program is essential for a successful pollution prevention effort. Most businesses are willing to buy into the philosophy of pollution prevention, but need assistance in actually implementing pollution prevention measures. This can be especially true of small businesses, which lack the specialized environmental expertise to develop an effective pollution prevention program. Pollution prevention technical assistance programs have been operated successfully within a number of types of agencies:

0-87371-654-X/93/$0.00+$.50
© 1993 by Lewis Publishers

89

- Nonprofit organizations. These organizations are free of government affiliations and can respond quickly to the different needs of clients.
- Universities and colleges. Universities have technical expertise, research facilities, and a ready source of labor (student interns).
- Government agencies. Agencies have close contact with regulatory agencies and funding sources.

8.2 PROGRAM COMPONENTS

A number of components should be in place to run an effective pollution prevention program. These components build upon each other and together create an effective and cohesive program. Components to include in an effective program are as follows.

8.2.1 A Library

A collection of references to refer to is essential when making pollution prevention recommendations. The EPA Pollution Prevention Information Exchange System data base offers an excellent source of pollution prevention references. This service is available to anyone with a PC and a modem (call the EPA at (202) 245-3557 for information). Along with standard reference materials, a library should also include lists of vendors of pollution prevention products and services.

8.2.2 An "800" Number

A great deal of marketing and promotion is required to start a technical assistance program. Businesses will need to be encouraged to make use of the services offered. An "800" number will provide free and quick access to a technical assistance program. It can be used to give waste reduction tips and referrals.

8.2.3 A Newsletter

A newsletter is an effective medium through which to promote pollution prevention. It can be used to advertise upcoming pollution prevention events as well as advertise the services of the technical assistance program. It can be used to keep the readers informed of recent developments in pollution prevention. Pollution prevention success stories can also be included in the newsletter. These types of articles will motivate the audience, give credit to active pollution preventers, and provide ideas for use in pollution prevention.

When writing a newsletter, it is important to know who makes up the audience and to write the newsletter to them. A newsletter with "something for everyone" will keep target audiences' reading interest. For example, if the audience is made up of management personnel, the articles might focus on policy and regulations; whereas if the audience is made up of small business owners and line workers, it might focus more on actual pollution prevention techniques.

8.2.4 Onsite Pollution Prevention Assessment Capability

Onsite assessments are an essential service for a program to provide. This is especially true for programs focusing on small business. A business without technical expertise can often benefit from an assessment. Performing assessments will also allow a program to build up a case file of pollution prevention problems and solutions. Before conducting pollution prevention assessments, a program should decide how to handle the issues concerning making regulatory interpretations for businesses and maintaining the confidentiality of the businesses assessed.

In addition, a program should consider its assessment approach. A small business may need technical support at the process level of its operation. However, a larger business may already have the technical expertise and staff to conduct ongoing assessments of the operation. In this case, technical assistance programs may want to focus on the company management in an effort to ensure pollution prevention is a part of management decision-making. To really understand company commitment to pollution prevention, technical assistance programs must determine whether prevention and environmental protection programs are a key part of company decisions, or merely rhetoric.

This information and understanding can be gathered, in part, by actually sitting down with company management and assessing their business philosophy and practice. The types of questions that could be asked include the following:

- Does the company have a written pollution prevention policy?
- How does the company demonstrate continual commitment to improving its environmental programs?
- How does the company incorporate pollution prevention into its day-to-day decisions?
- Does the company have actual pollution prevention staff?
- What is the budget for the pollution prevention program?
- Does the company provide for employee training in pollution prevention?
- How does the company evaluate its progress in reducing pollution?
- Does the company incorporate pollution prevention standards into management and employee performance reviews and job descriptions?

State and local pollution prevention programs can be effective agents for change by challenging companies (in a constructive way) to demonstrate their commitment to pollution prevention. Technical assistance programs should offer assistance to help motivate companies to adopt more prevention-oriented business policies.

Some programs use college students as interns to conduct assessments and write assessment reports. This will provide the program with inexpensive labor and a fresh outlook and will provide the students an invaluable introduction to practical pollution prevention. In addition, interns are sometimes less threatening to a company.

8.2.5 Outreach Capability

A continual effort needs to be made to market the advantages of pollution prevention and the services provided by the technical assistance program. This should include an attractive brochure describing the program's services.

A technical assistance program should also have the capability to conduct seminars and workshops. These events can be targeted to geographic areas to spread general pollution prevention information or to groups with common concerns to transfer specific pollution prevention information. It is important to target the audience with these activities and to provide specific, usable information as opposed to general, conceptual information. The workshop presenters should be prepared to tell the audience not just that they need a "solvent still," but that to distill 10 gallons a day of Solvo brand 328 stoddard solvent, they can use an Acme model 1486 solvent still, available from XYZ Service Company (206-000-0000) P.O. Box 0000, Albany, Oregon, 97321, and that the current list price is $2400. Presenters should also caution businesses to balance the information presented against their actual operations. Technological investments should always be made based upon actual workplace conditions.

8.3 RUNNING A TECHNICAL ASSISTANCE PROGRAM

A successfully run technical assistance program requires a marketing plan, a reputation for providing a respected and useful service, and a good working relationship with clients.

8.3.1 Marketing A Program

A technical assistance program must be aggressively marketed. While the idea of pollution prevention makes perfect sense to those working in the field, many businesses will take some convincing that it is worth time and investment. A technical assistance program should market both its services and the concept of pollution prevention. Workshops and a newsletter can be used to spread the word.

Workshops and presentations should be given to trade associations and conventions. Articles may also be written for trade association newsletters. Local Small Business Development Centers, Commerce and Economic Development Centers, and regulatory agencies are excellent resources to help a program make contacts with businesses.

A technical assistance program should also work with local colleges and trade associations to incorporate pollution prevention into their teaching and training. Student interns can be made an important part of a program, as previously mentioned.

A technical assistance program should strive to develop a positive, long-term working relationship with the businesses it is working with, as this will lead to a stable, productive program.

8.3.2 Establishing a Relationship with Business

Establishing a relationship with business is a critical facet of technical assistance and is often overlooked. There are two things to keep in mind when working with business:

- The overriding focus of any business is to make a profit. Business people are usually very helpful and most often want to do the right thing, but to reach them, a technical assistance program must appeal to their bottom line. They must be shown why pollution prevention will save them money or time.
- Business people know more about their own businesses than any technical assistance staff member will ever know. Technical assistance personnel need to use and respect business people's intimate knowledge of processes and the ins and outs of their business. In some instances, a business person will often become a more valuable resource to a technical assistance program than the program is to him/her. When business people are shown the respect they deserve, they can become valuable allies. Before giving businesses suggestions, technical assistance program personnel need to do their homework well. They must realize the many impediments that will be faced in implementing the pollution prevention approaches that sound so simple in the reference books. Technical assistance program personnel need to be aware that small changes in processes can affect the end quality of a product.

Businesses will want specific, usable information from a technical assistance program. They will want to know what exactly will work, how it works, where to get it, and how much it will cost. A technical assistance program should be prepared to deliver this type of information, to find it, or to tell them where to go to find it. Care should always be taken to make certain the business person knows that final decisions regarding pollution prevention options rest with the business itself. This will help reduce technical assistance program liability.

Businesses will often want regulatory interpretations from technical assistance programs, as any work in the environmental field invariably involves regulations. The technical assistance program should think this issue out carefully and establish exactly how these instances will be handled. By making regulatory interpretations, a technical assistance program will put itself in a position of liability. This issue should also be discussed with the regulatory agencies.

Businesses will want the work done with them to be confidential, both from other businesses and from regulatory agencies. A technical assistance program should be prepared to guarantee confidentiality. Many pollution prevention agencies have agreements with the regulators that the work they do will be confidential, with the exception of the reporting of gross violations.

A technical assistance program must protect its reputation carefully. One slip can ruin its reputation and its effectiveness. A technical assistance program is in a unique position to work with businesses in a positive way to achieve mutually beneficial goals. This potential should be a guiding principle in the work done.

8.3.3 Motivating Business

Technical assistance personnel must be continual advocates of pollution prevention. Program staffers should be cheerleaders of sorts to motivate businesses. An advantage of pollution prevention is it sells itself — it can be advocated by emphasizing cost savings, reduction of liability and regulation, and improvement of corporate image.

Public recognition can also be used as a motivator. Businesses like to receive recognition in a newsletter. An annual pollution prevention award can also motivate businesses to make pollution prevention improvements.

8.3.4 Conducting a Pollution Prevention Assessment

An assessment of pollution prevention opportunities within a business or department is a valuable tool. This assessment should be part of a recognized pollution prevention effort established in the business. This effort within a business should be supported by top level management and should include budget line items and personnel with specific pollution prevention duties. A technical assistance program can conduct pollution prevention assessments as a service to its clients. While providing these services, a technical assistance program should bear in mind the eventual goal is to establish a long-term, viable pollution prevention effort within the business itself. To conduct an assessment, follow the steps outlined below:

1.   Form an audit team. The team should include one of the technical assistance program staffers (preferably two) and members of the business. The business members should be from diverse backgrounds to involve many different points of view. A leader should be appointed. The team can then form the core of the long-range pollution prevention effort within the business.

2.   Review records. The team should then look at the entire business with the intention of preventing pollution. All aspects of a business should be considered including process technology, purchasing, accounting, record keeping, inventory, and materials handling. The records should be reviewed to establish procedures and to identify the amounts of material flowing through the business. The business should be broken into series of processes, and the materials' flow through each process then documented. A flow diagram/mass balance should be constructed for the different processes to determine the amounts of materials escaping as pollution.

Cost Analysis

Present System

Solvent used per year	$1500
Disposal Costs	$3000
Total Cost	$4500

Using a Solvent Still

Solvent used per year	$500
Disposal Costs	$800

Net Difference = $4500 - $800 = $3700

In this example the still (WITH A COST OF $4000) would pay itself off in slightly more than one year. It should be noted that there can be many other variables added to this example to determine its cost effectiveness. It is intended to be an example only.

Figure 1. Cost analysis.

3. Conduct a walk-through. After the operations of the business have been established, a walk-through of the facility should be conducted during working hours to observe the processes taking place. These processes should be observed with an open mind, as familiarity can be as much a hinderance as a help in trying to identify sources of waste and pollution. Look for air emissions, evaporative waste, wastewater, solid waste, heat/energy loss, poor maintenance, outdated stock, and spoiled production runs. Discuss procedures with line employees, as they are the most familiar with them. A walk-through should actually be conducted. What occurs on the floor is often quite different from the procedures described in the office by management.

4. Identify and analyze pollution prevention options. The data should then be analyzed to identify sources of waste and pollution. These sources can include obvious process sources as well as administrative procedures.

    Pollution that can be prevented should be identified and methods to achieve this prevention should be sought. The technical assistance library and other references can be used to identify pollution prevention approaches. "Media shifts" (taking pollution in one form and simply turning it into another) should be avoided. The goal should be to prevent or reduce the total amount of pollution as much as possible.

    The pollution prevention approaches used should be analyzed for the cost savings they will bring about. This can be a simple analysis as shown in Figure 1.

    Assume 600 gallons of solvent costing $2.50 per gallon are used per year. The solvent costs $5.00 per gallon to dispose. A solvent still would cost $4000 and would produce 400 gallons of usable solvent and 80 gallons of sludge per year that costs $10 per gallon to dispose.

5. Write a report of the findings. A report outlining the work accomplished should be given to the management. The report should include a statement of purpose, a summary, a process description (include flow diagrams), a table of pollution generated, and recommended pollution prevention options (including pros and cons, cost analyses, vendors, costs, etc.). It should be emphasized that the report provides suggestions only and that the final decisions on any changes are for the business to

make. The report should be made as user-friendly as possible, using graphs and charts. The report should also be written to a specific audience. If it is written to a small business owner with a high school education, it should be written in a format that he/she can readily understand and use.

8.4 CONCLUSION

A number of recommendations for providing pollution prevention technical assistance have been provided. Building a program with components that support each other and that provides businesses with tangible services will ensure long-term success. See Chapter 15 for additional resources.

8.4.1 A Word on Program Evaluation

Program evaluation is an important component of a technical assistance program. Here are a few methods to assess the effectiveness of program services:

*   follow-up assessments to measure changes in pollution or business policies
*   follow-up calls to "800" number users to determine if the information provided was useful and contributed to their prevention efforts
*   pretest and posttest evaluations can be used to measure training program effectiveness

Technical assistance programs may also want to conduct internal evaluation of their operation by performing the following:

*   tracking the number of calls fielded and the time it takes to respond
*   tracking the growth (or decline) of a programs budget and staff levels
*   measuring the level of staff expertise and improvement resulting from training
*   attempting to measure the actual reductions in pollution resulting from program efforts

Measuring pollution prevention program effectiveness is in the early stages of development. Federal, state, and local government agencies have not come to any agreement on appropriate measurement methodologies. Chapter 10 explores this question in more detail. Technical assistance programs are well advised to consider program evaluation as an integral component to the service they provide.

CHAPTER 9

Conducting Pollution Prevention Training Programs

Terry Foecke

9.1 INTRODUCTION

Many organizations develop and deliver training in order to speed implementation of pollution prevention. Local programs see this training as a natural outgrowth of efforts to inform industrial generators and the public of their obligations under many types of environmental regulations. Training is also outreach — teaching about pollution prevention and promoting pollution prevention as a preferred method of waste management.

This chapter will first describe the attributes of an "ideal" pollution prevention trainer. Second, the subject matter of pollution prevention training will be discussed along with the principal audiences for that training and their needs. Finally, some lessons learned about developing and delivering pollution prevention training will be presented.

9.2 THE POLLUTION PREVENTION TRAINER

There is no consensus yet on the issue of the "ideal" pollution prevention trainer. In fact, the only agreement may be that the ideal pollution prevention trainer does

0-87371-654-X/93/$0.00+$.50
© 1993 by Lewis Publishers

not exist. Perhaps, the best any organization can do is to assemble as many pieces as possible by using teams and continuing development of existing trainers. Nonetheless, there are several attributes to look for in the "ideal" pollution prevention trainer.

The first essential attribute of an ideal pollution prevention trainer seems to be that they be a trainer. That is, whatever this person's background or preparation for this work, they must be familiar with the principles of education (in this case, adult education), communications and presentation, and transfer of information. Furthermore, the subject matter often seems to require a person with some flair, someone who can "evangelize" a bit and persuade attendees to move away from old ways of acting and thinking.

The next attribute is competence at some level in the field of pollution prevention, and certainly a belief that pollution prevention is viable and important. This "field competence" helps during agenda development and debates over definition issues or the illustration of pollution prevention examples. While pollution prevention has a very large component of "common sense" to it, leading training in pollution prevention requires challenging the status quo, always a challenge.

The final attribute of an ideal pollution prevention trainer is that they be a "subject expert" for a particular topic. This seems to be very important in assessment training and certainly makes other training easier to deliver as well as more believable. This is probably the most difficult attribute to actually obtain or develop, but may also be the most important to the long-term success of training in pollution prevention.

A local program can assemble a team of people who will together provide many, if not all, of these attributes. A common approach is to have one or two program staff serve as training developers. They are responsible for gathering information about the audience and topic, drafting and distributing agenda, and gathering resource materials. These staff are supplemented by outside resource people such as industry association staff, industry representatives, and experienced program staff from elsewhere. The delivery of the training is done by having a "master of ceremonies" (usually someone from the local program) coordinate presentations and exercises. This way, no one person is burdened with the role of "master trainer."

9.3 POLLUTION PREVENTION AS A TRAINING SUBJECT

Many times training will target entire organizations with the intent of laying a base for more specific training sessions in the future. Training for pollution prevention is often an attempt to familiarize attendees with the assessment process used to discover opportunities for pollution prevention. By exposing attendees to the basics of the discovery and implementation of pollution prevention options, the ground will be prepared for the larger cultural change seen to be necessary. A further assumption is that at the orientation level, all attendees have some stake in pollution prevention.

Pollution prevention trainers can expect to cover four types of subject matter:

- introductory or orientation training
- technical training
  industry-specific
  use/waste/release-specific
  process-specific
- assessment training
- integration training
  strategic planning
  management seminars

9.3.1 Orientation Training

Orientation training in pollution prevention can be described as education outreach. This kind of training does not impart skills, but rather informs, persuades, promotes, or encourages in various measures about pollution prevention. Often lecture-based and short (four to six hour training time; sometimes as little as one h), these orientation sessions require minimal effort to meet the specific needs of a particular audience. A sample agenda is attached as Appendix 1.

9.3.2 Technical Training

Technical training is sought by a wide range of audiences. The material can cover anything from an entire industry group to specific processes and pollution prevention opportunities associated with them. The material is presented over one or two days and often draws on trainers from outside the sponsoring program. Considerable time may be invested in designing and delivering this type of training. A sample agenda is attached as Appendix 2.

9.3.3 Assessment Training

Assessment training prepares individuals or teams to review facilities, identify pollution prevention opportunities, and in some cases assist in implementation. Attendees often review a wide variety of facilities, waste streams, and chemical uses. The training includes a mixture of general pollution prevention orientation, role playing, and skill building in spotting pollution prevention opportunities. This training can take five days to complete. A sample agenda is attached as Appendix 3.

9.3.4 Integration Training

Integration training targets organizations for change — change that would allow for more implementation of pollution prevention. Topics covered include how to assess organizational structures, financial analysis, and strategic planning. The goal is to find a place for pollution prevention in each organization and in each individual's job. The length of training ranges from two hours for senior management to multiple two-day sessions for an entire staff. This training combines many of the agenda elements described above.

9.4 DEVELOPING A TRAINING PROGRAM

Sometimes no training "program" exists, but some sense of the framework for any particular training helps in agenda decisions. For example, it is easier to justify large up-front development costs for materials like resource packets if the program calls for later training of other groups. Key questions to consider when developing a training program include the following:

- Will the training be long-term or one-shot? A long-term commitment to pollution prevention means some attention needs to be paid to laying a good foundation for organizational change. This could be done, for example, by training managers first, along with a key group like inspectors or environmental coordinators. A one-shot training will be more concerned with reaching a group with high topical interest. This might include facilities with high air releases of solvents or enforcement staff charged with implementing a new directive to include pollution prevention conditions in settlements.
- Will there be multiple audiences? The next issue to consider is whether any particular training is intended to be given over a period of time, whether new audiences may be sought for the training (as can be the case with orientation training), and whether completely new audiences and topics will ever be considered.
- How much funding is available? The amount of money available will affect almost every decision from who the instructors will be to whether refreshments are provided, to how much time is spent developing the agenda and resources. Inexpensive (less than $500) training can be done as more "canned" materials become available, but only limited customizing will be possible.
- What is the time frame? Does all training have to be completed in a certain period for budgetary or project-related reasons? Is there latitude to create follow-up or refresher training at a later date? How much time can attendees reasonably be expected to devote to training and practice? Answers to these questions will determine how much time can be devoted to audience analysis and training development and will also determine the design of the training. For example, if only eight hours are available for presentation, after breaks and lunch there are only five-and-a-half to six hours available for delivery of the training materials. Furthermore, if the training must be presented in 90 days, this allows very little time for development, meaning the search for existing materials will be very important. Another rule of thumb is that a minimum of 30 days is required for attendees to get a training date on their calendars, and 60 days is far more realistic. In addition, an agenda must be developed before you can seek attendees.
- What are the barriers? Some common barriers encountered for pollution prevention training are as follows:

      lack of management commitment
      lack of resources
      lack of motivation on the part of trainees
      few materials available
      few experienced, local trainers available
      topics are seen as overwhelmingly large and complex
      regulations are media-specific, while pollution prevention focuses on cross-media transfers and cross-functional activities

- What are the opportunities? Some common opportunities encountered in pollution prevention training include the following:

      Management sees it as an opportunity to increase efficiency.
      Trainees see it as an opportunity to learn something new and "hot."
      All parties see it as an opportunity to do something good for the world.
      There is high public awareness of the issue.
      Pollution prevention builds heavily on issues such as quality management, communications, and team-building — issues already being discussed and implemented in many organizations.

9.4.1 Know Your Audience

Knowing the audience is important in the design and eventual success of a pollution prevention training effort. Typically the attendees will be a mixed audience, containing members with different functions, motivations, and needs, and very possibly observers who will stop in and out just to "see what is going on." There is no way to serve all members of a mixed audience. A "core" audience must be chosen, and decisions must be made related to the needs of that group. Try to learn as much as possible about the following basic attendee characteristics:

- Attendee function. The attendee's function (inspector, permit writer, process operator, plant manager, engineer) can influence selection of specific agenda items and give clues to the approach needed. For example, an inspector by definition will be more familiar with industrial facilities. Less time could then be spent becoming familiar with industry and more on examining and modifying current procedures. Or, a trainer could count on permit writers knowing rules very well and spend less time on the regulatory framework. This is also the place to determine whether attendees are from the public or private sector and what that means to the training.
- Attendee position. The position an attendee holds is important for broad agenda decisions. The type of information and style of presentation are different for an audience of managers than for an audience of staff or operators. Managers must understand the commitment required of the organization and of the employees of that organization to foster attention on pollution prevention. For public agency managers, a shift is required from reliance on command-and-control as the primary means of environmental protection to inclusion of such tools as promotion, persuasion, and encouragement. For private sector managers, recognition of environmental concerns is a key component of training, along with stressing the need to include all levels of the corporation in change (much along the lines of quality/quality improvement

training). A distinction can also be made between senior management and middle management in many organizations. Senior management usually receives shorter and more general training.

Staff require at least some orientation to pollution prevention, since they may be the primary agents of its implementation. Inspectors in public agencies are often the most directly affected and require time and information to integrate pollution prevention into their jobs. All other staff in an organization may very well receive only "lunch-hour" training. This is sufficient to begin establishing a sense that change is desirable, but not directed at any particular actions that need to be taken.

- Attendee experience. A training participant's experience in pollution prevention and industrial processes will drive the choice of technical content areas, the amount of time devoted to communications, and perhaps the amount of time required for the training to be effective.

- Attendee motivation. The motivation of attendees affects the delivery of the material and the amount of time spent developing the course. The most basic point to remember is that attendees who are told to be there or who feel forced to attend will not be "good" attendees. They will be less willing to engage fully in discussions and entertain creative solutions, key elements in pollution prevention training.

All these factors are analyzed to determine the training needs of a particular group of attendees. First, the goals of the training are determined. Then, agenda components are chosen and developed, taking into consideration the above factors. Finally, trainers are selected, and the delivery and site details completed. An important point to remember is that the needs attendees perceive for themselves are not always accurate. This is true of any training focused mostly on change, but especially true for training in pollution prevention. It may be helpful to think of information gathered directly from attendees not as "needs" but as "wants," subject to revision and expansion.

9.4.2 Determine Draft Training Goals

Goals serve to give attendees a sense of the content of the training, as well as what might be expected of them after the training. Goals also serve to focus training design and delivery discussions. Progress in meeting goals is often difficult to measure. Measurement should be attempted at a finer level of detail — that of objectives. For example, a training goal might focus on building greater understanding of pollution prevention. In this case, the training objective would focus on attendees being able to examine a list of activities, ask some questions, and be able to determine which were likely to be pollution prevention with 90% accuracy. The following list of goals is drawn from actual example training:

- Build awareness. Attendees could be made aware of pollution prevention as a possible course of action; the possibility for incorporating pollution prevention into their own activities; and the level of activity already occurring in the field of pollution prevention.

- Build competence. Skills can be gained in the delivery of pollution prevention training; communicating in or about unfamiliar situations; gathering and evaluating information; and thinking creatively.
- Build teams. Team-building is already a common focus in many organizations, especially when change is the focus. Pollution prevention cannot be fully implemented without a team effort. Practice in putting together and working on teams concerned with pollution prevention activities is very useful.
- Change jobs. Often attendees are asked to consider how they might do their jobs differently in order to promote pollution prevention.
- Change an organization. Most environmental programs focus on controlling pollution after it has been created. Therefore, it is critical that an attendee's organization change in order to promote pollution prevention, implement pollution prevention, or both.

9.4.3 Determine and Assess Potential Attendees

Sometimes the attendees are determined fairly early in the life of a training project (e.g., "We want to train all our fire inspectors to spot pollution prevention opportunities"). But often the attendee list needs to be narrowed and focused considerably before an agenda can be developed.

1. Survey attendees. Whether done formally or informally, some sort of assessment of attendees must be done in order to properly develop a training agenda. An informal assessment may simply be three to five phone calls to randomly selected representatives of the group. Training organizers should ask attendees what they know about pollution prevention and what they would like to know. This task requires a total time commitment of less than two hours. Done more formally, the assessment could require professional expertise in survey design and analysis and require several weeks to complete. One shortcut is to locate instances of similar training and "borrow" whatever assessment information seems applicable.
2. Analyze survey results. This analysis can be simple or complex, depending on time available and the survey itself. If the survey reveals information about any of the following, it can be used to design and deliver the training:
   special needs
   expectations that require management
   attendee skills/background that can be used
   identify believers
   attitudes about pollution prevention
   awareness of pollution prevention
3. Propose final training goals and draft agenda. Training goals and the draft agenda should:
   contain no more than five objectives
   show times and place
   give time for each component
   give purpose for each component
4. Check with sample group of potential attendees. A quick phone call to a few people who might attend the training can yield important reactions that can then be used for last-minute corrections to the agenda. Flexibility in the agenda should be considered

until the very last minute, as long as incorporating one comment does not eliminate other material seen as important by a significant number of the group.

9.5 TRAINING STYLE

Another early development decision has to do with the approach or style of the training. Two major training styles include lecture-based and interactive formats. A lecture-based training format is familiar to and probably most comfortable for attendees. Interactive (or cooperative, or learner-centered, or hands-on) training emphasizes the need to develop a "process" or "tools" each attendee will later customize to fit their personal situation. In addition, this approach to training involves attendees themselves (and their interactions) as much as possible. Attendees experience the concepts, rather than having them presented.

Because of its unfamiliarity and development needs, the interactive approach is almost always supplemented with some material delivered by lecture, as well as overheads/slides, hand-outs, and resource packets. At this point in agenda development, the most important decision to make is whether any interactive sessions will be included, so instructors and materials can be located. Some possible interactive approaches and materials will be described both in the discussion of agenda components and in the Resources section at the end of this chapter.

9.6 TRAINING LENGTH

There are many constraints that affect how much time certain groups of attendees will spend in training. This information will determine other training content decisions. Decisions about training length should consider the attendee's position and function. Some very rough rules of thumb about training length for selected audiences include the following:

- senior management — two hours
- managers without direct supervisory responsibility for line staff — two to four hours, depending on motivation
- managers charged with day-to-day direction of field or production staff — four to eight hours, depending on motivation and direction from top management
- field staff, production staff, managers charged with pollution prevention/environmental management — one to two days for any one training; a series of training may be necessary

Assessment training is a special case that, with practice and instruction, can require four to six days to complete.

9.7 MAKING AGENDA DECISIONS

Some basic components of a pollution prevention training program include the following:

- introduction
- background/historical review/current events
- communications
- technical content
- application/integration
- resources/next steps

Depending on the objectives of the training and the audience, different components will have different amounts of time devoted to their development and delivery. Senior management might receive mostly background and integration information, but very little technical material; other managers, a fairly even mix of all components, with a slight emphasis on communications; and implementation staff, a heavy emphasis on technical content and application, with only a brief background section. The decisions will be made using the audience analysis initially completed and by using a good training development team.

This is also a good point to determine other resource needs and the training "load" they will carry. For example, if technical content is deemed to be a very important training component, one or two case histories can be presented during the training, with the remainder of the content presented in a resource packet for use at the attendees' convenience. A substantial amount of time devoted to lecture on technical content might be a better choice for another training audience. Deciding the relative roles of printed and presented materials now rather than later will help clarify the budget (printing can be expensive and takes time) and direct the search for information and presenters.

9.8 TIPS FOR TRAINING PROGRAM DELIVERY

The following list provides training issues to consider:

- The definition. The definition of pollution prevention can vary by agency, level of government, and even by regulatory program. Take care to present at least the following:

    definition of pollution prevention from the federal Pollution Prevention Act of 1990

    waste management hierarchy

    state definition applicable to your location

    agency or program definition applicable to your training

    These statements of fact should be illustrated with examples, and time for discussion may be needed.

- Communication skills. Good communication is very important to the implementation of pollution prevention. However, communication skills are difficult to teach.
One common approach is to teach communication in application (e.g., role playing
exercises and onsite exercises). Attendees quickly see that listening and creative
thinking are very productive skills.
- Technical content. Technical training is high on the "wish list" of many attendees,
and for good reason. Yet materials are hard to find, and experienced trainers are
expensive. One approach is to de-emphasize technical content, urging instead a
focus on the process or the clients' own process. Another approach is to schedule
separate training that includes site visits. This training focuses on a particular
industrial process using industry and suppliers as speakers and resources. Technical
training for industry audiences can be sponsored by local programs using this model.
- Assessments. Pollution prevention assessment training is frequently requested. This
type of training is best left to trainers with experience in conducting onsite assessments. For most agenda developed and delivered for local programs, the best
approach is probably 30 to 60 minutes devoted to reviewing the basic principles of
pollution prevention opportunity assessments (as found in manuals such as the
EPA's Facility Pollution Prevention Guide).

The following suggestions can help a training session go well:

- The site. The training site should be secured well in advance, so the best location and
facility can be used. Whenever possible, a site away from the normal workplace is
very useful. This prevents attendees from slipping away to make phone calls or
check on projects. Appropriate advertising should be prepared and distributed,
giving all details including place, date, times, contacts, and site-specific information
such as driving directions and parking. A convenient way to gather models for this
sort of brochure or pamphlet is to save those prepared by other organizations.
- Breaks. Breaks should never be less than 15 minutes, and 30 minutes is much better.
The ill-will engendered by attempting to "herd" attendees back to work when they
are not finished with their conversations can seldom be overcome by even the most
well-liked trainer. Think of breaks as part of the training. Attendees will have a
chance to consider material and come back refreshed and ready for full participation.
Lunches should also be scheduled generously. Ninety minutes is usually sufficient
for all but the most remote situations. Providing lunch is often appreciated and
allows for more discussion among attendees.
- Administrative functions. Collecting fees and distributing forms and handouts can be
very distracting activities. Distributing resources during a training session often dis-
tracts attendees from the presenters and should only be done when the materials are
necessary for an exercise or when a point can be made no other way. Breaks are a good
time to leave materials at each attendees' place to minimize course disruption. An
excellent and much-appreciated alternative is to provide a resource table, convenient
for browsing before and after training sessions. Actual copies of resources should be
made available (marked "DISPLAY ONLY"). Ordering information and a request
sheet should be clearly visible.
- Attention to details. Finally, getting ready is probably the most important activity in
all of training — checking the room layout and audio-visual equipment, finding rolls
of masking tape and marking pens, setting out an attendance sheet, and determining

a place to put coats and bags. No amount of fussing over the details is wasted. Check standard trainer's checklists in the resources at the end of this chapter, and contact other experienced trainers for assistance. The training will go better and the trainers will be calmer if all the details are addressed before the training begins.

- Evaluations. Providing an evaluation form for completion immediately after the close of a training session is the most convenient way to gather feedback on that session, as well as guidance for developing future training sessions. Later follow-ups, such as interviews and surveys, can also be used to determine how well the training objectives were met and whether or not the skills presented were actually put into practice.

9.9 RESOURCES

1. Silberman, Mel, and Carol Auerbach. *Active Training — A Handbook of Techniques, Designs, Case Examples, and Tips* (New York: Lexington Books (An Imprint of Macmillan, Inc.), 1990).
2. Mill, C. R. *Activities for Trainers: 50 Useful Designs* (San Diego, CA: University Associates, Inc., 1980).
3. Brandt, R. C. *Flip Charts: How to Draw Them and How to Use Them* (San Diego, CA: University Associates, Inc., 1986).
4. "Fun Factory Exercise" (Minneapolis, MN: WRITAR).
5. Newstrom, J. W., and E. E. Scannell. *Games Trainers Play* (New York: McGraw Hill Book Company, 1980).
6. "Little Green Squares" (Minneapolis MN: WRITAR).
7. Newstrom, J. W., and E. E. Scannell. *More Games Trainers Play* (New York: McGraw Hill Book Company, 1983).
8. "Facility Pollution Prevention Guide," U.S. EPA, Office of Research and Development, EPA/600/R-92/088 (May 1992).
9. "Pollution Prevention Resources and Training Opportunities in 1992," U.S. EPA, Office of Pollution Prevention and Toxics (January 1992).
10. "Running a Conference as a Clean Product," U.S. EPA, Office of Research and Development (June 1991).
11. "The Oily Washers Game" (Minneapolis, MN: WRITAR).

9.10   APPENDICES

9.10.1 Appendix 1: Orientation Training Agenda

"Pollution Prevention — Description, Motivation, and Practice"

Description

This training program will present instruction and practice in techniques and information useful for promotion, persuasion, and encouragement in the area of industrial pollution prevention.

The goal of the training program will be that all attendees understand the following:

*   What is industrial pollution prevention?
*   What factors are important to successful discovery and implementation of pollution prevention practices?
*   What role can I (the attendee) play in the process of promotion of pollution prevention?

Sequence and Objectives (8-Hour Training Day)

Lesson 1:   Get acquainted

Activity: define terms
            introduce objectives
            conduct pretest
            outline activities
            define pollution prevention as a concept and an activity

Lesson 2:   Hands-on exercise

Activity: individual and group discussion
            perform and discuss a simple process
            analyze for pollution prevention opportunities
            analyze implementation

Lesson 3:   Role play

Activity: four repetitions
            two attendees per repetition

icebreaker
introduce attendees to different ways business may view pollution
  prevention

Lesson 4:   Hands-on exercise (1st half)

Activity: create teams
individuals assigned roles
perform and discuss complex process
experience pressures of business
experience importance of communication

Lesson 5:   Hands-on exercise (2nd half)

Activity: reassign roles
repeat Lesson 4, incorporating pollution prevention
apply principles
develop teamwork
experience putting opportunities into priority list
experience implementation

Lesson 6:   Discussion

Activity: pull together principles
allow time for feedback

9.10.2 APPENDIX 2: TECHNICAL TRAINING AGENDA

"Waste Minimization in Plating Operations"

Description

The audience for this course is engineers who are familiar with general metal finishing operations and procedures and who are familiar with waste minimization surveys. The intent of the course is to prepare these engineers for further waste minimization efforts, especially in the area of implementation. Emphasis is given to describing the "state-of-the-art" in each subject area, as well as methods and reasons for choosing particular techniques and technologies.

Day 1

8:30 – 9:00   Introduction

9:00 – 10:30   Principles of Pollution Prevention
Using a simple hands-on exercise, along with group discussion, vocabulary for the course and general principles are defined.

10:45 – 12:00   The Electroplating Process
The process of electroplating, from raw product to finish part, is described and discussed using visible examples in the classroom and a small demonstration model. Group discussion and questions are encouraged.

1:00 – 2:00   Plating Waste Minimization — Rinsing Processes
The importance of documenting and understanding rinsing needs is stressed, along with the impact of rinsing on waste generation.

2:15 – 3:00   Plating Waste Minimization — Rinsing Processes (cont'd)

3:00 – 4:30   Plating Waste Minimization — Product Substitution
Alternate plating processes including etchants and the use of deionized water are discussed. Pros and cons of each substitution are detailed.

Day 2

8:30 – 9:00   Review and Overview — Plating Waste Minimization —
                Solvent Use Reduction

Alternatives to solvent use are described with emphasis on understanding cleaning needs. Reuse possibilities and procedures are explored.

9:00 – 10:00   Plating Waste Minimization — Recovery Techniques/
                 Technologies
Beginning with dragout recovery/return, applicability of various approaches are discussed. A review of all recovery technologies currently in use is conducted, along with a summary of pros and cons of their use.

10:15 – 12:00   Plating Waste Minimization — Process Modification
Incorporating previous material as well as references from the literature, the implementation and effect of plating process changes such modifications as dwell time, transfer, and layout will be discussed.

1:00 – 2:00   Group Discussion
Using examples from the literature and attendee's experience, scenarios are examined critically for possible waste prevention alternatives.

2:15 – 4:30   Final Exercise
Working in groups of three to seven, attendees conduct a "survey" of an example shop presented by the instructor, select prevention options, and justify their choices to the group.

9.10.3 Appendix 3: Assessment Training Agenda

"Model Agenda"

Registration
Hospitality meeting
Dinner and Introductions

Day 1

      Overview of pollution prevention activities
      90 minutes

      Case study in the metal finishing industry
      45 minutes

      The need for pollution prevention
      75 minutes

      Creative problem solving
      4 hours

Day 2

      How to conduct an assessment of pollution prevention opportunities
      60 minutes

      Case study with metal working fluids
      60 minutes

      Pollution prevention resources
      90 minutes

      Mock industrial processes
      4 hours

Day 3

      Working with local regulators
      60 minutes

Developing and implementing a successful pollution prevention program
60 minutes

The importance of communications
30 minutes

Case study of solvent substitution
60 minutes

Small group brainstorming exercises in pollution prevention
90 minutes

Problem set
2 hours, 15 minutes

Day 4

Paperwork required to complete and document assessments
2 hours, 30 minutes

Time and phone logs
Expense reports
Conflicts of interest
60 minutes

Work hazards and confidentiality
60 minutes

Day 5

Onsite assessment training
4 hours

Group discussion of site visit
4 hours

CHAPTER **10**

Measuring Pollution Prevention Progress

David Dellarco

10.1 INTRODUCTION

This chapter presents a basic process that state and local governments can use to determine how to measure pollution prevention progress. This process should be viewed as guidance for decision-making that blends both individual pollution prevention program needs and measurement information found in pollution prevention literature. The pollution prevention measurement decision-making process is comprised of the following four steps:

1. identification of measurement needs
2. evaluation of measurement methodologies and approaches
3. matching needs with measurement methodologies and approaches
4. application of a selected methodology or approach

The remainder of this chapter discusses each step and describes a simplified example of how this guidance may be used by state and local governments.

0-87371-654-X/93/$0.00+$.50
© 1993 by Lewis Publishers

10.2 STEP 1 — IDENTIFICATION OF MEASUREMENT NEEDS

Measuring pollution prevention progress can be a complicated objective for any state or local government. To help simplify this activity, it is necessary to take the time to fully assess why the agency needs or wants to measure pollution prevention progress. It is difficult for a state or local government to determine how to measure progress without first knowing why measurement is desired.

Provided below are examples of pollution prevention measurement needs that may apply to any pollution prevention program. Prior to beginning an evaluation or design of pollution prevention measurement approaches, developing a comprehensive list of needs, tailored to a specific pollution prevention program, is recommended. Once this list has been developed, it should be sorted according to program priorities.

Examples of pollution prevention measurement needs include the following:

- evaluation of state or local government pollution prevention program effectiveness
- demonstration of pollution prevention progress
- tracking changes in pollutant releases
- targeting state or local government technical assistance efforts
- planning pollution prevention program initiatives

To help assist state and local governments formulate program specific needs, a questionnaire can be found in Appendix 1. This question form asks both general and specific questions about pollution prevention program activities and organizational experience with measurement. By taking the time to examine the results of this questionnaire, a pollution prevention program can gain insight into its "needs" for measuring pollution prevention. A list of program specific needs can then be developed and prioritized.

10.3 STEP 2 — EVALUATION OF MEASUREMENT METHODS AND APPROACHES

The second step of the decision-making process is to assess and understand available measurement methodologies or approaches. For any unique measurement approach, it is important to understand the following characteristics:

- assumptions upon which the methodology or approach is based
- complexity of the methodology or approach
- limitations inherent in the methodology or approach
- data necessary to drive the methodology or approach
- availability of these data

It is also important to grasp the evolutionary nature of pollution prevention measurement. Currently, measurement methodologies are being designed, tested, evaluated, and implemented. As environmental agencies and industry progress with measurement initiatives, more information is brought to light. The successes or failures, strengths or weaknesses of pollution prevention measurement programs provide invaluable information for any pollution prevention program attempting to establish its own component to measure progress.

In order to gain a more comprehensive understanding of pollution prevention measurement methodologies and approaches, state and local governments should become familiar with pollution prevention literature on this topic. Recommended reading on pollution prevention measurement is provided later in this chapter. It is also useful to become familiar with, and take advantage of, existing sources of information on pollution prevention such as the Pollution Prevention Information Clearinghouse (PPIC). To obtain information on the PPIC and how to gain access to this electronic support system, write to PPIC, 7600A Leesburg Pike, Falls Church, VA 22043.

In general, measurement methodologies can be segregated into five categories. State and local governments should become familiar with each category and develop an understanding of the advantages and disadvantages associated with each. While this chapter does not assess the advantages and disadvantages of each general category of measurement methodologies, a brief description of these types of measurement is presented below:

- Descriptive measure. A descriptive measure is a qualitative assessment of pollution prevention progress or activity — for example, a description of pollution prevention projects implemented at a facility.
- Absolute measure. An absolute measure is a quantitative measure of pollution prevention progress achieved by comparing the amounts of a specific pollutant released or generated over two time periods. The time period is usually from year to year or from any year to a baseline year — for example, the quantity of a specific hazardous waste generated in a year compared with the amount of the same waste generated the previous (or baseline) year.
- Relative measure. A relative measure is a quantitative measure of pollution prevention progress achieved by determining the change in the generation or release of a specific pollutant over a given time period (i.e., an absolute measure) and normalizing the quantity relative to a measure of the level of business activity (e.g., production) for a given time period — for example, the quantity of a specific pollutant released into the environment normalized for a specific production output during a time period. This is compared with the same measure for a previous time period or baseline. A result demonstrating that less of the pollutant was released to the environment per product for the earliest time period indicates pollution prevention progress. It is worth noting that the ability to normalize pollutant generation or release to production is the most difficult aspect of relative measures.
- Performance measure. A performance measure of pollution prevention progress is a qualitative or quantitative assessment of specific indicators of performance, rather than an assessment of change in the amount of a pollutant generated or released — for example, accounting the number and types of pollution prevention projects planned and/or implemented at a facility.

•   Degree of hazard measure. A degree of hazard measure, also called a risk-based measure, attempts to assess pollution prevention progress based on changes in the toxicity or other hazard for pollutants, which are generated or released — for example, changes in the composition of a waste from more toxic to less toxic constituents.

10.4 STEP 3 — MATCHING NEEDS WITH MEASUREMENT METHODS

When a state or local agency reaches Step 3 of the measurement decision-making process, two key elements should be clearly known:

•   The organization knows why it wants to measure pollution prevention progress and possesses a clear understanding of program measurement priorities.
•   The organization has developed a comprehensive understanding of how pollution prevention may be measured.

The prioritized needs for measuring pollution prevention progress can now be matched to available measurement methodologies and approaches. In making a needs-to-methodology match, state or local agencies can add criteria that can further help refine the selection of a particular measurement methodology or approach. Examples of these additional criteria are identified below:

•   identification of programmatic measurement needs that can, and cannot, be met with existing methodologies or approaches
•   data availability to drive a methodology or approach
•   data that has to be collected to drive a methodology or approach
•   program resource estimates necessary to establish a specific pollution prevention measurement initiative
•   limitations and uncertainties inherent in a methodology or approach

The needs-to-methodology match step in the decision-making process provides an agency with the opportunity to determine if its primary need(s) can be met through the application of an existing methodology or approach. In addition, the organization will gain a sense of the resource requirements necessary to satisfy its programmatic need(s). Finally, the agency will understand the limitations and uncertainties inherent in a particular methodology or approach.

In the instance where the programmatic measurement need outweighs availability of existing methodologies or approaches, a state or local agency may decide to satisfy this need through the design and development of a new or refined methodology that will satisfy this need. Because methodology design and development can be a time and resource intensive initiative, organizations considering this option may wish to consult with others with experience in this area. Two organizations that can help identify environmental agencies with experience in pollution prevention measurement methodology development are the National Roundtable of State Pollution Prevention Programs and the United States Environmental Protection Agency. See Chapter 15 for more information.

10.5 STEP 4 — APPLICATION OF SELECTED METHODS

The final step in the decision-making process is the application of the preferred methodology identified in Step 3. At this stage of the decision-making process, environmental agencies should do the following:

*   develop a complete measurement implementation plan
*   include testing the selected methodology or approach through field testing or a pilot project
*   develop and implement any necessary data collection

It may also be useful for the pollution prevention program to identify and contact other organizations using the same or similar methodology or approach for measurement. The experience of other environmental agencies or organizations that have already implemented a pollution prevention measurement initiative can provide invaluable knowledge and technical assistance.

10.6 DATA AVAILABILITY AND COLLECTION

Data collection efforts can be resource intensive activities for any organization. As a result, knowledge of existing data bases that can support measurement of pollution prevention progress is important. At this time, two mandated federal data collection efforts are implemented nationwide. These are the Toxics Release Inventory (TRI) and the Biennial Report (BR).

Both the BR and TRI data bases are evolving systems within the EPA. They possess strengths and weaknesses that should be understood prior to their use for measuring pollution prevention progress. State and local governments should learn more about these two national data bases by contacting the following EPA offices:

*   Biennial Report (BR)
    U.S. EPA
    Office of Solid Waste
    Information Management Branch
    OS-312
    401 M Street SW
    Washington, D.C. 20460

- Toxics Release Inventory (TRI)
  Emergency Planning and Community Right-to-Know Information Hotline
  OS-120
  401 M Street SW
  Washington, D.C. 20460

Due to the limitations of the TRI and BR data collection mechanisms, and/or the programmatic need(s) for pollution prevention measurement, environmental agencies may find it necessary to design and implement a unique data collection effort. Data collection options to consider are identified below:

- Mail surveys. Mail surveys are self-administrable, self-explanatory questionnaires mailed to a targeted group of respondents. Unless required by law, mail surveys generally have a low return rate of 20 to 40%. An advantage of mail surveys is that they can collect a large amount of data at a relatively low cost.
- Telephone surveys and personal interviews. Telephone surveys and personal interviews provide the opportunity to collect information through direct contact with the respondent. Structured telephone surveys and personal interviews can result in information and data that can be tabulated and analyzed.

10.7 CASE STUDIES

10.7.1 State or Local Environmental Agency

To illustrate how the pollution prevention decision-making process works, the following simplified example is provided. This discussion does not include a comprehensive analysis of available methodologies or approaches. It is only intended to serve as demonstration of how a state or local environmental agency can use the process described in this chapter to select or develop a particular methodology to meet a specific need.

Step 1 — Identification of Measurement Need

Suppose a local environmental agency concludes from the questionnaire found in Appendix 1 that its primary need is to measure the effectiveness of its pollution prevention program. This need is due to the fact that funding for this agency's pollution prevention program is directly related to a demonstration of pollution prevention progress or success to the city council.

Step 2 — Evaluation of Measurement Methodologies and Approaches

In 1992, the National Roundtable of State Pollution Prevention Programs developed a position paper, "Position Paper — Evaluating Pollution Prevention Program Effectiveness," on methodologies and approaches to measure pollution prevention

---

Evaluation by Clients

1. Questionnaires at time of service:
   - after on-site technical assistance, asking for an assessment of value
   - after training, conferences, etc., assessing content, style, and actual learning taking place;

2. Surveys/questionnaires as followup (by mail, phone, or in-person)
   - indicating pollution prevention program is in place
   - demonstrating "vision change"
   - assessing retention
   - asking for estimates of savings realized or wastes reduced as a result of service;

3. Number of requests for followup assistance or information;

4. Number of referrals by clients;

5. Presence of new internal programs as reported on data submission forms;

Independent Evaluation

Contractor/funder conducts reviews of client surveys, interviews, etc.:

- assessing relative value of program elements through rankings
- assessing impact and staying power of program
- assessing level of satisfaction of services provided
- assessing program targeting (if any)
- establishing who initiated contact and through what routes
- analyzing any reduction available data
- assessing program's value as a "change agent" acting on other institutions

---

Figure 1. Categories of internal evaluation.

program effectiveness. One key position expressed by the Roundtable is that, "no one yet knows how to correlate pollution prevention actions to *real* reductions in reported generation or release data." The Roundtable does acknowledge ongoing efforts to accomplish this objective by states with facility planning and reporting statutes. Because of the present inability to establish a cause and effect relationship between the application of a specific pollution prevention program element or activity and a quantifiable reduction in pollution, the local environmental agency in this case study will have to perform one of the following approaches:

- develop a methodology to calculate the cause and effect of program effectiveness
- wait until another state or local government program develops such a methodology
- rely on the best approaches that can currently be applied, while taking note of the inherent weaknesses

Because of time pressures, the local environmental agency decides the best available methodologies are to be utilized. Of the approaches currently available for evaluating program effectiveness, the National Roundtable of State Pollution Prevention Programs identifies both internal and external approaches. The internal approach is a basic accounting or assessment of the activities conducted by the program. The "categories of internal evaluation and methods" that the Roundtable identified as currently in use can be found in Figure 1.

Quantities of Services Provided by a Pollution Prevention Program

1. Raw Numbers of:
    - grants dispersed
    - on-site visits
    - reports generated
    - case studies written
    - newsletters written
    - policy statements written
    - permits granted
    - inspections completed
    - governor's awards given
    - workshops, conferences, training sessions delivered
    - pollution prevention programs established in industries

2. Raw hours spent:
    - on-site, on-phone, researching, promoting, writing reports and following up
    - preparing and delivering conferences, training, etc.

3. Rates of compliance with requirements for facility planning or payment of fees

4. Periodic reports to legislature/governor

Figure 2. Categories of external evaluation.

The external approach uses input from outside the pollution prevention program to evaluate the programs services. This can be provided from "clients" of the program or an independent source. The current types of external evaluation as described by the National Roundtable are outlined in Figure 2.

Step 3 — Matching Needs with Measurement Methods

Because of the need to evaluate program effectiveness in the near term, the local environmental agency decides to match its need for measurement to the approaches identified by the National Roundtable. It also establishes as one of its criteria a desire to utilize as much available internal data as possible. The agency determines that it can compile the number of hours in staff time spent onsite, on-phone, and promoting pollution prevention with industries. Because no external program data is available, the agency decides to hire a contractor to conduct a telephone survey in an attempt to estimate the amount of pollution prevented by the facilities receiving onsite technical assistance and/or customer satisfaction with program services.

Step 4 — Application of a Selected Method

The local environmental agency implements its contractor-supported data collection and compiles its internal data on program implementation. From these data, the agency develops a report that confirms that its time spent onsite, on-phone, and promoting pollution prevention with industries has resulted in pollution prevention (or pollution prevention activity) on the part of these industries. The agency is able to make a case to the city council that resources dedicated to pollution prevention are having their desired effect.

10.7.2 Pollution Prevention Measurement Efforts by Industry

Pollution prevention measurement is a focus of many industry pollution prevention programs. The ability to communicate pollution prevention progress to environmental agencies, the public, and within a company are a few of the incentives driving industry efforts. State and local agencies interested in pollution prevention measurement should contact local businesses and industries attempting to measure pollution prevention progress. A great deal of information and insight can be obtained from these industry measurement initiatives. At a minimum, it is strongly recommended that environmental agencies establish a dialogue with these industries in order to become more familiar with the practical pollution prevention measurement problems and solutions identified through industry efforts.

For example, a manufacturing company located in the Pacific Northwest has pollution prevention measurement goals to perform the following:

•   provide a common company-wide pollution prevention progress measurement
•   use existing data within the company
•   be obtainable in all product sectors
•   be useful at corporate, site, and process levels

In order to meet these objectives, the company decided to use a relative measure of pollution prevention, normalized by hourly labor hours (i.e., using hourly labor as its production activity index). Hourly labor hours was selected because of deficiencies in other possible indices such as raw material used, number of parts, weight of final product, and dollar value of final product.

Environmental agencies required to track the pollution prevention progress of this company will be much more successful through understanding the needs of, and decisions made by, the company in selecting its production activity index. Without this understanding, the agency could develop a pollution prevention measurement approach that conflicts with an industry program already designed and operational. This could in turn end up diverting each organization from successful pollution prevention measurement.

10.8 CONCLUSION

In conclusion, state or local environmental agencies interested in pollution prevention measurement should first know why they need/want to measure pollution prevention. Once the "why measure" question has been clearly answered, agencies should then take full advantage of available pollution prevention resources and expertise. At this time, pollution prevention measurement is a topic receiving a great deal of attention by both government and industry. Through the use of existing information and utilization of emerging pollution prevention measurement experiences, environmental agencies will be in a stronger position to identify a successful pollution prevention approach that meets their needs.

The U.S. EPA and selected state pollution prevention programs have formed a "measuring progress" working group to explore opportunities to measure waste minimization progress. Additional information on this work group can be obtained by contacting:

Ms. Donna Perla
Chief
Waste Minimization Branch
U.S. EPA
Office of Solid Waste
OS-320W
401 M Street SW
Washington, D.C. 20460

10.9 REFERENCES

1. U.S. EPA. "Minimization of Hazardous Waste," Report to Congress, Executive Summary and Fact Sheet (October 1986).
2. U.S. EPA, Office of Pollution Prevention and Toxics. "Toxic Chemical Release Inventory Reporting Form R and Instructions," (May 1992).
3. U.S. EPA. "1991 Hazardous Waste Report," (1991).
4. Industrial Economics, Inc. "Methodology for Pollution Prevention Assessment," prepared for U.S. EPA/OPPE/OPA (July 1992).
5. U.S. EPA. "Guidance for Capacity Assurance Planning," State Review Draft (June 29, 1992).
6. INFORM. "Environmental Dividends: Cutting More Chemical Wastes," draft (1992).

10.10 APPENDIX

10.10.1 Why Does Your Agency Want to Measure Pollution Prevention?

10.10 APPENDIX

WHY DOES YOUR AGENCY WANT TO MEASURE POLLUTION PREVENTION?

The questions in this form are generally directed to a particular program office, rather than to the agency as a whole. For example, if you are in the Hazardous Waste Bureau of the Department of Environmental Quality, emphasize the <u>Bureau's</u> activities and needs in your answers.

A.   **THIS SECTION INCLUDES SOME GENERAL QUESTIONS ABOUT YOUR PROGRAM OFFICE'S POLLUTION PREVENTION EFFORTS.**

A-1   **Which of the following is a focus of your program office's efforts?** (Please check all that apply)

_____   Regulating the generation and management of hazardous waste
_____   Monitoring environmental quality
_____   Minimizing the generation of hazardous waste
_____   Minimizing release of pollution to all media
_____   Minimizing the use of toxic materials
_____   Providing technical assistance to industry
_____   Other (Please specify) _____

A-2   **How did your program office become involved in pollution prevention?** (e.g., to implement state pollution prevention legislation, etc.)

A-3   **Have any of the following pollution prevention program options been considered or implemented by your program office?** (Please check all that apply)

_____   Technical assistance focusing on individual generators (e.g., on-site audits, telephone hotline, information clearinghouse, etc.)
_____   Technical assistance focusing on industries (e.g., publications, workshops)
_____   Economic incentives for pollution prevention (e.g., grants, loans, fees)
_____   Pollution prevention reporting
_____   Pollution prevention or toxics use reduction planning requirements
_____   Training on pollution prevention for agency personnel (e.g., regulatory personnel)
_____   Including pollution prevention information in inspections
_____   Incorporating pollution prevention into enforcement actions
_____   Targeting chemicals for phase-out
_____   Developing performance standards for industries
_____   Other (Please specify) _____

A-4   **Which of the following activities does your program office consider to be a part of pollution prevention?** (Please check all that apply)

_____   Change/reduction in use of input materials leading to less pollutant releases
_____   Change in industrial process leading to less pollution generated
_____   On-site (in-plant) recycling/reuse of waste materials
_____   Off-site recycling/reuse of waste materials
_____   Improved treatment of waste materials leading to less residuals
_____   Other (Please specify) _____

B.   **THE FOLLOWING QUESTIONS EXPLORE YOUR PROGRAM OFFICE'S NEED TO MEASURE
            GENERATORS' PROGRESS IN POLLUTION PREVENTION.**

B-1   **Does your program office have an interest in trying to measure generators'
          progress in pollution prevention?**

      ____ Y   ____ N

    If NO, please skip to Section *E*.
    If YES, please continue.

B-2   **The following is a list of possible reasons to measure pollution
          prevention progress. We are interested in knowing which (if any) of these
          needs apply to your program office.** Please note the following points of
          clarification.

    ·   Please think about the needs of your program office as <u>broadly</u> as
          possible, including both needs that are currently being addressed as
          well as needs that are <u>not</u> currently being addressed.

    ·   Some of the items on this list may not be needs of your program
          office at the present time, but may be needs you anticipate facing
          in the future. Please include these needs in your answers as well.

    ·   Finally, you may have needs that are not included on the list.
          Please feel free to add these needs at the end of the list, where
          there is a section for "other" needs.

<u>Instructions</u>: For each need provided on the list below, you will be asked
to complete two questions.

    ·   **First, please indicate if the need is an <u>externally imposed
          requirement</u> (i.e., the program office must address the need because
          of some requirement initiated outside of the program office).**

    ·   **Second, please indicate how much of an <u>internal priority</u> the need is
          to your program office <u>independent of external requirements</u>, using
          the following categories:**

    High   **=**   **Addressing this need is a high priority for my
                                program office**

    Med   **=**   **Addressing this need is a medium priority for my
                                program office**

    Low   **=**   **Addressing this need is a low priority for my
                                program office**

    Not-a-need **=**   **Not a need that has been identified by my program
                                office**

    Remember to keep your assessment of whether a need is an internal
    priority <u>separate</u> from whether it is an external requirement. For
    example, if a need is only important to your program office because it
    is externally required, you should rate it as a "low" priority.

Please think carefully about your answers, as they will form the basis of a
number of follow-up questions.

** Feel free to annotate your responses **

My program office needs to: **This need is an:**
                                       (Circle appropriate answer in each category)

	External Requirement:		**Internal Priority:**			

1. Track changes in hazardous waste generation levels: — Yes No — High Med Low Not-a-need

2. Track changes in pollution releases to all media: — Yes No — High Med Low Not-a-need

3. Track changes in hazardous substance usage: — Yes No — High Med Low Not-a-need

4. Assess changes in risk to the environment from pollution releases: — Yes No — High Med Low Not-a-need

5. Compare hazardous waste generation levels to state-wide or regional reduction goals: — Yes No — High Med Low Not-a-need

6. Assess the need for hazardous waste management capacity: — Yes No — High Med Low Not-a-need

7. Demonstrate progress in pollution prevention to city councils or state legislatures: — Yes No — High Med Low Not-a-need

8. Demonstrate progress in pollution prevention to the public: — Yes No — High Med Low Not-a-need

9. Demonstrate the economic or regulatory advantages of pollution prevention activities to generators: — Yes No — High Med Low Not-a-need

10. Compare pollution prevention progress among industries or generators: — Yes No — High Med Low Not-a-need

11. Evaluate the adequacy and/or accuracy of individual generators' pollution prevention reports (e.g., Toxics Release Inventory): — Yes No — High Med Low Not-a-need

12. Develop performance standards for industries or processes: — Yes No — High Med Low Not-a-need

13. Target agency regulatory efforts: — Yes No — High Med Low Not-a-need

14. Target agency pollution prevention technical assistance efforts: — Yes No — High Med Low Not-a-need

15. Plan agency pollution prevention initiatives: — Yes No — High Med Low Not-a-need

16. Evaluate the effectiveness of agency pollution prevention efforts: — Yes No — High Med Low Not-a-need

17. Research and evaluate specific pollution prevention techniques: — Yes No — High Med Low Not-a-need

18. Other (Please specify) — Yes No — High Med Low Not-a-need

    _____
    _____
    _____

19. Other (Please specify) — Yes No — High Med Low Not-a-need

    _____
    _____
    _____

20. Other (Please specify) — Yes No — High Med Low Not-a-need

    _____
    _____
    _____

B-3   Focusing only on the needs for measuring pollution prevention that you
        identified as <u>externally required</u> in Question B-2, please indicate
        below why each need is an external requirement of your program office.
        (Please list the number of the need in the space below, followed by a
        brief statement about the requirement.)

        <u>Number</u>:   <u>What is this external requirement</u>?

B-4   Focusing now only on the needs for measuring pollution prevention that
        you identified as <u>high priorities</u> in Question B-2, please indicate
        below why each need is a high priority to your program office.
        (Please list the number of the need in the space below, followed by a
        brief statement about why it is a priority.)

        <u>Number</u>:   <u>Why is this a priority</u>?

B-5   Given <u>all</u> of the needs that you identified as <u>external requirements</u>
        and/or as <u>priorities (high, med, or low)</u> in Question B-2, which do you
        consider to be the 2 or 3 most important? Please list the numbers of
        these needs and indicate why--based on your professional judgement--
        you think they are most important. (For example, Need #12--"Target
        agency regulatory efforts"--might be the most important need because
        regulations are the agency's primary tool for affecting change.)

        <u>Number</u>:   <u>Why is this need most important</u>?

B-6   Given <u>all</u> of the needs that you identified as <u>external requirements</u>
        and/or as <u>priorities (high, med, or low)</u> in Question B-2, which ones
        would you prefer that your program office not address? Please list
        these needs and indicate why--based on your professional judgement--
        you would prefer that your program office not address them. (For
        example, you might point to such reasons as technical feasibility of
        addressing the need, resource constraints of addressing the need, or
        difficulty in justifying the need).

        <u>Number</u>:   <u>Why would you prefer not to address this need</u>?

C.   THE FOLLOWING QUESTIONS EXPLORE THE INFORMATION YOU WOULD IDEALLY
        LIKE TO HAVE TO MEET YOUR NEEDS FOR MEASURING POLLUTION
        PREVENTION.

C-1   Given all the needs that you identified as <u>external requirements</u>
        and/or as <u>priorities (high, med, or low)</u> in Question B-2, indicate
        what specific information currently is being collected to address your
        needs, and then indicate which needs the information addresses. (For
        example, you might be using "quantity of waste managed in landfills"
        to address Need #2--"Assessing hazardous waste management capacity";
        or "the number of generators initiating pollution prevention
        activities" to address Need #7--"Demonstrating progress to the
        public".)

        What information is being collected   Number of the need this
        to address your needs?   information addresses:

C-2   Is the type of information that you personally would "ideally" like to know about pollution prevention currently available to you?

       ____ Y ____ N _____ Don't Know

       If YES, please skip to Section *D*.
       If NO or Don't Know, please continue.

C-3   What kind of information would you "ideally" like to know about pollution prevention that is NOT currently available to you? Ignore the feasibility of realizing this ideal.

C-4   Which of the needs identified above in Question B-2 would you use this "ideal" information to address?

       <u>Numbers</u>:

C-5   What are the barriers that prevent you from obtaining this "ideal" information? (Please check all that apply)

     ____ Resource constraints in collecting the information
     ____ Resource constraints in managing or analyzing the information
     ____ Technical constraints in collecting the information
     ____ Technical constraints in managing or analyzing the information
     ____ Insufficient authority to require the data from generators
     ____ Lack of coordination of data systems
     ____ Other (Please specify) _____

       Elaborate, if you wish:

D.   THE FOLLOWING QUESTIONS RELATE TO YOUR PROGRAM OFFICE'S EXPERIENCE WITH MEASURING POLLUTION PREVENTION.

This section provides an opportunity for you to relay your experiences with measuring hazardous pollution prevention. As many people are interested in the measurement of pollution prevention for different reasons, there are a broad range of measurement methods that are available. Measurement methods can range from qualitative assessments to quantitative assessments, from case studies to statistical analyses, and so forth. Please consider "measurement methods" as broadly or narrowly as is appropriate for your needs.

D-1   Has your program office used or investigated any method(s) to measure hazardous pollution prevention?

       ____ Y ____ N _____ Don't Know

       If NO or Don't Know, please skip to Section *E*.
       If YES, please continue.

D-2   Briefly describe the method(s) that your program office has used or investigated to measure pollution prevention. Feel free to use additional pages, or to attach a description of your methods in place of filling out this section. Please note any information you believe is important such as data sources used and how data are analyzed.

Don't feel obligated to provide a comprehensive description of these methods. Try to get a general indication of your methods.

Method 1:

Method 2:

D-3   **Which of the needs that you identified in Question B-2 are addressed by these measurement methods?** Please list the numbers.

Method 1:

Method 2:

D-4   **How would you rate the method's usefulness to you?** Please circle the appropriate code, and then briefly explain why you make that rating. (If the usefulness varies by need, please indicate which level of usefulness applies to which need.)

        High = highly useful
        Med   = moderately useful
        Low   = low usefulness
        DK   = Don't know

Method 1:   High   Med   Low   DK
Why do you make this rating?:

Method 2:   High   Med   Low   DK
Why do you make this rating?:

E.	**THE FOLLOWING ARE SOME CLOSING QUESTIONS.**

E-1   **Based on your experiences, what issues concern you most in the area of hazardous pollution prevention?** They can involve policy questions, regulatory issues, resource constraints, etc. Please don't hesitate to list whatever comes to mind.

E-2   **Are there any other agency personnel, companies, or individuals that you believe we should contact for further study?** Please provide name, affiliation, and address or phone number (if possible), and why you believe they should be contacted.

E-3   **Are there any other comments you would like to add?**

CHAPTER 11

Securing Resources to Support Pollution Prevention Programs

David T. Wigglesworth

11.1 INTRODUCTION

The scope and longevity of a state pollution prevention program correspond to the manner in which it is funded. A state program survey conducted in 1988 noted that base funding levels for "waste reduction" programs varied up to $1 million. It went on to note that annual program budgets were increasing for active, planned, and developing state programs "due mostly to the availability of federal funds." While many state programs are supported in part by state appropriation, some programs are supported with federal funding only. Developing and planned programs are "being supported with mixes of state and federal funds."[1]

A more recent EPA study (1992) underscores the importance of federal funding for state pollution prevention programs. The EPA Office of Pollution Prevention and Toxics reviewed its state pollution prevention grants program and found that these grants "have provided critical funding" for the establishment of state programs. The EPA report also stated that state programs "would not have achieved the prominence, stability, and visibility many currently enjoy without EPA grants."[2]

Unlike the established environmental media programs addressing air pollution, solid waste, and water quality, state pollution prevention programs do not
have a continuous source of federal operating funds many need to survive. Federal
pollution prevention funding is mostly available through grants issued on a
competitive basis. This fact raises serious concern about the long-term viability of
state pollution prevention efforts, especially since many states rely on these funds.

This chapter explores selected issues concerning state pollution prevention
funding, through a closer look at the state of Alaska's effort to secure pollution
prevention funding through the State/EPA Agreement (SEA) process. The SEA
process provides the mechanism for EPA to transfer federal funds to states to
support implementation of EPA programs. The pollution prevention set-aside
negotiated during the development of the 1993 SEA sets the state of Alaska on
course for a more stable funding base for its pollution prevention efforts.

11.2 INITIAL STATE FUNDING

Similar to many states, the Alaska Department of Environmental Conservation
(DEC) received a federal grant to initiate development of its pollution prevention
program. This grant is administered directly by the EPA Pollution Prevention
Division. (See Chapter 15 for details on these grant programs.) These grants are
issued on a competitive basis and often have a funding limit of approximately
$300,000 and now a 50% match requirement. The available funds for these grant
programs vary from year to year, from between $3 and 7 million.[3] These funds are
critical to fostering state and local attention to pollution prevention.

In 1989, the DEC received one of the first grants under the Source Reduction
& Recycling Technical Assistance (SRRTA) program. These initial funds provided the state with the opportunity to hire a pollution prevention staff person and
begin to build a program and conduct technical assistance activities in cooperation
with the Alaska Health Project — a private nonprofit group that provides pollution
prevention services.

11.2.1 Funding Scheme Drawbacks

The benefits of these federal grant funds are clear. The approximately $20
million in state grants distributed nationwide since 1989 have increased local,
state, and federal attention on pollution prevention.[4] More importantly, they have
been used to leverage additional state and private sector funding to support
prevention activities.

While there are demonstrated benefits, many drawbacks to this type of funding scheme exist. In Alaska's case, the SRRTA funds were successful in leveraging additional state contract and grant funds to support technical assistance
activities, but very little funding became available to support staff to implement
these activities and growing state legislative directives in this area. Public and

agency demand for pollution prevention services increased, but there were insufficient staff to fulfill these expectations. This scenario set the stage for program failure. Other state programs have experienced this dilemma and will continue to do so under the current funding scheme for pollution prevention. Other drawbacks to this scheme include the following:

- The funds generally support project-based activities, rather than overall program development.
- Competitive grant funding schemes require a large amount of initial investment (e.g., grant writing) without any funding guarantees and any assurances for additional funding after the grant completion.
- The noncontinuous nature of these grant programs does not support a sustained level of state or local pollution prevention activity.
- Programs will evolve in the direction of grant funding criteria and available sources of grant funds. These criteria may not meet the needs and priorities of individual states.
- State and local programs are now required to match these grant funds on a dollar for dollar basis. While this does force states to commit more funds to prevention, it puts unusually high demands on programs that have never had funding to build the internal support necessary to secure match funds and more importantly to build these funds into the base budget of their agencies. Moreover, most state legislatures will want to see immediate results, reinforcing this vicious cycle of supporting project-based programs with little emphasis on incorporating prevention into the fabric of the agency.
- Often, successful grants are those that incorporate a diverse group of private and public sector organizations. While this is important, it often spreads limited resources across many organizations. This creates a lot of momentum that soon slows down as resources dwindle. While volunteer efforts characterize many pollution prevention partnerships, even the best efforts cannot last without a sustained level of resources.
- Measuring pollution prevention progress and program effectiveness was not a high initial priority for securing federal funds. It is getting more attention today. This presents difficulties for state and local programs which were not initially asked to focus on this, do not have the resources for sustained program efforts, and have little or no guidance about criteria and methods to measure program effectiveness. It is extremely difficult for any pollution prevention program to measure its effectiveness when the majority of its time and energy is spent trying to sustain its funding base with uncertain funding sources.

11.2.2 Effort Toward Sustained Funding

The 1988 survey of state programs indicated that "state funding is provided to 95% of existing programs."[5] This suggests that state appropriations do contribute to the development of pollution prevention programs. The discussion of the North Carolina program in Chapter 2 underscores this point, but the survey does not indicate whether this funding is adequate. Moreover, 45% of the states surveyed did not respond to questions concerning resource levels.[6] A recent report prepared by the National Roundtable of State Pollution Prevention Programs shows increases in state program funding levels, but much of this increase is probably associated with new funds available for solid waste related activities.[7]

State efforts to adopt pollution prevention planning (or facility planning) laws (see Chapter 7) have the potential to secure a stable program resource base. While there are no guarantees, the passage of legislation typically carries with it funding that builds program support into the base budget of the agency. Other states have been successful in securing funding through a tax on the disposal and use of hazardous substances, fee for service, and private foundations. While clearly these efforts are useful and can help achieve sustained program support, they also require time and resources to develop and implement. This is a luxury many state programs do not have due to limited staff, lack of top management support, or existing funding stipulations that require attention to other aspects of a program (e.g., specific projects). Moreover, as environmental costs increase, emphasis is also being placed on reducing agency expenditures, downsizing, etc. While this trend certainly supports emphasis on pollution prevention as a cost reduction strategy, it will be harder and harder to justify new programs and secure adequate funding to implement pollution prevention programs. The difficulties in actually measuring reductions in pollution and the high expectations for these programs to produce immediate results underscore this point.

In an effort to secure a more stable funding base, state pollution prevention programs are now exploring opportunities to utilize existing resources enjoyed by the other environmental media programs. States (and EPA) are working to modify media program grants (see Chapter 1) to include pollution prevention deliverables or create pollution prevention set-asides that invest in the outright development of a state pollution prevention program.

11.2.3 Environmental Media Program Grants Offer Opportunity

The EPA is authorized to allocate funds to support the implementation of federal environmental programs.[8] The use of these funds is typically negotiated through the State/EPA Agreement Process (SEA). During this process, a state and EPA develop workplans and agree to grant terms and conditions. For example, a state hazardous waste program workplan might include a commitment to conduct 40 inspections of facilities that generate hazardous waste. The broader goal implicit in the SEA process is for states and the EPA to work toward continual improvement in a state's ability to protect the environment and in most instances, receive authorization to implement federal programs. Thus, traditional media programs have in place a funding mechanism that supports development of a sustained program versus a project-based approach that characterizes pollution prevention program funding.

Interest in media grant "flexibility" is also evident at the highest level within EPA. In early 1992, the Deputy EPA Administrator sought a legal opinion on this topic and also requested state input on the desirability of using media program grants to support pollution prevention efforts. The March 13, 1992 legal opinion[9] noted that EPA does have the authority to incorporate pollution prevention into many of its media program grants, though "grant eligible activities must be reasonably related to the authorized program." The opinion went on to imply that since these funds are "allotments," and not "entitlements," the EPA could modify program guidance to support more activities focusing on prevention. Since this opinion was determined, EPA staff have been evaluating media grant guidance in an effort to identify eligible pollution prevention activities to include in these documents.[10]

This trend toward grant flexibility is good news for state pollution prevention programs and for the subject of pollution prevention in general. Moreover, increasing focus on the need for stable pollution prevention funding is moving pollution prevention policy dialogue beyond "rhetoric" and challenging state and federal commitment to this issue. The following important themes emerge from this discussion:

- Existing law may limit grant flexibility in certain federal media program grants, and regulatory allotment requirements may need to be amended.[11]
- Grant flexibility is extremely threatening to existing media programs that also suffer from limited resources and have worked long and hard to develop their programs.
- There could be a tendency to make pollution prevention simply "just another single media deliverable" versus a core part of an environmental agency's mission.
- It may be difficult to embrace the multimedia nature of pollution prevention when grant flexibility is occurring in a single media environmental protection system.
- Grant flexibility requires trade-offs within media programs in order to fund pollution prevention activities. It is important to remember that funding levels remain the same. The activities just change.
- Grant flexibility will require commitment from state and federal managers and program staff. Even as guidance is written to support grant flexibility, program managers still need to give it priority over other required deliverables. Top level commitment and direction are key factors in developing pollution prevention programs within government, as is the case with the private sector.

11.3 ALASKA'S EXPERIENCE WITH GRANT FLEXIBILITY

Alaska has been successful in securing federal and state funds to support a variety of pollution prevention activities. These funds have assisted the state in building programs within the Department of Environmental Conservation and expanding commitment outside of the department (e.g., within local nonprofit organizations such as Alaska Health Project and Alaska Center for the Environment and business groups including the Anchorage Chamber of Commerce and the Alaska Support Industry Alliance). Increasingly the private sector in Alaska is contributing to these efforts by supporting programs such as the Green Star Program (see Chapter 12). With a few exceptions, these funds have not provided a sustained resource base to support permanent pollution prevention staff. This is especially true for the DEC Pollution Prevention Office and is one of the major obstacles to further advancement of pollution prevention in the state. Increasing demands for pollution prevention services, new emphasis placed on measuring progress, and available funding sources that focus on providing new deliverables versus building a stable program foundation create further concerns for the state's Pollution Prevention Office.

11.3.1 Limited Options

The DEC Pollution Prevention Office had very few options but to seek additional state appropriation and other federal grants to maintain program support. During fiscal year 1991, the state was successful in securing some personal service dollars and additional grant and contract funds. This increase primarily served to retain existing pollution prevention staff previously funded by an EPA grant. The most important aspect of this action was that pollution prevention staff funds became a part of the department's base budget, a first step in creating a sustained program.

During this same year, additional pollution prevention staff support was leveraged in the department's regional offices, primarily due to increasing management support for the pollution prevention concept. In addition, the office received additional staff support from EPA on a temporary basis (a two year contract with an EPA employee through the Intergovernmental Personnel Act — IPA).

In fiscal year 1992 (FY92), the DEC Pollution Prevention Office surfaced a proposal to set aside 1 to 2% of the state's SEA funds to provide staff support for the pollution prevention office. EPA Region 10 supported the set-aside in concept; however, varied support was voiced within the department. A compromise resulted in media programs incorporating pollution prevention language into FY92 SEA program workplans (language written by the DEC Pollution Prevention Office), but little or no funds were attached to these deliverables. As expected, very little additional prevention activity occurred since funding was not provided. However, this process was useful in fostering increased dialogue about the development of pollution prevention programs within the department.

As the fiscal year 1993 budget was being developed, the state of Alaska was (and continues to) experience many pressing financial problems. Declining oil revenues and increasing costs have created shortfalls in the DEC's operating budget. Efforts to secure additional state funds for pollution prevention became difficult. Regional pollution prevention activity (while still a policy priority) fell off due to shortfalls in all of their environmental programs. The FY93 SEA surfaced once again as a readily available option to secure additional pollution prevention funds. This time top management within both the EPA and the department supported the concept, providing the commitment necessary to pursue this funding option.

At first, 5% of all eligible federal grant and state match funds were proposed to be set aside to support the state's pollution prevention efforts. These funds would have been used to fund five positions, three of which would be placed in the department's major regional offices. The other two positions would join the existing two-person Pollution Prevention Office, providing additional administrative and technical support. After several months of negotiations and fine-tuning of actual eligible funds, the state and EPA agreed to a 3% pollution prevention set-aside for fiscal year 1993 (or a total of $168,000).[12] This resource level will increase to 4% in FY94 and 5% in FY95, contingent upon favorable evaluation of the initiative. By 1995, it is expected that the Pollution Prevention Office will have a stable annual budget to support PPO and regional office activity. This resource level (which includes other federal and state funds) is considered adequate for the office to deliver nonregulatory technical assistance services and conduct internal integration activities (especially since the recent creation of a senior management Pollution Prevention Policy Council within the department). These levels assume no new federal requirements and/or state legislative directives.

This set-aside agreement begins to move the state's pollution prevention efforts beyond a project-based program. The federal set-aside funds provide the needed resources to secure additional staff positions. The DEC is on record (per the SEA agreement) to pursue an additional state general fund increment to secure funds to make up for the declining one-time federal grant funds and IPA support that have been the mainstay of the state's Pollution Prevention Office. With these funds and current state general funds, the Pollution Prevention Office is now becoming more rooted in the budget structure of the department — central to becoming a sustained program.

Equally vital to success of this effort is to ensure the office does not become just another "compartmentalized" program, but uses its new resources to advance pollution prevention efforts within other media programs and throughout other sectors of Alaskan society. A true measure of success would be for the program to "disappear" over time as the entire department (and the private sector) embraces the pollution prevention philosophy and practice.

11.3.2 Observations

Whenever change occurs, it is always subject to intense scrutiny. The pollution prevention set-aside described herein is no exception, especially since this initiative had no model or preestablished process to follow. Policies and procedures were being developed as the process unfolded. Success measurement methods are still being fine-tuned. Perhaps most rewarding about this initiative is the fact that both EPA Region 10 and the state were willing to challenge the "status

quo" and take a strong step toward incorporating the pollution prevention paradigm into the budget process. The process of the set-aside is equally important as
any of its deliverables. The process required managers at the state and federal level
to assess their commitment to pollution prevention and their willingness to take
the "risks" necessary to advance pollution prevention within the department.
While formal evaluation of this initiative cannot be done at this time, several
observations may assist with similar efforts in the future:

*   The set-aside initiative benefitted from sustained top management commitment
    within the state and EPA Region 10.
*   Program level "champions" for the initiative existed within EPA and the state. They
    had access to decision-makers and participated in the decision-making process.
*   Some media program staff and managers within EPA and the state resisted the
    initiative. Many felt they "already do pollution prevention," or the impact of the set-
    aside would be too great on their program budgets and possibly threaten program
    authorization (legitimate concerns).
*   The negotiation of the set-aside workplan was challenging because of the constant
    tension between the media programs' desire for the Pollution Prevention Office to
    agree to perform specific deliverables to meet *their* program needs versus the
    funding needs to support ongoing efforts to build a core multimedia pollution
    prevention effort. A compromise resulted based upon the legitimate needs of the
    media programs and the Pollution Prevention Office.
*   EPA's willingness to support "trade-offs" in exchange for set-aside activities was
    central to this process and not always addressed. Media programs have spent years
    developing program activities. It is difficult to determine what activities will not get
    done.
*   An open negotiation process is important as well as good documentation of discussions.
    It is easy for emotions and "turf" issues to take over this process.
*   It is important to look at the set-aside process in the broadest context. Workplans can
    be refined during the course of the year if warranted. Alaska receives several million
    dollars of federal EPA funds each year to support the department's media programs;
    the FY93 set-aside totaled $168,000. Perspective is important.
*   The lack of a formal process for grant flexibility resulted in the state's Pollution
    Prevention Office negotiating workplan deliverables with over a dozen programs. It
    was inappropriate for the office to have to negotiate with so many programs. The
    expectations for program-specific deliverables far exceeded available funding.
*   EPA and states should develop a consistent procedure for conflict resolution during
    the negotiation process. EPA should establish a pollution prevention program con-
    tact to advocate the state's position within EPA, as is the case for other media
    programs.
*   State agencies with strong media programs may have an easier time negotiating a
    set-aside than those states with many other developing programs. Established media
    program staff may feel less threatened and may want to explore new activities.
*   States can expect considerable scrutiny if a pollution prevention set-aside is pursued.
    Some media programs will want to see the initiative fail while others will provide
    needed support. Success measurement will have to consider state-specific conditions

and set-aside terms. State pollution prevention programs can expect more emphasis placed on evaluating these programs than individual media programs receive. Moreover, success will most likely be measured both in terms of waste reduced or demonstrated progress toward integration and specific deliverables — the so called "bean count" that is used to judge the effectiveness of media programs.

- It is extremely important for states and EPA to pursue this issue with flexibility in mind. It could be very easy to develop grant flexibility guidance that is prescriptive and "program delegation" in tone. As with any industrial setting, pollution prevention implementation is site-specific, underscoring the need for states and EPA to consider local realities.

11.4 CONCLUSION

New efforts to build flexibility into media program grants confront the pollution prevention paradigm head on. The situation offers real opportunity for EPA and states to move beyond pollution prevention rhetoric and ad hoc program activities and build a sustained pollution prevention infrastructure. It is refreshing to see that EPA is making strong moves to support this type of flexibility. Time will tell whether their efforts will be sustained. The EPA has built pollution prevention into the FY93 state/EPA workplan guidance and is placing stronger emphasis on pollution prevention in the FY94 workplan guidance. The FY94 guidance goes as far as to sanction multimedia projects like the Blackstone Project in Massachusetts (see Chapter 4) and Alaska's set-aside initiative.[13]

As efforts to promote grant flexibility continue, it is important that states and EPA continue an open dialogue about several concerns posed by these events:

- Pollution prevention needs to be a core program function and a part of the overall agency mission. While pollution prevention should be an overall part of all activities and programs within a state environmental agency, there will always be a need for a core pollution prevention staff to provide internal and external technical assistance and conduct voluntary nonregulatory pollution prevention projects that single media regulatory programs cannot always conduct.
- The varying opinions about the pollution prevention definition may further confuse efforts to incorporate pollution prevention into media grant program activities.
- Consideration should be given to establishing pollution prevention base grant funding outside of the media grant programs. Funding guidance should be flexible enough to sustain current state activities. This will prevent potential "turf" and resources battles between pollution prevention programs and other programs — the programs that must work together to advance multimedia pollution prevention.
- Innovative multimedia pollution prevention activities may be difficult to foster since set-aside deliverables are subject to statutory and regulatory requirements within each program.

As the benefits of preventing pollution become more widespread, one can only hope all sectors of society will target more of our limited resources on efforts to increase industrial efficiency, develop clean technologies and products, and promote other programs to prevent pollution to all media. The willingness on the part of states and EPA to encourage grant flexibility to foster pollution prevention emphasis is important in its own right, and in leadership, it may provide to other sectors to do the same.

11.5 REFERENCES

1. Schecter, R. N. "Profile of State Waste Reduction Programs," in *Hazardous Waste Minimization,* H. M. Freeman, Ed. (New York: McGraw-Hill Publishing Co., 1990), p. 227.
2. U.S. EPA, Office of Pollution Prevention and Toxics. *Review of EPA's SRRTA and PPIS State Grants Program,* draft report, (October 1992), p. 3.
3. "Pollution Prevention Fact Sheet," U.S. EPA, Office of Pollution Prevention and Toxics, (February 1992).
4. Ibid.
5. Schecter, R. N. "Profile of State Waste Reduction Programs," in *Hazardous Waste Minimization*, H. M. Freeman, Ed. (New York: McGraw-Hill Publishing Co., 1990), p. 228.
6. Ibid, p. 227.
7. Hunt, G. Personal communication (September 1992).
8. Ludwiszewski, R. B. "Review of State Grant Authority," memorandum to F. Henry Habricht II, Deputy Administrator, U.S. EPA (March 13, 1992).
9. Ibid.
10. Habricht, F. H., II. "Integration of Pollution Prevention into Media State Grants," memorandum to Senior Policy Council, U.S. EPA (June 19, 1992).
11. Ludwiszewski, R. B. "Review of State Grant Authority," memorandum to F. Henry Habricht II, Deputy Administrator, U.S. EPA (March 13, 1992).
12. This resource level provides for three FTE. One technical and one support position will join the DEC Pollution Prevention Office. The remaining FTE is divided equally among the three main regional offices. The regional offices will conduct a pollution prevention project specific to their region.
13. Habricht, F. H., II. "Draft FY '94 State Grants Guidance: Integration of Pollution Prevention," memorandum to assistant administrators, U.S. EPA (October 15, 1992).

SECTION III:

POLLUTION PREVENTION PARTNERSHIPS

Introduction

In contrast to the previous section, Section III takes a look at efforts to foster cooperative pollution prevention programs outside of a government agency. Voluntary pollution prevention initiatives offer considerable value to both regulatory and nonregulatory pollution prevention programs. Pollution prevention partnerships help state and local programs to perform the following:

- build linkages between diverse organizations
- increase private and public sector resource opportunities to support prevention efforts
- create ownership and interest in pollution prevention across many sectors of society
- provide opportunity for regulatory agencies to move outside of specific program constraints and get involved in educational and multimedia pollution prevention initiatives

This section explores the factors contributing to successful pollution prevention partnerships as they operate in selected case study examples. As policymakers refine and further develop the pollution prevention framework, they are well advised to maintain the cooperative climate that allows these voluntary initiatives to exist. These efforts are central to building interest in and sustaining the pollution prevention paradigm.

CHAPTER 12

Fostering Voluntary Pollution Prevention Initiatives

Megan Benedict

12.1 INTRODUCTION

Voluntary pollution prevention efforts are driven by an entirely different set of incentives from those used in the regulatory approach. A look at these incentives as they have been found to operate through the Anchorage, Alaska Chamber of Commerce Green Star Program provides a model for development of similar efforts in other communities.

Businesses do not generally perceive that environmental regulations imposed from without make them more competitive, but rather, they feel that most such regulations are burdensome and costly. This perception is heightened in cases where a business may be aware that its competitors are not in compliance with certain regulations and therefore have gained an unfair economic advantage over those businesses that are in compliance. The main motivating factor to remain in compliance often has less to do with a desire to prevent pollution than it does with avoiding civil and/or criminal prosecution and the associated penalties and legal fees.

0-87371-654-X/93/$0.00+$.50
© 1993 by Lewis Publishers

On the other hand, businesses joining a voluntary pollution prevention effort are motivated by internal factors. For some companies, shareholders and/or employees may be demanding more environmentally sound practices. Others may decide to "prepare for the inevitable" by meeting a high environmental standard before it is imposed through regulations, so they will be "ahead of the game" when their competitors are faced with retooling their operations. Participation in a voluntary pollution prevention program can help develop the public perception of a company as capable of leadership and innovation in the environmental realm and therefore in other areas as well. And finally, the benefits to the bottom line become clearer as businesses learn about their opportunities to reduce costs and avoid liability through pollution prevention. The voluntary approach can be instrumental in bringing about the change in focus from pollution control to pollution prevention because it operates internally, within a business, and is pushed along by the same forces that motivate a business to seek a profit.

Voluntary and effective pollution prevention efforts now seem natural, whereas five, or even three years ago, such initiatives were exceedingly rare. Part of the reason for this is that the business community is now recognizing the advantages of taking a proactive role in this area. Extensive media coverage has informed the general public of the urgent need to address major environmental issues such as global warming, ozone depletion, and landfill scarcity, and this has helped lead to changing attitudes at the corporate level. Companies are now willing to look at ways to voluntarily reduce their use of hazardous materials, to cut waste disposal costs through reuse and recycling, and to minimize water and energy consumption.

12.2 GREEN STAR PROGRAM

In 1990, the Anchorage Chamber of Commerce established a Committee on Business and the Environment whose mission is to encourage businesses to see the compatibility of their profit-making and environmental objectives. This committee developed the Green Star Program, which demonstrates that pollution prevention is not only environmentally responsible, but also saves money and helps attract customers. Through the Green Star Program, businesses receive guidance and assistance in adopting environmentally sound practices and public recognition for their efforts. Within nine months of launching the program on Earth Day 1991, 80 businesses and nonprofit organizations representing more than 20,000 employees had enrolled. For these companies, participation in the Green Star Program has provided a framework for incorporating environmental goals into business policy. Clearly, the program has tremendous potential to influence Anchorage's voluntary efforts at pollution prevention and will play a major role in facilitating the convergence of corporate goals and environmental responsibility.

12.3 FORMING THE COMMITTEE

Two elements crucial to gaining the active participation of businesses in a voluntary pollution prevention program are feasible, attainable goals and credibility in the eyes of business and the public. These are also a requirement for earning and keeping the involvement of volunteer program organizers; the satisfaction of participating in such a program increases in direct proportion to its effectiveness.

The make-up of the Committee on Business and the Environment provides both these elements. Initiated by the 1990 chairman of the Anchorage Chamber of Commerce, the committee quickly became a diverse group, with representatives from both large and small businesses, from the nonprofit Alaska Center for the Environment, and from the State of Alaska Department of Environmental Conservation Pollution Prevention Office (PPO). In some cases, committee members had previously been adversaries, on opposite sides of the development versus conservation issue. But the group recognized from the start that in order to develop a credible program, cooperation between environmental activists and business interests was crucial. The involvement of the PPO in addition to business people and environmentalists was a key factor in developing a set of feasible pollution prevention goals, attainable by businesses of all sizes and types. The combined strengths and diversity of experience of the committee's various members enabled the group to work confidently toward its common goal — development of a forward-thinking, proactive pollution prevention program.

12.4 FUNCTIONING AS A GROUP

Initially, the committee held formal biweekly meetings at the Anchorage Chamber of Commerce office to devise a mission statement and explore ideas for program development. The committee chair, who was appointed by the overall chairman of the chamber of commerce, led these meetings, and volunteers took on administrative functions such as keeping minutes and coordinating meeting times. A paid staff member of the chamber of commerce sat in on these meetings to act as a liaison between the committee and the chamber itself and to inform the committee of services the chamber could offer and the structure of other chamber programs.

This early decision-making period was characterized by a hard-won consensus of opinion on most issues. Because of the diversity of the group, there was great potential for serious disagreement, and managing conflicts productively was of prime importance. That the group successfully aimed for and won consensus in most cases can be attributed to the fact that all of its members shared a common objective and were willing to put aside other differences in the interests of developing the program.

At one point a formal, 4-hour work session, led by a committee member who was a trained facilitator, became necessary in order to come to agreement on the program's broad goals and objectives and to devise a time line as a guide for meeting those goals. This session was extremely productive and gave participants the feeling they were making valuable contributions to a worthwhile project. As a result, committee members developed a strong team spirit and enjoyed the pleasure of working with other similarly dedicated people. When it came time to choose a name for the program, an informal brainstorming session was held at a local restaurant, and the name "Green Star" was coined. After many months of hard work, the entire group gathered for a potluck at one member's home, sharing a meal and getting to know one another beyond their roles on the committee. These social events helped to further motivate committee members to remain actively involved in their work.

12.5 DEFINING THE PROGRAM COMPONENTS

If the program was going to successfully motivate businesses to adopt real changes in their operations, it needed a cohesive framework. The committee identified the following necessary components:

- build awareness of pollution prevention opportunities
- define the specific steps to be taken
- provide education and assistance
- recognize and reward achievements

12.5.1 Building Awareness

The committee focused its first efforts on making the chamber membership aware of pollution prevention opportunities. A series of "environmental business tips" were compiled including illustrative examples drawn from local businesses. These one to two minute tips were presented verbally by various committee members at the weekly chamber of commerce luncheon forums, regularly attended by 100 to 250 people, and were subsequently printed in the chamber's monthly newsletter. Inclusion of these tips in the chamber's regular programs and publications served to inform the general chamber membership that local businesses had made commitments to address pollution prevention issues and to help legitimize these activities.

12.5.2 Defining The Standards

What exactly should the program ask businesses to do? How difficult should these tasks be? How could they be designed to be as flexible and yet as specific as possible? The Standards Subcommittee was formed and charged with the job of defining program standards which:

- address a range of pollution prevention strategies
- offer potential cost savings
- provide a challenge, but are not too daunting
- are attainable by businesses of any size or type

Green Star Standards

Complete all six of the following:
1. Adopt, post, and circulate to all employees the Green Star policy statement, or your version of it.
2. Designate a Green Star Coordinator or team.
3. Conduct an annual waste reduction assessment.
4. Provide three incentives or training opportunities to encourage management and employee participation.
5. Notify your customers about your environmental efforts by publicizing what your business is doing to meet the Green Star standards.
6. Assist at least one other business in learning the importance of becoming a Green Star business and encourage them to enroll in the Green Star program.

Complete any six of the following twelve:
7. Practice conservation of office paper.
8. Incorporate at least three energy-conserving changes in your business.
9. Monitor, record, and post utility usage and waste generation.
10. Incorporate waste reduction methods into materials and equipment purchases.
11. Purchase recycled/reusable materials for your business.
12. Enhance your business' maintenance program to improve equipment efficiency and reduce waste.
13. Segregate waste materials for recycling and reuse.
14. Promote proper handling and disposal of hazardous materials.
15. Reduce your business' use of toxic materials.
16. Establish a litter-free zone in the immediate vicinity of your place of business.
17. Establish a waste reduction, recycling, and energy efficiency library in your place of business.
18. Develop your own waste reduction method different from those listed above.

Figure 1. Green Star Standards.

Further, the standards must serve to institutionalize the program so it can become an ongoing, dynamic part of company policy.

The Standards Subcommittee worked as a team over several months to develop the standards. Many drafts were drawn, and suggestions for improvements solicited from a variety of people including engineers, university professors, and business people not involved in the committee. All this was accomplished with volunteer time, drawing on the expertise and commitment of committee members. The final product was 18 Green Star Standards that outline the activities to be undertaken in order to earn the Green Star Award. See Figure 1.

The first six of these standards are mandatory for all businesses enrolled in the program. Of the last 12, each business chooses to implement at least six, a flexible system that encourages businesses to identify their own opportunities for pollution prevention and allows all types of businesses to get involved.

12.5.3 Providing Education and Assistance

The Standards Subcommittee then developed guidance materials to provide to the businesses enrolled in the program. A standards booklet was written that offers detailed suggestions on how to implement the Green Star Standards and lists various sources of information on local pollution prevention programs and opportunities. Regularly scheduled workshops were planned to help orient enrolled businesses to the program and to encourage them to share information about their efforts. Two additional publications, produced by the State of Alaska Pollution Prevention Office and the Alaska Health Project, were chosen to round out the guidance packet. A Green Star Map of Anchorage was developed, showing locations of recycling centers and hazardous waste disposal sites and listing local pollution prevention resources such as antifreeze recyclers, waste auditors, and other information sources.

12.5.4 Recognizing Achievements

Once a business was convinced of the economic benefits of pollution prevention, what additional incentives would be required to win its participation in the program?

Public recognition is a powerful motivating tool for businesses and works in several ways to encourage enrollment in the Green Star Program including the following:

*   Green Star Award winners receive direct, positive publicity through the program's promotional campaign, which emphasizes specific achievements made by individual businesses.
*   Award winners earn the right to use the Green Star logo in their own marketing, thereby distinguishing themselves from their competitors (at least initially) and demonstrating to the public their commitment to environmental responsibility.
*   Peer pressure between businesses works to increase involvement.

Other tangible rewards include a Green Star Award certificate and window decals to display at the place of business and a special Green Star designation for chamber of commerce members in the organization's directory.

It is expected that a company's environmental efforts do not stop upon its achievement of the Green Star Award. Rather, the process of reviewing business policies and earning the award often serves to inspire members of the Green Star team to consider further measures to prevent pollution.

The Standards Subcommittee is charged with designing the next logical step for these businesses — the Earth Star level of the program. Earth Star, now in the final development phase, asks businesses to look beyond the limits of the Green Star Standards and to fully integrate an environmental ethic into every aspect of the operation. Rather than defining a prescriptive set of standards, Earth Star seeks a more comprehensive approach to environmental awareness and actions by a company. It is anticipated that this will require a thoroughness and dedication that initially only a few businesses will be able to achieve. It is hoped that Earth Star businesses will serve as models for the rest of the community and motivate other businesses to increase their commitment to pollution prevention.

12.6 SECURING CORPORATE SUPPORT

The committee drew on the incentives listed above to find the corporate support necessary for funding the Green Star Program. Certain key businesses were targeted to be approached with an offer to become a "founding sponsor" of the program. Appointments were made with the general manager of a major TV station and the publisher of a daily newspaper, both of which were asked to underwrite the cost of program publicity for one year through in-kind contributions. A local bank, known for its strong commitment to community affairs, was asked for a significant cash contribution to pay for the cost of part-time staff and for development of printed materials. The final lead sponsor, a refiner and retailer of petroleum products, came to the program out of interest in the activities of the committee and ended by committing to significant cash and in-kind contributions. This company's representative has since become chairman of the Committee on Business and the Environment and has been very active in promoting the program both in Anchorage and within his own company.

In the case of the first three companies, convincing them to sponsor the program was not easy. It required a number of meetings between the highest level of company management and the chair and vice chair of the committee, as well as the overall chairman of the chamber of commerce. In all three cases, personal relationships between these people helped achieve a positive outcome for the program. This peer influence was crucial in selling the Green Star concept and in convincing each of these business owners that their sponsorship of the program would pay off for them by increasing their stature and visibility in the community in a unique way. The benefits were discussed clearly, and a list of planned promotional opportunities was presented to each of the potential sponsors. Their names were to appear on all advertising (except PSAs — public service announcements), and they were to be credited by name and logo on all printed matter. Program sponsors were also to be recognized at the annual chamber of commerce luncheon forum scheduled to coincide with Earth Day and to mark the launching of the Green Star Program.

The fact that all four targeted businesses were secured as founding sponsors can be attributed both to the persuasiveness of the committee's chair and vice chair and the chamber's chairman and to the appeal of Green Star's innovative approach. This was something that these companies felt they *should* be doing, and if they did not, then some other business would lead the way.

12.7 LAUNCHING THE PROGRAM

With adequate corporate support pledged to fund the first year of the program's budgeted operations, the committee proceeded to design the format of the necessary printed materials. These included the following:

- introductory brochure to sell the program to potential enrollees
- standards summary
- enrollment card
- standards booklet

- achievement form
- award certificates and decals
- logo sheets
- press kit folder to hold enrollment packet
- letterhead and logo design

An advertising firm was retained to develop a program logo and come up with designs for some of the listed items. At all times, the committee members voiced strong opinions about the quality and design of the work, being certain to specify that all paper stocks have the highest possible content of post-consumer waste and that no superfluous materials were produced. Committee members wrote copy for the various pieces; this was not left to the advertisers, whose input was confined chiefly to design characteristics.

Members of the newly formed Marketing Subcommittee worked closely with a TV production crew to produce a series of informative commercials to stimulate interest in the program. One 10-second "teaser" spot and 4 separate 30-second informational spots were produced. These were initially aired on an intensive schedule on the sponsor station and then were later distributed to all stations as PSAs.

A bulk mailing of the introductory Green Star brochure was made to the 1200 members of the Anchorage Chamber of Commerce, accompanied by a cover letter signed by the chamber chairman urging them to enroll. Though the direct mail effort was limited to the chamber membership, enrollment in Green Star was open to any business.

12.8 SUSTAINING THE PROGRAM OVER THE LONG-TERM

The effort to develop and launch the Green Star Program was the work of a cohesive group of volunteers. Most of them were attracted by the opportunity to work with a diverse group of dedicated people to bring about the development of an environmental ethic in the business community — a sector of the community that has so far been slow to adopt these changes, but that bears a great potential impact on solutions to environmental problems.

Enthusiastic volunteerism continues to be a critical element in the success of the program. The subcommittees are run with volunteer effort, though some of the members (particularly those of the Standards Subcommittee) have built Green Star into the annual workplan activities of the various federal or state agencies they represent. Green Star's ability to maintain the long-term interest and involvement of these volunteers depends upon the continued success of the program to attract, educate, and serve the interests of the business community. The Green Star Program is designed to be flexible and dynamic; all elements of the program are open to change as needed.

A part-time program director was hired once the program began enrolling businesses, holding workshops, and responding to the public. As the program grew, a second part-time staffer was added. These positions are funded through a combination of corporate cash donations and enrollment fees and supplemented by a grant for program development from the U.S. EPA.

Office space and computer and clerical support were supplied by the Anchorage Chamber of Commerce. The State of Alaska's PPO has continuously provided many hours of staff time, including transportation expenses for PPO staff, in developing and helping to run the program. Alaska Center for the Environment initially provided a staff person to work on developing the program and has since funded a Green Star technical support position through a grant from the State of Alaska Energy Efficiency and Education Fund.

Other initial cash expenses of the Green Star Program included design and printing of materials and production costs of the first round of television commercials (air time was provided in-kind, as was advertising space in the daily newspaper). Printing expenses will be much lower in the future since the creative work is now done, and costs will be limited to reprints of the program materials. Television production costs will be ongoing as long as the committee feels that television remains an effective way to get the Green Star message across to the public. These costs will continue to be funded through corporate cash donations; all four of the original program sponsors have committed to a second year of support, and it is anticipated that other sponsors will come forward as the success of the program grows.

12.9 SPREADING THE WORD

As news of Green Star's innovative approach spreads, requests for information have come in from many communities both inside and outside Alaska. The original concept was to devise a program that could be easily replicated in other communities. As more frequent requests have been made for this information, the committee realized it needed a well-defined plan for transferring the program. A task force was formed to develop a step-by-step model for achieving such a transfer and to identify which communities might be best equipped to take it on. This model for the transfer process was completed over the course of three meetings of the task force and is now being shared with interested communities.

The model includes an agreement by the community to form a committee structured along the lines of the Anchorage Chamber of Commerce Committee on Business and the Environment, to include the business sector, environmental groups and representatives of the State PPO or its equivalent. It also requires signing of a contract that gives the community the right to use the

Green Star name, logo, and printed materials, that have been copyrighted by the Anchorage Chamber of Commerce, as long as it adheres to the policies and standards developed by the Green Star Program and does not undertake to make changes without consulting the program originators. These contingencies are meant to help build and maintain the integrity and credibility of the program in another community, while giving that group ownership of the program to the fullest extent possible.

CHAPTER 13

Regional Pollution Prevention Partnerships

David Teeter

13.1 INTRODUCTION

State and federal pollution prevention program development began approximately six years ago in the Pacific Northwest. The state environmental agencies in Alaska, Idaho, Oregon, and Washington, British Columbia, along with the U.S. EPA regional office in Seattle (hereafter noted as Region 10 EPA) decided to address regional hazardous waste management challenges. Pollution prevention assumed a central role in this effort, as well as in the overall environmental programs in each agency.

This chapter highlights some of the more important accomplishments of this regional effort. It also provides a brief historical account of this effort in order to provide some context. Third, it briefly raises some challenges that must be addressed if future collaboration is to be equally successful. Finally, it summarizes some lessons learned from this Pacific Northwest regional case study — lessons that may help transfer this effort to other regions. It is the collaborative nature of this effort that is worthy of note and central to achieving similar pollution prevention program development results elsewhere.

0-87371-654-X/93/$0.00+$.50
© 1993 by Lewis Publishers

A few author's caveats: In summarizing and drawing conclusions from several years of activity, I have probably omitted noteworthy items. I have also not attempted to highlight the many individual activities and accomplishments of each agency. My intent, rather, is to highlight how prevention was initially integrated into the collective decision-making and program operations of the Pacific Northwest federal and state environmental agencies. Overall, this chapter should highlight for the reader "why it worked here" and how it can elsewhere.

13.2 HISTORICAL CONTEXT AND HIGHLIGHTS

This section provides a brief history of the efforts to get pollution prevention "off the ground" and institutionalize it in legislation and programs. It also highlights some of the major accomplishments.

13.2.1 Building Policy-Level Pollution Prevention Support

Cooperative pollution prevention efforts among the four states and EPA date back to 1987. The four state EPA directors and the regional administrator of EPA Region 10 determined that the region should collectively address the basic question, "Do we have the right system in place to manage the (hazardous) wastes we generate in the Northwest?" The region was faced with new hazardous waste regulations[1] and the Capacity Assurance Planning process mandated by the Superfund Amendments and Reauthorization Act of 1986.[2] This overall commitment to address a commonly perceived regional issue represented a starting point for regional efforts. Executive management leadership proved critical to the development of various policy decisions including the endorsement of pollution prevention as an environmental program priority for participating agencies.[3]

Executive sponsorship had important consequences. Among them, it helped gain the attention of decision- and opinion-makers throughout the Northwest.[4] Two regional symposia addressing hazardous waste management were held in Seattle in 1987. These symposia targeted Northwest regional decision- and opinion-leaders[5] and resulted in a report and a series of recommendations. Two of these recommendations would strongly endorse pollution prevention: one calling for the creation of a Regional Hazardous Waste Advisory Council and one specifically endorsing development of a pollution prevention (waste reduction) strategy. This executive support also served to commit agency resources and key staff to this effort.[6]

13.2.2 Pollution Prevention Contributions of the Pacific Northwest Hazardous Waste Advisory Council

The council met approximately eight times between August 1988 and the summer of 1990. The council included members from industry, academia, public and environmental groups, and local and state elected officials who were appointed by the governors of the four states.[7] The EPA Region 10 administrator appointed four members representing the Province of British Columbia, federal facilities, the military, and Indian tribes. The council developed recommendations to the states on how they should approach difficult hazardous waste decisions within their area of responsibility including siting, need for capacity, and waste reduction. Three specific council recommendations reflected/influenced the growing pollution prevention mandate in each of the states:

- Resolution #2: Recommending a hierarchy of hazardous waste management options for the Pacific Northwest.[8] This affirmed the waste management hierarchy with pollution prevention at the top.
- Resolution #3: Recognizing the role of waste reduction as a source of capacity in the states' capacity assurance plans.[9]
- Resolution #4: Recommending to the states and EPA a comprehensive approach to waste reduction. This resolution accomplished several things:
  It endorsed the establishment of a waste reduction goal: reduction of hazardous waste generation in the Pacific Northwest by 50% by 1995.
  It endorsed waste reduction (pollution prevention) planning law elements such as those included in the Oregon Facility planning statute (see Chapter 7).
  It encouraged continued development of state and other technical assistance programs to provide information to industries and trade associations about pollution prevention opportunities.
  It endorsed the creation of a public-private Pollution Prevention Research Center to help address regional pollution prevention research needs, to set priorities and stimulate research, and to track and publicize results.

The council did one other thing to promote pollution prevention. At several of its meetings, the host state, or EPA, presented a company or facility with a "Waste Reduction Award" during a luncheon and issued a press release to publicize this success story.

The Pacific Northwest Hazardous Waste Advisory Council completed its work in the summer of 1990.[10] The four states, EPA, British Columbia, and Environment Canada signed, in January of 1991, a Memorandum of Understanding committing them to continued cooperation on hazardous waste management issues including pollution prevention.

It is worth noting that the council's resolutions, though significant, were only advisory. Council recommendations carry no legal force. The council did, however, draw together key public and private sector environmental leaders in each of the states to promote pollution prevention as a key part of the regional waste management system. The council, furthermore, helped promote the pollution prevention agenda in Alaska and Idaho, the two smaller waste generating states. Finally, council leadership was the key to the creation of the Pacific Northwest Pollution Prevention Research Center — a nonprofit organization located in Seattle, Washington.

The four states, EPA, and a committee of the council worked together through the summer of 1990 to secure funding support for the Pollution Prevention Research Center. Region 10 EPA was successful in securing two years of EPA headquarters funding support for the center in 1990.[11] This, in conjunction with significant private funding and commitments from each of the states, resulted in the creation of the center and hiring of a director in the spring of 1991.

13.2.3 Forging Staff and Program Alliances

Collaboration among state and EPA pollution prevention staff in 1987 and 1988 was both cause and consequence of some of the council accomplishments noted above. Staff were made available to support some of the council pollution prevention activities because of the commitment of their agency and program leadership. Conversely, the utility and relevance of the council's activities were due in part to the involvement of the state and EPA staff. Working together with skilled contractor support staff, the council work was relevant to agency program development needs.

Senior agency management and the process set up through the Hazardous Waste Advisory Council aided pollution prevention policy development in the region. Staff collaboration in several areas assured that equally important program development was being undertaken not only within their states but cooperatively among them.

13.2.4 The Habit of Working Together Pays Off

None of the four state environmental programs nor EPA Region 10 had pollution prevention programs in 1987.[12] This fact represented more of an opportunity than a problem to them, however. Success has come in large part because they had the following:

- a common sense plan — to "get some real pollution prevention activity going"
- agreed to identify opportunities where they might work together, particularly in the areas of technical assistance, training, and inter-program information exchange
- were able to exploit the policy support that the newly-placed pollution prevention emphasis afforded
- exhibited a "teamwork" approach, having gotten to know, work, and trust one another over the course of a year or two
- a willingness to creatively pursue EPA headquarters pollution prevention funding opportunities jointly[13]

Regional exchange and cooperation continue to evolve in support of pollution prevention program integration. For instance, the initial informal group of state and EPA (hazardous waste) pollution prevention staff advocates evolved into an ongoing organization. This organization, the Northwest Regional Roundtable for

Waste Reduction Programs, meets quarterly at different locations around the four-state region. Supported in part by EPA Region 10 resources, the Roundtable is an ongoing forum for pollution prevention program staff to accomplish the following:

•   exchange information about their programs, from program status to innovations, issues, and challenges
•   highlight central topics of common interest and concern
•   identify priorities for joint action and/or funding. For instance, pollution prevention assessment and inspector training courses have been offered under the auspices of the Roundtable, supported by state and EPA Region 10 funds. The Roundtable also hosted a Pollution Prevention Managers' Symposium in December of 1991 in order to promote pollution prevention integration into each of their agency programs.

A pollution prevention newsletter is also put out under the auspices of the Roundtable. Called the *Turning Point,* this publication promotes pollution prevention within the Northwest and shares information on current topics and developments of concern.

13.3 FUTURE CHALLENGES TO REGIONAL COLLABORATION

The cooperation that has marked Pacific Northwest state/EPA pollution prevention efforts has yielded meaningful dividends while not interfering with individual program efforts. These efforts developed pollution prevention "champions" to support pollution prevention integration, particularly when programs were in their infancy. Finally, state and EPA program linkages have been promoted through these efforts over the past four years.

Pollution prevention programs and program demands are evolving in the Northwest, as elsewhere. Increasing pollution prevention program development and integration will probably pose its own set of challenges for EPA and the states, given this model of cooperation.

Three years ago technical assistance was nearly a singular focus of most state pollution prevention programs. Now, federal and state programs are attempting to integrate pollution prevention into what have been traditional regulatory programs (e.g., using or "stretching" regulatory requirements). While presenting opportunities, this new emphasis on using all the tools poses challenges.

Traditional "turf" issues can crop up between EPA and the states over whether and how, for instance, EPA ought to best support prevention in the states. Should EPA, for instance, defer entirely to the state program and merely use grant monies to support fuller state efforts? An activist EPA pollution prevention presence in states with facility planning legislation (for instance, Oregon and Washington in the Northwest) can create confusion for generators and conflict over agency roles. States without their own pollution prevention programs or regulatory program authorization may, on the other hand, welcome this collaboration with EPA.[14]

13.4 LESSONS LEARNED FROM THE NORTHWEST REGIONAL CASE STUDY

A number of conclusions can be drawn from this case study. These are summarized so that the reader can perhaps learn from and perhaps apply some of the lessons from this Northwest example.

Commonly perceived interests were and are essential to such efforts:

*   Policy-makers must share a common interest and stake in pollution prevention — more than mere words. This common commitment has been a key element of the Northwest's efforts.
*   Commitment to prevention takes time and effort to build. This is true whether at the policy level or at the agency staff and program level.
*   The Northwest effort, with active teamwork, reinforced this commitment. Common commitment is maintained through such efforts as the Northwest Regional Roundtable, which has enhanced communication between programs and addressed some common needs and concerns.
*   Successful program development efforts can be due to unique opportunities present at one point in time. This was possibly the case for the Northwest effort. Interestingly, none of the state or EPA pollution prevention programs were in existence when this effort was undertaken — getting pollution prevention programs and projects under way had universal appeal and benefits.
*   Resource issues and challenges regarding agency roles are more likely as agencies' attention becomes more centered on integration of prevention into traditional regulatory programs.

Policy-level leadership and political will must exist to assure success. Policy level commitment has been critical to the successes noted in this case study. These efforts came from leadership through the respective organizations — from the agency director level down through the senior management chain.

Staff level champions are no less important to the success of successful pollution prevention development and integration efforts. Staff level leadership was both present and developed through the process. Without this, these efforts would not have been possible.

The respective roles and participation levels of agencies must be agreeable to others. The various organizations and agencies must also be comfortable with their roles and with those played by others:

*   The Northwest effort benefited from a very positive partnership. Distrust is easily engendered and quickly jeopardizes the best of efforts. Either roles should be spelled out, or participants should be drawn into an effort in a nonthreatening fashion. EPA's role, as a catalyst and supporter, demonstrated its commitment without threatening to "center stage" the other agencies in these efforts.
*   Major stakeholders' interests must be represented to assure the credibility of the process (here a council for the policy process) and buy in on the recommendations.

- Agencies have sought to keep the general public informed about the progress of pollution prevention efforts through the *Turning Point Newsletter*.

The collaborative efforts must complement the respective organizational priorities of the participants to assure ongoing participation. If they do not, support and interest will quickly evaporate:

- The council pollution prevention "policy" efforts, while pushing the prevention agenda, supported evolving programs or agenda in each of the states.
- Collaborative projects have consistently evolved around projects/needs that filled commonly perceived voids in the Northwest case study. For instance, joint training and technical assistance efforts have provided the states and EPA with desirable results and provided certain economies of scale, without getting in the way of other pressing pollution prevention responsibilities confronting each of the states.

Sufficient resources are necessary to support any such efforts — to assure an effective collaborative process and to assure successes are possible:

- The council effort, in particular, benefited enormously from the availability of EPA headquarters resources to support the policy-development process.
- Agency staff were involved, but sufficiently insulated from much of the council support work. Contractor support staffed the council. This enabled staff to concentrate their attention on specific individual program priorities, situations requiring their input, or those joint opportunities they might wish to explore.
- The EPA and the states have committed significant staff time and resources to these ongoing efforts. This reflected a genuine commitment to the effort and contributed to its success.

13.5 REFERENCES

1. Specific concerns included hazardous wastes that would be subject to the new "Land Disposal Restrictions" from the 1984 Amendments to the Resource Conservation and Recovery Act of 1976. See Hazardous and Solid Waste Amendments to RCRA; Public Law 98-616 (November 8, 1984).
2. Section 104 (c)(3)(9) of Public Law 99-499 (October 17, 1986).
3. Two Northwest states, Oregon and Washington, have specific pollution prevention facility planning legislation in effect, whereas Alaska and Idaho do not. The EPA has very limited authorities, these emanating from the Pollution Prevention Act of 1990.
4. The regional "capacity effort" was broadened to include British Columbia and Environment Canada.
5. Attendees included elected leaders from the four states at the state and local level, industry leaders, public interest group leaders, academia, and the media. For a summary of these symposia, see "Hazardous Waste Management in the Pacific Northwest: Final Report," U.S. EPA, Region 10 (March 1988).
6. Hazardous Waste Management in the Pacific Northwest: Final Report, (op. cit.).

7. Oregon and Washington had five members each; Alaska and Idaho, four.
8. "1989 Annual Report," Pacific Northwest Hazardous Waste Advisory Council.
9. "1989 Annual Report," This is the same source document for the following resolutions.
10. For a useful summary of the "lessons learned" from the council process, see Ross & Associates. *Lessons Learned: The Pacific Northwest Hazardous Waste Advisory Council's Approach to Regional Coordination and Policy Development,* prepared for EPA, Region 10 (February 1991). Ross & Associates provided support to council activities.
11. EPA funding for the center came through a competitive EPA process commonly referred to as the "2% Pollution Prevention Set-Aside."
12. The only organization in the Pacific Northwest offering technical assistance to business back in 1987 was the Alaska Health Project, a small nonprofit organization in Anchorage, Alaska.
13. For instance, the four states and EPA sent a "regional" proposal to the "RCRA Integrated Training and Technical Assistance" (RITTA) Grant in 1988. This was selected for headquarters funding. SARA 104 (c)(3)(9) funds were used to support capacity-related pollution prevention activities in the region through 1990.
14. Alaska's Department of Environmental Conservation (ADEC) has worked closely with EPA's program to promote pollution prevention in a few federal facility permits.

CHAPTER 14

Labor-Based Pollution Prevention Initiatives

Mark D. Catlin

14.1 WORKER INVOLVEMENT IN POLLUTION PREVENTION

Workers should be included as an integral part of pollution prevention programs. This recommendation, common to many pollution prevention manuals, has been supported by several recent studies citing worker involvement as an important feature of successful pollution prevention programs in industry.[1,2] The following are primary reasons for including workers (for this discussion production/maintenance, not managers/technical employees):

- Workers have detailed practical knowledge of the production processes where they work. This knowledge is needed to better identify, design, implement, and evaluate pollution prevention opportunities.
- Workers are affected by changes in the workplace resulting from pollution prevention activities. Worker involvement in program development and implementation can help to uncover obstacles to change and to resolve negative impacts of the changes.

Unfortunately, workers are not included in many pollution prevention programs, or their participation is very limited (such as offering suggestions through

0-87371-654-X/93/$0.00+$.50
© 1993 by Lewis Publishers

incentive award programs). Indeed, worker attitudes and behavior are sometimes perceived as one of the obstacles to successful pollution prevention.[3] Full worker participation in company pollution prevention programs is needed, during initial planning and opportunity assessments to implementation and ongoing evaluations. In addition, worker and union-based pollution prevention programs need to be established and supported by funding agencies.

This chapter discusses the interest workers have in pollution prevention programs, provides several examples of worker and union-based programs, and describes opportunities for state and local government agencies to incorporate worker and union participation into pollution prevention activities.

14.2 WORKERS' INTEREST IN POLLUTION PREVENTION

Most workers share similar concerns about the environment and the effects of pollution with the general public. But pollution prevention programs are of additional interest to workers. First, these programs often bring changes to the environment in which workers spend one quarter of their lives. Second, these efforts, if done properly, can improve health and safety conditions and productivity. And finally, these changes, if not carefully fitted into the complex physical and social environment of most workplaces, can make work more dangerous, more difficult, and less productive (with smaller paychecks or fewer jobs for workers).

14.2.1 Occupational Health and Safety Impacts

Workers can have unhealthy exposures to pollutants on their jobs. So they should benefit from the substitutions of safer chemicals or from the reduction in the use of more toxic chemicals. However, often pollution prevention "solutions" are implemented without fully considering the impact on worker health and safety. The following are examples:

• Workers at a manufacturing plant in the West became acutely ill after their company covered the exhaust ventilation system for solvent degreasing tanks with plastic sheeting. This pollution control technique (under the guise of pollution prevention) was made to reduce airborne emissions of solvents.

• After a citrus-based cleaner replaced an organic solvent for cleaning tools at a petroleum industry job-site in Alaska, workers experienced skin rashes and eye irritation. The workers and their supervisors had been told the new cleaner was "environmentally safe and nontoxic."

• A state of Washington employer set up an in-house recycling program. Workers lifting and carrying heavy loads, without the proper material handling equipment, had many back and shoulder injuries.

• Over a weekend, a tool manufacturer in the Midwest replaced the fluorescent lights in its production area with energy efficient sodium vapor lights. The glare from the lights made reading markings on tools and machines difficult. And a strobe effect caused by the lights created dangerous conditions in which it was not possible to determine if certain machines were spinning or stopped.

The National Institute for Occupational Health in Sweden has tried to anticipate the occupational health and safety implications of the chlorofluorocarbon ban scheduled for 1995.[4] They found that possible problems include worker exposure to new untested chemicals or known acutely toxic chemicals and higher levels of noise and vibration. Hopefully similar reviews will become more common in the pollution prevention literature.

Pollution prevention and occupational health and safety programs should be closely intertwined and both strive to improve conditions for workers. Worker participation helps to assure this will occur. Joint worker/management committees can be effective at improving health and safety conditions.[5] These are required in Washington and Oregon, and Congress is considering requiring these committees in all states.[6] These joint committees could be included in pollution prevention programs.

14.2.2 Other Impacts

In addition to the health and safety impacts, pollution prevention activities can impact many other aspects of a worker's job. Examples of some impacts that can create obstacles to worker acceptance of pollution prevention, if not recognized and addressed beforehand, include the following:

- The job becomes harder to accomplish.
- The job takes more time to finish.
- The job requires additional skills and training.
- Pay or job security is reduced.

These impacts can be temporary or permanent. Either way, a worker's productivity (and paycheck) can be affected. These impacts can be resolved by adjusting work rates and/or pay rates or providing training to match the changes. At worksites where collective bargaining agreements exist, the union and employer can work together to resolve the impacts of these changes. Because often programs have not fully considered their impacts on workers or permitted them to fully participate, some workers and their unions are very skeptical of pollution prevention activities.[7,8] Winning over workers and their unions, by trying to include their concerns, will strengthen state and local pollution prevention efforts.

14.3 WORKER AND UNION-BASED POLLUTION PREVENTION PROGRAMS

Several worker and union-based programs exist. These generally developed out of occupational health and safety programs and focused initially on education and training. The following briefly describes two such programs. Additional organizations interested in or developing worker and union-based programs are listed at the end of this chapter. This list is certainly not complete. (The author and editor would appreciate receiving information on other worker and union-based programs.)

14.3.1 International Brotherhood Of Painters & Allied Trades, Union Local 1555

Representing construction painters working for many contractors in the northern half of Alaska, this local union has integrated pollution prevention into three activities.[9] Funding to assist in the development of the second and third activities was provided by the Alaska DEC Pollution Prevention Office, Waste Reduction Matching Grant program. The three activities are listed below:

• Hazardous painting certification course. The course is a 16-hour class that covers basic concepts of worker health and safety and is required of all painters by the state of Alaska. The local union instructors build on this basic training and emphasize methods to reduce waste and pollution during painting.
• Apprentice training (joint labor/management program). Increased emphasis is being placed on teaching work practices that promote increased efficiency during painting. Additional training in the use of alternative technology has also been added such as HPLV (high pressure low velocity) spray guns.
• Solvent recycling and recovery. The local union and the Painters and Decorators Industry Advancement & Promotion Committee (a labor-management trust) purchase and operate a solvent recovery system to clean and recycle used solvent. Probably no single contractor could have attempted this project alone. State funds were used to design and evaluate this activity.

14.3.2 Boeing/International Association of Machinists Health and Safety Institute

This institute is a joint labor/management program with a mission to ensure continuous improvement of workplace health and safety.[10] It has an equal number of union and company representatives on staff, and decision-making is equal at all levels. One of its programs that could serve as a model for pollution prevention activities is its Process Material Change Coordination Team (PMCCT). The PMCCT consists of representatives from both the production and health and safety areas, with experienced workers from impacted areas used as advisors. The PMCCT is responsible for reviewing the safety and health impacts of changes in machines, processes, or materials. The team also helps explain to workers why changes are being made, the differences between the old materials and the new, and any health hazards posed by the changes.

14.4 OPPORTUNITIES FOR STATE OR LOCAL GOVERNMENT EFFORTS

State and local government pollution prevention agencies can play a key role in identifying, encouraging, and supporting innovative worker and union-based programs. Agencies should tap into the existing network of labor unions and joint labor/management organizations to promote pollution prevention. The following are some possibilities:

14.4.1 Identifying Opportunities

- Outreach to labor unions. This can best be done through state and local (usually county) labor councils. Local unions affiliate with these councils to work together on common goals. These councils often are represented on joint labor/management committees. They may have staff or committees for education, apprentice training, and workplace health and safety that would be interested in pollution prevention activities.[11] An agency labor liaison could assist in outreach with unions.
- Outreach to joint labor/management organizations. Many joint programs operate at the local, state, and regional level on issues such as workplace health and safety, training, productivity, and specific industry concerns. These can be located through state departments of labor and state and local labor councils.
- Outreach to state departments of labor. Programs common to most states include occupational health and safety consultation programs that provide information, assist with training, and conduct worksite inspections (nonregulatory); occupational safety and health enforcement agencies (in about half of states); and training and apprentice programs.

14.4.2 Encouraging Involvement

- Involve workers and unions. Establish a labor/management pollution prevention advisory board and include worker representatives on agency advisory committees and as reviewers of publications and applications for program funding. Add criteria for full worker and union participation in requests for proposals (RFPs) for pollution prevention grants. Encourage worker and union involvement in technical assistance and consulting services.
- Cross train agency consultants. Cross train pollution prevention staff in areas of occupational safety and health, labor unions, labor and management relations, and similar topics to assist them in recognizing impacts and obstacles and in communicating effectively with workers, unions, and joint labor/management programs.
- Sponsor conferences. Sponsor a workshop at a pollution prevention conference or a separate conference to address the issues of worker and union involvement and workplace impacts of change. A conference on *Labor Relations for Occupational Health Professionals* was planned at Cornell University in June of 1992 and could be a model for a similar pollution prevention conference.

14.4.3 Supporting Programs

- Labor and joint labor/management programs. Support these through funding, training, and technical assistance. Existing union and joint health and safety committees in specific industries or trades could be targeted to become involved in pollution prevention. Organizations experienced in providing training and technical services to workers and unions, such as Committees on Occupational Safety and Health (COSHs) and unions, could also be targeted.
- Education and training programs. Health and safety training programs required for hazard communication, hazardous waste and emergency response, asbestos abatement, lead paint abatement, and other topics have given tens of thousands of workers a basic knowledge to understand and begin to address hazardous materials and processes at their jobs. Pollution prevention concepts could be integrated into these programs. Many unions provide this training for their members jointly with their employers. Educational booklets and manuals could also be developed for workers that describe the concepts of pollution prevention and explain the role of workers and unions.
- Joint labor/management pollution prevention committees. These committees could be modeled after successful joint health and safety committees at specific worksites or within an industry or specific trade. The committees need to be structured to provide equal representation and participation by labor and management. The committee members will need to be trained in pollution prevention and have access to technical support.

14.5 SELECTED CONTACTS FOR DEVELOPING WORKER AND UNION-BASED PROGRAMS

- Workers' Institute for Safety and Health Division
  Occupational Health Foundation
  1126 16th Street, N.W., Suite 413
  Washington, D.C. 20036
  (202) 887-1980
- New York Committee on Occupational Safety and Health
  275 7th Avenue, 8th Floor
  New York, NY 10001
  (212) 627-9812
  (Can provide referrals to similar organizations in many states.)
- Toxic Use Reduction Institute
  University of Lowell
  1 University Avenue
  Lowell, MA 01854
  (508) 934-3275
- International Brotherhood of Painters & Allied Trades
  Mike Andrews, Director of Safety and Health
  1750 New York Avenue, N.W.
  Washington, D.C. 20006
  (202) 637-0700

- Boeing/Machinist Union Health and Safety Institute
  6840 Southcenter, Suite 200
  Seattle, WA 98188
  (206) 393-9289

14.6 REFERENCES

1. Huisingh, D., L. Martin, H. Hilger, and N. Seldman. *Proven Profits from Pollution Prevention: Case Studies in Resource Conservation and Waste Reduction* (Washington, D.C.: Institute for Local Self-Reliance, 1986), p. 17.
2. Dorfman, D. H., W. R. Muir, and C. G. Miller. *Environmental Dividends: Cutting More Chemical Wastes* (New York: INFORM, Inc., 1992), p. 32.
3. Hirschhorn, J. S. and K. U. Oldenburg. *Prosperity Without Pollution: The Prevention Strategy for Industry and Consumers* (New York: Van Nostrand Reinhold, 1991), pp. 82–83.
4. Olander, L., A. Colmsjo, B. Holmburg, S. Krantz, and U. Landstrom. "Occupational Implications of the Chlorofluorocarbon Ban in Sweden," *Am. J. Ind. Med.* 19:818–826 (1991).
5. Boden, L. I., J. A. Hall, C. Levenstein, and L. Punnett. "The Impact of Health and Safety Committees: A Study Based on Survey, Interview, and Occupational Safety and Health Administration Data," *J. Occup. Med.* 26(11):829–834 (1984).
6. Bureau of National Affairs. "Occupational Safety and Health Reporter," 21(39):1340–1341 (1992).
7. "Roundtable on OSHA at 20: What Now? Part 2," *New Solutions* 2(1):43–44 (1991).
8. "Que Pasa? A Canadian-Mexico "Free" Trade Deal," *New Solutions* 2(1):10–24 (1991).
9. Andrews, M., Business Manager Painters' Local 1555. Personal communication (1992).
10. IAM/Boeing Health and Safety Institute. "Annual Report" (1991).
11. Washington State Labor Council, AFL-CIO. "Working Together" (Seattle, WA: Washington State Labor Council).

SECTION IV:

POLLUTION PREVENTION RESOURCES

Introduction

Information and activity in the field of pollution prevention are changing rapidly. New pollution prevention technologies and techniques are being discovered, and their effectiveness is being evaluated. It is extremely difficult to stay current amidst the day-to-day responsibilities of state and local environmental officials. This section provides some useful resources for information, technical assistance, and funding.

As agencies develop and refine their pollution prevention programs, consideration should be given to building literature review and research into annual workplans. Travel funds should be set aside to support staff training opportunities. It is vital for all state and local pollution prevention professionals to establish a common knowledge base and a greater understanding of individual program needs and desires. Many environmental managers and staff are members of professional societies. Those interested in pollution prevention are encouraged to join the National Roundtable of State Pollution Prevention Programs. The National Roundtable (as it is commonly called) provides a useful forum for sharing and exchanging pollution prevention information and staying abreast of national policy issues in this area. The National Roundtable and other resources are described in greater detail in this section. **Readers should note this is not an exhaustive list of resources. Names, addresses, and phone numbers could have changed since publication of this book.**

CHAPTER 15

Selected Pollution Prevention Resources

David T. Wigglesworth

15.1 INTRODUCTION

This chapter provides a selected listing of contacts for additional pollution prevention information. In addition, a summary of potential EPA sources for pollution prevention funding is provided. State and local government officials should note that any resource listing is dynamic. Names and addresses may have changed since publication of this handbook. This chapter is divided into the following four sections:

* selected pollution prevention resources
* competitive federal pollution prevention grant resources
* state grants potentially flexible for pollution prevention activities
* EPA regional pollution prevention information network

0-87371-654-X/93/$0.00+$.50
© 1993 by Lewis Publishers

15.2 SELECTED POLLUTION PREVENTION RESOURCES[1,2]

15.2.1 Organizations and Agencies

State Pollution Prevention Programs

There are many programs at the state level providing a variety of pollution prevention technical assistance services. Refer to the Pollution Prevention Information Exchange System and/or the National Roundtable of State Pollution Prevention Programs for a detailed list of state and local programs.

National Roundtable of State Pollution Prevention Programs

The National Roundtable is a private, nonprofit organization promoting the development, implementation, and evaluation of efforts to avoid, eliminate, or reduce waste generation to all environmental media. The Roundtable believes such efforts are vital to the protection and enhancement of human health and the environment and conservation of natural resources. The Roundtable further believes such efforts are integral to the pursuit of environmentally responsible economic development.

The Roundtable offers state and local governments access to up-to-date pollution prevention information, annual pollution prevention roundtable meetings, and access to national policy dialogue regarding pollution prevention information. For more information contact:

David Thomas
Director
Illinois Hazardous Waste Research and Information Center
One East Hazelwood Drive
Champaign, Illinois 61820
(217) 333-8940

Northwest Regional Roundtable for State Waste Reduction Programs

The Northwest Regional Roundtable is an ad hoc forum for waste reduction programs to share and exchange information about pollution prevention activities. It meets quarterly. The states of Alaska, Idaho, Oregon, Washington, EPA Region 10, and British Columbia participate on the Roundtable. For more information contact:

Claire Rowlett
Pollution Prevention Specialist
U.S. EPA Region 10
1200 Sixth Avenue
Seattle, Washington 98101
(206) 553-1099

Waste Reduction Resource Center for the Southeast (WRRC)

The Resource Center provides pollution prevention technical assistance to states in the southeastern portion of the United States (U.S. EPA Region IV). Trained engineers respond to requests for technical assistance and conduct onsite technical assistance services. For more information contact:

Gary Hunt
Waste Reduction Resource Center
3825 Barrett Drive, Suite 300
P.O. Box 27687
Raleigh, NC 27611-7687
(919) 571-4100

Waste Reduction Institute for Training and Applications Research (WRITAR)

Founded in 1990, WRITAR is a nonprofit organization dedicated to facilitating implementation of innovative strategies, techniques, and technologies that prevent pollution at the source. Services provided by WRITAR include applications research, networks, training, facilitation, policy formulation, and education programs. For more information contact:

Terry Foecke
Executive Director
WRITAR
1313 5th Street SE
Minneapolis, MN 55414-4502
(612) 379-5995

American Institute for Pollution Prevention (AIPP)

The AIPP includes membership from approximately 20 individuals representing professional associations and industrial trade associations. The AIPP provides a liaison channel between the EPA and industry regarding a variety pollution prevention issues. The institute is sponsored by EPA and the University of Cincinnati. For more information contact:

Dr. Thomas Hauser
Department of Civil and Environmental Engineering
University of Cincinnati
Cincinnati, OH 45221
(513) 556-3693

The Local Government Commission

The Local Government Commission provides pollution prevention information and technical assistance to local governments in California. The organization has produced several useful publications for local governments considering pollution prevention programs. These publications are available to local governments outside the state of California. For more information contact:

Anthony Eulo
The Local Government Commission
909 12 Street #205
Sacramento, CA 95814
(916) 448-1198

EPA Office of Pollution Prevention and Toxics

This office sponsors and co-sponsors a number of pollution prevention activities including state grant programs, the pollution prevention information clearinghouse, the Administrator's Award for Excellence in Pollution Prevention, and pollution prevention research. OPPT also works to integrate pollution prevention into EPA programs and different sectors of society. For more information contact:

Lena Hann
United States Environmental Protection Agency
Office of Pollution Prevention and Toxics
Pollution Prevention Division
401 M Street SW
Washington, D.C. 20460
(202) 260-2237

EPA Risk Reduction Engineering Laboratory, Pollution Prevention Research Branch

The Pollution Prevention Research Branch is responsible for supporting projects that develop and demonstrate clean production technologies, clean products, and innovative approaches to reducing the generation of pollutants in all media. For more information contact:

Harry M. Freeman
Chief, Pollution Prevention Research Branch
United States Environmental Protection Agency
Risk Reduction Engineering Laboratory
Office of Research and Development
26 West Martin Luther King Drive

Cincinnati, OH 45268
(513) 569-7931

The Pacific Northwest Pollution Prevention Research Center (PPRC)

PPRC is a private, nonprofit organization established to advance pollution prevention research in the Pacific Northwest. It was established on April 22, 1991. PPRC is supported through private and public sector resources and has awarded over $200,000 in grant funds to support pollution prevention research. Request information on "Funders" of pollution prevention research. For more information contact:

Madeline M. Grulich
Pacific Northwest Pollution Prevention Research Center
1218 Third Avenue, Suite 1205
Seattle, WA 98101
(206) 223-1151

15.2.2 Hotlines and Clearinghouses[3]

Pollution Prevention Information Exchange System (PIES)

PIES is a computerized information network for the Pollution Prevention Information Clearinghouse (PPIC). PIES helps organizations identify grant programs and technical pollution prevention documents, contact experts in the field, and identify other pollution prevention resources. For more information contact:

Myles Morse
United States Environmental Protection Agency
Office of Environmental Engineering
  and Technology Demonstration
401 M Street SW
Washington, D.C. 20460
(202) 475-7161
  -or-
Pollution Prevention Information
Exchange System (PIES)
(703) 506-1025
(703) 821-4800 (technical support)

Pollution Prevention Information Clearinghouse (PPIC)

PPIC is a multimedia clearinghouse of technical, policy, programmatic, legislative, and financial information dedicated to promoting pollution prevention through efficient information transfer. PPIC is operated by the Pollution Prevention Division and Office of Research and Development. PPIC is composed of four different elements: (1) repository of technical information, (2) PIES — an electronic information exchange, (3) hotline for additional information, and (4) outreach. For more information contact:

Jocelyn Woodman
Pollution Prevention Division
United States Environmental Protection Agency
410 M Street SW (PM219)
Washington, D.C. 20460
(202) 382-4418

Other contacts to access PPIC include:

RCRA/Superfund Hotline: (800) 424-9346
Small Business Office Hotline: (800) 368-5888
PPIC Technical Assistance: (703) 821-4800

The Solid Waste Information Clearinghouse (SWICH)

SWICH was established by EPA to increase the availability of information on solid waste source reduction, recycling, composting, and other education and training issues. For more information contact:

SWICH
Box 7219
Silver Spring, MD 20910
(301) 585-2898
(800) 67-SWICH

Other EPA Hotlines

Emergency Planning and Community Right-to-Know: (800) 535-0202
Storm Water (NPDES Permitting): (703) 821-4660
Wetlands Information: (800) 832-7828
National Pesticide Network: (800) 858-7378

15.2.3 Publications

Pollution Prevention Review

The "Pollution Prevention Review" is an excellent quarterly periodical on issues concerning pollution prevention. Informative articles are presented in each edition and are relevant to state and local environmental agencies. For more information contact:

Pollution Prevention Review
c/o Executive Enterprises Publications Co., Inc.
22 West 21st Street
New York, NY 10010-6990
(212) 645-7880, ext. 248

Resource Recycling

"Resource Recycling" is another worthwhile publication that includes many articles concerning pollution prevention, waste reduction, and recycling. Topics addressing markets for recycling materials, plastics recycling, and development of local waste reduction and recycling programs are discussed. For more information contact:

Resource Recycling
P.O. Box 10540
Portland, OR 97210
(503) 227-1319

Facility Pollution Prevention Guide

This guide was developed by the EPA. It describes procedures for establishing a company-wide pollution prevention plan. Methods for conducting pollution prevention assessments, conducting a feasibility analysis, and evaluating a program are described. For more information contact:

Lisa Brown
U.S. Environmental Protection Agency
Pollution Prevention Research Branch
Risk Reduction Engineering Laboratory
26 West Martin Luther King Drive
Cincinnati, OH 45268
(513) 569-7215

Pollution Prevention Training Opportunities

This EPA publication is published to provide information on available pollution prevention training opportunities. The guide contains useful contacts for more information, listings of training courses by state, assessment manuals, and training videos. For more information contact:

Myles E. Morse
United States Environmental Protection Agency
Office of Research and Development
401 M Street SW
Washington, D.C. 20460
(202) 475-7161

15.3 POLLUTION PREVENTION GRANT RESOURCES[4]

Pollution Prevention Incentives for States (PPIS)

PPIS grant programs are intended to build and support state pollution prevention capabilities and to test innovative pollution prevention approaches and methodologies. For more information contact:

Lena Hann
Pollution Prevention Division
United States Environmental Protection Agency
401 M Street SW
Washington, D.C. 20460
(202) 260-4146

Agriculture in Concert with the Environment (ACE)

The EPA Office of Pollution Prevention and the Sustainable Agriculture Research and Education Program (SAREP) fund state-based projects involving education and training in sustainable agriculture, habitat protection, and sustainable farming practices. For more information contact:

Lena Hann
Office of Pollution Prevention
United States Environmental Protection Agency
401 M Street SW
Washington, D.C. 20460
(202) 260-4164
  -or-
Patrick Madden
United States Department of Agriculture
Cooperative State Research Service
(818) 242-0406

National Industrial Competitiveness Through Efficiency: Energy, Environment and Economics (NICE)

NICE is a joint project of the EPA and the Department of Energy designed to fund projects that improve energy efficiency, advance industrial competitiveness, and reduce toxic industrial emissions. For more information contact:

Brian Symmes (or Lena Hann)
Pollution Prevention Division

United States Environmental Protection Agency
401 M Street SW
Washington, D.C. 20460
(202) 260-4164

Risk Reduction Through Pollution Prevention (R2P2)

R2P2 is a grant program to foster integration of pollution prevention into EPA strategic planning efforts and to support state level pollution prevention efforts focused on high risk environmental problems. For more information contact:

Lena Hann (or Steven Keach)
Pollution Prevention Division
United States Environmental Protection Agency
401 M Street SW
Washington, D.C. 20460
(202) 260-4164
(202) 260-4908

Pollution Prevention in POTWs

The goal of this grant program is to support development of pollution prevention programs for publicly-owned treatment works and to encourage POTWs to develop source reduction efforts such as energy audits, water conservation, and reduction in toxic discharges into the sewer system. For more information contact:

Deborah Hanlon
Pollution Prevention Division
United States Environmental Protection Agency
410 M Street SW
Washington, D.C. 20460
(202) 260-2726

Municipal Solid Waste Innovative Technology Evaluation Program (MITE)

This program funds projects to evaluate and disseminate information on innovative technologies including those which foster waste reduction and recycling. For more information contact:

Lynnann Hitchens
EPA Risk Reduction Engineering Laboratory

Office of Research and Development
United States Environmental Protection Agency
26 West Martin Luther King Drive
Cincinnati, OH 45268
(513) 569-7672

EPA's Public Private Partnership Grant Program (P3)

P3 is designed to promote innovative methods for leveraging public and private resources to finance innovative environmental programs. This type of grant program can help promote pollution prevention projects with industry. For more information contact a regional pollution prevention contact listed in this chapter.

EPA Waste Reduction Evaluation at Federal Sites Program (WREAFS)

The objectives of this grant program is to (1) perform pollution prevention assessments at federal sites, (2) demonstrate pollution prevention technologies, (3) conduct pollution prevention workshops, and (4) enhance pollution prevention within the federal community. For more information contact:

James Bridges
Pollution Prevention Research Branch
Office of Research and Development
United States Environmental Protection Agency
26 West Martin Luther King Drive
Cincinnati, OH 45268
(513) 569-7931

Waste Reduction Innovative Technology Evaluation Grant Program (WRITE)

The WRITE program is designed to fund state activities to evaluate and document innovative pollution prevention technologies. For more information contact:

Lisa M. Brown
Pollution Prevention Research Branch
Office of Research and Development
United States Environmental Protection Agency
26 West Martin Luther King Drive

Cincinnati, OH 45268
(513) 569-7634

National Environmental Education Act Grants

The purpose of this grant program is to stimulate environmental education by supporting projects to design, demonstrate, or disseminate practices, methods, or techniques related to environmental education or training. These funds could potentially be used to support pollution prevention education activities. For more information contact the EPA regional pollution prevention contacts listed at the end of this chapter.

15.4 SELECTED "FLEXIBLE GRANTS" FOR POLLUTION PREVENTION[5]

Each year most states and EPA enter into cooperative agreements for conducting various environmental protection activities. These activities and corresponding workplans are made public through the State EPA Agreement process — known as the SEA. The SEA establishes a mechanism to transfer federal funds to support state implementation of federal environmental programs. The SEA process provides potential avenues to initiate special pollution prevention projects and/or establish core funding for development of state pollution prevention programs. Some traditional EPA grant programs offer flexibility for pollution prevention activity. While guidance is not yet explicit, many states and EPA are attempting to utilize these grant programs to redirect more funds toward pollution prevention. Grants with the greatest potential for incorporating pollution prevention include the Clean Air Act Section 105, Toxic Substances Control Act Section 28, Resource Conservation and Recovery Act Section 3011, Federal Insecticide, Fungicide, and Rodenticide Act Section 23, Section 313 of the Emergency Planning and Community Right-To-Know Act, and water program grants. Below is a selected listing of potentially flexible EPA grant programs. State and local governments are encouraged to pursue these possibilities as SEA's come up for renewal. See Chapter 11 for more details on this topic. **Additional guidance on grant flexibility may have been issued since publication of this book.**

Office of Air and Radiation (OAR)

The Clean Air Act Section 105 authorizes funding programs to prevent air pollution. Specific activities could include projects focused on alternative fuels,

Office of Wastewater Enforcement and Compliance (OWEC) Water Conservation Grants

Office of Waste/Office of Water (OWOW)

Surface Water Grant Program (Clean Water Act Section 106) offers possible funding encouraging states to identify source reduction options to prevent groundwater pollution.

Wetlands Grant Program (CWA 104(b)(3)) does not preclude pollution prevention activities, but no specific guidance has been developed.

National Estuary Program (CWA 320(g)/205(j)) identifies no specific guidance. Funds can be used to abate pollution that conceivably could mean pollution prevention activities.

Nonpoint Source Grant (CWA 319(h)/CWA 205(j)(5)/CWA 201(g)(1)(b)) abates nonpoint source pollution and prevents groundwater pollution. Funds could be used to focus on actual nonpoint source reduction activities.

Office of Ground Water/Drinking Water (OGWDW): UIC Grant Program

The purpose of these funds is to implement underground injection control programs. Grants under this program must be related to the mission of the UIC program. Additional guidance is needed to define options for flexible pollution prevention activities.

Public Water Systems Supervision Grant Program (SWDA) 1428(a)(b)

The purpose of this grant program is to identify wellhead protection areas and develop source management programs. Projects focusing on prevention pollution of drinking water are possible.

Office of Solid Waste and Emergency Response Core Programs Grant (CERCLA 117(e))

The purpose of this grant program is to fund the long-term remediation of environmental/health risks at hazardous waste sites. According to EPA, this program has been used in Georgia to develop a waste minimization program. Specific limitations on the use of these funds do exist.

Hazardous Waste Financial Assistance (RCRA 3011)

The purpose of this grant program is to support development and implementation of hazardous waste management programs. This grant program has traditionally allowed flexibility for pollution prevention activities to reduce hazardous wastes.

Hazardous Waste Financial Assistance (RCRA 3011)

The purpose of this grant program is to support development and implementation of hazardous waste management programs. This grant program has traditionally allowed flexibility for pollution prevention activities to reduce hazardous wastes.

Office of Underground Storage Tanks (OUST) State UST Program Grants

The purpose of this grant program is to support development and implementation of state underground storage tank programs. This grant program allows states to use funds in support of programs to reduce and prevent leaking underground storage tanks.

Office of Pesticides and Toxic Substances (OPTS) Pesticides Enforcement Grants (FIFRA 23(a)(1))

This grant program provides states with funds to implement a pesticide enforcement program, training, and applicator certification. Grant guidance encourages states to incorporate pollution prevention conditions in enforcement cases.

Pesticides Program Implementation (FIFRA 23(a)(1))

The purpose of this grant program is to provide training for applicators and to develop groundwater protection programs and worker protection programs. There appears to be flexibility for pollution prevention activities.

15.5 EPA REGIONAL POLLUTION PREVENTION INFORMATION NETWORK

The EPA regional pollution prevention contacts are useful resources to initiate further discussion on SEA grant flexibility for pollution prevention and to find out more about competitive pollution prevention grants. In addition, these contacts are useful resources for technical information and referral. **Following is a listing of the EPA contacts and phone numbers (names and phone numbers subject to change):**

Region	Name	Phone/Fax
EPA Region I	Abby Swaine	(617)565-4523/(617)565-3346
	Mark Mahoney	(617)565-1155/(617)565-3346
EPA Region II	Janet Sapadin	(212)264-1925/(212)264-9695
EPA Region III	Roy Denmark	(215)597-8327/(215)587-7906
EPA Region IV	Carol Monell	(404)347-7109/(404)347-1043

EPA Region V	Dolly Tong	(312)886-2910/(312)353-5374
EPA Region VI	Laura Townsend	(214)655-6580/(214)655-2146
EPA Region VII	Alan Wehmeyer	(913)551-7336/(303)293-7063
EPA Region VIII	Don Patton	(303)293-1456/(303)293-1198
EPA Region IX	Jesse Baskir Hilary Lauer	(415)744-2190/(415)744-1796 (415)744-2189/(415)744-1796
EPA Region X	Robyn Meeker Carolyn Gangmark	(206)553-8579/(206)553-4957 (206)553-4072/(206)553-4957

15.6 REFERENCES

1. "Pollution Prevention Training Opportunities in 1991," U.S. EPA, Office of Policy Planning and Evaluation (March 1991).
2. "Facility Pollution Prevention Guide," U.S. EPA, Office of Research and Development, EPA/600/R-92/088 (May 1992).
3. "Pollution Prevention Training Opportunities in 1991," U.S. EPA, Office of Policy Planning and Evaluation (March 1991).
4. "Pollution Prevention Fact Sheet," U.S. EPA, Office of Pollution Prevention (August 1991).
5. "Summary of EPA Grant Programs," U.S. EPA, draft (July 16, 1991).

INDEX